T0188367

Control Systems and Reinforcement Learning

A high school student can create deep Q-learning code to control her robot, without any understanding of the meaning of "deep" or "Q," or why the code sometimes fails. This book is designed to explain the science behind reinforcement learning and optimal control in a way that is accessible to students with a background in calculus and matrix algebra. A unique focus is algorithm design to obtain the fastest possible speed of convergence for learning algorithms, along with insight into why reinforcement learning sometimes fails. Advanced stochastic process theory is avoided at the start by substituting random exploration with more intuitive deterministic probing for learning. Once these ideas are understood, it is not difficult to master techniques rooted in stochastic control. These topics are covered in the second part of the book, starting with Markov chain theory and ending with a fresh look at actor-critic methods for reinforcement learning.

SEAN MEYN is a professor and holds the Robert C. Pittman Eminent Scholar Chair in the Department of Electrical and Computer Engineering, University of Florida. He is well known for his research on stochastic processes and their applications. His award-winning monograph *Markov Chains and Stochastic Stability* with R. L. Tweedie is now a standard reference. In 2015, he and Professor Ana Bušić received a Google Research Award recognizing research on renewable energy integration. He is an IEEE Fellow and IEEE Control Systems Society distinguished lecturer on topics related to both reinforcement learning and energy systems.

Control Systems and Reinforcement Learning

Sean Meyn
University of Florida

CAMBRIDGE
UNIVERSITY PRESS

University Printing House, Cambridge CB2 8BS, United Kingdom

One Liberty Plaza, 20th Floor, New York, NY 10006, USA

477 Williamstown Road, Port Melbourne, VIC 3207, Australia

314–321, 3rd Floor, Plot 3, Splendor Forum, Jasola District Centre, New Delhi – 110025, India

103 Penang Road, #05–06/07, Visioncrest Commercial, Singapore 238467

Cambridge University Press is part of the University of Cambridge.

It furthers the University's mission by disseminating knowledge in the pursuit of education, learning, and research at the highest international levels of excellence.

www.cambridge.org
Information on this title: www.cambridge.org/9781316511961
DOI: 10.1017/9781009051873

© Sean Meyn 2022

This publication is in copyright. Subject to statutory exception and to the provisions of relevant collective licensing agreements, no reproduction of any part may take place without the written permission of Cambridge University Press.

First published 2022

Printed in the United Kingdom by TJ Books Limited, Padstow Cornwall

A catalogue record for this publication is available from the British Library.

ISBN 978-1-316-51196-1 Hardback

Cambridge University Press has no responsibility for the persistence or accuracy of URLs for external or third-party internet websites referred to in this publication and does not guarantee that any content on such websites is, or will remain, accurate or appropriate.

March 9th of 2021 was one of the saddest days on record for me and I'm sure most of my colleagues. On this day, Kishan Baheti was taken from us by the COVID virus.
My dear friend Kishan, this book is dedicated to you.

Contents

Preface

During the spring semester of 2020, I was delivering my stochastic control course, for which the final weeks always focus on topics in reinforcement learning (RL). Throughout the semester, I was thinking ahead to crash courses on this topic to be delivered later in the year: two summer courses planned in Paris and Berlin, and another scheduled as part of the Simons Institute program on reinforcement learning.[1] A pandemic altered my travel plans, but it also gave me time to reflect on how to better teach this difficult material.

Soon after the spring semester ended, I was contacted by Diana Gillooly, then an editor at Cambridge University Press. She wrote "someone mentioned that you were scheduled to deliver lectures on reinforcement learning," and asked if I might be interested in writing a book on the topic. Her brief email set in motion the pages that lie in front of you.

There is of course a longer history: the book is a product of handouts I've prepared over more than a decade, and bits and pieces of papers and book chapters prepared over a longer period.

However, I promised my co-organizers of the Simons Institute RL program that I would present a crash course for true beginners, without heavy mathematics. I also promised myself I would write a book that would be accessible to senior undergraduates and graduate students, provided they came with sufficient motivation. These pandemic-induced contemplations led to two themes that I felt a need to spell out:

(i) Within the control systems literature, there are dynamic programming techniques to approximate the Q-function that appears in reinforcement learning. In particular, this "value function" is the solution to a simple convex program (an example is the "DPLP" appearing in Eq. (3.36)). Many of the algorithms in reinforcement learning are designed to approximate the same function but are based on root finding problems that are not well understood outside very special cases.

    This is just one example of the need to build better bridges between control and RL. I cannot claim the bridge is fully built. My hope is that the book will provide leads for future discoveries based on insights from each discipline.

(ii) *Stochastic approximation* (SA) is the most common method for analysis of recursive algorithms; this approach is commonly known as the *ordinary differential equations (ODE) method* [136, 229, 301, 357]. The relationship between RL and SA was recognized soon after Watkins introduced Q-learning [169, 352], and ODE methods for

[1] Video and slides from the 2020 Fall program are now available at `https://simons.berkeley.edu/programs/rl20`.

analysis of optimization algorithms have grown in sophistication over the past decade [198, 318, 335, 375]. Related ODE methods are part of a standard modeling framework in statistical mechanics, genetics, epidemiology (e.g., the SIR model), and even voting [24, 122, 225, 276].

The narrative is flipped in this book: rather than treating an ODE as simply an analytical tool, every algorithm in this book begins with an ideal ODE that is regarded as "step 1" in algorithm design. I believe this provides better insight into algorithm synthesis and analysis.

However, justification of this approach using SA is highly technical. In particular, the recent thesis and book chapter [107, 110] (which build on a similar narrative) assume significant background in the theory of stochastic processes. In this book, we lift the veil: there is nothing inherently *stochastic* about *stochastic approximation*, provided you are willing to work with sinusoids or other deterministic probing signals instead of stochastic processes. The ODE methods surveyed in Chapters 4 and 5 make no reference to probability theory.

This is my third book, and like the others the writing came with discoveries. While working on theme (i), my colleague Prashant Mehta and I found that *Convex Q-Learning* could be made much more practical by borrowing batch RL concepts that are currently popular. This led to the new work [246, 247] and new collaborations with Gergely Neu. You will find text and equations from these papers scattered throughout Chapters 3 and 5.

Chapter 4 on ODE methods and *quasi-stochastic approximation* was to be built primarily on [40, 41]. Over the summer of 2020, all of this material was generalized to create a complete theory of convergence and convergence rates for these algorithms, along with a better understanding of their application to both *gradient-free optimization* and *policy gradient* techniques for RL [85–87].

The second part of the book, such as *Zap Zero* for Q-learning, and insights on the rate of convergence for actor-critic methods. Each chapter ends with a "Notes" section that provides an overview of the origins of the main conclusions.

Many newcomers to reinforcement learning may be disappointed to see that the theory and algorithms in this book are far removed from the dream portrayed in the popular media: reinforcement learning is often described as an "agent" interacting in a physical environment, and maturing as it gains experience. Unfortunately, given today's technologies, the process of "learning from scratch while you control" is unlikely to succeed outside very special cases such as online advertising.

The tone of this book is entirely different: we pose an optimal control problem, and show how to obtain an approximate solution based on design of exploration strategies and tuning rules. This is not an eccentricity of the author but a disciplined and accepted approach to derive all of the standard approaches to reinforcement learning. In particular, the Q-learning algorithm of Watkins and its extensions are designed to solve or approximate the "dynamic programming" equations introduced in the 1950s.

The field is young, and its future may look something like the dream you had in mind before you read this preface. I hope that in the near future we will discover new paradigms for RL, perhaps drawing inspiration from intelligent living beings rather than optimality equations from the past century. I have confidence that the fundamental principles in this book will remain valuable without the shackles of the optimal control paradigm!

Acknowledgments

Let's begin three decades back. In the mid-1990s I (figuratively) won the lottery: a Fulbright fellowship that took me and my family, including my young daughters, Sydney and Sophie, to Bangalore, India. Those nine months at the Indian Institute of Science (IISc) with Vivek Borkar were the start of fruitful collaborations and a long-lasting friendship. Vivek's presence can be felt on nearly every page of the second half of this book.

I was also fortunate to have interactions with Ben Van Roy while he was completing his dissertation research at the Massachusetts Institute of Technology (MIT). His work with John Tsitsiklis is an absolute tour-de-force. Many aspects of the book draw from this early RL research. His current research is likely to have similar long-lasting impact.

Prashant Mehta once said to me, "I know how you do it! You surround yourself with amazing people!" Amazing is right, and he is right there at the top. This book is a product of collaborations with Vivek, Prashant, and many others, including Ana Bušić, Ken Duffy, Peter Glynn, Ioannis Kontoyiannis, Eric Moulines, and many old friends at the United Technologies Research Center (UTRC), including Amit Surana and George Mathew. My PhD advisor Peter Caines was my first and one of my all-time best colleagues, who enthusiastically supported my first investigations into Markov chain theory. This set the stage for collaborations with Richard Tweedie that began during my postdoctoral stay at the Australian National University. All amazing people, anyone will agree.

Younger stars that influenced my research include Shuhang Chen, who recently defended his dissertation in the math department and is lead author of [88] on finer ODE methods. Many thanks to current graduate student Fan Lu for comments on early drafts and assistance with numerical experiments.

Prabir Barooah helped to draw me to the University of Florida, from my former home at the University of Illinois. I've benefited from our interactions, and with his students including Naren Raman and Austin Coffman.

Max Raginsky helped me to navigate the literature outside of my usual orbit. In particular, his advice along with Polyak's recent survey [136] helped me to understand the contributions from the USSR in the early days of RL and SA. Max's research is also an inspiration: while references to his work are scattered throughout the book, much of this material is suited for a more advanced monograph.

Much of Chapters 2 and 3 is based on the state space control course created at the Decision and Control Laboratory at the University of Illinois. Many thanks to Bill Perkins, Tamer Basar, and Max Raginsky for allowing me to borrow material from the course manuscript [29], and laboratory manager Daniel Block for leading the design of innovative control experiments.

In 2018, I was fortunate to spend several months at the National Renewable Energy Laboratory (NREL), where I conducted research at the Autonomous Energy Systems laboratory. One outcome of these interactions was research on stochastic approximation, leading to the articles [40, 41, 85–87, 93]. The book would not be the same without collaborations at NREL with Andrey Bernstein, Marcello Colombino, Emiliano Dall'Anese, and my former graduate student Yue Chen.

In reviewing the literature on extremum seeking control for Chapter 4, I was skeptical of the common claim in the research literature that the idea began in the 1920s. The most convincing case for this history was made in [348]. I contacted coauthor Iven Mareels, who reassured me that this history was accurate. Then, with help from colleagues in France, I found and translated the 1922 document [217] that is considered the source of this optimization technique.

One of the great "bridge builders" at the intersection of RL and control theory is Frank Lewis, who has led the creation of several collected volumes on these topics. I was surprised when he thought of me one decade ago, leading to the contribution [165], and very enthusiastic when he invited me to contribute to a new volume one decade later [110].

Until recently, I have regarded RL as a hobby, as motivation for simplified models for complex systems (such as networks [254]), and as a vehicle to teach control theory. This changed with the arrival of Adithya Devraj to the University of Florida, where he pursued graduate studies with me until he graduated and departed for Stanford in the spring of 2020. His curiosity and intellect were an inspiration in many ways, and in particular drove me to learn more about the evolution of RL over the past decade. Many of the figures and much of the theory in the second part of this book are taken from his dissertation [107]. He also provided suggestions that improved many parts of the book.

I owe the Simons Institute a great debt. During the spring of 2018, I was a long-term visitor during its program on real-time decision making, and was doubly fortunate to be joined by Ana Bušić and Adithya Devraj. We learned a great deal from fellow visitors, and Peter Bartlett (along with other locals). Our discussions back then helped to motivate the 2020 program on RL, which provided a massive crash course on every aspect of the subject, with a strong emphasis on the sort of bridge building I am attempting to pursue with this book. In the fall of 2020, I watched tutorials on recent actor-critic techniques just before finishing Chapter 10 on this very topic. The book benefited from the `rltheory` virtual seminar series, organized by Gergely Neu, Ciara Pike-Burke, and Csaba Szepesvári,[2] which was also inspired by the 2020 RL program at Simons.

Returning to the present: in the spring of 2021, I created a new course based on Part I of this book. Many of the students were hungry for an accessible treatment of both control systems and RL, and survived the sometimes difficult and rocky three months. I appreciate all of the feedback I received over the semester, and did my best to respond. You can thank Arielle Stevens for correcting many confusing passages in the first three chapters, and for the gray boxes used to highlight important concepts. Many more improvements were made in response to input from other students, including Caleb Bowyer, Bo Chen, Austin Coffman, Chetan Dhulipalla, Weihan Shen, Zetong Xuan, Kei-Tai Yu, and Yongxu Zhang. Also on this list is the recent graduate Dr. Bob Moye and current graduate students conducting research with me on RL and related topics: Mario Baquedano Aguilar, Caio Lauand, and Amin Moradi.

I also received substantial feedback from current PhD candidate Vektor Dewanto soon after a draft manuscript was posted on Twitter in August of 2021.

Of course, I cannot forget my sponsors. Bob Bonneau at the Air Force Office for Scientific Research (AFOSR) encouraged funding for early research with Prashant Mehta on Q-learning, mean-field games, and nonlinear filtering. Derya Cansever and Purush Iyer at the Army Research Office (ARO) have funded more recent research on related topics. The National Science Foundation (NSF) has funded my most abstract and seemingly worthless

[2] `https://sites.google.com/view/rltheoryseminars/home`.

research topics, which hopefully led to something of value. My most reliable ally at NSF was Radhakisan (Kishan) Baheti, who recommended funding for my very first grant (on the topic of adaptive control, at the start of the 1990s). He was a fantastic mentor, alert to potentially foolish ideas, and also inspired by new if potentially useless research directions. He knew what everyone in the control community was up to! He also inspired all of us with his marathon runs and mastery of yoga.

– Sean Meyn, August 1, 2021

1

Introduction

To define *reinforcement learning* (RL), it is first necessary to define *automatic control*. Examples in your everyday life may include the cruise control in your car; the thermostat in your air conditioning, refrigerator, and water heater; and the decision-making rules in a modern clothes dryer. There are sensors that gather data, a computer to take the data to understand the state of the "world" (is the car traveling at the right speed? Are the towels still damp?), and based on these measurements an algorithm powered by the computer spits out commands to adjust whatever needs to be adjusted: throttle, fan speed, heating coil current, etc. More exciting examples include space rockets, artificial organs, and microscopic robots to perform surgery.

The dream of RL is automatic control that is truly automatic; without any knowledge of physics or biology or medicine, an RL algorithm tunes itself to become a super controller: the smoothest ride into space, and the most expert microsurgeon!

The dream is surely beyond reach in most applications, but recent success stories have inspired industry, scientists, and a new generation of students.

DeepMind's AlphaGo set the world on fire following the defeat of Go champion Fan Hui in 2015, and Lee Sedol the following year (a story told in the 2017 film [185]). Soon after was the astonishing sequel AlphaZero, which learns to play chess and Go by "self play" without any help from experts [150, 310, 322].[1]

1.1 What You Can Find in Here

Reinforcement learning today rests on two pillars of equal importance:

1. Optimal control: the two most famous RL algorithms, TD- and Q-learning, are all about approximating the *value function* that is at the heart of optimal control. Similarly, actor-critic methods are based on state feedback, which is motivated by optimal control theory.
2. Statistics and information theory, especially the topic of exploration, as in bandit theory. Consider the annoying ads on YouTube, which provide one example of Google's

[1] These success stories follow a longer history of demonstrations based on board games. An earlier breakthrough is Tesauro's implementation of TD-learning with neural network function approximation to obtain an RL algorithm for backgammon [350]. The 1997 victory of IBM's "Deep Blue" over chess champion Garry Kasparov was also front-page news [373]. While this algorithm resembles *model predictive control* rather than any RL algorithm described in this book, we will be liberal in our taxonomy of control and RL since we want to benefit from the best of both.

exploration: "will Diana click???" [171, 216, 307]. Exploration in RL is a rapidly evolving field – it will surely generate many new books in the years to come.

The big focus of the book is the first pillar, emphasizing the geometry of optimal control, and why it should not be difficult to create reliable algorithms for learning. We will not ignore the second pillar: motivation and successful heuristics will be explained without diving deeply into the theory. The reader will learn enough to begin experimenting with homemade computer code, and have a big library of options for algorithm design. Before completing half of the book, I hope that a student will have a solid understanding of why these algorithms are expected to be useful, and why they sometimes fail.

This is only possible through mastery of several fundamentals:

(i) The philosophical foundations of control design.
(ii) The theory of optimal control.
(iii) Ordinary differential equations (ODEs): stability and convergence. The ODE method, including translation to algorithm.
(iv) Basics of machine learning (ML): function approximation and optimization theory.

Any reader who knows the author will wonder why the list is so short! The following topics are seen as fundamental in RL theory, and are fundamental to much of my research:

(i) Stochastic processes and Markov chains.
(ii) Markov decision theory.
(iii) Stochastic approximation and convergence of algorithms.

Yes, we will get to all of this. However, I want to make it clear that there is no need for probability theory to understand many of the important concepts in RL.

The first half of the book contains RL theory and design techniques without any probability prerequisites. This means we pretend that the world is purely deterministic until the surname "Markov" appears in the second half of the book. Justification comes in part from the control foundations covered in Chapters 2 and 3. Do you think we modeled the probability of hitting a seagull when we designed a control system to take astronauts to the moon? The models used in traditional control design are often very simple, but good enough to get insight on how to control a rocket or a pancreas.

Beyond this, once you understand RL techniques in this simplified setting, it does not take much work to extend the ideas to the more complex probabilistic realm.

Among the highlights of Part I of the book are the following

► *ODE design.* The ODE method has been a workhorse for algorithm *analysis* since the introduction of the stochastic approximation technique of Robbins and Monro in the early 1950s [301]. In this book, we flip the narrative, and start off in the continuous time domain. There is tremendous motivation for this point of view:

(i) We will see that an ODE is much simpler to describe and analyze than the discrete-time noisy algorithm that is eventually implemented.
(ii) Remarkable discoveries in the optimization literature reinforce the value of this approach: first design an ODE with desirable properties, and then find a numerical analyst to implement this on a computer [318]. It is now known that the famous acceleration techniques of Polyak and Nesterov can be interpreted in this way.

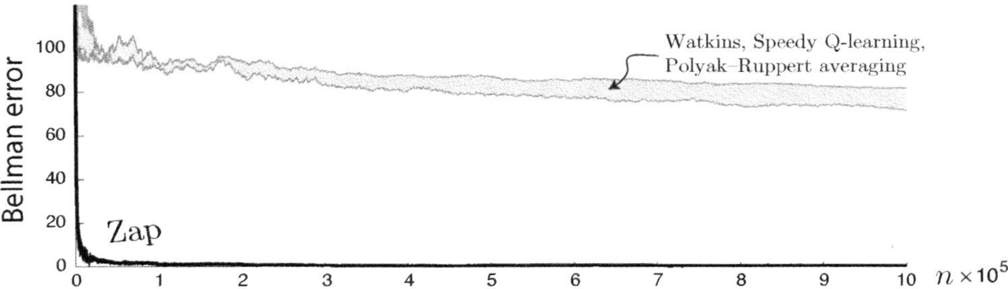

Figure 1.1 Maximum Bellman error $\{\overline{\mathcal{B}}_n : n \geq 0\}$ for various Q-learning algorithms [107].

(iii) Zap Q-learning will be one of many algorithms described in the book. It is a particular ODE design based on the Newton–Raphson flow introduced in the economics literature, and first analyzed by Smale in the 1970s [325]. The Zap ODE is universally stable and consistent, and hence when translated with care, provides new techniques for RL design [89, 107, 110, 112]. The power of Zap design is illustrated in Figure 1.1 – see Section 9.8.2 for details.

▸ *Quasistochastic approximation.* The theory of "stochastic approximation" amounts to justifying a discrete time algorithm based on an ODE approximation. An understanding of the general theory requires substantial mathematical background.

The reader will be introduced to stochastic approximation without any need to know the meaning of "stochastic." This is made possible by substituting mixtures of sinusoids for randomness, which is justified by an emerging science [11, 51, 52, 87, 93, 228]. Not only is this more accessible, but the performance in application to *policy gradient* methods in RL is remarkable.

The plots shown in Figure 1.2 are based on experiments described in Chapter 4, comparing exploration using sinusoids versus traditional random "independent and identically distributed (i.i.d.)" exploration. The histograms were generated through 1,000 independent experiments. The traditional approach labeled "1SPSA" requires additional training of many orders of magnitude when compared to quasistochatic approximation (QSA).

▸ *Batch RL methods and convex Q-learning.* One of the founders of AlphaGo admits that extension of these techniques is not trivial: "This approach won't work in more ill-structured problems like natural-language understanding or robotics, where the state space is more complex and there isn't a clear objective function" [150].

In applications to controlling building systems, the energy grid, robotic surgery, or autonomous vehicles, we need to think carefully about more structured learning and control architectures, designed so that we have a reliable outcome (hopefully with some guarantees on performance as well as the probability of disaster). The basic RL engine of AlphaZero is deep Q-learning (DQN) [259–261]: a batch Q-learning method that is easily explained, and offers great flexibility to allow the inclusion of "insights from experts." Completely new in this book are convex-analytic approaches to RL that have a far stronger supporting theory and can be designed to impose bounds on performance.

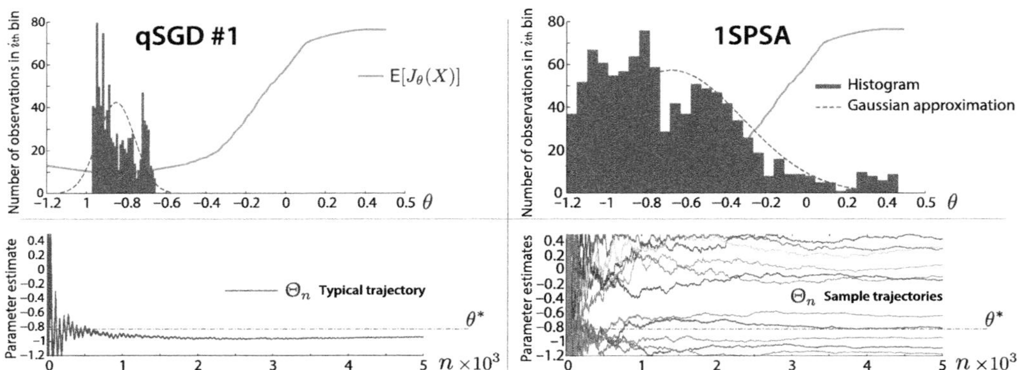

Figure 1.2 Error analysis for two policy gradient algorithms for Mountain Car, using QSA and traditional randomized exploration.

Part II might be considered a more traditional treatment of RL, since it begins with Markovian models and surveys the original TD methods developed in the 1990s. What is unique in this book is the attention to algorithm design, including ways to obtain insight in selecting "metaparameters" such as step-size gains. There is also new material, such as variance reduction methods (also known as *acceleration* techniques) for both Q-learning and actor-critic methods.

1.2 What's Missing?

The focus of the book is on control fundamentals that are most relevant to reinforcement learning, and a large collection of tools for RL algorithm design based on these fundamentals.

Some important topics will receive less attention:

(i) *Exploration.* This is a hot topic for research right now [171, 216, 244, 281, 307]. The theory is mature mainly within the subdiscipline of bandit theory. This book contains only a mention of bandit basics to explain the exploration/exploitation trade-off in RL.

(ii) *Data science.* Here I refer to the empirical side of statistics and computer engineering. Much success in RL may have been initially inspired by hardcore mathematical analysis, but success in applications requires clever computer engineers to create efficient code, and patience to test algorithms and hopefully improve them based on insight gained in particular examples.

   There are no large-scale empirical studies described in this book. Also, there is no attempt to catalog the growing list of RL algorithms.

(iii) *Machine learning topics.* The book will explain the meaning of neural networks and kernels, but ask the reader to go elsewhere for details.

Sample complexity theory is covered only briefly. There is no question that sample complexity theory is the bedrock of statistical learning theory, and the theory of bandits. However, I personally believe that its value in RL is limited: Bounds are typically loose, and

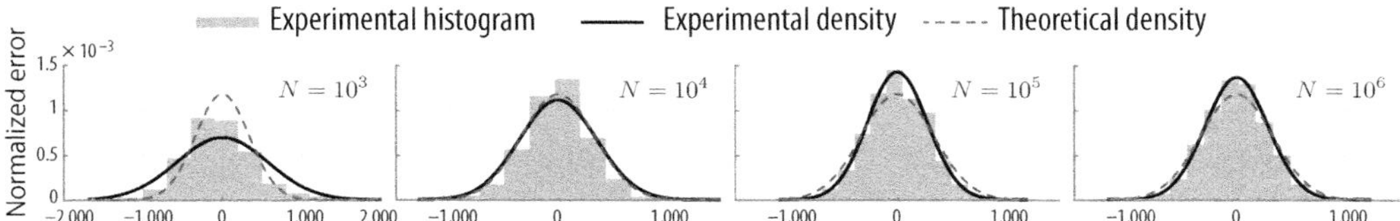

Figure 1.3 Comparison of Q-learning and relative Q-learning algorithms for the stochastic shortest path problem of [112]. The relative Q-learning algorithm is unaffected by large discounting.

to date they offer little insight for algorithm design. For example, I don't see how today's finite-n bounds will help DeepMind create better algorithms for Go or chess.

The value of asymptotic statistics is underappreciated in the RL literature. The best way to make this point is through images. Figure 1.3 is taken from [114] (many similar plots can be found in the thesis of A. Devraj [107]). Technical details regarding these plots may be found in Section 9.7.

The histograms show estimation error for a single parameter (one of many) using a particular implementation of *tabular Q-learning*. The integer N refers to the run length of the algorithm, and the histograms were obtained from 1,000 independent experiments. The "theoretical density" is what you can obtain from asymptotic statistics theory for stochastic approximation. This density is easily estimated based on limited data. In particular, in this experiment, it is clear after $N = 10^4$ samples that we have a very good variance estimate. This can then be used to obtain approximate confidence bounds after we run to $N = 10^7$ (we know how far we have to run once we have a variance estimate).

Variance theory for SA is used to decide run lengths. It is also used for algorithm *design*: for example, to adjust variables in an algorithm so that the asymptotic variance is minimized. Zap stochastic approximation and Polyak–Ruppert averaging are two examples of this approach. Outside of the bandits literature, *I am not aware of work in the sample complexity literature that can offer similar value for algorithm design in reinforcement learning.*

1.3 Resources

Many of the examples introduced in Chapters 2 and 3 are adapted from *Lecture Notes on Control System Theory and Design* [29]. The early chapters provide useful linear algebra background, but far more control theory than is needed to follow this book.

There are many great textbooks on deterministic control systems. See [15] and Murray's two-part online survey [268] for basics of modeling and design, and much more on linear control systems in [7, 76, 205]. Bertsekas [45, 46] provides a great treatment of optimal control for nonlinear systems, and an introduction to RL with a perspective that is similar to this book.

Luenberger [230] is my favorite introduction to optimization, and Boyd and Vandenberghe [73] is considered the bible, with far more depth in the domain of numerical methods. See also the new monograph of Bach [19].

The book of Sutton and Barto [338] is an encyclopedic introduction to RL. The books [44, 47, 347] are more foundational, and [289] is complementary to the treatment of RL here. The monographs [221, 360] contain essays by researchers at the intersection of RL and control. Finally, don't forget the resources at the Simons Institute website, `simons.berkeley.edu`. Videos and slides from the 2020 fall program on RL will be available whenever you have time to view a tutorial.

Part I

Fundamentals without Noise

2

Control Crash Course

A single chapter can hardly do justice to the amazing universe of control theory and practice. The textbook [15] gives an accessible introduction to the philosophy and practice of control, and is also full of history. I was fortunate to be at the Simons Institute at Berkeley, California, when one of the authors presented a two-part survey of ideas in the book.[1] These lectures are a great starting point if you are new to control systems and will inspire many old-timers.

2.1 You Have a Control Problem

You surely have encountered control problems in your daily life. If you know how to drive, then you know what it is like to be part of a control system:

y The *observations* (also called the "output") refers to the data you process in order to effectively maneuver the car through traffic: this includes your view of the streets and lights, and the sounds of angry drivers pleading with you to adjust your speed.

u You apply *inputs* to the system: steering wheel, brakes, and gas pedal are continuously adjusted based on your observations.

ϕ This symbol will be used to denote an algorithm that takes in the observations y and produces the response u. This mapping from y to u is known as a *policy*, and sometimes called a *feedback law* (the Greek letter is pronounced "*fee*").[2]

ff You are not simply reacting to horns and lights and the lines on the road. You started off with a plan: get to the farmers' market by 9 a.m. while avoiding the traffic downtown due to the demonstration. This planning is an example of *feedforward* control. Planning is based on forecasts, so inevitably plans will change as you gather information en route: traffic updates, or an invitation from a close friend to park your car and join the protest.

The feedforward component is typically defined with attention to a *reference signal* $\boldsymbol{r}$. The primary control objective is the *tracking problem*: construct a policy so that some object of interest $z(k)$ is approximately equal to $r(k)$ for all $k \geq 0$ (in control courses, it is often assumed that $z = y$).

The yelling and bumps on the road are collectively known as *disturbances*. Along with the reference signal, partial measurements of disturbances and their forecasts are taken into

[1] `https://simons.berkeley.edu/talks/murray-control-1`.

[2] My apologies to those accustomed to the symbol π. This is reserved for the irrational number.

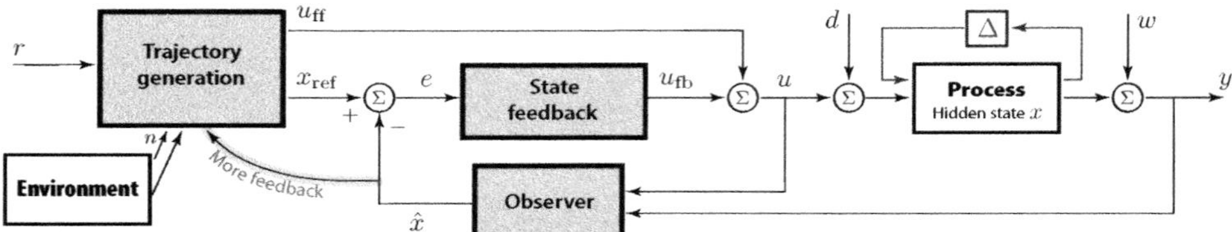

Figure 2.1 Control systems contain purely reactive feedback, as well as planning that is regularly updated. This represents two layers of feedback, differentiated in part by speed of response to new observations. These observations are often limited, so that we require estimates $\widehat{x}$ of a partially "hidden" state process x.

account in both the feedforward and the feedback components of the control system. The final input is often defined as the sum of two components:

$$u(k) = u_{\text{ff}}(k) + u_{\text{fb}}(k), \tag{2.1}$$

where in the shopping problem, u_{ff} quantifies the results of planning before heading to the market (perhaps with updates every 20 minutes), and u_{fb} is the second-by-second operation of the automobile.

The dream of RL is to mimic and surpass the skill using which humans create an internal algorithm ϕ to skillfully navigate through complex and unpredictable environments.

Figure 2.1 shows a block diagram typically used in model-based control design and illustrates a few common design choices: there is a state to be estimated using an **observer**, with state estimates denoted $\widehat{x}$. The block denoted **trajectory generation** constructs two signals: the feedforward component of the control, and also a reference x_{ref} that an internal state should track (the state is associated with the physical process). It is designed so that $x(k) = x_{\text{ref}}(k)$ for all k implies that the tracking problem is solved. The **state feedback** is designed to achieve this ideal.

There is a larger "world state" labeled **environment**, for which partial measurements are available, and forecasts of future events. Forecasts are of course important in the planning process that is part of trajectory generation.

The design of the three gray blocks is based on models of the process, the measurement (or sensor) noise w, the disturbances (such as the "input disturbance" d indicated in the figure), and a model of the environment. The "Δ-feedback loop" is a standard way to represent model uncertainty associated with the process to be controlled. This feature may be motivated by an unfortunate story.

2.1.1 Failure of an Adaptive Control System

Beginning in the 1950s, control theorists in partnership with the US Air Force looked for model-free approaches to flight control. From this came the "MIT rule," which may be regarded as an early attempt at adaptive control or "actor-only" reinforcement learning. Analysis of the MIT rule in [240] is based on techniques similar to the ODE method that is a foundation of this book. See [280] for a more recent study.

Preliminary simulations showed promise, as did field tests on the X-15 airplane. Some quotes from the 1970 report [300] hint at the enthusiasm of scientists and pilots involved:

> 1) Nearly invariant response was provided at essentially all aerodynamic flight conditions 2) accurate a priori knowledge of aircraft aerodynamic characteristics was not required to design a satisfactory system 3) aircraft configuration changes were adequately compensated for 4) the dual redundant concept provided a reliable and fail-safe system.

It was also noted that the adaptive control system "inspired confidence and allowed the pilot to spend time cross-checking flight instruments, checking subsystems, and 'sight-seeing.'"

These observations followed 65 test flights.

The control system was not robust enough to provide stable control in all situations encountered. Sadly, a pilot died in a crash attributed to oscillations induced by the adaptive system. The research program was shut down, but the tragedy inspired greater attention to robustness in control design.

It should go without saying that *every control engineer or practicing economist must study failures.* Airplanes and economies inevitably crash. In the long run, it is a greater tragedy if the experts do not bother to learn from disaster.

2.2 What to Do about It?

The vast literature on control solutions is built upon a model of input–output behavior that is used to design the policy ϕ. Modeling and control design are each an art form, with many possible solutions from vast statistics and control tool chests.

When we say *model*, we mean a sequence of mappings from inputs to outputs:

$$y(k) = \mathrm{G}_k(u(0),u(1),u(2),\ldots,u(k)), \qquad k \geq 0. \tag{2.2}$$

Each of the functions G_k may also depend on *exogenous variables* (outside of our control), such as the weather and traffic conditions. And here we come to one of the most vital principles of control design: *the model must capture essential properties of the system to be controlled*, and simultaneously *be simple enough to be useful.*

For example, aerospace engineers will create *absurdly simple models* for the design of flight control systems and from this create a policy ϕ designed to work well for the model. Of course, they do not stop there. The next step is to create an entirely new model for validation and simulate under a range of scenarios in order to answer a range of questions: What happens when the plane is full, empty, or flying through a thunderstorm? How does the control system perform after an engine detaches from a wing? If one of these tests fails, then the control engineer goes back to either improve the model, improve the policy, or *improve the airplane.* That's right, we may require additional sensors to measure pitch angles, or more powerful motors to control ailerons, flaps, or elevators.

I am writing without any knowledge of aerospace engineering. I am describing general principles for anyone interested in control design:

(1) Create a model for control.
(2) Design the policy ϕ based on the model.
(3) Simulate based on a high-fidelity model, and then revisit steps 1 and 2.

The success of this approach has been tremendous, as seen in the history recounted in [15].

Linear and Time Invariant Model. The most successful class of *absurdly simple models* are linear and time invariant (LTI). The general scalar LTI model is defined by a sequence of scalars $\{b_i\}$ (the *impulse response*), and for a given scalar input sequence $\boldsymbol{u}$, the model defines $y(k)$ as the sum

$$y(k) = \sum_{i=0}^{k} b_i u(k-i)\,, \qquad k \geq 0. \tag{2.3}$$

This is in fact too complex in many situations. A more tractable subclass of LTI models are autoregressive moving-average (ARMA): for scalar coefficients $\{a_i, b_i\}$,

$$y(k) = -\sum_{i=1}^{N} a_i y(k-i) + \sum_{i=0}^{M} b_i u(k-i)\,, \qquad k \geq 0. \tag{2.4}$$

A linear input–output model motivates the design of a policy ϕ that has a similar linear form. A common design technique based on optimization will be described in the following chapters, beginning in Section 3.6.

2.3 State Space Models

2.3.1 Sufficient Statistics and the Nonlinear State Space Model

In statistics, the term *sufficient statistic* is used to denote a quantity that summarizes all past observations. The *state* plays an analogous role in control theory.

A *state space model* requires the following ingredients: the *state space* X on which the state $\boldsymbol{x}$ evolves, and an *input space* (or *action space*) denoted U on which the input $\boldsymbol{u}$ evolves. We may have additional constraints coupling the state and the input, which is modeled via

$$u(k) \in \mathsf{U}(x)\,, \qquad \text{when } x(k) = x \in \mathsf{X}, \tag{2.5}$$

with $\mathsf{U}(x) \subseteq \mathsf{U}$ for each x. We might also want to model an observation process $\boldsymbol{y}$ evolving on a set Y. In the control theory literature, it is common to assume that X, U, and Y are subsets of Euclidean space, while in operations research and reinforcement learning it is more common to assume these are finite sets. Whenever possible, in this book we prefer the control perspective so that we can more easily search for structure of control solutions: For example, is an optimal input a continuous function of the state?

Next we require two functions $\mathrm{F}\colon \mathsf{X}\times\mathsf{U} \to \mathsf{X}$ and $\mathrm{G}\colon \mathsf{X}\times\mathsf{U} \to \mathsf{Y}$ that define the following state equations:

$$x(k+1) = \mathrm{F}(x(k), u(k)), \qquad x(0) = x_0, \tag{2.6a}$$

$$y(k) = \mathrm{G}(x(k), u(k)). \tag{2.6b}$$

An LTI model can often be transformed into a state space model in which the two functions F, G are linear in (x, u).

We might also allow F, G to depend upon the time variable k. It is argued in Section 3.3 that it is often more convenient to simply assume that the state $x(k)$ includes k as one component.

However, there is one example of a time-dependent model that highlights the role of state as a sufficient statistic. The general input–output model (2.2) always has a state space description, in which the state is the full history of the following inputs:

$$x(k+1) = [u(0),u(1),u(2),\ldots,u(k)]^{\intercal}. \tag{2.7}$$

We have $x(k+1) = \mathrm{F}_k(x(k),u(k))$, defined by concatenation, and $y(k) = \mathrm{G}_k(x(k),u(k))$ is a restatement of (2.2). For this deterministic model in which the input fully determines the output, (2.7) is called the (full) *history state*. A practical state space model can be regarded as a compression of the history state.[3]

In many cases, we can construct a good policy via *state feedback*, $u(k) = \phi(x(k))$, for some $\phi\colon \mathbb{R}^n \to \mathbb{R}$; in stochastic control, it is typical to say that ϕ is a *Markov policy* in this case. However, the power of this approach is fully realized only if we are flexible in our definition of the state. We won't be using the full history state because of complexity; what's more, *the "full history" may not be nearly rich enough.*

2.3.2 State Augmentation and Learning

Tracking and disturbance rejection are two of the basic goals in control design. Here we provide a brief glimpse of two tricks used to simultaneously track the reference $\boldsymbol{r}$ while rejecting disturbances:

(i) The definition of state is not sacred; invent a state process that simplifies control design.
(ii) Unknown quantities, including disturbances and even the state space model, can be learned based on input–output measurements.

Let's maintain our simplifying assumption that the input and output are scalar valued, and take $\mathsf{X} = \mathbb{R}^n$. The state evolution is also influenced by a scalar disturbance $\boldsymbol{d}$ that is outside our control, which requires a modification of (2.6a):

$$x(k+1) = \mathrm{F}(x(k),u(k),d(k)). \tag{2.8}$$

The ultimate goal is to achieve these three objectives simultaneously.

(a) Tracking: With $\tilde{y}(k) = y(k) - r(k)$,

$$\limsup_{k\to\infty} |\tilde{y}(k)| = e_\infty, \qquad \text{with } e_\infty = 0, \text{ or very small.} \tag{2.9}$$

(b) Disturbance rejection: The error e_∞ is not highly sensitive to the disturbance $\boldsymbol{d}$.
(c) Tuned transient response (you probably know what kind of acceleration "feels right" when driving a car).

A common special case is when the reference and disturbance are assumed independent of time (e.g., driving at constant speed with a steady headwind). In this special case, suppose in addition that the disturbance is known. We might choose $u(k) = \phi(x(k),r(0),d(0))$, where the policy ϕ is designed for success: $e_\infty = 0$. Typically, ϕ is designed so that the state is also convergent: $x(k) \to x(\infty)$ as $k \to \infty$. The limiting values must satisfy

[3] See [337] and its references.

$$x(\infty) = \mathrm{F}(x(\infty), u(\infty), d(0)),$$
$$u(\infty) = \phi(x(\infty), r(0), d(0)).$$

The outcome $e_\infty = 0$ is expressed as the final constraint:

$$r(0) = y(\infty) = \mathrm{G}(x(\infty), u(\infty)).$$

This approach is thus dependent on an accurate model, as well as direct measurements of $\boldsymbol{d}$.

Suppose that instead of exact measurements of the disturbance, we have a state space model whose output is $y_\mathrm{m}(k) = (r(k), d(k))^\intercal$:

$$z(k+1) = \mathrm{F_m}(z(k)), \tag{2.10a}$$
$$y_\mathrm{m}(k) = \mathrm{G_m}(z(k)), \tag{2.10b}$$

where $\boldsymbol{z}$ evolves on $\mathbb{R}^p$ for some integer $p \geq 1$. The functions $\mathrm{F_m} : \mathbb{R}^p \to \mathbb{R}^p$ and $\mathrm{G_m} : \mathbb{R}^p \to \mathbb{R}$ are assumed known. Part of this state description is $d(k+1) = d(k)$ if the disturbance is static.

Given the larger state space model (2.8, 2.10), we might opt for an *observer*-based solution:

$$u(k) = \phi(x(k), r(k), \hat{d}(k)),$$

where $\{\hat{d}(k)\}$ are estimates of the disturbance, based on input–output measurements up to time k (we might replace $x(k)$ with $\hat{x}(k)$ if we don't directly observe the state). Observer design makes up about 20% of a typical introductory course on state space control systems [7, 29, 76].

A second option, called the Internal Model Principle, is to create a different state augmentation that is entirely observed. For the sake of illustration, consider again the case of constant reference/disturbance. We have (2.10) in this case with $z(k) = y_\mathrm{m}(k)$, and $\mathrm{F_m}$ is the identity function:

$$z(k+1) = z(k).$$

State augmentation is performed based on this model: define for each k,

$$z'(k+1) = z'(k) + \tilde{y}(k), \tag{2.11}$$

with error $\tilde{y}(k+1)$ defined above (2.9). We regard $(x(k), z'(k))$ as the state for the purposes of control, and hence state feedback takes the form

$$u(k) = \phi(x(k), z'(k)). \tag{2.12}$$

The control design (2.12) is an example of *integral* control, since z' is the sum of errors (the discrete-time analog of integration).

Suppose that $z'(k)$ converges to some finite limit $z'(\infty)$, as $k \to \infty$; the value of the limit is irrelevant. This and (2.11) imply perfect tracking:

$$\lim_{k\to\infty} \tilde{y}(k) = \lim_{k\to\infty} [z'(k+1) - z'(k)] = 0.$$

This conclusion is remarkable: to obtain perfect tracking, we only require that the policy ϕ is designed so that $z'(k)$ converges to *some* finite limit. The secret to success is a hidden element of "learning" that comes with integral control.

State augmentation has many other dimensions. If we have forecasts of significant disturbances, then it may be wise to make use of these data: forecasts can be used in the design of the feedforward component $u_{\text{ff}}(k)$ in the decomposition (2.1), or they may be used for state augmentation.

2.3.3 Linear State Space Model

When F and G are linear, we obtain the linear state space model:

$$x(k+1) = Fx(k) + Gu(k), \qquad x(0) = x_0, \tag{2.13a}$$

$$y(k) = Hx(k) + Eu(k), \tag{2.13b}$$

where (F,G,H,E) are matrices of suitable dimension (in particular, F is $n \times n$ for an n-dimensional state space).

The state space model is not unique, in the sense that there are many choices for (F,G,H,E) that result in the same input–output behavior, even though the definition of the state process $\boldsymbol{x}$ will change depending on the model. And never forget, *we may add additional components to $x(k)$ as a means to solve a control problem.*

Linear State Feedback

The linear model (2.13) is often constructed so that the goal is to keep $x(k)$ near the origin – the *regulation problem*; consider, for example, flight control, where we wish to maintain velocity and altitude at some constant values. We first normalize the problem so that these constant values are *zero*. It is then common to apply a linear control law

$$u(k) = -Kx(k), \tag{2.14}$$

where K is called the *gain matrix*. To evaluate choice of gain, we tack on something like a reference signal:

$$u(k) = -Kx(k) + v(k).$$

The *closed-loop behavior* with new "input $\boldsymbol{v}$" has a similar state space description:

$$x(k+1) = (F - GK)x(k) + Gv(k), \qquad x(0) = x_0, \tag{2.15a}$$

$$y(k) = (C - EK)x(k) + Ev(k). \tag{2.15b}$$

The signal $v(k)$ appearing in (2.15a) is viewed as an "input disturbance." A goal of control is to choose K so that the closed-loop behavior is not very sensitive to this disturbance while simultaneously ensuring good tracking.

Realization Theory

The ARMA model (2.4) admits an infinite number of distinct state space descriptions. Let's begin with the scalar auto-regressive model:

$$y(k) = -\sum_{i=1}^{N} a_i y(k-i) + u(k), \qquad k \geq 0$$

which is (2.4), with $M = 0$ and $b_0 = 1$. We obtain the state space model (2.13) with $n = N$ by choosing $x(k) = (y(k), \dots, y(k-N+1))^{\intercal}$, and

$$F = \begin{bmatrix} -a_1 & -a_2 & -a_3 & \cdots & \cdots & -a_N \\ 1 & 0 & 0 & \cdots & \cdots & 0 \\ 0 & 1 & 0 & \cdots & \cdots & 0 \\ 0 & 0 & 1 & \cdots & \cdots & 0 \\ \vdots & & & \ddots & & \vdots \\ 0 & 0 & 0 & \cdots & 1 & 0 \end{bmatrix}, \qquad G = \begin{bmatrix} 1 \\ 0 \\ 0 \\ 0 \\ \vdots \\ 0 \end{bmatrix}, \tag{2.16}$$

$H = [1, 0, 0, \dots, 0]$, and $E = 0$.

This construction can be generalized: with $M = N - 1$ in (2.4), we first define an intermediate process

$$z(k) = -\sum_{i=1}^{N} a_i z(k-i) + u(k), \qquad k \geq 0. \tag{2.17}$$

So we arrive at a state space model with state space $x(k) = (z(k), \dots, z(k-N+1))^{\intercal}$ to describe the evolution of $\boldsymbol{z}$. We next use the assumption that $M = N - 1$: setting $u(k) = z(k) = 0$ for $k < 0$, it is possible to show that

$$y(k) = \sum_{i=0}^{N-1} b_i z(k-i) = Hx(k) + Eu(k),$$

where

$$H = [b_0, b_1, \dots, b_{N-1}], \qquad E = 0. \tag{2.18}$$

The state space description (2.16, 2.18) is known as *controllable canonical form*. There are many other "canonical forms," with special properties you can learn about in a linear systems course [7, 15, 29, 76, 205].

2.3.4 A Nod to Newton and Leibniz

In many engineering applications, it is best to start off in continuous time, with thanks to Newton and Leibnitz for bringing us calculus.

Some notational conventions reserved for continuous time: First, time is denoted using a subscript (such as u_t rather than $u(t)$) as a reminder that time is continuous. Moreover, it is often convenient to suppress time dependency altogether, so that $\frac{d}{dt}u$ represents the derivative at an unspecified time.

The state space model in continuous time has the form

$$\tfrac{d}{dt}x = \mathrm{f}(x, u), \tag{2.19}$$

where x is the state evolving in $\mathbb{R}^n$, and u the input evolving in $\mathbb{R}^m$. The motion of a typical solution to a nonlinear state space model in $\mathbb{R}^2$ is illustrated in Figure 2.2.

When the function f appearing in (2.19) is linear, then we obtain the linear state space model in continuous time. As in (2.13), this is accompanied by an observation process $\boldsymbol{y}$ evolving on $\mathbb{R}^p$:

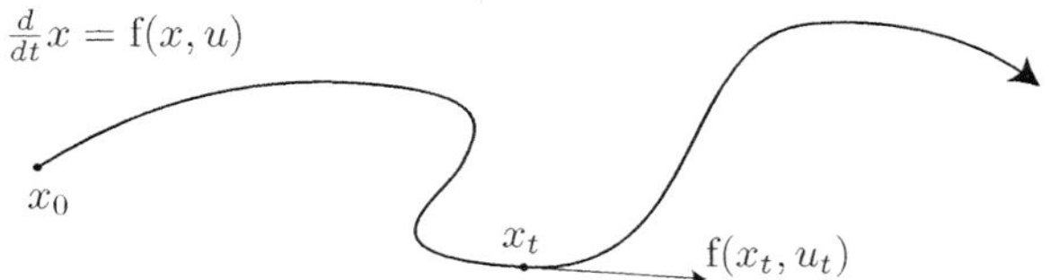

Figure 2.2 Trajectory of a nonlinear state space model in two dimensions: at any time t, the velocity $\frac{d}{dt}x_t$ is a function of the current state x_t and input u_t.

$$\frac{d}{dt}x = Ax + Bu, \tag{2.20a}$$

$$y = Cx + Du, \tag{2.20b}$$

and A,B,C,D are matrices of appropriate dimensions.

The geometry illustrated in Figure 2.2 is sometimes valuable in gaining intuition in control design (note that the vector $\mathrm{f}(x_t,u_t)$ is tangent to the state trajectory). Stability theory and optimal control theory are most attractive in the continuous time domain because of this simple geometry, and the simplicity that comes with calculus.

However, in the end we have to sample time to apply our control and learning algorithms. In this book, we will opt for an Euler approximation. For sampling interval Δ, the discrete time approximation of (2.19) is of the form (2.6a), with $\mathrm{F}(x,u) = x + \Delta\mathrm{f}(x,u)$. For the linear model (2.20a), this leads to $F = I + \Delta A$.

2.4 Stability and Performance

In this section, we consider the state space model (2.6a) in a *closed loop*: a policy ϕ is chosen, so that $u(k) = \phi(x(k))$ for each k. Since the feedback law is fixed, the state then evolves as a state space model without control. With just a slight abuse of notation, we write

$$x(k+1) = \mathrm{F}(x(k)), \qquad k \geq 0. \tag{2.21}$$

Our interest is in the long-run behavior of the state process; in particular, does it converge to an *equilibrium*? We also seek bounds on a particular performance metric called the *total cost*.

The following is assumed throughout:

$$\textit{The state space } \mathsf{X} \textit{ is equal to } \mathbb{R}^n\textit{, or a closed subset.} \tag{2.22}$$

For example, we allow the positive orthant, $\mathsf{X} = \mathbb{R}^n_+$. The restriction on the state space (2.22) is imposed so that any closed and bounded set $S \subset \mathsf{X}$ is necessarily a compact subset of X.

The definition of an equilibrium x^e is straightforward – it is a state at which the system is frozen:

$$x^e = \mathrm{F}(x^e). \tag{2.23}$$

The equilibrium will in fact be a part of the control design. Think of the cruise control in your car, in which "equilibrium" means traveling in a straight line at constant speed. The particular speed is something that you as the driver will choose. The control system then does the best it can to keep $x(k)$ near the desired value x^e.

2.4.1 Total Cost

This performance metric is based on a function $c\colon \mathsf{X} \to \mathbb{R}_+$, interpreted as the "cost function under policy ϕ," to be considered in greater depth in Chapter 3. Based on this, we arrive at a strange but ubiquitous definition: the total cost is a function of x, known as the (fixed policy) *value function*, and defined as the infinite sum:

$$J(x) = \sum_{k=0}^{\infty} c(x(k)), \qquad x(0) = x \in \mathsf{X}. \tag{2.24}$$

It is assumed that $c(x^e) = 0$, and we seek conditions ensuring that $x(k) \to x^e$ as $k \to \infty$, so there is some hope that J is finite valued. For the cruise control problem, the cost function is designed so that $c(x)$ is large if the state x corresponds to a speed that is far from desired.

Why Is the Controls Community So Excited about Total Cost? This metric for performance is not very intuitive, but there are compelling reasons for using it as a performance metric in control design:

(i) It is "forward looking." One might argue that (2.24) is looking too far foward (who cares about infinity?), but there is implicit "discounting" of the future since for a good policy we have $c(x(k)) \to 0$ quickly as $k \to \infty$.
(ii) Theory for total cost optimal control is often closely related to average cost optimal control – to be seen in Part II of the book.
(iii) If J is finite valued, then stability is typically guaranteed.

Benefit (iii) is the most abstract, but the most valuable aspect of this performance metric. Section 2.4.2 is dedicated to stability theory and its relationship to value functions. A part of this theory is based on the (fixed policy) dynamic programming equation:[4]

$$J(x) = c(x) + J(\mathrm{F}(x)). \tag{2.25}$$

This can be derived from the definition (2.24), written as

$$J(x) = c(x) + \sum_{k=0}^{\infty} c(x^+(k)),$$

where $\boldsymbol{x}^+$ is the solution to (2.21), starting at $x^+(0) = \mathrm{F}(x)$.

2.4.2 Stability of Equilibria

We survey here the most common definitions of stability for a nonlinear state space model. The first and most basic is a form of continuity near the equilibrium x^e. Let $\mathcal{X}(k; x_0)$ denote the state at time k with initial condition x_0: this is simply $x(k)$, obtained recursively from (2.21), starting at $x(0) = x_0$. In particular, the equilibrium property (2.23) implies that $\mathcal{X}(k; x^e) = x^e$ for all k.

[4] *Dynamic programming equation* and *Bellman equation* are used interchangeably, in reverence to [35].

Stable in the Sense of Lyapunov. The equilibrium x^e is stable in the sense of Lyapunov if for all $\varepsilon > 0$, there exists $\delta > 0$ such that if $\|x_0 - x^e\| < \delta$, then

$$\|\mathcal{X}(k;x_0) - \mathcal{X}(k;x^e)\| < \varepsilon \qquad \text{for all } k \geq 0.$$

In words, if an initial condition is close to the equilibrium, then it will stay close forever. An illustration is provided in Figure 2.3, with $B(r) = \{x \in \mathbb{R}^n : \|x - x^e\| < r\}$ for any $r > 0$.

This is a very weak notion of stability, since there is no guarantee that the state will ever approach the desired equilibrium. The next definitions impose convergence:

Asymptotic Stability. An equilibrium x^e is said to be *asymptotically stable* if x^e is stable in the sense of Lyapunov and for some $\delta_0 > 0$, whenever $\|x_0 - x^e\| < \delta_0$,

$$\lim_{k\to\infty} \mathcal{X}(k;x_0) = x^e. \tag{2.26}$$

The set of x_0 for which the preceding limit holds is called the *region of attraction* for x^e.

The equilibrium is *globally asymptotically stable* if the region of attraction is all of X: that is, $\delta_0 = \infty$, and hence $x(k) \to x^e$ from any initial condition.

It is common to say that the state space model is globally asymptotically stable. That is, it is often stressed that this is a property of the system (2.21) rather than the equilibrium $x^e \in \mathsf{X}$.

Sometimes we obtain a very fast rate of convergence: the state space model is said to be *globally exponentially asymptotically stable* if there are constants $\varrho_0 > 0$ and $B_0 < \infty$ such that for each initial condition and $k \geq 0$,

$$\|\mathcal{X}(k;x_0) - x^e\| \leq B_0\|x_0 - x^e\|e^{-\varrho_0 k}. \tag{2.27}$$

2.4.3 Lyapunov Functions

The construction of a *Lyapunov function* V is the most common approach to establishing asymptotic stability, as well as bounds on a value function (and more general bounds on the state process). In broad generality, V is a function on X taking nonnegative values, and the crucial property that makes it a Lyapunov function is that $V(x(k))$ is decreasing when $x(k)$ is large: this is formalized as a *drift inequality*. The Lyapunov function V is often regarded as a crude notion of "distance" to the "center of the state space."

For any scalar r, let $S_V(r)$ denote the *sublevel set*:

$$S_V(r) = \{x \in \mathsf{X} : V(x) \leq r\}. \tag{2.28}$$

In addition to the nonnegativity of V, we frequently assume it is *inf-compact*:

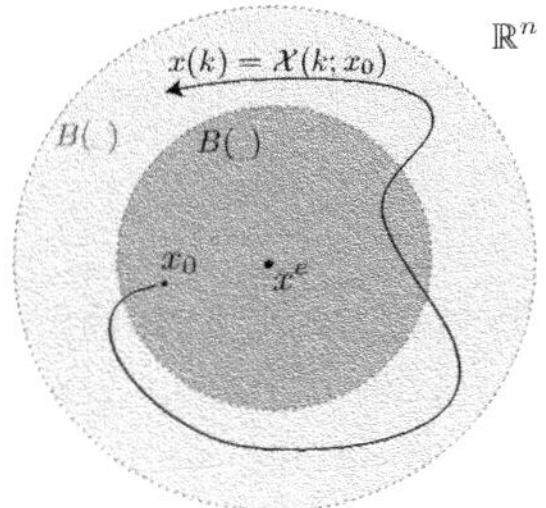

Figure 2.3 If $x_0 \in B(\delta)$, then $\mathcal{X}(k;x_0) \in B(\varepsilon)$ for all $k \geq 0$.

$$\{x \in \mathsf{X} : V(x) \le V(x^0)\} \text{ is a bounded set for each } x^0 \in \mathsf{X}.$$

That is, the set $S_V(r)$ takes on one of three forms for any r: the empty set, $S_V(r) = \mathsf{X}$, or $S_V(r) \subset \mathsf{X}$ is bounded.

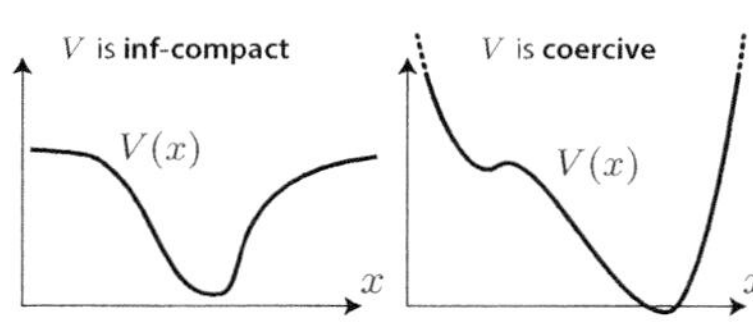

Figure 2.4 Inf-compact and coercive.

In most cases, we find that $S_V(r) = \mathsf{X}$ is impossible, so that we arrive at the stronger *coercive* assumption:

$$\lim_{\|x\|\to\infty} V(x) = \infty. \tag{2.29}$$

In this case, under our standing assumption (2.22), the set $S_V(r)$ is either empty or bounded for each r. Figure 2.4 illustrates the two classes of functions with $\mathsf{X} = \mathbb{R}$ (the function shown on the left is bounded). Here are three numerical examples:

(i) $V(x) = x^2$ is coercive since (2.29) holds.
(ii) $V(x) = x^2/(1+x^2)$ is inf-compact but not coercive: $S_V(r) = \mathbb{R}$ for $r \ge 1$, and $S_V(r) = [-a,a]$ (a bounded interval) for $0 \le r < 1$, with $a = \sqrt{r/(1-r)}$.
(iii) $V(x) = e^x$ is neither: $S_V(r) = (-\infty, \log(r)]$ is not a bounded subset of $\mathbb{R}$ for $r > 0$.

The value function J satisfies the intuitive properties of a Lyapunov function under mild conditions:

Lemma 2.1 *Suppose that the cost function* c *and the value function* J *defined in* (2.24) *are nonnegative and finite valued. Then,*

(i) $J(x(k))$ *is nonincreasing, and* $\lim_{k\to\infty} J(x(k)) = 0$ *for each initial condition.*
(ii) *Suppose in addition that* J *is continuous, inf-compact, and vanishes only at* x^e. *Then, for each initial condition,* $\lim_{k\to\infty} x(k) = x^e$.

The proof is postponed to Section 2.4.4, but we note here the first steps: the dynamic programming equation (2.25) implies that for each $k \ge 0$,

$$J(x(k+1)) = J(x(k)) - c(x(k)) \le J(x(k)). \tag{2.30}$$

That is, $J(x(k))$ is nonincreasing, so that $x(k) \in S_J(r)$ for each $k \ge 0$, with $r = J(x(0))$. The inf-compact assumption then implies that the state trajectory is "bottled-up" in the bounded set $S_J(r)$.

In the context of total-cost optimal control, the basic drift inequality considered in this book is *Poisson's inequality*: for nonnegative functions $V, c \colon \mathsf{X} \to \mathbb{R}_+$, and a constant $\overline{\eta} \ge 0$,

$$V(\mathrm{F}(x)) \le V(x) - c(x) + \overline{\eta}. \tag{2.31}$$

The reference to a French mathematician is explained in the notes. Poisson's inequality is a relaxation of the dynamic programming equation (2.25) through the introduction of $\overline{\eta}$, as well as the inequality.

Poisson's inequality is defined with attention to the dynamics: on combining (2.31) and (2.21), we obtain (similar to (2.30))

$$V(x(k+1)) \le V(x(k)) - c(x(k)) + \overline{\eta}, \qquad k \ge 0.$$

If $\overline{\eta} = 0$, it follows that the sequence $\{V(x(k) : k \geq 0\}$ is nonincreasing. Under mild assumptions on V, we obtain a weak form of stability:

Proposition 2.2 *Suppose that* (2.31) *holds with* $\overline{\eta} = 0$. *Suppose moreover that* V *is continuous, inf-compact, and has a unique minimum at* x^e. *Then the equilibrium is stable in the sense of Lyapunov.*

Proof From the definition of the sublevel sets, we obtain

$$\bigcap\{S_V(r) : r > V(x^e)\} = S_V(r)\Big|_{r=V(x^e)} = \{x^e\}.$$

The final equality follows from the assumption that x^e is the unique minimizer of V. The inf-compact assumption then implies the following inner and outer approximations: for each $\varepsilon > 0$, we can find $r > V(x^e)$ and $\delta < \varepsilon$ such that[5]

$$\{x \in \mathsf{X} : \|x - x^e\| < \delta\} \subset S_V(r) \subset \{x \in \mathsf{X} : \|x - x^e\| < \varepsilon\}.$$

If $\|x_0 - x^e\| < \delta$, then $x_0 \in S_V(r)$, and hence $x(k) \in S_V(r)$ for all $k \geq 0$ since $V(x(k))$ is nonincreasing. The preceding final inclusion then implies that $\|x(k) - x^e\| < \varepsilon$ for all k. Stability in the sense of Lyapunov follows. □

Bounds on the value function J are obtained by iteration: for example, the two bounds

$$V(x(2)) \leq V(x(1)) - c(x(1)) + \overline{\eta}, \quad V(x(1)) \leq V(x(0)) - c(x(0)) + \overline{\eta}$$

imply that $V(x(2)) \leq V(x(0)) - c(x(0)) - c(x(1)) + 2\overline{\eta}$. We can of course go further:

Proposition 2.3 ((Comparison Theorem)) *Poisson's inequality* (2.31) *implies the following bounds:*

(i) *For each* $\mathcal{N} \geq 1$ *and* $x = x(0)$,

$$V(x(\mathcal{N})) + \sum_{k=0}^{\mathcal{N}-1} c(x(k)) \leq V(x) + \mathcal{N}\overline{\eta}. \tag{2.32}$$

(ii) *If* $\overline{\eta} = 0$, *then* $J(x) \leq V(x)$ *for all* x.

(iii) *Suppose that* $\overline{\eta} = 0$, *and that* V, c *are continuous. Suppose moreover that* c *is inf-compact, and vanishes only at* x^e. *Then the equilibrium is globally asymptotically stable.* □

The proof is found in Section 2.4.4.

Proposition 2.3 raises a question: what if Poisson's inequality is tight, so that the inequality in (2.31) is replaced by equality? Consider this ideal with $\overline{\eta} = 0$, and use the more suggestive notation $V = J^\circ$ for the Lyapunov function:

$$J^\circ(\mathrm{F}(x)) = J^\circ(x) - c(x). \tag{2.33}$$

If J° is nonnegative valued, then we can take $V = J^\circ$ in Proposition 2.3 to obtain the upper bound $J(x) \leq J^\circ(x)$ for all x. Equality requires further assumptions:

[5] This conclusion requires a bit of topology: the characterization of compact sets in terms of "open coverings." If this is new to you, don't worry: topology is not a prerequisite for this book. In the future, you might want to take a first-year mathematical analysis course.

Proposition 2.4 *Suppose that* (2.33) *holds, along with the following assumptions:*

(i) *J is continuous, inf-compact, and vanishes only at x^e.*
(ii) *J° is continuous.*

Then, $J(x) = J^\circ(x) - J^\circ(x^e)$ for each x.

2.4.4 Technical Proofs

To establish Propositions 2.3 and 2.4, we first require Lemma 2.1.

Proof of Lemma 2.1 We begin with the sample path representation of (2.25):

$$J(x(k+1)) - J(x(k)) + c(x(k)) = 0. \tag{2.34}$$

Summing each side from $k = 0$ to $\mathcal{N} - 1$ gives for each $x = x(0)$, and each $\mathcal{N}$,

$$J(x) = J(x(\mathcal{N})) + \sum_{k=0}^{\mathcal{N}-1} c(x(k)).$$

On taking limits, we obtain

$$J(x) = \lim_{\mathcal{N}\to\infty} \Big\{ J(x(\mathcal{N})) + \sum_{k=0}^{\mathcal{N}-1} c(x(k)) \Big\} = \Big\{ \lim_{\mathcal{N}\to\infty} J(x(\mathcal{N})) \Big\} + J(x),$$

which implies (i) under the assumption that $J(x)$ is finite.

The inf-compact assumption in (ii) is imposed to ensure that the state trajectory evolves in a bounded set: (2.30) implies that $x(k) \in S_J(r)$ for the particular value $r = J(x(0))$, and each $k \geq 0$. Suppose that $\{x(k_i) : i \geq 0\}$ is a convergent subsequence of the state trajectory, with limit x^∞. Then $J(x^\infty) = \lim_{i\to\infty} J(x(k_i)) = 0$ follows by continuity of J.

The assumption that J vanishes only at x^e implies that $x^\infty = x^e$. Part (ii) follows, since every convergent subsequence reaches the same value x^e. □

Proof of Proposition 2.3 The bound (2.32) is established following the discussion preceding the proposition. We begin with the sample path representation of (2.31), similar to (2.34):

$$V(x(k+1)) - V(x(k)) + c(x(k)) \leq \overline{\eta}. \tag{2.35}$$

Summing each side from $k = 0$ to $\mathcal{N} - 1$ gives (i):

$$V(x(\mathcal{N})) - V(x(0)) + \sum_{k=0}^{\mathcal{N}-1} c(x(k)) \leq \overline{\eta}\mathcal{N}.$$

Part (ii) follows since $V(x(\mathcal{N})) \geq 0$ for each $\mathcal{N}$, so that when $\overline{\eta} = 0$ we obtain from the preceding bound

$$\sum_{k=0}^{\mathcal{N}-1} c(x(k)) \leq V(x(0)).$$

The proof of (iii) is identical to Lemma 2.1: part (ii) implies that $\lim_{k\to\infty} c(x(k)) = 0$, and the assumptions on c then imply that $x(k) \to x^e$ as $k \to \infty$.

It remains to show that x^e is stable in the sense of Lyapunov. To see this, first observe that with $\overline{\eta} = 0$, the bound (2.31) implies that $V \geq c$, so that V is also inf-compact. The bound (2.31), and conditions on $c, \overline{\eta}$, also imply that $V(x(k))$ is strictly decreasing when $x(k) \neq x^e$. Continuity of V implies that $V(x(k)) \downarrow V(x^e)$ for each $x(0)$, so that $V(x^e) < V(x(0))$ for all $x(0) \in \mathsf{X}$. Stability in the sense of Lypapunov then follows from Proposition 2.2. □

Proof of Proposition 2.4 The proof begins with iteration, as in Proposition 2.3:

$$J^\circ(x(\mathcal{N})) + \sum_{k=0}^{\mathcal{N}-1} c(x(k)) = J^\circ(x).$$

Lemma 2.1 (ii) and continuity of J° implies that $J^\circ(x(\mathcal{N})) \to J^\circ(x^e)$ as $\mathcal{N} \to \infty$, which implies the desired identity: $J^\circ(x^e) + J(x) = J^\circ(x)$. □

2.4.5 Geometry in Continuous Time

Let's briefly consider an analog of (2.21) in continuous time, with state evolving on $\mathsf{X} = \mathbb{R}^n$:

$$\frac{d}{dt}x_t = \mathrm{f}(x_t), \tag{2.36}$$

where $\mathrm{f}\colon \mathbb{R}^d \to \mathbb{R}^d$ is called the *vector field*. It is common to suppress the time index, writing $\frac{d}{dt}x = \mathrm{f}(x)$.

We let $\mathcal{X}(t; x_0)$ denote the solution to (2.36) at time t, when we need to emphasize dependency on the initial condition x_0. The definition of asymptotic stability of an equilibrium x^e is the same as for the state space model in discrete time (2.21). The equilibrium is globally asymptotically stable if, in addition,

$$\lim_{t\to\infty} \mathcal{X}(t; x_0) = x^e, \qquad \text{for all } x_0 \in \mathsf{X}.$$

Verification of global asymptotic stability invites the following assumptions, generalizing the theory in discrete time. Recall that $V\colon \mathbb{R}^n \to \mathbb{R}$ is *continuously differentiable* (or C^1) if the gradient ∇V exists and is continuous.

Lyapunov Function for Global Asymptotic Stability

- V is nonnegative valued and C^1.
- It is inf-compact (recall the definition that follows (2.28)).
- For any solution x, whenever $x_t \neq x^e$,

$$\frac{d}{dt}V(x_t) < 0. \tag{2.37}$$

Naturally, $\frac{d}{dt}V(x_t) = 0$ if $x_t = x^e$: in this case, $V(x_{t+s}) = V(x^e)$ for all $s \geq 0$.

Figure 2.5 illustrates the meaning of the vector field f for the special case $\mathsf{X} = \mathbb{R}^2$, and the figure is intended to emphasize the fact that $V(x_t)$ is nonincreasing when V is a Lyapunov function. The drift condition (2.37) can be expressed in functional form,

$$\langle \nabla V(x), \mathrm{f}(x) \rangle < 0, \qquad x \neq x^e. \tag{2.38}$$

This is illustrated geometrically in Figure 2.6.

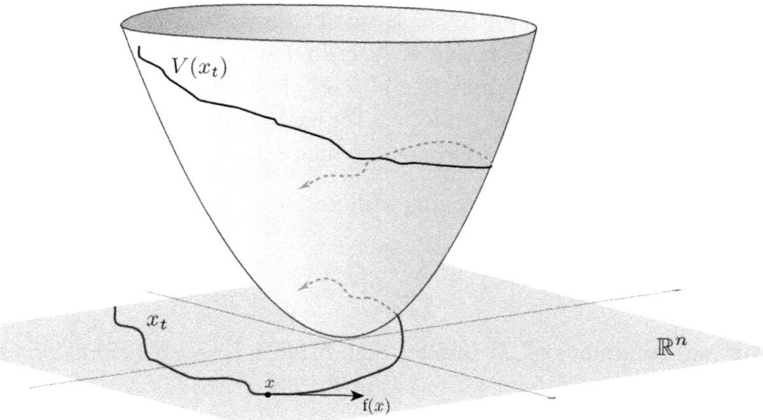

Figure 2.5 If V is a Lyapunov function, then $V(x_t)$ is nonincreasing with time.

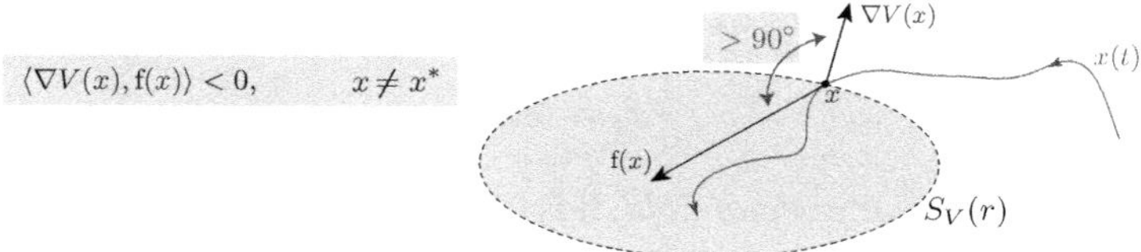

Figure 2.6 Geometric interpretations of a Lyapunov drift condition: the gradient $\nabla V(x)$ is orthogonal to the level set $\{y : V(y) = V(x)\}$, which is the boundary of the set $S_V(r)$ with $r = V(x)$.

Proposition 2.5 *If there exists a Lyapunov function V satisfying the assumptions for global asymptotic stability, then the equilibrium x^e is globally asymptotically stable.* □

Proposition 2.5 is a partial extension of Proposition 2.3 to the continuous time model. A full extension requires a version of Poisson's inequality. Suppose that $c\colon \mathbb{R}^n \to \mathbb{R}_+$ is continuous, $V\colon \mathbb{R}^n \to \mathbb{R}_+$ is continuously differentiable, and $\overline{\eta} \geq 0$ is a constant, jointly satisfying

$$\langle \nabla V(x), \mathrm{f}(x) \rangle \leq -c(x) + \overline{\eta}, \qquad x \in \mathsf{X}. \tag{2.39}$$

An application of the chain rule implies that this is a continuous time version of (2.31):

$$\frac{d}{dt} V(x_t) \leq -c(x_t) + \overline{\eta}, \qquad t \geq 0.$$

And with a bit more work, we reach the following conclusions:

Proposition 2.6 *If* (2.39) *holds for nonnegative $c, V, \overline{\eta}$, then*

$$V(x_T) + \int_0^T c(x_t)\, dt \leq V(x) + T\overline{\eta}, \qquad x_0 = x \in \mathsf{X}, \ T > 0.$$

If $\overline{\eta} = 0$, then the total cost is finite:

$$\int_0^\infty c(x_t)\, dt \leq V(x), \qquad x_0 = x \in \mathsf{X}. \tag{2.40}$$

Proof For any $T > 0$, we obtain by the fundamental theorem of calculus,

$$-V(x_0) \le V(x_T) - V(x_0) = \int_0^T \left(\tfrac{d}{dt}V(x_t)\right) dt \le T\overline{\eta} - \int_0^T c(x_t), \qquad T \ge 0.$$

If $\overline{\eta} = 0$, then the bound (2.40) follows on letting $T \to \infty$. □

Converse Theorems We have seen this implication:

Existence of Lyapunov function $\Longrightarrow$ *Stability and/or performance bound*

where the nature of stability depends on the nature of the Lyapunov function bound. What about a converse? That is, if the system is stable, can we infer that a Lyapunov function exists?

Assume moreover that the total cost is finite:

$$J(x) = \int_0^\infty c(x_t)\, dt, \qquad x_0 = x$$

with arbitrary initial condition. If J is differentiable, then we obtain a solution to (2.37) using $V = J$:

Proposition 2.7 *If J is finite valued, then for each initial condition x_0 and each t,*

$$\frac{d}{dt}J(x_t) = -c(x_t). \tag{2.41}$$

If J is continuously differentiable, the Lyapunov bound (2.37) *follows with equality:*

$$\nabla J(x) \cdot \mathrm{f}(x) = -c(x).$$

Proof We have a simple version of Bellman's principle (a focus of Chapter 3): for any $T > 0$,

$$J(x_0) = \int_0^T c(x_r)\, dr + J(x_T).$$

For $t \ge 0$, $\delta > 0$ given, apply this equation with $T = t + \delta$ and $T = t$:

$$J(x_0) = \int_0^{t+\delta} c(x_r)\, dr + J(x_{t+\delta}),$$
$$J(x_0) = \int_0^{t} c(x_r)\, dr + J(x_{t}).$$

On subtracting, and then dividing by δ, this gives

$$0 = \frac{1}{\delta}\int_t^{t+\delta} c(x_r)\, dr + \frac{1}{\delta}\big(J(x_{t+\delta}) - J(x_t)\big).$$

Letting $\delta \downarrow 0$, the first term converges to $c(x_t)$ because $c\colon \mathbb{R}^n \to \mathbb{R}$ is continuous, and the second term converges to the derivative of $J(x_t)$ with respect to time, which establishes (2.41). The final conclusion follows from the chain rule. □

2.4.6 Linear State Space Models

If the dynamics in (2.21) are linear, with $x(k) \in \mathsf{X} = \mathbb{R}^n$, then

$$x(k+1) = Fx(k), \qquad k \geq 0 \tag{2.42}$$

for an $n \times n$ matrix F, and by iteration

$$x(k) = F^k x, \qquad k \geq 0,\, x(0) = x.$$

This equation is valid with $k = 0$ since we take $F^0 = I$, the $n \times n$ identity matrix.

Suppose that the cost is also quadratic, $c(x) = x^{\intercal} S x$, for a symmetric and positive definite matrix S. It follows that $c(x(k))$ is a quadratic function of $x(0)$ for each k:

$$c(x(k)) = (F^k x)^{\intercal} S F^k x.$$

Hence the value function J defined in (2.24) is also quadratic:

$$J(x) = x^{\intercal} \Bigl[\sum_{k=0}^{\infty} (F^k)^{\intercal} S F^k \Bigr] x, \qquad x(0) = x \in \mathsf{X}.$$

That is, $J(x) = x^{\intercal} M x$, where M is the matrix within the brackets. It satisfies a linear fixed point equation, known as the (discrete-time) *Lyapunov equation*:

$$M = S + F^{\intercal} M F. \tag{2.43}$$

A proof of the following can be obtained based on these calculations:

Proposition 2.8 *The following are equivalent for the linear state space model* (2.42)*:*

(i) *The origin is locally asymptotically stable.*
(ii) *The origin is globally asymptotically stable.*
(iii) *The Lyapunov equation* (2.43) *admits a solution $M \geq 0$ for any $S \geq 0$.*
(iv) *Each eigenvalue λ of F satisfies $|\lambda| < 1$.*

$\square$

Controllable Canonical Form. Recall that this state space realization was based on the ARMA model (2.4), with $N = n$. If you have taken a course in signals and systems, you then know that stability of the ARMA model (in an input–output sense called bounded input, bounded output *[BIBO] stability*) is verified by examining the roots $\{p_i : 1 \leq i \leq n\}$ of the rational function

$$a(z) = 1 + \sum_{i=1}^{n} a_i z^{-i} = \prod_{i=1}^{n} (1 - p_i z^{-i}), \qquad z \in \mathbb{C}.$$

The system is BIBO stable if $|p_i| < 1$ for each i. The eigenvalues $\{\lambda_i : 1 \leq i \leq n\}$ of F are obtained as the solution to a root finding problem $\Delta_F(\lambda) = 0$, where

$$\Delta_F(\lambda) = \det(\lambda I - F) = \prod_{i=1}^{n} (\lambda - \lambda_i), \qquad \lambda \in \mathbb{C}.$$

For the state space model in controllable canonical form, it can be shown that $\Delta_F(z) = a(z) z^n$ for any $z \in \mathbb{C}$, and hence $\{p_i : 1 \leq i \leq n\} = \{\lambda_i : 1 \leq i \leq n\}$.

Example 2.4.1 (*Linear Model in Continuous Time*) Consider the linear ODE

$$\frac{d}{dt}x = Ax \tag{2.44}$$

whose solution is the matrix exponential:

$$x_t = e^{At}x(0), \qquad e^{At} = \sum_{m=0}^{\infty} \frac{1}{m!}t^m A^m. \tag{2.45}$$

Consequently, $x_t \to 0$ as $t \to \infty$ from each initial condition if and only if A is *Hurwitz*: each eigenvalue of A has strictly negative real part.

The solution to (2.41) is obtained with a quadratic $J(x) = x^{\intercal}Zx$, where the matrix Z can be found through a bit of linear algebra and calculus. The value function is nonnegative, so we may assume Z is positive semidefinite (hence in particular, symmetric: $Z = Z^{\intercal}$). Symmetry implies,

$$\tfrac{d}{dt}J(x_t) = 2x_t^{\intercal}ZAx_t = x_t^{\intercal}[ZA + A^{\intercal}Z]x_t$$

and from (2.41) this gives

$$x_t^{\intercal}[ZA + A^{\intercal}Z]x_t = -c(x_t) = -x_t^{\intercal}Sx_t.$$

This must hold for each t and each $x(0)$, giving the Lyapunov equation in continuous time:

$$0 = ZA + A^{\intercal}Z + S. \tag{2.46}$$

Euler Approximation If we sample, with constant sampling interval $\Delta > 0$, then from the continuous time model (2.44) we obtain the linear model (2.42): with $t_k = k\Delta$,

$$x(t_{k+1}) = e^{\Delta A}x(t_k), \qquad k \geq 0. \tag{2.47}$$

The Euler approximation of (2.44) also results in the linear model (2.42), but with $F = I + \Delta A$. The matrix F is precisely the first-order Taylor series approximation of the matrix exponential. While only an approximation, it is often good enough for control design.

A particular two-dimensional example is $A = \begin{pmatrix} -0.2, & 1 \\ -1, & -0.2 \end{pmatrix}$. The matrix is Hurwitz, with two eigenvalues $\lambda(A) = -0.2 \pm j$. With sampling interval $\Delta = 0.02$, we find that $F = I + \Delta A$ also has two complex eigenvalues:

$$\lambda(F) = 1 + \Delta\lambda(A) \approx 0.996 \pm 0.02j\,.$$

The eigenvalues satisfy $|\lambda(F)| < 1$, so we see that stability of the discrete-time approximation is inherited from the continuous-time model.

The Matlab command `M = dlyap(F',eye(2))` returns a solution to the Lyapunov equation (2.43) with $S = I$ (the identity matrix):

$$M = \begin{bmatrix} 131.9 & 0.0 \\ 0.0 & 131.9 \end{bmatrix}.$$

The fact that F has complex eigenvalues implies that the state process will exhibit rotational motion. The sample path of $\boldsymbol{x}$ shown on the left-hand side of Figure 2.7 spirals

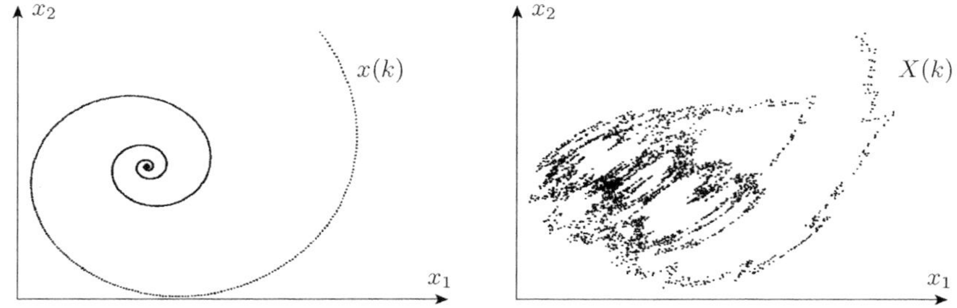

Figure 2.7 At the left is a sample path of the deterministic linear model (2.42). At the right is a sample path from the linear model with disturbance (2.48).

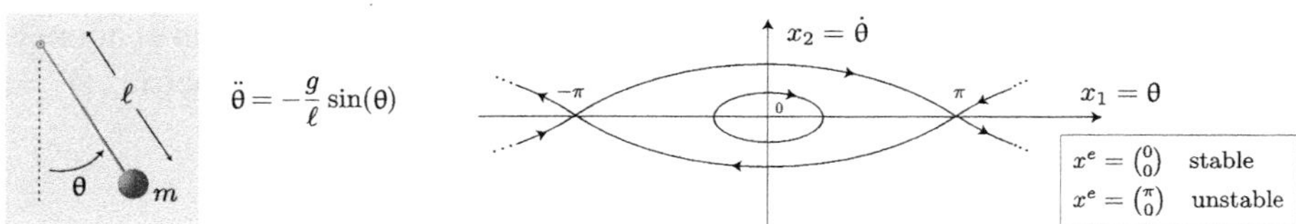

Figure 2.8 Frictionless pendulum: stable and unstable equilibria for the state space model.

toward the origin, and is intuitively "stable." The plot on the right is a simulation of the linear model subject to a "white noise" disturbance:

$$X(k+1) = FX(k) + N(k+1), \qquad k \geq 0. \tag{2.48}$$

See the discussion that follows (7.46) for details of the disturbance process $\boldsymbol{N}$. ■

Example 2.4.2 (*Frictionless Pendulum*) The *frictionless pendulum* illustrated on the left-hand side of Figure 2.8 is a favorite example in physics and undergraduate control courses. It is based on several simplifying assumptions:

- There is no friction or air resistance.
- The rod on which the bob swings is rigid and without mass.
- The bob has mass, but zero volume.
- Motion occurs only in two dimensions.
- The gravitational field is uniform.
- "F = MA" (apply classical mechanics, subject to the foregoing).

A nonlinear state space model is obtained in which x_1 is the angular position θ, and x_2 its derivative:

$$\frac{d}{dt}x = \mathrm{f}(x) = \begin{bmatrix} x_2 \\ -\frac{g}{\ell}\sin(x_1) \end{bmatrix}. \tag{2.49}$$

Shown on the right-hand side of Figure 2.8 are sample trajectories of x_t, and two equilibria.

An inspection of state trajectories shown on the right-hand side of Figure 2.8 reveals that the equilibrium $x^e = \binom{\pi}{0}$ is not stable in any sense, which agrees with physical intuition (the pendulum is sitting upright in this case). Trajectories that begin near the equilibrium $x^e = \mathsf{0}$ will remain near this equilibrium thereafter.

The origin is stable in the sense of Lyapunov. To see this, consider a Lyapunov function defined as the sum of potential and kinetic energy:

$$V(x) = \text{PE} + \text{KE} = mg\ell[1 - \cos(x_1)] + \tfrac{1}{2}m\ell^2 x_2^2.$$

The first term is potential energy relative to the height at the equilibrium $x^e = 0$, and the second is the classical "KE $= \frac{1}{2}mv^2$" formula for kinetic energy. It is not surprising that V is minimized at $x^e = 0$.

We have $\nabla V(x) = m\ell^2[(g/\ell)\sin(x_1), x_2]^\intercal$, and

$$\nabla V(x) \cdot \mathrm{f}(x) = m\ell^2\{(g/\ell)\sin(x_1) \cdot x_2 - x_2 \cdot (g/\ell)\sin(x_1)\} = 0.$$

This means that $\frac{d}{dt}V(x_t) = 0$, and hence $V(x_t)$ does not depend on time. For example, the periodic orbit shown in Figure 2.8 evolves in a level set of V:

$$\frac{g}{\ell}[1 - \cos(x_1(t))] + \tfrac{1}{2}x_2(t)^2 = \text{const.}$$

From this it follows that the origin is stable in the sense of Lyapunov.

Linearization: Using the first-order Taylor series approximation $\sin(\theta) \approx \theta$, the state space equation for the pendulum can be approximated by the LTI model (2.44): $\frac{d}{dt}x = Ax$, with

$$A = \begin{bmatrix} 0 & 1 \\ -g/\ell & 0 \end{bmatrix}. \tag{2.50}$$

The eigenvalues of A are obtained on solving the quadratic equation $0 = \det(I\lambda - A)$:

$$0 = \det\left(\begin{bmatrix} \lambda & -1 \\ g/\ell & \lambda \end{bmatrix}\right) = \lambda^2 + g/\ell \implies \lambda = \pm\sqrt{g/\ell}\,j.$$

The complex eigenvalues are consistent with the periodic behavior of the pendulum. ∎

2.5 A Glance Ahead: From Control Theory to RL

Here is a definition from Wikipedia, as seen on July 2020: "Reinforcement learning (RL) is an area of machine learning concerned with how software agents ought to take actions in an environment in order to maximize the notion of cumulative reward." Here is a translation of some of the key terms:

- ▲ **Machine learning** (ML) refers to prediction/inference based on sampled data.
- ▲ **Take actions** $\equiv$ feedback. That is, the choice of $u(k)$ for each k based on observations.[6]
- ▲ **Software agent** $\equiv$ policy ϕ. This is where the machine learning comes in: the creation of ϕ is based on a large amount of training data collected in "the environment."
- ▲ **Cumulative reward** $\equiv$ negative of the sum of cost, such as (2.24), but with the inclusion of the input:

$$\text{Cumulative reward} = -\sum_k c(x(k), u(k)).$$

[6] The term *features* is a common substitute for the observation process y shown in Figure 2.1.

An emphasis in the academic community is truly model-free RL, and most of the theory builds on the optimal control concepts reviewed in the next chapter. Some of the main ideas can be exposed right here.

What follows is background on how RL algorithms are currently formulated. Think hard about alternatives – remember, the field remains young!

2.5.1 Actors and Critics

The *actor-critic* algorithm of reinforcement learning is specifically designed within the context of stochastic control, so this is a topic for Part II. The origins of the terms are worth explaining here. We are given a parameterized family of policies $\{\phi^\theta : \theta \in \mathbb{R}^d\}$, which play the role of actors. For each θ, we (or our "software agents") can observe features of the state process $\boldsymbol{x}$ under chosen the policy. The ideal critic then computes exactly the associated value function J_θ, but in realistic situations we have only an estimate.

Since in this book we are minimizing cost rather than maximizing reward, the output of an actor-critic algorithm is the minimum

$$\theta^\star = \arg\min_\theta \langle \nu, J_\theta \rangle, \tag{2.51}$$

where $\nu \geq 0$ serves as a state weighting. This will be defined as a sum

$$\langle \nu, J_\theta \rangle = \sum_i J_\theta(x^i)\nu(x^i),$$

where $\nu(x^i)$ is relatively large for "important states."

Methods to solve the optimization problem (2.51) are explored in Section 4.6, using an approach known as *gradient free optimization*. These algorithms are intended to approximate the true gradient descent algorithms of optimization surveyed in Section 4.4, and are often called "actor-only methods." The meaning of actor-critic methods is explained in Chapter 10.

This is an example of ML: optimizing a complex objective function over a large function class for the purposes of prediction or classification (in this case, we are predicting the best policy). A very short introduction to ML can be found in Section 5.1.

2.5.2 Temporal Differences

Where do we find a critic? That is, how can we estimate a value function without a model? One answer lies in the sample path representation of the fixed policy dynamic programming equation, previously announced in (2.30). For any θ, we have

$$J_\theta(x(k)) = c(x(k),u(k)) + J_\theta(x(k+1)), \qquad k \geq 0, \quad u(k) = \phi^\theta(x(k)).$$

We might seek an approximation $\widehat{J}$ for which this identity is well approximated. This motivates the *temporal difference* (TD) sequence commonly used in RL algorithms:

$$\mathcal{D}_{k+1}(\widehat{J}) \stackrel{\text{def}}{=} -\widehat{J}(x(k)) + \widehat{J}(x(k+1)) + c(x(k),u(k)), \qquad k \geq 0, \quad u(k) = \phi^\theta(x(k)). \tag{2.52}$$

After collecting N observations, we obtain the mean-square loss:

$$\Gamma^{\varepsilon}(\widehat{J}) = \frac{1}{N}\sum_{k=0}^{N-1}\big[\mathcal{D}_{k+1}(\widehat{J})\big]^2. \tag{2.53}$$

We are then faced with another machine learning problem: minimize this objective function over all $\widehat{J}$ in a given class (for example, this is where neural networks frequently play a role).

If we can make (2.53) nearly zero, then we have a good estimate of a value function. Beyond its application to actor-critic methods, there are TD- and Q-learning techniques, designed to minimize (2.53) or a surrogate, that are part of a bigger RL toolbox.

2.5.3 Bandits and Exploration

Suppose that our policy is pretty good. Maybe not optimal in any sense, but $x(k) \to x^e$, $u(k) \to u^e$ rapidly as $k \to \infty$, where the limit satisfies $c(x^e,u^e) = 0$. We typically then have continuity:

$$\lim_{k\to\infty}\big[-\widehat{J}(x(k+1)) + \widehat{J}(x(k)) - c(x(k),u(k))\big] = -\widehat{J}(x^e) + \widehat{J}(x^e) - c(x^e,u^e) = 0. \tag{2.54}$$

It follows that we aren't observing very much via the temporal difference (2.52). If N is very large, then $\Gamma^{\varepsilon}(\widehat{J}) \approx 0$. This essentially destroys any hope for a reliable estimate of the value function. Expressed another way: a good policy does not lead to sufficient exploration of the state space.

There are many ways to introduce exploration. We can, for example, adapt our criterion as follows: denote by $\Gamma^{\varepsilon}(\widehat{J};x)$ the mean-square loss obtained with $x(0) = x$. Rather than take a very long run, perform many shorter runs, from many ($M > 1$) initial conditions. The loss function to be minimized is the average

$$\Gamma(\widehat{J}) = \frac{1}{M}\sum_{i=1}^{M}\Gamma^{\varepsilon}(\widehat{J};x^i). \tag{2.55}$$

The best way to choose the samples $\{x^i\}$ is a topic of research.

Another approach is to let the input do the exploring. The policy is modified slightly through the introduction of "noise":

$$u(k) = \breve{\phi}(x(k),\xi(k)).$$

For example, $\{\xi(k)\}$ might be a scalar signal, defined as a mixture of sinusoids. The noisy policy is defined so that

(i) $\breve{\phi}(x(k),\xi(k)) \approx \phi^{\theta}(x(k))$ for "most k."
(ii) The state process "explores." In particular, the policy is designed to avoid convergence of $(x(k),u(k))$ to any limiting value.

This is a crude approach, since by changing the input process, the associated value function also changes. More sensible approaches are contained in Chapters 4 and 5, and in the second part of the book: Q-learning and "off-policy SARSA" might be designed around an exploratory policy such as this one, but these algorithms are carefully designed to avoid bias from exploration.

The theory of exploration is mature only within a very special setting: multi-armed bandits. The term "bandit" refers to slot machines: you put money in the machine, pull an arm, and hope that more money pops out. A more rational application is in the advertisement industry, in which an "arm" is an advertisement (which costs money), and the advertiser hopes money will pop out as the ads encourage sales. There is a great history of heuristics and science to create successful algorithms to maximize profit, based only on noisy observations of the performance of candidate ads ([216] is a great reference on the theory of bandits, and a short survey is contained in Section 7.8). It is here that the "exploration/exploitation" trade-off is most clearly seen: you have to accept some loss of revenue through exploration in order to learn the best strategy, and then "exploit" as you gain confidence in your estimates.

The situation is much more complex in control applications: imagine that for each state $x(k)$, there is a multi-armed bandit. "Pulling arm a" at time k means choosing $u(k) = a \in \mathsf{U}$. Concepts from bandit theory have led to heuristics to best balance the exploration/exploitation trade-offs arising in RL. This is an exciting direction for future research [171, 307].

2.6 How Can We Ignore Noise?

It is hard to explain this precisely to a student without a background in probability theory. If you have some exposure to stochastic processes, then you might want to skim Section 7.2: you will learn how to construct a deterministic "fluid model" or "mean-field model" based on a more detailed and complex stochastic state space model, and find justification for control design based on the simpler model.

The pragmatic answer to this question is that we rarely have a reliable model of disturbances, so we leave them unmodeled but not ignored. That is, we attempt to create a control architecture that is not very sensitive to disturbances. There is an elegant theory of robust control for this purpose, though even here "robustness" is only with respect to disturbances within some uncertainty class. The most successful outcomes of this literature lean heavily on frequency domain concepts. For example, it is assumed that disturbances (the d shown in Figure 2.1) are largely limited to lower frequencies, and measurement noise (the w shown on the right-hand side of this figure) is limited to higher frequencies.

Justification for nonlinear control systems is based on Lyapunov function techniques. We establish stability of our control solution through a Lyapunov function V as outlined in Section 2.4.3, and then argue that V will continue to have "negative drift" in the form (2.31) even with error in the model F, or in the presence of the disturbance d.

Finally, the naive "disturbance-free" model obtained through physics, or through techniques surveyed in Section 7.2, often provides a great deal of insight for the structure of control solutions. We might use this insight to build architectures for reinforcement learning.

2.7 Examples

2.7.1 Wall Street

Let's begin with an example that clearly does not belong in this chapter. Search for "flash crash" on your internet browser to see images of the enormous volatility of stock prices on many time scales. While we have few tools for control design at this stage of the book, there are many interesting modeling questions that will help illustrate control and RL philosophy.

Where Is the Control Problem?

Let's consider the specific problem of stock portfolio management. The goal is to create a computer program that makes decisions second-by-second on which stocks to buy or sell. The goal is to "maximize profit," but there is also the notion of *risk*, which is not easily defined without tools from probability and statistics.

Perhaps more significant is that this control problem is not of the centralized variety. Consider how Figure 2.1 is interpreted for stock trading. The *process* is the global economy and everything that goes along with it! The two blocks *state feedback* and *observer* are the results of thousands of individual decision makers (the "agents") who forecast future prices (and other events), and employ optimization strategies for online decision making. *Trajectory generation* will also be local to each agent: this might represent decisions regarding purchase orders for new computers, new staff, or a new office closer to Wall Street.

In summary: stock trading is a game rather than a classical control problem, but this should not stop us. As an individual (or company designing software for others), we can treat the "process" along with the actions of all other players as a larger process. Reinforcement learning is an appealing approach to control design because the learning (or training) does not require a detailed model (though significant data are required for training).

This is a great example of the value of both measurements and actuation in control. The better your measurements, the more money you can expect to earn in an optimal control solution – there is no better example to illustrate this point. The book *Flash Boys* contains a popular treatment of the role of actuation – in particular, the cost of delay in the feedback loop [223] (see also [30]). It is claimed that millions of dollars can be made by reducing response delay by a millisecond!

State Feedback?

How do we interpret $u(k) = \phi(x(k))$? The input $u(k)$ is easy to understand, given the preceding description of the stock portfolio management problem.

What is the state $x(k)$? I don't know, and I would not trust anyone who claims to have an answer! It is traditional to view prices as a stochastic process that evolves according to the actions of millions of citizens and hundreds of corporations. There is modeling theory based on martingales and changes of measure, so theory from mathematical finance may provide intuition on how to construct a state process. A quick "gut reaction" might be this: $x(k) = x^0(k)$, the vector of all stock prices at time k. Without any knowledge of finance, my gut tells me that this would be a huge mistake. Here are examples of what many would add after further reflection:

(i) Past history of prices. It is important to visit recent performance in terms of both trends and volatility.
(ii) Forecasts of prices. You may have insider knowledge. You may realize that tweets from certain influential people provide insight on the decisions of others, which will then influence stock prices.
(iii) What is the objective? Once you have a formulation of reward and risk, make sure that these essential quantities are functions of your state process.

Figure 2.9 Mountain car.

You then have a very high-dimensional vector $x(k)$, and are left to find the feedback law ϕ.

There is no perfect state description. Even if a state space model were available, the full state would not be directly observed (and we would still want to use "side information," such as the tweets of CEOs and politicians). Appendix C contains a summary of *belief states* for partially observed control problems. This is an elegant way to create a fully observed state for the purposes of control, but comes with enormous cost in terms of complexity.

What follows are toy examples that will be useful for applying the methods to be developed over the course of this book. The models are presented in continuous time because of the elegance of calculus and classical mechanics.

2.7.2 Mountain Car

The goal is to drive a car with a very weak engine to the top of a very high mountain, as illustrated in Figure 2.9.

A two-dimensional state space model is obtained using position and velocity $x_t = (z_t, v_t)^{\intercal}$, and the input u is the throttle position (which is negative when the car is in reverse). In the following, the state space is defined to be a rectangular region,

$$\mathsf{X} = [z^{\text{min}}, z^{\text{goal}}] \times [-\overline{v}, \overline{v}]$$

in which z^{min} is a lower limit for the position z_t, and the target position is z^{goal}. The constraint $x_t \in \mathsf{X}$ means that the velocity v_t is bounded in magnitude by $\overline{v} > 0$.

Within the RL literature, this example was introduced in the dissertation [264], and has since become a favorite basic example [338].

What makes this problem interesting is that the engine is so weak that it is impossible to reach the hill directly from some initial conditions. A successful policy will sometimes put the car in reverse, and travel at maximal speed away from the goal to reach a higher elevation to the left. Several cycles back and forth may be required to reach the goal.

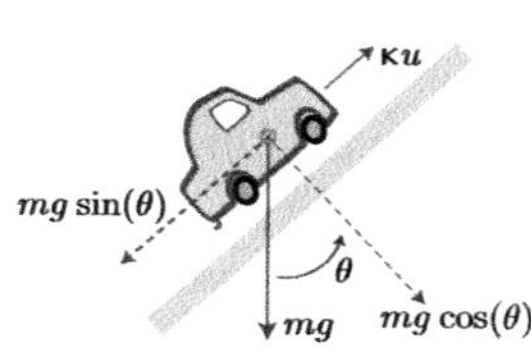

Figure 2.10 Two forces on the mountain car.

A continuous-time model can be constructed based on the two forces on the car, illustrated in Figure 2.10. To obtain a simple model, we need to be careful with our notion of distance: $z^{\text{goal}} - z_t$ denotes the *path distance* along the road to the goal, which is not the same as the distance along the *x-axis* in Figure 2.9. Subject to this convention, Newton's law gives

$$ma = m\frac{d^2}{dt^2}z = -mg\sin(\theta) + \kappa u.$$

With state $x = (z,v)^\intercal$, we arrive at the two-dimensional state space model,

$$\begin{aligned} \frac{d}{dt}x_1 &= x_2, \\ \frac{d}{dt}x_2 &= \frac{\kappa}{m}u - g\sin(\theta(x_1)), \end{aligned} \tag{2.56}$$

where $\theta(x_1)$ is the road grade at $z = x_1$.

An examination of the potential energy $\mathcal{U}$ tells us from which states we can reach the goal without control (setting $u = 0$ in (2.56)). The potential energy is proportional to elevation and can be computed by integrating the negative of force, $-F(z)$. For the control-free model, we have $-F(z) = mg\sin(\theta(z))$, and hence

$$\mathcal{U}(z) = \mathcal{U}(0) + mg\int_0^z \sin(\theta(z))\,dz. \tag{2.57}$$

The version of this model adopted in [338, ch. 10] uses these numerical values:

$$\kappa/m = 1, \quad g = 2.5, \quad \theta(z) = \pi + 3z.$$

In this case, (2.57) gives $\mathcal{U}(z) = \mathcal{U}(0) + mg\sin(3z)/3$. Figure 2.11 shows the potential energy as a function of z on the interval $[z^{\text{min}}, z^{\text{goal}}]$. It has a unique maximum at z^{goal}, which implies that it is necessary to apply external force to reach the goal for any initial condition satisfying $z(0) < z^{\text{goal}}$ and $v(0) \leq 0$.

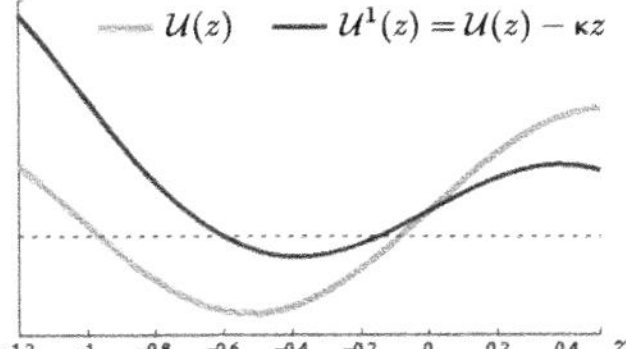

Figure 2.11 Potential energy for the mountain car.

Is the goal reachable? We again examine potential energy. Consider the force as a function of z with $u(k) = 1$ for all k. We obtain $-F(z) = mg\sin(\theta(z)) - \kappa$, and the resulting potential energy is the integral, denoted $\mathcal{U}^1(z) = \mathcal{U}(z) - \kappa z$ and shown in Figure 2.11. We now have $\mathcal{U}(z^{\text{min}}) > \mathcal{U}(z^{\text{goal}})$, so from $z(0) = z^{\text{min}}$ we will reach the goal with this open-loop control law.

Consider the initial position $z^0 = -0.6$, for which $\mathcal{U}^1(z^0)$ is indicated with a dashed line, and let z^1 denote the other value satisfying $z^1 > z^0$ and $\mathcal{U}^1(z^1) = \mathcal{U}^1(z^0)$. If $u(k) = 1$ for all k, then with initial condition $z(0) = -0.6$ and $v(0) = 0$, the car will initially move to the right, and stall at time t_1, for which $z(t_1) = z^1$. It will then reverse direction until it stalls at location z^0, and this process will repeat.

A discrete time model is adopted in [338, ch. 10], based on sampling the ODE with sampling interval $\Delta = 10^{-3}$: using the notation $x(k) = (z(k),v(k))^\intercal$,

$$z(k+1) = [\![z(k) + \Delta v(k+1)]\!]_1, \tag{2.58a}$$

$$v(k+1) = [\![v(k) + \Delta[u(k) - 2.5\cos(3z(k))]\,]\!]_2. \tag{2.58b}$$

This can be expressed in the form (2.6a) by substituting the expression for $v(k+1)$ in (2.58b) into the right-hand side of (2.58a).

The model is consistent with (2.56) using $\theta(z) = \pi + 3z$. The brackets denote projection of the values of $z(k+1)$ to the interval $[z^{\text{min}}, z^{\text{goal}}]$, and $v(k+1)$ to the interval $[-\overline{v}, \overline{v}]$. In addition, the constraint $v(k) \geq 0$ is imposed when $z(k) = z^{\text{min}}$, and $v(k) = 0$ when

$z(k) = z^{\text{goal}}$ (the car is parked once it reaches its target). The following values are chosen in numerical experiments:

$$z^{\text{min}} = -1.2, \ z^{\text{goal}} = 0.5, \text{ and } \overline{v} = 70. \tag{2.58c}$$

Here is an aggressive policy that will get you to the top: Whatever direction you are going, accelerate in that direction at maximum rate (provided this is feasible):

$$u(k) = \begin{cases} 0 & z(k) = z^{\text{goal}} \\ \text{sign}(v(k)) & \text{else} \end{cases}. \tag{2.59}$$

If $v(k) = 0$, then $\text{sign}(v(k))$ can be taken to be 1 or -1, subject to the constraint that $v(k+1) \neq 0$.

2.7.3 MagBall

The magnetically suspended metal ball illustrated in Figure 2.12 will be used to illustrate several important modeling concepts. In particular, it shows how to transform a set of nonlinear differential equations into a state space model, and how to approximate this by a linear state space model of the form (2.20). Further details from a control systems perspective may be found in the lecture notes [29].

The input u is the current applied to an electromagnet, and the output y is the distance between the center of the ball and the bottom edge of the magnet. Since positive and negative inputs are indistinguishable at the output of this system, it follows that this cannot be a linear system. The upward force due to the current input is approximately proportional to u^2/y^2, and hence from Newton's law for translational motion we adopt the model

$$ma = m\frac{d^2}{dt^2}y = mg - \kappa\frac{u^2}{y^2},$$

where g is the gravitational constant, and κ is some constant depending on the physical properties of the magnet and ball.

Control design goal: Maintain the distance to the magnet at some reference value r.

We obtain a state space model as a first step to control design. This input–output model can be converted to state space form to obtain something similar to the controllable canonical form description of the ARMA model in (2.16) and (2.18): using $x_1 = y$ and $x_2 = \frac{d}{dt}y$,

$$\frac{d}{dt}x_1 = x_2, \ \frac{d}{dt}x_2 = g - \frac{\kappa}{m}\frac{u^2}{x_1^2},$$

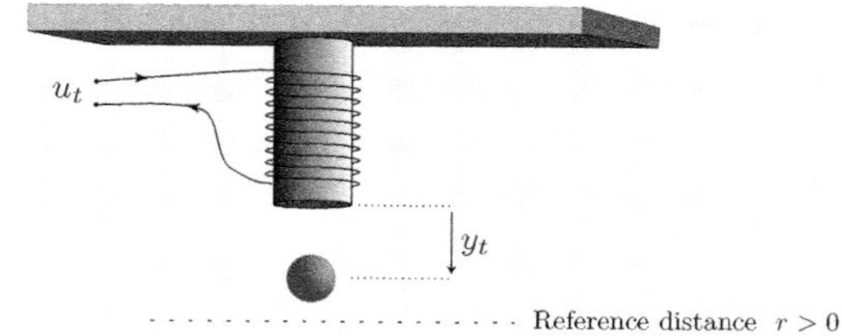

Figure 2.12 Magnetically suspended ball.

where the latter equation follows from the formula $\frac{d}{dt}x_2 = \frac{d^2}{dt^2}y$. This pair of equations defines a two-dimensional state space model of the form (2.19):

$$\frac{d}{dt}x_1 = x_2 = \mathrm{f}_1(x_1,x_2,u), \tag{2.60a}$$

$$\frac{d}{dt}x_2 = g - \frac{\kappa}{m}\frac{u^2}{(x_1)^2} = \mathrm{f}_2(x_1,x_2,u). \tag{2.60b}$$

It is nonlinear, since f_2 is a nonlinear function of x, and also the state space is constrained: $\mathsf{X} = \{x \in \mathbb{R}^2 : x_1 \geq 0\}$.

Suppose that a fixed current $u^\circ > 0$ is applied, and that the state x° is an equilibrium: $\mathrm{f}(x^\circ,u^\circ) = \mathsf{0}$. From the definition of f_1 in (2.60a), we must have $x_2^\circ = 0$, and setting $\mathrm{f}_2(x^\circ,u^\circ)$ equal to zero in (2.60b) gives

$$x_1^\circ = \sqrt{\frac{\kappa}{mg}}u^\circ > 0. \tag{2.61}$$

If we are *very* successful with our control design, and $x_t = (r,0)^\intercal$ for all t, then we must have

$$u_t = u^\circ, \quad t \geq 0, \qquad \text{where } u^\circ = r\sqrt{mg/\kappa} : \text{the solution to (2.61) with } x_1^\circ = r.$$

Of course, we don't expect that this "open-loop" approach will be successful. If we are realistically successful, so that $x_t \approx r$ for all t (perhaps after a transient), then we should expect that $u_t \approx u^\circ$ as well. The design of a feedback law to achieve this goal is often obtained through an approximate linear model, called a *linearization*.

Linearization about an Equilibrium State

The linearization is defined exactly as in the frictionless pendulum (2.49). Assume that the signals x_1, x_2, and u remain close to the fixed point $(x_1^\circ,x_2^\circ,u^\circ)$, and write

$$\begin{aligned} x_1 &= x_1^\circ + \tilde{x}_1, \\ x_2 &= x_2^\circ + \tilde{x}_2, \\ u &= u^\circ + \tilde{u}, \end{aligned}$$

where $\tilde{x}_1$, $\tilde{x}_2$, and $\tilde{u}$ are small-amplitude signals. From the state equations (2.60), we then have

$$\begin{aligned} \frac{d}{dt}\tilde{x}_1 &= x_2^\circ + \tilde{x}_2 = \tilde{x}_2, \\ \frac{d}{dt}\tilde{x}_2 &= \mathrm{f}_2(x_1^\circ + \tilde{x}_1, x_2^\circ + \tilde{x}_2, u^\circ + \tilde{u}). \end{aligned}$$

Applying a first-order Taylor series expansion to the right-hand side of the second equation gives

$$\begin{aligned} \frac{d}{dt}\tilde{x}_2 = \mathrm{f}_2(x_1^\circ,x_2^\circ,u^\circ) &+ \frac{\partial \mathrm{f}_2}{\partial x_1}\Big|_{(x_1^\circ,x_2^\circ,u^\circ)}\tilde{x}_1 + \frac{\partial \mathrm{f}_2}{\partial x_2}\Big|_{(x_1^\circ,x_2^\circ,u^\circ)}\tilde{x}_2 \\ &+ \frac{\partial \mathrm{f}_2}{\partial u}\Big|_{(x_1^\circ,x_2^\circ,u^\circ)}\tilde{u} + d. \end{aligned}$$

The final term d represents the error in the Taylor series approximation. After computing partial derivatives, we obtain

$$\frac{d}{dt}\tilde{x}_1 = \tilde{x}_2.$$

$$\frac{d}{dt}\tilde{x}_2 = \alpha\tilde{x}_1 + \beta\tilde{u} + d \qquad \text{with} \qquad \alpha = 2\frac{\kappa}{m}\frac{(u^\circ)^2}{(x_1^\circ)^3}, \qquad \beta = -2\frac{\kappa}{m}\frac{u^\circ}{(x_1^\circ)^2}.$$

This can be represented as a linear state space model with disturbance:

$$\frac{d}{dt}\tilde{x} = \begin{bmatrix} 0 & 1 \\ \alpha & 0 \end{bmatrix}\tilde{x} + \begin{bmatrix} 0 \\ \beta \end{bmatrix}\tilde{u} + \begin{bmatrix} 0 \\ 1 \end{bmatrix}d, \qquad \tilde{y} = \tilde{x}_1. \tag{2.62}$$

There is a hidden approximation in (2.62), since d is in fact a nonlinear function of (x,u). In control design, this approximation is taken one step further by setting $d \equiv 0$, to obtain the linear model (2.20). The approximate model is not very useful for simulations, but often leads to effective control solutions.

2.7.4 CartPole

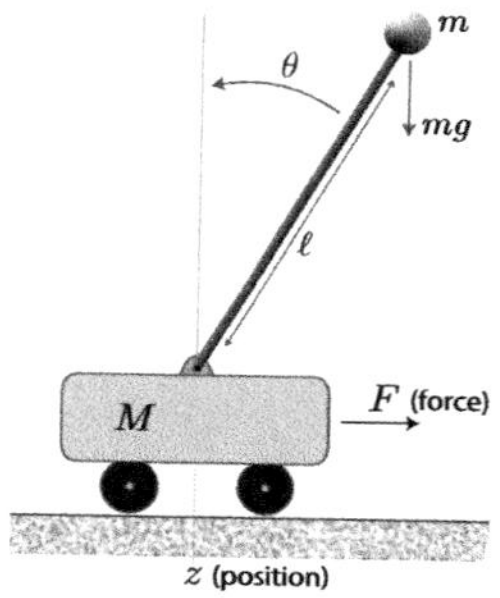

Figure 2.13 CartPole.

The next example has a long history within the control systems literature [14, 258, 331], and was introduced to the RL literature in early research of Barto et al. [26]. It is today a popular test example on `openai.com`. A history from the perspective of control education can be found in [385], which provides the dynamic equations with state $x = (z,\dot{z},\theta,\dot{\theta})$, where z is the horizontal position of the cart, and the angle θ is as shown in Figure 2.13.

The control design goal is regulation: Keep $\theta = 0$ while the cart is moving at some desired speed, or some desired fixed position. The aforementioned references describe several successful strategies to swing the pole up to a desired position without excessive energy. A normalized model used in [385] is given by

$$\begin{aligned} \tfrac{d}{dt}z &= \tfrac{d}{dt}x_1 = x_2, & \tfrac{d}{dt}x_2 &= u, \\ \tfrac{d}{dt}\theta &= \tfrac{d}{dt}x_3 = x_4, & \tfrac{d}{dt}x_4 &= \sin(x_3) - u\cos(x_3). \end{aligned} \tag{2.63}$$

The state equations are easily linearized near the equilibrium $u^e = 0$ and $x^e = (z^e,0,0,0)^{\intercal}$ for any z^e: using the first-order Taylor series approximations $\sin(x_3) \approx x_3$ and $\cos(x_3) \approx 1$, we obtain as in the derivation of (2.62)

$$\begin{aligned} \tfrac{d}{dt}\tilde{x}_1 &= \tilde{x}_2, & \tfrac{d}{dt}\tilde{x}_2 &= u, \\ \tfrac{d}{dt}\tilde{x}_3 &= \tilde{x}_4, & \tfrac{d}{dt}\tilde{x}_4 &= \tilde{x}_3 - u + d. \end{aligned} \tag{2.64}$$

Ignoring the "disturbance" (error term) d, the ODE (2.64) is a version of the state space model (2.20) with

$$A = \begin{bmatrix} 0 & 1 & 0 & 0 \\ 0 & 0 & 0 & 0 \\ 0 & 0 & 0 & 1 \\ 0 & 0 & 1 & 0 \end{bmatrix}, \qquad B = \begin{bmatrix} 0 \\ 1 \\ 0 \\ -1 \end{bmatrix}.$$

The matrix A is not Hurwitz, with eigenvalues at ± 1 and repeated eigenvalues at 0. This was anticipated at the start: it is unlikely that the pendulum will remain upright with a constant "open-loop" input, $u_t \equiv 0$. The linear model is of great value for insight, and for designing a linear feedback law to keep the system near the equilibrium:

$$\tilde{u} = -K\tilde{x}.$$

Methods to obtain the 4×1 matrix K through optimal control techniques will be investigated later in the book.

In conclusion, we know what to do locally, but the linearization provides no insight whatsoever on how to swing the pendulum up to the desired vertical position. The robotics community has developed ingenious specialized techniques for classes of nonlinear control problems that include CartPole as a special case (see [14, 82, 331, 385], and Exercise 3.10 for a survey of the approach of [14]). In the near future, we hope to marry existing control approaches with model-free techniques from RL to obtain reliable control designs in more complex settings.

2.7.5 *Pendubot and Acrobot*

Figure 2.14 shows a photograph of the *Pendubot* as it appeared in the robotics laboratory at the University of Illinois in the 1990s [29, 330] and a sketch indicating its component parts. It is similar to Sutton's Acrobot [341], which is another example that is currently popular on `openai.com`. The control objective is similar to CartPole: starting from any initial condition, swing the Pendubot up to a desired equilibrium, without excessive energy.

The value of this example is explained in the introduction of [330], where they compare to *CartPole*, and a variation of Furuta [137]:

> The balancing problem for the Pendubot may be solved by linearizing the equations of motion about an operating point and designing a linear state feedback controller, very similar to the classical cart-pole problem ... One very interesting distinction of the Pendubot over both the classical cart-pole system and Furuta's system is the continuum of balancing positions. This feature of the Pendubot is pedagogically useful in several ways, to show students how the Taylor series linearization is operating point dependent and for teaching controller switching and gain scheduling. Students can also easily understand physically how the linearized system becomes uncontrollable at $q_1 = 0, \pm\pi$. [This excerpt refers to the first and third illustrations shown in Figure 2.14b, with q_1, q_2 joint angles shown in Figure 2.15.]

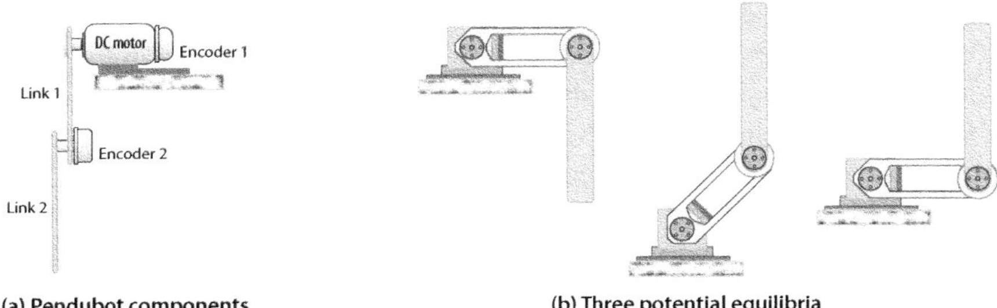

(a) Pendubot components (b) Three potential equilibria

Figure 2.14 (a) The Illinois Pendubot, showing component parts. (b) A continuum of equilibrium positions.

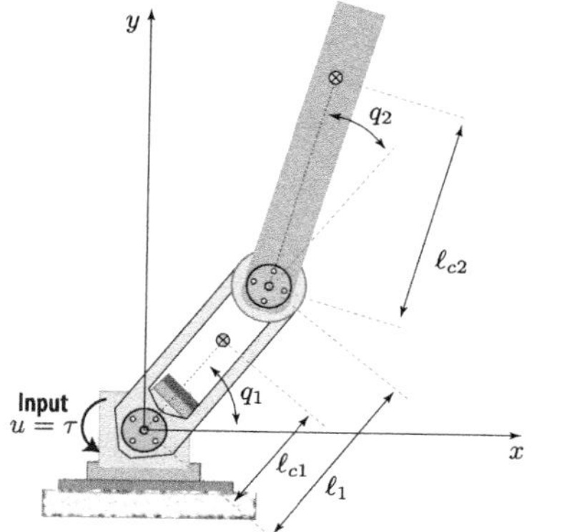

$$
\begin{aligned}
d_{11} &= m_1\ell_{c1}^2 + m_2(\ell_1^2 + \ell_{c2}^2 + 2\ell_1\ell_{c2}\cos(q_2)) + I_1 + I_2 \\
d_{22} &= m_2\ell_{c2}^2 + I_2 \\
d_{12} &= d_{21} = m_2(\ell_{c2}^2 + \ell_1\ell_{c2}\cos(q_2)) + I_2 \\
h_1 &= -m_2\ell_1\ell_{c2}\sin(q_2)\dot{q}_2^2 - 2m_2\ell_1\ell_{c2}\sin(q_2)\dot{q}_2\dot{q}_1 \\
h_2 &= m_2\ell_1\ell_{c2}\sin(q_2)\dot{q}_1^2 \\
\phi_1 &= (m_1\ell_{c1} + m_2\ell_1)g\cos(q_1) + m_2\ell_{c2}g\cos(q_1 + q_2) \\
\phi_2 &= m_2\ell_{c2}g\cos(q_1 + q_2)
\end{aligned}
$$

Figure 2.15 Coordinate description of the Pendubot: ℓ_1 is the length of the first link, and ℓ_{c1}, ℓ_{c2} are the distances to the center of mass of the respective links. The variables q_1, q_2 are joint angles of the respective links, and the input is the torque applied to the lower joint.

The Pendubot consists of two rigid aluminum links: Link 1 is directly coupled to the shaft of a DC motor mounted to the end of a table. Link 1 also includes the bearing housing for the second joint. Two optical encoders provide position measurements: One is attached at the elbow joint, and the other is attached to the motor. Note that no motor is directly connected to link 2 – this makes vertical control of the system, as shown in the photograph, extremely difficult!

The system dynamics can be derived using the so-called Euler–Lagrange equations found in robotics textbooks [332]:

$$d_{11}\ddot{q}_1 + d_{12}\ddot{q}_2 + h_1 + \phi_1 = \tau, \tag{2.65a}$$

$$d_{21}\ddot{q}_1 + d_{22}\ddot{q}_2 + h_2 + \phi_2 = 0, \tag{2.65b}$$

where the variables can be deduced from Figure 2.15. Consequently, this model may be written in state space form, $\frac{d}{dt}x = \mathrm{f}(x,u)$, where $x = (q_1, q_2, \dot{q}_1, \dot{q}_2)^\intercal$, and f is defined from the preceding equations.

This model admits various equilibria: For example, when $u^e = \tau^e = 0$, the vertical downward position $x^e = (-\pi/2, 0, 0, 0)$ is an equilibrium, as illustrated on the right-hand side of Figure 2.14. Three other possibilities are shown in Figure 2.14b, each with $\tau^e \neq 0$.

A fifth equilibrium is obtained in the upright vertical position, with $\tau^e = 0$ and $x^e = (+\pi/2, 0, 0, 0)^\intercal$. It is clear from the drawing shown on the left-hand side of Figure 2.14 that the upright equilibrium is strongly unstable in the sense that with $\tau = 0$, it is unlikely that the physical system will remain at rest. Nevertheless, the velocity vector vanishes, $\mathrm{f}(x^e, 0) = \mathsf{0}$, so by definition the upright position is an equilibrium when $\tau = 0$.

Although they are complex, we may again linearize these equations about the vertical equilibrium. With the input u equal to the applied torque, and the output y equal to the lower link angle, the resulting state space model is defined by the following set of matrices in the 1990s vintage system described in [330]:

$$A = \begin{bmatrix} 0 & 1.0000 & 0 & 0 \\ 51.9243 & 0 & -13.9700 & 0 \\ 0 & 0 & 0 & 1.0000 \\ -52.8376 & 068.4187 & 0 & 0 \end{bmatrix}, \quad B = \begin{bmatrix} 0 \\ 15.9549 \\ 0 \\ -29.3596 \end{bmatrix}, \tag{2.66}$$

$$C = \begin{bmatrix} 1 & 0 & 0 & 0 \end{bmatrix}, \qquad D = 0.$$

Postscripts

For those students who have had a course in undergraduate control systems, the corresponding transfer function has the general form

$$P(s) = k\frac{(s-\gamma)(s+\gamma)}{(s-\alpha)(s+\alpha)(s-\beta)(s+\beta)},$$

with $k > 0$ and $0 < \alpha < \gamma < \beta$. The variable "$s$" corresponds to differentiation. Writing

$$P(s) = k\frac{s^2-\gamma^2}{s^4 - 2(\alpha^2+\beta^2)s^2 + \alpha^2\beta^2},$$

the transfer function notation $Y(s) = P(s)U(s)$ denotes the ODE model:

$$\frac{d^4}{dt^4}\tilde{y} - 2(\alpha^2+\beta^2)\frac{d^2}{dt^2}\tilde{y} + \alpha^2\beta^2\tilde{y} = k[\frac{d^2}{dt^2}u - \gamma^2 u].$$

The roots of the denominator of $P(s)$ are $\{\pm\alpha, \pm\beta\}$, which correspond with the eigenvalues of A. The positive eigenvalues mean that A is not Hurwitz. The fact that $P(s_0) = 0$ for the positive value $s_0 = \gamma$ implies more bad news (a topic far beyond the scope of this book, but the impact of zeros in the right-half plane is worth reading about in basic texts, such as [7, 15, 76, 205]).

2.7.6 Cooperative Rowing

In a sculling boat, each rower has two oars or sculls, one on each side of the boat. The control system discussed here concerns coordination of N *individual scullers* (meaning just one rower per boat) that are part of a single team. You can see five of N teammates on the left-hand side of Figure 2.16. The team objective is to maintain constant velocity toward a target (let's say, the island of Kaua'i), and also maintain "social distance" between boats.

A state space model might be formulated as follows. Let z_t^i denote the distance from the origin, and u_t^i the force exerted by the rower at time t. Taking into account the fact that

Figure 2.16 Cooperative rowing with partial information.

drag increases with speed, and applying once more Newton's law, $f = ma$, results in the following system equations:

$$\frac{d^2}{dt^2} z^i = -a_i \frac{d}{dt} z^i + b_i u^i - d^i,$$

in which $\{a_i, b_i\}$ are positive scalars, and the disturbance $\{d^i_t\}$ is left unmodeled. If we ignore the disturbance (for the purposes of control design), we can pose the rowing game as a linear-quadratic optimal control problem: a topic covered in Sections 3.1 and 3.6. We will see that this will result in a policy of the form

$$u^i = K^i x + r^i,$$

where x is the $2N$-dimensional vector of positions and velocities for all the rowers, K^i is a $2N$-dimensional row vector, and r^i is a scalar function of time that depends upon the tracking goal. Implementation of this policy requires that each rower know the position and velocity of every other rower at each time. Let's think about how the rowers might cooperate without so much data.

Imagine that each rower only views the nearest neighbors to the left and right. This breaks the team of size N into (overlapping) subteams of size three that coordinate individually. Unfortunately, if N is large, it is known that this distributed control architecture can lead to large oscillations in the positions of the boats with respect to the distant island [130].

The theory of *mean-field games* suggests that a more robust strategy is obtained with just a bit of global information: Assume that at each time t, rower i has access to three scalar observations: her own position and velocity z^i_t, v^i_t, and the average position of all rowers:

$$\bar{z}_t = \frac{1}{N} \sum_{j=1}^{N} z^j_t . \tag{2.67}$$

One possibility is to *pretend* that $x^i_t = (z^i_t, v^i_t, \bar{z}_t)^\intercal$ evolves according to a state space model of the form (2.19), in which case it is appropriate to search for a state feedback policy $u^i_t = \phi^i(x^i_t)$.

Before fixing the architecture of the policy, it is essential to consider the goals. Since we have assumed that social distancing is managed through an independent control mechanism, there remain only two:

$$z^i_t \approx \bar{z}_t\,, \qquad v^i_t = \frac{d}{dt} z^i_t \approx v^{\text{ref}} \qquad \text{for all large } t.$$

Based on the discussion in Section 2.3.2, we might obtain better coordination through the introduction of a fourth variable, defined as the integral of the position error

$$z'^i_t = z'^i_0 + \int_0^t [z^i_r - \bar{z}_r]\, dr,$$

or the discounted approximation,

$$z'^i_t = z'^i_0 + \int_0^t e^{\varrho(t-r)} [z^i_r - \bar{z}_r]\, dr$$

with $\varrho > 0$. Once we have made our choice, we then search for a policy defined as a function of the four variables, $u^i_t = \phi^i(z^i_t, v^i_t, \bar{z}_t, z'^i_t)$.

However, *do not forget that this is a game* The "best" choice of ϕ^i will depend upon the choice of ϕ^j for all $j \neq i$. We might experiment with "best response" schemes designed to learn a collection of policies $\{\phi^i : 1 \leq i \leq N\}$ that work well for all. Best response is also behind the RL training in AlphaZero [322].

2.8 Exercises

2.1 *Controllable Canonical Form.* Consider the state space model (2.18) with $\mathsf{X} = \mathbb{R}^3$.

(a) If the input is defined by $u(k) = -Kx(k) + v(k)$ for a 1×3 gain matrix K, obtain a state space model in controllable canonical form (with new input v).

(b) For the special case $n = 3$ (so that F is a 3×3 matrix), design K so that the eigenvalues of $F - GK$ are each located at $1/2$. Perform this calculation by hand. Your answer will depend upon $\{a_1, a_2, a_3\}$. Based on your effort, explain why this is called controllable canonical form!

(c) Think a bit deeper: Have you solved a control problem? With state $x(k)$ defined via (2.17), would you say you are making good use of your output measurements?

If you are baffled, then seek advice from your professor, fellow students, and a good book on state feedback methods!

2.2 *Controllability and Observability.* Consider the linear state space model

$$\begin{aligned} x(k+1) &= Fx(k) + Gu(k), \quad x(0) = \binom{1}{1}, \\ y(k) &= Hx(k) \qquad \text{with } F = \begin{bmatrix} 0.5 & 1 \\ 0 & 2 \end{bmatrix}, \quad G = \begin{bmatrix} 1 \\ 0 \end{bmatrix}, \quad H^{\intercal} = \begin{bmatrix} 0 \\ 1 \end{bmatrix}. \end{aligned} \tag{2.68}$$

If you have taken a state space controls course, then you know that this system is not controllable and not observable. If you don't have this background, then you might be able to guess the definitions of these terms after completing this exercise.

(a) Can you find a feedback law $u(k) = \phi(x(k))$ that results in a bounded output $\boldsymbol{y}$?

(b) Does the situation improve if $H = [1\ 0]$?

(c) How about if $G = [0\ 1]^{\intercal}$?

2.3 *Stabilizability.* The state space model is called *stabilizable* if there is a feedback law $u(k) = \phi(x(k))$ that results in a closed-loop system that is globally asymptotically stable. The example in Exercise 2.2 is not stabilizable.

Perform the following calculations with $F = \begin{bmatrix} 2 & 1 \\ 0 & 0.5 \end{bmatrix}$ and $G = \begin{bmatrix} 1 \\ 0 \end{bmatrix}$:

(a) Design the gain in $u(k) = -Kx(k)$ so that $F - GK$ has repeated eigenvalues (you will see that you do not have choice in the value). Is K unique?

(b) Solve the Lyapunov equation (2.43) with F replaced by the closed-loop matrix $F - GK$ from (a), and with $S = I$.

(c) Denote $y(k) = x_1(k) = Hx(k)$. Suppose that our goal is to ensure that $y(k) \to r$ as $k \to \infty$, with r a constant. Modify your control design as follows:

$$u(k) = -K_1\tilde{y}(k) - K_2x_2(k) - K_3z^{\text{I}}(k),$$

where $\tilde{y}(k) = y(k) - r$ and $z^{\text{I}}(k+1) = z^{\text{I}}(k) + \tilde{y}(k)$ (review discussion surrounding (2.11)). Find $\bar{K}_3 > 0$ sufficiently small so that the system remains stable for $0 \leq K_3 \leq \bar{K}_3$. This is possible because of the inherent robustness of feedback (you verified stability when $K_3 = 0$).

(d) Obtain a state space model for the system in a closed loop, with augmented state $x^a = (x_1, x_2, z^I)$:

$$x^a(k+1) = F^a x^a(k) + G^a r,$$

where F^a is 3×3 and G^a is 3×1. Plot the eigenvalues of F^a for a range of values of $K_3 > 0$, and comment on your findings.

Solve the equilibrium equation (for your favorite control design): $x^a(\infty) = F^a x^a(\infty) + G^a r$. Is your equilibrium $x^a(\infty)$ consistent with your control goals?

Obtain a plot of $y(k)$ as a function of k, with initial condition $x_1(0) \gg r$, and verify that it converges to the desired limit and at the predicted rate.

2.4 Consider the scalar state space model, $x(k+1) = x(k) - \alpha x(k)^3$.

(a) Show that the origin is stable in the sense of Lyapunov, and estimate the region of attraction (which will depend upon α).

(b) Explain why this state space model is not globally asymptotically stable.

The state process $\boldsymbol{x}$ is in fact an Euler approximation of the ODE $\frac{d}{dt}x = -x^3$. See Exercise 2.15 for some interesting features of the solution.

Control Systems in Continuous Time

For simulating an ODE, you might try `ode45` in Matlab. There are several Python alternatives.

2.5 *Integral Control Design.* The temperature T in an electric furnace is governed by the linear state equation

$$\frac{d}{dt}T = u + w,$$

where u is the control (voltage) and w is a constant disturbance due to heat losses. It is not directly observed. It is desired to regulate the temperature to a steady-state value prescribed by the set-point $T = T^0$, where T^0 is your comfort temperature. The following should be solved by hand:

(a) Design a state-plus-integral feedback controller to *guarantee* that $T_t \to T^0$ as $t \to \infty$, for any constant w. This can take the form $u = -K_1(T - T^0) - K_2 z^I$ with

$$z^I_t = z^I_0 + \int_0^t [T_r - T^0]\, dr.$$

The closed-loop poles should have natural frequency $\omega_n \approx 1$ (that is, the eigenvalues of the 2×2 matrix that defines the closed-loop state space model should satisfy $|\lambda| \approx 1$.)

(b) To what value does the control u_t converge as $t \to \infty$? Has the controller "learned" w?

2.6 Solve the following based on the linear state space model $\frac{d}{dt}x = Ax$ with $A = \begin{bmatrix} -1 & 4 \\ 0 & -1 \end{bmatrix}$.

(a) Show that $V(x) = \|x\|^2 = x_1^2 + x_2^2$ is *not* a Lyapunov function.

(b) Find a quadratic function V that is.

(c) Consider the Euler approximation $x(k+1) = Fx(k)$ with $F = I + \Delta A$, and $\Delta > 0$. Estimate the range of $\Delta > 0$ for which your function V from part (b) is a Lyapunov function for this discrete time system. Is this range complete? That is, does it include all values for which the eigenvalues of F lie in the open unit disk in $\mathbb{C}$?

2.7 In this exercise, you will consider a particular control architecture for cooperative rowing, using a simplification of the model described in Section 2.7.6. Consider the homogeneous and disturbance-free system

$$\frac{d^2}{dt^2} z^i = -a \frac{d}{dt} z^i + u^i, \qquad 1 \le i \le N$$

with $a > 0$. The goal is to maintain $v_t^i \stackrel{\text{def}}{=} \frac{d}{dt} z_t^i \approx v^{\text{ref}}$ for all t, and $z_t^i \approx \bar{z}_t$ for each i,t, with $\bar{z}_t$ the average position (recall (2.67)). We wish to achieve these objectives without requiring that each rower have complete observations.

The following control architecture is of the category studied in [130]:

$$u^i = -K_-[z^i - z^{i-1}] - K_+[z^i - z^{i+1}] - K_v[\tfrac{d}{dt} z^i - v^{\text{ref}}], \qquad 1 \le i \le N,$$

where for notational convenience we interpret $z^0 = z^N$ and $z^{N+1} = z^1$. This architecture is well motivated in terms of goals, and the desire to make decisions based on only local information. Unfortunately, theory predicts problems when N is large.

(a) Describe the closed-loop dynamics as a $2N$-dimensional state space model, with constant input v^{ref}. This will have the form, for some matrix K and vector g,

$$\frac{d}{dt} x = (A - BK)x + g v^{\text{ref}}.$$

The remainder of the exercise is numerical, with $a = v^{\text{ref}} = 1$, $K_- = K_+$, and several values of N (say, 10, 500, 5,000):

(b) Choose nonnegative gains K_+, K_v so that the closed-loop system is stable, in the sense that the key error terms are bounded as functions of time and convergent:

$$e_z^i = \lim_{t \to \infty} (z_t^i - \bar{z}_t), \qquad e_v^i = \lim_{t \to \infty} (v_t^i - v^{\text{ref}}).$$

See if you can obtain gains so that $|e_v^i| \le 0.05$.

Note that you do not yet have any tools to efficiently compute the control gains. Just experiment until you find something that works.

(c) Obtain a plot of the eigenvalues of $A - BK$ for the chosen values of N. Do you find complex eigenvalues? Eigenvalues at zero?

(d) Simulate your control design for various nonideal initial conditions. Think hard about how to plot your results to display the poor behavior of these scullers. Discuss your findings.

2.8 Let's now consider the rowing game in which each rower has access to the average position (2.67), and the control architecture

$$u^i = -K_P[z^i - \bar{z}] - K_I z'^i - K_v[\tfrac{d}{dt} z^i - v^{\text{ref}}], \qquad 1 \le i \le N, \tag{2.69}$$

where in the notation of Section 2.7.6,

$$z_t'^i = z_0'^i + \int_0^t [z_r^i - \bar{z}_r]\, dr.$$

Repeat (a)–(d) of Exercise 2.7 based on this policy.

2.9 You are given a nonlinear input–output system defined by the nonlinear differential equation:

$$\ddot{y} = y^2(u - y) + 2\dot{u}. \tag{2.70}$$

(a) Obtain a two-dimensional nonlinear state space representation with output y, input u, and states $x_1 = y$ and $x_2 = \dot{y} - 2u$.

(b) Linearize this system of equations around its equilibrium output trajectory when $u \equiv 1$, and write it in state space form.

(c) *For those of you with background in classical control:* Find the transfer function for the linear system obtained in (b), and comment on the implications.

(d) Obtain a linear compensator $u = -K\tilde{x}$ for the linearization, where $\tilde{x} = (y-1, \dot{y})^{\intercal}$. To be successful, you want $\tilde{x}_t \to 0$ as $t \to \infty$ for each initial condition for which $\|\tilde{x}_0\|$ is sufficiently small.

2.10 We now consider (2.70) subject to a constant disturbance:

$$\ddot{y}(t) = y^2(u-y) + 2\dot{u} + d,$$

where the value of d is not known in advance. In this case, we cannot expect perfect tracking unless we introduce integral control:

$$u = -K\tilde{x}^a, \qquad \text{where} \quad \tilde{x}^a = (y-1, \dot{y}, z^I)^{\intercal}, \quad z^I_t = \int_0^t (y-1)\,dr.$$

Find a 1×3 row vector K so that this control design is stabilizing in the sense that $\tilde{x}^a$ is bounded, and $\tilde{x}$ vanishes for "small" initial conditions. Perform simulations to verify that perfect tracking is achieved for initial conditions near the equilibrium value and any fixed value of d satisfying $|d| \le 1$.

2.11 Consider the state space model $\frac{d}{dt}x = Ax + Bu$; $y = Cx$, where A is similar to a diagonal matrix. That is, $\Lambda = V^{-1}AV$ where Λ is a diagonal matrix, with each $\Lambda(i,i)$ an eigenvalue of A, and V is a matrix whose columns are eigenvectors.

(a) Obtain a state space model for $\overline{x} = V^{-1}x$, of the form $\frac{d}{dt}\overline{x} = \bar{A}\overline{x} + \bar{B}u$; $y = \bar{C}\overline{x}$, by finding representations for $(\bar{A}, \bar{B}, \bar{C})$. This state space representation is called *modal form.*

The remainder of the problem is numerical, using

$$A = \begin{bmatrix} 8 & -7 & -2 \\ 8 & -10 & -4 \\ -4 & 5 & 2 \end{bmatrix}, \qquad B = \begin{bmatrix} 0 \\ 0 \\ 1 \end{bmatrix}, \qquad C = [1\ 0\ 0].$$

(b) Find the eigenvalues and eigenvectors of A, and verify that the matrix $\Lambda = V^{-1}AV$ is indeed diagonal when V is the matrix of eigenvectors.

(c) Obtain a state space model in modal form.

2.12 *Foster's Criterion.* Suppose that $\frac{d}{dt}x = \mathrm{f}(x)$ is a nonlinear state space model on $\mathbb{R}^n$. Assume also that there is a C^1 function $V\colon \mathbb{R}^n \to \mathbb{R}_+$, and a set S such that

$$\langle \nabla V(\theta), \mathrm{f}(\theta)\rangle \le -1, \qquad \theta \in S^c. \tag{2.71}$$

Foster introduced a version of this stability criterion for Markov chains in the middle of the last century [135].

(a) Show that $T_K(x) \le V(x)$ for $x \in \mathbb{R}^n$, where

$$T_K(x) = \min\{t \ge 0 : x_t \in K\}, \qquad x_0 = x \in \mathbb{R}^n.$$

(b) In the special case of a stable linear system [$\mathrm{f}(x) = Ax$, with A Hurwitz], show that a solution to (2.71) is given by $V(x) = \log(1 + x^{\intercal}Mx)$ for some matrix $M > 0$, and with $S = \{x : \|x\| \le k\}$ for some scalar k.

(c) Find an explicit V, S for $A = \begin{bmatrix} -1 & 4 \\ 0 & -1 \end{bmatrix}$ (the matrix used in Exercise 2.6).

2.13 Consider the nonlinear state space model on the real line,

$$\frac{d}{dt}x = \mathrm{f}(x) = \frac{1-e^x}{1+e^x} = -\tanh(x/2).$$

(a) Sketch f as a function of x, and from this plot explain why $x^e = 0$ is an equilibrium, and this equilibrium is globally asymptotically stable.
(b) Find a solution to the Poisson inequality (2.39): $\langle \nabla V, f\rangle \leq -c + \overline{\eta}$, with $c(x) = x^2$ and $\overline{\eta} < \infty$. You might try a polynomial, or a log of a polynomial of $|x|$. See if you can find a solution with $\overline{\eta} = 0$.
(c) Find a solution V to Foster's criterion (2.71), with $S = [-k,k]$ for some $k > 0$. Also, explain why $T_S(x)$ is not finite valued using $S = \{0\}$ (that is, $k = 0$).

2.14 Suppose that one wants to minimize a C^1 function $V\colon \mathbb{R}^n \to \mathbb{R}_+$. A necessary condition for a point $x^\circ \in \mathbb{R}^n$ to be a minimum is that it be a *stationary point*: $\nabla V(x^\circ) = 0$.
Consider the steepest descent algorithm $\frac{d}{dt}x = -\nabla V(x)$. Find conditions on the function V to ensure that a given stationary point x° will be asymptotically stable for this equation. *One approach*: Find conditions under which the function V is a Lyapunov function for this state space model. We will return to this topic in Section 4.4.

2.15 Consider the nonlinear state space model on the real line,

$$\frac{d}{dt}x = \mathrm{f}(x) = -x^3.$$

(a) Sketch f as a function of x, and from this plot explain why $x^e = 0$ is an equilibrium, and this equilibrium is globally asymptotically stable.
(b) Find a solution to the Poisson inequality (2.39) with $c(x) = x^2$: $\langle \nabla V, f\rangle \leq -c + \overline{\eta}$ with $\overline{\eta} < \infty$. You might try a polynomial, or a log of a polynomial in of $|x|$. See if you can find a solution with $\overline{\eta} = 0$.
(c) Find a bounded solution to Foster's criterion (2.71).

2.16 Consider the Van der Pol oscillator, described by the pair of equations

$$\begin{aligned}\frac{d}{dt}x_1 &= x_2,\\ \frac{d}{dt}x_2 &= -(1 - x_1^2)x_2 - x_1.\end{aligned} \tag{2.72}$$

(a) Obtain a linear approximate model $\frac{d}{dt}\tilde{x} = A\tilde{x}$ around the unique equilibrium $x^e = 0$.
(b) Verify that A is Hurwitz, and obtain a quadratic Lyapunov function V for the linear model.
(c) Show that V is also a Lyapunov function for (2.72) on the set $S_V(r)$ defined in (2.28), for some $r > 0$. That is, show that the drift inequality (2.37) holds whenever $x_t \in S_V(r)$.
Conclude that the set $S_V(r) \subset \Omega \equiv$ *the region of attraction for* x^e.
(d) *Can we find the entire region of attraction?* Take a box around the origin $B = \{x : -m \leq x_1 \leq m, \ -m \leq x_2 \leq m\}$ for some integer m (definitely larger than 1, but less than 10 will suffice). Choose N values $\{x^i\} \subset B$ (say, $N = 10^3$), and simulate the ODE for each i, with $x_0 = x^i$, to test to see if $x_t \in S_V(r)$ for some $t < \infty$, and hence $x^i \in \Omega$.
Why does entry to $S_V(r)$ guarantee that x_0 is in the region of asymptotic stability?

2.17 *Inverted Pendulum with Friction.* Consider the pendulum with applied force u, and "damping force" $b\dot{\theta}$:

θ u

$$\tfrac{d}{dt}x = \mathrm{f}(x,u) = \begin{bmatrix} x_2 \\ g\sin(x_1) - u\cos(x_1)\end{bmatrix},$$

where $x = (\theta, \dot{\theta})^{\intercal}$, and $a,b > 0$. Note that the location of $\theta = 0$ is now at the top, in contrast to what is shown in Figure 2.8. This is because our goal here is to swing the pendulum up and stabilize in the unstable upward position (corresponding to $\theta = 0$ in this exercise).
Envision the state space as an infinite tube: equate θ and $\theta + 2\pi n$ for any n.

(a) Obtain a linearized state space model with equilibrium (x^e, u^e) for each possible equilibrium (you will find that $x_2^e = 0$ is required). Comment on the challenge for $x_1^e = \pm\pi/2$.
(b) Obtain a linear feedback law that results in $x^e = 0$ asymptotically stable (locally).

You will obtain a control solution that is globally asymptotically stable in Exercise 3.10 after you learn a few concepts from optimal control in the next chapter.

2.18 *Linear Control Design for MagBall.* Our goal is to maintain the ball at rest at some preassigned distance r from the magnet.

(a) Find u° so that $x^\circ = (r, 0)^\intercal$ is an equilibrium: $f(x^\circ, u^\circ) = 0$. Based on the linearization (2.62), design a linear control law for (2.62), of the form

$$\tilde{u} = -K\tilde{x} = -K_1\tilde{x}_1 - K_2\tilde{x}_2$$

with $\tilde{x}_1 = x - x^\circ$ and $\tilde{x}_2 = x_2$. Make sure that your solution results in $A - BK$ Hurwitz.

(b) A difficulty with this design is that u° depends on c/m, which may not be known. Modify your design as follows:

$$\tilde{u} = -K\tilde{x}^a, \qquad \text{where} \quad \tilde{x}^a = (\tilde{x}_1, \tilde{x}_2, z^I)^\intercal, \quad z_t^I = \int_0^t \tilde{x}_1\, dr \tag{2.73}$$

with $K = [K_1, K_2, K_3]$. This is known as proportional-integral-derivative (PID) control. Obtain a third-order linear state space model, and choose $K_3 > 0$ so that the 3×3 matrix remains Hurwitz, and the transient behavior remains "good" (you decide what that means). Observe that the equilibrium condition $\frac{d}{dt} z^I = 0$ implies that $x_1^e = r$.

(c) Simulate as in Exercise 2.16 to estimate the region of attraction (you may restrict the simulation to initial conditions with zero velocity).

2.19 *Feedback Linearization for MagBall.* For systems with simple nonlinearities, there is a "brute-force" approach to obtain a linear model. For MagBall, we may view $\nu = u^2/x_1^2$ as an input, from which we obtain a linear system via (2.60):

$$\frac{d}{dt}x_1 = x_2,$$
$$\frac{d}{dt}x_2 = g - \frac{\kappa}{m}\nu.$$

(a) As in the previous exercise, obtain a control law $\nu = -K\tilde{x}$, where K_1 and K_2 are parameters chosen for stability and good transient response.

(b) Obtain an expression for the equilibrium x^e for the closed-loop system using the gain K obtained in (a). This is obtained by setting $\frac{d}{dt}x_i = 0$ for $i = 1, 2$.

(c) Modify your design as in (2.73): $\nu = -K\tilde{x}^a$. Find $K_3 > 0$ so that the transient behavior remains "good."

(d) You will need to modify your policy in (c) so ν is nonnegative valued, say $\nu = \phi(\tilde{x}^a) = \max(0, K\tilde{x} + K_3 z^I)$. The current applied to the magnet using this policy is then

$$u = x_1\sqrt{\phi(\tilde{x}^a)}. \tag{2.74}$$

Simulate, and estimate the region of attraction. You may restrict the simulation to zero initial velocity.

How does the region of attraction change when κ is doubled? κ divided by 2? Do not change your policy! The point is to check if your solution is robust to an inaccurate model.

Warning: Recall that it is not possible to achieve convergence to x° from any initial condition.

Note: See [199] for a survey on feedback linearization – a topic that has far more depth than is obvious from this example.

Matrix Algebra

2.20 Let A be an $n \times n$ matrix, and suppose that the following infinite sum exists:

$$U = I + A + A^2 + A^3 + \cdots ,$$

where I denotes the identity matrix. Verify that U is the inverse of the matrix $I - A$.

Note that this coincides with the Taylor series expansion of $f(x) = 1/(1-x)$ when $n = 1$.

2.21 Two square matrices A and $\bar{A}$ are called *similar* if there is an invertible matrix M such that

$$A = M^{-1}\bar{A}M.$$

Obtain the following for two similar matrices A and $\bar{A}$.

(a) Show that A^m is similar to $\bar{A}^m$ for any $m \ge 1$, where the superscript "m" denotes matrix product,

$$A^1 = A, \qquad A^m = A(A^{m-1}), \qquad m \ge 1.$$

(b) Show that v is an eigenvector for A if and only if Mv is an eigenvector for $\bar{A}$.

(c) Suppose that $\bar{A}$ is diagonal ($\bar{A}_{ij} = 0$ if $i \neq j$). Suppose moreover that $|\bar{A}_{ii}| < 1$ for each i. Conclude that $I - A$ admits an inverse by applying Exercise 2.20.

2.22 *Matrix Exponential.* Compute e^{At} for all t for the 2×2 matrix

$$A = aI + bJ\,, \qquad I = \begin{bmatrix} 1 & 0 \\ 0 & 1 \end{bmatrix} \quad J = \begin{bmatrix} 0 & 1 \\ -1 & 0 \end{bmatrix}.$$

The notation is intended to be suggestive: $J^2 = -I$.

It is not difficult to obtain a formula for A^m for each m, as required in the definition (2.45). With $a < 0$ and $b \neq 0$, describe the solution to $\frac{d}{dt}x = Ax$ with a nonzero initial condition.

2.9 Notes

The notion of "state" is flexible in both control theory [15] and reinforcement learning [337, 338]. The motivation is the same in each field: For the purposes of online decision making, replace the full history of observations at time k by some finite-dimensional "sufficient statistic" $x(k)$. One constraint that arises in RL is that the state process must be directly observable; in particular, the belief state that arises in partially observed Markov decision processes (MDPs) requires the (model-based) nonlinear filter, and is hence not directly useful for model-free RL. In practice, the "RL state" is specified as some compression of the full history of observations – see [338, section 17.3] for further discussion.

For more on linear models see [7, 80] and [118] for more advanced and recent material.

Textbook treatments on Lyapunov theory can be found in [45] (nonlinear) and [7, 205] (linear). The Electrical and Computer Engineering (ECE) Department at the University of Illinois had a great course on state space methods – the lecture notes are now available online [29]. The first section of [165] contains a brief crash course on Lyapunov theory, written in the style of this book, and with applications to reinforcement learning.

Poisson's inequality (2.31) is far removed (roughly two centuries) from the celebrated equation introduced by mathematician Siméon Poisson. The motivation back then was potential theory, as defined in theoretical physics. About one century later, Poisson's equation arose as a central player in studying the evolution of the density of Brownian motion (a particular Markov process). The terminology *Poisson inequality* and *Poisson equation* is today applied to any Markov chain, with *generator* playing the role of the Laplacian. The generator takes any function $h\colon \mathsf{X} \to \mathbb{R}$ to a new function denoted $\mathcal{A}h$. In particular, the deterministic state space model (2.21) can be regarded as a Markov chain [257], and the associated generator is defined as

$$\mathcal{A}h\,(x) = h(\mathrm{F}(x)) - h(x).$$

In this notation, (2.31) becomes $\mathcal{A}V \le -c + \overline{\eta}$.

3

Optimal Control

The chapter surveys optimization techniques for design of the feedback loop in Figure 2.1.

The feedforward component of the input is often designed based on optimization techniques, but without the dynamic programming equations that are the focus of this chapter and much of RL theory. Keep the larger feedback loops in mind when you apply RL to real-world control problems.

3.1 Value Function for Total Cost

To begin, we recall some notation: $x(k)$ is the state at time k, which evolves in a state space X; $u(k)$ is input at time k, which evolves in the input (or action) space U (the sets X and U may be Euclidean space, a finite set, or something more exotic). There may also be an output $\boldsymbol{y}$ as shown in Figure 2.1, but it is usually ignored in this chapter. The input and state are related through the dynamical system (2.6a)

$$x(k+1) = \mathrm{F}(x(k), u(k)), \tag{3.1}$$

where $\mathrm{F}\colon \mathsf{X} \times \mathsf{U} \to \mathsf{X}$.

Design of a state feedback policy $u(k) = \phi(x(k))$ is based on a cost function c. It is assumed throughout that it takes on nonnegative values:

$$c\colon \mathsf{X} \times \mathsf{U} \to \mathbb{R}_+ .$$

The total cost J associated with a particular control input $\boldsymbol{u} \stackrel{\text{def}}{=} u_{[0,\infty)}$ is defined by the sum

$$J(\boldsymbol{u}) = \sum_{k=0}^{\infty} c(x(k), u(k)).$$

The *value function* is defined to be the minimum over all inputs, which is a function of the initial condition:

$$J^\star(x) = \min_{\boldsymbol{u}} \sum_{k=0}^{\infty} c(x(k), u(k)), \quad x(0) = x \in \mathsf{X}. \tag{3.2}$$

The goal of optimal control is to find an input sequence that achieves the minimum in (3.2). We settle for an approximation in the majority of cases.

Why should we care? It is rare in our everyday lives that we think about solving a decision problem over an infinite horizon. It is favored in the control theory literature because an optimal policy often comes with stability guarantees: Theorem 3.1 implies this identity for the optimal input–output process:

$$J^\star(x^\star(k)) = c(x^\star(k),u^\star(k)) + J^\star(x^\star(k+1)),$$

which is a version of Poisson's inequality (2.31) with $\overline{\eta} = 0$ (and inequality replaced by equality). Mild conditions laid out in Proposition 2.3 then imply that x^e is globally asymptotically stable under the optimal policy.

What's more, once you understand the total cost formulation, other standard optimal control objectives can be treated as special cases. This is explained in Section 3.3.

Under our assumption that c is nonnegative, the value function is also nonnegative. The following are minimal assumptions to ensure that $J^\star$ is finite:

(i) There is a target state x^e that is an equilibrium for some input u^e:

$$\mathrm{F}(x^e,u^e) = x^e.$$

(ii) The cost function c is nonnegative and vanishes at this equilibrium, $c(x^e,u^e) = 0$.

(iii) For any initial condition x_0, there is an input sequence $\boldsymbol{u}_0$ and a time T^0 such that with this initial condition and this input we have $x(T^0) = x^e$.

Condition (iii) is a weak form of *controllability*. Under these three assumptions, it follows that $J^\star(x) < \infty$ for each x.

Example 3.1.1 (*Linear Quadratic Regulator*) The Linear Quadratic Regulator problem refers to the special case of linear dynamics (2.13), with quadratic cost:

$$c(x,u) = x^\intercal S x + u^\intercal R u. \tag{3.3}$$

It is always assumed that $S \geq 0$ (positive semidefinite) and $R > 0$ (positive definite). If there is one policy for which $J^\star$ is finite valued, then the value function is quadratic: $J^\star(x) = x^\intercal M^\star x$, where $M^\star \geq 0$. The optimal policy is obtained by linear state feedback: $\phi^\star(x) = -K^\star x$ for a matrix $K^\star$ that is a function of $M^\star$ and other system parameters. A bit more on this special case is contained in Section 3.6, where it will be clear why we impose $R > 0$.

■

3.2 Bellman Equation

Let $x = x(0)$ be an arbitrary initial state, and let k_m be an intermediate time, $0 < k_m < \infty$. We regard $J^\star(x(k_m))$ as the *cost to go* at time k_m: This is the optimal total cost over the remaining lifetime of the optimal state-input trajectory.

Based on this interpretation, we obtain the following:

$$\begin{aligned} J^\star(x) &= \min_{u_{[0,\infty)}} \Big[\sum_{k=0}^{k_m-1} c(x(k),u(k)) + \sum_{k=k_m}^{\infty} c(x(k),u(k)) \Big] \\ &= \min_{u_{[0,k_m]}} \Big[\sum_{k=0}^{k_m-1} c(x(k),u(k)) + \underbrace{\min_{u_{[k_m,\infty)}} \Big(\sum_{k=k_m}^{\infty} c(x(k),u(k)) \Big)}_{J^\star(x(k_m))} \Big], \end{aligned}$$

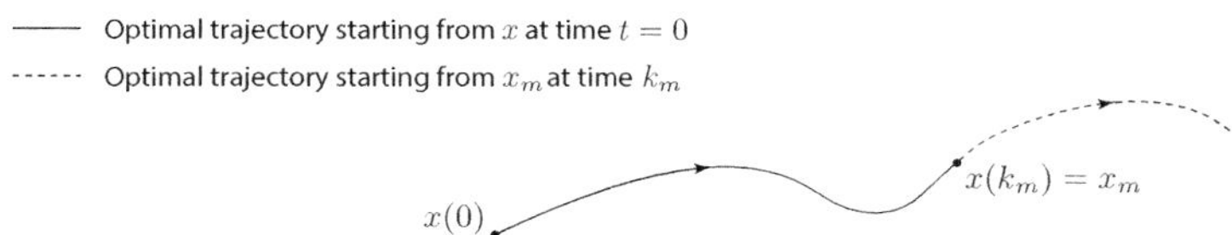

Figure 3.1 Principle of optimality: If a better control existed on $[k_m,\infty)$, we would have chosen it.

which gives the functional "fixed point equation":

$$J^\star(x) = \min_{u_{[0,k_m-1]}} \Big[\sum_{k=0}^{k_m-1} c(x(k),u(k)) + J^\star(x(k_m)) \Big]. \tag{3.4}$$

As a consequence, the optimal control over the whole interval has the property illustrated in Figure 3.1: If the optimal trajectory passes through the state x_m at time $x(k_m)$ using the control $\boldsymbol{u}^\star = u_{[0,\infty)}$, then the control $u^\star_{[k_m,\infty)}$ must be optimal for the system starting at x_m at time k_m. If a better $u^\star$ existed on $[k_m,\infty)$, we would have chosen it. This concept is called the *principle of optimality*.

Analysis in continuous time proceeds by letting $k_m \downarrow 0$ to obtain a partial differential equation. Theory is far simpler in discrete time: We set $k_m = 1$ to obtain the following celebrated result.

Theorem 3.1 *Suppose that the value function $J^\star$ is finite valued, and an optimal input $\boldsymbol{u}^\star$ solving* (3.2) *exists. Then the value function satisfies*

$$J^\star(x) = \min_u \{ c(x,u) + J^\star(\mathrm{F}(x,u)) \}. \tag{3.5}$$

Suppose that the minimum in (3.5) *is unique for each x, and let $\phi^\star(x)$ denote the minimum. Then the optimal input is expressed as state feedback,*

$$u^\star(k) = \phi^\star(x^\star(k)). \tag{3.6}$$

□

Equation (3.5) is often interpreted as a *fixed point equation* in the unknown "variable" $J^\star$. It goes by the name *Bellman equation* or *dynamic programming (DP) equation*: the two terms are used interchangeably in this book.

Q-Function. The function of two variables within the minimum in (3.5) is the *Q-function* of reinforcement learning:

$$Q^\star(x,u) \stackrel{\text{def}}{=} c(x,u) + J^\star(\mathrm{F}(x,u)). \tag{3.7a}$$

The Bellman equation is expressed

$$J^\star(x) = \min_u Q^\star(x,u) \tag{3.7b}$$

and the optimal feedback law any minimizer is expressed as follows:

$$\phi^\star(x) \in \arg\min_u Q^\star(x,u), \qquad x \in \mathsf{X}. \tag{3.7c}$$

The Q-function solves the fixed point equation,

$$Q^\star(x,u) = c(x,u) + \underline{Q}^\star(\mathrm{F}(x,u)), \qquad x \in \mathsf{X},\, u \in \mathsf{U}, \tag{3.7d}$$

where $\underline{Q}(x) \stackrel{\text{def}}{=} \min_u Q(x,u)$, $x \in \mathsf{X}$, for any function Q.

Equation (3.7d) is obtained by eliminating $J^\star$ in (3.7a) via the identity (3.7b). Applications of this dynamic programming equation appear throughout the book, starting in Section 3.7.

The term *dynamic programming* also refers to recursive algorithms designed to obtain the solution to a Bellman equation. However, dynamic programming is only practical when X is finite, or the system has special structure (such as for linear state space models and quadratic cost). The two most popular algorithms are value iteration and policy iteration (also known as policy *improvement*).

3.2.1 Value Iteration

Given an initial approximation V^0 for $V^\star$ appearing in (3.5), a sequence of approximations is defined recursively via

$$V^{n+1}(x) = \min_u \{c(x,u) + V^n(\mathrm{F}(x,u))\}, \qquad x \in \mathsf{X},\, n \ge 0. \tag{3.8}$$

Recursions like this to solve fixed point equations are generally known as *successive approximation*. In Exercise 3.5, you will establish the following interpretation:

$$V^{n+1}(x) = \min_{u_{[0,n]}} \Big\{\sum_{k=0}^{n} c(x(k),u(k)) + V^0(x(n+1))\Big\}, \quad x(0) = x \in \mathsf{X}. \tag{3.9}$$

The recursion (3.8) is known as the value iteration algorithm (VIA). It is convergent under very general conditions: for each x,

$$\lim_{n\to\infty} [V^n(x) - V^n(x^e)] = J^\star(x).$$

Here is the simplest result of this kind:

Proposition 3.2 *Consider the VIA under the following assumptions:*

(i) *The state space* X *and input space* U *are finite.*
(ii) *The cost function* c *is nonnegative and vanishes only at* (x^e,u^e)*, and* $J^\star$ *is finite valued.*
(iii) *The initialization* V^0 *is chosen with nonnegative entries, and* $V^0(x^e) = 0$.

Then there is $n_0 \ge 1$ *such that*

$$V^n(x) = J^\star(x), \quad x \in \mathsf{X},\ n \ge n_0.$$

Proof Let $\phi^\star$ be an optimal policy, and let $n_0 \ge 1$ denote a value such that $(x^\star(k),u^\star(k)) = (x^e,u^e)$ for $k \ge n_0$. Such an integer exists because $J^\star$ is finite valued.

We have from (3.9),

$$V^n(x) \le \sum_{k=0}^{n-1} c(x(k),u(k)) + V^0(x(n)), \text{when } u(k) = \phi^\star(x(k)) \text{ for each } k, \quad x(0) = x \in \mathsf{X}.$$

The right-hand side is precisely $J^\star(x) + V^0(x^e) = J^\star(x)$ for $n \ge n_0$. And for such n, the inequality must then be equality due to (3.9) and optimality of $\phi^\star$. □

The VIA generates a sequence of policies, defined as minimizers in (3.8). For each $n \ge 0$,

$$\phi^n(x) \in \arg\min_u \{c(x,u) + V^n(\mathrm{F}(x,u))\}, \qquad x \in \mathsf{X}. \tag{3.10}$$

Each of these policies is stabilizing, subject to an assumption on the initial value function: The function V^0 is nonnegative, and satisfies for some $\overline{\eta} \ge 0$,

$$\min_u \{c(x,u) + V^0(\mathrm{F}(x,u))\} \le V^0(x) + \overline{\eta}, \qquad x \in \mathsf{X}. \tag{3.11}$$

This can be interpreted as a version of Poisson's inequality (2.31) for the system controlled using the policy ϕ^0:

$$V^0(\mathrm{F}(x,\phi^0(x))) \le V^0(x) - c(x,\phi^0(x)) + \overline{\eta}.$$

Proposition 3.3 *Suppose that* (3.11) *holds, with* V^0 *nonnegative. That is,*

$$\{c(x,u) + V^0(\mathrm{F}(x,u))\}\Big|_{u=\phi^0(x)} \le V^0(x) + \overline{\eta}, \qquad x \in \mathsf{X}.$$

Then a similar bound holds for each n*:*

$$\{c(x,u) + V^n(\mathrm{F}(x,u))\}\Big|_{u=\phi^n(x)} \le V^n(x) + \overline{\eta}_n, \qquad x \in \mathsf{X},$$

where the upper bounds are nonnegative and nonincreasing:

$$\overline{\eta} \ge \overline{\eta}_0 \ge \overline{\eta}_1 \ge \cdots.$$

The conclusions of Proposition 3.3 are most interesting when $\overline{\eta} = 0$ so that, for each n,

$$\{c(x,u) + V^n(\mathrm{F}(x,u))\}\Big|_{u=\phi^n(x)} \le V^n(x).$$

The following bound then follows from Proposition 2.3:

$$J^n(x) \le V^n(x), \qquad x \in \mathsf{X},$$

where J^n is the total cost using policy ϕ^n.

Proof of Proposition 3.3 Denote for $n \ge 0$,

$$\mathcal{B}^n(x) = V^{n+1}(x) - V^n(x), \qquad \overline{\eta}_n = \sup_x \mathcal{B}^n(x).$$

The VIA recursion (3.8) gives, for any x,

$$\min_u \{c(x,u) + V^n(\mathrm{F}(x,u))\} = V^{n+1}(x) = V^n(x) + \mathcal{B}^n(x).$$

For this reason, the function $\mathcal{B}^n$ is known as the *Bellman error* (associated with the approximation of $J^\star$ by V^n). The Lyapunov bound then follows from the definition of ϕ^n:

$$\big\{c(x,u) + V^n(\mathrm{F}(x,u))\big\}\Big|_{u=\phi^n(x)} = \min_u \big\{c(x,u) + V^n(\mathrm{F}(x,u))\big\} \le V^n(x) + \overline{\eta}_n.$$

It remains to obtain bounds on $\{\overline{\eta}_n\}$. First observe that by (3.11),

$$V^1(x) \le \big\{c(x,u) + V^0(\mathrm{F}(x,u))\big\}\Big|_{u=\phi^0(x)} \le V^0(x) + \overline{\eta},$$

from which we conclude that $\mathcal{B}_0(x) \le \overline{\eta}$ for all x, and hence also $\overline{\eta}_0 \le \overline{\eta}$.

The next steps are similar: For $n \ge 1$,

$$V^{n+1}(x) \le \big\{c(x,u) + V^n(\mathrm{F}(x,u))\big\}\Big|_{u=\phi^{n-1}(x)},$$

$$V^n(x) = \big\{c(x,u) + V^{n-1}(\mathrm{F}(x,u))\big\}\Big|_{u=\phi^{n-1}(x)}.$$

On subtracting,

$$\mathcal{B}^n(x) = V^{n+1}(x) - V^n(x) \le \big\{V^n(\mathrm{F}(x,u)) - V^{n-1}(\mathrm{F}(x,u))\big\}\Big|_{u=\phi^{n-1}(x)} \le \overline{\eta}_{n-1}.$$

Hence $\overline{\eta}_n = \sup_x \mathcal{B}^n(x) \le \overline{\eta}_{n-1}$ as claimed. □

3.2.2 Policy Improvement

The policy improvement algorithm (PIA) starts with an initial policy ϕ^0, and updates recursively as follows: For policy ϕ^n, the associated total cost is computed:

$$J^n(x) = \sum_{k=0}^{\infty} c(x(k),u(k)), \qquad u(k) = \phi^n(x(k)) \text{ for each } k, \quad x(0) = x \in \mathsf{X}. \tag{3.12}$$

This solves the fixed-policy Bellman equation,

$$J^n(x) = \big\{c(x,u) + J^n(\mathrm{F}(x,u))\big\}\Big|_{u=\phi^n(x)}. \tag{3.13}$$

This is followed by the policy improvement step to obtain the next policy:

$$\phi^{n+1}(x) \in \arg\min_u \{c(x,u) + J^n(\mathrm{F}(x,u))\}, \qquad x \in \mathsf{X}. \tag{3.14}$$

The proof of the following is similar to the proof of Proposition 3.3. The proof that the value functions are nonincreasing is an application of Proposition 2.3.

Proposition 3.4 *Suppose that ϕ^0 is stabilizing, in the sense that J^0 is finite valued. Then for each $n \ge 0$,*

$$\big\{c(x,u) + J^n(\mathrm{F}(x,u))\big\}\Big|_{u=\phi^{n+1}(x)} \le J^n(x), \qquad x \in \mathsf{X}.$$

Consequently, the value functions are nonincreasing:

$$J^0(x) \ge J^1(x) \ge J^2(x) \ge \cdots.$$

□

3.2.3 Perron–Frobenius Theory: A Gentle Introduction*

One step in the PIA requires a subroutine: how to solve the fixed policy dynamic programming equation (3.13)? The purpose here is to present an efficient approach to computing the value function when the state space is finite; this is also a prelude to theory for Markov chains, as well as spectral graph theory that arises in ML.

Let's return for a moment to the setting of Section 2.4, where we considered the state space model without control:

$$x(k+1) = \mathrm{F}(x(k))\,, \qquad k \geq 0,$$

and associated value function (2.24), recalled here:

$$J(x) = \sum_{k=0}^{\infty} c(x(k))\,, \qquad x(0) = x \in \mathsf{X}.$$

The value function satisfies a version of (3.13), which in (2.25) is expressed in the simpler form

$$J(x) = c(x) + J(\mathrm{F}(x))\,, \qquad x \in \mathsf{X}. \tag{3.15}$$

Much of Perron–Frobenius theory concerns calculation of fixed point equations involving matrices. To apply this theory, we need a matrix. Assume the state space is finite, and to simplify notation, suppose that the state space is a sequence of positive integers: $\mathsf{X} = \{1,2,3,\dots,N\}$ for some $N > 1$. Assume that $x^e = N$, which satisfies $\mathrm{F}(N) = N$ by the equilibrium property. Assume also that $c(N) = 0$, and that the value function is finite valued.

Define an $N \times N$ *transition matrix* P as follows: $P(i,j) = 0$ or 1 for each i and j, and $P(i,j) = 1$ means that $j = \mathrm{F}(i)$. Consequently, the ith row of P has exactly one nonzero element. In particular, $P(N,N) = 1$ characterizes the equilibrium property. With this notation, we have a new way of thinking about the fixed-policy dynamic programming equation:

$$J(i) = c(i) + \sum_{j=1}^{N} P(i,j)J(j)\,, \qquad 1 \leq i \leq N. \tag{3.16}$$

Now, dear reader: *please accept a new way of thinking about the notation:*

$$\vec{J} = \vec{c} + P\vec{J}. \tag{3.17}$$

That is, we view $\vec{J}$ is an N-dimensional column vector whose ith element is $J(i)$, and the definition of $\vec{c}$ is analogous. I am pleading with you here, because I know from experience that young graduate students feel uncomfortable going from (3.15) to (3.17).

At first glance, it seems clear that we can solve this equation by inversion:

$$\vec{J} = [I - P]^{-1}\vec{c}.$$

The problem, however, is that $I - P$ is never invertible. To see this, take $v \in \mathbb{R}^N$ with constant nonzero entries ($v(i) = v(1) \neq 0$ for all i), and observe that by construction of P,

$$Pv = v.$$

That is, v is an eigenvector of P with eigenvalue 1. It follows that v is in the null space of $I - P$.

You might try a pseudo inverse. In Matlab, this is computed using the command `J=(I-P)\c`. But if you do this, you may not understand what is going on behind Matlab's curtain. Also, how do you know if you have obtained the boundary constraint $J(x^e) = 0$?

Here is one ingenious idea behind the theory of Perron and Frobenius: Choose two vectors $s, \nu \in \mathbb{R}^N$ with nonnegative entries, and satisfying

$$P(i,j) \geq s(i)\nu(j), \qquad 1 \leq i,j \leq N. \tag{3.18}$$

This is called a *minorization condition*. Letting $s \otimes \nu$ denote the "outer product" of these two vectors, this is equivalently expressed

$$P(i,j) \geq [s \otimes \nu](i,j), \qquad 1 \leq i,j \leq N.$$

We then play with the fixed point equation:

$$\vec{c} = [I - P]\vec{J} = [I - (P - s \otimes \nu)]\vec{J} - [s \otimes \nu]\vec{J},$$

and note that the final term is just a constant times s, represented as a column vector:

$$[s \otimes \nu]\vec{J} = \delta s, \qquad \delta = \sum_j \nu(j)J(j)$$

so that

$$\vec{c} = [I - (P - s \otimes \nu)]\vec{J} - \delta s. \tag{3.19}$$

Under very mild conditions, we can invert the matrix multiplying $\vec{J}$ in (3.19). The inverse is known as the *fundamental matrix*:

$$G = [I - (P - s \otimes \nu)]^{-1} = \sum_{n=0}^{\infty} (P - s \otimes \nu)^n, \tag{3.20}$$

with $(P - s \otimes \nu)^k$ the kth matrix power for $k \geq 1$, and with $(P - s \otimes \nu)^0 = I$ (the identity matrix). Here is where the minorization condition comes in: The matrix $(P - s \otimes \nu)^k$ has nonnegative entries for each $k \geq 0$, so that the infinite sum is always meaningful. If it is finite valued, then from (3.19) we obtain

$$\vec{J} = G\vec{c} + \delta G s.$$

To find δ, you must apply the boundary condition for J,

$$0 = J(N) = \sum_k G(N,k)c(k) + \delta \sum_k G(N,k)s(k),$$

and then obtain δ by division.

Alternatively, think harder about your choice of ν! Here is a simple consequence of the Perron–Frobenius construction:

Proposition 3.5 *Consider the state space model with* $\mathsf{X} = \{1,2,3,\dots,N\}$. *Suppose that* $c\colon \mathsf{X} \to \mathbb{R}_+$ *vanishes at the state* N*, and suppose that the total cost* J *is finite valued. Define the matrix* G *using* $s = \nu = e^N$ *(the* N*th basis vector in* $\mathbb{R}^N$*).*

Then $\vec{J} = G\vec{c}$. That is, for each $i \in \mathsf{X}$,

$$J(i) = \sum_{j=1}^{N} G(i,j)c(j) = \sum_{n=0}^{\infty}\sum_{j=1}^{N}(P - s\otimes\nu)^n(i,j)c(j).$$

Proof The minorization condition holds because $P(N,N) = 1 = [s\otimes\nu](N,N)$, and $[s\otimes\nu](i,j) = 0$ for all other i, j. Applying the boundary constraint $J(N) = 0$ gives

$$\delta = \sum_j \nu(j)J(j) = J(N) = 0.$$

To see that G is finite valued, we establish an interpretation for each term in the sum: for $j < N$,

$$(P - s\otimes\nu)^n(i,j) = \mathbb{1}\{x(n) = j\}, \qquad \text{when } x(0) = i.$$

The left-hand side is zero for any i and $n \geq 1$ when $j = N$. Let $n_0 \geq 1$ denote an integer for which $x(n) = N$ for $n \geq n_0$ and any initial condition. Then G can be expressed as a finite sum:

$$G = \sum_{n=0}^{n_0}(P - s\otimes\nu)^n. \qquad \square$$

3.3 Variations

The total cost problem (3.2) is the standard in the control literature, and opens the door to many other possibilities.

3.3.1 Discounted Cost

A more popular objective within the operations research literature is the *discounted-cost* problem:

$$J^\star(x) = \min_{\boldsymbol{u}} \sum_{k=0}^{\infty} \gamma^k c(x(k),u(k)), \quad x(0) = x \in \mathsf{X}, \tag{3.21}$$

with $\gamma \in (0,1)$ the *discount factor*. This solves the discounted-cost optimality equation

$$J^\star(x) = \min_u \{c(x,u) + \gamma J^\star(\mathrm{F}(x,u))\}.$$

The Q-function becomes $Q^\star(x,u) \stackrel{\text{def}}{=} c(x,u) + \gamma J^\star(\mathrm{F}(x,u))$, so that $J^\star(x) = \min_u Q^\star(x,u)$.

3.3.2 Shortest Path Problem

Given a subset $A \subset \mathsf{X}$, define

$$\tau_A = \min\{k \geq 1 : x(k) \in A\}.$$

The discounted shortest path problem (SPP) is defined to be the minimal discounted cost incurred before this time:

$$J^\star(x) = \min_{\boldsymbol{u}} \sum_{k=0}^{\tau_A - 1} \gamma^k c(x(k), u(k)), \qquad x(0) = x. \tag{3.22}$$

Proposition 3.6 *If $J^\star$ is finite valued, then it is the solution to the DP equation:*

$$J^\star(x) = \min_u \Big\{ c(x,u) + \gamma \mathbb{1}\{\mathrm{F}(x,u) \in A^c\} J^\star(\mathrm{F}(x,u)) \Big\}, \qquad x \in \mathsf{X}. \tag{3.23}$$

Proof As in the total cost problem, we begin with

$$J^\star(x) = \min_{\boldsymbol{u}} \Big\{ c(x,u(0)) + \sum_{k=1}^{\tau_A - 1} \gamma^k c(x(k), u(k)) \Big\},$$

with the understanding that $\sum_{k=1}^{0} = 0$: The upper limit in the sum is equal to 0 when $\tau_A = 1$ (equivalently, $x(1) \in A$). Consequently,

$$\begin{aligned} J^\star(x) &= \min_{u(0)} \Big\{ c(x,u(0)) + \gamma \mathbb{1}\{x(1) \in A^c\} \min_{u_{[1,\infty]}} \sum_{k=1}^{\tau_A - 1} \gamma^{k-1} c(x(k), u(k)) \Big\} \\ &= \min_{u(0)} \Big\{ c(x,u(0)) + \gamma \mathbb{1}\{x(1) \in A^c\} J^\star(x(1)) \Big\}, \qquad x(1) = \mathrm{F}(x,u(0)) \\ &= \min_u \Big\{ c(x,u) + \gamma \mathbb{1}\{\mathrm{F}(x,u) \in A^c\} J^\star(\mathrm{F}(x,u)) \Big\}. \end{aligned}$$

□

For the purposes of unifying the control techniques that follow, it is useful to recast (3.22) as an instance of the total cost problem (3.21). This requires the definition of a new state process $\boldsymbol{x}^a$ with dynamics F^a, and a new cost function c^a defined as follows:

(i) Modified state dynamics: $\mathrm{F}^a(x,u) = \begin{cases} \mathrm{F}(x,u) & x \in A^c \\ x & x \in A \end{cases}$
so that $x^a(k+1) = x^a(k)$ if $x^a(k) \in A$ (called a *graveyard set* for the control system).

(ii) Modified cost function: $c^a(x,u) = \begin{cases} c(x,u) & x \in A^c \\ 0 & x \in A \end{cases}$.

From these definitions, it follows that the value function (3.22) can be expressed as follows:

$$J^\star(x) = \min_{\boldsymbol{u}} \sum_{k=0}^{\infty} \gamma^k c^a(x^a(k), u(k)), \qquad x \in A^c.$$

Example 3.3.1 (*Mountain Car*) Recall the Mountain Car example introduced in Section 2.7.2. The control objective is a shortest path problem: to reach the goal in minimal time. Let $c(x,u) = 1$ for all x,u with $x \neq z^{\text{goal}}$, and $c(z^{\text{goal}},u) = 0$ for any u. The SPP can be expressed as a total-cost optimal control problem based on the model and this cost function. The optimal total cost (3.2) is finite for each initial condition, and the Bellman equation (3.5) becomes

$$J^\star(x) = 1 + \min_u J^\star(\mathrm{F}(x,u)), \quad x_1 < z^{\text{goal}}$$

and with $J^\star(z^{\text{goal}}, x_2) = 0$ for any value of x_2.

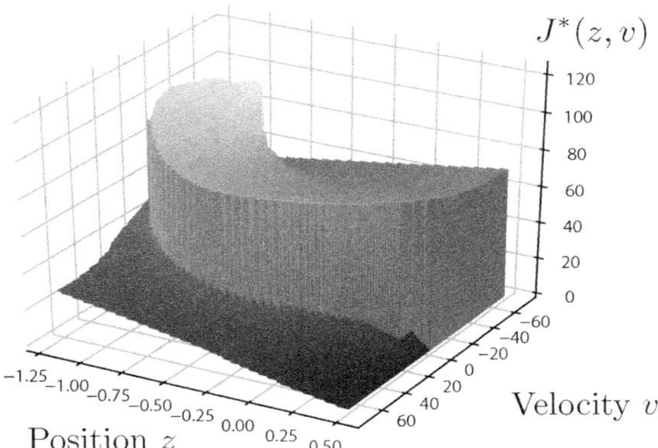

Figure 3.2 $J^\star$ for Mountain Car.

Figure 3.2 shows the value function obtained using value iteration, based on a finite state space approximate model (details may be found in Section 3.9.1). The total cost is relatively low with initial condition $x_0 = (z,v)$ satisfying $v \geq 0.2$, because the car can reach the goal without stalling, using $u(k) = 1$ whenever $z(k) < z^{\text{goal}}$. ■

3.3.3 *Finite Horizon*

Your choice of discount factor is based on how concerned you are with the distant future. Motivation is similar for the *finite horizon* formulation: Fix a horizon $\mathcal{N} \geq 1$, and denote

$$J^\star(x) = \min_{u_{[0,\mathcal{N}]}} \sum_{k=0}^{\mathcal{N}} c(x(k),u(k)), \quad x(0) = x \in \mathsf{X}. \tag{3.24}$$

This can be interpreted as the total-cost problem (3.2), following two modifications of the state description and the cost function, similar to the SPP:

(i) Enlarge the state process to $x^a(k) = (x(k),\tau(k))$, where the second component is "time" plus an offset: $\tau(k) = \tau(0) + k, \qquad k \geq 0.$
(ii) Extend the definition of the cost function as follows:

$$c^a((x,\tau),u) = \begin{cases} c(x,u) & \tau \leq \mathcal{N} \\ 0 & \tau > \mathcal{N} \end{cases}.$$

That is, $c^a((x,\tau),u) = c(x,u)\mathbb{1}\{\tau \leq \mathcal{N}\}$ for all x,τ,u.

If these definitions are clear to you, then you understand that we have succeeded in the transformation:

$$J^\star(x) = \min_{\boldsymbol{u}} \sum_{k=0}^{\infty} c^a(x^a(k),u(k)), \quad x^a(0) = (x,\tau),\ \tau = 0. \tag{3.25}$$

However, to write down the Bellman equation it is necessary to consider all values of τ (at least values $\tau \leq \mathcal{N}$), and not just the desired value $\tau = 0$. Letting $J^\star(x,\tau)$ denote the right-hand side of (3.25) for arbitrary values of $\tau \geq 0$, the Bellman equation (3.5) becomes

$$J^\star(x,\tau) = \min_u \{c(x,u)\mathbb{1}\{\tau \leq \mathcal{N}\} + J^\star(\mathrm{F}(x,u),\tau+1)\}. \tag{3.26}$$

The similarity with (3.8) is explored in Exercise 3.5.

Based on (3.25) and the definition of c^a, we know that $J^\star(x,\tau) \equiv 0$ for $\tau > \mathcal{N}$. This is considered a *boundary condition* for the recursion (3.26), which is put to work as follows: First, since $J^\star(x,\mathcal{N}+1) \equiv 0$,

$$J^\star(x,\mathcal{N}) = \underline{c}(x) \stackrel{\text{def}}{=} \min_u c(x,u).$$

Applying (3.26) once more gives

$$J^\star(x,\mathcal{N}-1) = \min_u \{c(x,u) + \underline{c}(\mathrm{F}(x,u))\}.$$

These steps can be repeated until we obtain the finite horizon value function $J^\star(\,\cdot\,) = J^\star(\,\cdot\,,0)$.

What about the policy? It is again obtained via (3.26), but the optimal policy depends on the extended state:

$$\phi^\star(x,\tau) \in \arg\min_u \{c(x,u) + J^\star(\mathrm{F}(x,u),\tau+1)\}, \qquad \tau \le \mathcal{N}. \tag{3.27}$$

This means that the feedback is no longer time homogeneous:[1]

$$u^\star(k) = \phi^\star(x^\star(k),k). \tag{3.28}$$

3.3.4 Model Predictive Control

An extremely successful control technique in many fields (such as in manufacturing and building operations) is model predictive control (MPC). This is a slight variant of (3.28) to obtain a *stationary* policy:

$$u(k) = \phi^{\text{MPC}}(x^\star(k)) = \phi^\star(x(k),0), \tag{3.29}$$

where the right-hand side is defined in (3.27) using $\tau = 0$. However, MPC is never presented as state feedback because the policy ϕ^{MPC} is not computed and stored in memory. Rather, for each k, when the state $x = x(k)$ is observed, the finite horizon optimization is performed to obtain the value $u(k) = \phi^\star(x,0)$ That is, the policy is only evaluated for those states that are observed [242, 243].

Nevertheless, the general optimal control theory surveyed here provides techniques to ensure that the total cost associated with (3.29) is finite. Denote for $x \in \mathsf{X}$,

$$J^{\text{MPC}}(x) = \sum_{k=0}^{\infty} c(x(k),u(k)),$$

subject to $x(0) = x$, and $u(k) = \phi^{\text{MPC}}(x(k))$ for all k.

Proposition 3.7 *Consider the policy* (3.29), *obtained with modified objective:*

$$J^\star(x;0) = \min_{u_{[0,\mathcal{N}]}} \sum_{k=0}^{\mathcal{N}-1} c(x(k),u(k)) + V^0(x(\mathcal{N})), \quad x(0) = x \in \mathsf{X}, \tag{3.30}$$

where $V^0 \colon \mathsf{X} \to \mathbb{R}_+$ *satisfies* (3.11) *with* $\overline{\eta} = 0$*:*

$$\min_u \{c(x,u) + V^0(\mathrm{F}(x,u))\} \le V^0(x), \qquad x \in \mathsf{X}.$$

Then the total cost J^{MPC} *is everywhere finite.*

[1] Substituting $\tau^\star(k) = k$ is justified because we cannot control time!

Proof From the definitions (3.9) and (3.30), we conclude that $J^\star(x;0) = V^{\mathcal{N}}(x)$ (the outcome of $\mathcal{N}$ iterations of VIA). Proposition 3.3 then gives a version of Poisson's inequality

$$\{c(x,u) + V(\mathrm{F}(x,u))\}\Big|_{u=\phi^{\mathrm{MPC}}(x)} \le V(x), \qquad x \in \mathsf{X}$$

with $V = V^{\mathcal{N}}$. The conclusion that J^{MPC} is finite valued follows from Proposition 2.3 (the Comparison Theorem). □

3.4 Inverse Dynamic Programming

An alternative to dynamic programming is to change the problem: In optimal control, we are given c, and then face the (often daunting) task of computing $J^\star$. Here we reverse the computational task: Given any function J, find a cost function c^J so that (3.5) is satisfied.

To proceed in a way that respects our original goal, we consider the *Bellman error*:

$$\mathcal{B}(x) = -J(x) + \min_u[c(x,u) + J(\mathrm{F}(x,u))]. \tag{3.31}$$

This is precisely the error in the Bellman equation (3.5). Based on this, we obtain a solution to a Bellman equation, with a modified cost function:

$$J(x) = \min_u[c^J(x,u) + J(\mathrm{F}(x,u))], \tag{3.32a}$$

$$c^J(x,u) = c(x,u) - \mathcal{B}(x). \tag{3.32b}$$

The minimizer in (3.32a) defines a policy, denoted ϕ^J:

$$\phi^J(x) \in \arg\min_u[c^J(x,u) + J(\mathrm{F}(x,u))] = \arg\min_u[c(x,u) + J(\mathrm{F}(x,u))]. \tag{3.33}$$

This procedure is known as *inverse dynamic programming* (IDP). It is one formulation of the *control-Lyapunov function* approach to control design. Minimizing the Bellman error is a goal of many approaches to reinforcement learning. Motivation is provided in the following:

Proposition 3.8 *Suppose that the following hold:*

(i) *J is nonnegative, continuous, and vanishes only at x^e.*
(ii) *The function $c^J(x) = c(x,\phi^J(x))$ satisfies the following: It is nonnegative, continuous, inf-compact, and vanishes only at x^e.*
(iii) *There is a constant ϱ satisfying $0 \le \varrho < 1$, and*

$$\mathcal{B}(x) = c(x,u) - c^J(x,u) \ge -\varrho c(x,u) \qquad \textit{for all } x,u.$$

Let J^{IDP} denote the value function under the policy ϕ^J:

$$J^{\mathrm{IDP}}(x) = \sum_{k=0}^{\infty} c(x(k),u(k)), \qquad x(0) = x,\ u(k) = \phi^J(x(k)) \textit{ for all } k. \tag{3.34}$$

This admits the pair of bounds:

$$J^\star(x) \le J^{\mathrm{IDP}}(x) \le (1+\varrho)J^\star(x).$$

The proof of Proposition 3.8 requires a deeper look at the dynamic programming equation (3.5). The following is an extension of Proposition 2.4:

Proposition 3.9 *Suppose that the value function $J^\star$ is finite valued, and the optimal policy $\phi^\star$ is stabilizing, in the sense that $x^\star(k) \to x^e$ as $k \to \infty$ for any initial condition.*

Suppose that $J\colon \mathsf{X} \to \mathbb{R}_+$ is continuous, vanishes at x^e, and solves

$$J(x) \le \min_u \{c(x,u) + J(\mathrm{F}(x,u))\}\,, \quad x \in \mathsf{X}. \tag{3.35}$$

Then $J = J^\star$.

Proof We adopt the same notation as in inverse dynamic programming: $\phi^J(x)$ is defined as a minimizer in (3.35) for each x, and J^{IDP} the associated value function (3.34). We have the bound $J^{\text{IDP}} \le J$ by the Comparison Theorem, Proposition 2.3. We can also establish the following bound by induction on $\mathcal{N}$ (starting with (3.35)):

$$\begin{aligned} J(x) &\le \min_{u_{[0,\mathcal{N}]}} \Big\{ \sum_{k=0}^{\mathcal{N}-1} c(x(k),u(k)) + J(x(\mathcal{N})) \Big\} \\ &\le \sum_{k=0}^{\mathcal{N}-1} c(x^\star(k),u^\star(k)) + J(x^\star(\mathcal{N}))\,, \qquad x(0) = x\,,\ u^\star(k) = \phi^\star(x^\star(k)) \ \text{ for all } k, \end{aligned}$$

with the second inequality obtained because we have replaced the minimum with a specific policy. We have $J(x^\star(\mathcal{N})) \to 0$ as $\mathcal{N} \to \infty$ by the assumptions on J and $\phi^\star$, and hence $J \le J^\star$.

Putting these bounds together gives for all x,

$$J^\star(x) \le J^{\text{IDP}}(x) \le J(x) \le J^\star(x),$$

which implies that these functions coincide, and in particular $J = J^\star$. □

Proof of Proposition 3.8 The assumptions on J and c^J are imposed so that we may apply Proposition 2.3 for the state space model subject to $u(k) = \phi^J(x(k))$. Part (i) implies that $J^{\text{IDP}}(x) \le J(x)$ for all x, and (iii) tells us that x^e is globally asymptotically stable under this policy. We can then apply Proposition 3.9 to establish equality:

$$J(x) = J^{\text{IDP}}(x) = \min_{\boldsymbol{u}} \sum_{k=0}^{\infty} c^J(x(k),u(k)).$$

As in the proof of Proposition 3.9, the right-hand side can only be increased by replacing the minimum with the optimal policy: With $x(0) = x$,

$$J^{\text{IDP}}(x) \le \sum_{k=0}^{\infty} c^J(x^\star(k),u^\star(k)) \le (1+\varrho)J^\star(x),$$

where the second inequality uses $c^J \le (1+\varrho)c$. □

3.5 Bellman Equation Is a Linear Program

One approach to control design is to introduce a family of candidate value function approximations $\{J^\theta : \theta \in \mathbb{R}^d\}$, and compute the parameter θ^* that minimizes the Bellman error, such as through minimizing the mean-square criterion (2.53). A significant challenge is that the loss function $\Gamma^\varepsilon(J^\theta)$ is not convex, even when J^θ depends linearly on θ.

We obtain a convex optimization problem that is suitable for RL implementation by applying a common trick in optimization: Overparameterize the search space. The first step is to regard $J^\star$ and $Q^\star$ as independent variables, and regard (3.7a) as a linear constraint. Following this approach, we obtain a linear program that lends itself to RL algorithm design.

Naturally, we obtain a finite-dimensional linear program only if the state space and action space are finite. In this case, as part of the algorithm we choose a *weighting function* ν, and denote for any candidate approximation J,

$$\langle \nu, J\rangle \stackrel{\text{def}}{=} \sum_{x\in\mathsf{X}} \nu(x)J(x).$$

It is assumed that $\nu(x) > 0$ for each x. In most cases, this will be a probability mass function (pmf), meaning that in addition we assume $\sum_x \nu(x) = 1$.

Even when the state space is not finite, say $\mathsf{X} = \mathbb{R}^n$, we continue to assume that ν has finite support $\{x^i : 1 \le i \le M\}$. In this case, the definition becomes

$$\langle \nu, J\rangle \stackrel{\text{def}}{=} \sum_{i} \nu(x^i)J(x^i).$$

Proposition 3.10 states that the Bellman equation can be cast as a linear program.

Proposition 3.10 *Suppose that the value function* $J^\star$ *defined in* (3.2) *is continuous, inf-compact, and vanishes only at* x^e. *Then the pair* $(J^\star, Q^\star)$ *solves the following linear program (LP) in the "variables"* (J,Q):

$$\max_{J,Q} \ \langle \nu, J\rangle \tag{3.36a}$$

$$\text{s.t.} \ \ Q(x,u) \le c(x,u) + J(\mathrm{F}(x,u)), \tag{3.36b}$$

$$Q(x,u) \ge J(x), \qquad x\in\mathsf{X},\ u\in\mathsf{U}(x), \tag{3.36c}$$

$$J \textit{ is continuous, and } J(x^e) = 0. \tag{3.36d}$$

□

The linear program will be called the *dynamic programming linear program* (DPLP). It reappears in Section 5.5 as 5.62, followed by several approaches to approximately solve a DP equation.

We can without loss of generality strengthen (3.36b) to equality: $Q(x,u) = c(x,u) + J(\mathrm{F}(x,u))$. Based on this substitution, the variable Q is eliminated:

$$\max_{J} \ \langle \nu, J\rangle \tag{3.37a}$$

$$\text{s.t.} \ \ c(x,u) + J(\mathrm{F}(x,u)) \ge J(x), \qquad x\in\mathsf{X},\ u\in\mathsf{U}(x). \tag{3.37b}$$

This more closely resembles what you find in the stochastic control literature (see [10] for a survey). The more complex LP (3.36) is introduced because it is easily adapted to RL applications.

3.6 Linear Quadratic Regulator

For the linear system model (2.13), with quadratic cost (3.3), it is known that the value function is quadratic, $J^\star(x) = x^\intercal M^\star x$ for each x. The Q-function is also quadratic: Combining the definition (3.7a) with the system model (2.13a),

$$Q^\star(x,u) = c(x,u) + J^\star(Fx + Gu). \tag{3.38}$$

A more explicit quadratic representation can be found in (3.41).

The optimal policy is obtained by minimizing the Q-function over u, which is easily done via the first-order condition for optimality:

$$0 = \nabla_u Q^\star(x,u) = 2Ru^\star + 2G^\intercal M^\star(Fx + Gu^\star).$$

Under the assumption that $R > 0$, it follows that $R + G^\intercal M^\star G > 0$ (and hence invertible). The minimizer $u^\star = \phi^\star(x)$ defines the optimal policy as linear state feedback:

$$\phi^\star(x) = -K^\star x \quad \text{with} \quad K^\star = [R + G^\intercal M^\star G]^{-1} G^\intercal M^\star F. \tag{3.39}$$

To obtain $\phi^\star$, we must compute the value function, since the gain $K^\star$ depends on $M^\star \geq 0$. This matrix solves a fixed point equation known as the *algebraic Riccati equation* (ARE):

$$M^\star = F^\intercal \left(M^\star - M^\star G[R + G^\intercal M^\star G]^{-1} G^\intercal M^\star \right) F + S. \tag{3.40}$$

The derivation of the ARE for the linear quadratic regulator (LQR) model in continuous time is found in Section 3.9.4.

To understand the LP (3.36) in this special case, it is most convenient to express all three functions appearing in (3.36b) in terms of the variable $z^\intercal = (x^\intercal, u^\intercal)$:

$$J^\star(x,u) = z^\intercal M^{J^\star} z, \qquad Q^\star(x,u) = z^\intercal M^{Q^\star} z, \qquad c(x,u) = z^\intercal M^c z, \tag{3.41a}$$

$$M^{J^\star} = \begin{bmatrix} M^\star & 0 \\ 0 & 0 \end{bmatrix}, \qquad M^c = \begin{bmatrix} S & 0 \\ 0 & R \end{bmatrix}, \tag{3.41b}$$

$$M^{Q^\star} = M^c + \begin{bmatrix} F^\intercal M^\star F & F^\intercal M^\star G \\ G^\intercal M^\star F & G^\intercal M^\star G \end{bmatrix}. \tag{3.41c}$$

Justification of the formula for $M^{Q^\star}$ is contained in the proof of Proposition 3.11 that follows.

Proposition 3.11 *Suppose that $J^\star$ is everywhere finite. Then the value function and Q-function are each quadratic: $J^\star(x) = x^\intercal M^\star x$ for each x, where $M^\star \geq 0$ is a solution to the algebraic Riccati equation* (3.40), *and the quadratic Q-function is given in* (3.41c). *The matrix $M^\star$ is also the solution to the following convex program:*

$$M^\star \in \arg\max \ \operatorname{trace}(M) \tag{3.42a}$$

$$\text{s.t.} \quad \begin{bmatrix} S & 0 \\ 0 & R \end{bmatrix} + \begin{bmatrix} F^\intercal M F & F^\intercal M G \\ G^\intercal M F & G^\intercal M G \end{bmatrix} \geq \begin{bmatrix} M & 0 \\ 0 & 0 \end{bmatrix}, \tag{3.42b}$$

where the maximum is over symmetric matrices M, and the inequality constraint (3.42b) *is in the sense of symmetric matrices.* □

Despite its linear programming origins, (3.42) is not a linear program: It is an example of a semidefinite program (SDP) [364].

Proof of Proposition 3.11 The reader is referred to standard texts for the derivation of the ARE [7, 76]. The following is a worthwhile exercise: postulate that $J^\star$ is a quadratic function of x, and you will find that the Bellman equation implies the ARE.

Now, on to the derivation of (3.42). The variables in the linear program introduced in Proposition 3.10 consist of functions J and Q. For the LQR problem, we restrict to quadratic functions

$$J(x) = x^{\intercal} M x\,, \qquad Q(x,u) = z^{\intercal} M^{Q} z$$

and treat the symmetric matrices (M, M^{Q}) as variables.

To establish (3.42), we are left to show (1) the objective functions (3.36a) and (3.42a) coincide for some ν, and (2) the functional constraints (3.36b, 3.36c) are equivalent to the matrix inequality (3.42b). The first task is the simplest:

$$\operatorname{trace}(M) = \sum_{i=1}^{n} J(e^{i}) = \langle \nu, J \rangle,$$

with $\{e^{i}\}$ the standard basis elements in $\mathbb{R}^{n}$, and $\nu(e^{i}) = 1$ for each i.

The equivalence of (3.42b) and (3.36b, 3.36c) is established next, and through this we also obtain (3.41c). In view of the discussion preceding (3.37), the inequality constraint (3.36b) can be strengthened to equality:

$$Q^{\star}(x,u) = c(x,u) + J^{\star}(Fx + Gu).$$

It remains to establish the equivalence of (3.42b) and (3.37).

Applying (3.38), we obtain a mapping from M to M^{Q}. Denote

$$M^{J} = \begin{bmatrix} M & 0 \\ 0 & 0 \end{bmatrix}, \qquad \Xi = \begin{bmatrix} F & G \\ F & G \end{bmatrix},$$

giving for all x and $z^{\intercal} = (x^{\intercal}, u^{\intercal})$,

$$J(x) = x^{\intercal} M x = z^{\intercal} M^{J} z\,, \qquad J(Fx + Gu) = z^{\intercal} \Xi^{\intercal} M^{J} \Xi z.$$

This and (3.38) gives, for any z,

$$\begin{aligned} z^{\intercal} M^{Q} z = Q(x,u) &= c(x,u) + J(Fx + Gu) \\ &= z^{\intercal} M^{c} z + z^{\intercal} \Xi^{\intercal} M^{J} \Xi z. \end{aligned}$$

The desired mapping from M to M^{Q} then follows, under the standing assumption that M^{Q} is a symmetric matrix:

$$M^{Q} = M^{c} + \Xi^{\intercal} M^{J} \Xi = \begin{bmatrix} S & 0 \\ 0 & R \end{bmatrix} + \begin{bmatrix} F^{\intercal} M F & F^{\intercal} M G \\ G^{\intercal} M F & G^{\intercal} M G \end{bmatrix}.$$

The constraint (3.37) is thus equivalent to

$$z^{\intercal} M^{J} z = J(x) \le Q(x,u) = z^{\intercal} M^{Q} z\,, \quad \text{for all } z.$$

This is equivalent to the constraint $M^{J} \le M^{Q}$, which is (3.42b). □

3.7 A Second Glance Ahead

In Section 2.5, it was only possible to talk about RL within the framework of policy selection within a parameterized family. We can broaden our discussion now that we know something about optimal control.

Let's turn to a common approach to RL in which we choose a parameterized family of functions $\{Q^\theta : \theta \in \mathbb{R}^d\}$, and seek among them an approximation to the Q-function $Q^\star$ defined in (3.7a). We frequently use a linear parameterization

$$Q^\theta(x,u) = \theta^\intercal \psi(x,u), \quad \theta \in \mathbb{R}^d, \tag{3.43}$$

in which $\psi_i : \mathsf{X} \times \mathsf{U} \to \mathbb{R}$ is called the ith basis function, $1 \le i \le d$. For any θ, we obtain a policy by mimicking (3.7c):

$$\phi^\theta(x) \in \arg\min_u Q^\theta(x,u), \qquad x \in \mathsf{X}. \tag{3.44}$$

Consider how we might approximate PIA from Section 3.2.2: Given an initial policy ϕ^0, generate a sequence of policies $\{\phi^n\}$ and parameter estimates $\{\theta_n\}$ as follows:

(i) Obtain a parameter θ_n to achieve the approximation $Q^{\theta_n} \approx Q_n$, where the latter is the fixed-policy Q-function that satisfies

$$Q_n(x,u) = c(x,u) + Q_n(x^+,u^+), \qquad x^+ = \mathrm{F}(x,u), \ u^+ = \phi^n(x^+). \tag{3.45}$$

(ii) Define a new policy $\phi^{n+1} = \phi^{\theta_n}$.

Variations of this approximation of PIA are explored in greater depth in Section 5.3 and in Part II.

An alternative is to build an approximation algorithm based on the dynamic programming equation for the Q-function introduced in (3.7d):

$$Q^\star(x,u) = c(x,u) + \underline{Q}^\star(\mathrm{F}(x,u)), \qquad \underline{Q}^\star(x) = \min_u Q^\star(x,u),$$

which admits the model-free representation, for any state-input trajectory:

$$Q^\star(x(k),u(k)) = c(x(k),u(k)) + \underline{Q}^\star(x(k+1)). \tag{3.46}$$

Just as in (2.52), for any approximation $\widehat{Q}$ we can observe the Bellman error:

$$\mathcal{D}_{k+1}(\widehat{Q}) \stackrel{\text{def}}{=} -\widehat{Q}(x(k),u(k)) + c(x(k),u(k)) + \underline{\widehat{Q}}(x(k+1)). \tag{3.47}$$

This is zero for every k if $\widehat{Q} = Q^\star$.

Q-learning is broadly defined as algorithms to choose θ^* so that $|\mathcal{D}_{k+1}(Q^\theta)|$ is in some sense minimized over all θ, based on observations of the system for $k = 0$ to N. The first approach that might come to mind is to mimic the mean-square criterion (2.53):

$$\Gamma^\varepsilon(\theta) = \frac{1}{N}\sum_{k=0}^{N-1} \big[\mathcal{D}_{k+1}(Q^\theta)\big]^2. \tag{3.48}$$

The LP approach of Section 3.5 suggests alternatives, and other approaches are investigated in Chapter 5.

3.8 Optimal Control in Continuous Time*

Hopefully it was made clear in Section 2.3.4 that calculus can bring clarity to theory of state space models. For example, the discrete-time counterpart of Figure 2.2 is far less enlightening. Further motivation was given in prior examples and in Section 2.6: In many cases, the system model is based on laws of physics. The value of calculus is even greater when we come to optimal control, since it is frequently simpler to pose and approximate optimal control problems in continuous time.

The nonlinear state space model was previously introduced in (2.19), and is repeated here for convenience: $\frac{d}{dt}x = \mathrm{f}(x,u)$. The total cost J associated with a particular control input $\boldsymbol{u} \stackrel{\text{def}}{=} u_{[0,\infty)}$ is defined by the integral

$$J(\boldsymbol{u}) = \int_0^\infty c(x_t,u_t)dt,$$

where c is a scalar-valued function of (x,u) as before, and as before our goal is to minimize J over all inputs. This will require assumptions if we expect J to be finite. A minimal assumption is that there is a target state x^e that is an equilibrium for some input u^e, and the cost vanishes at this equilibrium:

$$\mathrm{f}(x^e,u^e) = 0, \qquad c(x^e,u^e) = 0.$$

The value function is defined as in (3.2):

$$J^\star(x) = \min_{u_{[0,\infty)}} \Big[\int_0^\infty c(x_t,u_t)dt\Big], \quad x_0 = x \in \mathsf{X}.$$

Under general conditions, it satisfies a differential equation known as the *Hamilton–Jacobi–Bellman (HJB) equation*. Its derivation proceeds as in the construction of the Bellman equation in Section 3.2.

Let x be an arbitrary initial state, and let t_m be an intermediate time, $0 < t_m < \infty$. As in the discrete-time development, we regard $J^\star(x_{t_m})$ as the *cost to go*. Based on this interpretation, we obtain the following:

$$\begin{aligned} J^\star(x) &= \min_{u_{[0,\infty)}} \Big[\int_0^{t_m} c(x_t,u_t)dt + \int_{t_m}^\infty c(x_t,u_t)dt\Big] \\ &= \min_{u_{[0,t_m]}} \Big[\int_0^{t_m} c(x_t,u_t)dt + \underbrace{\min_{u_{[t_m,\infty)}} \Big(\int_{t_m}^\infty c(x_t,u_t)dt\Big)}_{J^\star(x_{t_m})}\Big]. \end{aligned}$$

That is,

$$J^\star(x) = \min_{u_{[0,t_m]}} \Big[\int_0^{t_m} c(x_t,u_t)dt + J^\star(x_{t_m})\Big], \qquad x_0 = 0. \tag{3.49}$$

This identity is the continuous-time extension of the Bellman equation, as illustrated in Figure 3.1. It is known as the *principle of optimality*: If the optimal trajectory passes through the state x_m at time x_{t_m} using the control $u^\star$, then the control $u^\star_{[t_m,\infty)}$ must be optimal for the system starting at x_m at time t_m. As remarked in the caption of Figure 3.1: *If a better u^* existed on $[t_m,\infty)$, we would have chosen it.*

The HJB equation is obtained on letting $t_m \downarrow 0$. Define Δ_x via

$$\Delta_x = x_{t_m} - x_0 = x_m - x.$$

Assuming that the value function is continuously differentiable, we may perform a Taylor series expansion using the optimality equation (3.49) to obtain

$$J^\star(x) = \min_{u_{[0,t_m]}} \{c(x,u_0)t_m + J^\star(x) + \nabla J^\star(x) \cdot \Delta_x\} + o(t_m).$$

The "little oh" notation $o(t_m)$ is recalled in Appendix A. Subtracting $J^\star(x)$ from each side and dividing through by t_m then gives

$$0 = \min_{u_{[0,t_m]}} \left\{ c(x,u_0) + \nabla J^\star(x) \cdot \frac{\Delta_x}{t_m} \right\} + o(1).$$

Letting $t_m \to 0$, we obtain $o(1) \to 0$ by definition, and the ratio Δ_x/t_m can be replaced by a derivative:

$$\lim_{t_m \downarrow 0} \frac{\Delta_x}{t_m} = \frac{d}{dt}x_t\Big|_{t=0} = \mathrm{f}(x_0,u_0).$$

This gives the following celebrated equation:

$$0 = \min_u \left[c(x,u) + \nabla J^\star(x) \cdot \mathrm{f}(x,u)\right]. \tag{3.50}$$

Theorem 3.12 *If the value function $J^\star$ has continuous derivatives, then it satisfies the HJB equation* (3.50). *Suppose that the minimum in* (3.50) *exists and is unique for each x, to form a continuous function $\phi^\star$. Then the optimal control is expressed as state feedback:*

$$u_t^\star = \phi^\star(x_t^\star) = \arg\min_u \left[c(x_t^\star,u) + \nabla J^\star(x_t^\star) \cdot \mathrm{f}(x_t^\star,u)\right]. \qquad \square$$

The term in brackets in (3.50) has an important interpretation in terms of the *Hamiltonian*,

$$H(x,p,u) \stackrel{\text{def}}{=} c(x,u) + p^\intercal \mathrm{f}(x,u). \tag{3.51}$$

The function of two variables $Q(x,u) \stackrel{\text{def}}{=} H(x,\nabla_x J^\star(x),u)$ is the Q-function of reinforcement learning for models in continuous time.

The following result is a version of the *minimum principle* of optimal control.

Theorem 3.13 *Suppose that an optimal input–state pair exists, and that the value function $J^\star$ has continuous derivatives. Then the optimal control $u_t^\star$ must minimize the Hamiltonian for each time t,*

$$\min_u H(x_t^\star,p_t^\star,u) = H(x_t^\star,p_t^\star,u_t^\star) \tag{3.52}$$

with $p_t^\star = \nabla_x J^\star(x_t^\star)$. $\square$

The standard minimum principle does not start with the HJB equation. Rather, the vector valued "co-state" process $\{p_t^\star\}$ is defined by another differential equation. This can provide enormous reduction in complexity since we do not need to compute the value function.

3.9 Examples

3.9.1 Mountain Car

This is an optimal control problem with infinite state space. The steps used to obtain the value function shown in Figure 3.2 are summarized here, beginning with an approximate model:

Quantized State Space

A continuous state space model is commonly approximated through a partition of the state space into a finite collection of bins $\mathsf{X} = \cup_{i=1}^{n} B_i$. This step is called quantization or binning. The next step is to choose a representative state $x^i \in B_i$ for each i, and define approximate dynamics on the state space consisting of the n states $\mathsf{X}_\diamond \stackrel{\text{def}}{=} \{x^i : 1 \le i \le n\}$.

In this two-dimensional example, it is convenient to choose bins based on a rectangular grid: For an integer $N > 1$, choose $n = N^2$, and select $\mathsf{X}_\diamond = \{x^{i,j} = (z^i, u^j)^\intercal : 1 \le i \le N, 1 \le j \le N\}$, where the position and velocity values are equally spaced and satisfy

$$-1.2 = z^1 < z^2 < \cdots < z^N = 0.5, \qquad -\overline{v} = v^1 < v^2 < \cdots < v^N = \overline{v}.$$

Each state $x^{i,j}$ belongs to a bin denoted $B_{i,j}$: The bins are disjoint, with union equal to X. The value $N = 160$ was used to obtain the approximation shown in Figure 3.2.

The state space model with state space $\mathsf{X}_\diamond$ is denoted

$$x_\diamond(k+1) = F_\diamond(x_\diamond(k), u(k)), \tag{3.53}$$

where $x_\diamond(k) \in \mathsf{X}_\diamond$ and $u(k) \in \mathsf{U} = \{-1,1\}$ for each k. The next step is to define the dynamics (i.e., $F_\diamond$) which requires some care.

We define $F_\diamond(x^{N,j}, u) = (z^N, 0)$ for any u and j, since in this case $x^{N,j} = (0.5, v^j)$ (so the car is parked).

Consider now $x^{i,j} \in \mathsf{X}_\diamond$ with $i < N$ and $u \in \mathsf{U}$. Denote $x_+^{i,j}(u) = F(x^{i,j}, u)$, the two-dimensional vector with components

$$z_+^{i,j}(u) = F_1(x^{i,j}, u), \qquad v_+^{i,j}(u) = F_2(x^{i,j}, u).$$

Define indices i_+ and j_+ uniquely by the constraint $x_+^{i,j}(u) \in B_{i_+, j_+}$. The specification of velocity dynamics is straightforward:

$$F_{\diamond 2}(x^{i,j}, u) = v^{j+}.$$

The position dynamics are modified slightly as follows:

$$F_{\diamond 1}(x^{i,j}, u) = \begin{cases} z^{i_+ + 1}, & z_+^{i,j}(u) \ge z^i \text{ and } z^{i_+} = z^i \\ z^{i_- - 1}, & z_+^{i,j}(u) < z^i \text{ and } z^{i_+} = z^i \\ z^{i_+}, & \text{else} \end{cases}. \tag{3.54}$$

These dynamics are defined so that $F_{\diamond 1}(x^{i,j}, u) \ne z^i$ for any $i < N$. *Rationale:* to avoid the existence of state $x_\diamond = x^{i,j}$ satisfying $i < N$ and $x_\diamond = F(x_\diamond, u)$ for any $u \in \mathsf{U}$.

VIA and PIA Implementation

VIA will be successful for any initialization V^0 in this finite state space model. The choice $V^0 \equiv 0$ was used in the numerical experiments described in the following.

Successful implementation of PIA requires an initial policy that is stabilizing, in the sense that the goal is reached from each initial condition. A variant of (2.59) was chosen: For each $x = (z, v)^\intercal \in \mathsf{X}_\diamond$,

$$\phi^0(x) = \begin{cases} \text{sign}(v) & z + v \ge \text{Tol} \\ 1 & \text{else} \end{cases}.$$

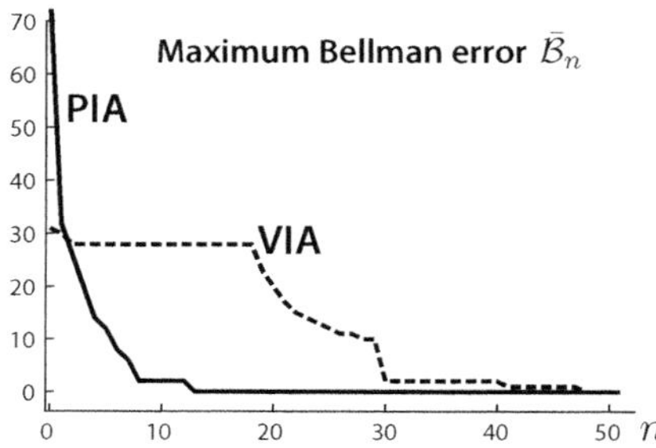

Figure 3.3 Convergence of the two basic dynamic programming algorithms for the mountain car.

The value Tol $= -0.8$ was found to work well.

Computation of the fixed-policy value function J^n for the policy ϕ^n was performed using the numerical technique surveyed in Section 3.2.3. The fact that the computation was successful to compute J_0 implies that the policy ϕ^0 is stabilizing. Proposition 3.4 then implies that each of the polices $\{\phi^n\}$ obtained using PIA is also stabilizing.

Recall the Bellman error defined in (3.31). The maximal absolute error at iteration n is denoted

$$\bar{\mathcal{B}}_n = \max_x \Bigl| -J^n(x) + \min_u [c(x,u) + J^n(\mathrm{F}(x,u))] \Bigr|.$$

The same notation is used for VIA, with J^n replaced by V^n. Plots of the maximal Bellman error as a function of iteration n are shown for each algorithm in Figure 3.3. While PIA requires far fewer iterations to achieve $\bar{\mathcal{B}}_n = 0$, the complexity per iteration for PIA is far greater than VIA: Recall that in the former, the fixed point equation (3.12) must be solved to obtain J^n in each iteration.

3.9.2 Spiders and Flies

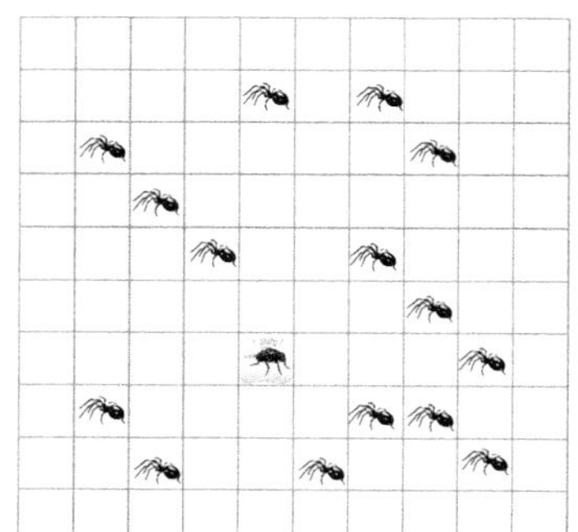

Figure 3.4 A multi-agent control problem: 15 spiders cooperate to kill a single fly.

In the example illustrated in Figure 3.4, there are 15 "agents" (the spiders) that are cooperating to capture a single fly. In any "realistic" version of this example, the fly will hop around the grid in an unpredictable fashion. This realism requires a stochastic model that is beyond our reach at this stage in the book. For now, let's assume that the fly is stationary, and the spiders move to their desired position without error.

At each time k, each spider can move to the next square (horizontally or vertically), or stay in its current position. There are five possible moves per spider: Hence with 15 spiders, the input space U is massive: $|\mathsf{U}| = 5^{15}$ (over 10^{10} elements). The minimization step (3.8) in the value iteration algorithm is infeasible.

The state space is also large: If we define the state as the location of squares inhabited by spiders, then $|\mathsf{X}| = \binom{100}{15}$ (over 10^{17} elements). Let's not worry about this complexity right now. We will develop approximation techniques to effectively compress a complex state space.

The size of the input space can be reduced dramatically through a modification of the definition of state, and a minor modification of dynamics. This system as described evolves in discrete time, with an increment from k to $k+1$ representing T_s seconds in "real time." In the new system description, we divide this sampling time by 15, and enforce that only one spider changes position at each time step on this new time scale. For this, we assume that there is a unique number $1, \ldots, 15$ associated with each spider, and the spiders move in this given order.

The new state space is represented as a product space $\mathsf{X} = \mathsf{Z} \times \{1,\dots,15\}$. If $x(k) = (z,m)$, then $z \in \mathsf{Z}$ specifies the position of each of the 15 labeled spiders on the grid at time k, and m is the label for the spider who will make a decision at this time. At time $k+1$, the new state $x(k+1) = (z',m')$ is specified: z' denotes the new positions of spiders after spider-m is moved based on the decision at time k, and $m' = m+1$, with the convention that "16" represents "1." That is, $m' - 1 = m$ (modulo 15).

The size of the state space is increased because we are now considering ordered subsets of the grid, and also because we are keeping track of the label. The number of ordered subsets of size 15 is $|\mathsf{Z}| = 15! \times \binom{100}{15}$, giving

$$|\mathsf{X}| = |\mathsf{Z}| \times 15 \approx 5 \times 10^{30}.$$

This is *massive*, but remains finite. The input space U consists of only five elements.

Hence if we have an approximation Q of the Q-function that defines the optimal policy via (3.7c), then on observing the state $x = x(k)$ at time k, the input $u(k)$ is obtained by minimizing over only five elements:

$$\phi(x) \in \mathop{\arg\min}_{u \in \mathsf{U}} Q(x,u).$$

3.9.3 Contention for Resources and Instability

Shown in Figure 3.5 is an example of a queueing network with multiple arrivals. The model is inspired by applications to semiconductor manufacturing plants in which many different types of component are created, but many share similar needs in terms of raw materials and processing steps. The figure shows a caricature of this application in which there are two final products emerging from buffers 2 and 4. Raw material arrives to buffers 1 and 3, so that each of the two products requires attention at each of the two stations.

Queueing networks are subject to significant volatility and uncertainty: processors break down, arrivals are not predictable, and there may be spikes in demand. For these reasons, it may seem silly to consider a deterministic model for an application that so obviously fits in later chapters.

This example will serve to show that significant insight can be obtained by first considering an ideal model without disturbances. There is also some theoretical justification for considering total-cost optimal control as an approximation for average-cost optimal control for stochastic control systems – more on this topic can be found in Section 7.2 and in [254].

It is simplest to begin in continuous time.

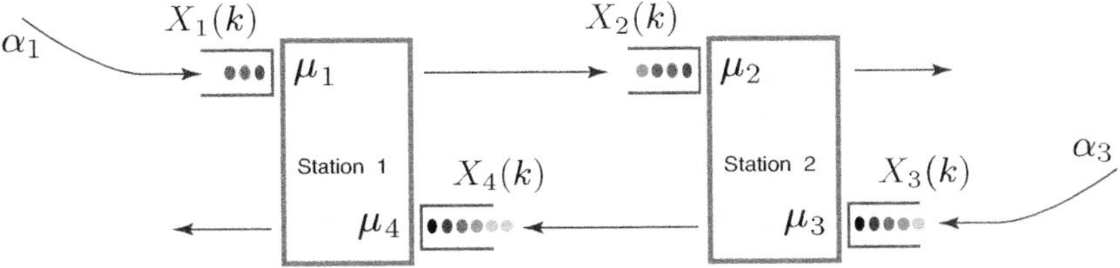

Figure 3.5 A multiclass queueing network: At each of the two stations, the scheduling problem amounts to determine processing rates for each of the two materials waiting in the queue.

Fluid Model

In this simplest model, the buffer levels take on nonnegative but continuous values. Raw material flows into buffers 1 and 3 continuously at rates α_1 and α_3, respectively. Each of the two stations has a single server. For example, at station 1 the server may work on buffer 1 or buffer 4. During a time interval during which server 1 devotes its capacity to buffer 1, material flows continuously from buffer 1 to buffer 2 at rate μ_1. The evolution of the queue lengths can be described by the linear state space model, with state $\boldsymbol{q}$ evolving in $\mathsf{X} = \mathbb{R}^4_+$:

$$\frac{d^+}{dt} q_t = F q_t + G u_t + \alpha.$$

The right derivative "$\frac{d^+}{dt}$" is used since state trajectories are typically piecewise smooth. The system parameters are $\alpha = (\alpha_1, 0, 0, \alpha_4)^\intercal$,

$$F = 0_{4\times 4} \qquad G = \begin{bmatrix} -\mu_1 & 0 & 0 & 0 \\ \mu_1 & -\mu_2 & 0 & 0 \\ 0 & 0 & -\mu_3 & 0 \\ 0 & 0 & \mu_3 & -\mu_4 \end{bmatrix}.$$

The four-dimensional input is subject to several constraints:

- $u_t(i) \geq 0$ for each i (it isn't possible to "un-do" processing at a buffer).
- $u_t(1) + u_t(4) \leq 1$ and $u_t(2) + u_t(3) \leq 1$ (station constraints).
- $\frac{d^+}{dt} q_t(i) \geq 0$ whenever $q_t(i) = 0$ (enforces nonnegativity of the four buffers).

Collectively these constraints define the region $\mathsf{U}(x)$ for each $x \in \mathsf{X} = \mathbb{R}^4_+$.

Stabilizability and Load

Is the origin an equilibrium for some input? This is an easy question to answer because the dynamics are linear. If $q_t \equiv q^e = \mathsf{0}$ for some input u^e_t, and all t, then

$$\mathsf{0} = \frac{d}{dt} q^e_t = F q^e_t + G u^e_t + \alpha = G u^e_t + \alpha.$$

This gives $u^e_t = u^e \stackrel{\text{def}}{=} -G^{-1}\alpha$. The matrix $-G^{-1}$ exists and has nonnegative entries. To see if $u^e \in \mathsf{U}$, we must consider the station constraints, expressed as $C u^e \leq \mathsf{1}$, where C is known as the constituency matrix:

$$C = \begin{bmatrix} 1 & 0 & 0 & 1 \\ 0 & 1 & 1 & 0 \end{bmatrix}.$$

The 2×4 dimensional matrix obtained as the product is known as the *workload matrix*:

$$\Xi \stackrel{\text{def}}{=} -CG^{-1} = \begin{bmatrix} 1/\mu_1 & 0 & 1/\mu_4 & 1/\mu_4 \\ 1/\mu_2 & 1/\mu_2 & 1/\mu_3 & 0 \end{bmatrix}.$$

The two-dimensional vector $\rho \stackrel{\text{def}}{=} C u^e = -CG^{-1}\alpha$ is obviously important, since $\rho_i \leq 1$ for each i is equivalent to feasibility of u^e. The network load is defined to be the maximum, $\rho_\bullet = \max_i \rho_i$.

There is also a dynamic notion of workload, $w_t = \Xi q_t$, which evolves as

$$\frac{d^+}{dt} w_t = -CG^{-1}\{G u_t + \alpha\} = -C u_t + \rho.$$

Letting $\iota_t = 1 - Cu_t$ denote the *idleness rate* at time t gives

$$\frac{d}{dt}w_t = -(1-\rho) + \iota_t.$$

The idleness rate is nonnegative: $\iota_t \in \mathbb{R}^2_+$ whenever $u_t \in \mathsf{U}$. This explains why a strict bound is imposed:

$$\rho_\bullet \stackrel{\text{def}}{=} \max_i \rho_i < 1. \tag{3.55}$$

Under this load condition, there are many stabilizing policies: $u_t = \phi(q_t)$ designed so that the origin is reached in finite time, from any initial condition.

One stabilizing policy is defined by a control-Lyapunov function design:

$$u_t \in \arg\min\{\tfrac{d}{dt}V(q_t) : u_t \in \mathsf{U}(q_t)\},$$

where $V : \mathsf{X} \to \mathbb{R}_+$ vanishes only at the origin. Consider for example $V(q_t) = \frac{1}{2}\|q_t\|^2$. The chain rule gives

$$\frac{d}{dt}\tfrac{1}{2}\|q_t\|^2 = q_t^{\intercal}\frac{d}{dt}q_t = q_t^{\intercal}[Gu_t + \alpha].$$

The control-Lyapunov function design is thus

$$\begin{aligned}\phi(x) &= \arg\min_{u\in\mathsf{U}(x)} x^{\intercal}Gu = \arg\max_{u\in\mathsf{U}(x)} x^{\intercal}(-Gu)\\ &= \arg\max_{u\in\mathsf{U}(x)}\big(u_1\mu_1(x_1 - x_2) + u_2\mu_2x_2 + u_3\mu_3(x_3 - x_4) + u_4\mu_4x_4\big).\end{aligned}$$

This results in a policy $u_t = \phi(q_t)$, with state-dependent priorities. For example:

$$\begin{aligned} u_t(1) &= 1 \quad \text{if } \mu_1(q_t(1) - q_t(2)) > \mu_4 q_t(4),\\ u_t(3) &= 1 \quad \text{if } \mu_3(q_t(3) - q_t(4)) > \mu_2 q_t(2).\end{aligned}$$

This is known as the MaxWeight policy in the queueing network literature. It is not difficult to show that the policy is stabilizing: V serves as a Lyapunov function, provided $\rho_\bullet < 1$.

A Well-Motivated but Unstable Policy

A common cost function is the total customer population $c(x,u) = c(x) = \sum_i x_i$. This motivates the *last buffer first served* (LBFS) policy, in which strict priority is given to exit buffers:

$$u_t(4) = 1 \text{ whenever } q_t(4) > 0, \qquad u_t(2) = 1 \text{ whenever } q_t(2) > 0.$$

The preference to exit buffers is motivated by the desired to make $c(q_t)$ decrease quickly.

Depending upon the system parameters, this policy may be *destabilizing* for the fluid model, even when load condition (3.55) is met. An example is found when the service rates satisfy

$$\mu_1 > \mu_2 \text{ and } \mu_3 > \mu_4. \tag{3.56}$$

From the initial condition $q_0 = x = (1,0,0,0)^{\intercal}$, the state trajectory under the LBFS policy can be computed for small t:

$$q_t = x + t(\alpha_1 - \mu_1, \mu_1 - \mu_2, \alpha_3, 0)^{\intercal}.$$

At time $T_1 = (\mu_1 - \alpha_1)^{-1}$, the first buffer empties, and we then have, for $t > T_1, t \approx T_1$,

$$q_t = q_{T_1} + t(0, \alpha_1 - \mu_2, \alpha_3, 0)^{\intercal}.$$

At time $T_2 = T_1 + q_{T_1}/(\mu_2 - \alpha_1)$, the second buffer will drain, and all of the work will be at buffer three. Note that over the time interval $[T_1, T_2]$, buffer 1 remains empty: the arrivals to buffer 1 at rate α_1 are passed directly to buffer 2.

The main point is that during the entire time interval $[0, T_2]$, the exit buffer at Station 1 is starved. Starting from time T_2, an analogous situation arises, where now the exit buffer at Station 2 is temporarily starved. We can conclude that either $u_t(4) = 0$ or $u_t(2) = 0$ for all $t \geq 0$. This implies that

$$u_t(2) + u_t(4) \leq 1, \tag{3.57}$$

so that buffers 2 and 4 behave as if they are located at a single station. The inequality (3.57) resulting from this policy is known as the *virtual station* constraint. The *virtual load* and *virtual workload* process are defined by the following:

$$\rho_v = \frac{\alpha_1}{\mu_2} + \frac{\alpha_3}{\mu_4}, \tag{3.58}$$

$$w_t^v = \frac{q_t(1) + q_t(2)}{\mu_2} + \frac{q_t(3) + q_t(4)}{\mu_4}, \qquad t \geq 0. \tag{3.59}$$

We can compute

$$\frac{d^+}{dt} w_t^v = \frac{\alpha_1 - \mu_2 u_t(2)}{\mu_2} + \frac{\alpha_3 - \mu_4 u_t(4)}{\mu_4} = \rho_v - [u_t(2) + u_t(4)].$$

If $\rho_v > 1$ then $\frac{d^+}{dt} w_t^v \geq -(1 - \rho_v) > 0$ for all t, so that $\|q_t\| \to \infty$ as $t \to \infty$.

A specific example is given by

$$\mu_1 = \mu_3 = 10; \qquad \mu_2 = \mu_4 = 3; \qquad \alpha_1 = \alpha_3 = 2.$$

The network load is given by $\rho_\bullet = 2(1/3 + 1/10) < 1$, which implies that there are many stabilizing policies. However, $\rho_v = 2(1/3 + 1/3) > 1$, so that the fluid model controlled using LBFS is unstable in the strongest possible sense.

Figure 3.6 shows two simulations of the network model based on these parameters with common initial condition. The evolution of buffer levels for the fluid model are shown on the right, where it is evident that $\|q_t\| \to \infty$ as $t \to \infty$. The left-hand side shows the behavior of

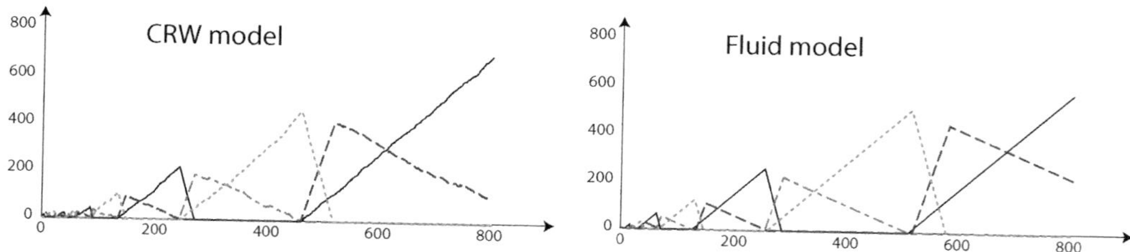

Figure 3.6 Sample paths of the multiclass network. Each plot shows a simulation of the four buffer levels in the network using the LBFS policy for identical initial conditions. Shown at the left are results for a stochastic model, and on the right results for a fluid model.

a stochastic model in which average arrival and service rates match those of the fluid model; details can be found in Section 7.6. Solidarity of the two models is clear in this simulation.

3.9.4 Solving the HJB Equation

These final examples illustrate optimal control solutions for models in continuous time.

Example 3.9.1 (*LQR*) The formulation of the *linear quadratic regulator* problem is as expected:

$$\begin{aligned} \frac{d}{dt}x &= Fx + Gu, \qquad x(0) = x_0, \\ c(x,u) &= x^{\intercal} S x + u^{\intercal} R u, \end{aligned} \tag{3.60}$$

where S is a positive semidefinite matrix, and $R > 0$. Provided the value function $J^\star$ is finite valued, it follows that it is a quadratic function of x, and an optimal policy is obtained via linear state feedback. The proof of these statements is exactly the same as in Section 3.6.

In particular, once we know that $J^\star(x) = x^{\intercal} M^\star x$ for each x, then the HJB equation gives

$$\begin{aligned} \phi^\star(x) &= \arg\min_u \{x^{\intercal} S x + u^{\intercal} R u + [2M^\star x]^{\intercal} [Fx + Gu]\} \\ &= \arg\min_u \{u^{\intercal} R u + 2x^{\intercal} M^\star G u\}, \end{aligned}$$

where in the second equation we imposed symmetry of $M^\star$, giving $[M^\star x]^{\intercal} = x^{\intercal} M^\star$. The minimum of this quadratic function of u is obtained by solving the linear equation:

$$\nabla_u \{u^{\intercal} R u + 2x^{\intercal} M^\star G u\}\Big|_{u=\phi^\star(x)} = 0,$$

which gives $\phi^\star(x) = -R^{-1} G^{\intercal} M^\star x$.

The closed-loop dynamics are given by

$$\frac{d}{dt}x^\star = [F - GR^{-1}G^{\intercal} M^\star] x^\star.$$

The HJB equation (3.50) gives

$$\begin{aligned} \frac{d}{dt}J^\star(x_t^\star) &= -c_{\phi^\star}(x_t^\star), \\ c_{\phi^\star}(x) &= c(x,\phi^\star(x)) = x^{\intercal}\{S + M^\star G R^{-1} G^{\intercal} M^\star\}x, \quad x \in \mathsf{X}. \end{aligned}$$

A fixed point equation for $M^\star$ is also obtained from (3.50):

$$\begin{aligned} 0 &= \{x^{\intercal} S x + u^{\intercal} R u + [2M^\star x]^{\intercal} [Fx + Gu]\}\Big|_{u=\phi^\star(x)} \\ &= x^{\intercal}\{S + M^\star G R^{-1} G^{\intercal} M^\star\}x + x^{\intercal}\left\{2M^\star F - 2M^\star G R^{-1} G^{\intercal} M^\star\right\}x. \end{aligned}$$

Substitute $2x^{\intercal} M^\star F x = x^{\intercal}[M^\star F + F^{\intercal} M^\star]x$, and after canceling terms this results in

$$0 = x^{\intercal}\left\{S + M^\star F + F^{\intercal} M^\star - M^\star G R^{-1} G^{\intercal} M^\star\right\}x.$$

Since this holds for any x, and since the matrix within the brackets is symmetric, it follows that $M^\star$ is a positive semidefinite solution to the ARE:

$$0 = S + F^{\intercal} M^\star + M^\star F - M^\star G R^{-1} G^{\intercal} M^\star. \tag{3.61}$$

■

Example 3.9.2 (*Linear System with Polynomial Cost*) Consider a scalar integrator model, with polynomial cost:

$$\frac{d}{dt}x = \mathrm{f}(x,u) = u\,, \qquad c(x,u) = u^2 + x^4. \tag{3.62}$$

The HJB equation becomes $0 = \min_u \{u \frac{d}{dx} J^\star(x) + u^2 + x^4\}$. Minimizing with respect to u defines the state feedback solution,

$$\phi^\star(x) \stackrel{\text{def}}{=} -\tfrac{1}{2}\frac{d}{dx} J^\star(x)\,.$$

The closed-loop system has the appealing form

$$\frac{d}{dt}x_t^\star = -\tfrac{1}{2}\frac{d}{dx} J^\star(x_t^\star).$$

Substituting the formula for $u^\star$ back into the HJB equation gives the differential equation

$$0 = \{u\tfrac{d}{dx} J^\star(x) + u^2 + x^4\}\big|_{u=\phi^\star(x)} = -\tfrac{1}{4}\left(\tfrac{d}{dx} J^\star(x)\right)^2 + x^4,$$

giving $\frac{d}{dx}J^\star(x) = \pm 2x^2$. The unique nonnegative and continuously differentiable solution is $J^\star(x) = \frac{2}{3}|x|^3$, and hence the optimal policy is

$$\phi^\star(x) = -\frac{1}{2}\frac{d}{dx} J^\star(x) = -x^2 \mathrm{sign}(x).$$

■

3.10 Exercises

3.1 *Solving the ARE* Consider the two-dimensional linear state space model discussed following (2.47), now with input:

$$x(x) = Fx(k) + Gu(k)\,, \qquad F = I + 0.02\begin{bmatrix} -0.2 & 1 \\ -1 & -0.2 \end{bmatrix}, \quad G = 0.02\begin{bmatrix} 1 \\ 0 \end{bmatrix}.$$

Solve the ARE with $c(x,u) = x_1^2 + u^2$ to obtain the value function and the optimal policy. Is $J^\star$ coercive?

3.2 The following is an example of a routing model as considered in computer networking courses:

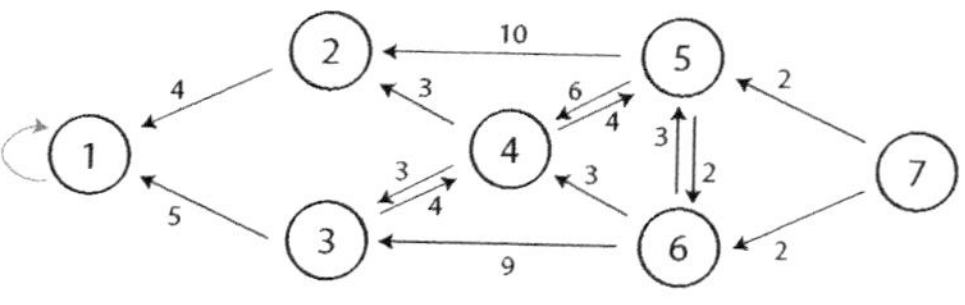

This is a network with seven nodes, and directed weighted edges as shown. Associated with any path there is a cost. For example, the path $7 \to 6 \to 3 \to 1$ has cost $2 + 9 + 5 = 16$. The goal is to obtain the path to node 1 with minimal cost, for each node.

Formulate this shortest path problem as an infinite horizon optimal control problem by specifying the state space X, the input space U, the model $\mathrm{F}(x,u)$, and cost $c(x,u)$. The "self loop" shown at node 1 may help you to conceptualize your optimal control formulation. Describe VIA and PIA for this example, and solve the SPP using each algorithm.

Plot the error of your estimates as a function of iteration n for various initial conditions. It is interesting to see what happens when $V^n(i) < 0$ for each $i \neq 1$ in VIA (but remember to use $V^n(1) = 0$, which is motivated by the representation (3.9)).

Standard solution methods are the Bellman–Ford algorithm and Dijkstras algorithm. The former is regarded as a special case of VIA.

3.3 *Box Constrained LQR* Consider the optimal control problem in Exercise 3.1 in which the input is subject to the box constraint: $u(k) \in \mathsf{U} = \{u \in \mathbb{R} : -1 \le u \le 1\}$. LQR theory will not give you the optimal policy unless the initial condition $x(0)$ is sufficiently close to the origin. Numerical methods are the only answer [369].

Use VIA to approximate the optimal policy on the bounded domain $\{x \in \mathbb{R}^2 : -10 \le x_i \le 10\,,\ i = 1{,}2\}$. Compare your solution to the projected optimal policy:

$$\phi(x) = \max(-1, \min(1, K^\star x)), \qquad \text{with } K^\star \text{ obtained in Exercise 3.1.}$$

3.4 Consider the scalar optimal control problem with linear dynamics:

$$x(k+1) = x(k) - u(k), \tag{3.63}$$

with $x(k)$ and $u(k)$ constrained to $\mathsf{X} = \mathbb{R}_+$.

(a) With cost function $c(x,u) = x^2 + Ru^2$, show that the LQR solution solves the total cost optimization problem (3.2). *You must check that your policy is feasible*, which means that $0 \le u^\star(k) \le x^\star(k)$ for each k. Obtain your solution by hand (no computer, since you must obtain the solution as a function of R).

In the remainder of this exercise, you will consider the more general cost $c(x,u) = x^p + Ru^q$. Assume that $p,q \ge 1$ so that c is a convex function on $\mathbb{R}^2_+$. Linearity of (3.63) then implies that $J^\star$ is also convex.

(b) Write code to approximate $J^\star$ and $\phi^\star$ using VIA and/or PIA on a finite set $\mathsf{X}_\diamond = \{i\delta : 0 \le i \le n-1\}$, with $n\delta = 10$ and $\delta \le 0.1$. Obtain plots of the value function and optimal policy for a few choices of (p,q,R). Include the special case $p = 1$ and $q = 2$.

(c) You might guess that $J^\star$ is approximated by $J(x) = Sx^s$, with $S > 0$ and $s \ge 1$. Estimate the Bellman error (3.31) for arbitrary R, keeping in mind that u is constrained:

$$\mathcal{B}(x) = -J(x) + \min_{0 \le u \le x} \left[c(x,u) + J(\mathrm{F}(x,u))\right], \qquad \mathrm{F}(x,u) = x - u.$$

If you find yourself stuck, you may instead resort to computation: Plot $\mathcal{B}$ as a function of x for various values of p,q,R,s,S. For a few values of p,q,R, what is the best value of s,S? You might also first solve the problem for a model in continuous time to gain intuition (see Exercise 3.8).

3.5 The similarity between (3.26) and (3.8) is explored in this exercise.

To get started, assume that $J^0 \equiv 0$ for the initialization of value iteration, and compute J^1 using (3.8). Verify that $J^1(x) = J^\star(x,\mathcal{N})$ for each x. Repeat: Write down the formula for J^2 using (3.8), and verify that $J^2(x) = J^\star(x,\mathcal{N}-1)$ (recall (3.26)). This procedure leads to a proof by induction that $J^{k+1}(x) = J^\star(x,\mathcal{N}-k)$ for each $k \le \mathcal{N}$.

Now a mild generalization: For general J^0, show that the function J^n obtained from the VIA algorithm (3.8) satisfies (3.9) (and observe the similarity with (3.4)). The proof of (3.9) is an instance of the *principle of optimality* illustrated in Figure 3.1.

Continuous Time

3.6 Consider the double integrator $\ddot{y} = u$. Perform the following calculations by hand:

(a) Obtain a state space model with $x_t = (y_t, \dot{y}_t)^\intercal$.

(b) Compute the value function

$$J^\star(x) = \min_u \int_0^\infty y_t^2 + u_t^2\, dt\,, \qquad x(0) = x.$$

3.7 *Comparing LQR in Continuous and Discrete Time* Let's revisit Exercise 3.1, but in its original continuous time setting:

$$\frac{d}{dt}x = Ax + Bu, \qquad A = \begin{bmatrix} -0.2 & 1 \\ -1 & -0.2 \end{bmatrix}, \quad B = \begin{bmatrix} 1 \\ 0 \end{bmatrix}.$$

Compute the value function and the optimal policy with $c(x,u) = x_1^2 + u^2$. How does the policy compare with what was obtained in Exercise 3.1? Are the value functions related (approximately) in any way?

3.8 Consider the variant of 3.63 in continuous time:

$$\frac{d}{dt}x = \mathrm{f}(x,u) = -u, \qquad c(x,u) = x^p + Ru^q. \tag{3.64}$$

Estimate the following Bellman error (3.31):

$$\mathcal{B}(x) = \min_{u \geq 0}[c(x,u) + \nabla J(x) \cdot \mathrm{f}(x,u)],$$

where $J(x) = Sx^s$, with $S > 0$ and $s \geq 1$. What values of s, S do you recommend? (Provide an answer for arbitrary p, q, R.)

3.9 *Optimization of the Rowing Game* We now return to Exercise 2.8, and design (K_p, K_I, K_v) in (2.69) using LQR. Rather than consider the full $3N$-dimensional system, we *pretend* that the signal $\bar{z}$ defined in (2.67) is entirely exogenous (rather than a function of the state).

(a) Obtain a state space model under this idealization, with augmented state $x^{ai} = (z^i, v^i, z'^i)$, and $\bar{z}$ treated as an *exogenous* input:

$$\frac{d}{dt}x^{ai} = A^i x^{ai} + B^i u^i + E\bar{z} \qquad \text{with } A^i \in \mathbb{R}^{3\times 3} \ B^i, E \in \mathbb{R}^3.$$
$$\frac{d}{dt}\bar{z} = \overline{v}^z.$$

For this to approximate the actual dynamics, the constant $\overline{v}^z$ will depend upon the feedback gains that determine u^i.

(b) Obtain $(K_p^\star, K_I^\star, K_v^\star)$ using LQR based on this (A^i, B^i) and with quadratic cost

$$c^i(x^a, u) = c_0^i(x^a) + Ru^2,$$
$$c_0^i(z^i, z'^i, v^i) = [z^i - \bar{z}]^2 + S_v[v^i - v^{\mathrm{ref}}]^2$$

in which $S_v, R > 0$. Note that you may calculate the gains using $v^{\mathrm{ref}} = 0$, but your policy uses nonzero values:

$$u^i = -K_p^\star(z^i - \bar{z}) - K_I^\star z'^i - K_v^\star(v^i - v^{\mathrm{ref}}). \tag{3.65}$$

(c) *We now stop pretending*: Analyze the closed-loop system in which each sculler uses (3.65), with $\bar{z} = \bar{z}_t$ the average position. The N-dimensional vector input (with ith component (3.65)) has the form

$$u = -Kx + K^0 v^{\mathrm{ref}} \qquad \text{with } K, K^0 \in \mathbb{R}^{3N}.$$

Compute the value function $J\colon \mathbb{R}^{3N} \to \mathbb{R}_+$ associated with your policy, and compare it to $J^\star$ using full state feedback (both value functions are defined with $c(x,u) = \sum_i c^i(x^{ai}, u^i)$). Note that each value function is a quadratic function of the full $3N$-dimensional state, so your comparison is in terms of the respective matrices. One should be larger than the other. What is the "loss" from using limited information? You might consider

$$\text{Loss} = \frac{1}{\text{trace}(M^\star)} \text{trace}\left(M - M^\star\right)$$

with $J(x) = x^\intercal M x$ when $v^{\text{ref}} = 0$.

Or, propose your own definition of loss and provide justification.

(d) Repeat (c) for several values of N, and in each case obtain the three eigenvalues in closed loop for your three-dimensional model. Compare these to the eigenvalues for the true closed-loop system, which takes the form

$$\frac{d}{dt}x = (A - BK)x + Ev^{\text{ref}}, \qquad \text{with } B, E \in \mathbb{R}^{3N},$$

and A, B, E obtained from part (a). The theory of *mean-field games* predicts stability and approximate optimality of (3.65) when N is large [81].

Note: If $(A - BK)$ has eigenvalues in the right half plane, you may need to reconsider your choice of R or S_v.

3.10 *Energy Control Design for the Inverted Pendulum [14]* We return to the control system described in Exercise 2.17. Once you have completed parts (a) and (b), solve the following.

Unnormalized kinetic and potential energy are functions of the state:

$$\text{KE}(x) = \tfrac{1}{2}(\dot\theta)^2, \qquad \text{PE}(x) = \cos(\theta) - 1,$$

where the potential energy is relative to $\theta = 0$, where it is maximal.

In the seminal paper of Åström and Furuta, the control-Lyapunov function approach is applied using total energy:

$$E(x) = \text{KE}(x) + s_p \text{PE}(x),$$

with $s_p > 0$. You can look at the paper, but I suggest you discover for yourself what value will result in a stabilizing feedback law.

The goal is to steer energy to some target value E_0. We will take $E_0 = 0$, which corresponds to the upright position (as in the paper, we do not include friction in the model). You may pretend that $g = 1$ in your simulations.

(c) To obtain a control-Lyapunov function consistent with our goals, choose

$$J(x) = \tfrac{1}{2}[E(x) - E_0]^2 = \tfrac{1}{2}[\tfrac{1}{2}x_2^2 + s_p(\cos(x_1) - 1)]^2. \tag{3.66}$$

Define a feedback law ϕ_J and cost function c as follows (with $R > 0$ fixed):

$$\phi_J(x) = \arg\min_u \{\tfrac{1}{2}Ru^2 + \text{f}(x,u)\cdot\nabla J\,(x)\},$$
$$c(x,u) = \tfrac{1}{2}Ru^2 - \min_\nu \{\tfrac{1}{2}R\nu^2 + \text{f}(x,\nu)\cdot\nabla J\,(x)\}.$$

Verify that J solves the HJB equation with this c, and choose parameters for J in (3.66) so that c is nonnegative, with $c(x,u) > 0$ whenever $x_2^2 + u^2 > 0$, $x_1 \neq \pm\pi/2$, and $E(x) \neq 0$.

(d) Try out your control design from (c). Obtain plots as a function of time (including state-input trajectories, and $E(x_t)$). Include these scenarios:

- An initial condition x_0 satisfying $J(x_0) = 0$ but $x_0 \neq 0$.
- The initial condition $x_0 = (\pi, 0)^\intercal$, with two or more values of R. In the case of large R, does the pendulum require many swings to reach its target?

3.11 In Exercise 3.10, you learned how to control a pendulum to obtain $E(x_t) \to 0$ as $t \to \infty$. You likely saw the pendulum swing around, periodically reaching $x_t \sim 0$, and then flying away from this desired position.

In this exercise, you will attempt to catch the pendulum and more carefully steer it to the upright position. You will consider the normalized dynamics:

$$0 = \ddot{\theta} - \sin(\theta) + u\cos(\theta), \qquad \text{that is, } m = g = \ell \text{ (for convenience).}$$

(a) For $x = (\theta, \dot{\theta})^{\intercal} \approx 0$, a Taylor series expansion gives

$$0 \approx \ddot{\theta} - \theta + u.$$

Based on this linear approximation, obtain a linear state space model, and from this a feedback law $u = -K^{\star}x$ based on LQR with cost $c(x,u) = \|x\|^2 + ru^2$ (you may need to experiment with r to obtain a good design).

(b) Given a threshold $\tau_E > 0$, consider the following policy:

$$u_t = \begin{cases} -K^{\star}x_t & \|x_t\| \le \tau_E \\ \phi^E(x_t) & \text{else} \end{cases},$$

where ϕ^E is the policy you obtained in the previous assignment. Global asymptotic stability may require a weighted norm, such as

$$\|x\|^2 = J^{\star}(x) = x^{\intercal}M^{\star}x, \qquad \text{where } M^{\star} \text{ solves the ARE (continuous time version).}$$

Conjecture conditions under which this policy results in a closed-loop system that is globally asymptotically stable on the restricted state space $\mathsf{X} = \{x \in \mathbb{R}^2 : -2 < E(x) < 1\}$ (this includes all states of the form $x = (\theta, 0)$ with $|\theta| < \pi$).

(c) Simulate! Obtain a successful control design, and provide plots and discussion.

Note that the definition of u_t doesn't make much sense unless you convert to physical units. In Matlab, use `theta = wrapToPi(theta)` (so that $|\theta| \le \pi$).

3.12 Solve an adaptation of Exercise 3.10 for the mountain car, which requires the following modifications:

(i) The state space model (2.56).

(ii) $E(x) = \text{KE}(x) + \text{PE}(x)$, where kinetic and potential energy are

$$\text{KE}(x) = \tfrac{1}{2}mv^2 \qquad \text{PE}(x) = \mathcal{U}(z) - \mathcal{U}(z^{\text{goal}}), \qquad x = (z, v) \in \mathsf{X}, \tag{3.67}$$

with $\mathcal{U}$ defined in (2.57). Obtain a formula for $\frac{d}{dt}E(x_t)$, and based on this propose a control law (perhaps based on a control-Lyapunov function design) that will drive $E(x_t)$ to zero. For simulations, use the numerical values given in Section 2.7.2.

3.13 Obtain an energy-based policy (along with an adaptation of Exercise 3.10) for MagBall, based on the description in Section 2.7.3.

Some ideas to get you started: The kinetic energy of the ball as a function of state is $\frac{1}{2}mv^2$, with $v = x_2$. We next introduce potential energy, following the arguments used to justify the two plots in Figure 2.11. The right-hand side of (2.60b) was obtained from Newton's law, with force

$$F(y,u) = mg - \kappa(u/y)^2.$$

Integrate the force with fixed $u = u^{\circ}$ to obtain the potential energy associated with this static input:

$$\mathcal{U}(y) = -\int_r^y F(y, u^{\circ})dz.$$

This function is strictly concave, with maximum at $y = r$, where evidently $\mathcal{U}(r) = 0$. The total energy is then defined by

$$E(x) = \tfrac{1}{2}mx_2^2 + \mathcal{U}(x_1).$$

It is easily established that $\nabla E\,(x) = (-F(x_1, u^\circ), mx_2)^{\intercal}$.

3.11 Notes

There are many excellent books on the theory and history of nonlinear optimal control, such as [45, 386]. Inverse dynamic programming and the control-Lyapunov function approach have a long history in the control theory literature [121, 283, 369]. It also lurks behind the curtains in the RL literature: To be seen in Chapter 5, minimization of the Bellman error is a common goal in RL that is closely aligned with the IDP approach to control

This chapter has provided only a brief survey of the LQR problem. See the books [7, 80, 205] for much more theory and history, the December 1971 special issue of the *IEEE Transactions on Automatic Control*, and early work of Kalman [175, 176]. If you have the Control System Toolbox from Matlab, then you have available some brilliant tools for computation:

`lqr`, `lqrd` solve the LQR problem using the data A, B, Q, and R.
`are`, `ared` solve the algebraic Riccati equation in continuous or discrete time.
`conv`, `rlocus` are used to graph the "symmetric root locus" [7, 76] (worth knowing about, but this book is not the best reference!).

See [126] for a recent control-theoretic approach to accelerate value iteration.

The linear programming approach to dynamic programming goes back to Manne in the 1960s [10, 63, 106, 237]. There is an ongoing research program on LP approaches to optimal control for deterministic systems [67, 68, 132, 139, 140, 160, 161, 177, 215, 349, 367], and SDPs in linear optimal control [71, 369].

Figure 3.4 is taken from [42] to illustrate the potential complexity of control problems with large input space, and how the complexity can be reduced via a clever choice of model. The example is posed in a stochastic setting, so of course the fly is not frozen in place.

The network shown in Figure 3.5 is called the Kumar–Seidman–Rybko–Stolyar model in [254]: the potential instability of this model was discovered in [203], which led to further investigation in [100, 308], followed by a burst of interest in stability and control theory for stochastic networks. See [254] for more history.

The book is entirely focused on the standard performance objectives, focusing on total cost, discounted cost, and average cost. This leaves out objectives such as variance-penalized objectives, risk-sensitive control [374], or more exotic functions of the occupancy pmf introduced in Section 5.7. In such cases the objective in (5.82a) is replaced with $\mathcal{C}(\varpi)$ in which $\mathcal{C}$ is convex. See [152, 383] for treatments of this more general setting.

4

ODE Methods for Algorithm Design

For our purposes, an *algorithm* is a finite sequence of computer-implementable instructions, designed to compute or approximate a policy, its performance, a value function, or related quantities. In algorithm *design*, it is useful to throw away the constraints of computers, and pretend that they can operate with infinite clock speed. An ordinary differential equation (ODE) will be regarded as an example of an algorithm operating on this imaginary computer.

The motivation comes from two sources. First, we want to know if our algorithm will eventually lead to a good approximation. This is easily couched in the theory of stability of ODEs, for which there is a far richer theory than stability of recursions in discrete time. Secondly, once we have constructed an ODE with desirable properties, including stability, we can then get advice from experts to provide the translation from calculus to a practical recursive algorithm. In this chapter, the translation step is performed using an Euler approximation, but it is hoped that the reader will experiment with more efficient ODE solvers based on an evolving theory of numerical methods [79].

Throughout the remainder of the book, we apply the following steps in algorithm design:

ODE Method

1. Formulate the algorithmic goal as the root finding problem:
$$\bar{f}(\theta^*) = 0, \quad \text{where } \bar{f} \colon \mathbb{R}^d \to \mathbb{R}^d.$$
2. Refine the design of $\bar{f}$, if necessary, to ensure that the associated ODE is globally asymptotically stable:
$$\frac{d}{dt}\vartheta = \bar{f}(\vartheta). \tag{4.1a}$$
3. Is an Euler approximation appropriate?
$$\theta_{n+1} = \theta_n + \alpha_{n+1}\bar{f}(\theta_n), \quad n \geq 0. \tag{4.1b}$$
See Section 4.1 for conditions under which (4.1b) is a good approximation.
4. Design an algorithm to approximate (4.1b) based on whatever observations are available.

4.1 Ordinary Differential Equations

Let's start with a question we should probably have posed earlier: *What is an ODE?* The question was taken for granted many times in the preceding pages. Up to now, the state space model in continuous time considered in Section 2.4.5 is the most significant example.

In this chapter, the "state variable" often represents the output of an algorithm rather than anything directly related to a control system. For this reason, throughout this chapter we use $\boldsymbol{\vartheta} = \{\vartheta_t : t \geq 0\}$ to denote the state process for the ODE, and restrict to the Euclidean setting: $\vartheta_t \in \mathbb{R}^d$ for an integer d. The state space model (2.36) in this notation is

$$\frac{d}{dt}\vartheta = \mathrm{f}(\vartheta), \qquad \vartheta_0 = \theta_0 \text{ given,} \tag{4.2}$$

where $\mathrm{f}\colon \mathbb{R}^d \to \mathbb{R}^d$ is the vector field as in (2.36). Two examples with $d = 1$:

$\mathrm{f}(\theta) = a\theta$ and $\vartheta_t = \theta_0 e^{at}$.
$\mathrm{f}(\theta) = \theta^{-2}$ and $\vartheta_t = [\theta_0^{-1} - t]^{-1}$.

The ODE (4.2) is called *time homogeneous* since f does not depend upon t. See Section 3.3 for hints on how to apply state augmentation to create homogeneity for a model in which the vector field f depends on time.

In every application of the ODE approach to algorithm design, the first step is to construct the vector field so that ϑ_t converges to some desired value $\theta^* \in \mathbb{R}^d$. In particular, if $\vartheta_0 = \theta^*$, then the solution to the ODE should stay put: $\vartheta_t = \theta^*$ for all $t \geq 0$. This requires that $\frac{d}{dt}\vartheta_t = \mathsf{0}$ for all t, which by (4.2) implies that θ^* is an *equilibrium*: $\mathrm{f}(\theta^*) = \mathsf{0}$. Advanced material on stability theory for ODEs is contained in Section 4.8. Some of this can be anticipated from the Lyapunov theory contained in Section 2.4.5.

Understanding theory surrounding existence of solutions of (4.2) is the first step toward understanding ODE principles for algorithm design in this chapter and in Part II of the book. Much like the Bellman equation (3.5) is regarded as a fixed point equation, the ODE (4.2) is a fixed point equation in the variable $\boldsymbol{\vartheta} = \{\vartheta_t : t \geq 0\}$. *Perhaps we can mirror the success of the value iteration algorithm* (3.8) (an instance of successive approximation)? Writing (4.2) as $\vartheta = \vartheta - \frac{d}{dt}\vartheta + \mathrm{f}(\vartheta)$, an analog would be

$$\vartheta_t^{n+1} = \vartheta_t^n - \frac{d}{dt}\vartheta_t^n + \mathrm{f}(\vartheta_t^n), \qquad t \geq 0,\, n \geq 0,$$

with $\boldsymbol{\vartheta}^0 = \{\vartheta_t^0 : t \geq 0\}$ given as initial condition. Sorry to say, this approach is doomed to failure! One source of difficulty is the repeated differentiation in this recursion, which means we have to be very careful with our selection of $\boldsymbol{\vartheta}^0$. Also, this recursion does not respect the requirement that the initial condition θ_0 is specified.

The Fundamental Theorem of Calculus motivates a more sensible approach. That is,

$$\vartheta_t = \theta_0 + \int_0^t \mathrm{f}(\vartheta_\tau)d\tau\,, \qquad 0 \leq t \leq \mathcal{T}, \tag{4.3}$$

where the finite time horizon $\mathcal{T}$ is chosen for the sake of analysis. Successive approximation is defined as before: Take an initial guess $\boldsymbol{\vartheta}^0 = \{\vartheta_t^0 : 0 \leq t \leq \mathcal{T}\}$, and define for $n \geq 0$,

$$\vartheta_t^{n+1} = \theta_0 + \int_0^t \mathrm{f}(\vartheta_\tau^n)d\tau\,, \qquad 0 \leq t \leq \mathcal{T}. \tag{4.4}$$

This recursion is known as *Picard iteration*. It is successful under mild assumptions:

Proposition 4.1 *Suppose that the function* f *is globally* Lipschitz continuous*: there is $L > 0$ such that for each $x,y \in \mathbb{R}^d$,*

$$\|\mathrm{f}(x) - \mathrm{f}(y)\| \leq L\|x - y\|. \tag{4.5}$$

Then for each θ_0 there exists a unique solution to (4.3) *on the infinite time horizon. Moreover, successive approximation is uniformly convergent:*

$$\lim_{n\to\infty} \max_{0\le t\le \mathcal{T}} \|\vartheta_t^n - \vartheta_t\| = 0. \qquad \square$$

A key component of the proof of Proposition 4.1 is Grönwall's Inequality, which commonly appears in the theory of stochastic approximation, as well as ordinary differential equations. Note that Bellman had early influence here [34], which is why Proposition 4.2 is often called the Bellman–Grönwall lemma.

Proposition 4.2 (Grönwall Inequality) *Let α, β and z be nonnegative functions defined on an interval $[0,\mathcal{T}]$, with $\mathcal{T} > 0$. Assume that β and z are continuous, and the integral inequality holds:*

$$z_t \le \alpha_t + \int_0^t \beta_s z_s \, ds, \qquad 0 \le t \le \mathcal{T}. \tag{4.6a}$$

(i) *The Grönwall Inequality holds:*

$$z_t \le \alpha_t + \int_0^t \alpha_s \beta_s \exp\Bigl(\int_s^t \beta_r \, dr\Bigr) \, ds, \qquad 0 \le t \le \mathcal{T}. \tag{4.6b}$$

(ii) *If, in addition, the function α is nondecreasing, then*

$$z_t \le \alpha_t \exp\Bigl(\int_0^t \beta_s \, ds\Bigr), \qquad 0 \le t \le \mathcal{T}. \tag{4.6c}$$

$\square$

The proof can be found in Section 4.8, or if you have background in linear state space models, you might want to work it out on your own. Hint: First solve the problem with equality:

$$z_t = \alpha_t + \int_0^t \beta_s z_s \, ds. \tag{4.7}$$

You can construct a state space model, with state $x_t = z_t - \alpha_t$, and because it is a scalar linear system you obtain an explicit solution. The solution leads to something like (4.6b), but with equality.

The following simple lemma is also frequently required in ODE analysis.

Lemma 4.3 *Suppose that $\{\gamma_t : t \in \mathbb{R}\}$ is a nonnegative function satisfying the following:* (i) $|\gamma_t - \gamma_s| \le L|t-s|$ *for a constant L and all t,s and* (ii) $\int_0^\infty \gamma_t \, dt < \infty$. *Then,* $\lim_{t\to\infty} \gamma_t = 0$.

Proof Assumption (i) implies that for any t_0 we have the bound $\gamma_t \ge \gamma_{t_0} - L(t-t_0)$ for $t_0 \le t \le t_0 + \gamma_{t_0}/L$. This, combined with (ii), then gives

$$\frac{1}{2L} \lim_{t_0\to\infty} \gamma_{t_0}^2 = \lim_{t_0\to\infty} \int_{t_0}^{t_0+\gamma_{t_0}/L} \bigl(\gamma_{t_0} - L(t-t_0)\bigr) \, dt \le \lim_{t_0\to\infty} \int_{t_0}^{\infty} \gamma_t \, dt = 0. \qquad \square$$

4.2 A Brief Return to Reality

This entire chapter considers ODE approaches to algorithm design: This means design of the function f appearing in (4.2), or design of the more exotic "quasistochastic" ODEs for which theory and applications are developed in Sections 4.5–4.7.

There is the inevitable translation step: Any design formulated in continuous time must be translated to create a practical algorithm. If you have taken a first-year calculus course, then you probably have predicted the most common approach: select a sequence of times $\{0 = t_0 < t_1 < \cdots\}$, and replace the derivative in (4.2) by a finite difference: With $\bar{\vartheta}_0 = \theta_0$ given, define for each $n \geq 0$,

$$\alpha_{n+1}^{-1}[\bar{\vartheta}_{t_{n+1}} - \bar{\vartheta}_{t_n}] = \mathrm{f}(\bar{\vartheta}_{t_n}),$$

where $\alpha_{n+1} = t_{n+1} - t_n > 0$. The recursive nature is evident after rearranging terms:

$$\bar{\vartheta}_{t_{n+1}} = \bar{\vartheta}_{t_n} + \alpha_{n+1}\mathrm{f}(\bar{\vartheta}_{t_n}). \tag{4.8}$$

In our final algorithm, we simplify notation, writing $\theta_n = \bar{\vartheta}_{t_n}$, and $\{\alpha_n\}$ is known as the step-size sequence. This is known as the Euler approximation of an ODE, or simply *Euler's method.*

This approximation is successful under the assumptions of Proposition 4.1: It can be shown that

$$\max_{0 \leq t \leq \mathcal{T}} \|\bar{\vartheta}_t - \vartheta_t\| \leq K(L, \mathcal{T})\bar{\alpha}, \tag{4.9}$$

where $\bar{\alpha} = \max\{\alpha_k : t_k \leq \mathcal{T}\}$, and L was introduced in (4.5). Grönwall's Inequality is used in the proof of (4.9), which leads to upper bounds on $K(L, \mathcal{T})$ that at first appear frightening (growing exponentially fast in L and $\mathcal{T}$).

Fortunately, asymptotic stability of the ODE often implies stability of (4.8), and in this case we obtain the bound (4.9) with $K(L, \mathcal{T})$ independent of $\mathcal{T} > 0$. Theorem 4.9 is an important special case for applications to optimization.

4.2.1 *Euler Approximation for a Linear System*

The Euler approximation for the LTI model in continuous time (2.44), with $\mathrm{f}(x) = Ax$, results in the discrete time model (2.42), with $F = (1 + \alpha A)$ (with constant step-size $\alpha_n \equiv \alpha > 0$).

Consider the scalar case $\frac{d}{dt}\vartheta = a\vartheta$, which admits the solution $\vartheta_t = \theta_0 e^{at}$. The Euler approximation results in a similar solution, as a function of the initial condition:

$$\bar{\vartheta}_{t_{n+1}} = F^n \bar{\vartheta}_0, \qquad F = (1 + \alpha a).$$

The approximation $\bar{\vartheta}_{t_n} = \vartheta_{t_n} + O(\alpha)$ follows from the Taylor series approximation for the exponential, $(1 + \alpha a)^n \approx (e^{\alpha a})^n = e^{a t_n}$.

If $a < 0$ and $\alpha < |a|^{-1}$, then the approximation holds on the infinite time interval, since both $\bar{\vartheta}_{t_n}$ and ϑ_{t_n} converge to zero geometrically fast, as $n \to \infty$. This bound on the step-size α may be regarded as a special case of a more general theory – see Theorem 4.9. □

Those interested in a high-fidelity approximation of an ODE usually abandon the Euler approximation for more sophisticated techniques, such as the midpoint method or more general Runge–Kutta methods [79, 168, 384]. The update equations are more complex, but this complexity is often offset by the tighter approximation. However, remember in this chapter our goal is to estimate a stationary point, the solution $\theta^* \in \mathbb{R}^d$ to

$$\mathrm{f}(\theta^*) = 0, \tag{4.10}$$

and not accurately track solutions to the ODE (4.2). The best way to perform an ODE approximation for this relatively modest goal is an open field for research.

4.3 Newton–Raphson Flow

This section concerns an approach to ODE design in which the goal is to solve the root finding problem (4.10). The parameter θ^* is regarded as an equilibrium condition for the ODE (4.2). The problem we face here is that this ODE may not be stable in any sense. In this section, we describe a general approach to modify the dynamics and ensure stability.

Section 4.4 concerns root finding problems for the special case in which $\mathrm{f} = -\nabla_\theta \Gamma$, where $\Gamma \colon \mathbb{R}^d \to \mathbb{R}_+$ is a loss function associated with some optimization problem. The root finding problem is then equivalent to the first-order condition for optimality, $\nabla_\theta \Gamma\,(\theta^*) = 0$. If Γ has nice properties (such as convexity), then it is not difficult to establish stability of (4.2) using Lyapunov function techniques (such results are surveyed in Section 4.4). The techniques in this section may prove useful in applications for which stability of (4.2) fails.

Our starting point is to regard $\mathrm{f}(\vartheta_t)$ as the "state variable," and our next step is to define dynamics so that $\lim_{t\to\infty} \mathrm{f}(\vartheta_t) = 0$ for each initial condition. Under mild additional assumptions on f, it will follow that $\lim_{t\to\infty} \vartheta_t = \theta^*$, which is our design objective.

If $\mathrm{f}(\vartheta_t)$ is a state variable, this means there is an associated vector field $\mathcal{V} \colon \mathbb{R}^d \to \mathbb{R}^d$, with

$$\frac{d}{dt}\mathrm{f}(\vartheta_t) = \mathcal{V}(\mathrm{f}(\vartheta_t)). \tag{4.11}$$

One way to ensure that $\mathrm{f}(\vartheta_t)$ converges to zero is to choose $\mathcal{V}(f) = -f$, giving

$$\frac{d}{dt}\mathrm{f}(\vartheta_t) = -\mathrm{f}(\vartheta_t). \tag{4.12}$$

The solution is $\mathrm{f}(\vartheta_t) = e^{-t}\mathrm{f}(\vartheta_0)$, which converges to zero exponentially quickly. *Achieving these dynamics would be an amazing feat!*

Well, it isn't really so difficult. Apply the chain rule:

$$\frac{d}{dt}\mathrm{f}(\vartheta_t) = A(\vartheta_t)\frac{d}{dt}\vartheta_t, \qquad \text{with} \quad A(\theta) = \partial_\theta \mathrm{f}\,(\theta)\,, \quad \theta \in \mathbb{R}^d,$$

where $\partial_\theta \mathrm{f}$ denotes the $d \times d$ Jacobian matrix with entries

$$A_{i,j}(\theta) = \frac{\partial}{\partial \theta_j} f_i\,(\theta). \tag{4.13}$$

This means that achieving the dynamics (4.11) is equivalent to

$$\frac{d}{dt}\vartheta_t = [A(\vartheta_t)]^{-1}\mathcal{V}(\mathrm{f}(\vartheta_t)).$$

Application of this identity for the special case $\mathcal{V}(f) = -f$ results in a famous ODE:

Newton–Raphson Flow

$$\frac{d}{dt}\vartheta_t = -\big[A(\vartheta_t)\big]^{-1}\mathrm{f}(\vartheta_t). \tag{4.14a}$$

The function on the right-hand side is the *Newton–Raphson vector field*

$$\mathrm{f}^{\mathsf{NRf}}(\theta) = -\big[A(\theta)\big]^{-1}\mathrm{f}(\theta). \tag{4.14b}$$

In most applications, it is not possible to determine a priori if the matrix $A(\theta) = \partial_\theta \mathrm{f}(\theta)$ is full rank, which motivates a *regularized Newton–Raphson flow*: For fixed $\varepsilon > 0$,

$$\frac{d}{dt}\vartheta_t = \mathcal{G}(\vartheta_t)\mathrm{f}(\vartheta_t), \tag{4.15}$$

where $\mathcal{G}(\theta) \stackrel{\text{def}}{=} -[\varepsilon I + A(\theta)^{\intercal}A(\theta)]^{-1}A(\theta)^{\intercal}$ is an approximation of the pseudo-inverse of $-A(\theta)$. It is shown in Proposition 4.4 that solutions to (4.15) are bounded in time, provided $V = \|\mathrm{f}\|^2$ is a coercive function on $\mathbb{R}^d$. Mild additional conditions imply that V serves as a Lyapunov function for (4.15), giving

$$\lim_{t\to\infty} \mathrm{f}(\vartheta_t) = 0. \tag{4.16}$$

Proposition 4.4 *Consider the following conditions for the function* f*:*

(a) f *is globally Lipschitz continuous and continuously differentiable. Hence* $A(\cdot)$ *is a bounded and continuous matrix-valued function.*
(b) $\|\mathrm{f}\|$ *is coercive. That is, the set* $\{\theta : \|\mathrm{f}(\theta)\| \le n\}$ *is bounded for each* n*.*
(c) *The function* f *has a unique root* θ^**, and* $A^{\intercal}(\theta)\mathrm{f}(\theta) \neq 0$ *for* $\theta \neq \theta^*$*. Moreover, the matrix* $A^* = A(\theta^*)$ *is nonsingular.*

The following hold for solutions to the ODE (4.15) *under increasingly strong assumptions:*

(i) *If (a) holds, then for each* t*, and each initial condition,*

$$\frac{d}{dt}\mathrm{f}(\vartheta_t) = -A(\vartheta_t)[\varepsilon I + A(\vartheta_t)^{\intercal}A(\vartheta_t)]^{-1}A(\vartheta_t)^{\intercal}\mathrm{f}(\vartheta_t). \tag{4.17}$$

(ii) *If in addition (b) holds, then the solutions to the ODE are bounded, and*

$$\lim_{t\to\infty} A(\vartheta_t)^{\intercal}\mathrm{f}(\vartheta_t) = 0. \tag{4.18}$$

(iii) *If (a)–(c) hold, then* (4.15) *is globally asymptotically stable.* □

Proof The result (i) follows from the chain rule and the definitions.

The proof of (ii) is based on the Lyapunov function $V(\vartheta) = \frac{1}{2}\|\mathrm{f}(\vartheta)\|^2$ combined with (a):

$$\frac{d}{dt}V(\vartheta_t) = -\mathrm{f}(\vartheta_t)^{\intercal}A(\vartheta_t)[\varepsilon I + A(\vartheta_t)^{\intercal}A(\vartheta_t)]^{-1}A(\vartheta_t)^{\intercal}\mathrm{f}(\vartheta_t).$$

The right-hand side is nonpositive when $\vartheta_t \neq \theta^*$. Integrating each side gives for any $T > 0$,

$$V(\vartheta_T) = V(\vartheta_0) - \int_0^T \mathrm{f}(\vartheta_t)^{\intercal}A(\vartheta_t)[\varepsilon I + A(\vartheta_t)^{\intercal}A(\vartheta_t)]^{-1}A(\vartheta_t)^{\intercal}\mathrm{f}(\vartheta_t)dt, \tag{4.19}$$

so that $V(\vartheta_T) \le V(\vartheta_0)$ for all T. Under the coercive assumption, it follows that solutions to (4.15) are bounded. Also, letting $T \to \infty$, we obtain from (4.19) the bound

$$\int_0^\infty \mathrm{f}(\vartheta_t)^\intercal A(\vartheta_t)[\varepsilon I + A(\vartheta_t)^\intercal A(\vartheta_t)]^{-1} A(\vartheta_t)^\intercal \mathrm{f}(\vartheta_t) dt \le V(\vartheta_0).$$

Boundedness of ϑ_t and continuity of A imply the existence of $B(\vartheta_0) < \infty$ such that

$$\int_0^\infty \gamma_t \, dt \le B(\vartheta_0) < \infty, \qquad \gamma_t \stackrel{\text{def}}{=} \|A(\vartheta_t)^\intercal \mathrm{f}(\vartheta_t)\|^2.$$

The functions f and A are Lipschitz continuous, and boundedness then implies that γ_t satisfies the Lipschitz condition in Lemma 4.3. Hence $\lim_{t\to\infty} A(\vartheta_t)^\intercal \mathrm{f}(\vartheta_t) = 0$ as claimed.

We next prove (iii). While this follows from Proposition 2.5, we have the ingredients for a short alternative proof that hopefully also offers additional insight.

Global asymptotic stability of (4.15) requires that solutions converge to θ^* from each initial condition, and also that θ^* is stable in the sense of Lyapunov. Assumption (c) combined with (ii) gives the former, that $\lim_{t\to\infty} \vartheta_t = \theta^*$. A convenient sufficient condition for the latter is obtained by considering $A_\varepsilon = \partial_\theta[\mathcal{G}(\theta)\mathrm{f}(\theta)] \,|_{\theta=\theta^*}$. Stability in the sense of Lyapunov holds if this matrix is Hurwitz (all eigenvalues are in the strict left-half plane in $\mathbb{C}$) [181, theorem 4.7].

Applying the definitions, we obtain $A_\varepsilon = -[\varepsilon I + M]^{-1} M$ with $M = A(\theta^*)^\intercal A(\theta^*) > 0$ (recall that $A(\theta^*)$ is assumed to be nonsingular). The eigenvectors of A_ε coincide with those of M, and for each eigenvector–eigenvalue pair (v,λ) for M, we have

$$A_\varepsilon v = \lambda_A v, \qquad \lambda_A = -\frac{\lambda}{\varepsilon + \lambda} < 0.$$

This establishes that A_ε is Hurwitz. □

4.4 Optimization

Here we turn to minimization of a loss function $\Gamma\colon \mathbb{R}^d \to \mathbb{R}_+$, for which we would like to compute a global minimum:

$$\theta^* \in \arg\min \Gamma(\theta).$$

This section contains a very brief survey of optimization theory and ODE techniques to estimate θ^*. In particular, we establish conditions under which the steepest-descent ODE is convergent:

$$\frac{d}{dt}\vartheta = -\nabla_\theta \Gamma(\vartheta). \tag{4.20}$$

This is also known as the *gradient flow*.

Recall that the gradient $\nabla\Gamma\,(\theta_0)$ at a vector $\theta_0 \in \mathbb{R}^d$ is orthogonal to the level set $\{\theta \in \mathbb{R}^d : \Gamma(\theta) = \Gamma(\theta_0)\}$, in the sense illustrated in Figure 4.1. For a given time t_0, denote $\theta_0 = \vartheta_{t_0}$, $r_0 = \Gamma(\theta_0)$, and recall from (2.28) the definition of the sublevel set:

$$S_\Gamma(r_0) = \{\theta \in \mathbb{R}^d : \Gamma(\theta) \le r_0\}.$$

If the gradient at θ_0 is nonzero, as in the example shown, then the gradient flow drives the solution into the interior of this set: $\Gamma(\vartheta_t) < r_0$ for all $t > t_0$. In particular, each sublevel set is *absorbing*: once a solution to the gradient flow enters the set $S_\Gamma(r_0)$, it can never exit.

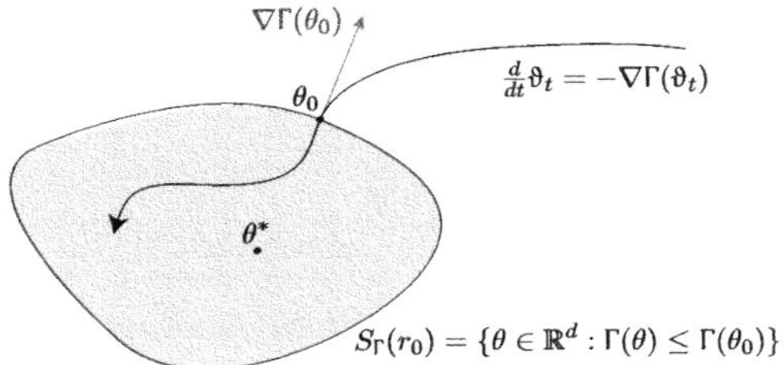

Figure 4.1 Gradient flow: $\Gamma(\vartheta_t)$ is nonincreasing because each sublevel set $S_\Gamma(r_0)$ is absorbing.

This intuition is the starting point toward finding conditions under which the gradient flow is convergent using Lyapunov function techniques. Two typical choices for a Lyapunov function are

$$V(\theta) = \tfrac{1}{2}\|\theta - \theta^*\|^2 \qquad \text{or} \qquad V(\theta) = \tfrac{1}{2}[\Gamma(\theta) - \Gamma^\star], \tag{4.21}$$

where $\Gamma^\star = \min_\theta \Gamma(\theta)$. The latter is most natural, based on the intuition obtained from Figure 4.1 and the similarity between this figure and Figure 2.6.

The Polyak–Łojasiewicz (PL) condition considered in Section 4.4.2 is one minimal criterion for convergence. When we are ready to approximate the gradient flow using an Euler approximation, it is standard to impose the following *L-smooth* condition: for some $L > 0$, and all θ, θ',

$$\Gamma(\theta') \le \Gamma(\theta) + [\theta' - \theta]^\intercal \nabla\Gamma(\theta) + \tfrac{1}{2}L\|\theta' - \theta\|^2. \tag{4.22}$$

The usefulness of this bound is explained in Section 4.4.3.

Please do not feel you have to prove a theorem before you can experiment: The algorithms we obtain are frequently successful in practice, even when our assumptions are violated. For example, the optimization problems arising in training neural networks do not satisfy any of the assumptions presented here, but practitioners commonly apply the gradient descent algorithm described in Section 4.4.3, which is nothing but an Euler approximation of the gradient flow.

4.4.1 Role of Convexity

The term has come up in casual discussion in preceding chapters, but now requires a formal definition:

Convexity

► A set $S \subset \mathbb{R}^d$ is convex if it contains, all line segments with endpoints in S. That is, $(1-\alpha)\theta^0 + \alpha\theta^1 \in S$ for $\theta^0, \theta^1 \in S$, and any $\alpha \in (0,1)$.

► A function $\Gamma\colon S \to \mathbb{R}$, with convex domain S, is called convex if the following bound holds: For any pair $\theta^0, \theta^1 \in S$ and $\rho \in (0,1)$:

$$\Gamma((1-\rho)\theta^0 + \rho\theta^1) \le (1-\rho)\Gamma(\theta^0) + \rho\Gamma(\theta^1). \tag{4.23}$$

It is *quasiconvex* if the sublevel set $S_\Gamma(r)$ is convex (or empty) for any $r \in \mathbb{R}$.

A convex function is always quasi-convex. With $S = \mathbb{R}$, any continuous nondecreasing function is quasiconvex, since in this case $S_\Gamma(r) = (-\infty, a(r)]$ for each r, where $a(r) = \max\{\theta : \Gamma(\theta) \le r\}$ (continuity isn't required to ensure quasiconvexity, but is required to arrive at this representation for the sublevel set).

The following characterization has a stronger geometric flavor:

Lemma 4.5 *For any convex set S, a function $\Gamma\colon S \to \mathbb{R}$ is convex if and only if for each $\theta^0 \in \mathbb{R}^d$, there is a vector $v^0 \in \mathbb{R}^d$ satisfying*

$$\Gamma(\theta) \ge \Gamma(\theta^0) + \langle v^0, \theta - \theta^0 \rangle, \qquad \textit{for all } \theta \in S. \tag{4.24}$$

The right-hand side of (4.24) is regarded as an affine function of θ, and the bound means that the graph of Γ is always above the graph of the affine function. The vector v^0 is called a *subgradient*. If Γ is differentiable at θ^0, then it is an ordinary gradient $v^0 = \nabla\Gamma(\theta^0)$.

There are also several stronger conditions:

▲ The function Γ is *strictly convex* if the inequality (4.23) is strict whenever $\theta^1 \neq \theta^0$.
▲ If Γ is differentiable, then it is called *strongly convex* if for a constant $\delta_0 > 0$,

$$\langle \nabla\Gamma(\theta) - \nabla\Gamma(\theta^0), \theta - \theta^0 \rangle \ge \delta_0 \|\theta - \theta^0\|^2 \qquad \text{for all } \theta, \theta^0 \in \mathbb{R}^d. \tag{4.25}$$

Strong convexity is used to establish nice numerical properties of the gradient flow. The value of convexity and strict convexity is made clear in the following.

Proposition 4.6 *Suppose that $\Gamma\colon \mathbb{R}^d \to \mathbb{R}_+$ is convex. Then, for given $\theta^0 \in \mathbb{R}^d$,*

(i) *if θ^0 is a local minimum, then it is also a global minimum;*
(ii) *if Γ is differentiable at θ^0, with $\nabla\Gamma(\theta^0) = 0$, then θ^0 is a global minimum;*
(iii) *if either of (i) or (ii) holds, and if Γ is strictly convex, then θ^0 is the unique global minimum.* □

The gradient flow is convergent under mild conditions. See Exercise 4.7 for generalization to matrix gain.

Proposition 4.7 *Suppose that Γ is continuously differentiable, convex, and coercive, with unique minimizer θ^*. Then the gradient flow* (4.20) *is globally asymptotically stable, with unique equilibrium θ^*. If Γ is strongly convex, then the rate of convergence is exponential:*

$$\|\vartheta_t - \theta^*\| \le e^{-\delta_0 t}\|\vartheta_0 - \theta^*\|, \tag{4.26}$$

where δ_0 appears in (4.25).

Proof We adopt the Lyapunov function approach, using $V(\theta) = \frac{1}{2}\|\theta - \theta^*\|^2$. From the chain rule,

$$\frac{d}{dt}V(\vartheta_t) = -\nabla_\theta\Gamma(\vartheta_t)^\intercal[\vartheta_t - \theta^*].$$

Convexity implies that $\Gamma(\theta^*) \ge \Gamma(\vartheta_t) + \nabla_\theta\Gamma(\vartheta_t)^\intercal[\theta^* - \vartheta_t]$, giving

$$\frac{d}{dt}V(\vartheta_t) \le -[\Gamma(\vartheta_t) - \Gamma(\theta^*)] \le 0,$$

where the inequality is strict when $\vartheta_t \neq \theta^*$. Proposition 2.5 then implies global asymptotic stability.

Under strong convexity, we apply $\nabla_\theta \Gamma(\theta^*) = 0$ to obtain the stronger bound:

$$\frac{d}{dt} V(\vartheta_t) = -\{\nabla_\theta \Gamma(\vartheta_t) - \nabla_\theta \Gamma(\theta^*)\}^\intercal [\vartheta_t - \theta^*] \le -\delta_0 \|\vartheta_t - \theta^*\|^2.$$

That is, $\frac{d}{dt} V(\vartheta_t) \le -2\delta_0 V(\vartheta_t)$. This implies that $V(\vartheta_t) \le V(\vartheta_0) \exp(-2\delta_0 t)$ for any t, which establishes (4.26). □

4.4.2 Polyak–Łojasiewicz Condition

The use of the Euclidean norm to define a Lyapunov function in Proposition 4.7 relied heavily on convexity. An alternative is known as the Polyak–Łojasiewicz (PL) inequality: For some $\mu > 0$ and all θ,

$$\tfrac{1}{2}\|\nabla\Gamma(\theta)\|^2 \ge \mu[\Gamma(\theta) - \Gamma^\star]. \tag{4.27}$$

We do not assume here that Γ is convex, or that there is a unique optimizer.

Theorem 4.8 *If the PL inequality holds, then the gradient flow satisfies, for each initial* ϑ_0 :

$$\Gamma(\vartheta_t) - \Gamma^\star \le e^{-\mu t}[\Gamma(\vartheta_0) - \Gamma^\star].$$

If in addition Γ *is coercive, then the solutions are bounded, and any limit point* θ_∞ *of* $\{\vartheta_t\}$ *is an optimizer:* $\Gamma(\theta_\infty) = \Gamma^\star$.

Proof We adopt the second option in (4.21) for a Lyapunov function:

$$V(\theta) = \tfrac{1}{2}[\Gamma(\theta) - \Gamma^\star] \quad \Longrightarrow \quad \tfrac{d}{dt} V(\vartheta_t) = -\tfrac{1}{2}\|\nabla_\theta \Gamma(\vartheta_t)\|^2 \le -\mu V(\vartheta_t).$$

This implies the desired inequality $\Gamma(\vartheta_t) - \Gamma^\star = V(\vartheta_t) \le e^{-\mu t} V(\vartheta_0)$.

If Γ is coercive, then trajectories of $\boldsymbol{\vartheta}$ evolve in the compact set $S = \{\theta : V(\theta) \le V(\vartheta_0)\}$. If θ_∞ is a limit point, this means $\theta_\infty = \lim_{n\to\infty} \vartheta_{t_n}$, with $t_n \uparrow \infty$. Continuity of the loss function then implies optimality: $\Gamma(\theta_\infty) = \lim_{n\to\infty} \Gamma(\vartheta_{t_n}) = \Gamma^\star$. □

4.4.3 Euler Approximation

The standard Euler approximation of the gradient flow (4.20) is known as steepest descent:

$$\theta_{k+1} = \theta_k - \alpha \nabla\Gamma(\theta_k). \tag{4.28}$$

To obtain convergence from each initial condition, we suppose that the objective function is L-smooth (recall (4.22)). This is one of two crucial bounds in the proof of the following cousin of Theorem 4.8:

Theorem 4.9 *Suppose that* Γ *satisfies two bounds: the* L*-smooth inequality* (4.22), *and the PL inequality* (4.27). *Then, provided* $\alpha \le 1/L$, *the following bound holds for* (4.28):

$$\Gamma(\theta_k) - \Gamma^* \le (1 - \alpha\mu)^k [\Gamma(\theta_0) - \Gamma^*].$$

Proof The L-smooth inequality applied to the gradient descent recursion (4.28) gives

$$\Gamma(\theta_{k+1}) - \Gamma(\theta_k) \le [\theta_{k+1} - \theta_k]^\intercal \nabla\Gamma(\theta_k) + \tfrac{1}{2} L\|\theta_{k+1} - \theta_k\|^2 = (-\alpha + \tfrac{1}{2} L\alpha^2)\|\nabla\Gamma(\theta_k)\|^2.$$

The bound $-\alpha + \frac{1}{2}L\alpha^2 \leq -\frac{1}{2}\alpha$ holds when $\alpha \leq 1/L$. This and the PL inequality (4.27) imply

$$\Gamma(\theta_{k+1}) - \Gamma(\theta_k) \leq -\alpha\tfrac{1}{2}\|\nabla\Gamma(\theta_k)\|^2 \leq -\alpha\mu[\Gamma(\theta_k) - \Gamma^\star].$$

Rearranging and subtracting $\Gamma^\star$ from both sides gives

$$\Gamma(\theta_{k+1}) - \Gamma^\star \leq (1 - \alpha\mu)[\Gamma(\theta_k) - \Gamma^\star].$$

Iterating this inequality gives the result. □

In practice, the L-smooth inequality for Γ is usually verified via a global Lipschitz condition on its gradient:

$$\|\nabla\Gamma(\theta') - \nabla\Gamma(\theta)\| \leq L\|\theta' - \theta\|. \tag{4.29}$$

Lemma 4.10 *Suppose that* (4.29) *holds for all* $\theta,\theta' \in \Theta$*, where* $\Theta \subseteq \mathbb{R}^d$*. We then have:*

(i) $|\langle\nabla\Gamma(\theta') - \nabla\Gamma(\theta),\theta' - \theta\rangle| \leq L\|\theta' - \theta\|^2$ *for all* $\theta,\theta' \in \Theta$.
(ii) *If* Θ *is convex, then* Γ *is* L*-smooth.*

Proof Part (i) is immediate from (4.29):

$$|\langle\nabla\Gamma(\theta') - \nabla\Gamma(\theta),\theta' - \theta\rangle| \leq \|\nabla\Gamma(\theta') - \nabla\Gamma(\theta)\|\|\theta' - \theta\| \leq L\|\theta' - \theta\|^2.$$

To establish (ii), for $\theta,\theta' \in \Theta$ denote $\theta_t = \theta + t[\theta' - \theta]$ and $\xi_t = \Gamma(\theta_t)$. We have $\theta_t \in \Theta$ for $0 \leq t \leq 1$ under the convexity assumption. The function is differentiable on this domain, with $\frac{d}{dt}\xi_t = \langle\nabla\Gamma(\theta_t),\theta' - \theta\rangle$. Applying (i),

$$\tfrac{d}{dt}\xi_t - \tfrac{d}{dt}\xi_0 = \langle\nabla\Gamma(\theta_t) - \nabla\Gamma(\theta_0),\theta' - \theta\rangle \leq tL\|\theta' - \theta\|^2.$$

Integrating from $t = 0$ to $t = 1$ gives (4.22):

$$\begin{aligned}\Gamma(\theta') = \xi(1) &= \xi_0 + \int_0^1 \tfrac{d}{dt}\xi_t\,dt \\ &\leq \xi_0 + \tfrac{d}{dt}\xi_0 + \tfrac{1}{2}L\|\theta' - \theta\|^2 \\ &= \Gamma(\theta) + \langle\nabla\Gamma(\theta),\theta' - \theta\rangle + \tfrac{1}{2}L\|\theta' - \theta\|^2.\end{aligned}$$

□

4.4.4 Constrained Optimization

Consider the optimization problem with equality constraints:

$$\begin{aligned}\Gamma^\star \stackrel{\text{def}}{=} \min \quad & \Gamma(\theta) \\ \text{s.t.} \quad & g(\theta) = 0,\end{aligned} \tag{4.30}$$

where $g\colon \mathbb{R}^d \to \mathbb{R}^m$ (so there are $m \geq 1$ constraints). The constraints are convex if and only if g is an affine function of θ: For an $m \times d$ matrix D and vector $d \in \mathbb{R}^m$,

$$g(\theta) = D\theta + d. \tag{4.31}$$

One approach to the solution of these problems is through a *Lagrangian relaxation*, defined through a sequence of steps. Introduce the Lagrangian $\mathcal{L}\colon \mathbb{R}^d \times \mathbb{R}^m \to \mathbb{R}$:

$$\mathcal{L}(\theta,\lambda) = \Gamma(\theta) + \lambda^\intercal g(\theta), \qquad \theta \in \mathbb{R}^d, \quad \lambda \in \mathbb{R}^m. \tag{4.32}$$

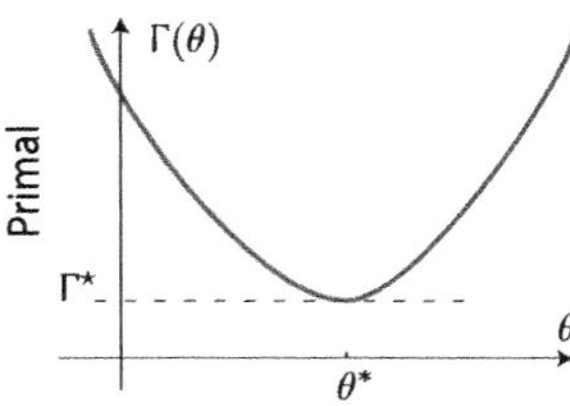

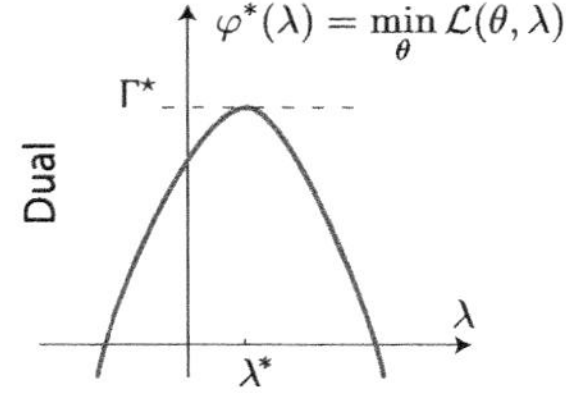

Figure 4.2 Primal and dual optimization problems.

The so-called dual function is the minimum of the Lagrangian, with constraints removed:

$$\varphi^*(\lambda) = \min_\theta \mathcal{L}(\theta,\lambda). \tag{4.33}$$

The value $-\infty$ is possible: Consider what happens when Γ is a linear function of θ.

For any $\lambda \in \mathbb{R}^m$, we obtain a lower bound on $\Gamma^\star$ as follows:

$$\varphi^*(\lambda) \leq \min_\theta\{\mathcal{L}(\theta,\lambda) : g(\theta) = 0\} = \min_\theta\{\Gamma(\theta) : g(\theta) = 0\} = \Gamma^\star,$$

where the inequality holds because we have reintroduced the constraints, which means we are minimizing $\mathcal{L}$ over a potentially smaller set. The dual problem is defined to be the maximum of φ^* over all λ:

$$\max_\lambda \min_\theta \mathcal{L}(\theta,\lambda) = \max_\lambda \varphi^*(\lambda) \leq \Gamma^\star. \tag{4.34}$$

We say there is a *duality gap* if the inequality is strict. The left-hand side is called a min-max (or saddle point) problem. Figure 4.2 shows a typical example of convex optimization without duality gap.

There is a simple ODE to obtain a solution to the saddle point problem (4.34), known as the *primal-dual flow*:

$$\frac{d}{dt}\vartheta = -\nabla_\theta \mathcal{L}(\vartheta,\lambda) = -\nabla_\theta \Gamma(\vartheta) - [\partial_\theta g(\vartheta)]^\intercal \lambda, \tag{4.35a}$$

$$\frac{d}{dt}\lambda = \nabla_\lambda \mathcal{L}(\vartheta,\lambda) = g(\vartheta), \tag{4.35b}$$

where, under the affine assumption, $[\partial_\theta g(\vartheta)]^\intercal \lambda = D^\intercal \lambda$.

Proposition 4.11 *Suppose that the following hold: (i) Γ is strictly convex and coercive, and (ii) the function g is affine, of the form (4.31), in which the $m \times d$ matrix D has rank m. Then the primal-dual flow converges to the unique solution $(\theta^*,\lambda^\star)$ of the dual: $\mathcal{L}(\theta^*,\lambda^\star) = \varphi^*(\lambda^\star) = \Gamma^\star$.* □

The proof can be found in Section 4.8.3. The first step is to exploit convexity to show that $V(\theta,\lambda) = \frac{1}{2}\|\theta - \theta^*\|^2 + \frac{1}{2}\|\lambda - \lambda^\star\|^2$ is a Lyapunov function. This part of the proof is very similar to the proof of Proposition 4.7.

The case of *inequality constraints* is considered next, where similar analysis can be applied.

Inequality Constraints

We again have a function $g\colon \mathbb{R}^d \to \mathbb{R}^m$ that defines the constraints, but replace equality with inequality in the primal:

$$\begin{aligned} \Gamma^\star \stackrel{\text{def}}{=} \min \quad & \Gamma(\theta) \\ \text{s.t.} \quad & g(\theta) \le 0. \end{aligned} \tag{4.36}$$

If g_i is a convex function for each i (or simply quasiconvex), then the constraint region $S = \{\theta : g(\theta) \le 0\}$ is a convex set.

The Lagrangian and dual function φ^* are defined exactly as before, but we must restrict to $\lambda \in \mathbb{R}^m_+$ to obtain the prior upper bound:

$$\varphi^*(\lambda) \le \min_\theta \{\mathcal{L}(\theta,\lambda) : g(\theta) \le 0\} \le \min_\theta \{\Gamma(\theta) : g(\theta) \le 0\} = \Gamma^\star,$$

where the second inequality is based on the bound $\lambda^\intercal g(\theta) \le 0$, whenever $g(\theta) \le 0$ and $\lambda \ge 0$. The saddle point problem is defined as before:

$$\max_{\lambda \ge 0} \min_\theta \mathcal{L}(\theta,\lambda) = \max_{\lambda \ge 0} \varphi^*(\lambda) \le \Gamma^\star. \tag{4.37}$$

Subject to convexity and minor additional assumptions, there is no duality gap (the inequality is replaced with equality).

A pure steepest ascent algorithm to compute λ^* would be of the form $\frac{d}{dt}\lambda_t = \nabla\varphi^*(\lambda_t)$. In the case of inequality constraints considered here, we must include a reflection process to ensure that $\lambda_t(i) \ge 0$ for each i (details to follow shortly).

A representation of the gradient is easily found. Suppose that for each $\lambda \in \mathbb{R}^m_+$, there is $\theta^s(\lambda)$ satisfying

$$\varphi^*(\lambda) = \min_\theta \{\Gamma(\theta) + \lambda^\intercal g(\theta)\} = \Gamma(\theta^s(\lambda)) + \lambda^\intercal g(\theta^s(\lambda)).$$

Proposition 4.12 *For any $\lambda^0 \in \mathbb{R}^m_+$, a subgradient of the dual function is given by $\nabla\varphi^*(\lambda^0) = [g(\theta^s(\lambda^0))]^\intercal$. That is, for all $\lambda \in \mathbb{R}^m_+$,*

$$\varphi^*(\lambda) \le \varphi^*(\lambda^0) + [g(\theta^s(\lambda^0))]^\intercal(\lambda - \lambda^0).$$

Proof We have by the definitions

$$\begin{aligned} \varphi^*(\lambda) = \min_\theta \{\Gamma(\theta) + \lambda^\intercal g(\theta)\} &\le \Gamma(\theta^s(\lambda^0)) + \lambda^\intercal g(\theta^s(\lambda^0)) \\ &= [\Gamma(\theta^s(\lambda^0)) + \lambda^{0\intercal} g(\theta^s(\lambda^0))] + (\lambda - \lambda^0)^\intercal g(\theta^s(\lambda^0)) \\ &= \varphi^*(\lambda^0) + [g(\theta^s(\lambda^0))]^\intercal(\lambda - \lambda^0). \end{aligned}$$ □

This inspires the primal-dual flow that is almost the same as (4.35). The ODE for the parameter estimate is identical:

$$\frac{d}{dt}\vartheta_t = -\nabla\Gamma(\vartheta_t) - [\partial g(\vartheta_t)]^\intercal \lambda_t.$$

The ODE for the dual variable λ must be modified to impose nonnegativity. This comes in the form of an m-dimensional *reflection process* γ. It is easiest to express the new dual dynamics in integral form

$$\lambda_t = \lambda_0 + \int_0^t g(\vartheta_r)dr + \gamma_t\,, \tag{4.38}$$

where $\lambda_0 \geq 0$ is the initial condition. The reflection process is defined by three constraints (for each $1 \leq i \leq m$):

(1) $\gamma_0(i) = 0$.
(2) $\gamma(i)$ is nondecreasing, and the solution to (4.38) is nonnegative ($\lambda_t(i)$ is nonnegative for each i and t).
(3) It is the *minimal* function of time satisfying 1 and 2. This is equivalently expressed

$$\int_0^T \lambda_t(i)d\gamma_t(i) = 0\,, \qquad \text{for all } T > 0. \tag{4.39}$$

The integral (4.39) is defined in the sense of Riemann and Stieltjes, and on combining (1)–(3), we see that

$$\lambda_t(i) > 0 \Longrightarrow \frac{d}{dt}\gamma_t(i) = 0.$$

Proposition 4.11 extends easily to this primal-dual flow, and the proof is almost identical: The property (4.39) allows us to disregard the reflection process in a crucial part of the Lyapunov function analysis found in Section 4.8.3.

Proposition 4.13 *Suppose that Γ is strictly convex and coercive, that g is convex, and suppose that $\partial g\,(\theta^*)$ has rank m. Then the primal-dual flow converges to the unique solution $(\theta^*,\lambda^\star)$ of the dual:*

$$\mathcal{L}(\theta^*,\lambda^\star) = \varphi^*(\lambda^\star) = \Gamma^\star.$$

□

Euler Approximation

A remaining question is how to translate the primal-dual flow with reflection into a discrete-time algorithm, since (4.38) is no longer an ODE. A standard primal-dual algorithm is defined by the pair of recursions:

$$\theta_{n+1} = \theta_n - \alpha_{n+1}\{\nabla\Gamma(\theta_n) + [\partial g\,(\theta_n)]^\intercal\lambda_n\}, \tag{4.40a}$$
$$\lambda_{n+1} = \big[\lambda_n + \alpha_{n+1}g(\theta_n)\big]_+, \tag{4.40b}$$

where $\big[\,\cdot\,\big]$ is the componentwise maximum with zero. Hence (4.40b) can be expressed

$$\begin{aligned}\lambda_{n+1} &= \lambda_n + \alpha_{n+1}g(\theta_n) + \Delta_n^+,\\ \Delta_n^+ &= \big[\lambda_n + \alpha_{n+1}g(\theta_n)\big]_+ - [\lambda_n + \alpha_{n+1}g(\theta_n)] \geq 0\end{aligned}$$

so that Δ_n^+ may be interpreted as an increment of a reflection process.

4.5 Quasistochastic Approximation

We are interested in solving a root-finding problem of a special form, which requires an adjustment of notation. Given a function $f\colon \mathbb{R}^d \times \Omega \to \mathbb{R}^d$, and a random vector Φ taking values in a set Ω (assumed to be a subset of Euclidean space), we denote the average (or expectation) by

$$\bar{f}(\theta) \stackrel{\text{def}}{=} \mathsf{E}[f(\theta,\Phi)], \qquad \theta \in \mathbb{R}^d. \tag{4.41}$$

Our goal is then to solve $\bar{f}(\theta^*) = 0$ for this exotic function $\bar{f}\colon \mathbb{R}^d \to \mathbb{R}^d$. In this section, we introduce algorithms to achieve this goal by adapting the ODE approaches in previous sections of this chapter, so that $\bar{f}$ sometimes plays the role of the vector field f used to define the ODE (4.2):

$$\frac{d}{dt}\vartheta_t = \bar{f}(\vartheta_t). \tag{4.42}$$

The big challenge is that we may know little about f or Φ.

If you don't know what is meant by random, or expectations, you don't have to worry. We avoid any mention of probability in this section by replacing "random variables" with sinusoids, or other "bouncy" functions of time.

For those of you with a background in probability theory. The stochastic approximation (SA) method of Robbins and Monro [301] amounts to a variation of the Euler scheme (4.8), in which we replace $\bar{f}$ by samples from f:

$$\theta_{n+1} = \theta_n + \alpha_{n+1} f(\theta_n, \Phi_n), \qquad n \ge 0, \tag{4.43}$$

where $\{\Phi_n\}$ are random vectors, whose distributions approximate those of Φ for large n, and $\{\alpha_n\}$ is a nonnegative step-size sequence.

We say that an ODE approximation holds if $\theta_n \approx \vartheta_{t_n}$, where ϑ is the solution to (4.42), and the sampling times $\{t_n\}$ are defined as in (4.8). The assumptions required for a good approximation are not very different from what is required to successfully apply the deterministic Euler approximation (4.8).

The upshot of stochastic approximation is that it can be implemented without knowledge of the function f or of the distribution of Φ; rather, it can rely on observations of the sequence $\{f(\theta_n, \Phi_n)\}$. This is one reason why these algorithms are valuable in the context of reinforcement learning.

In much of the SA and RL literature, it is assumed that $\boldsymbol{\Phi}$ is a *Markov chain*: a topic considered in depth in Chapter 6. A motivating observation in the present chapter is that Markov chains need not be stochastic: The deterministic state space model (2.21) (without control) always satisfies the *Markov property* used in Part II of this book. For example, for given $\omega > 0$, the sequence $\Phi_n = [\cos(\omega n), \sin(\omega n)]$ is a Markov chain on Ω (the unit circle in $\mathbb{R}^2$). This motivates the *quasi-stochastic approximation* (QSA) ODE:

$$\frac{d}{dt}\Theta_t = a_t f(\Theta_t, \xi_t). \tag{4.44}$$

We use the terms *gain* and *step-size* interchangeably for the nonnegative process $\boldsymbol{a}$, and $\boldsymbol{\xi}$ is called the *probing signal*.

The expectation in (4.41) is defined by the sample path average:

$$\bar{f}(\theta) = \lim_{T\to\infty} \frac{1}{T} \int_0^T f(\theta, \xi_t)dt, \ \text{ for all } \theta \in \mathbb{R}^d. \tag{4.45}$$

Of course, the existence of this limit requires assumptions on f and the probing signal.

The probing signal is deterministic in the QSA theory developed in this chapter. Two canonical choices with $\Omega \subset \mathbb{R}^m$ are the m-dimensional mixtures of periodic functions:

$$\xi_t = \sum_{i=1}^{K} v^i [\phi_i + \omega_i t]_{(\text{mod } 1)}, \tag{4.46a}$$

$$\xi_t = \sum_{i=1}^{K} v^i \sin(2\pi[\phi_i + \omega_i t]) \tag{4.46b}$$

for fixed $K \geq 1$, vectors $\{v^i\} \subset \mathbb{R}^m$, phases $\{\phi_i\}$, and frequencies $\{\omega_i\}$. Such signals have well-defined steady-state means and covariance matrices. Consider for example (4.46b) in the special case

$$\xi_t(i) = \sqrt{2}\sin(\omega_i t), \qquad 1 \leq i \leq m \tag{4.47}$$

with $\omega_i \neq \omega_j$ for all $i \neq j$. The steady-state mean and covariance then satisfy

$$\lim_{T\to\infty} \frac{1}{T} \int_{t=0}^{T} \xi_t \, dt = 0, \tag{4.48a}$$

$$\lim_{T\to\infty} \frac{1}{T} \int_{t=0}^{T} \xi_t \xi_t^{\intercal} \, dt = I, \tag{4.48b}$$

where I is the identity matrix.

For a function $g\colon \mathbb{R}^K \to \mathbb{R}$, we can expect the following asymptotic independence, provided the frequencies $\{\omega_i\}$ are distinct:

$$\begin{aligned} &\lim_{T\to\infty} \frac{1}{T} \int_0^T g\big(\sin(2\pi[\phi_1 + \omega_1 t]), \dots, \sin(2\pi[\phi_K + \omega_K t])\big)\, dt \\ &\qquad = \int_0^1 \cdots \int_0^1 g\big(\sin(2\pi[\phi_1 + t_1]), \dots, \sin(2\pi[\phi_K + t_K])\big)\, dt_1 \cdots dt_K. \end{aligned} \tag{4.49}$$

See Lemma 4.37 for a precise statement based on another general class of probing signals.

The following subsections contain examples to illustrate theory of QSA, and also a glimpse at applications.

4.5.1 Quasi Monte-Carlo

Consider the problem of obtaining the integral over the interval $[0,1]$ of a function $y\colon \mathbb{R} \to \mathbb{R}$. In a standard Monte-Carlo approach we would draw independent random variables $\{\Phi(k)\}$, with distribution uniform on the interval $[0,1]$, and then average:

$$\theta_n = \frac{1}{n} \sum_{k=0}^{n-1} y(\Phi(k)). \tag{4.50}$$

In one QSA approach, the probing signal is the one-dimensional *sawtooth function*, $\xi_t \overset{\text{def}}{=} t$ (modulo 1), and estimates are defined by the average

$$\Theta_t = \frac{1}{t} \int_0^t y(\xi_r) dr. \tag{4.51}$$

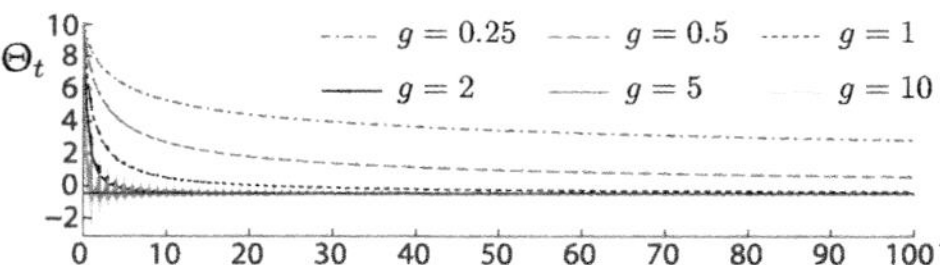

Figure 4.3 Sample paths of quasi Monte Carlo estimates.

Alternatively, we can adapt the QSA model (4.44) to this example, with

$$f(\theta, \xi) \stackrel{\text{def}}{=} y(\xi) - \theta. \tag{4.52}$$

The mean vector field is given by

$$\bar{f}(\theta) = \lim_{T\to\infty} \frac{1}{T} \int_0^T f(\theta, \xi_t)dt = \int_0^1 y(\xi_t)dt - \theta,$$

so that $\theta^* = \int_0^1 y(\xi_t)dt$ is the unique root of $\bar{f}$. The QSA ODE (4.44) gives

$$\tfrac{d}{dt}\Theta_t = a_t[y(\xi_t) - \Theta_t]. \tag{4.53}$$

The Monte Carlo approach (4.51) can be transformed into something resembling (4.53). Taking derivatives of each side of (4.51), we obtain using the product rule of differentiation, and the fundamental theorem of calculus,

$$\frac{d}{dt}\Theta_t = -\frac{1}{t^2}\int_0^t y(\xi_r)dr + \frac{1}{t}y(\xi_t) = \frac{1}{t}[y(\xi_t) - \Theta_t].$$

This is precisely (4.53) with $a_t = 1/t$ (not a great choice for an ODE design, since it is not bounded as $t \downarrow 0$).

The numerical results that follow are based on $y(\theta) = e^{4t}\sin(100\theta)$, whose mean is $\theta^* \approx -0.5$. The differential equation (4.53) was approximated using a standard Euler scheme with sampling interval 10^{-3}. Several variations were simulated, differentiated by the gain $a_t = g/(1+t)$. Figure 4.3 shows typical sample paths of the resulting estimates for a range of gains, and common initialization $\Theta_0 = 10$. In each case, the estimates converge to the true mean $\theta^* \approx -0.5$, but convergence is very slow for $g > 0$ significantly less than one. Recall that the case $g = 1$ is very similar to what was obtained from the Monte Carlo approach (4.51).

Independent trials were conducted to obtain variance estimates. In each of 10^4 independent runs, the common initial condition was drawn randomly,[1] and the estimate was collected at time $T = 100$. Figure 4.4 shows three histograms of estimates for standard Monte Carlo (4.50) and QSA using gains $g = 1$ and 2. An alert reader must wonder: *Why is the variance reduced by four orders of magnitude when the gain is increased from* 1 *to* 2*?* The relative success of the high-gain algorithm is explained in Section 4.5.

Buyer Beware

The remainder of this chapter is based on extensions of quasi Monte Carlo, which is traditionally framed in discrete time. The sawtooth function used in (4.51) is a common choice in this research area, defined more generally in discrete time as follows:

[1] $N(0, 10)$ (Gaussian with zero mean and variance 10).

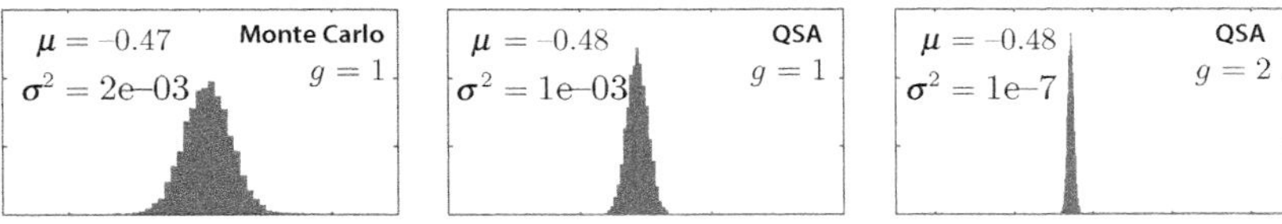

Figure 4.4 Histograms of Monte Carlo and quasi Monte Carlo estimates after 10^4 independent runs. The optimal parameter is $\theta^* \approx -0.4841$.

$$\xi(k) = \xi(0) + \omega k \pmod 1. \tag{4.54}$$

Subject to conditions on the parameter ω and function $y\colon \mathbb{R} \to \mathbb{R}$, we have the Law of Large Numbers:

$$\lim_{N\to\infty} \frac{1}{N} \sum_{k=1}^{N} y(\xi(k)) = \int_0^1 y(r)dr.$$

This is known as the Equidistribution Theorem (see [33], and [149, p. 87] for more history). The quasi Monte Carlo literature contains more sophisticated techniques to define well-behaved "probing sequences."

Sinusoids and sawtooth functions are used in this chapter for simplicity (and because of my own ignorance of the substantial literature on pseudorandomness). An expert on quasi Monte Carlo methods might suggest a two-step process in translating a QSA ODE to discrete time:

(1) A discrete-time approximation of the QSA ODE.
(2) Careful selection of the probing sequence in discrete time.

I am hopeful that step 2 can be avoided, as long as we are careful with step 1. We are not bound to Euler here: Remember that Matlab's `ode45` is based on more efficient numerical methods.

4.5.2 System Identification

The next example illustrating QSA techniques concerns system identification. Consider the nonlinear state space model in continuous time:

$$\begin{aligned} \tfrac{d}{dt} x_t &= \mathrm{f}(x_t, u_t) + d_t\,, \qquad x_0 \text{ given} \\ y_t &= \mathrm{g}(x_t, u_t) + w_t \end{aligned} \tag{4.55}$$

with state $x_t \in \mathbb{R}^n$ and input $u_t \in \mathbb{R}^m$, and the output taken scalar for simplicity: $y_t \in \mathbb{R}$. The signals $\{d_t\}$ and $\{w_t\}$ are known respectively as the *disturbance* and *measurement noise*.

The functions f and g that define the dynamics are not known. We are given observations of the input and output (and possibly also the state), and wish to find a model that fits these measurements. One approach is to propose a parameterized family of models:

$$\begin{aligned} \tfrac{d}{dt} x_t^\theta &= \mathrm{f}(x_t^\theta, u_t; \theta)\,, \qquad x_0^\theta = x_0 \\ y_t^\theta &= \mathrm{g}(x_t^\theta, u_t; \theta). \end{aligned}$$

The goal is to estimate $\theta^* \in \mathbb{R}^d$ based on input–output measurements, where this "best parameter" corresponds to a model that best reflects input–output observations.

In the prediction error method, we introduce a loss function $\Gamma\colon \mathbb{R}^d \to \mathbb{R}_+$ defined by

$$\Gamma(\theta) = \frac{1}{\mathcal{T}} \int_0^{\mathcal{T}} \ell(y_t - y_t^\theta)dt,$$

in which y_t is observed at time t, and y_t^θ is obtained from the model with identical input $\boldsymbol{u}$, and initial state $x_0^\theta = x_0$. The function $\ell\colon \mathbb{R} \to \mathbb{R}_+$ satisfies $\ell(0) = 0$ and $\ell(z) > 0$ for $z \neq 0$.

Consider the typical quadratic loss, $\ell(z) = z^2$. We might hope to apply gradient descent to find the minimizer θ^* of Γ, where the gradient can be expressed

$$\begin{aligned} \nabla_\theta \Gamma(\theta) &= \frac{1}{\mathcal{T}} \int_0^{\mathcal{T}} \nabla_\theta \ell(y_t - y_t^\theta)dt \\ &= -2\frac{1}{\mathcal{T}} \int_0^{\mathcal{T}} (y_t - y_t^\theta)\nabla_\theta y_t^\theta \, dt. \end{aligned}$$

We are then faced with finding a model for the gradient of the observations.

We might design the model so that this is an easy task:

$$y_t^\theta = \theta^\intercal \phi_t,$$

where the *regression vector* $\phi_t \in \mathbb{R}^d$ is a function of observations and not the model. Hence the gradient is expressed in terms of observables, $\nabla_\theta y_t^\theta = \phi_t$, and the gradient of the loss function is linear: $\frac{1}{2}\nabla_\theta \Gamma(\theta) = M\theta - b$, with

$$M = \frac{1}{\mathcal{T}} \int_0^{\mathcal{T}} \phi_t \phi_t^\intercal \, dt \quad \text{and} \quad b = \frac{1}{\mathcal{T}} \int_0^{\mathcal{T}} y_t \phi_t \, dt.$$

These representations are one motivation for ARMA models (see Section 2.2 for a definition in discrete time).

In the absence of such a simple description, we look more closely at the state space model. Assume that x_t^θ and y_t^θ are each continuously differentiable in (t,θ). Let $S_t^\theta = \partial_\theta x_t^\theta$ denote the $n \times d$ matrix of partial derivatives of the state:

$$[S_t^\theta]_{i,k} = \frac{\partial}{\partial \theta_k} x_t^\theta(i), \qquad 1 \le i \le n, \quad 1 \le k \le d.$$

Recalling the calculus convention $\nabla_\theta y_t^\theta = [\partial_\theta y_t^\theta]^\intercal$, we obtain by the chain rule

$$\begin{aligned} \frac{d}{dt} S_t^\theta &= \mathrm{f}_x(x_t^\theta, u_t; \theta) S_t^\theta + \mathrm{f}_\theta(x_t^\theta, u_t; \theta), \\ \partial_\theta y_t^\theta &= \mathrm{g}_x(x_t^\theta, u_t; \theta) S_t^\theta + \mathrm{g}_\theta(x_t^\theta, u_t; \theta), \end{aligned}$$

where each subscript on the right-hand side represents a partial derivative. For example, $\mathrm{f}_x(x,u;\theta)$ is the $n \times n$ matrix with entries

$$[\mathrm{f}_x(x,u;\theta)]_{i,j} = \frac{\partial}{\partial x_j} \mathrm{f}_i\,(x,u;\theta).$$

There are two challenges with this approach: One is potential numerical instability of the differential equation generating $\{S_t^\theta\}$. Another is the complexity of this ODE, especially when the dimension n is large: *Do we really have to generate* $\{S_t^\theta : 0 \le t \le \mathcal{T}\}$ *in order to obtain* $\nabla_\theta \Gamma(\theta)$ *for a single value of* θ*?* This is a massive burden if we require many iterations of steepest descent. This is ample motivation for the gradient-free approaches to optimization surveyed in Section 4.6.

4.5.3 Approximate Policy Improvement

Consider again a nonlinear state space model in continuous time,

$$\tfrac{d}{dt}x_t = \mathrm{f}(x_t,u_t), \qquad t \ge 0,$$

with $x_t \in \mathbb{R}^n$, $u_t \in \mathbb{R}^m$. Given a cost function $c\colon \mathbb{R}^{n+m} \to \mathbb{R}$, our goal is to approximate the optimal value function

$$J^\star(x) = \min_{\boldsymbol{u}} \int_0^\infty c(x_t,u_t)dt, \qquad x = x_0$$

and approximate the optimal policy. For this, we first explain how policy improvement extends to the continuous time setting.

For any feedback law $u_t = \phi(x_t)$, denote the associated value function by

$$J^\phi(x) = \int_0^\infty c(x_t,\phi(x_t))dt, \qquad x = x_0.$$

It follows from Proposition 2.7 that this solves a dynamic programming equation:

$$0 = c(x,\phi(x)) + \nabla J^\phi(x) \cdot \mathrm{f}(x,\phi(x)).$$

The policy improvement step in this continuous time setting defines the new policy as the minimizer:

$$\phi^+(x) \in \arg\min_u \{c(x,u) + \nabla J^\phi(x) \cdot \mathrm{f}(x,u)\}.$$

Consequently, approximating the term in brackets is key to approximating PIA.

An RL algorithm is constructed through the following steps (which were first proposed in Section 3.7). First, add J^ϕ to each side of the fixed-policy dynamic programming equation:

$$J^\phi(x) = J^\phi(x) + c(x,\phi(x)) + \nabla J^\phi(x) \cdot \mathrm{f}(x,\phi(x)).$$

The right-hand side motivates the following definition of the fixed-policy Q-function:

$$Q^\phi(x,u) = J^\phi(x) + c(x,u) + \mathrm{f}(x,u) \cdot \nabla J^\phi(x).$$

The policy update can be equivalently expressed $\phi^+(x) \in \arg\min_u Q^\phi(x,u)$, and this Q-function solves the fixed point equation

$$Q^\phi(x,u) = \underline{Q}^\phi(x) + c(x,u) + \mathrm{f}(x,u) \cdot \nabla \underline{Q}^\phi(x), \tag{4.56}$$

where $\underline{H}^\phi(x) = H(x,\phi(x))$ for any function H (note that this is a substitution, rather than the minimization appearing in (3.7d)).

Consider now a family of functions for approximation $\{Q^\theta : \theta \in \mathbb{R}^d\}$, and consider the *Bellman error*:

$$\mathcal{B}^\theta(x,u) = -Q^\theta(x,u) + \underline{Q}^\theta(x) + c(x,u) + \mathrm{f}(x,u) \cdot \nabla \underline{Q}^\theta(x). \tag{4.57}$$

A model-free representation is obtained, on recognizing that for any state-input pair (x_t, u_t),

$$\mathcal{B}^\theta(x_t, u_t) = -Q^\theta(x_t, u_t) + \underline{Q}^\theta(x_t) + c(x_t, u_t) + \tfrac{d}{dt}\underline{Q}^\theta(x_t). \tag{4.58}$$

The error $\mathcal{B}^\theta(x_t, u_t)$ can be observed without knowledge of the dynamics f or even the cost function c. The goal is to find θ^* that minimizes the mean-square error:

$$\|\mathcal{B}^\theta\|^2 \stackrel{\text{def}}{=} \lim_{T\to\infty} \frac{1}{T}\int_0^T \big[\mathcal{B}^\theta(x_t, u_t)\big]^2\, dt. \tag{4.59}$$

We choose a feedback law with "exploration" of the form introduced in Section 2.5.3:

$$u_t = \breve{\phi}(x_t, \xi_t), \tag{4.60}$$

chosen so that the resulting state trajectories are bounded for each initial condition, and the joint process $(\boldsymbol{x}, \boldsymbol{u}, \boldsymbol{\xi})$ admits an "ergodic steady state" (meaning that the existence of sample path averages such as (4.59) is guaranteed).

This approximation technique defines an approximate version of PIA: Given a policy ϕ and approximation $\widehat{Q}$, the policy is updated:

$$\phi^+(x) = \arg\min_u \widehat{Q}(x, u). \tag{4.61}$$

This procedure is repeated to obtain a recursive algorithm.

Least Squares Solution

Consider the loss function

$$\Gamma(\theta) = \lim_{T\to\infty} \Gamma_T(\theta) = \lim_{T\to\infty} \frac{1}{T}\int_0^T \tfrac{1}{2}\big[\mathcal{B}^\theta(x_t, u_t)\big]^2\, dt.$$

Suppose that the function approximation architecture is linear (3.43), so that Γ_T is a quadratic function of θ:

$$\Gamma_T(\theta) = \theta^\intercal M_T \theta - 2b_T^\intercal\theta + \Gamma_T(0) = (\theta - \theta^*)^\intercal M_T(\theta - \theta^*) + \Gamma_T(\theta^*).$$

We leave it to the reader to find expressions for M_T, b_T, and $\Gamma_T(0)$.

In this special case, we do not need gradient descent techniques: The matrices M_T and b_T are obtained as sample-path averages – the Monte Carlo approach surveyed in Section 4.5.1 – and then $\theta_T^* = M_T^{-1} b_T$ is the unique minimizer of Γ_T.

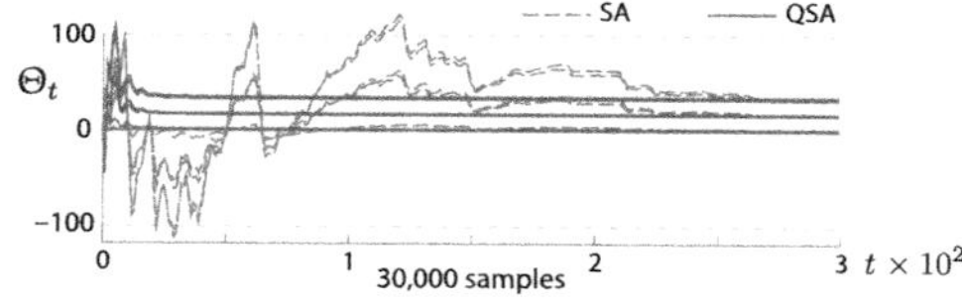

Figure 4.5 Comparison of QSA and stochastic approximation (SA) for policy evaluation.

Gradient Descent

Without a linear parameterization, we turn to gradient descent to minimize Γ, with gradient

$$\nabla\Gamma(\theta) = \lim_{T\to\infty}\frac{1}{T}\int_0^T [\mathcal{B}^\theta(x_t,u_t)]\nabla_\theta\mathcal{B}^\theta(x_t,u_t)dt.$$

The first-order condition for optimality is expressed as the root-finding problem $\nabla_\theta\Gamma(\theta) = 0$, and the standard gradient descent algorithm in ODE form is

$$\tfrac{d}{dt}\vartheta_t = -\nabla_\theta\Gamma(\vartheta_t).$$

Its QSA counterpart (4.44) is

$$\tfrac{d}{dt}\Theta_t = -a_t\mathcal{B}^{\Theta_t}(x_t,u_t)\zeta_t^{\Theta_t}, \tag{4.62a}$$

$$\zeta_t^\theta \stackrel{\text{def}}{=} \nabla_\theta\mathcal{B}^\theta(x_t,u_t) = -\nabla_\theta Q^\theta(x_t,u_t) + \Big\{\nabla_\theta Q^\theta(x_t,\phi(x_t)) + \tfrac{d}{dt}\nabla_\theta Q^\theta(x_t,\phi(x_t))\Big\}, \tag{4.62b}$$

where (4.62b) follows from (4.58), provided we can justify the exchange of differentiation with respect to time and with respect to θ.

The QSA gradient descent algorithm (4.62) is best motivated by a nonlinear function approximation, but it is instructive to see how the ODE simplifies for the linearly parameterized family (3.43). We have in this case

$$\zeta_t = -\psi(x_t,u_t) + \psi(x_t,\phi(x_t)) + \tfrac{d}{dt}\psi(x_t,\phi(x_t))$$

and $\mathcal{B}^\theta(x_t,u_t) = c_t + \zeta_t^\intercal\theta$ using $c_t = c(x_t,u_t)$, so that (4.62a) becomes

$$\tfrac{d}{dt}\Theta_t = -a_t\left[\zeta_t\zeta_t^\intercal\,\Theta_t + c_t\zeta_t\right]. \tag{4.63}$$

The convergence of (4.63) may be very slow if the matrix

$$R^\zeta \stackrel{\text{def}}{=} \lim_{t\to\infty}\frac{1}{t}\int_0^t \zeta_\tau\zeta_\tau^\intercal\,d\tau \tag{4.64}$$

has eigenvalues close to zero. This can be resolved through the introduction of a larger gain $\boldsymbol{a}$, or a matrix gain. One approach is to estimate R^ζ from data and invert: $G_t = [\widehat{R}_t^\zeta]^{-1}$ with

$$\widehat{R}_t^\zeta = \frac{1}{t+1}\Big\{\widehat{R}_0^\zeta + \int_0^t \zeta_\tau\zeta_\tau^\intercal\,d\tau\Big\}, \qquad \widehat{R}_0^\zeta > 0 \tag{4.65a}$$

$$\tfrac{d}{dt}\Theta_t = -a_tG_t\left[\zeta_t\zeta_t^\intercal\,\Theta_t + c_t\zeta_t\right], \qquad t \ge 0. \tag{4.65b}$$

Numerical Example

Consider the LQR problem in which $\frac{d}{dt}x = Ax + Bu$, and $c(x,u) = x^\intercal Sx + u^\intercal Ru$, with $S \ge 0$ and $R > 0$. The fixed-policy Q-function associated with any stable linear policy $\phi(x) = -Kx$, takes the form

$$Q^\phi(x,u) = \begin{bmatrix}x\\u\end{bmatrix}^\intercal\left(\begin{bmatrix}S & 0\\0 & R\end{bmatrix} + \begin{bmatrix}A^\intercal M + MA + M & MB\\B^\intercal M & 0\end{bmatrix}\right)\begin{bmatrix}x\\u\end{bmatrix},$$

where M solves the Lyapunov equation (2.46) with S replaced by $K^\intercal RK + S$:

$$A^\intercal M + MA + K^\intercal RK + S = 0.$$

This motivates a quadratic basis, which for the special case $n = 2$, and $m = 1$ becomes

$$\psi(x,u) = (x_1^2, x_2^2, x_1 x_2, x_1 u, x_2 u, u^2)^{\mathsf{T}}.$$

In order to implement the algorithm (4.65b), we begin with selecting an input of the form

$$u_t = -K_e x_t + \xi_t, \tag{4.66}$$

where K_e is a stabilizing feedback gain (which need not be the same K whose value function we wish to approximate).

The numerical results that follow are based on a double integrator with friction:

$$\ddot{y} = -0.1\dot{y} + u,$$

which can be expressed in state space form using $x = (y, \dot{y})^{\mathsf{T}}$:

$$\dot{x} = \begin{bmatrix} 0 & 1 \\ 0 & -0.1 \end{bmatrix} x + \begin{bmatrix} 0 \\ 1 \end{bmatrix} u. \tag{4.67}$$

A relatively large cost was imposed on the input: $S = I$ and $R = 10$.

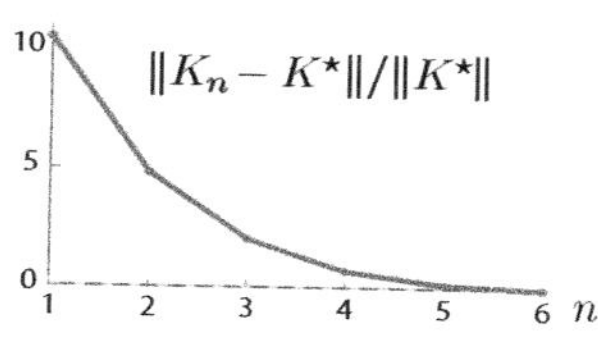

Figure 4.6 Iterations of PIA.

Figure 4.5 shows the evolution of the QSA ODE (4.65) for the evaluation of the policy with gain $K = [1,0]$, in which the input (4.66) used $K_e = [1,2]$ and ξ the sum of 24 sinusoids with random phase shifts and whose frequency was sampled uniformly between 0 and 50 rad/s. The gain was $a_t = 1/(1+t)$. The QSA ODE is compared with the related SA algorithm in which ξ is "white noise" instead of a deterministic signal.[2]

The gain K was chosen as an initialization in approximate policy iteration: With $K_0 = K$, we obtain an approximation Q^{θ^0} for the associated fixed policy Q-function for this linear policy, and then $\phi^1(x) = K_1 x$ is obtained via the policy improvement step (4.61) with $\widehat{Q} = Q^{\theta^0}$. These steps are repeated to generate a sequence of parameter estimates $\{\theta^n\}$ and feedback gains $\{K_n\}$. Figure 4.6 shows the weighted error for the feedback gains, where the optimal gain $K^\star$ is obtained from the ARE derived in Section 3.9.4. The PIA algorithm indeed converges to the optimal control gain $K^\star$.

4.5.4 A Brief Tour of QSA Theory

While QSA theory is far simpler than stability of its stochastic ancestor, the technicalities are best left to the end of the chapter – see Section 4.9 for details. Contained here is an overview, and some guidelines for algorithm design.

Our interest is not just in convergence of QSA, but convergence rates, and intuition regarding the choice of algorithm parameters. We say that the rate of convergence is $1/t^{\varrho_0}$ if

$$\limsup_{t\to\infty} t^{\varrho} \|\widetilde{\Theta}_t\| = \begin{cases} \infty & \varrho > \varrho_0 \\ 0 & \varrho < \varrho_0 \end{cases}, \tag{4.68}$$

where $\widetilde{\Theta}_t \stackrel{\text{def}}{=} \Theta_t - \theta^*$ is the estimation error. By careful design, we can achieve $\varrho_0 = 1$, which is optimal in most cases. Exercise 4.18 shows that convergence may be much faster

[2] For implementation, both (4.65) and the linear system (4.67) were approximated using Euler's method, with time step of 0.01 s.

if the probing signal acts purely multiplicatively, rather than additively as in the Monte Carlo example.

QSA-ODE Solidarity

The *apparent noise* plays a crucial role in the analysis:

$$\widetilde{\Xi}_t = f(\Theta_t, \xi_t) - \bar{f}(\Theta_t), \tag{4.69}$$

so that

$$\tfrac{d}{dt}\Theta_t = a_t[\bar{f}(\Theta_t) + \widetilde{\Xi}_t]. \tag{4.70}$$

While this is similar to the ODE (4.42), an apparent discrepancy is that the gain $\boldsymbol{a}$ is absent. In the continuous time theory, it is simplest to introduce a gain for the purposes of comparison:

$$\tfrac{d}{dt}\overline{\Theta}_t = a_t\bar{f}(\overline{\Theta}_t)\,, \qquad t \ge t_0\,, \overline{\Theta}_{t_0} = \Theta_{t_0}, \tag{4.71}$$

where the choice of t_0 depends on the stability properties of the associated ODE (4.42) with constant gain.

We are left with two steps:

(1) Understand the relationship between the solution to the original ODE (4.42), and the solution to (4.71).
(2) Obtain bounds on the error between solutions to the QSA ODE (4.70) and the ODE (4.71) in which the apparent noise is removed. In this step, we consider the scaled error:

$$Z_t = \frac{1}{a_t}\left(\Theta_t - \overline{\Theta}_t\right), \qquad t \ge t_0. \tag{4.72}$$

It is shown that this is a bounded function of time under mild assumptions.

Most of Section 4.9 is devoted to step 2. Step 1 is addressed easily through the following change of variables:

$$\tau = s_t \stackrel{\text{def}}{=} \int_0^t a_r\, dr, \qquad t \ge 0. \tag{4.73}$$

Lemma 4.14 *Let* $\{\vartheta_\tau : \tau \ge \tau_0\}$ *denote the solution to* (4.42) *initialized at time* $\tau_0 = s_{t_0}$, *with* $\vartheta_{\tau_0} = \Theta_{t_0}$. *The solution to* (4.71) *is then given by*

$$\overline{\Theta}_t = \vartheta_\tau\,, \quad t \ge t_0. \qquad \square$$

Gain Selection

Consider the standard choice of gain

$$a_t = g/(1+t)^\rho, \tag{4.74}$$

in which $g > 0$ and $0 < \rho \le 1$ are fixed. The time scaling reveals a significant difference between $\rho < 1$ and $\rho = 1$:

$$\tau = \begin{cases} g\log(1+t) & \rho = 1 \\ g\dfrac{1}{1-\rho}(1+t)^{1-\rho} & 0 < \rho < 1 \end{cases}. \tag{4.75}$$

It is here that we arrive at an apparent conflict in choice of gain. To make this clear, suppose that the ODE (4.42) satisfies the following form of exponential asymptotic stability: there exists $\varrho_0 > 0$, $B_0 < \infty$ such that for any solution to (4.42), and any $t \geq 0$,

$$\|\vartheta_t - \theta^*\| \leq B_0 \|\vartheta_0 - \theta^*\| \exp(-\varrho_0 t). \tag{4.76}$$

From the identity $\|\overline{\Theta}_t - \theta^*\| = \|\vartheta_\tau - \theta^*\|$, we come to very different conclusions, depending on ρ:

$\rho < 1$: $\{\overline{\Theta}_t\}$ to converges to θ^* *very quickly*. However, in this case boundedness of $\{Z_t\}$ implies a suboptimal rate:

$$\|\Theta_t - \overline{\Theta}_t\| \leq B_Z \frac{1}{(1+t)^\rho}, \tag{4.77}$$

where B_Z is a function of the initial condition Θ_0.

$\rho = 1$: The bound (4.77) is ideal, but the rate of convergence of $\{\overline{\Theta}_t\}$ may not be: an application of (4.75) gives

$$\|\overline{\Theta}_t - \theta^*\| \leq B_0 \|\overline{\Theta}_0 - \theta^*\| \frac{1}{(1+t)^{g\varrho_0}}.$$

To obtain the optimal $1/t$ convergence rate for QSA requires $g \geq 1/\varrho_0$. This high gain may lead to other problems, such as large transients.

It is here that the averaging technique of Polyak, Juditsky, and Ruppert (PJR averaging) comes to the rescue. We use $\rho < 1$ to exploit the fast convergence of $\{\overline{\Theta}_t\}$ to θ^*, and then reduce volatility by simply averaging some fraction of the estimates:

$$\Theta_T^{\mathrm{PR}} \stackrel{\mathrm{def}}{=} \frac{1}{T - T_0} \int_{T_0}^{T} \Theta_t \, dt. \tag{4.78}$$

For example, $T_0 = T - T/5$ means that we average the final 20%. This approach will achieve the optimal $1/T$ convergence rate under very mild assumptions. Section 4.5.5 provides a gentle introduction to the theory for a special case.[3]

Basic Assumptions and Conclusions

It is simplest to adopt a "Markovian" setting in which the probing signal is itself the state process for a dynamical system:

$$\tfrac{d}{dt}\xi = \mathrm{H}(\xi), \tag{4.79}$$

where $\mathrm{H}\colon \Omega \to \Omega$ is continuous, with Ω a bounded subset of Euclidean space. A canonical choice is the K-dimensional torus: $\Omega = \{x \in \mathbb{C}^K : |x_i| = 1,\ 1 \leq i \leq K\}$, and $\boldsymbol{\xi}$ defined to allow modeling of excitation as a mixture of sinusoids:

$$\xi_t = [\exp(j\omega_1 t), \ldots, \exp(j\omega_K t)]^{\intercal}, \tag{4.80}$$

with distinct frequencies, ordered for convenience: $0 < \omega_1 < \omega_2 < \cdots < \omega_K$. The dynamical system (4.79) is linear in this special case. It is ergodic, in a sense made precise in Lemma 4.37.

[3] The "J" is omitted from the superscript in (4.78): This is to keep notation compact, and also because of Polyak's independent work before Juditsky. See Section 4.11 for history.

The following assumptions are imposed throughout the remainder of the chapter:

(QSA1) The process $\boldsymbol{a}$ is nonnegative, monotonically decreasing, and

$$\lim_{t\to\infty} a_t = 0, \qquad \int_0^\infty a_r\,dr = \infty. \tag{4.81}$$

(QSA2) The functions $\bar{f}$ and f are Lipschitz continuous: for a constant $L_f < \infty$,

$$\begin{aligned}\|\bar{f}(\theta') - \bar{f}(\theta)\| &\le L_f\|\theta' - \theta\|,\\ \|f(\theta',z) - f(\theta,z)\| &\le L_f\|\theta' - \theta\|, \quad \theta',\theta \in \mathbb{R}^d,\ z\in\Omega.\end{aligned}$$

There exists a Lipschitz continuous function $b_0\colon \mathbb{R}^d \to \mathbb{R}_+$, such that for all $\theta \in \mathbb{R}^d$,

$$\Big\|\int_{t_0}^{t_1} \tilde{f}_t(\theta)dt\Big\| \le b_0(\theta), \quad 0\le t_0 \le t_1, \qquad \text{where} \quad \tilde{f}_t(\theta) = f(\theta,\xi_t) - \bar{f}(\theta). \tag{4.82}$$

(QSA3) The ODE (4.42) has a globally asymptotically stable equilibrium θ^*.

The Lipschitz conditions on $\bar{f}$ and f in (QSA2) are what you would expect if you have been exposed to theory for stochastic approximation. General sufficient conditions on both f and ξ for the ergodic bound (4.82) are given in Lemma 4.37.

A fourth *assumption* is that the QSA ODE is ultimately bounded in the following sense: There exists $b < \infty$ such that for each $\theta \in \mathbb{R}^d$ and $z \in \Omega$, there is a $T_{\theta,z}$ such that

$$\|\widehat{\Theta}_\tau\| \le b \ \text{ for all } \tau \ge T_{\theta,z}, \quad \text{when } \widehat{\Theta}_0 = \theta,\ \xi_0 = z. \tag{4.83}$$

Verification of ultimate boundedness is the subject of Section 4.9.3. For example, (4.83) can be established using a Lyapunov drift condition similar to (2.39).

The proof of Theorem 4.15 is also found in Section 4.9.

Theorem 4.15 (Boundedness Implies Convergence) *Suppose that (QSA1)–(QSA3) hold, along with the ultimate boundedness assumption* (4.83). *Then the solution to* (4.44) *converges to θ^* for each initial condition.*

Coupling

The following partial integrals play a central role when we turn to rates of convergence: For $\theta \in \mathbb{R}^d$ and $T \ge 0$,

$$\Xi^{\text{I}}_T(\theta) = \int_0^T \tilde{f}_t(\theta)dt. \tag{4.84}$$

This is a bounded function of T under (QSA2) (recall (4.82)). The coupling to be established is expressed as the limit,

$$\lim_{t\to\infty} \|Z_t - \Xi^{\text{I}}_t(\theta^*)\| = 0. \tag{4.85}$$

This implies precise bounds on the rate of convergence of Θ_t to θ^*, since by the definition (4.72),

$$\Theta_t = \theta^* + a_t Z_t.$$

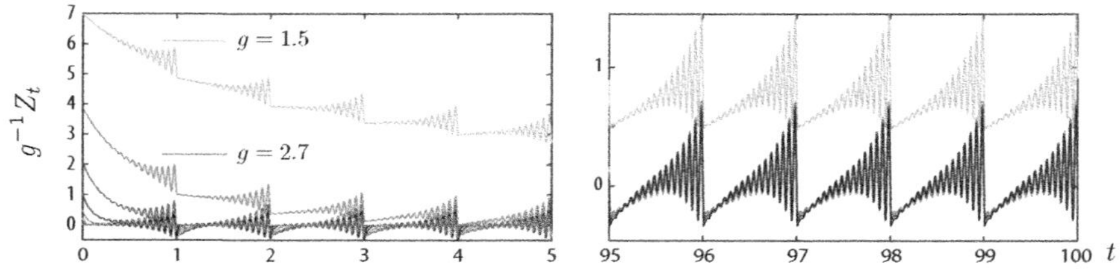

Figure 4.7 Evolution of $Z_t = (1+t)\widetilde{\Theta}_t$ using quasi Monte Carlo estimates for a range of gains.

Details of this theory are postponed to Section 4.9. Here we simply illustrate the conclusion with a simple example.

Consider the linear QSA ODE with vector field

$$f(\theta, z) = A(\theta - \theta^*) + Bz, \qquad \theta \in \mathbb{R}^d, \ z \in \Omega. \tag{4.86}$$

In this special case, (4.84) is independent of θ:

$$\Xi^{\mathrm{I}}_T(\theta) = \Xi^{\mathrm{I}}_T = B \int_0^t \xi_r \, dr.$$

The coupling result (4.85) is illustrated using the simple Monte Carlo example, whose plots are shown in Figure 4.3. The representation (4.53) is easily modified to take the form (4.86). First, denote by $\boldsymbol{\xi}^0$ a periodic function of time whose sample paths define the uniform distribution on $[0,1]$: For any continuous function c,

$$\lim_{T\to\infty} \frac{1}{T} \int_0^T c(\xi_t^0) dt = \int_0^1 c(x) dx.$$

We previously used the sawtooth function, $\xi_t^0 = t \pmod 1$. Introduce a gain $g > 0$, and consider

$$\frac{d}{dt}\Theta_t = \frac{g}{1+t}[y(\xi_t^0) - \Theta_t]. \tag{4.87}$$

This is of the form (4.86) with $A = -1$, $B = 1$, and $\xi_t = [y(\xi_t^0) - \theta^*]$.

Theorem 4.24 implies the coupling result (4.85) only for $g > 1$. Figures 4.3 and 4.4 illustrate the qualitative conclusion of Theorem 4.24. Coupling is illustrated in Figure 4.7.

The scaled error $g^{-1}Z_t$ is compared since $\boldsymbol{\xi}$ grows linearly with g: We expect $g^{-1}Z_t \approx \int_0^t y(\xi^0(r)) - \theta^* \, dr$ for large t.

The figure compares results using 10 gains, approximately equally spaced on a logarithmic scale. The smallest gain is $g = 1.5$, and all other gains satisfy $g \geq 2$. Theorem 4.24 asserts that $|Z_t - \Xi_t^I| = O\big([1+t]^{-\delta_S}\big)$, where $\delta_S < 0.5$ for $g = 1.5$, and $\delta_S = 1$ for $g \geq 2$. The initial condition was set to $\Theta_0 = 10$ in each experiment. The scaled errors $\{g^{-1}Z_t : 95 \leq t \leq 100\}$ are nearly indistinguishable when $g \geq 2$.

4.5.5 Constant Gain Algorithm

The choice $a_t = \alpha$ (independent of time) is often favored in practice. For the linear model (4.86), this is not unreasonable, as we shall see in the following. The highlight is Corollary 4.17, establishing the optimal rate of convergence when using PJR averaging.

However, please be warned: the conclusions that follow are highly sensitive to the precise modeling assumption (4.86). Consider the minor variant, using

$$f(\theta,z) = [A_0 + \varepsilon z A_1]\theta\,, \qquad \theta \in \mathbb{R}^d\,,\ z \in \mathbb{R}. \tag{4.88}$$

Stability of the constant gain algorithm is characterized in [36] for this and more general linear systems with multiplicative "quasidisturbance." The characterizations have little resemblance to any other theory in this book – in particular, the average vector field $\bar{f}(\theta) = A_0\theta$ is often useless for stability analysis. See Exercise 4.18 for a short tour of this theory.

Convergence theory for vanishing gain algorithms is far more intuitive, even when subject to multiplicative disturbances as in (4.88).

Analysis for the linear model (4.86) is simplified since QSA is a time-invariant linear system:

$$\tfrac{d}{dt}\Theta_t = \alpha[A\widetilde{\Theta}_t + B\xi_t],$$

where $\widetilde{\Theta}_t \stackrel{\text{def}}{=} \Theta_t - \theta^*$ is the error at time t. We can solve this ODE when the probing signal is the mixture of sinusoids (4.46b), whose derivation is simplified by applying the *principle of super-position*. To put this to work, we restrict to the probing signal (4.46b), and for each i, consider the ODE

$$\tfrac{d}{dt}\widetilde{\Theta}^i_t = \alpha\bigl[A\widetilde{\Theta}_t + v^i \sin(2\pi[\phi_i + \omega_i t])\bigr)\,, \qquad \widetilde{\Theta}^i_0 = 0.$$

The principle states that the solution to this ODE can be represented as the sum

$$\widetilde{\Theta}_t = e^{\alpha A t}\widetilde{\Theta}_0 + B\sum_{i=1}^{K}\widetilde{\Theta}^i_t. \tag{4.89}$$

The response to the initial error $\widetilde{\Theta}_0 = \Theta_0 - \theta^*$ decays to zero exponentially quickly. Consequently, to understand the steady-state behavior of the algorithm, it suffices to fix a single value of i.

For more complex probing signals we can again justify consideration of sinusoids, provided we can justify a Fourier series approximation. Let's keep things simple, and stick to sinusoids. And it is much easier to work with complex exponentials:

$$\tfrac{d}{dt}\widetilde{\Theta}_t = \alpha[A\widetilde{\Theta}_t + v\exp(j\omega t)]\,, \qquad \widetilde{\Theta}_0 = 0,$$

with $\omega \in \mathbb{R}$ and $v \in \mathbb{R}^d$ (dropping the scaling 2π and the phase ϕ for simplicity). We can express the solution as a convolution:

$$\begin{aligned}\widetilde{\Theta}_t &= \alpha\int_0^t \exp\bigl(\alpha A r\bigr)v\exp\bigl(j\omega(t-r)\bigr)\,dr \\ &= \alpha\Bigl(\int_0^t \exp\bigl([\alpha A - j\omega I]r\bigr)\,dr\Bigr)v\exp\bigl(j\omega t\bigr).\end{aligned}$$

Writing $D = [\alpha A - j\omega I]$, the integral of the matrix exponential is expressed:

$$\int_0^t e^{Dr}\,dr = D^{-1}\bigl[e^{Dt} - I\bigr].$$

Using linearity once more, and the fact that the imaginary part of $e^{j\omega t}$ is $\sin(\omega t)$, we arrive at a complete representation for (4.89):

Proposition 4.16 *Consider the linear model with A Hurwitz, and probing signal* (4.46b), *for which the constant gain QSA ODE has the solution* (4.89). *Then $\widetilde{\Theta}_t^i = \alpha W_t^i v^i$ for each i and t, with*

$$W_t^i = \mathrm{Im}\Big([\alpha A - j\omega_i I]^{-1}\big[\exp(\alpha A t) - \exp\big(2\pi j[\phi_i + \omega_i t]\big)I\big]\Big). \tag{4.90}$$

□

Proposition 4.16 illustrates a challenge with fixed gain algorithms: If we want small steady-state error, then we require small α (or large ω_i, but this brings other difficulties for computer implementation: *Never forget Euler, and the limitations imposed by a large Lipschitz constant!*). However, if $\alpha > 0$ is very small, then the impact of the initial condition in (4.89) will persist for a long time.

The PJR averaging technique can be used to improve the steady-state behavior:

Corollary 4.17 *Suppose that the assumptions of Proposition 4.16 hold, so in particular f is linear. Consider the averaged estimates* (4.78) *in which $T_0 = T - T/\kappa$ for fixed $\kappa > 1$. Then,*

$$\Theta_T^{\mathsf{PR}} = \theta^* + \frac{1}{T}\Big(\kappa M_T \theta_0 + \alpha B \sum_{i=1}^{K} M_T^i v^i\Big),$$

where

$$M_T = A^{-1}\Big[\exp(\alpha A T) - \exp(\alpha A T_0)\Big]$$

and M_T^i is equal to the integral of W_t^i appearing in (4.90)*:*

$$\begin{aligned} M_T^i = {} & \kappa \mathrm{Im}\Big([\alpha A]^{-1}[\alpha A - j2\pi\omega_i I]^{-1}\Big[\exp(\alpha A T) - \exp(\alpha A T_0)\Big]\Big) \\ & + \kappa \mathrm{Im}\Big(\frac{j}{2\pi\omega_i}[\alpha A - j2\pi\omega_i I]^{-1}\Big[\exp(2\pi[\phi_i + \omega_i T]j) - \exp(2\pi[\phi_i + \omega_i T_0]j)\Big]\Big). \end{aligned}$$

Hence Θ_T^{PR} converges to θ^* at rate $1/T$. □

4.5.6 Zap QSA

The convergence theory surveyed in Section 4.9 requires that the ODE (4.42) have a globally asymptotically stable equilibrium θ^*. A tight bound on the rate of convergence requires that the linearization matrix A^* is Hurwitz.

What if A^* is not Hurwitz? Or worse, what if the crucial stability assumption fails? Consider the two time-scale algorithm:

$$\begin{aligned} \tfrac{d}{dt}\Theta_t &= \frac{1}{1+t}[-\widehat{A}_t]^{-1} f(\Theta_t, \xi_t), \\ \tfrac{d}{dt}\widehat{A}_t &= \frac{g}{(1+t)^\rho}[A_t - \widehat{A}_t], \qquad A_t = \partial_\theta f(\Theta_t, \xi_t). \end{aligned} \tag{4.91}$$

This is called Zap-QSA, designed to mimic the Newton–Raphson flow.

The second ODE is introduced so that $\widehat{A}_t \approx A(\Theta_t) \stackrel{\text{def}}{=} \partial_\theta \bar{f}(\Theta_t)$ (following a transient). This requires $0 < \rho < 1$, meaning we use high gain for the matrix estimate. Provided we can ensure a bounded inverse, we arrive at something more closely resembling the Newton–Raphson flow:

$$\frac{d}{dt}\Theta_t = \frac{1}{1+t}[-A(\Theta_t)]^{-1}\big[\bar{f}(\Theta_t) + \Xi_t\big],$$

where $\Xi_t = f(\Theta_t, \xi_t) - \bar{f}(\Theta_t) + \varepsilon_t$: The error ε_t comes from the approximation $\widehat{A}_t \approx A(\Theta_t)$.

The most important motivation for the matrix gain in (4.91) is stability, by appealing to theory for the Newton–Raphson flow. Zap QSA typically shows very fast convergence whenever the assumptions required for convergence of the Newton–Raphson flow are satisfied.

4.6 Gradient-Free Optimization

How can we find the minimum of a function without computing its gradient? There are gradient-free variants of stochastic approximation available that provide an answer. Fortunately, we do not have to wait until Chapter 8, since these algorithms can be cast within the framework of QSA theory.

This section concerns the unconstrained minimization problem

$$\min_{\theta \in \mathbb{R}^d} \Gamma(\theta). \tag{4.92}$$

It is assumed that $\Gamma \colon \mathbb{R}^d \to \mathbb{R}$ has a unique minimizer, denoted as θ^*. To apply QSA techniques, we relax our goal: Find a solution to $\bar{f}(\theta^*) = 0$, where this represents the first-order necessary condition for optimality:

$$\bar{f}(\theta) \stackrel{\text{def}}{=} \nabla \Gamma(\theta), \qquad \theta \in \mathbb{R}^d. \tag{4.93}$$

This is equivalent to our original objective if Γ is convex (recall Proposition 4.6).

The algorithms described here are based on the following architecture:

- ▲ Create rules that determine a d-dimensional signal $\boldsymbol{\Psi}$, with $\Gamma(\Psi_t)$ measured for each t.
- ▲ Construct an ODE of the form

$$\tfrac{d}{dt}\Theta_t = -a_t \breve{\nabla}_\Gamma(t) \tag{4.94}$$

in which $\breve{\nabla}_\Gamma(t)$ is designed to approximate (4.93) in an average sense:

$$\int_{T_0}^{T_1} a_t \breve{\nabla}_\Gamma(t)dt \approx \int_{T_0}^{T_1} a_t \nabla\Gamma(\Theta_t)dt, \qquad \text{for } T_1 \gg T_0 \geq 0.$$

Terminology

See the "Notes" section for the history of gradient-free optimization techniques. It is noted there that there are two distinct approaches. The first is strongly rooted in stochastic approximation theory, and commonly goes by the name *simultaneous perturbations stochastic approximation* (SPSA). The second and much older approach is called *extremum-seeking*

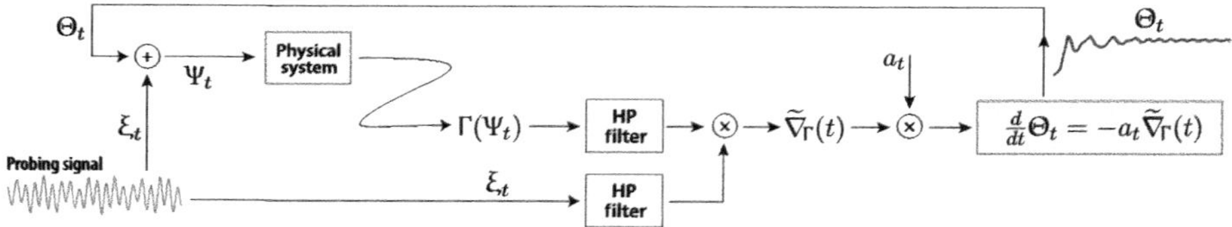

Figure 4.8 Extremum seeking control for gradient free optimization.

control (ESC), which is formulated in a purely deterministic setting. The similarity between SPSA and ESC becomes clearer when cast as QSA.

Within the machine learning community, algorithms of the form (4.94) are known as *stochastic gradient descent* (SGD). This motivates the use of the terminology *quasi stochastic gradient descent* (qSGD) in this book. Algorithm qSGD #1, shown later in this chapter, is a QSA interpretation of the one-measurement form of SPSA introduced in [329], and qSGD #2 is a very special case of ESC – to be explained based on the general architecture illustrated in Figure 4.8.

4.6.1 Simulated Annealing

The primary motivation for SPSA and ESC algorithms is that they can be run based purely on observations of the loss function. A secondary motivation is that the probing can be designed to emulate a "simulated annealing" algorithm for optimization of functions that are not convex: The probing can help the algorithm avoid local minima. The example described here was designed to illustrate this point.

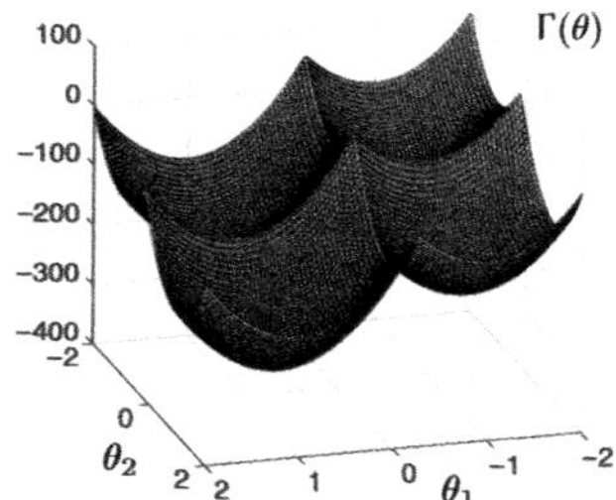

Figure 4.9 A highly nonconvex loss function.

Figure 4.9 shows a plot of a highly nonconvex function, defined as the "soft min" of convex quadratic functions:

$$\Gamma(\theta) = -\log\Big(\sum_{i=1}^{4} \exp(-\{z_i + \|\theta - \theta^i\|^2\}/\sigma^2)\Big)$$

with $\sigma = 1/10$, and

$$\{[\theta^i, z_i]\} = \big\{[\binom{-1}{-1}, -1],\ [\binom{-1}{1}, -2],\ [\binom{1}{-1}, -2],\ [\binom{1}{1}, -3]\big\}.$$

The minimizer is $\theta^* \approx \binom{1}{1}$, with $\Gamma(\theta^*) \approx -300$.

The algorithm qSGD #1 is defined in (4.96). It was tested in this special case:

$$\frac{d}{dt}\Theta_t = -a_t \frac{1}{\varepsilon}\xi_t \Gamma(\Theta_t + \varepsilon\xi_t)$$

using $\varepsilon = 0.15$, $a_t = \min\{\overline{a}, (1+t)^{-\rho}\}$ with $\rho = 0.9$ and $\overline{a} = 10^{-3}$. The probing signal was chosen to satisfy (4.48):

$$\xi_t = \sqrt{2}[\sin(t\omega_1), \sin(t\omega_2)]^{\intercal},$$

with $\omega_1 = 1/4$ and $\omega_2 = 1/e^2$ chosen to obtain attractive plots – higher frequencies lead to faster convergence.

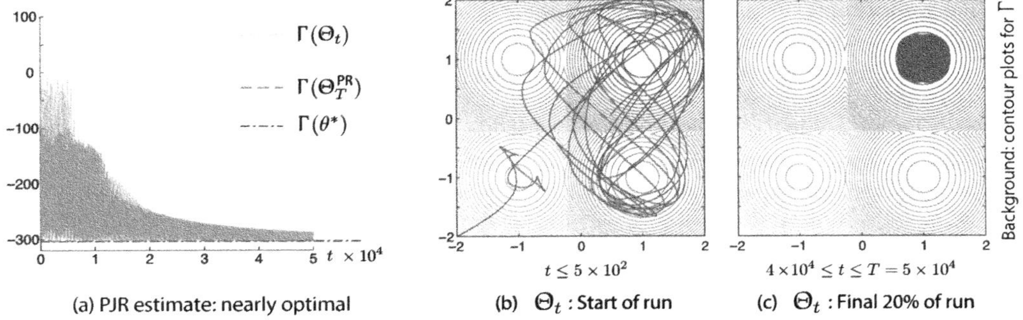

Figure 4.10 Minimizing a loss function with multiple local minima: While $\Gamma(\Theta_t)$ is highly oscillatory, the estimate Θ_T^{PR} is nearly optimal (obtained by averaging the final 20% of parameter estimates).

These metaparameters were obtained by trial and error: If $\overline{a}$ or ε is too small, then we are sometimes trapped in a local minima.

The ODE was approximated using a standard Euler scheme with 1s sampling interval: The crude ODE approximation led to the requirement that ω_1/ω_2 is irrational.

The two plots on the right-hand side in Figure 4.10 show the evolution of Θ_t in $\mathbb{R}^2$ for $0 \le t \le 5 \times 10^4$, with $\Theta_0 = (-2, -2)^{\intercal}$. The plots indicate that the estimates exhibit significant variation throughout the run, but in plot (c) it is clear that they are trapped within the region of attraction of the global minimum.

What's more, averaging is highly successful: The estimate Θ_T^{PR} was obtained as the average of Θ_t over the final 20% of the run. It is found that $\Gamma(\Theta_T^{PR})$ is only a small fraction of 1% greater than $\Gamma(\theta^*)$.

4.6.2 A Menu of Algorithms

In each of the algorithms defined here, it is assumed that the process $\boldsymbol{\Psi}$ is the sum of two terms: $\Psi_t = \Theta_t + \varepsilon\xi_t$, $t \ge 0$, where $\varepsilon > 0$, and $\boldsymbol{\xi}$ is a d-dimensional probing signal. For simplicity, we impose the normalization conditions (4.48) unless stated otherwise:

$$\lim_{T\to\infty} \frac{1}{T}\int_{t=0}^{T} \xi_t \, dt = 0, \qquad \lim_{T\to\infty} \frac{1}{T}\int_{t=0}^{T} \xi_t \xi_t^{\intercal} \, dt = I. \tag{4.95}$$

This is easily arranged using a mixture of sinusoids.

The first algorithm is the simplest:

qSGD #1

For a given $d \times d$ positive definite matrix G, and $\Theta_0 \in \mathbb{R}^d$,

$$\tfrac{d}{dt}\Theta_t = -a_t \frac{1}{\varepsilon} G \xi_t \Gamma(\Psi_t), \tag{4.96a}$$

$$\Psi_t = \Theta_t + \varepsilon \xi_t. \tag{4.96b}$$

This algorithm takes the form (4.44), with

$$f(\theta, \xi_t) = -\frac{1}{\varepsilon} G \xi_t \Gamma(\theta + \varepsilon \xi_t). \tag{4.97}$$

If $\Gamma\colon \mathbb{R}^d \to \mathbb{R}$ is twice continuously differentiable, then a second-order Taylor expansion of the objective function gives

$$\Gamma(\theta + \varepsilon\xi_t) = \Gamma(\theta) + \varepsilon \xi_t^{\intercal} \nabla\Gamma(\theta) + \tfrac{1}{2}\varepsilon^2 \xi_t^{\intercal} \nabla^2\Gamma(\theta)\xi_t + o(\varepsilon^2)$$

$$\text{and hence} \quad f(\theta, \xi_t) = -\frac{1}{\varepsilon} G\Gamma(\theta)\xi_t - G\xi_t\xi_t^{\intercal}\nabla\Gamma\,(\theta) + O(\varepsilon),$$

where the error notation $o(\,\cdot\,)$ and $O(\,\cdot\,)$ notation is reviewed in Appendix A. Under (4.95), this implies the following approximation for the averaged vector field:

$$\bar{f}_\varepsilon(\theta) \stackrel{\text{def}}{=} \lim_{T\to\infty} \frac{1}{T}\int_{t=0}^{T} f(\theta, \xi_t)dt = -G\nabla\Gamma(\theta) + O(\varepsilon). \tag{4.98}$$

QSA theory predicts that qSGD #1 will approximate the steepest descent algorithm for the choice $G = I$.

The next algorithm requires differentiation of measurements. It is motivated by the representation

$$\frac{d}{dt}\Gamma(\Psi_t) = \varepsilon\nabla\Gamma\,(\Psi_t)^{\intercal}\xi_t',$$

where the prime denotes a derivative: $\xi_t' = \frac{d}{dt}\xi_t$.

qSGD #2

For a given $d \times d$ positive definite matrix G, and initial condition Θ_0,

$$\tfrac{d}{dt}\Theta_t = -a_t \frac{1}{\varepsilon} G \xi_t' \tfrac{d}{dt}\Gamma(\Psi_t), \tag{4.99a}$$

$$\Psi_t = \Theta_t + \varepsilon\xi_t. \tag{4.99b}$$

This algorithm fits neatly in the ESC architecture illustrated in Figure 4.8, in which the high-pass (HP) filters are chosen to be pure differentiation:

$$\breve{\nabla}_\Gamma(t) = \tfrac{d}{dt}\xi_t \times \tfrac{d}{dt}\Gamma(\Psi_t).$$

Algorithm (4.99) can also be cast as a QSA ODE, in which we view $\xi_t^\bullet \stackrel{\text{def}}{=} (\xi_t, \frac{d}{dt}\xi_t) \in \mathbb{R}^{2m}$ as the exploration signal. Equation (4.99a) gives

$$f(\theta, \xi_t^\bullet) = \frac{1}{\varepsilon} G\xi_t'\{\xi_t'\}^{\intercal}\nabla\Gamma\,(\theta + \varepsilon\xi_t).$$

Analysis of each of these two algorithms presents challenges. A challenge with qSGD #2 is differentiation of the observations $\{\Gamma(\Psi_t)\}$. This is motivation for replacing differentiation with a high-pass filter.

For qSGD #1, the challenge is presented by the form of f in (4.97). In many problems, we know that $\nabla\Gamma$ is globally Lipschitz continuous, but Γ is *not*. In such cases, f is not Lipschitz continuous in θ, which will be a standing assumption in the theory. This is not an enormous challenge, since we can modify the algorithm to obtain convergence (say, using a projection of parameter estimates onto a bounded set).

Lipschitz continuity is easily established for the next algorithm.

qSGD #3

For a given $d \times d$ positive definite matrix G, and initial condition Θ_0,

$$\frac{d}{dt}\Theta_t = -a_t \frac{1}{2\varepsilon} G\xi_t \Big\{ \Gamma(\Theta_t + \varepsilon\xi_t) - \Gamma(\Theta_t - \varepsilon\xi_t) \Big\}. \tag{4.100}$$

Denoting by $a_t f(\Theta_t, \xi_t)$ the right-hand side of (4.100), we can show that f is Lipschitz in its first variable whenever $\nabla\Gamma$ is Lipschitz, and in this case $f(\theta,\xi) = -G\xi\xi^\intercal \nabla\Gamma(\theta) + O(\varepsilon)$.

The mean vector field $\bar{f}_\varepsilon$ for (4.100) admits the same approximation (4.98) under slightly milder conditions on the probing signal, with the zero-mean assumption (4.48a) dropped. Moreover, the following global consistency result holds:

Proposition 4.18 *Suppose that the following hold for the function Γ and algorithm parameters in qSGD #3:*

(i) *Assumption (QSA1) holds.*
(ii) *The probing signal satisfies* (4.48b).
(iii) *$\nabla\Gamma$ is globally Lipschitz continuous, and Γ is strongly convex (review Section 4.4.1 for definitions), with unique minimizer $\theta^* \in \mathbb{R}^d$.*

Then there exists $\bar{\varepsilon} > 0$ such that for each $\varepsilon \in (0,\bar{\varepsilon})$, there is a unique root θ^*_ε of $\bar{f}_\varepsilon$, satisfying $\|\theta^*_\varepsilon - \theta^*\| \le O(\varepsilon)$. Moreover, convergence holds from each initial condition: $\lim_{t\to\infty} \Theta_t = \theta^*_\varepsilon$. □

Proof The hypotheses of the proposition imply that Assumptions (QSA1)–(QSA2) of Section 4.5.4 hold for $f(\theta,\xi) = -G\xi\xi^\intercal\nabla\Gamma(\theta) + O(\varepsilon)$ and $\bar{f}_\varepsilon$ defined in (4.98). Since Γ is strongly convex, it holds that there is $\varepsilon_0 > 0$ such that there is a unique solution to $G\nabla\Gamma(\theta) = z$ whenever $\|z\| \le \varepsilon_0$, from which Assumption (QSA3) may be established for $\varepsilon > 0$ sufficiently small. Theorem 4.15 then implies that for each $\varepsilon > 0$, Θ_t converges to the unique root θ^*_ε of $\bar{f}_\varepsilon$ satisfying $\|\nabla\Gamma(\theta^*_\varepsilon)\| = O(\varepsilon)$. Due to strong convexity, we have the following:

$$\Gamma(\theta^*) \ge \Gamma(\theta^*_\varepsilon) + (\nabla\Gamma(\theta^*_\varepsilon))^\intercal(\theta^* - \theta^*_\varepsilon) + \frac{\eta}{2}\|\theta^*_\varepsilon - \theta^*\|^2,$$

for some $\eta > 0$. Therefore,

$$\begin{aligned}\frac{\eta}{2}\|\theta^*_\varepsilon - \theta^*\|^2 &\le \Gamma(\theta^*) - \Gamma(\theta^*_\varepsilon) + (\nabla\Gamma(\theta^*_\varepsilon))^\intercal(\theta^*_\varepsilon - \theta^*)\\ &\le \|\nabla\Gamma(\theta^*_\varepsilon)\|\|\theta^*_\varepsilon - \theta^*\|,\end{aligned}$$

implying that $\|\theta^*_\varepsilon - \theta^*\| \le O(\varepsilon)$. □

4.7 Quasi Policy Gradient Algorithms

It is not difficult to apply these techniques to the "tamer" examples considered in Chapter 2.

4.7.1 Mountain Car

We return to the example introduced in Section 2.7.2, and the simple policy (2.59). This cannot be optimal since it is clear the state will remain near z^{min} far longer than necessary from certain initial conditions. A more sensible policy will avoid this "western frontier." Here is one suggestion, based on a threshold θ in the interval $[z^{\text{min}}, z^{\text{goal}}]$.

With $z(k) = x_1(k)$ and $v(k) = x_2(k)$ denoting position and velocity at time-step k, consider

$$u(k) = \phi^\theta(x(k)) = \begin{cases} 1 & \textit{if } z(k) \le \theta \\ \text{sign}(v(k)) & \text{else} \end{cases}. \tag{4.101}$$

The policy "panics" and accelerates the car towards the goal whenever $z(k)$ is at or below the threshold θ.

The range of acceptable θ can be estimated by examining the graph of potential energy shown in Figure 2.11, in the case of static input $u(k) \equiv 1$. Its minimum is at $z^\circ \approx -0.48$. Denoting $v(1) = \text{F}_2(x,u)$, we have by definition of z°,

$$0 = \tfrac{d}{dz}\mathcal{U}^1(z^\circ) = mg\sin(\theta(z^\circ)) - \kappa = v(0) - v(1), \qquad u = 1,\, x = (z^\circ, 0)^{\intercal}.$$

That is, $v(1) = v(0) = 0$, which implies that the mountain car has stalled: $x(1) = x(0)$. We therefore cannot allow a policy for which $\phi(x^\circ) = 1$, which means that the policy ϕ^θ is not acceptable if $\theta > z^\circ$. We don't observe infinite total cost in experiments that follow because we artificially bound the value function, as explained later.

Figure 4.11 shows trajectories of position as a function of time from three initial conditions, each with $v(0) = 0$, and with two instances of this policy: $\theta = -0.8$, and $\theta = -0.2$. The former is a much better choice from initial position $z(0) = -0.6$: We see that the time to reach the goal is nearly twice as long when using $\theta = -0.2$ as compared to $\theta = -0.8$.

Let's see how to adapt qSGD #1 to find the optimal value of θ. A discrete-time approximation of the recursion (4.96) is

$$\Theta_{n+1} = \Theta_n - \alpha_{n+1}\frac{1}{\varepsilon}G\xi_{n+1}\Gamma(\Psi_{n+1}), \tag{4.102a}$$

$$\Psi_{n+1} = \Theta_n + \varepsilon\xi_{n+1}. \tag{4.102b}$$

The question is, how do we define Γ?

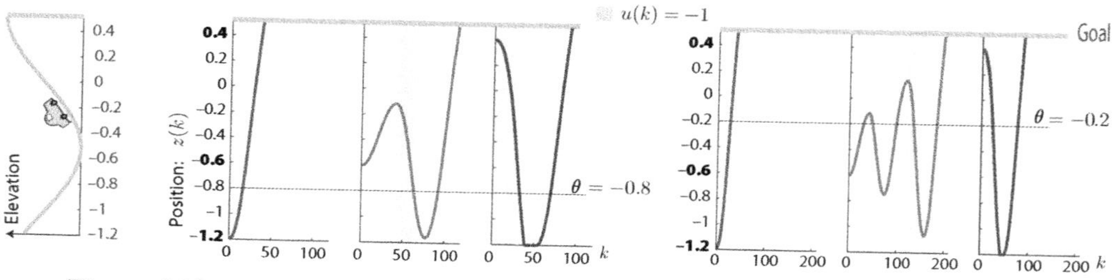

Figure 4.11 Trajectories for the mountain car for two policies, and three initial conditions.

The total cost in this example coincides with the time to reach the goal. For fixed initial condition $x_0 \in \mathbb{R}^d$, we might estimate the minimum of the corresponding total cost $J_\theta(x_0)$ over θ. A natural approach is episodic: at stage n of the algorithm, we initialize the car at state x_0, and run the policy ϕ^θ using $\theta = \Psi_{n+1} = \Theta_n + \varepsilon\xi_{n+1}$. On reaching the goal state, we have a measurement of $J_\theta(x_0)$ for this value of θ.

We make two modifications to this objective function. First, because we don't know if the policy is stabilizing for all θ, we introduce a maximal value $J^{\max}$ of our choosing. Second, we are interested in more than one initial condition. Let ν denote a pmf on X, and define as our objective function

$$\Gamma(\theta) = \sum \nu(x^i) \min\{J^{\max}, J_\theta(x^i)\},$$

where the sum is over the support of ν. If ν has K points of support, then K experiments are required to obtain the measurement $\Gamma(\Psi_{n+1})$ at stage $n+1$ of the algorithm.

The value $J^{\max} = 5{,}000$ was used in all of the numerical experiments that follow.

A second option is to introduce a second probing signal to generate a quasirandom sequence of initial conditions $\{x_0^n : n \geq 0\}$ that admit an ergodic average: For any subset $S \subset \mathsf{X}$,

$$\nu(S) = \lim_{N\to\infty} \sum_{n=1}^{N} \mathbb{1}\{x_0^n \in S\}.$$

In this case, we don't require that ν have finite support, so our objective requires the general notation,

$$\Gamma(\theta) = \int \min\{J^{\max}, J_\theta(x)\}\, \nu(dx). \tag{4.103}$$

In this case, the recursion (4.102a) is modified as follows:

$$\begin{aligned} \Theta_{n+1} &= \Theta_n - \alpha_{n+1}\frac{1}{\varepsilon} G\xi_{n+1}\Gamma_{n+1}, \\ \Gamma_{n+1} &\stackrel{\text{def}}{=} \min\{J^{\max}, J_\theta(x_0^{n+1})\}\big|_{\theta=\Psi_{n+1}}. \end{aligned} \tag{4.104}$$

The experiments that follow are based on (4.104) option 2, though the first option (using K experiments per iteration of the algorithm) is most likely preferable in terms of accelerating convergence. The sequence $\{x_0^n = (z_0^n, v_0^n)^\intercal\}$ was chosen to cover the state space uniformly. This was achieved by introducing a second probing signal $\xi_n^x = (\xi_n^z, \xi_n^v)$ with

$$\xi_n^z = \text{frac}(nr_z), \qquad \xi_n^v = \text{frac}(nr_v),$$

where "frac" denotes the fractional part of a real number, r_v, r_z are irrational, and their ratio is also irrational. The values $r_v = \pi$ and $r_z = e$ were chosen in all experiments. Then define

$$v_0^n = \overline{v}(2\xi_n^v - 1) \qquad \text{and} \qquad z_0^n = z^{\min} + [z^{\text{goal}} - z^{\min}]\xi_n^z. \tag{4.105}$$

Figure 4.12 shows one run using the constant step-size $\alpha_n \equiv 0.1$, $\varepsilon = 0.05$, and $\xi_n = \sin(n)$. The large fixed step-size was chosen simply to illustrate the exotic nonlinear dynamics that emerge from this algorithm. It would seem that the algorithm has failed, since the estimates oscillate between -1.2 and -0.3 in steady state, while the actual optimizer is $\theta^* \approx -0.8$. The dashed line shows the average of $\{\Theta_n\}$ over the final 20% of estimates. This average is very nearly optimal, since the objective function is nearly flat for θ near the optimizer.

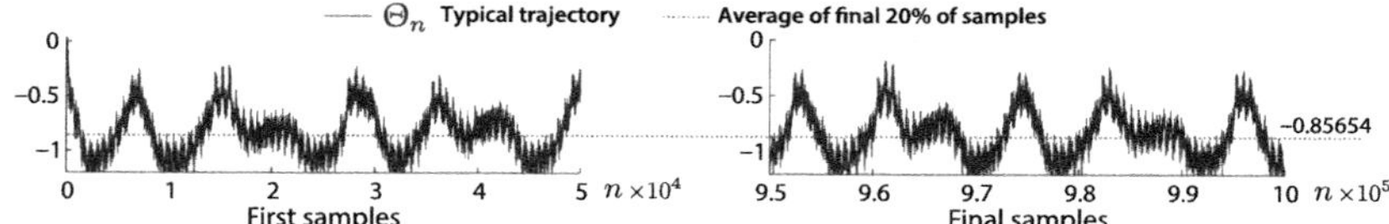

Figure 4.12 qSGD #1 for the mountain car: the gradient-free optimization algorithm (4.102) using a large constant step-size.

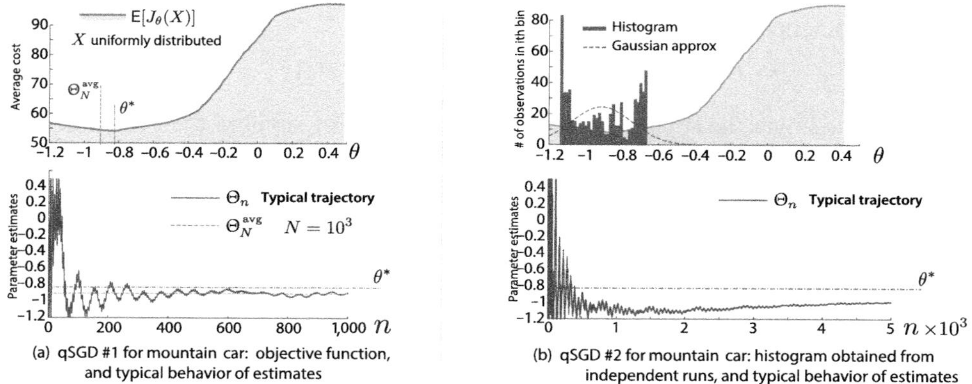

Figure 4.13 qSGD for the mountain car: (a) qSGD #1; (b) qSGD #2 implemented using (4.107).

Figure 4.13a shows results from an experiment with decaying step-size $\alpha_n = 1/n^{0.75}$, small $\varepsilon > 0$, and a minor change in the probing signal:

$$\xi_n = \sin(2\pi\phi + n). \tag{4.106}$$

The phase variable ϕ was selected uniformly at random in $[0,1]$ when repeated experiments were performed. The upper plot in Figure 4.13a shows the average cost (4.103), with $N = 10^4$ for a range of θ. The value of θ^* was obtained by computing the minimum of this function. This approach to estimate the optimal threshold is simpler and more reliable than QSA techniques! Brute-force methods make sense if the dimension of θ is one or two; in complex situations, we need a more clever search strategy.

Figure 1.2 shows results from 10^3 independent runs, each with horizon length $\mathcal{T} = 10^4$. In each case, the parameter estimates evolve according to (4.104), to obtain estimates $\{\Theta_n^i : 1 \le n \le \mathcal{T}, 1 \le i \le 10^3\}$. The two columns are distinguished by the probing signals. For QSA, the probing signal $\boldsymbol{\xi}$ was a sinusoid, with phase ϕ selected independently in the interval $[0,1)$, in each of the 10^3 runs. The results displayed in the second column are based on an experiment with random probing signals, each uniform and independent on its respective range. The distribution of ξ_n was chosen uniform on the interval $[-1,1]$ for each n. The label "1SPSA" refers to Spall's single observation algorithm based on random (i.i.d.) exploration (see the "Notes" section at the end of this chapter for history).

qSGD #2 is easily adapted to this application:

$$\Theta_{n+1} = \Theta_n - \alpha_{n+1} G \xi'_{n+1} \Gamma'_{n+1}, \tag{4.107a}$$

$$\Psi_{n+1} = \Theta_n + \varepsilon \xi_{n+1}, \tag{4.107b}$$

where the primes denote approximations of the derivatives appearing in (4.99a):

$$\xi'_{n+1} = \frac{1}{\delta}(\xi_{n+1} - \xi_n), \quad \Gamma'_{n+1} = \frac{1}{\delta}(\Gamma_{n+1} - \Gamma_n),$$

where $\delta > 0$ is the sampling interval, and Γ_{n+1} is defined by (4.104) if using option 2.

A histogram and sample path of parameter estimates are shown in Figure 4.13b, based on algorithm (4.107) with $\delta^2 = 0.5$, and all of the same choices for parameters, except that the step-size was reduced to avoid large initial transients: $\alpha_n = \min(1/n^{0.75}, 0.05)$. This results in $\alpha_n = 1/n^{0.75}$ for $n \geq 55$.

Based on the histogram, the performance appears slightly worse than observed for qSGD # 1 in Figure 1.2, but these outcomes are a product of particular choices for algorithm parameters.

4.7.2 LQR

The linear quadratic regulator (LQR) optimal control problem was introduced in Section 3.6 for models in discrete time, and revisited again in Section 3.9.4 for the continuous-time model,

$$\tfrac{d}{dt} x = Ax + Bu.$$

The value function is defined as the minimum total cost

$$J^\star(x) = \min_{\boldsymbol{u}} \int_0^\infty c(x_t, u_t)\, dt\,, \quad x_0 = x \in \mathsf{X}$$

with quadratic cost (3.3): $c(x,u) = x^\intercal S x + u^\intercal R u$. If finite valued, then this value function is quadratic, $J^\star(x) = x^\intercal M^\star x$, with matrix $M^\star \geq 0$ solving the algebraic Riccati equation (3.61), and the optimal input is linear state feedback:

$$u_t^\star = -K^\star x_t^\star = -R^{-1} B^\intercal M^\star x_t^\star.$$

For simplicity, we restrict to the single-input model, so that $K^\star$ is a row vector ($1 \times n$).

If we do not have a model available, then we can approximate the optimal policy by first estimating (A, B) through system identification, and then proceed to solve the ARE to obtain the estimate of the optimal gain. Alternatively, we can use gradient-free methods to estimate $K^\star$ directly, identifying a feedback gain K with $\theta^\intercal$. One great benefit of the latter approach is that we are free to impose structure on the gain matrix. For example, for a system with n states and n inputs, we might search for the $n \times n$ gain matrix that is optimal over all *diagonal* matrices. This means we consider $u_t(i) = -\theta_i x_t(i)$ for each i and t, and optimize over $\theta \in \mathbb{R}^n$. Exercise 4.17 provides an example to test qSGD on a particular example of this flavor.

Consider the unstructured problem in which $u_t = -\theta^\intercal x_t$, in which the goal is to minimize the objective function

$$\Gamma(\theta) = \sum \nu(x_0^i) J_\theta(x_0^i),$$

where ν is a pmf on the state space, and J_θ is the infinite horizon cost with the feedback law determined by θ:

$$J_\theta(x_0) = \int_0^\infty c(x_t, u_t)\,dt\,, \qquad x_0 \in \mathbb{R}^n.$$

To apply qSGD, it would be necessary to approximate by the finite horizon objective

$$J_\theta(x_0) = \int_0^{\mathcal{T}} c(x_t, u_t)\,dt + x_{\mathcal{T}}^\intercal S_0 x_{\mathcal{T}}\,,$$

with $S_0 > 0$ included to encourage a stable control solution.

Before considering qSGD, we should first see if the gradient flow will be successful:

$$\frac{d}{dt}\vartheta = -\nabla\Gamma\,(\vartheta).$$

It is simplest to return to the infinite horizon setting, so that $\mathcal{T} = \infty$ and $S_0 = 0$. Analysis is based on the correlation matrix

$$\Sigma_0 = \sum \nu(x_0^i) x_0^i \{x_0^i\}^\intercal$$

and the solution X_θ to the Lyapunov equation

$$(A - B\theta^\intercal)X_\theta + X_\theta(A - B\theta^\intercal)^\intercal + \Sigma_0 = 0,$$

from which we obtain $\Gamma(\theta) = \text{trace}\,(SX_\theta) + R\theta^\intercal X_\theta\theta$.

We begin with bad news: It is known that Γ may be nonconvex in θ. An example in [77] shows that the domain on which $\Gamma(\theta)$ is finite is not convex, but this paper also brings good news. It has been known since the 1980s that $\nabla\Gamma\,(\theta)$ vanishes only at $\theta = \theta^\star$, and that $V(\theta) = \Gamma(\theta) - \Gamma(\theta^*)$ is coercive (even though it is not everywhere finite valued). Hence this serves as a Lyapunov function:

$$\frac{d}{dt}V(\vartheta_t) = -\|\nabla\Gamma\,(\vartheta_t)\|^2 < 0\,, \qquad \text{whenever } \vartheta_t \neq \theta^*.$$

In conclusion, based on this theory we can expect success using qSGD provided we project parameter estimates (possibly required since neither Γ or its gradient is Lipschitz continuous).

4.7.3 What about High Dimensions?

The qSGD algorithms are easy to code, and quickly converge to an approximately optimal parameter for the example considered in this section. In high dimensions, we can't expect to blindly apply any of these algorithms. For example, consider the choice of probing signal (4.47), where i ranges from 1 to $d = 1{,}000$. If the frequencies $\{\omega_i\}$ are chosen in a narrow range, then the limit (4.48b) will converge very slowly. The rate will be faster if the frequencies are widely separated, but we then need a much higher resolution ODE approximation to implement an algorithm.

This challenge is well understood in the optimization literature. One approach to create a reliable algorithm is to employ *block coordinate descent*. This requires two ingredients:

(i) A sequence of time points $T_0 = 0 < T_1 < T_2 < \cdots$.
(ii) A sequence of "parameter blocks" $B_k \subset \{1,\ldots,d\}$ for each $k \geq 0$, where the number of elements d_B in B_i is far smaller than d.

The qSGD ODE (4.94) is modified so that $\Theta_t(i)$ is held constant on the interval $[T_k, T_{k+1})$ for $i \notin B_k$, and

$$\frac{d}{dt}\Theta_t(i) = -a_t[\breve{\nabla}_\Gamma(t)]_i, \qquad i \in B_k\,,\ t \in [T_k, T_{k+1}).$$

See [19, 72, 282] for this and more sophisticated approaches.

4.8 Stability of ODEs*

This asterisk at the end of this section title indicates that it contains advanced material. The stability theory here is needed if you want to fully understand why the ODE methods surveyed in this chapter are "well behaved," and the concepts will be extended to QSA in the following section.

We begin with the proof of a central result and a simple corollary.

4.8.1 Grönwall's Inequality

Proof of Grönwall's Inequality, Proposition 4.2 Consider first the simpler equality (4.7):

$$z_t = \gamma_t + \int_0^t \beta_s z_s \, ds.$$

Observe that γ is continuous, under the assumption that z and β are continuous. We can "solve" this equation through the construction of a state space model with state $x_t = z_t - \gamma_t$, and output z_t. From the integral equation

$$x_t = \int_0^t \beta_s \big[x_s + \gamma_s\big] \, ds,$$

we obtain the time-varying linear state space model

$$\frac{d}{dt}x_t = \beta_t x_t + \beta_t \gamma_t\,, \qquad z_t = x_t + \gamma_t$$

with initial condition $x_0 = z_0 - \gamma_0 = 0$. This scalar linear state space model, with "input" $u_t = \beta_t \gamma_t$, has an explicit solution:

$$x_t = \int_0^t u_s \exp\Big(\int_s^t \beta_r \, dr\Big) \, ds.$$

We next turn to the inequality (4.6a), which we can write as

$$z_t = \alpha_t + \int_0^t \beta_s z_s \, ds - \delta_t,$$

where $\delta_t \geq 0$ for each t. Define $\gamma_t = \alpha_t - \delta_t$ and obtain, with $u_t = \beta_t \gamma_t$ as before,

$$x_t = \int_0^t u_s \exp\Big(\int_s^t \beta_r \, dr\Big) \, ds \leq \int_0^t \beta_s \alpha_s \exp\Big(\int_s^t \beta_r \, dr\Big) \, ds.$$

Using $z_t = x_t + \gamma_t \leq x_t + \alpha_t$ then gives (i).

We now establish (ii): If the function $\boldsymbol{\alpha}$ is nondecreasing, then from part (i) and the assumption that $\boldsymbol{\beta}$ is nonnegative,

$$z_t \leq \alpha_t + \alpha_t \int_0^t \beta_s \exp\Big(\int_s^t \beta_r \, dr\Big) \, ds, \qquad 0 \leq t \leq \mathcal{T}.$$

This bound implies (ii) on substituting

$$\int_0^t \beta_s \exp\Big(\int_s^t \beta_r \, dr\Big) \, ds = \exp\Big(\int_0^t \beta_r \, dr\Big) - 1. \qquad \square$$

Grönwall's Inequality implies a crude bound that is needed in approximations:

Proposition 4.19 *Consider the ODE* (4.2), *subject to the Lipschitz condition* (4.5). *Then,*

(i) *There is a constant* B_f *depending only on* f *such that*

$$\|\vartheta_t\| \leq \big(B_f + \|\vartheta_0\|\big)e^{Lt} - B_f, \tag{4.108a}$$

$$\|\vartheta_t - \vartheta_0\| \leq (B_f + L\|\vartheta_0\|)te^{Lt}, \qquad t \geq 0. \tag{4.108b}$$

(ii) *If there is an equilibrium* θ^*, *then for each initial condition,*

$$\|\vartheta_t - \theta^*\| \leq \|\vartheta_0 - \theta^*\|e^{Lt}, \qquad t \geq 0.$$

Proof We present a complete proof of (ii) and (4.108a) (the proof of (4.108b) is similar).

If there is an equilibrium θ^*, this means that $\mathrm{f}(\theta^*) = \mathbf{0}$. The proof of (ii) then begins with (4.3), in the form

$$\vartheta_t - \theta^* = \vartheta_0 - \theta^* + \int_0^t \mathrm{f}(\vartheta_\tau) d\tau, \qquad 0 \leq t \leq T.$$

Under the equilibrium condition and the Lipschitz assumption,

$$\|\mathrm{f}(\vartheta_\tau)\| = \|\mathrm{f}(\vartheta_\tau) - \mathrm{f}(\theta^*)\| \leq L\|\vartheta_\tau - \theta^*\|.$$

Writing $z_t = \|\vartheta_t - \theta^*\|$, this bound combined with (4.3) gives

$$z_t \leq z_0 + L\int_0^t z_\tau \, d\tau, \qquad 0 \leq t \leq T.$$

Grönwall's Inequality then gives (ii): Apply Proposition 4.2 (ii) using $\beta_t \equiv L$ and $\alpha_t \equiv z_0$.

To establish (4.108a), take any $\theta^\bullet \in \mathbb{R}^d$ and use the Lipschitz condition to obtain

$$\begin{aligned}\|\mathrm{f}(\theta)\| &\leq \|\mathrm{f}(\theta) - \mathrm{f}(\theta^\bullet)\| + \|\mathrm{f}(\theta^\bullet)\| \\ &\leq L\|\theta - \theta^\bullet\| + \|\mathrm{f}(\theta^\bullet)\| \\ &\leq L\|\theta\| + L\|\theta^\bullet\| + \|\mathrm{f}(\theta^\bullet)\|.\end{aligned}$$

With $\theta^\bullet$ fixed, define $B_f = [\|\theta^\bullet\| + \|\mathrm{f}(\theta^\bullet)\|]/L$, so that

$$\|\mathrm{f}(\theta)\| \le L[\|\theta\| + B_f], \qquad \theta \in \mathbb{R}^d.$$

Applying (4.3) then gives

$$\|\vartheta_t\| + B_f \le \|\vartheta_0\| + B_f + L\int_0^t [\|\vartheta_\tau\| + B_f]\, d\tau.$$

Grönwall's Inequality establishes (4.108a), using $z_t = \|\vartheta_t\| + B_f$ for each t, and $\alpha_t = z_0$. □

4.8.2 Lyapunov Functions

The survey contained in Section 2.4.5 tells us much of what we need to know about Lyapunov functions. Given the goals of algorithm design, our interest is global asymptotic stability, so that the drift condition of interest is (2.38) with x^e replaced by θ^*:

$$\langle \nabla V(\theta), \mathrm{f}(\theta)\rangle < 0, \qquad \theta \neq \theta^*.$$

This (and a few additional assumptions) allows application of Proposition 2.5 to establish convergence of $\boldsymbol{\vartheta}$.

Often the first step to establishing consistency of an ODE or algorithm is to show that the estimates do not "blow up." The ODE is called *ultimately bounded* if there is a bounded set $S \subset \mathbb{R}^d$ such that for each initial condition θ_0, there is a time $T(\theta_0)$ such that $\vartheta_t \in S$ for $t \ge T(\theta_0)$. This concept appeared in (4.83) in our treatment of QSA.

There is naturally a Lyapunov condition to check:

$$\langle \nabla V(\theta), \mathrm{f}(\theta)\rangle \le -\delta_0, \qquad \theta \in S^c. \tag{4.109}$$

Proposition 4.20 *Assume that there is a continuously differentiable function $V\colon \mathbb{R}^d \to \mathbb{R}_+$ satisfying* (4.109) *for some $\delta_0 > 0$ and set $S \subset \mathbb{R}^d$. Then $T_S(\theta) \le \delta_0^{-1} V(\theta)$ for $\theta \in \mathbb{R}^d$, where*

$$T_S(\theta) = \min\{t \ge 0 : \vartheta_t \in S\}, \qquad \vartheta_0 = \theta \in \mathbb{R}^d.$$

If in addition S is compact, and V is inf-compact, then the ODE (4.2) *is ultimately bounded.*

Proof We take $\delta_0 = 1$ without loss of generality (obtained by scaling the function V if necessary).

The bound on the first entrance time T_S is part of Exercise 2.12! It follows easily from the sample path interpretation of (4.109):

$$\frac{d}{dt}V(\vartheta_t) \le -1, \qquad 0 \le t \le T_S(\theta), \qquad \vartheta_0 = \theta \in \mathbb{R}^d. \tag{4.110}$$

Integrate each side from time $t = 0$ to $t = T_N = \min(N, T_S(\theta))$ (the minimum with N is required since we don't yet know if $T_S(\theta) < \infty$). Next, apply the fundamental theorem of calculus

$$-V(\vartheta_0) \le V(\vartheta_{T_N}) - V(\vartheta_0) \le -T_N,$$

giving $\min(N, T_S(\theta)) \le V(\vartheta_0)$, and the desired bound on choosing $N > V(\vartheta_0)$.

The crucial part of the proposition requires that we modify the set S. Since it is compact, and V is inf-compact, there exists $N < \infty$ such that $S \subset S_V(N) = \{\theta : V(\theta) \le N\}$, with $S_V(N)$ also compact. Hence,

$$\langle \nabla V(\theta), \mathrm{f}(\theta)\rangle \le -1, \qquad \theta \in \mathbb{R}^d,\ V(\theta) \ge N.$$

In fact, we should write $V(\theta) > N$, since this corresponds to $\theta \in S_V(N)^c$, but remember the left-hand side is continuous. Because $V(\vartheta_t)$ is decreasing whenever $\vartheta_t \in S_V(N)^c$, it follows that the set $S_V(N)$ is *absorbing*, which means that $\vartheta_t \in S_V(N)$ for all $t \ge T_S(\theta)$. □

4.8.3 Gradient Flows

The proofs of Propositions 4.11 and 4.13 rely on Lyapunov techniques and the following:

Lemma 4.21 (Arzelà–Ascoli Theorem) *Consider a sequence of vector-valued functions $\{\gamma^n : n \ge 0\}$ that satisfy these two conditions on a bounded time interval $[a,b]$:*

(i) *Uniformly bounded: There is a constant B such that $\|\gamma_t^n\| \le B$ for all n and $a \le t \le b$.*
(ii) *Equicontinuity: For each $\varepsilon > 0$, there exists $\delta > 0$ such that $\|\gamma_t^n - \gamma_s^n\| \le \varepsilon$ for every n, and every $t,s \in [a,b]$ satisfying $|t-s| \le \delta$.*

Then there exists a subsequence $\{n_k\}$ and a continuous function γ^∞ such that

$$\lim_{k\to\infty} \max_{a\le t\le b} \|\gamma_t^{n_k} - \gamma_t^\infty\| = 0.$$

Equicontinuity holds under a uniform Lipschitz bound: $\|\gamma_t^n - \gamma_s^n\| \le L|t-s|$ for fixed L, and all t,s,n.

Proof of Proposition 4.11 We first note that the existence of an optimizer follows from the assumptions: The optimizer θ^* for the primal exists because of the assumptions on Γ. It remains coercive and convex when its domain is restricted to the set $\{\theta : g(\theta) = 0\}$. The dual optimizer λ^* is then obtained via the first-order conditions for optimality:

$$0 = \nabla_\theta \mathcal{L}(\theta^*,\lambda^*) = \nabla\Gamma(\theta^*) + D^\intercal \lambda^*.$$

Multiplying each side by D and inverting gives $\lambda^* = -[DD^\intercal]^{-1} D\nabla\Gamma(\theta^*)$, and then by construction

$$\varphi^*(\lambda^*) = \min_\theta \mathcal{L}(\theta,\lambda^*) = \mathcal{L}(\theta^*,\lambda^*) = \Gamma(\theta^*) + \lambda^{*\intercal} g(\theta^*) = \Gamma^\star.$$

The proof of convergence is similar to Proposition 4.7. Consider the Lyapunov function

$$V(\theta,\lambda) = \tfrac{1}{2}\|\theta-\theta^*\|^2 + \tfrac{1}{2}\|\lambda-\lambda^*\|^2. \tag{4.111}$$

Applying the chain rule,

$$\begin{aligned}\tfrac{d}{dt} V(\vartheta_t,\lambda_t) &= \langle \vartheta_t - \theta^*, \tfrac{d}{dt}\vartheta_t\rangle + \langle \lambda_t - \lambda^\star, \tfrac{d}{dt}\lambda_t\rangle \\ &= -\langle \vartheta_t - \theta^*, \nabla_\theta \mathcal{L}(\vartheta_t,\lambda_t)\rangle + \langle \lambda_t - \lambda^\star, \nabla_\lambda \mathcal{L}(\vartheta_t,\lambda_t)\rangle.\end{aligned}$$

Convexity of $\mathcal{L}$ in θ and linearity in λ gives, respectively,

$$\begin{aligned}\mathcal{L}(\theta^*,\lambda_t) &\ge \mathcal{L}(\vartheta_t,\lambda_t) + \langle \theta^* - \vartheta_t, \nabla_\theta \mathcal{L}(\vartheta_t,\lambda_t)\rangle, \\ \mathcal{L}(\vartheta_t,\lambda_t) &= \mathcal{L}(\vartheta_t,\lambda^*) + \langle \lambda_t - \lambda^\star, \nabla_\lambda \mathcal{L}(\vartheta_t,\lambda_t)\rangle.\end{aligned}$$

This implies the derivative bound

$$\begin{aligned}\tfrac{d}{dt}V(\vartheta_t,\lambda_t) &\le [\mathcal{L}(\theta^*,\lambda_t) - \mathcal{L}(\vartheta_t,\lambda_t)] + [\mathcal{L}(\vartheta_t,\lambda_t) - \mathcal{L}(\vartheta_t,\lambda^*)] \\ &= [\mathcal{L}(\theta^*,\lambda_t) - \mathcal{L}(\theta^*,\lambda^*)] + [\mathcal{L}(\theta^*,\lambda^*) - \mathcal{L}(\vartheta_t,\lambda^*)].\end{aligned}$$

The first term on the right-hand side can be simplified:

$$\mathcal{L}(\theta^*,\lambda_t) - \mathcal{L}(\theta^*,\lambda^*) = (\lambda_t - \lambda^*)^{\intercal} g(\theta^*).$$

This is zero since θ^* is feasible. The second term is nonpositive by the saddle point property (4.34), giving

$$\tfrac{d}{dt}V(\vartheta_t,\lambda_t) \le \mathcal{L}(\theta^*,\lambda^*) - \mathcal{L}(\vartheta_t,\lambda^*) \le 0.$$

The inequality is strict when $\vartheta_t \ne \theta^*$ since Γ, and hence $\mathcal{L}(\,\cdot\,,\lambda^*)$ is strictly convex.

From this, we obtain the following conclusions:

(i) $V(\vartheta_t,\lambda_t)$ is nonincreasing, which implies that $\{\vartheta_t,\lambda_t\}$ evolve in a compact set.

(ii) The bound $0 \le \int_0^T \{\mathcal{L}(\vartheta_t,\lambda^*) - \mathcal{L}(\theta^*,\lambda^*)\}\,dt \le V(\vartheta_0,\lambda_0)$ is obtained for all $T > 0$ by integration. This and (i) implies that $\lim_{t\to\infty} \mathcal{L}(\vartheta_t,\lambda^*) = \mathcal{L}(\theta^*,\lambda^*) = \Gamma(\theta^*)$ (see Lemma 4.3).

(iii) $\lim_{t\to\infty} \vartheta_t = \theta^*$ as $t \to \infty$ since $\mathcal{L}(\,\cdot\,,\lambda^*)$ is strictly convex.

To establish convergence of the dual variable, we revisit (4.35a). Applying Lemma 4.21 with $\gamma_t^n = (\vartheta_{n+t}, \tfrac{d}{dt}\vartheta_{n+t})$, we can establish equicontinuity on $[a,b]$ for any $a < b$, and any subsequential limit γ^∞ is identically constant: $\gamma_t^\infty = (\theta^*,\mathbf{0})$. Hence from the derivative equation (4.35a),

$$0 = \lim_{t\to\infty} \tfrac{d}{dt}\vartheta_t = \lim_{t\to\infty} \{-\nabla\Gamma(\vartheta_t) - D^{\intercal}\lambda_t\}.$$

It follows that any limit point λ_∞ of $\{\lambda_t\}$ satisfies $0 = \nabla\Gamma(\theta^*) + D^{\intercal}\lambda_\infty$, and, on multiplying each side by D,

$$0 = D\nabla\Gamma(\theta^*) + DD^{\intercal}\lambda_\infty.$$

Under the full rank assumption, $\lambda_\infty = -[DD^{\intercal}]^{-1}D\nabla\Gamma\,(\theta^*) = \lambda^*$. □

Proof of Proposition 4.13 We present a shorter proof, highlighting the differences with the proof of Proposition 4.13.

We first obtain a representation for the Lagrange multiplier: from the first-order criterion for optimality, we have $\nabla_\theta\mathcal{L}(\theta,\lambda) = \mathbf{0}$ at $(\theta,\lambda) = (\theta^*,\lambda^*)$. That is,

$$\nabla\Gamma(\theta^*) + D^{\intercal}\lambda^* = 0, \qquad \text{with } D = \partial g\,(\theta^*),$$

and thus by the full rank assumption,

$$\lambda^* = -[DD^{\intercal}]^{-1}D\nabla\Gamma(\theta^*).$$

Based on this representation, the proposition is established once we have shown that $\{\vartheta_t,\lambda_t\}$ is bounded, and $\lim_{t\to\infty}\vartheta_t = \theta^*$. As in the previous proposition this then implies that, with $D_t \stackrel{\text{def}}{=} \partial g\,(\vartheta_t)$,

$$0 = \lim_{t\to\infty} \tfrac{d}{dt}\vartheta_t = \lim_{t\to\infty} \{-\nabla\Gamma(\vartheta_t) - D_t^{\intercal}\lambda_t\}.$$

Under convergence of $\{\vartheta_t\}$ and the full rank condition, this implies that $\{\lambda_t\}$ is also convergent:

$$\lim_{t\to\infty} \lambda_t = -\lim_{t\to\infty} \{D_t D_t^{\intercal}\}^{-1} D_t \nabla\Gamma(\vartheta_t) = \lambda^*.$$

To complete the proof, we use the quadratic Lyapunov function (4.111) to establish convergence of $\{\vartheta_t\}$. Apply the chain rule to obtain

$$V(\vartheta_T,\lambda_T) = V(\vartheta_0,\lambda_0) + \int_0^T -\{\langle \vartheta_t - \theta^*, \nabla_\theta \mathcal{L}(\vartheta_t,\lambda_t)\rangle + \langle \lambda_t - \lambda^*, \nabla_\lambda \mathcal{L}(\vartheta_t,\lambda_t)\rangle\}\, dt$$
$$+ \int_0^T (\lambda_t - \lambda^\star)^{\intercal} d\gamma_t.$$

The final integral can be bounded as follows:

$$\int_0^T (\lambda_t - \lambda^\star)^{\intercal} d\gamma_t = -\lambda^{\star\intercal} \int_0^T d\gamma_t \le 0.$$

The equality follows from (4.39), and the inequality follows from the assumption that the integral and $\lambda^\star$ are each n-dimensional vectors with nonnegative entries.

Preceding as in the case of equality constraints,

$$V(\vartheta_T,\lambda_T) - V(\vartheta_0,\lambda_0) \le \int_0^T [\mathcal{L}(\theta^*,\lambda_t) - \mathcal{L}(\theta^*,\lambda^*)] + [\mathcal{L}(\theta^*,\lambda^*) - \mathcal{L}(\vartheta_t,\lambda^*)]\, dt$$
$$= \int_0^T \{\lambda_t^{\intercal} g(\theta^*) + [\mathcal{L}(\theta^*,\lambda^*) - \mathcal{L}(\vartheta_t,\lambda^*)]\}\, dt.$$

This implies that $V(\vartheta_T,\lambda_T)$ is nonincreasing, since each term in the integrand is nonpositive:

$$\lambda_t^{\intercal} g(\theta^*) \le 0 \qquad \text{and} \qquad \mathcal{L}(\theta^*,\lambda^*) - \mathcal{L}(\vartheta_t,\lambda^*) \le 0.$$

Moreover, the second inequality is strict whenever $\vartheta_t \ne \theta^*$. From here, we may follow the steps of Proposition 4.11 to conclude that ϑ_t is convergent to $\theta^\star$. □

4.8.4 The ODE at ∞

We consider here an entirely different way to verify that the ODE (4.2) is ultimately bounded.

The idea is pretty simple: To see if the ODE is ultimately bounded, we only need to consider values of ϑ that are "very big." Rather than bring out a telescope to examine these big states, we scale the state and examine the resulting dynamics. To make this explicit requires that we make dependency on the initial condition explicit, writing $\vartheta(t;\theta_0)$ for the solution to (4.2) with initial condition $\vartheta_0 = \theta_0$.

Let $r \ge 1$ by a scaling parameter (assumed large), consider the solution of the ODE with $\vartheta_0 = r\theta_0$, and scale the solution to obtain

$$\vartheta_t^r \stackrel{\text{def}}{=} r^{-1}\vartheta(t; r\theta_0).$$

We have $\vartheta_0^r = \theta_0$ for any $r \ge 1$, and we obtain from (4.2),

$$\tfrac{d}{dt}\vartheta_t^r = r^{-1}\tfrac{d}{dt}\vartheta(t;r\theta_0) = r^{-1}\mathrm{f}(\vartheta(t;r\theta_0)).$$

On denoting $\mathrm{f}_r(\theta) = r^{-1}\mathrm{f}(r\theta)$ for $\theta \in \mathbb{R}^d$, this becomes

$$\tfrac{d}{dt}\vartheta^r_t = \mathrm{f}_r(\vartheta^r_t). \tag{4.112}$$

Suppose that a limiting vector field exists:

$$\mathrm{f}_\infty(\theta) \stackrel{\text{def}}{=} \lim_{r\to\infty} \mathrm{f}_r(\theta) = \lim_{r\to\infty} r^{-1}\mathrm{f}(r\theta)\,, \qquad \theta \in \mathbb{R}^d\,, \tag{4.113}$$

and define the ODE at ∞ as the limiting case of (4.112):

$$\tfrac{d}{dt}\vartheta^\infty_t = \mathrm{f}_\infty(\vartheta^\infty_t)\,, \qquad \vartheta^\infty_0 \in \mathbb{R}^d. \tag{4.114}$$

We have $\mathrm{f}_\infty(\mathsf{0}) = \mathsf{0}$ by (4.113), so the origin is an equilibrium of (4.114).

Proposition 4.22 *Suppose that* f *is globally Lipshitz continuous, with Lipschitz constant L. Suppose that the limit* (4.113) *exists for all θ to define a continuous function $\mathrm{f}_\infty : \mathbb{R}^d \to \mathbb{R}^d$. Then, if the origin is asymptotically stable for* (4.114)*, it follows that the ODE* (4.2) *is ultimately bounded.*

To prove the proposition, we first need to better understand the special properties of the solution to (4.114):

Lemma 4.23 *Suppose that the assumptions of Proposition 4.22 hold, so in particular the origin is asymptotically stable for* (4.114)*. Then the following hold:*

(i) *For each $\theta \in \mathbb{R}^d$ and $s \ge 0$,*

$$\mathrm{f}_\infty(s\theta) = s\mathrm{f}_\infty(\theta).$$

(ii) *If $\{\vartheta^\infty_t : t \ge 0\}$ is any solution to the ODE* (4.114)*, and $s > 0$, then $\{y_t = s\vartheta^\infty_t : t \ge 0\}$ is also a solution, starting from $y_0 = s\vartheta^\infty_0 \in \mathbb{R}^d$.*

(iii) *The origin is* globally *asymptotically stable for* (4.114)*, and convergence to the origin is exponentially fast: For some $R < \infty$ and $\rho > 0$,*

$$\|\vartheta^\infty_t\| \le Re^{-\rho t}\|\vartheta^\infty_0\|\,, \qquad \vartheta^\infty_0 \in \mathbb{R}^d.$$

Proof Consider first the scaling result in part (i): from the definition (4.113), with $s > 0$,

$$\mathrm{f}_\infty(s\theta) = \lim_{r\to\infty} r^{-1}\mathrm{f}(rs\theta) = s \lim_{r\to\infty} (sr)^{-1}\mathrm{f}(rs\theta) = s\mathrm{f}_\infty(\theta).$$

The case $s = 0$ is trivial, since it is clear that $\mathrm{f}_\infty(\mathsf{0}) = 0$. This establishes (i).

Next, write

$$\vartheta^\infty_t = \vartheta^\infty_0 + \int_0^t \mathrm{f}_\infty(\vartheta^\infty_\tau)d\tau.$$

Multiplying both sides by s and applying (i) gives (ii).

Asymptotic stability of the origin implies the following: (i) There exists $\varepsilon > 0$ such that $\lim_{t\to\infty}\vartheta^\infty_t = \mathsf{0}$ whenever $\|\vartheta^\infty_0\| \le \varepsilon$ and (ii) the convergence is uniform in the initial condition. Consequently, there exists $T_0 > 0$ such that

$$\|\vartheta^\infty_t\| \le \tfrac{1}{2}\varepsilon \qquad \text{for } t \ge T_0 \text{ whenever } \|\vartheta^\infty_0\| \le \varepsilon.$$

Next, apply scaling: For any initial condition ϑ_0^∞, consider $y_t = s\vartheta_t^\infty$ using $s = \varepsilon/\|\vartheta_0^\infty\|$, chosen so that $\|y_0\| = \varepsilon$. Then $\|y_t\| \le \frac{1}{2}\varepsilon = \frac{1}{2}\|y_0\|$ for $t \ge T_0$, implying

$$\|\vartheta_{T_0}^\infty\| \le \tfrac{1}{2}\|\vartheta_0^\infty\|, \qquad t \ge T_0\,,\ \vartheta_0^\infty \in \mathbb{R}^d.$$

This easily implies (iii) by iteration, as follows: For any t, we can write $t = nT_0 + t_0$, with $0 \le t_0 < T_0$, so that

$$\|\vartheta_t^\infty\| \le \tfrac{1}{2}\|\vartheta_{nT_0+t_0}^\infty\| \le 2^{-n}\|\vartheta_{t_0}^\infty\|.$$

Proposition 4.19 gives $\|\vartheta_{t_0}^\infty\| \le e^L\|\vartheta_0^\infty\|$, so that

$$\|\vartheta_t^\infty\| \le 2e^L\, 2^{-(n+1)}\|\vartheta_0^\infty\|,$$

where the right-hand side has been arranged to make use of the bound $t \le (n+1)T_0$, giving $2^{-(n+1)} \le \exp(-\log(2)t/T_0)$. We arrive at the bound in (iii) with $R = 2e^L$ and $\rho = \log(2)/T_0$. □

Proof of Proposition 4.22 Denote

$$\mathcal{E}(\theta) = \|\mathrm{f}(\theta) - \mathrm{f}_\infty(\theta)\|$$

so that by Lemma 4.23, with $s = \|\theta\|$,

$$\tfrac{1}{\|\theta\|}\mathcal{E}(\theta) = \|\mathrm{f}_s(\theta/s) - \mathrm{f}_\infty(\theta/s)\|.$$

Because the functions $\{\mathrm{f}_s : s \ge 1\}$ are uniformly Lipschitz continuous, and $\|\theta/s\| = 1$ by definition, the right-hand side converges to zero uniformly as $\|\theta\| \to \infty$. That is, $\mathcal{E}(\theta) = o(\|\theta\|)$.

Let's think about what this means: For any $\varepsilon > 0$, there exists $N(\varepsilon) < \infty$, such that $\mathcal{E}(\theta) \le \varepsilon\|\theta\|$ whenever $\|\theta\| \ge N(\varepsilon)$. From this, we get the simpler-looking bound:

$$\mathcal{E}(\theta) \le B_\varepsilon + \varepsilon\|\theta\|\,, \qquad \text{where } B_\varepsilon = \max\{\mathcal{E}(\theta) : \|\theta\| \le N(\varepsilon)\}. \tag{4.115}$$

For any initial condition ϑ_0, we compare two solutions based on this bound:

$$\vartheta_t = \vartheta_0 + \int_0^t \mathrm{f}(\vartheta_\tau)d\tau,$$
$$\vartheta_t^\infty = \vartheta_0 + \int_0^t \mathrm{f}_\infty(\vartheta_\tau^\infty)d\tau.$$

Write $z_t = \|\vartheta_t - \vartheta_t^\infty\|$ and use the preceding definition to obtain

$$z_t \le \int_0^t \|\mathrm{f}_\infty(\vartheta_\tau) - \mathrm{f}_\infty(\vartheta_\tau^\infty)\|\, d\tau + \int_0^t \mathcal{E}(\vartheta_\tau)d\tau \le L\int_0^t z_\tau\, d\tau + \int_0^t \mathcal{E}(\vartheta_\tau)d\tau.$$

Grönwall's Inequality in its second form (4.6c) holds, with $\beta_t \equiv L$, and α_t the second integral, giving

$$z_t \le e^{Lt} \int_0^t \mathcal{E}(\vartheta_\tau) d\tau \le e^{Lt} \int_0^t \{B_\varepsilon + \varepsilon \|\vartheta_\tau\|\} d\tau,$$

where the second inequality uses (4.115), with $\varepsilon > 0$ to be chosen. Proposition 4.19 gives $\|\vartheta_\tau\| \le \{B_f + \|\vartheta_0\|\} e^{L\tau}$, so that

$$\|\vartheta_t - \vartheta_t^\infty\| = z_t \le t e^{Lt} B_\varepsilon + \varepsilon e^{Lt} \{B_f + \|\vartheta_0\|\}\{L^{-1} e^{Lt}\}.$$

And applying the triangle inequality once more,

$$\|\vartheta_t\| \le \|\vartheta_t^\infty\| + \varepsilon L^{-1} e^{2Lt} \|\vartheta_0\| + B_{\varepsilon,t},$$

where the value $B_{\varepsilon,t}$ can be identified by rearranging terms. Finally we can bring in Lemma 4.23, which implies the existence of T_0 such that $\|\vartheta_t^\infty\| \le \frac{1}{2}\|\vartheta_0^\infty\| = \frac{1}{2}\|\vartheta_0\|$ when $t \ge T_0$. Hence,

$$\|\vartheta_{T_0}\| \le \left(\tfrac{1}{2} + \varepsilon L^{-1} e^{2LT_0}\right) \|\vartheta_0\| + B_{\varepsilon,T_0}.$$

Choose $\varepsilon > 0$ so small that the term in parentheses is no greater than $3/4$:

$$\|\vartheta_{T_0}\| \le \rho \|\vartheta_0\| + B_{\varepsilon,T_0}, \qquad \rho = 3/4.$$

Arguing as in the proof of Lemma 4.23, we can iterate to obtain for each integer n, and $t_0 \le T_0$,

$$\|\vartheta_{nT_0 + t_0}\| \le \rho^n \|\vartheta_{t_0}\| + \frac{1}{1-\rho} B_{\varepsilon,T_0} \le \rho^n \{B_f + \|\vartheta_0\|\} e^{LT_0} + \frac{1}{1-\rho} B_{\varepsilon,T_0}.$$

This establishes ultimate boundedness, and we can choose $S = \left\{\theta : \|\theta\| \le \frac{1}{1-\rho} B_{\varepsilon,T_0} + 1\right\}$.

□

4.9 Convergence Theory for QSA*

We consider in this section the general nonlinear ODE (4.44), subject to Assumptions (QSA1)–(QSA3) (introduced in Section 4.5.4). The proof of Theorem 4.15 is mainly a straightforward application of Grönwall's Inequality, as stated in Proposition 4.2. Stability theory for QSA follows closely the stability theory of ODEs surveyed in Section 4.8.

It is only when we come to convergence rates that we encounter mathematical challenges. These results also require further assumptions. First, a slight strengthening of (QSA2):

(QSA4) The vector field $\bar{f}$ is differentiable, with derivative denoted

$$A(\theta) = \partial_\theta \bar{f}(\theta). \tag{4.116}$$

That is, $A(\theta)$ is a $d \times d$ matrix for each $\theta \in \mathbb{R}^d$, with $A_{i,j}(\theta) = \dfrac{\partial}{\partial \theta_j} \bar{f}_i(\theta)$.

Moreover, the derivative A is Lipschitz continuous, and $A^* = A(\theta^*)$ is Hurwitz.

The matrix-valued function A is uniformly bounded over $\mathbb{R}^d$, subject to the global Lipschitz assumption on $\bar{f}$ imposed in (QSA2). The Hurwitz assumption implies that the ODE (4.42) is (locally) exponentially asymptotically stable.

The final assumption is a substantial strengthening of the ergodic limit (4.82):

(QSA5) The probing signal is the solution to (4.79), with Ω a compact subset of Euclidean space. It has a unique invariant measure μ on Ω, and satisfies the following for each initial condition $\xi_0 \in \Omega$:

(i) For each θ there exists a function $\hat{f}(\theta, \cdot)$ satisfying

$$\hat{f}(\theta,\xi_{t_0}) = \int_{t_0}^{t_1} [f(\theta,\xi_t) - \bar{f}(\theta)]\,dt + \hat{f}(\theta,\xi_{t_1}), \qquad \text{for all } 0 \le t_0 \le t_1 \tag{4.117}$$

$$\text{with} \quad \bar{f}(\theta) = \int_\Omega f(\theta,x)\,\mu(dx) \qquad \text{and} \qquad 0 = \int_\Omega \hat{f}(\theta,x)\,\mu(dx).$$

(ii) The function $\hat{f}$, and derivatives $\partial_\theta \bar{f}$ and $\partial_\theta f$ are C^1 and Lipschitz continuous in θ. In particular, $\hat{f}$ admits a derivative $\widehat{A}$ satisfying

$$\widehat{A}(\theta,\xi_{t_0}) = \int_{t_0}^{t_1} [A(\theta,\xi_t) - A(\theta)]\,dt + \widehat{A}(\theta,\xi_{t_1}), \qquad 0 \le t_0 \le t_1,$$

where $A(\theta,\xi) = \partial_\theta f(\theta,\xi)$ and $A(\theta) = \partial_\theta \bar{f}(\theta)$ was defined in (4.116). Lipschitz continuity is assumed uniform with respect to the exploration process: For $L_f < \infty$,

$$\begin{aligned}
\|\hat{f}(\theta',\xi) - \hat{f}(\theta,\xi)\| &\le L_f\|\theta' - \theta\|,\\
\|A(\theta',\xi) - A(\theta,\xi)\| &\le L_f\|\theta' - \theta\|,\\
\|\widehat{A}(\theta',\xi) - \widehat{A}(\theta,\xi)\| &\le L_f\|\theta' - \theta\|, \qquad \theta',\theta \in \mathbb{R}^d,\ \xi \in \Omega.
\end{aligned}$$

(iii) Denote $\Upsilon_t = [\widehat{A}(\theta^*,\xi_0) - \widehat{A}(\theta^*,\xi_t)]f(\theta^*,\xi_t)$. The following limit exists:

$$\overline{\Upsilon} \stackrel{\text{def}}{=} \lim_{T\to\infty} \frac{1}{T}\int_0^T \Upsilon_t\,dt = -\int_\Omega \widehat{A}(\theta^*,x)f(\theta^*,x)\,\mu(dx)$$

and the following partial integral is bounded in t:

$$\widetilde{\Upsilon}_t^I = \int_0^t [\widetilde{\Upsilon}_r - \overline{\Upsilon}]\,dr, \qquad \text{where} \quad \widetilde{\Upsilon}_t = \Upsilon_t - \overline{\Upsilon}. \tag{4.118}$$

Assumption (QSA5) (iii) is imposed because the vector $\overline{\Upsilon}$ arises in an approximation of the scaled error Z_t. This assumption is not much stronger than the others. In particular, the partial integral in (4.118) will be bounded if there is a bounded solution $\{\widehat{\Upsilon}_t\}$ to

$$\widehat{\Upsilon}_{t_0} = \int_{t_0}^{t_1} [\widetilde{\Upsilon}_t - \overline{\Upsilon}]\,dt + \widehat{\Upsilon}_{t_1}, \qquad \text{for all } 0 \le t_0 \le t_1.$$

The remainder of this section is organized into five subsections:

- ▲ The first subsection summarizes bounds on the rate of convergence for QSA – found in Theorems 4.24 and 4.25 – along with an overview of their proofs.
- ▲ Section 4.9.2 concerns bounds between (4.42) and the QSA ODE (4.44), which is the foundation for much of the remainder of this section.
- ▲ Criteria for ultimate boundedness for QSA are contained in Section 4.9.3.

▲ Section 4.9.4 contains theory to justify Assumption (QSA5).
▲ Section 4.9.5 contains proofs of the main results related to rates of convergence.

4.9.1 Main Results and Some Insights

The notation $\hat{f}$ in (4.117) is used to emphasize the parallels with Markov process and stochastic approximation theory: This is precisely the solution to *Poisson's equation* (with forcing function $\tilde{f}(\cdot) = f(\theta,\cdot) - \bar{f}(\cdot)$) that appears in theory of simulation of Markov processes, average-cost optimal control, and stochastic approximation [12, 39, 144, 250]. For the one-dimensional probing signal defined by the sawtooth function $\xi_t \stackrel{\text{def}}{=} t \pmod 1$, $t \geq 1$, a solution to Poisson's equation has a simple form:

$$\hat{g}(z) = -\int_0^z [g(x) - \bar{g}]\, dx + \hat{g}(0) \qquad z \in [0,1),$$
$$\text{where} \quad \bar{g} = \int_0^1 g(x)dx.$$

It will be useful to introduce new notation: For $\theta \in \mathbb{R}^d$ and $T \geq 0$,

$$\Xi^{\mathrm{I}}_T(\theta) = \int_0^T [f(\theta,\xi_t) - \bar{f}(\theta)]\, dt = \hat{f}(\theta,\xi_0) - \hat{f}(\theta,\xi_T), \tag{4.119}$$

where the second equality follows from (4.117). The special case $\theta = \theta^*$ deserves special notation:

$$\Xi^{\mathrm{I}}_T = \Xi^{\mathrm{I}}_T(\theta^*) = \int_0^T f(\theta^*,\xi_t)dt,$$

where the right-hand side is justified by the equilibrium condition $\bar{f}(\theta^*) = 0$.

Theorem 4.24 *Suppose that (QSA1)–(QSA5) hold, and the gain is* $a_t = 1/(1+t)^\rho$.

(i) $\rho < 1$. *The following hold:*

$$\begin{aligned} \Theta_t &= \theta^* + a_t Z_t + o(a_t), \\ Z_t &= \bar{Y} + \Xi^{\mathrm{I}}_t + o(1), \end{aligned} \tag{4.120a}$$

where

$$\bar{Y} = [A^*]^{-1}\Upsilon. \tag{4.120b}$$

(ii) $\rho = 1$. *If* $I + A^*$ *is Hurwitz, then the convergence rate is* $1/t$:

$$\begin{aligned} \Theta_t &= \theta^* + a_t Z_t + o(a_t), \\ Z_t &= \bar{Y} + \Xi^{\mathrm{I}}_t + o(1), \qquad \textit{with} \quad \bar{Y} = [I + A^*]^{-1}\Upsilon. \end{aligned} \tag{4.120c}$$

□

We turn next to PJR averaging (4.78). This is often presented as a two time-scale algorithm:

$$\frac{d}{dt}\Theta_t = a_t f(\Theta_t,\xi_t), \tag{4.121a}$$

$$\frac{d}{dt}\Theta^{\mathrm{PR}}_t = \frac{1}{1+t}[\Theta_t - \Theta^{\mathrm{PR}}_t]. \tag{4.121b}$$

What is crucial in this estimation technique is that the first gain is relatively large: $\lim_{t\to\infty}(1+t)a_t = \infty$. The solution to (4.121b) can be expressed as an approximate average:

$$\Theta_T^{\text{PR}} = \frac{1}{1+T}\Theta_0^{\text{PR}} + \frac{1}{1+T}\int_0^T \Theta_t\,dt\,, \qquad T \ge 0.$$

It may not make sense to average over the entire history, since this may include wild initial transients. This is why (4.78) is usually preferred, which is restated here: For $\kappa > 1$,

$$\Theta_T^{\text{PR}} = \frac{1}{T-T_0}\int_{T_0}^T \Theta_t\,dt\,, \qquad T \ge 0\,,\ T_0 = T - T/\kappa. \tag{4.121c}$$

The choice of T_0 is made so that $1/(T-T_0) = \kappa/T$. The set of equations (4.121) will be called Polyak–Ruppert averaging, but the theory that follows is restricted to (4.121c).

Theorem 4.25 *Suppose that the assumptions of Theorem 4.24 hold, so that in particular $a_t = 1/(1+t)^\rho$ with $\rho \in (\frac{1}{2},1)$. Then, with Θ_T^{PR} defined by* (4.121c), *with $\kappa > 1$, we have*

$$\Theta_T^{\text{PR}} = \theta^* + a_T c(\rho,\kappa)\bar{Y} + \Phi_T/T, \tag{4.122}$$

where $\bar{Y}$ is defined in (4.120b), *$c(\rho,\kappa) = \kappa[1-(1-1/\kappa)^{1-\rho}]/(1-\rho)$, and where $\{\Phi_t\}$ is a bounded function of time. Consequently, the convergence rate is $1/T$ if and only if $\bar{Y} = 0$.* □

Exercise 4.11 provides a simple example for which $\bar{Y} \neq 0$, and averaging might actually slow convergence. Exercise 4.12 contains a more positive message: When using qSGD #1, we might have $\bar{Y} \neq 0$, but its norm is of order ε (the scaling used in the algorithm).

Proof Outline

The first step is to explain why we can replace $\overline{\Theta}_t$ with θ^* in the definition (4.72) of the scaled error Z_t. Proposition 4.26 provides justification, and makes clear the enormous difference between the choice of $\rho = 1$ or $\rho < 1$ when using the gain $a_t = 1/(1+t)^\rho$:

Proposition 4.26 *Suppose that (QSA3) holds, and that $\bar{f}$ is C^1 with A^* Hurwitz. Fix $\varrho_0 > 0$ satisfying Real$(\lambda) < -\varrho_0$ for every eigenvalue λ for A^*. Then there exists $b > 0$, $B < \infty$ such that whenever $\|\vartheta_{\tau_0} - \theta^*\| \le b$, the solution $\{\vartheta_\tau : \tau \ge \tau_0\}$ of the ODE* (4.42) *satisfies*

$$\|\vartheta_\tau - \theta^*\| \le B\|\vartheta_{\tau_0} - \theta^*\|\exp(-\varrho_0[\tau - \tau_0])\,, \qquad \tau \ge \tau_0.$$

Consequently, the following hold for the solution to the ODE (4.71) *using the gain $a_t = 1/(1+t)^\rho$: If $\|\overline{\Theta}_{t_0} - \theta^*\| \le b$, then*

(i) *If $\rho = 1$ then $\|\overline{\Theta}_t - \theta^*\| \le B\|\vartheta_{\tau_0} - \theta^*\|[(1+t_0)/(1+t)]^{\varrho_0}$ for $t \ge t_0$.*
(ii) *Using any $0 < \rho < 1$,*

$$\|\overline{\Theta}_t - \theta^*\| \le \bar{B}_{t_0}\|\vartheta_{\tau_0} - \theta^*\|\exp\bigl(-\varrho_0(1-\rho)^{-1}(1+t)^{1-\rho}\bigr)\,, \qquad t \ge t_0, \tag{4.123}$$

where $\bar{B}_{t_0} = B\exp\bigl(\varrho_0(1-\rho)^{-1}(1+t_0)^{1-\rho}\bigr)$. □

A significant conclusion is that when $\rho < 1$, so that 4.123 holds, then

$$Z_t = \frac{1}{a_t}(\Theta_t - \theta^*) + \varepsilon_t^z, \tag{4.124}$$

with $\varepsilon_t^z = [\theta^* - \overline{\Theta}_t]/a_t$ vanishing *quickly* as $t \to \infty$.

Proposition 4.27 shows how the nonlinear ODE is naturally "linearized," provided it is convergent.

Proposition 4.27 *Suppose that (QSA1)–(QSA4) hold, and that solutions to* (4.44) *converge to θ^* for each initial condition. Then the scaled error admits the representation*

$$\frac{d}{dt} Z_t = \big[r_t I + a_t A(\overline{\Theta}_t)\big] Z_t + a_t \Delta_t + \widetilde{\Xi}_t \,, \qquad Z_{t_0} = 0, \tag{4.125a}$$

where $r_t = -\frac{d}{dt}\log(a_t)$, $\widetilde{\Xi}_t = f(\Theta_t, \xi_t) - \bar{f}(\Theta_t)$, and bounds on Δ_t are distinguished in the following cases: Setting $A^* = A(\theta^*)$,

(i) *With $a_t = 1/(1+t)$,*

$$\frac{d}{dt} Z_t = a_t \big[I + A^*\big] Z_t + a_t \Delta_t + \widetilde{\Xi}_t, \tag{4.125b}$$

where

$$\|\Delta_t\| = O\big(\frac{1}{a_t} \|\Theta_t - \overline{\Theta}_t\|^2\big) = o(\|Z_t\|). \tag{4.125c}$$

(ii) *For any $\rho \in (0,1)$, using the gain $a_t = 1/(1+t)^\rho$ gives*

$$\frac{d}{dt} Z_t = a_t A^* Z_t + a_t \Delta_t + \widetilde{\Xi}_t, \tag{4.125d}$$

where $\Delta_t = \Delta_t^{(\rho)} + (r_t/a_t) Z_t$, with

$$\|\Delta_t^{(\rho)}\| = O\Big(\frac{1}{a_t} \|\Theta_t - \overline{\Theta}_t\|^2\Big). \tag{4.125e}$$

Once again $\|\Delta_t\| = o(\|Z_t\|)$, since $r_t = \rho/(1+t)$ in this case.

Note that $r_t = -\frac{d}{dt}\log(a_t)$ is always nonnegative under (QSA1).

The challenge in applying Proposition 4.27 is that the "noise" process $\widetilde{\Xi}_t$ appearing in (4.125a) is nonvanishing, and is not scaled by a vanishing term. This is resolved through the change of variables: Denote for $t \geq 0$,

$$Y_t \stackrel{\text{def}}{=} Z_t - \Xi_t^{\text{I}}(\Theta_t), \tag{4.126}$$

where $\Xi_t^{\text{I}}(\Theta_t)$ is defined in (4.119). It is shown in Proposition 4.38 that Y_t solves the differential equation

$$\frac{d}{dt} Y_t = a_t \big[A^* Y_t + \Delta_t^Y - \Upsilon_t + A^* \Xi_t^{\text{I}}\big] + r_t [Y_t + \Xi_t^{\text{I}}],$$

where $\Xi_t^{\text{I}} = \Xi_t^{\text{I}}(\theta^*)$, and $\|\Delta_t^Y\| = o(1 + \|Y_t\|)$ as $t \to \infty$.

It will be shown that this implies convergence: $\lim_{t\to\infty} Y_t = \bar{Y}$. This leads easily to the proof of Theorem 4.24, from which Theorem 4.25 then follows – the details are established in the remainder of this section.

4.9.2 ODE Solidarity

The proof of Theorem 4.15 requires a precise ODE approximation, which is explained in this subsection. For this, we recall the "averaged" vector field introduced in (4.45):

$$\bar{f}(\theta) = \lim_{T\to\infty} \frac{1}{T}\int_0^T f(\theta,\xi_t)dt, \text{ for all } \theta \in \mathbb{R}^d. \tag{4.127}$$

The first step in the theory is to find assumptions to ensure that the limit exists. Following this, the solutions to the ODE (4.42) and the QSA ODE (4.44) are compared and shown to converge to the same limit provided both have bounded solutions.

Recall that the starting point in an ODE approximation is the temporal transformation (4.73). The time-scaled process is then defined by

$$\widehat{\Theta}_\tau \stackrel{\text{def}}{=} \Theta(s^{-1}(\tau)) = \Theta_t\Big|_{t=s^{-1}(\tau)}. \tag{4.128}$$

The chain rule of differentiation (and using $d\tau = a_t\, dt$) gives

$$\frac{d}{d\tau}\Theta(s^{-1}(\tau)) = f\big(\Theta(s^{-1}(\tau)),\xi(s^{-1}(\tau))\big).$$

That is, the time-scaled process solves the ODE:

$$\frac{d}{d\tau}\widehat{\Theta}_\tau = f\big(\Theta(s^{-1}(\tau)),\xi(s^{-1}(\tau))\big). \tag{4.129}$$

The two processes $\boldsymbol{\Theta}$ and $\widehat{\boldsymbol{\Theta}}$ differ only in time scale, and hence, proving convergence of one proves that of the other. In this subsection, we deal exclusively with $\widehat{\boldsymbol{\Theta}}$; it is on the "right" time scale for comparison with $\boldsymbol{\vartheta}$, the solution of (4.42).

Define ϑ^τ_w, $w \ge \tau$, to be the unique solution to (4.42) "starting" at $\widehat{\Theta}_\tau$:

$$\frac{d}{dw}\vartheta^\tau_w = \bar{f}(\vartheta^\tau_w),\ w \ge \tau,\ \vartheta^\tau_\tau = \widehat{\Theta}_\tau. \tag{4.130}$$

We have the following suggestive representations:

$$\begin{aligned} \widehat{\Theta}_{\tau+v} &= \widehat{\Theta}_\tau + \int_\tau^{\tau+v} f\big(\widehat{\Theta}_w,\xi(s^{-1}(w))\big)\, dw, \\ \vartheta^\tau_{\tau+v} &= \widehat{\Theta}_\tau + \int_\tau^{\tau+v} \bar{f}(\vartheta^\tau_w)dw, \qquad \tau,v \ge 0. \end{aligned} \tag{4.131}$$

Proposition 4.28 *Assume that $\widehat{\boldsymbol{\Theta}}$ is bounded. Then, for any $T > 0$,*

$$\lim_{\tau\to\infty} \sup_{v\in[0,T]} \Big\| \int_\tau^{\tau+v} \big[f\big(\widehat{\Theta}_w,\xi(s^{-1}(w))\big) - \bar{f}(\widehat{\Theta}_w)\big]\, dw \Big\| = 0, \tag{4.132a}$$

$$\lim_{\tau\to\infty} \sup_{v\in[0,T]} \|\widehat{\Theta}_{\tau+v} - \vartheta^\tau_{\tau+v}\| = 0. \tag{4.132b}$$

The proposition easily establishes Theorem 4.15:

Proof of Theorem 4.15 Under the assumptions of the theorem, there exists $b < \infty$ such that $\|\vartheta^{\tau}_{\tau}\| = \|\widehat{\Theta}_{\tau}\| \le b$, for $\tau \ge T_{\theta,z}$. By the definition of global asymptotic stability, for every $\varepsilon > 0$, there exists $\mathcal{T}_{\varepsilon} > 0$ such that

$$\|\vartheta^{\tau}_{\tau+v} - \theta^*\| < \varepsilon \quad \text{for all } v \ge \mathcal{T}_{\varepsilon}, \quad \text{whenever } \|\vartheta^{\tau}_{\tau}\| \le b.$$

Proposition 4.28 gives

$$\limsup_{\tau\to\infty} \|\widehat{\Theta}_{\tau+\mathcal{T}_{\varepsilon}} - \theta^*\| \le \limsup_{\tau\to\infty} \|\widehat{\Theta}_{\tau+\mathcal{T}_{\varepsilon}} - \vartheta^{\tau}_{\tau+\mathcal{T}_{\varepsilon}}\| + \limsup_{\tau\to\infty} \|\vartheta^{\tau}_{\tau+\mathcal{T}_{\varepsilon}} - \theta^*\| \le \varepsilon.$$

We obtain the desired limit, since $\varepsilon > 0$ is arbitrary. □

The following pages are devoted to the proof of Proposition 4.28. We begin with a crude bound, generalizing Proposition 4.19 to the QSA ODE. The proof of Proposition 4.19 extends to Lemma 4.29 with only notational changes.

Lemma 4.29 *Consider the ODE* (4.129), *subject to the Lipschitz condition in (QSA2). Then there is a constant B_f depending only on f such that*

$$\|\widehat{\Theta}_t - \widehat{\Theta}_0\| \le (B_f + L_f\|\widehat{\Theta}_0\|)te^{L_f t}, \qquad t \ge 0. \tag{4.133}$$

□

The next step is to obtain a version of (4.132a) with $\widehat{\Theta}_w$ frozen. The bound (4.134) in Lemma 4.30 is a strong version of the Law of Large Numbers (LLN) for the time-scaled process $\{\xi(s^{-1}(\tau))\}_{\tau\ge 0}$. Notice the difference with a conventional LLN. Here, the interval of integration is some arbitrary fixed T, and the averaging becomes more accurate as the interval is shifted toward infinity.

Lemma 4.30 *For any $T > 0$ and $\theta \in \mathbb{R}^d$,*

$$\Big\|\int_{\tau}^{\tau+T} [f(\theta,\xi(s^{-1}(w))) - \bar{f}(\theta)]\,dw\Big\| \le b_0(\theta)\varepsilon^f_{\tau}, \qquad \varepsilon^f_{\tau} \stackrel{\text{def}}{=} 3a_t\Big|_{t=s^{-1}(\tau)}, \tag{4.134}$$

where $b_0(\theta)$ is given in 4.82.

Proof With $\tilde{f}_w(\theta) = f(\theta,\xi_w) - \bar{f}(\theta)$ for each w and θ, denote $\mathcal{E}_t \stackrel{\text{def}}{=} \int_0^t \tilde{f}_w(\theta)dw$. By the assumed bound (4.82),

$$\|\mathcal{E}_t\| \le b_0(\theta), \qquad t \ge 0. \tag{4.135}$$

The following integral is simplified using integration by parts:

$$\int_{t_0}^{t_1} a_t\tilde{f}_t(\theta)dt = a_t\mathcal{E}_t\Big|_{t_0}^{t_1} - \int_{t_0}^{t_1} a_t'\mathcal{E}_t\,dt.$$

Taking the norm of each side gives, by the triangle inequality,

$$\Big\|\int_{t_0}^{t_1} a_t\tilde{f}_t(\theta)dt\Big\| \le a_{t_0}\|\mathcal{E}_{t_0}\| + a_{t_1}\|\mathcal{E}_{t_1}\| + \int_{t_0}^{t_1} |a_t'|\|\mathcal{E}_t\|\,dt.$$

Applying (4.135) gives

$$\left\| \int_{t_0}^{t_1} a_t \tilde{f}_t(\theta)dt \right\| \le 2a_{t_0} b_0(\theta) - b_0(\theta) \int_{t_0}^{t_1} a_t'\, dt \le 3a_{t_0} b_0(\theta),$$

where, in the first inequality, we have used the fact that a_t is nonincreasing, so that $|a_t'| = -a_t'$.

Letting $t_0 = s^{-1}(\tau)$, $t_1 = s^{-1}(\tau + T)$, $t = s^{-1}(w)$ (giving $dw = a_t dt$), yields by a change of variables in integration:

$$\left\| \int_{\tau}^{\tau+T} [f(\theta, \xi(s^{-1}(w))) - \bar{f}(\theta)]\, dw \right\| = \left\| \int_{t_0}^{t_1} a_t \tilde{f}_t(\theta)dt \right\| \le 3a_{t_0} b_0(\theta) = \varepsilon_\tau^f b_0(\theta). \quad \square$$

Proof of Proposition 4.28 The two parts of the proof establish the two limits in the proposition. Recall that these two limits are subject to the assumption that $\boldsymbol{\Theta}$ is bounded.

Proof of (4.132a) Denote

$$\mathcal{E}_{\tau+v}^{\tau} = \int_{\tau}^{\tau+v} [f(\widehat{\Theta}_w, \xi(s^{-1}(w))) - \bar{f}(\widehat{\Theta}_w)]\, dw.$$

To establish (4.132a), we must show that this converges to zero as $\tau \to \infty$, uniformly for v in bounded intervals.

Fix $\delta > 0$ and denote $\tau_k = \tau + k\delta$ for $k \ge 0$. As in the theory of Riemannian integration, the Lipschitz conditions in (QSA2) imply the following bound:

$$\mathcal{E}_{\tau+v}^{\tau} = \sum_{k=0}^{n_v - 1} \int_{\tau_k}^{\tau_k + \delta} [f(\widehat{\Theta}_{\tau_k}, \xi(s^{-1}(w))) - \bar{f}(\widehat{\Theta}_{\tau_k})]\, dw + \varepsilon_v^{\tau},$$

where n_v denotes the integer part of v/δ, and $\|\varepsilon_v^{\tau}\| \le b_L v\delta$ for some constant $b_L < \infty$. The bound is uniform in τ under the assumption that $\boldsymbol{\Theta}$ is bounded.

Lemma 4.30 and the triangle inequality imply the bound

$$\|\mathcal{E}_{\tau+v}^{\tau}\| \le \sum_{k=0}^{n_v-1} \varepsilon_{\tau_k}^f b_0(\widehat{\Theta}_{\tau_k}) + b_L v\delta \le \varepsilon_\tau^f \sum_{k=0}^{n_v-1} b_0(\widehat{\Theta}_{\tau_k}) + b_L v\delta.$$

Let $b_\bullet < \infty$ denote a constant satisfying $b_0(\widehat{\Theta}_\tau) \le b_\bullet$ for all τ. Then,

$$\|\mathcal{E}_{\tau+v}^{\tau}\| \le b_\bullet \frac{v}{\delta} \varepsilon_\tau^f + b_L v\delta.$$

Lemma 4.30 then implies that for any $T > 0$,

$$\limsup_{\tau \to \infty} \sup_{v \in [0,T]} \|\mathcal{E}_{\tau+v}^{\tau}\| \le b_L T\delta.$$

This completes the proof of (4.132a), since $\delta > 0$ was arbitrary.

Proof of (4.132b) The result is very similar to lemma 1 in chapter 2 of [65]. It is a refinement of Lemma 4.31, and its proof begins with the representation (4.137) for $\mathcal{E}_w^{\tau} = \vartheta_w^{\tau} - \widehat{\Theta}_w$, $w \ge \tau$.

The Lipschitz conditions in (QSA2) imply the bound:

$$\|\mathcal{E}^{\tau}_{\tau+v}\| \le \delta^{\tau} + L_f \int_{\tau}^{\tau+v} \|\mathcal{E}^{\tau}_{w}\| \, dw,$$

where

$$\delta^{\tau} \stackrel{\text{def}}{=} \sup_{\tau' \ge \tau} \max_{0 \le v \le T} \Big\| \int_{\tau'}^{\tau'+v} [\bar{f}(\widehat{\Theta}_w)) - f(\widehat{\Theta}_w, \xi(s^{-1}(w)))] \, dw \Big\|.$$

Proposition 4.2 then gives $\|\mathcal{E}^{\tau}_{\tau+v}\| \le e^{L_f} \delta^{\tau}$ for all τ, and all $0 \le v \le 1$. The error term δ^{τ} vanishes as $\tau \to \infty$ due to (4.132a). □

Local Solidarity

We conclude this subsection with a weak but general bound on the difference between $\widehat{\boldsymbol{\Theta}}$ and $\boldsymbol{\vartheta}^{\tau}$. The inequality does not require boundedness of solutions to the ODEs and is useful for small $T > 0$ to establish a Lyapunov drift condition for $\widehat{\boldsymbol{\Theta}}$.

Lemma 4.31 *For some $\bar{b} < \infty$ and any $0 < T \le 1$,*

$$\|\widehat{\Theta}_{\tau+T} - \vartheta^{\tau}_{\tau+T}\| \le e^{L_f} b_0(\widehat{\Theta}_{\tau}) \varepsilon^{f}_{\tau} + \bar{b}(1 + \|\widehat{\Theta}_{\tau}\|) T^2, \tag{4.136}$$

where $b_0(\theta)$ is given in (4.82), and L_f is the Lipschitz constant introduced in Assumption (QSA2).

Proof Denote $\mathcal{E}^{\tau}_{w} = \vartheta^{\tau}_{w} - \widehat{\Theta}_w$ for $w \ge \tau$. The pair of identities (4.131) give

$$\mathcal{E}^{\tau}_{\tau+T} = \int_{\tau}^{\tau+T} [\bar{f}(\widehat{\Theta}_w) - f(\widehat{\Theta}_w, \xi(s^{-1}(w)))] \, dw + \int_{\tau}^{\tau+T} [\bar{f}(\vartheta^{\tau}_{w}) - \bar{f}(\widehat{\Theta}_w)] \, dw \,, \ \tau, T \ge 0. \tag{4.137}$$

The Lipschitz conditions in (QSA2) are used to bound the integrands:

$$\begin{aligned}
&\|\bar{f}(\widehat{\Theta}_w)) - \bar{f}(\widehat{\Theta}_{\tau}))\| \le L_f \|\widehat{\Theta}_w - \widehat{\Theta}_{\tau}\|, \\
&\|f(\widehat{\Theta}_w, \xi(s^{-1}(w))) - f(\widehat{\Theta}_{\tau}, \xi(s^{-1}(w)))\| \le L_f \|\widehat{\Theta}_w - \widehat{\Theta}_{\tau}\|, \\
&\|\bar{f}(\vartheta^{\tau}_{w}) - \bar{f}(\widehat{\Theta}_w)\| \le \|\mathcal{E}^{\tau}_{w}\|.
\end{aligned}$$

Consequently, for any $T \ge 0$,

$$\begin{aligned}
\|\mathcal{E}^{\tau}_{\tau+T}\| &\le \Big\| \int_{\tau}^{\tau+T} [\bar{f}(\widehat{\Theta}_{\tau})) - f(\widehat{\Theta}_{\tau}, \xi(s^{-1}(w)))] \, dw \Big\| \\
&\quad + 2L_f \int_{\tau}^{\tau+T} \|\widehat{\Theta}_w - \widehat{\Theta}_{\tau}\| \, dw + L_f \int_{\tau}^{\tau+T} \|\mathcal{E}^{\tau}_{w}\| \, dw \\
&\le \alpha^{\tau}_{T} + L_f \int_{\tau}^{\tau+T} \|\mathcal{E}^{\tau}_{w}\| \, dw \,, \qquad \alpha^{\tau}_{T} \stackrel{\text{def}}{=} b_0(\widehat{\Theta}_{\tau}) \varepsilon^{f}_{\tau} + 2L_f \int_0^T \|\widehat{\Theta}_{\tau+w} - \widehat{\Theta}_{\tau}\| \, dw.
\end{aligned}$$

Hence by Grönwall's lemma, in the form (4.6c),

$$\|\mathcal{E}^{\tau}_{\tau+T}\| \le \alpha^{\tau}_{T} e^{L_f T}.$$

Using the same proof to derive (4.108b) via Grönwall's lemma, we have

$$\|\widehat{\Theta}_{\tau+w} - \widehat{\Theta}_{\tau}\| \le (B_f + L_f \|\widehat{\Theta}_{\tau}\|) w e^{L_f w}.$$

Increasing $e^{L_f w}$ to $e^{L_f T}$ for the range of integration gives

$$2\int_0^T \|\widehat{\Theta}_{\tau+w} - \widehat{\Theta}_\tau\| \, dw \le 2(B_f + L_f\|\widehat{\Theta}_\tau\|)e^{L_f T}\int_0^T w\, dw = (B_f + L_f\|\widehat{\Theta}_\tau\|)T^2 e^{L_f T}.$$

Hence

$$\alpha_T^\tau \le b_0(\widehat{\Theta}_\tau)\varepsilon_\tau^f + L_f(B_f + L_f\|\widehat{\Theta}_\tau\|)T^2 e^{L_f T},$$

which completes the proof, since $0 \le T \le 1$ by assumption. □

4.9.3 Criteria for Stability

The first step in establishing convergence of QSA is to show that the solutions are bounded in time. Two approaches can be borrowed from the dynamical systems literature: Lyapunov function techniques, or the ODE at ∞ introduced in Section 4.8.4.

Lyapunov Criterion and (QSV1)

There exists a continuous function $V\colon \mathbb{R}^d \to \mathbb{R}_+$ and constants $c_0 > 0$, $\delta_0 > 0$ such that, for any initial condition ϑ_0 of (4.42), and any $0 \le T \le 1$, the following bounds hold whenever $\|\vartheta_s\| > c_0$:

$$V(\vartheta_{s+T}) - V(\vartheta_s) \le -\delta_0 \int_0^T \|\vartheta_t\| \, dt.$$

The Lyapunov function is Lipschitz continuous: There exists a constant $L_V < \infty$ such that $\|V(\theta') - V(\theta)\| \le L_V\|\theta' - \theta\|$ for all θ, θ'.

Assumption (QSV1) ensures that $V(\vartheta_t)$ is strictly decreasing whenever ϑ_t escapes a ball of radius c_0. If V is differentiable, then this assumption implies

$$\frac{d}{dt}V(\vartheta_t) \le -\delta_0\|\vartheta_t\|, \quad \text{whenever } \|\vartheta_t\| > c_0.$$

The integral form is chosen since sometimes it is easier to establish a bound in this form. In particular, the proof of Proposition 4.34 is based on the construction of a solution to (QSV1).

Verifying (QSV1) for a Linear System

Consider the ODE (4.42), in which $\bar{f}(x) = Ax$ with A a Hurwitz $d \times d$ matrix. There is a quadratic function $V_2(x) = x^\intercal M x$ with $M \in \mathbb{R}^{d\times d}$ satisfying the Lyapunov equation $MA + A^\intercal M = -I$, with $M > 0$. Consequently, solutions to (4.42) satisfy

$$\frac{d}{dt}V_2(\vartheta_t) = -\|\vartheta_t\|^2.$$

Choose $V = \sqrt{V_2}$, so that by the chain rule

$$\frac{d}{dt}V(\vartheta_t) = -\frac{1}{2}\frac{1}{\sqrt{V_2(\vartheta_t)}}\|\vartheta_t\|^2 \le -\frac{1}{2\sqrt{\lambda_{\max}}}\|\vartheta_t\|,$$

where $\lambda_{\max}$ is the largest eigenvalue of M. This V is a Lipschitz solution to (QSV1), for any $c_0 > 0$. □

We first establish ultimate boundedness under a variant of (QSV1):

Lemma 4.32 *The solution to* (4.129) *is ultimately bounded if, for some* $T > 0$, $0 < \delta_1 < 1$, *and* $\uptau_0, b < \infty$,

$$V(\widehat{\Theta}_{\uptau+T}) - V(\widehat{\Theta}_\uptau) \le -\delta_1 \|\widehat{\Theta}_\uptau\|,$$

for all $\uptau \ge \uptau_0$, $\|\widehat{\Theta}_\uptau\| > b$. □

Proof For each initial condition $\widehat{\Theta}_0 = \theta$ and $\uptau \ge \uptau_0$, denote

$$\tau = \tau(\theta,\uptau) \stackrel{\text{def}}{=} \min(v \ge 0 : \|\widehat{\Theta}_{\uptau+v}\| \le b),$$

where $\uptau_0$ and b are defined in the lemma. If $\|\widehat{\Theta}_\uptau\| \le b$, then $\tau = 0$, and if $\|\widehat{\Theta}_{\uptau+v}\| > b$ for all $v \ge 0$, set $\tau = \infty$. For $m \in \mathbb{Z}_+$, define $\tau_m = \min\{\tau, m\}$. Then,

$$\begin{aligned}
-\tau_m b\delta_1 &\ge -\delta_1 \int_\uptau^{\uptau+\tau_m} \|\widehat{\Theta}_w\|\, dw \\
&\ge \int_\uptau^{\uptau+\tau_m} (V(\widehat{\Theta}_{w+T}) - V(\widehat{\Theta}_w))dw \\
&= \int_{\uptau+\tau_m}^{\uptau+\tau_m+T} V(\widehat{\Theta}_w)dw - \int_\uptau^{\uptau+T} V(\widehat{\Theta}_w)dw \\
&\ge -\int_\uptau^{\uptau+T} V(\widehat{\Theta}_w)dw.
\end{aligned}$$

The right-hand side is independent of m, which establishes the upper bound

$$\tau \le \frac{1}{b\delta_1}\int_\uptau^{\uptau+T} V(\widehat{\Theta}_w)dw.$$

Under the Lipschitz assumption on V, Proposition 4.19 can be applied to establish that for some finite constant b_V,

$$\tau \le b_V(1 + \|\widehat{\Theta}_\uptau\|).$$

Hence $\tau(\theta,\uptau)$ is everywhere finite.

Denote $b_1 = \sup\{\|\widehat{\Theta}_{\uptau+v}\| : \uptau \ge \uptau_0,\ v \le \tau(\theta,\uptau), \|\widehat{\Theta}_\uptau\| \le b+1\}$. That is, b_1 bounds the maximum norm of any excursion of $\boldsymbol{\Theta}$ that begins at time $\uptau$ if $\widehat{\Theta}_\uptau \in S = \{\theta : \|\theta\| \le b+1\}$, and ends at the arrival time to the set $S_0 = \{\theta : \|\theta\| \le b\}$, denoted $\uptau + \tau(\theta,\uptau)$. Since every trajectory enters $S_0 \subset S$ for some time $\uptau \ge \uptau_0$, it follows that $\|\widehat{\Theta}_\uptau\| \le b_1$ for all $\uptau$ sufficiently large. □

Proposition 4.33 *Under (QSV1), the solution to* (4.129) *is ultimately bounded: there exists* $b < \infty$ *such that for any* $\widehat{\Theta}_0 = \widehat{\Theta}$, $\limsup_{\uptau\to\infty} \|\widehat{\Theta}_\uptau\| \le b$.

Proof Recall that V is the Lyapunov function and $c_0 > 0$ is the constant introduced in (QSV1). For $0 \le T \le 1$, $\|\widehat{\Theta}_\uptau\| \ge c_0 + 1$,

$$\begin{aligned}
V(\widehat{\Theta}_{\uptau+T}) - V(\widehat{\Theta}_\uptau) &= V(\widehat{\Theta}_{\uptau+T}) - V(\vartheta^\uptau_{\uptau+T}) + V(\vartheta^\uptau_{\uptau+T}) - V(\vartheta^\uptau_\uptau) \\
&\le |V(\widehat{\Theta}_{\uptau+T}) - V(\vartheta^\uptau_{\uptau+T})| + V(\vartheta^\uptau_{\uptau+T}) - V(\vartheta^\uptau_\uptau) \\
&\le L_f\|\widehat{\Theta}_{\uptau+T} - \vartheta^\uptau_{\uptau+T}\| - \delta_0 T\|\widehat{\Theta}_\uptau\| \\
&\le \{e^{L_f} b_0(\widehat{\Theta}_\uptau)\varepsilon^f_\uptau + \bar{b}(1 + \|\widehat{\Theta}_\uptau\|)T^2\} - \delta_0 T\|\widehat{\Theta}_\uptau\|,
\end{aligned}$$

where the second inequality follows from the Lipschitz assumption on V and the last inequality uses Lemma 4.31. Recall that b_0 is Lipschitz continuous, and $\varepsilon_\tau^f = o(1)$. It follows that we can choose $T > 0$ sufficiently small and τ_0 sufficiently large so that

$$V(\widehat{\Theta}_{\tau+T}) - V(\widehat{\Theta}_\tau) \le -\tfrac{1}{2}\delta_0 T\|\widehat{\Theta}_\tau\|, \qquad \tau \ge \tau_0 \quad \|\widehat{\Theta}_\tau\| \ge c_0 + 1 .$$

Lemma 4.32 completes the proof. □

ODE@∞

When extending the techniques of Section 4.8.4, we require the vector field at ∞ associated with the average vector field:

$$\bar{f}_\infty(\theta) \stackrel{\text{def}}{=} \lim_{r\to\infty} r^{-1}\bar{f}(r\theta), \qquad \theta \in \mathbb{R}^d. \tag{4.138}$$

Proposition 4.34 *Suppose that the following hold:*

(i) *The limit* (4.138) *exists for all* θ *to define a continuous function* $\bar{f}_\infty \colon \mathbb{R}^d \to \mathbb{R}^d$.
(ii) *The origin is globally asymptotically stable for the ODE at* ∞:

$$\frac{d}{dt}\vartheta_t^\infty = \bar{f}_\infty(\vartheta_t^\infty), \qquad \theta \in \mathbb{R}^d. \tag{4.139}$$

Then there is a Lipschitz continuous function V *that satisfies (QSV1).*

The main step in the proof of Proposition 4.34 is to show that the assumptions of the theorem imply that the ODE (4.42) is ultimately bounded. Lemma 4.23 is repeated here in the new notation for convenience:

Lemma 4.35 *Suppose that (QSA2) holds, and the limit* (4.138) *exists for all* θ *to define a continuous function* $\bar{f}_\infty \colon \mathbb{R}^d \to \mathbb{R}^d$. *Suppose moreover that the origin is asymptotically stable for* (4.139). *Then the following hold:*

(i) $\bar{f}_\infty(s\theta) = s\bar{f}_\infty(\theta)$ *for each* $\theta \in \mathbb{R}^d$ *and* $s \ge 0$.
(ii) *If* $\{\vartheta_t^\infty : t \ge 0\}$ *is any solution to the ODE* (4.139), *and* $s > 0$, *then* $\{y_t = s\vartheta_t^\infty : t \ge 0\}$ *is also a solution, starting from* $y_0 = s\vartheta_0^\infty \in \mathbb{R}^d$.
(iii) *The origin is* globally *asymptotically stable for* (4.139), *and convergence to the origin is exponentially fast: For some* $R < \infty$ *and* $\rho > 0$,

$$\|\vartheta_t^\infty\| \le \mathrm{R}e^{-\rho t}\|\vartheta_0^\infty\|, \qquad \vartheta_0^\infty \in \mathbb{R}^d.$$ □

The following is essentially one step in the proof of Proposition 4.22.

Lemma 4.36 *Under the assumptions of Lemma 4.35, for each* $T < \infty$ *and* $\varepsilon \in (0,1]$, *there exists* $K_T < \infty$ *independent of* ε, *and* $B_T(\varepsilon) < \infty$ *such that for all solutions to* (4.42) *and* (4.139) *from common initial condition* ϑ_0,

$$\|\vartheta_t - \vartheta_t^\infty\| \le B_T(\varepsilon) + K_T[1 + \|\vartheta_0\|]\varepsilon.$$ □

Proof of Proposition 4.34 Choose $T > 0$ so that $\|\vartheta_t^\infty\| \le \frac{1}{2}\|\theta\|$ when $t \ge T$, for any solution to (4.139), from any initial condition $\vartheta_0^\infty = \theta$. We then define

$$V^\infty(\theta) = \int_0^T \|\vartheta_t^\infty\|\, dt\,, \qquad \vartheta_0^\infty = \theta,$$

$$V(\theta) = \int_0^T V^\infty(\vartheta_t) dt\,, \qquad \vartheta_0 = \theta.$$

The Grönwall Inequality implies that each is a Lipschitz continuous function of θ. Moreover, applying Lemma 4.35 it follows that the first is radially homogeneous, $V^\infty(s\theta) = sV^\infty(\theta)$ for each θ and $s > 0$, and satisfies the lower bound for some $\delta > 0$:

$$V^\infty(\theta) \ge \delta\|\theta\|.$$

Consequently, this is a Lyapunov function for the ODE@∞: For each initial condition $\vartheta_0^\infty = \theta$,

$$V^\infty(\vartheta_T^\infty) = \int_0^T \|\vartheta_{t+T}^\infty\|\, dt \le \tfrac{1}{2}V^\infty(\theta) \le V^\infty(\theta) - \tfrac{1}{2}\delta\|\theta\|.$$

The next step is to show that a similar bound holds with ϑ_T^∞ replaced by ϑ_T. Let L_V denote the Lipschitz constant for V^∞. The preceding bound combined with Lemma 4.36 gives

$$V^\infty(\vartheta_T) \le V^\infty(\theta) - \tfrac{1}{2}\delta\|\theta\| + L_V\Big(B_T(\varepsilon) + K_T[1 + \|\theta\|]\varepsilon\Big).$$

Fix $\varepsilon \in (0,1)$ so that

$$L_V K_T \varepsilon \le \delta/4,$$

giving

$$V^\infty(\vartheta_T) \le V^\infty(\theta) - \tfrac{1}{4}\delta\|\theta\| + K'_V$$

with $K'_V = L_V(B_T(\varepsilon) + K_T)$.

To complete the proof, write

$$V(\vartheta_s) = \int_s^T V^\infty(\vartheta_t) dt + \int_0^s V^\infty(\vartheta_{T+t})\, dt.$$

The preceding bound gives

$$V^\infty(\vartheta_{T+t}) \le V^\infty(\vartheta_t) - \tfrac{1}{4}\delta\|\vartheta_t\| + K'_V$$

so that

$$V(\vartheta_s) \le V(\vartheta_0) - \tfrac{1}{4}\delta \int_0^s \|\vartheta_t\|\, dt + sK'_V.$$

This bound implies (QSV1). □

4.9.4 Deterministic Markovian Model

The goal here is to understand Assumption (QSA5) in a simple setting. For this, we suppress the variable θ in the function $\hat{f}(\theta,\xi)$ appearing in (4.117), and adopt the new notation:

$$\hat{g}(\xi_{t_0}) = \int_{t_0}^{t_1} [g(\xi_t) - \bar{g}]\, dt + \hat{g}(\xi_{t_1}), \qquad 0 \le t_0 \le t_1. \tag{4.140}$$

We are essentially fixing a single index i and parameter θ, and setting $g(\xi_t) \stackrel{\text{def}}{=} f_i(\theta,\xi_t)$.

This is a version of *Poisson's equation* – see Section 4.9.1 for further discussion. The function $\hat{g}$ is the solution (known as the relative value function in some applications), g is the *forcing function*, and $\bar{g}$ its steady-state mean. Lemma 4.37 concerns the special case (4.80) for which H is a linear function of $z \in \mathbb{C}^K$.

Lemma 4.37 *Suppose that $g\colon \mathbb{C}^K \to \mathbb{R}$ admits the Taylor series representation,*

$$g(z) = \sum_{n_1,\dots,n_K} a_{n_1,\dots,n_K} z_1^{n_1} \cdots z_K^{n_K}, \qquad z \in \Omega, \tag{4.141}$$

where the sum is over all K-length sequences in $\mathbb{Z}_+^K$, and the coefficients $\{a_{n_1,\dots,n_K}\} \subset \mathbb{C}^K$ are absolutely summable:

$$\sum_{n_1,\dots,n_K} |a_{n_1,\dots,n_K}| < \infty. \tag{4.142}$$

Then, with ξ defined in (4.80),

(i) *The ergodic limit holds:*

$$\bar{g} = \lim_{T\to\infty} \frac{1}{T}\int_0^T g(\xi_t)dt = \int_0^1 \cdots \int_0^1 g\big(e^{2\pi j t_1},\dots,e^{2\pi j t_K}\big)\, dt_1 \cdots dt_K,$$

where $\bar{g} = a_0$ (the coefficient when $n_i = 0$ for each i).

(ii) *There exists a solution $\hat{g}\colon \mathbb{C}^K \to \mathbb{R}$ to* (4.140). *It is of the form* (4.141)*:*

$$\hat{g}(x) = \sum_{n_1,\dots,n_K} \hat{a}_{n_1,\dots,n_K} x_1^{n_1} \cdots x_K^{n_K}, \tag{4.143}$$

in which $|\hat{a}_{n_1,\dots,n_K}| \le |a_{n_1,\dots,n_K}|/\omega_1$ for each coefficient.

Proof Complex exponentials are used to obtain the following simple formula:

$$g(\xi_t) = \sum_{n_1,\dots,n_K} a_{n_1,\dots,n_K} \exp\big(\{n_1\omega_1 + \cdots + n_K\omega_K\}jt\big).$$

The absolute-summability assumption (4.142) justifies Fubini's theorem:

$$\begin{aligned}\int_{t_0}^{t_1} [g(\xi_t) - \bar{g}]\, dt &= \sum_{n_1,\dots,n_K} a_{n_1,\dots,n_K} \int_{t_0}^{t_1} \exp\big(\{n_1\omega_1 + \cdots + n_K\omega_K\}jt\big)\, dt \\ &= \hat{g}(\xi_{t_0}) - \hat{g}(\xi_{t_1}),\end{aligned}$$

where $\hat{g}$ is given by (4.143) with $\hat{a}_0 = 0$ (that is, $n_k = 0$ for each k), and for all other coefficients, $\hat{a}_{n_1,\dots,n_K} = a_{n_1,\dots,n_K}\{n_1\omega_1 + \cdots + n_K\omega_K\}^{-1}j$. □

The lemma then justifies (QSA5) provided $f_i(\theta,\cdot)$ satisfies the Taylor series bound for each i and θ, along with the derivatives $\frac{\partial}{\partial\theta_j} f_i(\theta,\cdot)$, for each i,j. While an explicit formula for $\hat{f}$ is not required in any algorithm, bounds may be valuable in finer convergence rate analysis of QSA ODEs. In particular, the approximation of the scaled error $Z_t \stackrel{\text{def}}{=} \frac{1}{a_t}(\Theta_t - \overline{\Theta}_t)$ obtained in Theorem 4.24 depends on $\hat{f}(\theta^*, \xi_t)$.

4.9.5 Convergence Rates

We begin with a proof of Proposition 4.27. Recall from Lemma 4.14 the identity $\overline{\Theta}_t = \vartheta_\tau$ for $t \ge t_0$ and $\tau \stackrel{\text{def}}{=} s_t \ge \tau_0$.

Proof of Proposition 4.27 Taking derivatives of each side of (4.72) gives, by the product rule,

$$\begin{aligned}\frac{d}{dt} Z_t &= \frac{d}{dt}\Big(\frac{1}{a_t}(\Theta_t - \overline{\Theta}_t)\Big) \\ &= \Big(-\frac{1}{a_t^2}\frac{d}{dt}a_t\Big)(\Theta_t - \overline{\Theta}_t) + f(\Theta_t, \xi_t) - \bar{f}(\overline{\Theta}_t) \\ &= r_t Z_t + f(\Theta_t, \xi_t) - \bar{f}(\overline{\Theta}_t),\end{aligned}$$

where in the final equation we used the chain rule for the derivative of a logarithm (recall that $r_t = -\frac{d}{dt}\log(a_t)$) and the definition of Z_t.

On adding and subtracting $\bar{f}(\Theta_t)$, we arrive at a suggestive decomposition:

$$\frac{d}{dt} Z_t = r_t Z_t + \underbrace{\big[\bar{f}(\Theta_t) - \bar{f}(\overline{\Theta}_t)\big]}_{R_t\text{: almost linear}} + \underbrace{\big[f(\Theta_t, \xi_t) - \bar{f}(\Theta_t)\big]}_{\widetilde{\Xi}_t\text{: bounded disturbance}}.$$

That is, under the assumptions of Proposition 4.27,

$$R_t = A(\overline{\Theta}_t)\big[\Theta_t - \overline{\Theta}_t\big] + \varepsilon_t^1,$$

where, under the Lipschitz condition on $A = \partial_\theta \bar{f}$,

$$\|\varepsilon_t^1\| = O(\|\Theta_t - \overline{\Theta}_t\|^2) = o(a_t\|Z_t\|).$$

This completes the proof of (4.125a), with $\Delta_t = \varepsilon_t^1/a_t$.

If $a_t = 1/(1+t)$, we obtain $r_t = 1/(1+t) = a_t$. Equation (4.125a) thus implies the approximation (4.125b), where the definition of $\|\Delta_t\|$ is modified to include the error from replacing $A(\overline{\Theta}_t)$ with its limit $A^* = A(\theta^*)$.

Consider next the "larger gain" $a_t = 1/(1+t)^\rho$, with $\rho \in (0,1)$, so that $r_t = \rho/(1+t)$. The simpler approximation (4.125d) follows, in which $\|\Delta_t\|$ has an additional term: once again, we replace $A(\overline{\Theta}_t)$ with its limit A^*, and also use the approximation $r_t = O(1/t)$. □

Recall the change of variables: $Y_t \stackrel{\text{def}}{=} Z_t - \Xi_t^{\text{I}}(\Theta_t)$ was introduced as a means to remove the nonvanishing noise $\widetilde{\Xi}_t$ in (4.125a). Proposition 4.38 establishes a differential equation for $\boldsymbol{Y}$, similar to the QSA ODE (4.44).

The ratio r_t/a_t is bounded in t for the standard choice $a_t = g/(1+t)^\rho$ (recall from the definition in Proposition 4.27).

Proposition 4.38 *Under the assumptions of Theorem 4.24, suppose that $r_t/a_t \le b$ for a constant b, and all $t \ge 0$. Then, the vector-valued process $\mathbf{Y}$ satisfies the differential equation,*

$$\frac{d}{dt}Y_t = a_t\left[A^*Y_t + \Delta_t^Y - \Upsilon_t + A^*\Xi_t^{\mathrm{I}}\right] + r_t[Y_t + \Xi_t^{\mathrm{I}}], \tag{4.144}$$

where $\Xi_t^{\mathrm{I}} = \Xi_t^{\mathrm{I}}(\theta^*)$, and $\|\Delta_t^Y\| = o(1+\|Y_t\|)$ as $t\to\infty$. That is, for scalars $\{\varepsilon_t^Y\}$,

$$\|\Delta_t\| \le \varepsilon_t^Y\{1+\|Y_t\|\}, \qquad t \ge t_0,$$

with $\varepsilon_t^Y \to 0$ as $t\to\infty$.

Proof Using the chain rule, we have

$$\begin{aligned}\frac{d}{dt}\{\Xi_t^{\mathrm{I}}(\Theta_t)\} &= \{f(\Theta_t,\xi_t) - \bar{f}(\Theta_t)\} + \partial_\theta\Xi_t^{\mathrm{I}}(\Theta_t)\cdot\{\frac{d}{dt}\Theta_t\} \\ &= \widetilde{\Xi}_t + \partial_\theta\Xi_t^{\mathrm{I}}(\Theta_t)\cdot\{a_t f(\Theta_t,\xi_t)\},\end{aligned}$$

where the second equation follows from the definition $\widetilde{\Xi}_t \stackrel{\text{def}}{=} f(\Theta_t,\xi_t) - \bar{f}(\Theta_t)$, and the dynamics (4.44). Rearranging terms, we obtain

$$\widetilde{\Xi}_t = \frac{d}{dt}\{\Xi_t^{\mathrm{I}}(\Theta_t)\} - a_t\Upsilon_t(\Theta_t), \tag{4.145}$$

where $\Upsilon_t(\Theta_t) = \partial_\theta\Xi_t^{\mathrm{I}}(\Theta_t)\cdot f(\Theta_t,\xi_t)$.

The following is then obtained on substitution into (4.125a):

$$\tfrac{d}{dt}Y_t = a_t\left[A(\overline{\Theta}_t)Y_t + \Delta_t - \Upsilon_t(\Theta_t) + A(\overline{\Theta}_t)\Xi_t^{\mathrm{I}}(\Theta_t)\right] + r_t[Y_t + \Xi_t^{\mathrm{I}}(\Theta_t)].$$

To go from this ODE to (4.144), we must bound the error:

$$\begin{aligned}\Delta_t^Y &\stackrel{\text{def}}{=} \Delta_t^{\mathrm{a}} + \Delta_t^{\mathrm{b}}, \\ \text{where}\quad \Delta_t^{\mathrm{a}} &= \Delta_t + \left[A(\overline{\Theta}_t) - A^*\right](Y_t + \Xi_t^{\mathrm{I}}), \\ \Delta_t^{\mathrm{b}} &= A(\overline{\Theta}_t)(\Xi_t^{\mathrm{I}}(\Theta_t) - \Xi_t^{\mathrm{I}}) - (\Upsilon_t(\Theta_t) - \Upsilon_t) + \frac{r_t}{a_t}(\Xi_t^{\mathrm{I}}(\Theta_t) - \Xi_t^{\mathrm{I}}).\end{aligned}$$

We have $\|\Delta_t\| = o(1+\|Y_t\|)$ because of the prior assertion that $\|\Delta_t\| = o(\|Z_t\|)$ as $t\to\infty$, and the assumption that $\Xi_t^{\mathrm{I}}(\Theta_t)$ is bounded in t (recall (4.117) and (4.119)). Proposition 4.26 combined with Lipschitz continuity of A then implies that $\|\Delta_t^{\mathrm{a}}\| = o(1+\|Y_t\|)$.

To complete the proof, we must bound the error in replacing Θ_t with θ^* in each appearance in Δ_t^{b}. The representation (4.119) combined with (QSA5) implies that for a constant L,

$$\|A(\overline{\Theta}_t) - A^*\| \le L\|\overline{\Theta}_t - \theta^*\| \quad\text{and}\quad \|\Xi_t^{\mathrm{I}}(\Theta_t) - \Xi_t^{\mathrm{I}}\| \le L\|\Theta_t - \theta^*\|, \qquad t \ge 0,$$

and hence both error terms are vanishing, and also $\|\Upsilon_t(\Theta_t) - \Upsilon_t\| = o(1)$ by Lipschitz continuity of $\partial_\theta\Xi_t^{\mathrm{I}}(\theta)$: From (4.119) and (QSA5):

$$\partial_\theta\Xi_t^{\mathrm{I}}(\theta) = \widehat{A}(\theta,\xi_0) - \widehat{A}(\theta,\xi_t).$$

These bounds show that $\|\Delta_t^{\mathrm{b}}\| = o(1)$. □

Proof of Theorem 4.24 First rewrite (4.144) as

$$\frac{d}{dt}Y_t = a_t\Big[(A^* + \frac{r_t}{a_t}I)Y_t + \Delta_t^Y - \Upsilon_t + (A^* + \frac{r_t}{a_t}I)\Xi_t^{\rm I}\Big],$$

where $r_t/a_t = o(1)$ for $\rho < 1$, and $r_t/a_t \equiv 1$ if $\rho = 1$. The preceding can be regarded as a linear QSA ODE with vanishing disturbance. Let $\kappa(\rho) = \mathbb{1}\{\rho = 1\}$ (equal to zero for $\rho < 1$, and $\kappa(1) = 1$). Under the condition that $A^* + \kappa(\rho)I$ is Hurwitz, the proof of Theorem 4.15 can be used with no significant changes to establish convergence:

$$\bar{Y} = \lim_{t\to\infty} Y_t = \lim_{T\to\infty}\frac{1}{T}\int_0^T \big[\Xi_t^{\rm I} + [A^* + \kappa(\rho)I]^{-1}\partial_\theta \Xi_t^{\rm I}\cdot f(\theta^*,\xi_t)\big]\,dt = [A^* + \kappa(\rho)I]^{-1}\overline{\Upsilon},$$

where the second equality holds because $\lim_{T\to\infty}\frac{1}{T}\int_0^T \Xi_t^{\rm I}\,dt = 0$ under (4.119), and from the definition of $\overline{\Upsilon}$ in (QSA5). This gives the coupling result $Z_t = \bar{Y} + \Xi_t^{\rm I} + o(1)$.

The second approximation in (4.120a) follows from the first: Applying the definition (4.72) gives

$$\Theta_t = \overline{\Theta}_t + a_t[\bar{Y} + \Xi_t^{\rm I}] + o(a_t).$$

For $\rho < 1$, we have $\overline{\Theta}_t = \theta^* + o(a_t)$ since $\overline{\Theta}_t$ converges to θ^* faster than t^{-N} for any N.

For $\rho = 1$, Proposition 4.26 (i) implies that $\overline{\Theta}_t = \theta^* + O(t^{-\varrho_0})$ where $\mathrm{Real}(\lambda) < -\varrho_0$ for every eigenvalue λ for A^*. Therefore, $\overline{\Theta}_t = \theta^* + o(t^{-1})$ if $I + A^*$ is Hurwitz. □

The proof of Theorem 4.25 is broken into three lemmas that follow. The assumptions of the theorem are assumed throughout. In particular, in the definition (4.121c) of $\Theta_T^{\rm PR}$, it is assumed that $a_t = 1/(1+t)^\rho$ with $\rho \in (\frac{1}{2},1)$, and $T_0 = (1 - 1/\kappa)T$.

The first step is to approximate the estimation error as

$$\Theta_T^{\rm PR} - \theta^* \stackrel{\rm def}{=} \frac{1}{T - T_0}\int_{T_0}^T [\Theta_t - \theta^*]\,dt = \frac{1}{T - T_0}\int_{T_0}^T [\Theta_t - \overline{\Theta}_t]\,dt + o(1/T^p), \qquad (4.146)$$

where $p > 1$ is fixed but arbitrary. This bound follows from Proposition 4.26 (ii) (recall (4.124)).

The vector-valued process Φ_T appearing in (4.122) is constructed as part of the proof. It is the sum

$$\Phi_T = [A^*]^{-1}\{Y_T - Y_{T_0} + \Psi_T^a + \Psi_T^b\} + o(1) \qquad (4.147a)$$

$$\text{with} \qquad \Psi_T^a \stackrel{\rm def}{=} -\int_{T_0}^T r_t Z_t\,dt \quad \text{and} \quad \Psi_T^b \stackrel{\rm def}{=} \int_{T_0}^T a_t\widetilde{\Upsilon}_t\,dt = \int_{T_0}^T a_t\,d\widetilde{\Upsilon}_t^I, \qquad (4.147b)$$

where, from (4.118),

$$\widetilde{\Upsilon}_t = \Upsilon_t - \overline{\Upsilon} \quad \text{and} \quad \widetilde{\Upsilon}_t^I = \int_0^t [\Upsilon_r - \overline{\Upsilon}]\,dr$$

with $\overline{\Upsilon}$ the ergodic mean introduced in (QSA5). The first term $\{\Psi_T^a\}$ is bounded because $\{Z_t\}$ is bounded, and $r_t = 1/(1+t)$, giving

$$\|\Psi_T^a\| \le \log(T/T_0)\sup_t \|Z_t\| = \log(\kappa/(\kappa - 1))\sup_t \|Z_t\| < \infty.$$

A proof that $\{\Psi^b_T\}$ is bounded is postponed to Lemma 4.41.

Lemma 4.39 *Under the assumptions of Theorem 4.25,*

$$\int_{T_0}^{T} [\Theta_t - \overline{\Theta}_t]\, dt = [A^*]^{-1}\Big\{Z_T - Z_{T_0} - \int_{T_0}^{T} \widetilde{\Xi}_t\, dt + \Psi^a_T + o(1)\Big\}. \tag{4.148}$$

Proof Combining the definition $a_t Z_t = \Theta_t - \overline{\Theta}_t$ and

$$\tfrac{d}{dt} Z_t = a_t A^* Z_t + a_t \Delta_t + \widetilde{\Xi}_t$$

(see (4.125d)) gives, by the Fundamental Theorem of Calculus,

$$Z_T - Z_{T_0} = A^* \int_{T_0}^{T} [\Theta_t - \overline{\Theta}_t]\, dt + \int_{T_0}^{T} [a_t \Delta_t + \widetilde{\Xi}_t]\, dt. \tag{4.149}$$

Applying Proposition 4.27, the scaled error term can be expressed

$$a_t \Delta_t = a_t \Delta^{(\rho)}_t + r_t Z_t.$$

Theorem 4.24 (i) implies that $r_t \|Z_t\| = O(1/t)$ and $a_t \|\Delta^{(\rho)}_t\| = O(\|\Theta_t - \overline{\Theta}_t\|^2) = O(a_t^2)$, so that (4.148) follows on rearranging terms in (4.149) and using the definition (4.147b). □

Lemma 4.40 *Under the assumptions of Theorem 4.25,*

$$\Theta^{\rm PR}_T - \theta^* = \frac{1}{T - T_0}[A^*]^{-1}\Big\{Y_T - Y_{T_0} + \int_{T_0}^{T} a_t \Upsilon_t\, dt + \Psi^a_T + o(1)\Big\}. \tag{4.150}$$

Proof Recall (4.145) and (4.119), which give

$$\begin{aligned}
\int_{T_0}^{T} \widetilde{\Xi}_t\, dt &= [\Xi^{\rm I}_T(\Theta_T) - \Xi^{\rm I}_{T_0}(\Theta_{T_0})] - \int_{T_0}^{T} a_t \Upsilon_t(\Theta_t) dt \\
&= [\Xi^{\rm I}_T(\Theta_T) - \Xi^{\rm I}_{T_0}(\Theta_{T_0})] - \int_{T_0}^{T} a_t \Upsilon_t\, dt + \int_{T_0}^{T} a_t O(\|\Theta_t - \overline{\Theta}_t\|) dt,
\end{aligned}$$

where $\int_{T_0}^{T} a_t O(\|\Theta_t - \overline{\Theta}_t\|) dt = o(1)$ for $\rho \in (\frac{1}{2}, 1)$. Recalling the definition $Y_t \stackrel{\rm def}{=} Z_t - \Xi^{\rm I}_t(\Theta_t)$ in (4.126) gives

$$Z_T - Z_{T_0} - \int_{T_0}^{T} \widetilde{\Xi}_t\, dt = Y_T - Y_{T_0} + \int_{T_0}^{T} a_t \Upsilon_t\, dt + o(1). \tag{4.151}$$

Combining (4.148) and (4.151) completes the proof:

$$\begin{aligned}
\Theta^{\rm PR}_T - \theta^* &= \frac{1}{T - T_0} \int_{T_0}^{T} [\Theta_t - \overline{\Theta}_t]\, dt + o(1/T) \\
&= \frac{1}{T - T_0}[A^*]^{-1}\Big\{Y_T - Y_{T_0} + \int_{T_0}^{T} a_t \Upsilon_t\, dt + \Psi^a_T + o(1)\Big\}.
\end{aligned}$$
□

The integral on the right-hand side of (4.150) is the crucial term, which can be expressed as

$$\int_{T_0}^{T} a_t \Upsilon_t\, dt = \overline{\Upsilon} \int_{T_0}^{T} a_t\, dt + \Psi^b_T, \tag{4.152}$$

with Ψ^b_T defined in (4.147b).

Lemma 4.41 *Under the assumptions of Theorem 4.25, the process* $\{\Psi^b_T\}$ *is bounded, and the integral in the first term in* (4.152) *admits the approximation*

$$\kappa \int_{T_0}^{T} a_t \, dt = a_T[T + O(1)]c(\rho,\kappa), \qquad \text{with } c(\rho,\kappa) = \frac{\kappa}{1-\rho}\big(1 - (1 - 1/\kappa)^{1-\rho}\big).$$

Proof The bound on the integral of $a_t = 1/(1+t)^\rho$ is a calculus exercise. It remains to bound $\{\Psi^b_T\}$. Using integration by parts,

$$\Psi^b_T \stackrel{\text{def}}{=} \int_{T_0}^{T} a_t \, d\widetilde{\Upsilon}^I_t = a_t \widetilde{\Upsilon}^I_t \Big|_{t=T_0}^{T} - \int_{T_0}^{T} [\tfrac{d}{dt} a_t] \widetilde{\Upsilon}^I_t \, dt$$
$$= [a_T \widetilde{\Upsilon}^I_T - a_{T_0} \widetilde{\Upsilon}^I_{T_0}] + \rho \int_{T_0}^{T} \frac{1}{(1+t)^{1+\rho}} \widetilde{\Upsilon}^I_t \, dt.$$

This is bounded in T because $\{\widetilde{\Upsilon}^I_T\}$ is bounded under the assumptions of the theorem. □

Proof of Theorem 4.25 Lemma 4.40 combined with (4.152) and Lemma 4.41 establishes (4.122). □

4.10 Exercises

4.1 Consider the scalar ODE $\frac{d}{dt}\vartheta = \mathsf{f}(\vartheta) = -\vartheta^3$ (previously explored in Exercise 2.15).

(a) Verify that it is globally asymptotically stable.

(b) Simulate using the standard Euler approximation:

$$\theta_{n+1} = \theta_n + \alpha_{n+1}\mathsf{f}(\theta_n).$$

Verify analytically or through simulation that the discrete-time recursion is unstable for any choice of fixed step-size (that is, $\alpha_n = \alpha_0$ for each n, and also α_0 independent of θ_0).

(c) Propose a step-size rule that is successful. For what values of t_n is $\theta_n \approx \vartheta_{t_n}$?

4.2 Compute the Newton–Raphson vector field f^{NRf} defined in (4.14b) for the three scalar examples: $\mathsf{f}(x) =$

(a) $-\nabla\Gamma(x)$ with $\Gamma(x) = x^2(1 + (x+10)^2)$

(b) $-\nabla\Gamma(x)$ with $\Gamma(x) = \log(e^x + e^{-x})$

(c) $\sin(x)$

In each case:

- Obtain overlapping plots of $\mathsf{f}(\theta)$ and $\mathsf{f}^{\text{NRf}}(\theta)$ as a function of θ. Which of the six functions is globally Lipschitz continuous?
- Obtain the roots of f and f^{NRf}.
- *Identify the regions of attraction*: We say that θ is in the *region of attraction* an equilibrium θ° for the Newton–Raphson flow if

$$\lim_{t\to\infty} \vartheta_t = \theta^\circ,$$

where ϑ_t is the solution to (4.14a) at time t, with initial condition $\Theta_0 = \theta$. Describe the region of attraction for each root of f^{NRf}.

4.3 Consider the root-finding problem $\mathsf{f}(\theta^*) = 0$ with $\mathsf{f}_1(\theta) = \theta_1 - 2\theta_2$ and $\mathsf{f}_2(\theta) = \|\theta\|^2 - 5$. You can compute the two solutions $\{\theta^{*+}, \theta^{*-}\}$ by substituting $\theta_1 = 2\theta_2$ into the quadratic equation $\theta_1^2 + \theta_2^2 = 5$.

(a) A normalized ODE is promising:

$$\tfrac{d}{dt}\vartheta(1) = -\mathrm{f}_1(\vartheta), \qquad \tfrac{d}{dt}\vartheta(2) = -\mathrm{f}_2(\vartheta)/\sqrt{1+\|\theta\|^2},$$

where the scaling of f_2 is imposed so that the right-hand side is Lipschitz continuous. The minus signs are used in the hopes of achieving stability.

Verify through analysis or simulation that this approach fails.

(b) Apply the Newton–Raphson flow and plot the resulting trajectories. You can obtain trajectories using an ODE solver, or compute them explicitly using $\mathrm{f}(\vartheta_t) = e^{-t}\mathrm{f}(\vartheta_0)$ and then solving for ϑ_t. Compute or estimate the region of attraction for each of the two equilibria.

(c) Verify that the regularized Newton–Raphson flow (4.15) satisfies conditions (a) and (b) of Proposition 4.4. Condition (c) fails: Find all solutions to $A^{\intercal}(\theta)\mathrm{f}(\theta) = 0$ and discuss the implications.

4.4 The monkey saddle is the two-dimensional surface defined by

$$h(x,y) = x^3 - 3xy^2.$$

A saddle point is a pair (x^s, y^s) at which the gradient ∇h vanishes.

(a) Verify that the origin is the unique saddle point.

(b) Derive the Newton–Raphson flow to find the saddle point.

(c) Plot $\nabla h(x_t, y_t)$ as a function of t from various initial conditions to see that it does follow a line from $h(x_0, y_0)$ to the origin.

4.5 The monkey saddle in polar coordinates is expressed $h(r,\phi) = r^3\cos(3\phi)$. Repeat Exercise 4.4 for this function of two variables.

4.6 Suppose that the following hold for the function $\mathrm{f}\colon \mathbb{R}^d \to \mathbb{R}$ (just slightly stronger than assumptions (b) and (c) of Proposition 4.4): f is continuously differentiable, $\|\mathrm{f}\|$ is coercive, and $A(\theta)$ is full rank for each θ. Conclude that the function f is *onto*: For each $z \in \mathbb{R}^d$, there is $\theta^z \in \mathbb{R}^d$ for which $\mathrm{f}(\theta^z) = z$. Suggested approach: Consider the Newton–Raphson flow using $\mathrm{f}_z(\theta) = \mathrm{f}(\theta) - z$, resulting in $\tfrac{d}{dt}\mathrm{f}_z(\vartheta) = -\mathrm{f}_z(\vartheta)$. Be sure to explain how you use the coercive condition.

4.7 We can include a matrix gain in the gradient flow if deemed desirable:

$$\tfrac{d}{dt}\vartheta = -\nabla_\theta G\Gamma(\vartheta). \tag{4.153}$$

Suppose that G is positive definite and the assumptions of Proposition 4.7 hold. Design a new Lyapunov function so that the conclusions of Proposition 4.7 continue to hold using (4.153). You might consider a weighted norm $V(\theta) = \tfrac{1}{2}\|\tilde{\theta}\|_M^2 = \tfrac{1}{2}\tilde{\theta}^{\intercal}M\tilde{\theta}$, with $M > 0$.

4.8 Let's explore some of the difficulties minimizing the function $\Gamma(x) = x^2(1+(x+10)^2)$ using gradient descent. One problem is that it is not convex, and also has multiple local minima. Another is that its gradient has cubic growth, which introduces potential numerical problems, as in Exercise 4.1.

(a) Code an Euler approximation of gradient descent $\tfrac{d}{dt}\Theta = -\nabla\Gamma(\Theta)$. Perform multiple runs, with varying initial conditions (it will eventually fail when you choose an initial condition too large).

(b) Introduce a weighting function $w\colon \mathbb{R} \to [1,\infty)$, and consider the normalized algorithm:

$$\tfrac{d}{dt}\vartheta = -w(\vartheta)\nabla\Gamma(\vartheta).$$

Choose a continuous weighting function so that the right-hand side is globally Lipschitz continuous, while ensuring that the origin remains a (locally) asymptotically stable equilibrium (prove stability using a Lyapunov function).

(c) Test the Euler approximation for the modified ODE with a range of initial conditions.

This example reappears in Exercises and 8.2 and 4.13.

4.9 *Oja's Algorithm.* This is a famous ODE technique, designed to estimate the eigenvectors of an $N \times N$ matrix W. Suppose that the matrix is positive definite, so that the eigenvalues of W are nonnegative. Fix an integer $N_m \leq N$, and suppose there is a "spectral gap" in the following sense: If the eigenvalues of W are ordered so that $\lambda_1 \geq \lambda_2 \geq \cdots \lambda_n$, then $\lambda_{N_m} > \lambda_{N_m+1}$. Our goal is to identify these first eigenvalues, along with the subspace S spanned by the first N_m eigenvectors.

Let m_t denote an $N \times N_m$ matrix whose columns are intended to approximate elements of S. Oja's subspace algorithm is expressed as the polynomial differential equation:

$$\tfrac{d}{dt} m_t = [I - m_t m_t^{\intercal}] W m_t, \tag{4.154}$$

where m_0 is given as initial condition. It is known that, for "most" initial conditions, the solution to the ODE is convergent and the limit m_∞ lies in S (see [91] and also [59, 278, 321]).

(a) Review Exercise 4.8, and observe that Oja's algorithm poses a similar challenge since the right-hand side of the ODE (4.154) is not Lipschitz. Propose a modified ODE through the introduction of a scalar weighting function.

(b) Experiment with this method to compute the first few singular values of a matrix A of your choosing ($\sigma_i(A) = \sqrt{\lambda_i(A^{\intercal} A)}$).

4.10 *Analysis of Oja's Algorithm.* Consider the case $N_m = 1$, so that m_t is a column vector. Assume as before that W is positive definite.

(a) Using the Lyapunov function $V(x) = \frac{1}{2}\|x\|^2$, show that there is $c_0 > 0$ such that

$$\tfrac{d}{dt} V(m_t) \leq -V(m_t), \qquad \text{whenever } V(m_t) > c_0.$$

Conclude that the trajectories are ultimately bounded, in the sense that $V(m_t) \leq c_0$ for each initial condition, and all t sufficiently large.

(b) Take a second look at your expression for $\frac{d}{dt} V(m_t)$, and establish that in fact $\|m_t\| \to 1$ as $t \to \infty$ from each initial condition.

(c) Let $\{v^i\}$ denote an orthonormal basis of eigenvectors of W, and write

$$m_t = \sum_{i=1}^{N} \alpha_t(i) v^i.$$

From the foregoing, we have $1 = \lim_{t\to\infty} \|m_t\| = \lim_{t\to\infty} \sum_{i=1}^{N} [\alpha_t(i)]^2$. Establish the following ODE for the coefficients:

$$\tfrac{d}{dt}\alpha(i) = [\lambda_i - \bar{\lambda}]\alpha(i), \qquad \bar{\lambda}_t = \sum_{i=1}^{N} [\alpha_t(i)]^2 \lambda_i.$$

(d) Verify that the solution to the ODE from (c) has the following representation:

$$\alpha_t(i) = \exp\Big(\int_0^t [\lambda_i - \bar{\lambda}_r] dr\Big) \alpha_0(i).$$

(e) Assume that λ_1 is the maximal eigenvalue of W that is not repeated, so that $\lambda_i < \lambda_1$ for $i \geq 2$. Show that $\alpha_1(t) \to 1$ exponentially quickly in this case. For this, it is useful to write

$$\alpha_t(i) = \exp([\lambda_i - \lambda_1]t) \exp\Bigl(\int_0^t [\lambda_1 - \bar{\lambda}_r]dr\Bigr)\alpha_0(i).$$

4.11 *Failure of PJR Averaging.* Theorem 4.25 tells us that PJR averaging will lead to the optimal $1/T$ convergence rate, provided the vector $\overline{\Upsilon}$ defined above (4.118) is null. In this exercise, you will see that this assumption cannot be taken for granted. Consider the scalar QSA ODE $\frac{d}{dt}\vartheta_t = a_t f(\vartheta_t, \xi_t)$, in which

$$f(\vartheta_t, \xi_t) = -(1 + \sin(t))\vartheta_t + \xi_t^0, \qquad \vartheta_0 \in \mathbb{R},$$

where $\xi_t = (\xi_t^0, \sin(t))^\intercal$, and the scalar signal $\{\xi_t^0\}$ has zero mean.

(a) Obtain $\bar{f}$, θ^*, and expressions for the time-varying quantities of interest in (QSA5):

$$f(\theta, \xi_t), \ A(\theta, \xi_t), \ \widehat{A}(\theta, \xi_t).$$

(b) Choose ξ_t^0 so that it has mean zero, yet $\overline{\Upsilon} = 1$.

(c) Verify numerically that PJR averaging fails for this example, but (4.122) does hold. It is enough to verify through simulation that

$$a_T^{-1}\{\Theta_T^{\mathsf{PR}} - \theta^*\} \approx c(\rho, \kappa)\overline{\Upsilon}/A^*, \quad \text{for } T \text{ very large.}$$

Take ρ and κ of your choosing, respecting the assumptions of Theorem 4.25.

4.12 *Exploration in qSGD.* This problem concerns qSGD #1: $\frac{d}{dt}\Theta_t = -a_t \frac{1}{\varepsilon} \xi_t \Gamma(\Theta_t + \varepsilon\xi_t)$. You may assume $a_t = (1+t)^\rho$ (respecting QSA theory).

The domain of the objective function is $\mathbb{R}^2$, and in this problem you will assume it is quadratic:

$$\Gamma(\theta) = \tfrac{1}{2}\theta^\intercal M \theta, \quad \theta \in \mathbb{R}^2, \qquad \text{with } M > 0.$$

The origin is the unique minimizer (by definition of the positive definite condition $M > 0$).

In this exercise, you would be wise to apply a variant of Lemma 4.37 (see also (4.49)): For any polynomial function $g\colon \mathbb{R}^2 \to \mathbb{R}$,

$$\lim_{T\to\infty} \frac{1}{T}\int_0^T g(\cos(t), \sin(\pi t))dt = \int_0^1\int_0^1 g(\cos(2\pi t_1), \sin(2\pi t_2))dt_1 dt_2.$$

(a) Consider a simple probing signal $\xi_t = p_t v$ where $p_t = \cos(t) + \sin(\pi t)$ and $v \in \mathbb{R}^2$ are fixed. Obtain $\bar{f}$ in the ODE approximation $\frac{d}{dt}\vartheta_t = \bar{f}(\vartheta_t)$, and *conclude that this approach fails.*

(b) Consider now $\xi_t = \cos(t)v^1 + \sin(\pi t)v^2$ with $v^1 = (1,0)^\intercal$ and $v^2 = (0,1)^\intercal$. Obtain $\bar{f}$ in the ODE approximation $\frac{d}{dt}\vartheta_t = \bar{f}(\vartheta_t)$ and identify its stationary points.
Is Θ_t convergent in this case? If so, does the limit approximate the minimizer $\theta^* = 0$?

(c) Continuing with the special case (b), obtain expressions for the time-varying quantities of interest in (QSA5):

$$f(\theta, \xi_t), \ A(\theta, \xi_t), \ \widehat{A}(\theta, \xi_t).$$

Based on this, obtain an expression for $\overline{\Upsilon}$.

(d) How do you expect your conclusions will extend to an objective function that is not quadratic? You should be able to find conditions under which $\|\overline{\Upsilon}\| = O(\varepsilon)$.

4.13 Use qSGD combined with PJR-averaging to obtain the minimum of $\Gamma(x) = x^2(1 + (x+10)^2)$. Test your algorithms for a range of ε, and initial conditions $\Theta_0 < -10$ and also $\Theta_0 > 2$.

Review Exercise 4.8 before proceeding: Success will require projection or some other mechanism to ensure boundedness of your estimates (neither Γ nor its derivative is Lipschitz continuous).

(a) Experiment with each of the three qSGD algorithms, provide plots of the estimates as a function of time, and comment on your initial findings. Decide on your favorite algorithm for the remainder of the exercise.

(b) Comment on how the rate of convergence is impacted by ε for $\Theta_0 > 2$, and the likelihood of becoming trapped with $\Theta_0 < -10$ (here $\varepsilon > 0$ scales the probing signal in each of the qSGD algorithms).

Obtain a plot of your estimate of θ^*_ε as a function of $\varepsilon > 0$ for $\Theta_0 > 2$, and comment on observed bias.

(c) See if you can design a time-varying process $\{\varepsilon_t\}$ that results in a reliable algorithm that is convergent for any initial condition Θ_0.

Test your final design with the modified function $\Gamma_m(x) = x^2(1+(x+m)^2)$ for a range of values of m (say, $m \in \{-4,4,8\}$).

4.14 Consider again the MagBall example introduced in Section 2.7.3. This exercise is a follow-up to Exercise 2.19. Our goal is to maintain the ball at rest at some preassigned distance r_0 from the magnet.

Our approach is to use gradient-free optimization: Let $c(x,u) = \tilde{y}^2 + u^2$, where $\tilde{y} = x_1 - r_0$. Propose a family of policies $u = \phi^\theta(x)$, based on your insight from Exercise 2.19, and minimize $\mathsf{E}[J_\theta(X)]$ using qSGD (see (4.103) and surrounding discussion).

4.15 Revisit Exercise 3.10, now with the introduction of a cost function $c(x,u) = \|x\|^2 + u^2$.

Based on your insight from Exercise 3.10, propose a family of policies $u = \phi^\theta(x)$, $\theta \in \mathbb{R}^d$ (choose $d \leq 4$). Obtain an approximation of the minimum of $\mathsf{E}[J_\theta(X)]$ using qSGD.

4.16 *Optimization of the Rowing Game.* Rather than apply LQR, as in Exercise 3.9, optimize (K_p, K_I, K_v) using qSGD. Are your results similar to what was obtained in Exercise 3.9 when N is large?

4.17 This exercise (as well as Exercise 4.16) might clarify the remarks at the close of Section 4.7.2: When we search for policies that are optimal within a specific class, we are often forced to abandon dynamic programming and instead use optimization techniques such as qSGD.

The state evolves on $\mathsf{X} = \mathbb{R}^n$, in continuous time, in which the derivative of each state is directly influenced only by the local input and a single neighbor:

$$\tfrac{d}{dt} x_t(i) = x_t(i-1) + u_t(i), \qquad 1 \leq i \leq n,$$

where for notational convenience we set $x_t(0) \equiv 0$. The cost function is quadratic, of the special form $c(x,u) = \|x\|^2 + r\|u\|^2$ with $r > 0$.

(a) Obtain the $n \times n$ feedback gain $K^\star$ for a range of n, and see if you discover any special structure. You might also see what happens for very small or very large r.

(c) We next obtain an optimal gain over a restricted class of policies: $u_t(i) = -\theta x_t(i)$ for each i and t. Devise a QSA ODE to find θ^*, and for a range of r compare the performance of your solution to what was obtained in (a). For this, you must compute the value function J associated with your policy and compare it to $J^\star$.

4.18 Consider the linear QSA ODE with multiplicative noise (4.88):

$$\tfrac{d}{dt}\Theta_t = a_t f(\Theta_t, \xi_t) = a_t[A_0 + \varepsilon \xi_t A_1]\Theta_t,$$

with $\xi_t = \sin(\omega t + \phi)$.

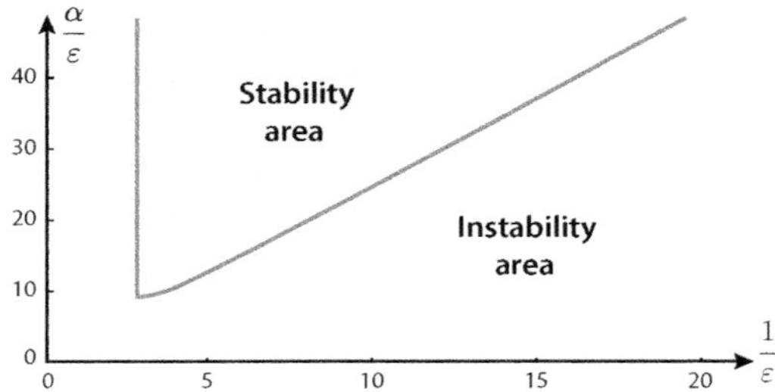

Figure 4.14 Stabilization by noise (from [36]).

(a) What is θ^*? What is the apparent noise (4.69) in this case? Conjecture on the rate of convergence of the QSA ODE (4.44) with A_0 Hurwitz and $a_t = 1/(1+t)$, and see if you can verify your conjecture in the scalar case $d = 1$.
Theory for the constant gain algorithm $a_t \equiv \alpha$ is a bit trickier:

(b) Consider this scalar example,

$$\tfrac{d}{dt}\Theta_t = -[\alpha + \varepsilon\xi_t]\Theta_t.$$

Estimate the range of (α,ε) for which the ODE is stable. You might see if you can obtain analytical results: The scalar linear ODE $\frac{d}{dt}\Theta_t = \beta_t\Theta_t$ admits a closed-form solution (skim Exercise 4.10 to see the solution for a different application).

(c) Suppose that there are n linearly independent eigenvectors $\{v^i\}$ for $A_0^{\intercal}$, and that these are also eigenvectors for $A_1^{\intercal}$: For possibly complex numbers $\{\lambda_i, \mu_i\}$,

$$A_0^{\intercal}v^i = \lambda_i v^i, \qquad A_1^{\intercal}v^i = \mu_i v^i.$$

Explain how in this special case you can use your results from (b) to obtain conditions for stability in the constant gain algorithm.
The next part shows that stability is not so simple when this eigenvector assumption fails.

(d) *Stabilization by Noise.* The article [36] contains a characterization of stability for the general linear algorithm with constant gain. The theory is illustrated with this numerical example:

$$\tfrac{d}{dt}\Theta_t = [\alpha A_0 + \varepsilon\xi_t A_1]\Theta_t$$

$$\text{using} \qquad A_0 = \begin{bmatrix} 0 & 1 \\ 0 & 0 \end{bmatrix} \quad A_1 = \tfrac{1}{10}\begin{bmatrix} 6 & 13 \\ 8 & -16 \end{bmatrix}.$$

The eigenvalues of A_0 are each zero, and those of A_1 are $\{1, -2\}$, so neither matrix is Hurwitz.

For a nonzero initial condition Θ_0, the Lyapunov exponent is defined as the limit

$$\Lambda(\alpha,\varepsilon) = \lim_{t\to\infty} t^{-1}\log(\|\Theta_t\|).$$

Fix $\varepsilon = 1/5$ and obtain a plot of estimates of $\Lambda(\alpha,\varepsilon)$ for $\alpha > 0$. Are your results consistent with the stability region shown in Figure 4.14?

4.11 Notes

These notes consist of many components, reflecting the breadth of the chapter.

4.11.1 ODE Methods for Algorithm Design

The ODE (4.14a) was introduced in the economics literature, which led to the comprehensive analysis by Smale [325]. The term *Newton–Raphson flow* for (4.14a) was introduced in the deterministic control literature [320, 370]. The Zap SA algorithm was introduced at the same time, and based on the same ODE [90, 110, 112]. Within the optimization literature, the term "Newton–Raphson dynamical system" is used: see [5] for history.[4] Much more on this technique will appear in the second half of the book. See Section 8.5.2 for a variant that does not require matrix inversion.

The paper [335] sparked new appreciation for ODE methods within the optimization community (with particular interest in applications to ML). The goal was to understand the dynamics of two common optimization algorithms with "acceleration":

(i) Polyak's heavy-ball method:

$$x_{k+1} - x_k = \delta_{k+1}[x_k - x_{k-1}] - \alpha_{k+1}\nabla\Gamma(x_k). \tag{4.155}$$

(ii) Nesterov's accelerated gradient algorithm:

$$x_{k+1} = y_k - \alpha_{k+1}\nabla\Gamma(y_k), \qquad y_k = x_k + \delta_k[x_k - x_{k-1}]. \tag{4.156}$$

Either recursion reduces to the gradient descent algorithm (4.28) when $\delta_k \equiv 0$. Polyak's algorithm takes $\delta_k = \delta > 0$; Nesterov's algorithm uses $\delta_k = (k-1)/(k+2)$. Theory behind these algorithms typically requires $\alpha_k \equiv \alpha$ independent of k.

An ODE approximation for Polyak's algorithm (4.155) with $\delta_k \equiv \delta$ is easily anticipated on denoting $\theta_k = x_k$, and $D_{k+1} = \theta_{k+1} - \theta_k$ [16]. For simplicity, take $\alpha = 1$ and write (4.155) as

$$D_{k+1} - D_k = -(1-\delta)D_k - \nabla\Gamma(\theta_k).$$

This is an Euler approximation of the second-order ODE:

$$\tfrac{d^2}{dt^2}\vartheta = -(1-\delta)\tfrac{d}{dt}\vartheta - \nabla\Gamma(\vartheta).$$

Nesterov's algorithm (4.156) is considered in [335], using the favored time-varying choice of δ_k. A similar ODE approximation is established:

$$\tfrac{d^2}{dt^2}\vartheta = -\beta_t\tfrac{d}{dt}\vartheta - \nabla\Gamma(\vartheta), \qquad \beta_t = 3/t.$$

The appearance of "3" is explained by the representation $\delta_k = 1 - 3/(k+2)$.

Better understanding of the dynamics of these ODEs led to a much fuller understanding of why Polyak and Nesterov were so successful [16, 198, 335]. This work was part of the inspiration for growing interest in ODE and stochastic differential equation (SDE) approximations for more efficient recursive algorithms [200, 294, 318, 375, 384], for neural network approximation [84, 358], and ODE design based on concepts from robust control theory [127, 163, 164].

[4] Many thanks to Vivek Borkar for alerting me to Smale's early contributions, and to Francis Bach for passing on [5].

4.11.2 Optimization

Luenberger has been my favorite source for teaching optimization [230, 231], but the best encyclopedic treatment is probably [73] together with the recent book [19].

A version of Theorem 4.9 is found in Polyak [286]. The main assumption (4.27) is a restricted form of a bound introduced by mathematician Łojasiewicz, which is why this is called the Polyak–Łojasiewicz (PL) condition in the optimization literature. The simple proof of Theorem 4.9 is taken from [179] (which contains much more insight and many applications).

The conclusions of Proposition 4.11 can be improved with a modified algorithm and a more carefully constructed Lyapunov function [116, 292].

It is worth looking over the field of online optimization with application to control [96, 263]. The goals are similar to those of qSGD and policy gradient algorithms.

4.11.3 QSA

Section 4.5 was initially conceived as an early introduction to stochastic approximation for algorithm design – a topic explored in Chapter 8. Over the course of writing this book, the mission evolved to become a stand-alone toolkit for optimization and control.

Much of Sections 4.5–4.7 is adapted from [40, 41, 87], which was inspired by the prior results in [245, 319]; [93] contains applications to gradient-free optimization with constraints. The QSA concept was first introduced in [212, 213] for applications to finance.

The theory of two time-scale stochastic approximation enjoys a parallel history with the theory of singular perturbations for differential equations, which has played an important role in control theory and applications [186]. A simple example is the dynamical system described by the following set of differential equations:

$$\begin{aligned} \tfrac{d}{dt} x_1 &= \mathrm{f}_1(x_1, x_2), \\ \varepsilon \tfrac{d}{dt} x_2 &= \mathrm{f}_2(x_1, x_2). \end{aligned}$$

It is assumed that $0 < \varepsilon \ll 1$, so that the dynamics of x_2 are much faster than that of x_1. Suppose that this is a function of time, with $\varepsilon_t \downarrow 0$ as $t \uparrow \infty$. Assume moreover that there is a continuous function ϕ satisfying $\mathrm{f}_2(x_1, \phi(x_1)) = 0$ for each x_1. Under further conditions, there is a tight approximation between the preceding ODE and

$$\tfrac{d}{dt} x_1 = \mathrm{f}_1(x_1, \phi(x_1)).$$

This is the thinking behind Zap QSA (4.91).

PJR averaging was introduced independently by their namesakes [287, 288, 306] (note that Polyak had independent contributions prior to his collaboration with Juditsky). This work has nothing to do with QSA, but concerns optimizing the covariance Σ_θ appearing in (6.40) for stochastic approximation – see the "Notes" section of Chapter 8 for more background. The application of averaging techniques for rate optimization in QSA appears to be new.

The function $\hat{g}$ in Lemma 4.37 (ii) is precisely the solution to Poisson's equation, with forcing function $\tilde{g} = g - a_0$, that appears in theory of simulation of Markov processes, average-cost optimal control, and stochastic approximation [12, 39, 144, 250].

The phrase *ODE method* is frequently tributed to Ljung [229], though most authors use this to mean a method of analysis rather than a technique for algorithm design. Polyak in

[136] credits Tsypkin [357] for the realization that stochastic approximation is an invaluable ingredient in the creation of algorithms for learning.

The ODE@∞ (4.113) was introduced in [69] for stability verification in stochastic approximation: Proposition 4.22 is a very special case of the Borkar–Meyn theorem [66, 69], which has been refined considerably in recent years [296, 297]. The use of abstract ODE models to verify stability of stochastic recursions also appears in queueing networks [98, 99, 254] and Markov chain Monte Carlo (MCMC) [134]. We will revisit this approach to stability verification in Chapter 8.

Assumption (QSA5) is analogous to common assumptions in the study of simulation or stochastic approximation algorithms when $\boldsymbol{\xi}$ is a Markov process [38, 144]. Conditions for a well-behaved solution to Poisson's equation are available, subject to conditions on the Markov process and the function. In particular, for SDEs, a nondegeneracy condition known as hypoellipticity is a first step, and then a solution to Poisson's equation exists subject to a Lyapunov function drift condition [144]. While the process $\boldsymbol{\xi}$ defined by (4.79) is Markovian, it is purely degenerate in the sense that Poisson's equation (4.140) in differential form is a first-order PDE:

$$g(z) + \partial \hat{g}(z) \cdot \mathrm{H}(z) = \bar{g}\,, \qquad z \in \Omega.$$

There is little theory available for well-behaved solutions beyond the simple special case considered in Section 4.9.4.

4.11.4 SGD and Extremum Seeking Control

In gradient-free optimization, the goal is to minimize a loss function $\Gamma(\theta)$ over $\theta \in \mathbb{R}^d$. It is possible to observe the loss function at any desired value, but no gradient information is available.

The topic has been studied in two seemingly disconnected research communities: techniques intended to directly approximate gradient descent through perturbation techniques, known as simultaneous perturbations stochastic approximation (SPSA), and extremum-seeking control (ESC), which is formulated in a purely deterministic setting. Algorithm (4.99) is a stylized version of the ESC approach. Much of Sections 4.5 and 4.6 is taken from [40, 41, 85, 86]; [52] also develops SPSA using a specially designed class of deterministic probing sequences.

See [202] for history of gradient-free optimization in adaptive control, and [11, 228, 348] for the nearly century-old history of ESC (and [298, 299] for the Russian perspective). The following text from [348] is striking:

> In his 1922 paper, or invention disclosure, Leblanc describes a mechanism to transfer power from an overhead electrical transmission line to a tram car using an ingenious non-contact solution. In order to maintain an efficient power transfer in what is essentially a linear, air-core, transformer/capacitor arrangement with variable inductance, due to the changing air-gap, he identifies the need to adjust a (tram based) inductance (the input) so as to maintain a resonant circuit, or maximum power (the output).
>
> *Leblanc explains a control mechanism of how to maintain the desirable maximum power transfer using what is essentially an extremum seeking solution* (emphasis added).

This discussion refers to the 1922 disclosure [217], which amounts to an analog implementation of gradient-free optimization. A schematic from this document is shown in Figure 4.15.

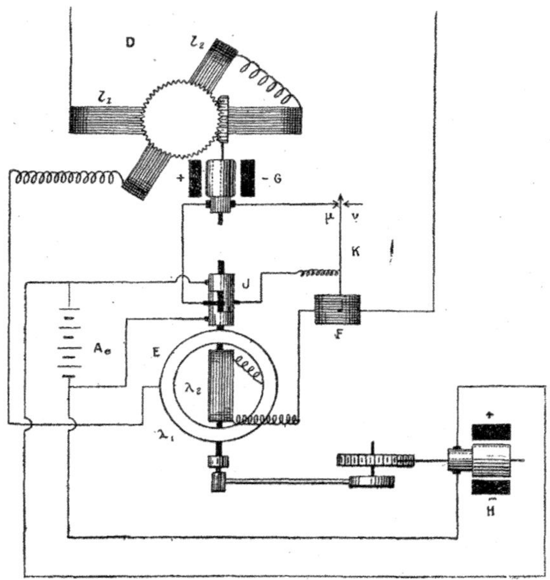

Figure 4.15 Schematic taken from Leblanc's 1922 disclosure [217], which is considered the birth of extremum-seeking control.

Theory for SPSA began with the algorithm of Keifer–Wolfowitz [182], which requires at each iteration access to two perturbations per dimension to obtain a stochastic gradient estimate, as in qSGD #3. This computational barrier was addressed in the work of Spall, which sparked further research [50–52, 54, 148, 327–329]. Most valuable for applications in RL is the one-measurement form of SPSA introduced in [329]: This can be expressed in the form (4.43), in which

$$f(\theta_n, \Phi_{n+1}) = \Gamma(\theta_n + \varepsilon\Phi_{n+1})\Phi_{n+1}, \tag{4.157}$$

where $\mathbf{\Phi}$ is a zero-mean and i.i.d. vector-valued sequence. The qSGD #1 algorithm (4.96) is a continuous-time analog.

The introduction of [274] suggests that there is an older history of improvements to SPSA in the Russian literature: see (2) of that paper and surrounding discussion. Beyond history, the contributions of [274] include rates of convergence results for standard and new SPSA algorithms. Information-theoretic lower bounds for optimization methods that have access to noisy observations of the true function were derived in [170]. This class of algorithms also has some history in the bandits literature [1, 78].

In all of the SPSA literature surveyed in this section, a gradient approximation is obtained through the introduction of an i.i.d. probing signal. For this reason, the best possible rate is of order $1/\sqrt{n}$, which is far slower than can be obtained using QSA techniques.

Policy gradient techniques are traditionally posed in a stochastic setting, in which $\boldsymbol{\xi}$ is i.i.d. (independent and identically distributed). The most popular approach is the actor-critic method, in which a value function approximation algorithm such as TD-learning acts as a subroutine. There is an enormous literature, and it is best to refer to [44, 338] for history, as well as the recent work [236].

5

Value Function Approximations

We now have all the preliminaries necessary to describe reinforcement learning algorithms designed for value function approximation.

The approximation techniques are built around a family of functions denoted $\mathcal{H}$. Standard examples discussed in Section 5.1 include neural networks and kernels, as well as linear approximation using a basis (an example of this can be found in Section 4.5.3). In most cases, the function class is finite dimensional, with dimension denoted d. For example, to approximate the Q-function $Q^\star$ defined in (3.7a), the family is denoted $\{Q^\theta : \theta \in \mathbb{R}^d\}$.

Most algorithms are based on optimization: An algorithm designed to compute the *optimal* parameter θ^* will be based on some loss function $\Gamma(\theta)$, with $\theta^* = \arg\min_\theta \Gamma(\theta)$. The algorithm may be recursive, in which case it generates a sequence of parameter estimates $\{\theta_n\}$, designed so that $\theta_n \to \theta^*$ as $n \to \infty$. It should come as no surprise that concepts from Chapter 4 will guide algorithm design.

Reinforcement learning algorithms are typically designed to be *model free*, in which the inputs to the algorithm consist of three terms: $\{u(k)\}$ the input sequence to the control system, the sequence of observed costs $c(x(k),u(k))$, and observed *features* that depend on the class of algorithms. For the linear parameterization $Q^\theta(x,u) = \sum_i \theta_i \psi_i(x,u)$, the sequence of features is the d-dimensional sequence $\{\psi(x(k),u(k))\}$.

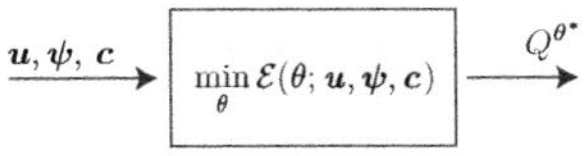

$\boldsymbol{u}, \boldsymbol{\psi}, \boldsymbol{c}$ → $\min_\theta \mathcal{E}(\boldsymbol{\theta}; \boldsymbol{u}, \boldsymbol{\psi}, \boldsymbol{c})$ → Q^{θ^*}

Figure 5.1 Online Q-learning: Inputs are observed features, and costs or rewards.

Figure 5.1 is included to emphasize that these are the only inputs to the algorithm. We don't require a model, and the state sequence $\{x(k)\}$ may not be fully observed. For any approximation Q^θ, we define a policy inspired by optimal control theory (in particular, (3.7c)):

$$\phi^\theta(x) = \arg\min_u Q^\theta(x,u), \qquad x \in \mathsf{X}. \tag{5.1}$$

In standard control textbooks, there is a two-step process: (1) identify a model, such as the ARMA model (2.4) and (2) design a control solution based on this model (perhaps through optimal control techniques). Step (2) is often a significant computational challenge. One of the great achievements of RL is to sidestep this challenge by estimating the Q-function directly.

System identification and value function approximation share common challenges and remedies. The notion of *exploration* that is so important in this chapter is entirely analogous to the *persistence of excitation* requirement in system identification [80, 207, 293].

What's a Good Approximation? If you have read Chapter 3 on optimal control, you surely want to learn how to approximate the Q-function $Q^\star$. However, you are more eager to obtain an estimate of the optimal policy:

$$\phi^\star(x) = \mathop{\arg\min}_{u \in \mathsf{U}(x)} Q^\star(x,u)\,, \qquad x \in \mathsf{X}.$$

A few things to keep in mind as we evaluate an algorithm:

(i) *Approximation fidelity.* We do not need a highly accurate approximation of the Q-function if our goal is to obtain a policy that is approximately optimal. Rather, the goal is that the performance of the policy ϕ^{θ^*} is approximately optimal. Ideally, then, $\Gamma(\theta)$ would be some measure of policy performance. The mean-square Bellman error (5.5) is a common surrogate.

(ii) *Policy evaluation.* Suppose it is computationally feasible to compute or approximate $\Gamma(\theta_n)$ (perhaps based on a model). In this case, we can keep a tally of performance for selected iterations $\{\Gamma(\theta_{n_k}) : k \geq 1\}$. We then select those policies among $\{\phi^{\theta_{n_k}} : k \geq 1\}$ with the best performance. Most likely we will do further testing, following the guidelines in Section 2.2 and suggestions found in Section 5.1.5.

5.1 Function Approximation Architectures

This section might be viewed as the briefest crash course on machine learning. See [57] for a more leisurely introduction to the function approximation concepts covered here.

The goal is to approximate a function $H^*\colon \mathsf{Z} \to \mathbb{R}$, where interpretation of H^* and the definition of the set of points Z depend on context. This is regarded as a *learning* problem when the estimate is based on data gathered in an experiment. For example, H^* might be the Q-function defined in (3.7a), and $\mathsf{Z} = \mathsf{X} \times \mathsf{U}$. In this case, the data will be obtained from experiments on the control system: the input applied to the system, along with functions of the resulting input-state process.

The techniques described here for function approximation require a few ingredients:

(i) A *function class* $\mathcal{H}$. Three examples are described in this chapter: a d-dimensional linear function class, d-dimensional nonlinear function class defined by a neural network, and one infinite-dimensional class: the *reproducing kernel Hilbert space* (RKHS).

(ii) For each $h \in \mathcal{H}$, we associate a nonnegative "loss" denoted $\Gamma(h)$. The loss function is designed so that $\Gamma(h)$ is small when $h = H^*$; our approximation is lousy if $\Gamma(h)$ is very large. We impose just one requirement on this loss function: Assumed given are samples $\{z_i : 1 \leq i \leq N\} \subset \mathsf{Z}$, and Γ depends only on h evaluated at the samples. Consequently, rather than thinking of the domain of Γ as the abstract collection $\mathcal{H}$, it is a mapping $\Gamma\colon \mathbb{R}^N \to \mathbb{R}$, with

$$\Gamma(h) = \Gamma(h(z_1), \ldots, h(z_N)). \tag{5.2}$$

(iii) An algorithm to obtain the minimizer of $\Gamma(h)$ over $h \in \mathcal{H}$. This book is filled with techniques for constructing algorithms, and techniques to obtain insight on their rate of convergence.

The objective Γ in (5.2) is known as the *empirical risk*, and its minimization over a function class $\mathcal{H}$ is known as *empirical risk minimization* (ERM).

We begin with two examples of loss functions, and three examples of the function class $\mathcal{H}$.

5.1.1 Function Approximation Based on Training Data

Curve Fitting

Suppose that we have noisy observations of a function $H^* : \mathbb{R} \to \mathbb{R}$:

$$y_i = H^*(z_i) + d_i,$$

where the noise $\{d_i\}$ is not too large and has nice statistical properties (for example, its average is close to zero). The sequence $\{(z_i, y_i) : 1 \le i \le N\}$ is called *training data*. The quadratic loss function is defined by

$$\Gamma(h) = \frac{1}{N}\sum_{i=1}^{N}[y_i - h(z_i)]^2, \qquad h \in \mathcal{H}. \tag{5.3}$$

If $\Gamma(h^*) = 0$, then the function exactly matches the observations: $h^*(z_i) = y_i$ for each i. This looks like good news in the disturbance-free setting ($d_i \equiv 0$), so that $h^*(z_i) = H^*(z_i)$ for each i.

Figure 5.2 shows function approximation outcomes from three different algorithms: Each algorithm constructs the function h based on the training samples $\{(z_i, y_i)\}$. The first plot illustrates typical results when we put too much trust in the data: We achieved $\Gamma(h) = 0$, which should be good news. However, it is unlikely that the true function exhibits so many peaks and valleys – this behavior is most likely the product of a bad algorithm. The term *overfitting* is used to describe this undesirable behavior when $\Gamma(h) \approx 0$. A good algorithm produces the smooth approximation shown in the middle. This is achieved using a regularizer. With too much regularization, you obtain a poor approximation, as shown on the right.

The preference for the middle plot in Figure 5.2 is based on a *smoothness prior* for the underlying data; that is, a substitute for the probabilistic priors used in Bayesian statistics.

Mean-Square Bellman Error

In Section 5.3, we begin a survey of techniques to estimate the optimal Q-function $Q^\star$ defined in (3.7a). This is a function approximation problem in which $H = Q^\star$ and $\mathsf{Z} = \mathsf{X} \times \mathsf{U}$. Our *second glance ahead* in Section 3.7 provided a roadmap, inspired by

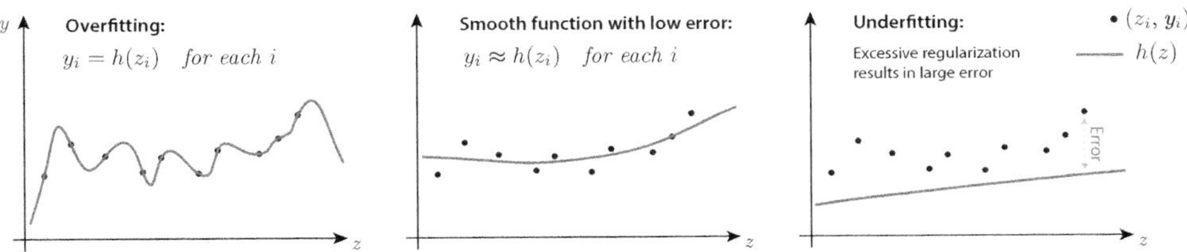

Figure 5.2 Three attempts to approximate the data $\{z_i, y_i\}$ with a smooth function.

the Bellman error (3.7d). For any function $Q\colon \mathsf{X}\times\mathsf{U}\to\mathbb{R}$, and any input-state sequence $(\boldsymbol{u},\boldsymbol{x})$, the temporal difference is defined in (3.47), and recalled here:

$$\mathcal{D}_{k+1}(Q) \stackrel{\text{def}}{=} -Q(x(k),u(k)) + c(x(k),u(k)) + \underline{Q}(x(k+1)), \tag{5.4}$$

with $\underline{Q}(x) \stackrel{\text{def}}{=} \min_u Q(x,u)$.

Given a time horizon $\mathcal{N}\geq 1$, and the input-state sequence $\{u(k),x(k) : 0\leq k\leq \mathcal{N}\}$, we must take $N=\mathcal{N}+1$ and observations $z_i = (x(i-1),u(i-1))$ to match the notation (5.2), and from this define the loss function

$$\Gamma(h) = \frac{1}{N}\sum_{i=1}^{N}\big[D_i(h(z_i),h(z_{i+1}))\big]^2, \tag{5.5a}$$

$$D_i(h(z_i),h(z_{i+1})) = -h(x(i-1),u(i-1)) + c(x(i-1),u(i-1)) + \underline{h}(x(i)) \tag{5.5b}$$

with $\underline{h}(x) = \min_u h(x,u)$ for any function h. The complex-looking term (5.5b) is the temporal difference, $D_i(h(z_i),h(z_{i+1})) = \mathcal{D}_i(h)$, as defined in (5.4).

Empirical Distributions

In the RL literature, you will find the term *experience replay buffer* in reference to training data, and from this the *empirical distribution* (or *empirical pmf*) generated from these data:

$$\varpi^N(x,u,x^+) = \frac{1}{N}\sum_{k=0}^{N-1}\mathbb{1}\{x(k)=x\,,\ u(k)=u\,,\ x(k+1)=x^+\}\,, \qquad x,x^+\in\mathsf{X},\ u\in\mathsf{U}. \tag{5.6}$$

This is a pmf on $\mathsf{X}\times\mathsf{U}\times\mathsf{X}$ for any sequence $\{x(k),u(k)\}$ and any $N\geq 1$. Simple accounting leads to the following alternate expression for (5.5a):

$$\Gamma(h) = \sum_{x,u,x^+}\varpi^N(x,u,x^+)\{-h(x,u)+c(x,u)+\underline{h}(x^+)\}^2, \tag{5.7}$$

where the sum is over all $(x,u,x^+)\in\mathsf{X}\times\mathsf{U}\times\mathsf{X}$ for which $\varpi^N(x,x^+)>0$. This interpretation of $\Gamma(h)$ as an *empirical mean* is useful for both intuition and theory (such as the LP approach to RL that is surveyed over the final sections of this chapter).

5.1.2 Linear Function Approximation

This refers to a family of functions, linearly parameterized by $\theta\in\mathbb{R}^d$:

$$h^\theta(z) = \sum_{i=1}^{d}\theta_i\psi_i(z)\,, \qquad z\in\mathsf{Z}, \tag{5.8}$$

where $\{\psi_i\}$ are the basis functions. It is convenient to stack these together to form a function $\psi\colon\mathsf{Z}\to\mathbb{R}^d$, and then write $h^\theta = \theta^{\intercal}\psi$. For any smooth loss function, the first-order condition for optimality is $0 = \nabla_\theta\Gamma(h^\theta)$. For the mean-square Bellman error (5.5a), this becomes

$$0 = \frac{1}{N}\sum_{k=1}^{N} D_k(h^\theta(z_k),h^\theta(z_{k+1}))\zeta^\theta(k) \qquad \text{where} \quad \zeta^\theta(k) = \nabla_\theta D_k(h^\theta(z_k),h^\theta(z_{k+1})). \tag{5.9}$$

The choice of basis can be informed by some understanding of the control problem. For example, if $\mathsf{Z} = \mathbb{R}^2$ and it is known that H^* is convex, then it may be sufficient to choose h^θ quadratic, with $d = 6$:

$$\begin{aligned}&\psi_1(z) = z_1\,,\ \psi_2(z) = z_2\,,\\ &\psi_3(z) = z_1^2\,,\ \psi_4(z) = z_1 z_2\,,\ \psi_5(z) = z_2^2\,, \qquad \text{and } \psi_6(z) = 1 \text{ for all } z \in \mathbb{R}^2.\end{aligned}$$

Tabular and Binning

A common choice in the theory of RL is the *tabular* setting in which z denotes a typical pair (x,u). It is assumed that X and U are finite, and an ordering is chosen: $\mathsf{X} \times \mathsf{U} = \{z^i = (x^i,u^i) : 1 \le i \le d\}$, in which d is the total number of state-input pairs. The tabular basis is the family of indicator functions

$$\psi_i(x,u) = \mathbb{1}\{(x,u) = (x^i,u^i)\}\,, \qquad (x,u) \in \mathsf{X} \times \mathsf{U}\,,\ 1 \le i \le d. \tag{5.10}$$

If $\mathsf{Z} = \mathsf{X} \times \mathsf{U}$ is not finite, then we can apply binning. Recall from Section 3.9.1 how binning was applied to obtain an approximate model for the mountain car example through first "quantizing" the state space, and then computing the optimal policy for the approximate model using VIA. In RL, we do not approximate the model, but we can perform binning through an extension of the tabular basis. Given a disjoint decomposition $\mathsf{Z} = \bigcup_{i=1}^d B_i$, the ith basis is the indicator function:

$$\psi_i(x,u) = \mathbb{1}\{(x,u) \in B_i\}\,, \qquad (x,u) \in \mathsf{X} \times \mathsf{U}\,,\ 1 \le i \le d. \tag{5.11}$$

This is also written $\psi_i = \mathbb{1}_{B_i}$. Exercise 9.3 is designed to show how this can be a good choice in RL, in the sense that it leads to a consistent algorithm for value function approximation.

Galerkin Relaxation

The term *Galerkin relaxation* appears throughout the book as a means to approximate equality constraints, and sometimes also inequality constraints. As an example of this technique, consider again the loss function (5.5) associated with the mean-square Bellman error. An alternative approximation of the DP equation is obtained by constructing a d_ζ-dimensional sequence $\{\zeta(k)\}$, and search for a function h that satisfies the constraint:

$$0 = \frac{1}{N}\sum_{k=1}^{N} D_k(h(z_k),h(z_{k+1}))\zeta_i(k)\,, \qquad 1 \le i \le d_\zeta. \tag{5.12}$$

This is called a Galerkin relaxation, and certainly a relaxation of our ultimate if unrealistic goal: to find a function h for which the temporal difference $D_k(h(z_k),h(z_{k+1}))$ is zero for each k. In the context of RL, the vectors $\{\zeta(k)\}$ appear as *eligibility vectors* in standard algorithms (see Section 5.4).

For a finite-dimensional function class, we take $d_\zeta = d$, so that (5.12) represents d constraints, which is consistent with the d unknowns, $\{\theta_i^* : 1 \le i \le d\}$.

Equation (5.12) appears similar to (5.9). However, $\zeta(k) = \zeta^\theta(k)$ is not a valid choice, since the Galerkin relaxation does not allow $\zeta(k)$ to depend on the θ. In practice, we might design $\{\zeta(k)\}$ so that $\zeta(k) \approx \zeta^\theta(k)$ for θ in a region of interest.

We are not always so fortunate to have intuition regarding the shape of H^*, and binning may be too complex, which is why there has been so much attention focused on the "black box" function approximation architectures discussed next.

5.1.3 Neural Networks

Neural networks can be used to define a parameterized family of approximations $\{h^\theta\}$ that are highly nonlinear in θ. The purpose of this very brief introduction is to explain how a neural network can be used for function approximation, and especially for applications to value function approximation.

Figure 5.3 shows an example of a feedforward neural network with a single input layer, a single output layer, and three *hidden layers* (the optional *bias* terms are not included). For our purposes, this figure represents a function approximation $h\colon \mathbb{R}^3 \to \mathbb{R}$, so that the input layer is $z = (z_1, z_2, z_3)^\intercal$.

This is called a feedforward network because calculation of y as a function of z is performed sequentially, moving from left to right. For given weight vectors $\{w_k^j\}$ (whose dimensions will be clear from the definitions), the calculations proceed as follows:

The first step is to calculate values $s^1 \in \mathbb{R}^4$ in hidden layer one, via

$$s_k^1 = \sigma(\langle w_k^1, z\rangle), \qquad 1 \le k \le 4,$$

where the notation $\langle w_k^1, z\rangle$ represents the usual dot product of two vectors, and $\sigma\colon \mathbb{R} \to \mathbb{R}$ is known as the *activation function*. There are two standard choices:

$$\textit{Sigmoid:}\quad \sigma(r) = 1/(1+e^{-r}), \qquad\qquad \textit{ReLu:}\quad \sigma(r) = \max(0,r).$$

Calculation of $s^2, s^3 \in \mathbb{R}^4$ is similar:

$$s_k^2 = \sigma(\langle w_k^2, s^1\rangle), \quad s_k^3 = \sigma(\langle w_k^3, s^2\rangle), \qquad 1 \le k \le 4.$$

The output is then defined by $y = \langle w_k^4, s^3\rangle$, which is a linear function of the third hidden layer, but a complex nonlinear function of the input z. The weights are identified with the parameter θ: We may write $y = h^\theta(z)$, with

$$\{\theta_i : 1 \le i \le d\} = \{w_k^j\}, \qquad d = 3\times 4 + 4\times 4 + 4\times 4 + 4 = 48.$$

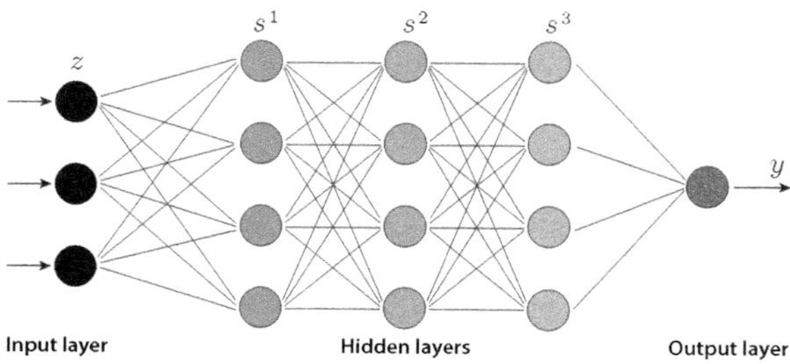

Figure 5.3 Neural network with three hidden layers.

5.1.4 Kernels

Let's start at the conclusion: When applying kernel methods, our approximation of H^* takes the form:

$$h^\theta(z) = \sum_{i=1}^{N} \theta_i \mathbb{k}(z, z_i), \qquad z \in \mathsf{Z}, \tag{5.13}$$

where $\mathbb{k}$ is the kernel function that we choose from a large library.

You might argue that this is simply the linear function approximation approach described earlier, with $d = N$ and $\psi_i(z) = \mathbb{k}(z, z_i)$ for each i and z. Your argument is absolutely correct! To appreciate the kernel method, you need to see how we arrive at this particular form for h^θ.

We return to the "beginning," which is the choice of kernel.

Choice of Kernel, and Requirements

Three standard examples are

$$\begin{aligned}
&\text{Gaussian:} && \mathbb{k}(z, z') = \exp\Bigl(\frac{-\|z - z'\|^2}{2\sigma^2}\Bigr), \\
&\text{Laplacian:} && \mathbb{k}(z, z') = \exp\Bigl(\frac{-\|z - z'\|}{\sigma}\Bigr), \\
&\text{Polynomial:} && \mathbb{k}(z, z') = (r\langle z, z'\rangle + 1)^m, \qquad z, z' \in \mathsf{Z},
\end{aligned}$$

where $\sigma > 0$, $r > 0$ and $m \geq 1$ are design parameters.

Recall that in some control applications we may know that H^* is convex and nonnegative. In this case, the polynomial kernel is attractive because h^θ in (5.13) is convex if m is even, and $\{\theta_i\}$ are nonnegative.

Each of these three examples has the symmetry property, $\mathbb{k}(x, y) = \mathbb{k}(y, x)$. This is one of the several required properties of a kernel. A crucial requirement is that it is *positive definite*: For every $n \geq 1$, every collection $\{z_i : 1 \leq i \leq n\} \subset \mathsf{Z}$, and every $\alpha \in \mathbb{R}^n$,

$$\sum_{i,j=1}^{n} \alpha_i \alpha_j \mathbb{k}(z_i, z_j) \geq 0, \tag{5.14}$$

with equality if and only if $\alpha = 0$.

Function Class for Approximation

Once we have selected a kernel, we arrive at a function class $\mathcal{H}$: an infinite-dimensional analog of the set of functions $\{h^\theta : \theta \in \mathbb{R}^d\}$ defined in (5.8). There is no space in this book to give a full definition of $\mathcal{H}$, and the norm $\|\cdot\|_{\mathcal{H}}$ that is a critical part of the theory.

For our purposes, it is enough to know that $\mathcal{H}$ contains every function of the form (5.13). That is, for any integer n, scalars $\{\alpha_i\}$, and $\{z_i\} \subset \mathsf{Z}$, the following function lies in $\mathcal{H}$:

$$h^\alpha(z) = \sum_{i=1}^{n} \alpha_i \mathbb{k}(z, z_i), \qquad z \in \mathsf{Z}.$$

The primitive functions h^α are also *dense* in $\mathcal{H}$. That is, if $h \in \mathcal{H}$, then for each $\varepsilon > 0$, there is h^α of this form (for some integer n, scalars $\{\alpha_i\}$, $\{z_i\} \subset \mathsf{Z}$, all depending on ε), satisfying $\|h - h^\alpha\|_\mathcal{H} \le \varepsilon$.

For any two functions h^α, h^β of this form, an inner product is introduced that is consistent with the norm:

$$\langle h^\alpha, h^\beta \rangle_\mathcal{H} = \sum_{i,j=1}^{n} \alpha_i \beta_j \Bbbk(z_i, z_j), \tag{5.15a}$$

$$\|h^\alpha\|_\mathcal{H} = \sqrt{\langle h^\alpha, h^\alpha \rangle_\mathcal{H}}. \tag{5.15b}$$

The positivity assumption (5.14) ensures that $\langle h^\alpha, h^\alpha \rangle_\mathcal{H}$ is nonnegative. The definition of the inner product and norm can be extended to the larger collection of functions $\mathcal{H}$, and endowed with this inner product it is known as a *reproducing kernel Hilbert space* (*RKHS*).

Details regarding $\mathcal{H}$ are not required in applications because the *Representer Theorem* tells us we can restrict to the primitive functions in the function approximation problems of interest to us. To present this theorem requires one more ingredient.

Regularized Loss Function

In addition to the loss function Γ, we require a *regularizer* of the form $G(\|h\|_\mathcal{H})$, where $G\colon \mathbb{R}_+ \to \mathbb{R}_+$ is nondecreasing. Typical choices are $G(r) = \delta r^2$ or $G(r) = \delta r$, with $\delta > 0$. Our interest is solving the regularized optimization problem:

$$h^* = \arg\min\{\Gamma(h) + G(\|h\|_\mathcal{H}) : h \in \mathcal{H}\}. \tag{5.16}$$

The regularizer is introduced to manage the overfitting problem illustrated in Figure 5.2.

Theorem 5.1 (Representer Theorem) *Suppose that* $\{z_i : 1 \le i \le N\}$ *are given, along with a loss function of the form* (5.2). *Then any minimizer of the optimization problem* (5.16) *can be expressed, for some* $\alpha^* \in \mathbb{R}^N$,

$$h^*(\cdot) = \sum_{i=1}^{N} \alpha_i^* \Bbbk(\cdot, z_i). \tag{5.17}$$

We return to the two examples.

Curve Fitting

Consider the quadratic loss (5.3). If the regularizer is also quadratic, $G(r) = \delta r^2$, then the Representer Theorem provides an explicit solution to (5.16). We are left to obtain the optimal parameter:

$$\alpha^* = \arg\min_\alpha \{\sum_{i=1}^{N} [y_i - h^\alpha(z_i)]^2 + \delta \|h^\alpha\|_\mathcal{H}^2\}.$$

Let K denote the $n \times n$ matrix with entries $K_{i,j} = \Bbbk(z_i, z_j)$. We then have $\|h^\alpha\|_\mathcal{H}^2 = \alpha^\intercal K \alpha$, and $h^\alpha(z_i) = \sum_j \alpha_j \Bbbk(z_i, x_j) = [K\alpha]_i$. To compute α^*, we set the partial derivatives of the loss equal to zero:

$$0 = \frac{\partial}{\partial \alpha_j} \{\sum_{i=1}^{N} [y_i - [K\alpha]_i]^2 + \delta \alpha^\intercal K \alpha\} = -2 \sum_{i=1}^{N} [y_i - [K\alpha]_i] K_{i,j} + 2\delta [K\alpha]_j.$$

With $y, \alpha^* \in \mathbb{R}^N$ column vectors, this gives

$$\alpha^* = (K^{\intercal}K + \delta K)^{-1}K^{\intercal}y. \tag{5.18}$$

The transpose in (5.18) is not necessary, since $K = K^{\intercal}$ by assumption.

Mean-Square Bellman Error

We no longer have an explicit solution to (5.16), even with G quadratic, but we know that h^* is of the form (5.17) for some vector α^*. Hence finding h^* is a finite-dimensional optimization problem. Exercises 5.10 and 5.11 provide a roadmap to approximations of this complex nonlinear optimization by a sequence of quadratic optimization problems.

A more successful approach may proceed using a convex loss function $\Gamma\colon \mathbb{R}^N \to \mathbb{R}_+$, constructed by applying the representations in Section 3.5; more on this approach may be found in Section 5.5.

5.1.5 Are We Done Yet?

Let's think about how to answer the question within the context of minimizing the mean-square Bellman error using linear function approximation, which results in the root-finding problem (5.9). That is, $\bar{f}_N(\theta_N^*) = 0$, with

$$\bar{f}_N(\theta) = \frac{1}{N}\sum_{k=1}^{N} D_k(h^\theta(z_k), h^\theta(z_{k+1}))\zeta^\theta(k).$$

While it may take you a long time to compute θ_N^*, you are far from done.

Some experiments you can perform to obtain more confidence that you have a useful solution:

Is Your Parameterization Redundant?

Consider $Q^\theta = \theta^{\intercal}\psi$, an approximate Q-function. Along with estimates of the best value of θ, obtain the sample correlation matrix:

$$\widehat{R}^\psi = \frac{1}{N}\sum_{i=1}^{N} \psi(z_i)\psi(z_i)^{\intercal}. \tag{5.19}$$

Look at the eigenvalues of this positive semidefinite matrix – if there is a nontrivial null space, then there may be a problem with your basis or your choice of data.

If $\widehat{R}^\psi v = 0$ for some nonzero vector v, then obviously $v^{\intercal}\widehat{R}^\psi v = 0$, meaning that

$$0 = v^{\intercal}\widehat{R}^\psi v = \frac{1}{N}\sum_{i=1}^{N}\big(v^{\intercal}\psi(z_i)\big)^2.$$

It follows that Q^θ, with $\theta = v$, is identically zero on the samples observed. And it means your basis is redundant, in the sense that one ψ_k is a linear combination of the others: If $v_k \neq 0$, then

$$\psi_k(z_i) = -\frac{1}{v_k}\sum_{j\neq k} v_j\psi_j(z_i), \qquad 1 \le i \le N.$$

There are two potential explanations: (1) your basis is truly linearly dependent in an algebraic sense: $v^{\intercal}\psi(z) = 0$ for every $z \in \mathsf{Z}$ or (2) *insufficient exploration*: The samples $\boldsymbol{z}$ evolve in a small subset of Z.

Is Your Parameter Predictive Using Fresh Data?

Obtain $M \gg 1$ more batches of data $\{\boldsymbol{z}^m : 1 \le m \le M\}$, and compute $\bar{f}_N^m(\theta_N^*)$ for each m, with

$$\bar{f}_N^m(\theta) = \frac{1}{N}\sum_{k=1}^{N} D_k(h^\theta(z_k^m), h^\theta(z_{k+1}^m))\zeta^\theta(k), \qquad 1 \le m \le M.$$

You need to increase N, if there is large variability in $\{\bar{f}_N^m(\theta_N^*) : 1 \le m \le M\}$.

Is the Output of Your Algorithm Predictive of What Really Matters?

This will take some work, but it is truly essential. With $M \gg 1$ batches of data, estimate the performance you obtain with the output of your algorithm. This means that for each $m = 1, \ldots, M$, you must:

(i) Obtain an estimate θ^{*m} using your algorithm.
(ii) Obtain $\phi^{*m}(x) = \arg\min_u Q^{\theta^{*m}}(x,u)$.
(iii) Run more experiments to estimate the performance. For the total cost problems considered here, choose a pmf ν with finite support. For each initial condition x^i satisfying $\nu(x^i) > 0$, run a simulation to estimate $J(x^i)$ under policy ϕ^{*m}, and then obtain $\Gamma_m = \sum_i \nu(x^i)\widehat{J}_m(x^i)$. Look at the sample mean and variance of $\{\Gamma_m : 1 \le m \le M\}$. High variance means you need a longer run.
Or, you might decide to look more closely at those policies for which Γ_m is smallest – maybe you got lucky! To know for sure, you need a deeper investigation of performance, using data independent of what was used for training.

For many readers, the preceding discussion is mainly a guide to receive a passing grade on upcoming simulation assignments! If we are talking about *real life*, rather than a homework problem, then you need advice from experts. For example, if your θ^* is supposed to define an optimal policy for an autonomous car, then you need experts in sociology as well as highway engineering to conduct realistic experiments to validate your control design.

5.2 Exploration and ODE Approximations

The success of the RL algorithms surveyed in this chapter depends in part on the choice of input $\boldsymbol{u}$ used for training. The purpose of this section is to make this precise, and present our main assumption on the input designed for generating data to train the algorithm (that is, exploration, as first surveyed in Section 2.5.3). Throughout this chapter, it is assumed that the input used for training is state feedback with perturbation, of the form

$$u(k) = \breve{\phi}(x(k), \xi(k)), \tag{5.20}$$

where ξ is a bounded sequence evolving on a set $\Omega \subset \mathbb{R}^p$ for some $p \geq 1$. It plays the same role as the probing signal introduced for gradient-free optimization in Section 4.6, with applications to policy gradient algorithms in Section 4.7.

In the theoretical development of QSA it was convenient to assume that the exploration itself evolves according to the autonomous state space model (4.79). In discrete time, we make the change of notation

$$\xi(k+1) = \mathrm{H}(\xi(k)), \tag{5.21}$$

in which $\mathrm{H}\colon \Omega \to \Omega$ is continuous. Subject to the policy (5.20), it follows that the triple $\Phi(k) = (x(k), u(k), \xi(k))^{\intercal}$ has a similar recursive form, evolving on the larger state space Z. In some cases, such as in TD(λ) learning, it is necessary to add additional components to $\Phi(k)$ and extend the state space Z. This is the reason for the abstract description of $\boldsymbol{\Phi}$ in Assumption (Aξ).

A Few Words on Ergodic Averages

Assumption (Aξ) that follows is similar to Assumption (QSA5) appearing in Section 4.9, in that both concern averages of observations. In the discrete-time setting of this chapter, we denote

$$\bar{g}_N = \frac{1}{N}\sum_{k=1}^{N} g(\Phi(k))$$

for $g\colon \mathsf{Z} \to \mathbb{R}$ continuous, and $N \geq 1$. The main assumption is the existence of a limit, known as the ergodic mean (also known as ergodic *average* or *expectation*):

$$\mathsf{E}_{\varpi}[g(\Phi)] \stackrel{\text{def}}{=} \lim_{N\to\infty} \bar{g}_N. \tag{5.22}$$

The expression $\mathsf{E}_{\varpi}[g(\Phi)]$ may be regarded as convenient notation, but in many cases it is represented as an integral: The *probability measure* ϖ has a density ρ, so that

$$\mathsf{E}_{\varpi}[g(\Phi)] = \int_{\mathsf{Z}} g(z)\rho(z)dz.$$

Here is a simple result to illustrate the origin of a density:

Lemma 5.2 *Consider the scalar probing signal $\xi(k) = \sin(2\pi k/T)$, $k \geq 0$. Provided T is an irrational number, for any continuous function $g\colon \mathbb{R} \to \mathbb{R}$, we have*

$$\lim_{N\to\infty} \frac{1}{N}\sum_{k=1}^{N} g(\xi(k)) = \int_0^1 g(\sin(2\pi r))dr = \int_{-1}^{1} g(t)\rho(t)dt, \tag{5.23}$$

where $\rho(t) = [\pi\sqrt{1-t^2}]^{-1}$ is known as the arcsine density.

Proof Consider first the signal $\xi^0(k) = [k/T]_1$, where $[r]_1$ denotes the fractional part of a scalar $r \in \mathbb{R}_+$. This signal samples points uniformly in the interval $[0,1]$, giving for continuous functions $h\colon \mathbb{R} \to \mathbb{R}$,

$$\lim_{N\to\infty} \frac{1}{N}\sum_{k=1}^{N} h(\xi^0(k)) = \int_0^1 h(r)dr.$$

The first equality in (5.23) follows on taking $h(\xi^0(k)) = g(\sin(2\pi\xi^0(k))) = g(\xi(k))$. The second equality is a calculus exercise. □

It will simplify some analysis to impose uniformity of the limit (5.22) over Lipschitz continuous functions. For any $L > 0$, denote

$$\mathcal{G}_L = \{g : \|g(z') - g(z)\| \le L\|z - z'\|, \text{ for all } z, z' \in \mathsf{Z}\}.$$

Assumption (Aξ) The state and action spaces X and U are each closed subsets of Euclidean space; F defined in (3.1), $\breve{\phi}$ defined in (5.20), and H in (5.21) are each continuous on their domains. There is a larger state process $\boldsymbol{\Phi}$ with the following properties:

(i) $\boldsymbol{\Phi}$ evolves on a closed subset of Euclidean space, denoted Z, and $(x(k), u(k), \xi(k)) = w(\Phi(k))$ for each k, where $w\colon \mathsf{Z} \to \mathsf{X} \times \mathsf{U} \times \Omega$ is Lipschitz continuous.
(ii) There is a probability measure ϖ such that for any continuous function $g\colon \mathsf{Z} \to \mathbb{R}$, the ergodic mean (5.22) exists for each initial condition $\Phi(0)$.
(iii) The limit in (5.22) is uniform on $\mathcal{G}_L$, for each $L < \infty$:

$$\lim_{N\to\infty} \sup_{g\in\mathcal{G}_L} |\bar{g}_N - \mathsf{E}_\varpi[g(\Phi)]| = 0.$$

The "quasirandomized" policy structure defined by (5.20) and (5.21) is imposed so that the ergodic limit (5.22) can be expected to exist. Please remember that these assumptions are *not* essential for successful implementation of algorithms. They are introduced only to simplify analysis.

ODE Approximations

Just as in the previous chapter, ergodicity allows for approximation of algorithms by simpler ODE approximations. In particular, consider a recursion of the form

$$\theta_{n+1} = \theta_n + \alpha_{n+1} f_{n+1}(\theta_n), \qquad n \ge 0, \tag{5.24}$$

in which $\{f_n\}$ is a sequence of functions that admits an ergodic limit:

$$\bar{f}(\theta) \stackrel{\text{def}}{=} \lim_{N\to\infty} \frac{1}{N} \sum_{k=1}^{N} f_k(\theta), \qquad \theta \in \mathbb{R}^d.$$

The associated ODE is defined using this vector field:

$$\frac{d}{dt}\vartheta_t = \bar{f}(\vartheta_t). \tag{5.25}$$

An ODE approximation is defined by mimicking the usual Euler construction: the time scale for the ODE is defined by the nondecreasing time points $\tau_0 = 0$ and $\tau_n = \sum_0^n \alpha_k$ for $n \ge 1$. Define a continuous time process by $\Theta_{\tau_n} = \theta_n$ for each n, and extend to all t through piecewise linear interpolation. Let $\{\vartheta^n_t : t \ge \tau_n\}$ denote the solution to the ODE (5.25) with initial condition $\vartheta^n_{\tau_n} = \theta_n$. We then say that the algorithm (5.24) admits an *ODE approximation* if for each initial θ_0 and $\mathcal{N} > 0$,

$$\lim_{n\to\infty} \sup_{\tau_n \le \tau \le \tau_n + \mathcal{N}} \|\Theta_\tau - \vartheta^n_\tau\| = 0. \tag{5.26}$$

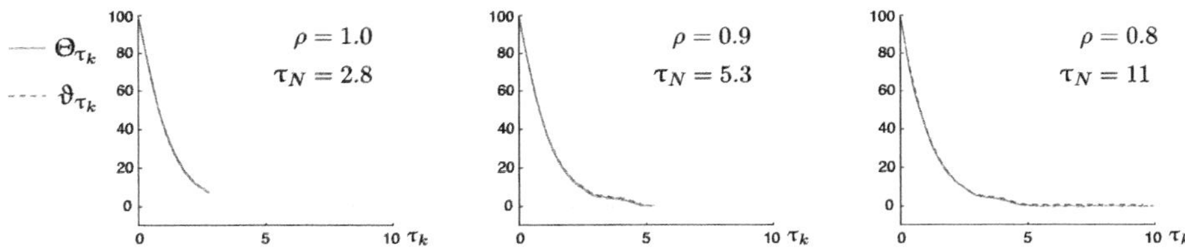

Figure 5.4 ODE approximations for root finding.

If the parameter sequence $\{\theta_n\}$ is bounded, then it is often easy to establish (5.26) by following the steps of Proposition 4.28. We can then follow the proof of Theorem 4.15 to establish convergence of the parameter sequence whenever (5.25) is globally asymptotically stable.

Figure 5.4 is adapted from Figure 8.5, illustrating a version of (5.24) in which $f_{n+1}(\theta)$ is *random* for each n, with mean equal to $\bar{f}(\theta)$. The definition of an ODE approximation (5.26) is unchanged in this stochastic approximation setting.

The three plots each compare $\Theta_{\tau_k} = \theta_k$ with ϑ_{τ_k} ($\vartheta^n_{\tau_k}$ with $n = 0$), and are distinguished by choice of step-size: $\alpha_n = 1/n^\rho$, with $\rho = 1.0, 0.9, 0.8$. In each case, the algorithm (5.24) was run for a common choice of $\{f_n\}$, and common time horizon $1 \le n \le N = 10^5$. The significant difference observed in these plots is how ρ influences the range of τ_n: The value $N = 10^5$ corresponds to $\tau_N < 3$ for $\rho = 1$, while $\tau_N > 10$ for $\rho = 0.8$.

The approximation $\theta_k \approx \vartheta_{\tau_k}$ is unusually tight in this example. The explanation is the large initial condition: The compression of the vertical axis masks volatility of the parameter estimates.

The more aggressive high gain obtained with larger ρ leads to faster convergence of $\{\vartheta_\tau : \tau \ge 0\}$, but in some cases this introduces unacceptable volatility in the parameter estimates $\{\theta_n : n \ge 0\}$. These remarks echo the theory of QSA outlined in Section 4.5.4 and formalized in Theorem 4.24.

5.3 TD-Learning and Linear Regression

TD-learning refers to methods to approximate a value function for a fixed-policy ϕ. This may be just one step in an approximation of the policy improvement algorithm introduced in Section 3.2.2, which requires estimation of J^n to be used in the policy improvement step (3.14).

5.3.1 Fixed-Policy Temporal Difference

The *second glance ahead* discussion, contained in Section 3.7, included an informal introduction to approximate policy improvement. This approach requires estimates of the fixed-policy Q-function to obtain the policy update:

$$\phi^{n+1}(x) = \arg\min_u Q_n(x,u), \qquad x \in \mathsf{X},$$

in which Q_n solves or approximates (3.45). Section 4.5.3 contains an example intended to illustrate this approach.

For any policy ϕ with associated value function J^ϕ, the fixed policy Q-function is denoted

$$Q^\phi(x,u) = c(x,u) + J^\phi(\mathrm{F}(x,\phi(x))).$$

In this notation, the fixed-point equation (3.45) becomes

$$Q^\phi(x,u) = c(x,u) + Q^\phi(x^+,u^+), \qquad x^+ = \mathrm{F}(x,u), \ u^+ = \phi(x^+). \tag{5.27}$$

For any approximation Q, we can observe the error in this fixed-point equation as another temporal difference: For any input-state sequence $(\boldsymbol{u},\boldsymbol{x})$, denote

$$\mathcal{D}_{k+1}(Q) \stackrel{\text{def}}{=} -Q(x(k),u(k)) + c(x(k),u(k)) + \underline{Q}_\phi(x(k+1)), \tag{5.28a}$$

$$\underline{Q}_\phi(x) \stackrel{\text{def}}{=} Q(x,\phi(x)), \qquad x \in \mathsf{X}. \tag{5.28b}$$

The temporal difference (5.28a) is zero for all k if we substitute Q^ϕ for Q.

Algorithms to approximate Q^ϕ based on the temporal difference sequence (5.28a) are called SARSA. These algorithms are only a minor variation on the TD-learning algorithms designed to estimate J^ϕ, so we opt for the simpler terminology "TD-learning" throughout the book.

There are two distinct flavors of TD-learning: *on policy* and *off policy*. The on-policy versions choose $u(k) = \phi(x(k))$ in the definition (5.28a). The difficulties with on-policy algorithms should be clear following the discussion regarding exploration in Section 2.5.3: If ϕ is a good policy, in the sense that $x(k) \to x^e$, $u(k) = \phi(x(k)) \to u^e$ as $k \to \infty$, then for any function Q,

$$\begin{aligned}\lim_{k\to\infty} \mathcal{D}_{k+1}(Q) &= \lim_{k\to\infty} \{-Q(x(k),u(k)) + c(x(k),u(k)) + Q(x(k+1),\phi(x(k+1))\} \\ &= c(x^e,u^e), \qquad \textit{if}\ u(k) = \phi(x(k)) \text{ for each } k.\end{aligned} \tag{5.29}$$

Consequently, under the convention $c(x^e,u^e) = 0$, the temporal difference error approaches zero for any choice of Q.

In this part of the book, we focus mainly on off-policy algorithms designed to allow for exploration. The elegant theory for on-policy algorithms in stochastic control is explored in Part II.

5.3.2 Least Squares and Linear Regression

Consider the linear parameterization introduced previously in (3.43):

$$Q^\theta(x,u) = \theta^{\intercal}\psi(x,u), \quad \theta \in \mathbb{R}^d. \tag{5.30}$$

Given the assumption that $Q(x^e,u^e) = 0$, it is important to construct the function class with this in mind:

$$\psi_i(x^e,u^e) = 0 \quad 1 \le i \le d. \tag{5.31}$$

From the definition (5.28a), we obtain

$$\mathcal{D}_{k+1}(Q^\theta) = -Q^\theta(x(k),u(k)) + c(x(k),u(k)) + \underline{Q}^\theta_\phi(x(k+1)).$$

This can be expressed in a form that will inspire a budding statistician. On denoting

$$\gamma_k = c(x(k),u(k)), \tag{5.32a}$$

$$\Upsilon_{k+1} = \psi(x(k),u(k)) - \psi(x(k+1),\phi(x(k+1))), \tag{5.32b}$$

we obtain the representation

$$\gamma_k = \Upsilon_{k+1}^{\intercal}\theta + \mathcal{D}_{k+1}(Q^\theta). \tag{5.32c}$$

This is the form of a standard regression problem:

$$\gamma_k = \Upsilon_{k+1}^{\intercal}\theta^* + \varepsilon_k,$$

where $\{\varepsilon_k = \mathcal{D}_{k+1}(Q^{\theta^*}) : k \geq 0\}$ is regarded as "noise," and θ^* is typically defined as the minimum variance parameter: $\theta^* = \arg\min_\theta \Gamma(\theta)$, with

$$\Gamma(\theta) = \mathsf{E}_\varpi\big[[\gamma_0 - \Upsilon_1^{\intercal}\theta]^2\big] \stackrel{\text{def}}{=} \lim_{N\to\infty} \frac{1}{N}\sum_{k=0}^{N-1}[\gamma_k - \Upsilon_{k+1}^{\intercal}\theta]^2. \tag{5.33}$$

This is the mean-square error for the temporal difference sequence: Applying (5.32c),

$$\Gamma(\theta) = \lim_{N\to\infty} \frac{1}{N}\sum_{k=1}^{N}[\mathcal{D}_k(Q^\theta)]^2.$$

Convergence of this limit requires conditions on the input, and further conditions are required so that this loss function is meaningful. In particular, for the on-policy approach in which (5.29) holds, $\Gamma(\theta) = 0$ for every θ! This is why exploration is needed. Exercise 5.2 illustrates design of the probing signal for the special case of LQR.

Least Squares Temporal Difference Learning (LSTD)

For a given $d \times d$ matrix $W > 0$, integer N, and observed samples $\{u(k),x(k) : 0 \leq k \leq N\}$, the minimizer is obtained:

$$\theta_N^{\text{LSTD}} = \arg\min_\theta \Gamma_N(\theta), \qquad \Gamma_N(\theta) = \theta^{\intercal}W\theta + \sum_{k=0}^{N-1}[\gamma_k - \Upsilon_{k+1}^{\intercal}\theta]^2. \tag{5.34}$$

This defines the approximation of the Q-function: $Q^{\theta_N^{\text{LSTD}}} = \sum_i \theta_N^{\text{LSTD}}(i)\psi_i$.

The objective is a positive-definite quadratic, so the solution to (5.34) is obtained on setting the gradient of the objective to zero: $\nabla\Gamma_N(\theta) = 0$ for $\theta = \theta_N^{\text{LSTD}}$.

Proposition 5.3 $\theta_N^{\text{LSTD}} = [N^{-1}W + R_N]^{-1}\overline{\psi}_N^{\gamma}$, *with*

$$R_N = \frac{1}{N}\sum_{k=1}^{N}\Upsilon_k\Upsilon_k^{\intercal}, \quad \overline{\psi}_N^{\gamma} = \frac{1}{N}\sum_{k=0}^{N-1}\Upsilon_{k+1}\gamma_k. \qquad \square$$

The regularizer $\theta^{\intercal}W\theta$ is introduced to ensure a unique solution. It is worth investigating the implications if R_N is not invertible.

Proposition 5.4 *Suppose that R_N has rank less than d. Then there is a nonzero vector $v \in \mathbb{R}^d$ for which the following hold, for each $0 \le k \le N-1$:*

(i) *For any $\theta \in \mathbb{R}^d$ and $r \in \mathbb{R}$,*

$$\mathcal{D}_{k+1}(Q^\theta) = \mathcal{D}_{k+1}(Q^{\theta'}), \quad \text{with } \theta' = \theta + rv.$$

(ii) *For the on-policy implementation,*

$$v^\intercal \psi(x(0),u(0)) = v^\intercal \psi(x(k),u(k)).$$

Hence the basis falls into the "redundant" category discussed in Section 5.1.5.

Proof If R_N does not have full rank, it then follows that there is a nonzero vector v satisfying $v^\intercal R_N v = 0$. By definition,

$$0 = v^\intercal R_N v = \frac{1}{N}\sum_{k=0}^{N-1}\bigl(v^\intercal \Upsilon_{k+1}\bigr)^2.$$

That is, $v^\intercal \Upsilon_k = 0$ for every observed sample, which means

$$0 = v^\intercal \psi(x(k),u(k)) - v^\intercal \psi(x(k+1),\phi(x(k+1))), \qquad 0 \le k \le N-1. \tag{5.35}$$

Part (i) then follows from (5.35) and the definition (5.28a): for any scalar r, with $\theta' = \theta + rv$,

$$\begin{aligned}\mathcal{D}_{k+1}(Q^{\theta'}) &= -Q^{\theta'}(x(k),u(k)) + c(x(k),u(k)) + Q^{\theta'}(x(k+1)),\phi(x(k+1))) \\ &= c(x(k),u(k)) + [\theta + rv]^\intercal[-\psi(x(k),u(k)) + \psi(x(k+1),\phi(x(k+1)))] \\ &= c(x(k),u(k)) + \theta^\intercal[-\psi(x(k),u(k)) + \psi(x(k+1),\phi(x(k+1)))] = \mathcal{D}_{k+1}(Q^\theta).\end{aligned}$$

If $u(k) = \phi(x(k))$ for all k, then (5.35) becomes

$$v^\intercal \psi(x(k),u(k)) = v^\intercal \psi(x(k+1),u(k+1)), \qquad 0 \le k \le N-1,$$

which implies (ii). □

On-policy algorithms are sometimes preferred because of ease of analysis (mainly in the context of stochastic control). To ensure sufficient exploration, it may be best to go with the restart option introduced in (2.55):

Least Squares Temporal Difference Learning (with Restart)

Assumed given are $d \times d$ matrix $W > 0$, integers N and M, and observed samples

$$\{u^i(k), x^i(k) : 0 \le i \le N, 1 \le i \le M\} \tag{5.36a}$$

with user-defined initial conditions $\{x^i(0) : 1 \le i \le M\}$, and with input $u^i(k) = \breve{\phi}(x^i(k), \xi^i(k))$.

The approximation of the Q-function $Q^{\theta_N^{\text{LSTD}}} = \psi^\intercal \theta_N^{\text{LSTD}}$ is obtained, in which the optimal parameter is defined by the following steps:

(i) Introduce a per-batch loss function $\Gamma^i_N(\theta)$: Defined by (5.34) using the ith batch, $B^i = \{u^i(k), x^i(k) : 0 \le k \le N\}$.
(ii) Define $\theta^{\text{LSTD}}_N = \arg\min_\theta \Gamma_N(\theta)$, with

$$\Gamma_N(\theta) = \frac{1}{M}\sum_{i=1}^{M} \Gamma^i_N(\theta). \tag{5.36b}$$

This approach does not rule out $u^i(k) = \phi(x^i(k))$ for each i and k (on-policy).

Note that analysis of RL algorithms with restart require a modification of Assumption (Aξ).

5.3.3 Recursive LSTD and Zap

LSTD learning is often presented as a recursive algorithm:

Proposition 5.5 *LSTD learning in the form* (5.34) *admits the recursive representation:*

$$\theta^*_{N+1} = \theta^*_N + G_{N+1}\Upsilon_{N+1}\big[\gamma_N - \Upsilon^{\intercal}_{N+1}\theta^*_N\big], \tag{5.37a}$$

$$G_{N+1} = G_N - \frac{1}{k_{N+1}} G_N \Upsilon_{N+1}\Upsilon^{\intercal}_{N+1} G_N, \qquad N \ge 0 \tag{5.37b}$$

with $k_{N+1} = 1 + \Upsilon^{\intercal}_{N+1} G_N \Upsilon_{N+1}$.

Proof The recursion is an application of Proposition 5.3: Letting $G_N = [W + NR_N]^{-1}$, the proposition implies that for $N \ge 0$,

$$G^{-1}_{N+1}\theta^*_{N+1} = (N+1)\bar{\psi}^{\gamma}_{N+1}$$
$$\text{and} \quad G^{-1}_{N+1} = G^{-1}_N + \Upsilon_{N+1}\Upsilon^{\intercal}_{N+1}.$$

The recursion (5.37b) follows from the Matrix Inversion Lemma (A.1).

To obtain (5.37a), we apply this recursion for $\bar{\psi}^{\gamma}_N$, also implied by Proposition 5.3:

$$(N+1)\bar{\psi}^{\gamma}_{N+1} = N\bar{\psi}^{\gamma}_N + \Upsilon_{N+1}\gamma_N.$$

Consequently,

$$\begin{aligned} G^{-1}_{N+1}\theta^*_{N+1} &= (N+1)\bar{\psi}^{\gamma}_{N+1} \\ &= N\bar{\psi}^{\gamma}_N + \Upsilon_{N+1}\gamma_N \\ &= G^{-1}_N\theta^*_N + \Upsilon_{N+1}\gamma_N \\ &= \{G^{-1}_{N+1} - \Upsilon_{N+1}\Upsilon^{\intercal}_{N+1}\}\theta^*_N + \Upsilon_{N+1}\gamma_N. \end{aligned}$$

Multiplying each side by G_{N+1} and rearranging terms establishes (5.37a). □

The algorithm (5.37) can be represented as a QSA recursion with matrix gain:

$$\theta^*_{N+1} = \theta^*_N + \alpha_{N+1}R_{N+1}\Upsilon_{N+1}\big[\gamma_N - \Upsilon^{\intercal}_{N+1}\theta^*_N\big]$$

in which $\alpha_N = 1/N$ and

$$R_N^{-1} = \frac{1}{N}\Big[W + \sum_{k=1}^{N} \Upsilon_k \Upsilon_k^{\intercal}\Big].$$

Back to Zap

We might have arrived at this algorithm through the ODE method, in which the recursive algorithm is designed to approximate a matrix-gain ODE:

$$\tfrac{d}{dt}\vartheta_t = M\bar{f}(\vartheta_t).$$

Given our objective to minimize the loss function (5.33), it is natural to take $\bar{f}(\theta) = -\frac{1}{2}\nabla\Gamma(\theta)$ and M positive definite. The recursion (5.37a) is an approximation of this ODE using $M = \mathsf{E}_{\varpi}[\Upsilon_k \Upsilon_k^{\intercal}]^{-1}$.

We can also write

$$M^{-1} = \mathsf{E}_{\varpi}[\Upsilon_k \Upsilon_k^{\intercal}] = \tfrac{1}{2}\partial_\theta^2 \mathsf{E}_{\varpi}[(\gamma_{k-1} - \Upsilon_k^{\intercal}\theta)^2] = \tfrac{1}{2}\partial_\theta^2 \Gamma(\theta) = -\partial_\theta \bar{f}(\theta).$$

Hence LSTD is a single time-scale approximation of Zap QSA.

5.4 Projected Bellman Equations and TD Algorithms

LSTD learning suffers from two computational challenges:

(i) What do you do if $d = 10^6$? Practitioners in machine learning often face high-dimensional optimization problems and claim that dimensions of one million are no longer a concern. This success story is attributed to advances in optimization theory, computer engineering, and computing power.

(ii) How can LSTD be extended to nonlinear function approximation, such as when each θ_i is a weight in a neural network?

In the RL research community, it is typical to modify the objective in order to reduce computational complexity. A favored approach is to create algorithms that obtain solutions to a *projected* dynamic programming equation. While there is little supporting theory, the algorithms inspired by this viewpoint have been highly successful with neural network function approximation.

The motivation behind these algorithms requires a bit more background on function approximation, described here using the notation of Section 5.1. We begin with an abstraction: Find a function h^* that solves a fixed point equation:

$$h^* = T(h^*). \tag{5.38}$$

The specifics of the domain and range of h^*, and the meaning of the mapping T, depend on the problem we would like to solve. The DP equation (3.5) is one example, with $h^* = J^\star$. If solving (5.38) is intractable, we might seek an approximation.

We choose a function class $\mathcal{H}$ and a mapping $P_{\mathcal{H}}\colon \mathcal{H} \to \mathcal{H}$. That is, $P_{\mathcal{H}}(h) \in \mathcal{H}$ for any $h \in \mathcal{H}$. More conditions on this mapping will be imposed later. We then introduce an approximation of (5.38):

$$\hat{h} = \widehat{T}(\hat{h}) \stackrel{\text{def}}{=} P_{\mathcal{H}}\{T(\hat{h})\}. \tag{5.39}$$

In some cases, this approach fails or is too complex, so we consider an alternative: Given a second function class $\mathcal{G}$, find a function $\hat{h} \in \mathcal{H}$ solving

$$0 = P_{\mathcal{G}}\{\hat{h} - T(\hat{h})\}. \tag{5.40}$$

This is a generalization of (5.39):

Proposition 5.6 *Suppose that the following hold:*

(i) $\mathcal{H} = \mathcal{G}$.
(ii) *$\mathcal{H}$ is a linear function class: $a_1 h_1 + a_2 h_2 \in \mathcal{H}$ whenever $h_1, h_2 \in \mathcal{H}$ and $a_1, a_2 \in \mathbb{R}$.*
(iii) *The mapping $P_{\mathcal{H}}$ is linear: For $h_1, h_2 \in \mathcal{H}$ and $a_1, a_2 \in \mathbb{R}$,*

$$P_{\mathcal{H}}(a_1 h_1 + a_2 h_2) = a_1 P_{\mathcal{H}}(h_1) + a_2 P_{\mathcal{H}}(h_2).$$

Then the solutions to (5.39) *and* (5.40) *coincide.* □

When we put these ideas to practice in control, the mappings $P_{\mathcal{H}}$ and $P_{\mathcal{G}}$ are defined to be projections (formally defined later). $\widehat{T}$ will define the *projected Bellman operator*, and (5.40) is called the *projected Bellman equation.*

5.4.1 Galerkin Relaxations and Projection

We begin with assumptions on $\mathcal{G}$ and the mapping $P_{\mathcal{G}}$.

It is assumed that each $g \in \mathcal{G}$ is a function $g\colon \mathsf{Z} \to \mathbb{R}$, and with Z the larger state space used in Assumption (Aξ). The function class $\mathcal{G}$ is also assumed to be linear: $a_1 g_1 + a_2 g_2 \in \mathcal{G}$ whenever $g_1, g_2 \in \mathcal{G}$ and $a_1, a_2 \in \mathbb{R}$. To define what is meant by projection requires geometry: The expectation introduced in (Aξ) is used to define an inner product and norm on functions $h_1, h_2\colon \mathsf{Z} \to \mathbb{R}$:

$$\langle h_1, h_2 \rangle_{\varpi} = \mathsf{E}_{\varpi}[h_1(\Phi) h_2(\Phi)], \qquad \|h_1\|_{\varpi} = \sqrt{\mathsf{E}_{\varpi}[(h_1(\Phi))^2]} = \sqrt{\langle h_1, h_1 \rangle_{\varpi}}.$$

The function class $L_2(\varpi)$ is defined to be all functions h for which $\|h\|_{\varpi}$ is finite. For any $h \in L_2(\varpi)$, the projection onto $\mathcal{G}$ is defined as

$$\hat{h} = P_{\mathcal{G}}(h) \stackrel{\text{def}}{=} \arg\min_{g} \{\|g - h\|_{\varpi} : g \in \mathcal{G}\}.$$

The optimizer $\hat{h} \in \mathcal{G}$ satisfies the orthogonality principle:

$$\langle h - \hat{h}, g \rangle_{\varpi} = 0, \qquad g \in \mathcal{G}. \tag{5.41}$$

We henceforth assume that $\mathcal{G}$ has finite dimension: We choose d functions $\{\zeta_i : 1 \le i \le d\}$, stack these together to define a function $\zeta\colon \mathsf{Z} \to \mathbb{R}^d$, and then define $\mathcal{G} = \{g = \theta^{\intercal} \zeta : \theta \in \mathbb{R}^d\}$. We denote $\zeta(k) = \zeta(\Phi(k))$, and call this the sequence of *eligibility vectors*, since they will play a role in a Galerkin relaxation (first introduced in (5.12)).

Proposition 5.7 *Suppose that $\zeta_i \in L_2(\varpi)$ for each i, and that these functions are* linearly independent *in $L_2(\varpi)$. That is, $\|\theta^{\intercal} \zeta\|_{\varpi} = 0$ implies that $\theta = 0$.*

For each $h \in L_2(\varpi)$, the projection exists, is unique, and given by $\hat{h} = \theta^{*\intercal} \zeta$ with

$$\theta^* = [R^{\zeta}]^{-1} \bar{\psi}^h, \tag{5.42}$$

where $\bar{\psi}^h \in \mathbb{R}^d$ *and the* $d \times d$ *matrix* R^ζ *are defined by*

$$\begin{aligned}\bar{\psi}_i^h &= \langle \zeta_i, h \rangle_\varpi, \\ R^\zeta(i,j) &= \langle \zeta_i, \zeta_j \rangle_\varpi, 1 \le i,j \le d.\end{aligned} \tag{5.43}$$

Proof The orthogonality principle (5.41) tells us that for each i,

$$\langle h - \hat{h}, \zeta_i \rangle_\varpi = 0.$$

Combining this identity with the representation $\hat{h} = \theta^{*\intercal}\zeta$ completes the proof. □

Proposition 5.7 is the motivation for Galerkin approaches to root finding, generalizing the sample path definition (5.12):

Proposition 5.8 *Equation* (5.40) *holds if and only if*

$$0 = \langle \zeta_i, \hat{h} - T(\hat{h}) \rangle_\varpi, \qquad 1 \le i \le d. \tag{5.44}$$

This is by definition the Galerkin relaxation of (5.38) *in this* L_2 *setting.* □

5.4.2 TD(λ)-Learning

The fixed point equation (5.27) is of the form (5.38): Define for any function $h\colon \mathsf{X} \times \mathsf{U} \to \mathbb{R}$,

$$T(h)\Big|_{(x,u)} = c(x,u) + h(x^+,u^+), \qquad x^+ = \mathsf{F}(x,u), \; u^+ = \phi(x^+)$$

so that $Q^\phi = T(Q^\phi)$.

Galerkin relaxations lead to the oldest and most celebrated RL algorithms. Consider specification of $\mathcal{H}$ as a finite-dimensional function class $\{h = \theta^\intercal \psi : \theta \in \mathbb{R}^d\}$, where $\psi_i\colon \mathsf{X} \times \mathsf{U} \to \mathbb{R}$ for each i. We arrive at the projected Bellman equation by applying the approximation (5.39) to this problem, in its equivalent form (5.44): For each i,

$$0 = \mathsf{E}_\varpi\big[\zeta_i(k)\{\hat{h}(x(k),u(k)) - [c(x(k),u(k)) + \hat{h}(x(k+1),\phi(x(k+1)))]\}\big],$$

where we have used the definition of the inner product, along with the notation $\zeta(k) = \zeta(\Phi(k))$. The solution of this root-finding problem defines $Q^{\theta^*} \in \mathcal{H}$.

Recalling the definition (5.29), the projected Bellman equation is equivalently expressed

$$0 = \mathsf{E}_\varpi\big[\zeta(k)\mathcal{D}_{k+1}(Q^\theta)\big]\Big|_{\theta=\theta^*}. \tag{5.45}$$

Given N observations, an approximation is obtained via

$$0 = \frac{1}{N}\sum_{k=0}^{N-1} \zeta(k)\mathcal{D}_{k+1}(Q^\theta)\Big|_{\theta=\theta^*}, \tag{5.46}$$

which is precisely of the form (5.12).

We can now define the meaning of "λ" in TD(λ) learning, which depends entirely on the choice of $\mathcal{G}$. To keep notation more compact, denote

$$\psi_{(k)} \stackrel{\text{def}}{=} \psi(x(k),u(k)), \qquad c_k \stackrel{\text{def}}{=} c(x(k),u(k)), \qquad k \ge 0, \tag{5.47}$$

and when possible use ζ_k instead of $\zeta(k)$ for the eligibility vector, and we denote $\underline{Q}^\theta_\phi(x) = Q^\theta(x,\phi(x))$.

TD(λ) Learning

For a given $\lambda \in [0,1]$, nonnegative step-size sequence $\{\alpha_n\}$, initial conditions θ_0, ζ_0, and observed samples $\{u(k), x(k) : 0 \le k \le N\}$, the sequence of estimates is defined by the coupled equations:

$$\theta_{n+1} = \theta_n + \alpha_{n+1}\mathcal{D}_{n+1}\zeta_n, \tag{5.48a}$$
$$\mathcal{D}_{n+1}(Q) = -Q^{\theta_n}(x(n),u(n)) + c_n + \underline{Q}_{\Phi}^{\theta_n}(x(n+1)), \tag{5.48b}$$
$$\zeta_{n+1} = \lambda\zeta_n + \psi_{(n+1)}. \tag{5.48c}$$

This defines the approximation of the Q-function $Q^{\theta_N} = \sum_i \theta_N(i)\psi_i$.

For the purposes of analysis, we require an extension of the state process:

$$\Phi(k) = (x(k), u(k), \xi(k), \zeta(k))^{\intercal}$$

so that $\zeta(k)$ is a linear function of $\Phi(k)$.

Denote $\bar{f}_\lambda(\theta) = \mathsf{E}_\varpi\big[\zeta(k)\mathcal{D}_{k+1}(Q^\theta)\big]$. TD($\lambda$) is an approximation of the ODE

$$\tfrac{d}{dt}\vartheta = \bar{f}_\lambda(\vartheta).$$

The right-hand side is linear: $\bar{f}_\lambda(\theta) = A(\theta - \theta^*)$, in which

$$A = \mathsf{E}_\varpi\big[\zeta(k)[-\psi_{(k)} + \psi(x(k+1), \phi(x(k+1))]^{\intercal}\big]. \tag{5.49}$$

Convergence of TD(λ) learning is not guaranteed in the off-policy setting, even with $\lambda = 0$. A famous example is described after Figure 5.5.

What about neural networks? If $\mathcal{H}$ is not a linear function class, then we lose much of the convergence theory, but the algorithm can be salvaged:

TD(λ) Learning (with Nonlinear Function Approximation)

For a given $\lambda \in [0,1]$, nonnegative step-size sequence $\{\alpha_n\}$, initial conditions θ_0, ζ_0, and observed samples $\{u(k), x(k) : 0 \le k \le N\}$, the sequence of estimates is defined by the coupled equations:

$$\theta_{n+1} = \theta_n + \alpha_{n+1}\mathcal{D}_{n+1}\zeta_n, \tag{5.50a}$$
$$\zeta_{n+1} = \lambda\zeta_n + \zeta^0_{n+1}, \tag{5.50b}$$
$$\zeta^0_n = \nabla_\theta Q^\theta(x(n),u(n))\big|_{\theta=\theta_n} \tag{5.50c}$$

and with $\mathcal{D}_{n+1}$ defined as in (5.48b).

Figure 5.5 Baird's star problem.

This is a generalization of (5.48) since $\zeta_n^0 = \psi_{(n)}$ if $\mathcal{H}$ is a d-dimensional linear function class.

Unstable Dynamics with Perfect Exploration

Figure 5.5 shows Baird's counterexample, which provides an example of instability when using TD(λ). There are six states and no control, with cost identically zero. From any initial condition, the state remains at $x(k) = 7$ for all $k \geq 1$. Hence $Q^\star(x,u) = h^\star(x) = 0$ for each x. Note that here θ^i denotes the ith index of the vector θ.

The example violates two conventions in this chapter:

(i) $\psi(x^e) = (0,\dots,0,1,2)^\intercal \neq \mathsf{0}$ with $x^e = 7$, so that (5.31) is violated.
(ii) There are only seven states, yet the basis is eight dimensional. This implies that the sample correlation matrix (5.19) is never full rank, for any value of N.

The degenerate correlation matrix shouldn't be such a concern, since $h^{\theta^*} = h^\star$ and also $\mathcal{D}_{n+1}^{\theta^*} = 0$ for all n with $\theta^* = \mathsf{0}$. Rank degeneracy implies that θ^* is not unique.

The example was introduced in the discounted cost setting, with discount factor $\gamma \leq 1$. This is maintained here, and since there is no control we use value function notation to define the temporal difference:

$$\mathcal{D}_{n+1}^{\theta} = -h^\theta(x(n)) + \gamma h^\theta(x(n+1)) = -h^\theta(x(n)) + \gamma h^\theta(7), \tag{5.51}$$

where the second equality holds because of the trivial dynamics. The definition of the eligibility vector is modified slightly in the discounted setting:

$$\zeta_{n+1} = \lambda\gamma\zeta_n + \psi(x(n+1)).$$

So-called perfect exploration is based on a version of restart, in which episodes allow only a single transition, and each of seven initial conditions is sampled uniformly. A periodic implementation is described as follows: For $n = 0,1,\dots,6$, choose $x(n) = n+1$ and obtain

$$\mathcal{D}_{n+1} = -h^{\theta_n}(n+1) + \gamma h^{\theta_n}(7),$$

where $\{\theta_n\}$ are updated using TD(λ): $\theta_{n+1} = \theta_n + \alpha_{n+1}\mathcal{D}_{n+1}\zeta_n$. This procedure is repeated so that $x(n) - 1 = n$ modulo 7 for all $n \geq 1$.

The algorithm diverges for $\gamma \leq 1$ sufficiently large and some initial conditions (under our standing assumption that $\sum \alpha_n = \infty$). To see this requires a closer look at the temporal difference:

$$\mathcal{D}_{n+1} = \begin{cases} -[\theta_n^8 + 2\theta_n^k] + \gamma[2\theta_n^8 + \theta_n^7] & x(n) = k \leq 6 \\ -[2\theta_n^8 + \theta_n^7] + \gamma[2\theta_n^8 + \theta_n^7] & x(n) = 7 \end{cases}.$$

The source of instability is revealed by looking at the evolution of the last entry of the parameter estimate:

$$\theta_{n+1}^8 = \theta_n^8 + \begin{cases} \alpha_{n+1}\{(2\gamma - 1)\theta_n^8 + \gamma\theta_n^7 - 2\theta_n^k\}\zeta_n^8 & x(n) = k \leq 6 \\ \alpha_{n+1}\{-(1-\gamma)[2\theta_n^8 + \theta_n^7]\}\zeta_n^8 & x(n) = 7 \end{cases}.$$

Suppose that $\gamma > \frac{1}{2}$ and $\theta_0^8 > 0$ is large relative to the other parameters. Whenever $x(n) = k \leq 6$, the estimate θ_{n+1}^8 tends to increase, because of the positive coefficient $(2\gamma - 1)$.

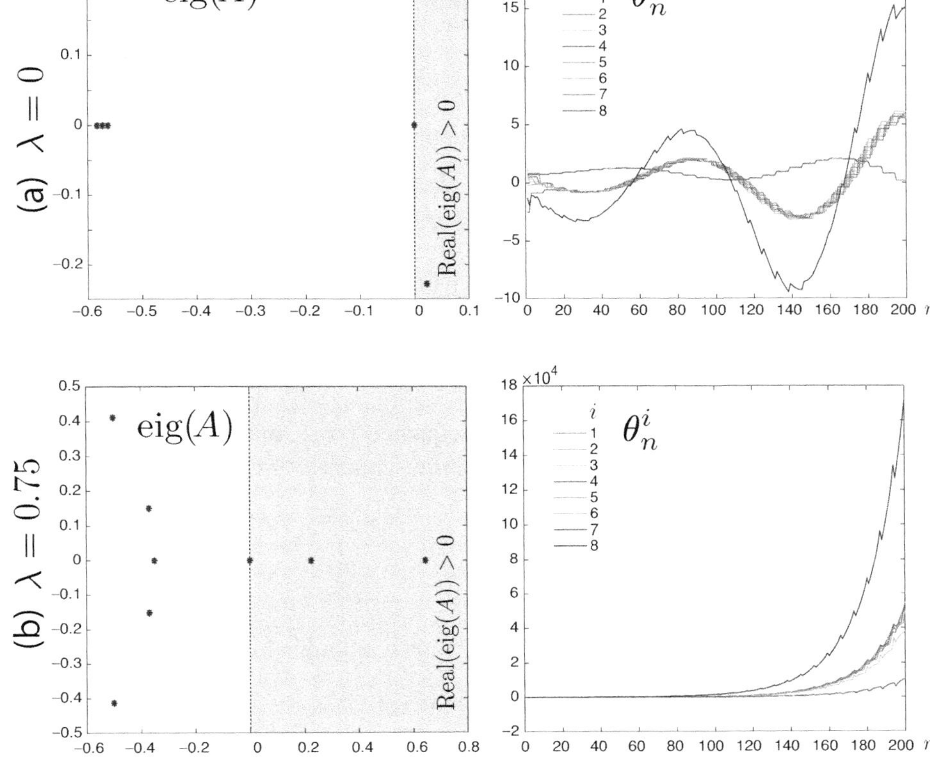

Figure 5.6 Baird's star problem: parameter estimates and eigenvalues of A with $\gamma = 0.9$. (a) $\lambda = 0$ (b) $\lambda = 0.75$.

If $x(n) = 7$, then the coefficient of θ_n^8 becomes negative, but remember $x(n) = 7$ occurs only 1/7 of the time.

In this example, TD(λ) can be expressed as the linear recursion

$$\theta_{n+1} = \theta_n + \alpha_{n+1} A_{n+1} \theta_n\,, \qquad A_{n+1} = \zeta_n \{-\psi(x(n)) + \gamma\psi(7)\}^{\intercal}.$$

The matrix (5.49) becomes

$$A = \mathsf{E}_\varpi[A_{n+1}] = \frac{1}{7}\sum_{n=1}^{7} A_n.$$

Based on the recursion for θ_n^8, it may not be surprising that A is not Hurwitz for all values of γ. Figure 5.6 shows results from two experiments with $\gamma = 0.9$, two values of λ, and fixed step-size $\alpha_n \equiv \alpha_0$.

The parameter estimates diverge in these two experiments, and the behavior is as predicted from the eigenvalues of A. With $\lambda = 0$, the eigenvalues in the right half plane are complex, and in this case the estimates oscillate to infinity.

In the remainder of this section, we turn to approximation of $Q^\star$: the Q-function associated with the optimal control problem.

5.4.3 Projected Bellman Operator and Q-Learning

The Q-function for the total cost optimal control problem solves the fixed point equation (3.7d), copied here for convenience:

$$Q^\star(x,u) = c(x,u) + \underline{Q}^\star(\mathrm{F}(x,u)),$$

with $\underline{Q}(x) = \min_u Q(x,u)$ for any Q. For a parameterized family of approximations $\{Q^\theta : \theta \in \mathbb{R}^d\}$, recall that for each θ we define a policy via (3.44):

$$\phi^\theta(x) = \arg\min_u Q^\theta(x,u)\,, \qquad x \in \mathsf{X}.$$

We obtain an algorithm for approximation via "pattern matching" with (5.48). The algorithm with linear function approximation is presented here:

Q(λ) Learning

For a given $\lambda \in [0,1]$, nonnegative step-size sequence $\{\alpha_n\}$, initial conditions θ_0, ζ_0, and observed samples $\{u(k),x(k) : 0 \le k \le N\}$, the sequence of estimates is defined by the coupled equations:

$$\theta_{n+1} = \theta_n + \alpha_{n+1}\mathcal{D}_{n+1}\zeta_n, \tag{5.52a}$$

$$\zeta_{n+1} = \lambda\zeta_n + \psi_{(n+1)}, \tag{5.52b}$$

$$\mathcal{D}_{n+1} = -Q^{\theta_n}(x(n),u(n)) + c_n + Q^{\theta_n}(x(n+1),\phi^{\theta_n}(x(n+1))), \tag{5.52c}$$

with $\psi_{(n+1)} = \psi(x(n+1),u(n+1))$, $c_n = c(x(n),u(n))$.

The algorithm has significant similarities as well as differences with TD-learning:

▲ The major change is (5.52c): The current policy estimate ϕ^{θ_n} is used, rather than the fixed policy ϕ in TD(λ). Note that in (5.52c) we can substitute

$$Q^{\theta_n}(x(n+1),\phi^{\theta_n}(x(n+1))) = \underline{Q}^{\theta_n}(x(n+1)) \stackrel{\text{def}}{=} \min_u Q^{\theta_n}(x(n+1),u).$$

▲ QSA theory predicts that a limit θ^* for Q(λ)-learning will solve $\bar{f}(\theta^*) = 0$, with

$$\bar{f}(\theta) = \mathsf{E}_\varpi\big[f_{n+1}(\theta)\big]\,, \qquad f_{n+1}(\theta) = \mathcal{D}_{n+1}(Q^\theta)\zeta_n. \tag{5.53}$$

This appears the same as TD(λ) until you recognize the different definition for $\mathcal{D}_{n+1}(Q^\theta)$ obtained from (5.52c):

$$\mathcal{D}_{n+1}(Q^\theta) = -Q^\theta(x(n),u(n)) + c_n + \min_u Q^\theta(x(n+1),u).$$

▲ For the special case $\lambda = 0$, we can apply Proposition 5.6 to conclude that Q^{θ^*} solves the projected Bellman equation:

$$Q^{\theta^*} = P_{\mathcal{H}}\{T(Q^{\theta^*})\},$$

in which the Bellman operator is redefined: $T(Q)\big|_{(x,u)} = c(x,u) + \underline{Q}(\mathrm{F}(x,u))$.

Sadly, these observations bring us to a dead-end. An ODE analysis of Q(λ)-learning requires that we look at global asymptotic stability of the ODE with vector field $\bar{f}$ defined in (5.53). As a first step, we must find conditions under which the root finding problem admits a solution! Unfortunately, very little is known about existence, even in the case $\lambda = 0$. And, if an equilibrium does exist, stability theory is nearly absent.

5.4.4 GQ-Learning

If we are concerned that $\bar{f}(\theta^*) = 0$ does not admit a solution, then we might turn to the next best option: For a given $d \times d$ matrix $M > 0$, solve

$$\min_{\theta} \Gamma(\theta) = \min_{\theta} \tfrac{1}{2} \bar{f}(\theta)^{\intercal} M \bar{f}(\theta). \tag{5.54}$$

We can then apply the ODE method to devise an algorithm. One approach is gradient descent:

$$\frac{d}{dt}\vartheta_t = -[\partial_\theta \bar{f}\,(\vartheta_t)]^{\intercal} M \bar{f}(\vartheta_t). \tag{5.55}$$

The GQ-learning algorithm of [234] can be regarded as a discrete-time translation of this ODE, using $M = \mathsf{E}[\zeta_n \zeta_n^{\intercal}]^{-1}$. Matrix inversion is avoided through a two-time-scale algorithm: an ODE approximation of $M\bar{f}(\vartheta_t)$ is obtained using the solution to the "high-gain" ODE

$$\frac{d}{dt}\omega_t = b_t\big[\bar{f}(\vartheta_t) - R\omega_t\big],$$

where $R = M^{-1} = \mathsf{E}[\zeta_n \zeta_n^{\intercal}]$. Provided $\{b_t\}$ is chosen very large and $\{\vartheta_t\}$ is bounded, it is not difficult to establish that the approximation $\omega_t \approx M\bar{f}(\vartheta_t)$ will hold after a transient period.

These ODEs are motivation for the two-time-scale GQ algorithm, presented here for linear function approximation:

GQ(λ) Learning

With the same starting point as Q(λ) learning, and an additional initialization $\omega_0 \in \mathbb{R}^d$:

$$\theta_{n+1} = \theta_n - \alpha_{n+1} A_{n+1}^{\intercal} \omega_n, \tag{5.56a}$$

$$\omega_{n+1} = \omega_n + \beta_{n+1}\{ f_{n+1}(\theta_n) - \zeta_{n+1}\zeta_{n+1}^{\intercal}\omega_n \}, \tag{5.56b}$$

$$\zeta_{n+1} = \lambda\zeta_n + \psi_{(n+1)},$$

$$\mathcal{D}_{n+1} = -Q^{\theta_n}(x(n),u(n)) + c_n + \underline{Q}^{\theta_n}(x(n+1)),$$

$$f_{n+1}(\theta_n) = \mathcal{D}_{n+1}\zeta_n, \qquad A_{n+1} = \partial_\theta f_{n+1}(\theta_n) = \zeta_n\{-\psi_{(n)} + \underline{\psi}_{(n+1)}\}^{\intercal} \tag{5.56c}$$

with $\psi_{(n+1)} = \psi(x(n+1),u(n+1))$, and $\underline{\psi}_{(n+1)} = \psi(x(n+1),\phi^{\theta_n}(x(n+1)))$.

As always, the output of the algorithm defines the final approximation Q^{θ_N}. The ODE approximation is successful provided the second step-size sequence is relatively large:

$$\lim_{n\to\infty} \frac{\beta_n}{\alpha_n} = \infty. \tag{5.57}$$

There are several challenges and questions:

- We may have difficulty obtaining a global minimum of (5.54) because the objective Γ is not convex.
- Suppose that in fact $\bar{f}(\theta^*) = 0$ *does have a solution*. Challenges remain with any approximation of the ODE (5.55), beyond lack of convexity of the objective function. Nesterov discusses this approach to root finding in his monograph [273, section 4.4.1]. He warns that it can lead to numerical instability: "*. . . if our system of equations is linear, then such a transformation squares the condition number of the problem.*"[1] He goes on to warn that it can lead to a "*squaring the number of iterations*" to obtain the desired error bound. To see this, consider the second-order approximation of the loss function at θ^*:

$$\Gamma(\theta) \approx \Gamma(\theta^*) + (\theta - \theta^*)^{\intercal}[A^* M A^{*\intercal}](\theta - \theta^*),$$

  which uses $\bar{f}(\theta^*) = 0$. The appearance of $A^* M A^{*\intercal}$ is the "squaring" that Nesterov warns about. If A^* has a large condition number, then we may make things much worse by squaring. The numerical challenge can be addressed with an alternative choice for M, provided this can be done without introducing additional complexity.
- Last but not least, it is not obvious that minimizing (5.54) is a worthwhile goal. Further research is needed to explain why $Q(\lambda)$ and GQ algorithms are often successful in practice, and to predict when these algorithms might fail.

5.4.5 Batch Methods and DQN

The *Deep Q Network* (DQN) algorithm was designed for neural network function approximation; the term "deep" refers to a large number of hidden layers. The basic algorithm is summarized here, without imposing any particular form for Q^θ.

One component of this approach is to abandon the purely recursive form of the preceding RL algorithms. In a batch RL algorithm, the time-horizon N is broken into B batches of more reasonable size, defined by the sequence of intermediate times $T_0 = 0 < T_1 < T_2 < \cdots < T_{B-1} < T_B = N$. The potential benefits are more obvious when we come to RL design using kernels for function approximation, or for stochastic control systems.

DQN

With $\theta_0 \in \mathbb{R}^d$ given, along with a sequence of positive scalars $\{\alpha_n\}$, define recursively,

$$\theta_{n+1} = \arg\min_\theta \Big\{ \Gamma_n^\varepsilon(\theta) + \frac{1}{\alpha_{n+1}} \|\theta - \theta_n\|^2 \Big\}, \qquad 0 \le n \le B-1, \tag{5.58a}$$

[1] More on the curse of condition number can be found in Section 8.6.1, along with definitions.

where for each n, with $r_n = T_{n+1} - T_n$,

$$\Gamma_n^\varepsilon(\theta) = \frac{1}{2}\frac{1}{r_n}\sum_{k=T_n}^{T_{n+1}-1}\big[-Q^\theta(x(k),u(k)) + c_k + \underline{Q}^{\theta_n}(x(k+1))\big]^2. \tag{5.58b}$$

The elegance and simplicity of DQN is clear when Q^θ is defined via linear function approximation, so that (5.58a) is the unconstrained minimum of a quadratic. The following summarizes obvious yet suggestive properties of the solution to (5.58a) for both linear and nonlinear function approximation:

Proposition 5.9 *Suppose that $\{Q^\theta(x,u) : \theta \in \mathbb{R}^d\}$ is continuously differentiable in θ for each x,u. Then*

(i) *The solution to* (5.58a) *solves the fixed point equation*

$$\theta_{n+1} = \theta_n + \alpha_{n+1}\frac{1}{r_n}\sum_{k=T_n}^{T_{n+1}-1}\big[-Q^\theta(x(k),u(k)) + \gamma_n(k)\big]\nabla_\theta Q^\theta(x(k),u(k))\Big|_{\theta=\theta_{n+1}} \tag{5.59}$$

with $\gamma_n(k) = c_k + \underline{Q}^{\theta_n}(x(k+1))$.

(ii) *If the parameterization is linear, so that $\nabla_\theta Q^\theta(x(k),u(k)) = \psi_{(k)}$, then*

$$\theta_{n+1} = \theta_n + \alpha_{n+1}\{A_n\theta_{n+1} - b_n\} \tag{5.60a}$$

$$\textit{with}\quad A_n = -\frac{1}{r_n}\sum_{k=T_n}^{T_{n+1}-1}\psi_{(k)}\psi_{(k)}^{\intercal}, \tag{5.60b}$$

$$b_n = -\frac{1}{r_n}\sum_{k=T_n}^{T_{n+1}-1}\gamma_n(k)\psi_{(k)}. \tag{5.60c}$$

The linear case is particularly simple since we can solve (5.60a) by rearranging terms and inverting:

$$\theta_{n+1} = [I - \alpha_{n+1}A_n]^{-1}\{\theta_n - \alpha_{n+1}b_n\}.$$

The approximation $[I - \alpha_{n+1}A_n]^{-1} \approx I + \alpha_{n+1}A_n$ holds if α_{n+1} is sufficiently small, and from this we obtain

$$\theta_{n+1} \approx [I + \alpha_{n+1}A_n]\{\theta_n - \alpha_{n+1}b_n\} \approx \theta_n + \alpha_{n+1}\{A_n\theta_n - b_n\}.$$

For nonlinear function approximation, it is not clear why the optimization problem should be solved at each iteration. Under the assumptions of Proposition 5.9, we have $\|\theta_{n+1} - \theta_n\| \le K\alpha_{n+1}$ for some fixed $K < \infty$, whenever the parameter sequence $\{\theta_n\}$ is bounded. Consequently,

$$\theta_{n+1} = \theta_n + \alpha_{n+1}\frac{1}{r_n}\sum_{k=T_n}^{T_{n+1}-1}\bigl[-Q^{\theta_n}(x(k),u(k)) + \gamma_n(k) + \mathcal{E}_{n+1}\bigr]\nabla_\theta Q^{\theta_n}(x(k),u(k)),$$

where $\|\mathcal{E}_{n+1}\| \le O(\alpha_{n+1})$. This motivates the *batch QSA* approximation of DQN:

Batch Q(0) Learning

With $\theta_0 \in \mathbb{R}^d$ given, along with a sequence of positive scalars $\{\alpha_n\}$, define recursively,

$$\begin{aligned}\theta_{n+1} &= \theta_n + \alpha_{n+1}\frac{1}{r_n}\sum_{k=T_n}^{T_{n+1}-1}\mathcal{D}_{k+1}(\theta_n)\nabla_\theta Q^{\theta_n}(x(k),u(k)),\\ \mathcal{D}_{k+1}(\theta_n) &= -Q^{\theta_n}(x(k),u(k)) + c_k + \underline{Q}^{\theta_n}(x(k+1)).\end{aligned} \tag{5.61}$$

While DQN is easy to implement, it does not resolve the issues surrounding Q(λ)-learning:

Proposition 5.10 *Consider the DQN algorithm with possibly nonlinear function approximation. Assume that Q^θ is continuously differentiable, and its gradient $\nabla Q^\theta(x,u)$ is globally Lipschitz continuous, with Lipschitz constant independent of (x,u). Suppose that $B = \infty$, the nonnegative step-size sequence, satisfies*

$$\sum \alpha_n = \infty, \qquad \sum \alpha_n^2 < \infty,$$

and suppose that the sequence $\{\theta_n\}$ defined by the DQN algorithm is convergent to some $\theta_\infty \in \mathbb{R}^d$. Then

(i) $\bar{f}(\theta_\infty) = 0$, *with $\bar{f}$ defined via* (5.53) *using* $\zeta_n = \nabla_\theta Q^\theta(x(n),u(n))\Big|_{\theta=\theta_n}$.

(ii) *The algorithm admits the ODE approximation* $\frac{d}{dt}\vartheta_t = \bar{f}(\vartheta_t)$. □

These conclusions should raise a warning, since we do not know if $\bar{f}$ defined in (5.53) has a root. If we manage to establish the existence of a solution to $\bar{f}(\theta_\infty) = 0$, we do not know if the ODE is stable, or if θ_∞ has desirable properties.

On the other hand, DQN is used every day with success, so it should not be ignored.

5.5 Convex Q-Learning

We have surveyed three classes of algorithms within the "TD taxonomy":

(i) Approximate PIA using LSTD or TD(λ). We can be assured success under two conditions: (a) The function class is linear, and (b) the function class is *complete* in the sense that we can be assured that $Q^{\theta_n} = Q^{\phi^n}$ for each n.

(ii) GQ learning to obtain the minimal mean-square Bellman error. We are assured success if $Q^\star$ lies in our function class, and the objective function satisfies conditions aligned with gradient descent (such as the PL condition introduced in Section 4.4.2).

(iii) Galerkin relaxations of the DP equation are obtained using Q(λ) learning, DQN, or Batch Q(0) learning. Here theory is almost nonexistent.

The RL algorithms surveyed in this section are all motivated by the DPLP(3.36). We begin with a direct approach based on a joint parameterization: In the notation of Section 5.1, $\mathcal{H} = \{h^\theta = (J^\theta, Q^\theta) : \theta \in \mathbb{R}^d\}$. The value θ_i might represent the ith weight in a neural network function approximation architecture, but to justify the adjective *convex*, we require a linearly parameterized family:

$$J^\theta(x) = \theta^\intercal \psi^J(x), \qquad Q^\theta(x,u) = \theta^\intercal \psi(x,u).$$

The function class is normalized with $J^\theta(x^e) = 0$ for each θ. For the linear approximation architecture, this requires $\psi_i^J(x^e) = 0$ for each $1 \le i \le d$; for a neural network architecture, this normalization is imposed through definition of the output of the network. Convex Q-learning algorithms based on an RKHS are described in Section 5.5.2.

Consider the translation of (3.36) based on a parameterized family:

$$\begin{aligned} &\max_\theta \ \langle \mu, Q^\theta \rangle \\ &\text{s.t.} \ \ Q^\theta(x,u) \le c(x,u) + J^\theta(\mathrm{F}(x,u)), \\ &\qquad Q^\theta(x,u) \ge J^\theta(x), \qquad x \in \mathsf{X},\ u \in \mathsf{U}(x), \end{aligned} \tag{5.62}$$

where μ is now a weighting function on $\mathsf{X} \times \mathsf{U}$.

We can if we wish strengthen the first constraint to equality: $Q^\theta(x,u) = c(x,u) + J^\theta(\mathrm{F}(x,u))$. This is reasonable if we have a good model: First create a parameterized family $\{J^\theta\}$, and then *define* $Q^\theta(x,u) = c(x,u) + J^\theta(\mathrm{F}(x,u))$ for each θ, x,u.

However, if we don't have a highly accurate model, it is then better to relax the equality constraint, which is why (5.62) is our preferred starting point.

Another inequality that might be removed from (5.62) is $Q^\theta \ge J^\theta$, since the optimal solution for the DPLP results $J^\star = \underline{Q}^\star$. We can remove J^θ from (5.62) by imposing this constraint:

$$\begin{aligned} &\max_\theta \ \langle \mu, Q^\theta \rangle \\ &\text{s.t.} \ \ Q^\theta(x,u) \le c(x,u) + \underline{Q}^\theta(\mathrm{F}(x,u)), \qquad x \in \mathsf{X},\ u \in \mathsf{U}(x) \end{aligned} \tag{5.63}$$

or even

$$\max_\theta \ \langle \nu, \underline{Q}^\theta \rangle \quad \text{subject to the inequality constraints in (5.63),}$$

with ν a weighting function on X. With either objective function, this remains a convex program provided the function class is linear in θ. And through design, we must ensure that $\underline{Q}^\theta(x^e) = 0$ for each θ. This might be achieved by imposing $\psi_i(x^e,u) = 0$ for all i and u, and recognizing that it is reasonable to assume that $\mathsf{U}(x^e) = \{u^e\}$ (once we are at the equilibrium with zero cost, there is no reason to leave).

The algorithms in this section are based on approximations of (5.63). Several options are surveyed in the following.

5.5.1 Convex Q-Learning with a Finite-Dimensional Function Class

We begin with the linear function class:

$$Q^\theta(x,u) = \theta^\intercal \psi(x,u). \tag{5.64}$$

While this is required for convergence theory, any of the algorithms to come can be applied using a nonlinear function approximation architecture.

An approximation of the inequality constraint in (5.63) is given by $\Gamma^{\varepsilon}(\theta) \le 0$, where

$$\Gamma^{\varepsilon}(\theta) \stackrel{\text{def}}{=} \lim_{N\to\infty} \frac{1}{N} \sum_{k=0}^{N-1} \big[\mathcal{D}^{\circ}_{k+1}(\theta)\big]_{-}, \tag{5.65a}$$

$$\mathcal{D}^{\circ}_{k+1}(\theta) \stackrel{\text{def}}{=} -Q^{\theta}(x(k),u(k)) + c_k + \underline{Q}^{\theta}(x(k+1)), \tag{5.65b}$$

and $[z]_{-} = \max(0, -z)$ for any $z \in \mathbb{R}$, and $c_k = c(x(k),u(k))$. Subject to (5.64), the function Γ^{ε} is convex, so that $\{\theta : \Gamma^{\varepsilon}(\theta) \le 0\}$ is a convex subset of $\mathbb{R}^d$.

This motivates the first algorithm:

Convex Q-Learning

Choose a pmf μ on $\mathsf{X} \times \mathsf{U}$, a convex regularizer $\mathcal{R}_N(\theta)$, tolerance $\text{Tol} \ge 0$, and solve

$$\theta^* = \arg\min_{\theta} \; -\langle \mu, Q^{\theta}\rangle + \mathcal{R}_N(\theta) \tag{5.66a}$$

$$\text{s.t.} \;\; \Gamma^{\varepsilon}_N(\theta) \stackrel{\text{def}}{=} \frac{1}{N} \sum_{k=0}^{N-1} \big[\mathcal{D}^{\circ}_{k+1}(\theta)\big]_{-} \le \text{Tol}. \tag{5.66b}$$

The choice of regularizer might be based on computational efficiency. The introduction of the tolerance "Tol" is also in anticipation of computational challenges to be discussed shortly.

The next algorithm is inspired by the batch architecture of DQN: Choose intermediate times $T_0 = 0 < T_1 < T_2 < \cdots < T_{B-1} < T_B = N$, and a sequence of regularizers: $\mathcal{R}_n(Q,\theta)$ is a convex functional of Q,θ, that may depend on θ_n. Examples follow.

Batch Convex Q-Learning #1

With $\theta_0 \in \mathbb{R}^d$ given, define recursively

$$\theta_{n+1} = \arg\min_{\theta} \Big\{ -\langle \mu, Q^{\theta}\rangle + \mathcal{R}_n(Q^{\theta},\theta) \Big\} \tag{5.67a}$$

$$\text{s.t.} \;\; \Gamma^{\varepsilon}_n(\theta) \le \text{Tol}, \tag{5.67b}$$

where for $0 \le n \le B-1$, with $r_n = T_{n+1} - T_n$,

$$\Gamma^{\varepsilon}_n(\theta) = \frac{1}{r_n} \sum_{k=T_n}^{T_{n+1}-1} \big[\mathcal{D}^{\circ}_{k+1}(\theta)\big]_{-}. \tag{5.67c}$$

It is expected that $\mathcal{R}_n$ will be designed to avoid discarding previous data, such as

$$\mathcal{R}_n(Q^{\theta},\theta) = \mathcal{R}^0_n(\theta) + \frac{1}{2}\frac{1}{\beta_{n+1}} \|\theta - \theta_n\|^2, \tag{5.68}$$

in which $\mathcal{R}^0_n$ is convex and $\{\beta_n\}$ are positive scalars.

The next variant is inspired by a primal-dual algorithm. Recall that $[z]_+ = \max(0,z)$ for $z \in \mathbb{R}$.

Batch Convex Q-Learning #2

With $\theta_0 \in \mathbb{R}^d$ and $\lambda_0 \geq 0$ given, and a step-size sequence $\{\alpha_n\}$, define recursively:

$$\theta_{n+1} = \arg\min_\theta \Big\{ -\langle \mu, Q^\theta \rangle + \lambda_n [\Gamma_n^\varepsilon(\theta) - \text{Tol}] + \mathcal{R}_n(Q^\theta,\theta) \Big\}, \tag{5.69a}$$

$$\lambda_{n+1} = [\lambda_n + \alpha_{n+1}(\Gamma_n^\varepsilon(\theta_{n+1}) - \text{Tol})]_+. \tag{5.69b}$$

The introduction of Tol > 0 (strictly positive) in (5.69b) is crucial: $\Gamma_n^\varepsilon(\theta_{n+1}) \geq 0$ for any n by definition, so $\{\lambda_n\}$ is a nondecreasing sequence if Tol $= 0$.

This formulation is best suited to approximation as a QSA recursion, as in the batch Q(0)-learning algorithm (5.61). Consider the choice of regularizer (5.68), with $\mathcal{R}_n^0$ convex for each n. The first-order condition for optimality in (5.69a) results in the fixed point equation:

$$0 = \nabla_\theta \Big\{ -\langle \mu, Q^\theta \rangle + \lambda_n [\Gamma_n^\varepsilon(\theta) - \text{Tol}] + \mathcal{R}_n^0(\theta) \Big\} \Big|_{\theta=\theta_{n+1}} + \frac{1}{\beta_{n+1}} [\theta_{n+1} - \theta_n].$$

This motivates a primal-dual algorithm:

Batch Convex Q-Learning #3

With $\theta_0 \in \mathbb{R}^d$ and $\lambda_0 \geq 0$ given, define recursively

$$\theta_{n+1} = \theta_n - \beta_{n+1} \nabla_\theta \Big\{ -\langle \mu, Q^\theta \rangle + \lambda_n [\Gamma_n^\varepsilon(\theta) - \text{Tol}] + \mathcal{R}_n^0(\theta) \Big\} \Big|_{\theta=\theta_n}, \tag{5.70a}$$

$$\lambda_{n+1} = [\lambda_n + \alpha_{n+1}(\Gamma_n^\varepsilon(\theta_{n+1}) - \text{Tol})]_+, \tag{5.70b}$$

where $\{\alpha_n, \beta_n\}$ satisfy (5.57).

Any of these algorithms can be improved through attention to the concepts in Section 4.5. In particular, convergence might be accelerated using PJR averaging.

Numerical Instability with Fast Sampling. Real-life control problems typically involve a system operating in continuous time. Care must be taken with sampling, because the temporal difference may not be very informative.

This challenge arises in every algorithm based on temporal differences, but is most pronounced with convex Q-learning. It is best explained through an example.

Example 5.5.1 (*Convex Q for the Mountain Car*) The system equations (2.58) for the mountain car represent an Euler approximation for the ODE (2.56), with sampling interval $\Delta = t_{k+1} - t_k = 10^{-3}$, so that $x(k) \approx x_{t_k}$ with $t_k = k \times 10^{-3}$, and where $\{x_t\}$ is the solution to the ODE. In applying convex Q-learning with the basis (5.11), it is observed that $\mathcal{D}^\circ_{n+1} = c_n$ for many values of n, where

$$\mathcal{D}^\circ_{n+1} \stackrel{\text{def}}{=} -Q^{\theta_n}(x(n),u(n)) + c_n + \underline{Q}^{\theta_n}(x(n+1)).$$

The desired constraint $\mathcal{D}^\circ_{n+1} \geq 0$ is vacuous in this case. This is purely an artifact of fast sampling, resulting in very small values $\|x(n+1) - x(n)\|$.

We can choose to increase the sampling interval, or we can adopt state-dependent sampling. Suppose that we are given data $\{x(k)\}$ that is obtained from sampling at a very quick rate. One approach to subsampling is through binning $\mathsf{X} = \bigcup_{i=1}^d B_i$ (a disjoint union), and choosing sampling times $\{\tau_k\}$ so that adjacent sampled states lie in distinct bins: $\text{Bin}(x(\tau_{k+1})) \neq \text{Bin}(x(\tau_k))$ for all k.

Here is one successful approach: Choose an upper limit $\overline{n}$, take $\tau_0 = 0$, and for $k \geq 0$,

$$\tau_{k+1} = \min\{\tau_k + \overline{n}, \tau^0_{k+1}\}, \qquad \tau^0_{k+1} = \min\{j \geq \tau_k + 1 : \text{Bin}(x(j)) \neq \text{Bin}(x(\tau_k))\}.$$

To apply any of the algorithms in this chapter, we assume the input takes a constant value on the interval $[\tau_k, \tau_{k+1})$ for each k, and introduce the cumulative cost,

$$\mathcal{C}_{\tau_k} = \sum_{j=\tau_k}^{\tau_{k+1}-1} c(x(j),u(\tau_k)).$$

For the mountain car this becomes $\mathcal{C}_{\tau_k} = \tau_{k+1} - \tau_k$ if the goal is not reached before time τ_{k+1}. The temporal difference sequence is then redefined:

$$\mathcal{D}^\circ_{n+1} \stackrel{\text{def}}{=} -Q^{\theta_n}(x(\tau_n),u(\tau_n)) + \mathcal{C}_{\tau_n} + \underline{Q}^{\theta_n}(x(n+1)).$$

An alternative is to apply one of the specialized algorithms for continuous time data described in Section 5.6. ■

5.5.2 BCQL and Kernel Methods

Batch methods are featured in this book because they are currently popular with practitioners, and also because of kernel methods are anticipated. In this setting, we no longer have a fixed d-dimensional basis. Rather, due to Theorem 5.1 (the Representer Theorem), an effective basis emerges from the observed samples in which the dimension of θ is equal to the number of observations N. Even in simple examples, the value of N for a reliable estimate may be larger than 1 million.

Suppose that $\mathcal{H}$ is defined based on a RKHS. BCQL #2 is easily adapted to this setting with a change in notation. In particular, we redefine the loss function (5.67c):

$$\Gamma^\varepsilon_n(Q) = \frac{1}{r_n} \sum_{k=T_n}^{T_{n+1}-1} \big[\mathcal{D}^\circ_{k+1}(Q)\big]_-,$$

$$\mathcal{D}^\circ_{k+1}(Q) = -Q(x(k),u(k)) + c(x(k),u(k)) + \underline{Q}(x(k+1)), \qquad Q \in \mathcal{H}.$$

Kernel Batch Convex Q-Learning

With $\theta_0 \in \mathbb{R}^d$ and $\lambda_0 \geq 0$ given, define recursively

$$Q^{n+1} = \arg\min_{Q \in \mathcal{H}} \Big\{ -\langle \mu, Q \rangle + \lambda_n [\Gamma_n^{\varepsilon}(Q) - \mathrm{Tol}] + \mathcal{R}_n(Q) \Big\}, \tag{5.71a}$$

$$\lambda_{n+1} = [\lambda_n + \beta_{n+1}(\Gamma_n^{\varepsilon}(Q_{n+1}) - \mathrm{Tol})]_+. \tag{5.71b}$$

A candidate regularizer similar to (5.68) is the quadratic

$$\mathcal{R}_n(Q) = \tfrac{1}{2}\frac{1}{\alpha_{n+1}} \|Q - Q^n\|_{\mathcal{H}}^2.$$

However, this choice presents a challenge: To apply the Representer Theorem, we must make a change of variables $h = Q - Q^n$, and our BCQL algorithm will produce the optimizer $h^{n+1} \in \mathcal{H}$. The Representer Theorem tells us that the function $h^{n+1}(\,\cdot\,,\cdot\,)$ is a linear combination of the functions $\{\Bbbk((x(k),u(k)),(\,\cdot\,,\cdot\,))\}$, where k ranges over the nth batch (of size r_n). The Q-function approximation is the sum $Q^{n+1} = Q^n + h^{n+1}$, and so by induction,

$$Q^{n+1} = Q^0 + h^1 + \cdots + h^{n+1}.$$

This estimate is entirely too complex: Each h^i depends on r_i observations.

A regularizer that avoids this complexity is defined by the sum of two quadratics:

$$\mathcal{R}_n(Q) = \frac{1}{\alpha_{n+1}} \tfrac{1}{2} \|Q - Q^n\|_n^2 + \delta \|Q\|_{\mathcal{H}}^2, \tag{5.72}$$

where $Q^n \in \mathcal{H}$ is the estimate at stage n, and

$$\|Q - Q^n\|_n^2 = \frac{1}{r_n} \sum_{k=T_n}^{T_{n+1}-1} \big(Q(x(k),u(k)) - Q^n(x(k),u(k))\big)^2.$$

With this choice of regularizer, the Representer Theorem tells us that for each n, the optimizer takes the following form: For some $\theta^{n*} \in \mathbb{R}^{r_n}$,

$$Q^n(x,u) = \sum_{i=1}^{r_n} \theta_i^{n*} \Bbbk(z_i, z), \qquad z = (x,u),$$

where $\{z_i = (x_i,u_i)\}$ are the state-input pairs observed on the time interval $\{T_{n-1} \leq k < T_n\}$.

5.6 Q-Learning in Continuous Time*

Recall from Section 3.8 the HJB equation $0 = \min_u \{c(x,u) + \nabla J^\star(x) \cdot \mathrm{f}(x,u)\}$. The term in brackets doesn't lead to a useful definition of the Q-function. Instead, we fix a scalar $\sigma > 0$ and denote

$$H^\star(x,u) \stackrel{\text{def}}{=} \{c(x,u) + \nabla J^\star(x) \cdot \mathrm{f}(x,u)\} + \sigma J^\star(x).$$

A similar construction was introduced in Section 4.5.3 using $\sigma = 1$. The addition of a function of x doesn't change the minimizer, so that whenever the conditions of Theorem 3.12 hold,

$$\phi^\star(x) = \arg\min_u H^\star(x,u).$$

The identity $\underline{H}^\star(x) = \min_u H^\star(x,u) = \sigma J^\star(x)$ follows from the HJB equation, which on substituting into the definition of $H^\star$ gives

$$H^\star(x,u) = c(x,u) + \sigma^{-1}\nabla\underline{H}^\star(x)\cdot \mathrm{f}(x,u) + \underline{H}^\star(x). \tag{5.73}$$

The component involving the model can be eliminated using the chain rule, $\frac{d}{dt}\underline{H}^\star(x_t) = \partial\underline{H}^\star(x_t)\frac{d}{dt}x_t$, and then substituting the dynamics $\frac{d}{dt}x_t = \mathrm{f}(x_t,u_t)$ gives for any input-state trajectory

$$\tfrac{d}{dt}\underline{H}^\star(x_t) = \nabla\underline{H}^\star(x_t)\cdot \mathrm{f}(x_t,u_t).$$

We can follow the same steps as in discrete time: Substituting the derivative formula into (5.73) gives the sample path representation:

$$H^\star(x_t,u_t) = c(x_t,u_t) + \sigma^{-1}\tfrac{d}{dt}\underline{H}^\star(x_t) + \underline{H}^\star(x_t).$$

This is valid for any input and resulting state satisfying $\frac{d}{dt}x_t = \mathrm{f}(x_t,u_t)$ for all t.

Rearranging terms, $\underline{H}^\star(x_t)$ is expressed as the output of a first-order, stable linear system:

$$\tfrac{d}{dt}\underline{H}^\star(x_t) = -\sigma\underline{H}^\star(x_t) + \sigma\mathcal{U}_t, \tag{5.74}$$

with "input" $\mathcal{U}_t \stackrel{\text{def}}{=} H^\star(x_t,u_t) - c(x_t,u_t)$, whose solution is

$$\underline{H}^\star(x_t) = e^{-\sigma t}\underline{H}^\star(x_0) + \sigma\int_0^t e^{-\sigma(t-\tau)}[H^\star(x_\tau,u_\tau) - c(x_\tau,u_\tau)]\,d\tau. \tag{5.75}$$

It is convenient to use compact notation for the "smoothed" processes on the right-hand side:

$$\mathcal{H}_t^\star \stackrel{\text{def}}{=} \sigma\int_0^t e^{-\sigma(t-\tau)}H^\star(x_\tau,u_\tau)d\tau, \qquad \mathcal{C}_t \stackrel{\text{def}}{=} \sigma\int_0^t e^{-\sigma(t-\tau)}c(x_\tau,u_\tau)d\tau. \tag{5.76}$$

Each satisfies a first-order differential equation:

$$\tfrac{d}{dt}\mathcal{H}_t^\star = -\sigma[\mathcal{H}_t^\star - H^\star(x_t,u_t)], \qquad \tfrac{d}{dt}\mathcal{C}_t = -\sigma[\mathcal{C}_t - c(x_t,u_t)].$$

Given a parameterized family of approximations $\{H^\theta : \theta\in\mathbb{R}^d\}$, we define $\underline{H}^\theta$ and $\mathcal{H}_t^\theta$ as before, and then duplicate any of the algorithms proposed for discrete time.

Two batch algorithms are introduced in the following. Either can be replaced with a QSA ODE similar to (5.61). The two algorithms are distinguished by the goal. In the first and simpler case, we are considering the standard total cost problem, and assume we are observing (x_t,u_t) for a long period of time. In the second algorithm, we are using restart, which is well motivated in path-finding problems, such as in the mountain car example.

If t is large, then it is reasonable to neglect the term $e^{-\sigma t}\underline{H}^\theta(x_0)$ in (5.75), and define the temporal difference as follows:

$$\mathcal{D}_t(\theta) = \underline{H}^\theta(x_t) - [\mathcal{H}_t^\theta - \mathcal{C}_t]. \tag{5.77}$$

This is a concave function of θ if the parameterization is linear.

We arrive at a generalization of (5.66) to choose θ^*:

Convex Q-Learning

Choose a pmf μ on $\mathsf{X} \times \mathsf{U}$, a time horizon $[T_0,T]$, a convex regularizer $\mathcal{R}(\theta)$, tolerance $\text{Tol} \geq 0$, and solve

$$\theta^* = \arg\min_\theta \quad -\langle \mu, H^\theta \rangle + \mathcal{R}(\theta) \tag{5.78a}$$

$$\text{s.t.} \quad \int_{T_0}^{T} \{\mathcal{D}_t(\theta)\}_- \, dt \leq \text{Tol}. \tag{5.78b}$$

Consider next a batch setting based on independent trials (as in the mountain car, in which we reach the goal at time T_n, and then reinitialize to a state x_{T_n}). For simplicity, we simply state a translation of DQN, in which one appearance of the parameter is fixed at the previous value θ_n. Define the following for $t \geq T_n$:

$$\mathcal{D}_t^n(\theta) = \underline{H}^{\theta_n}(x_t) - e^{-\sigma(t-T_n)}\underline{H}^{\theta_n}(x_{T_n}) - \sigma \int_{T_n}^{t} e^{-\sigma(t-\tau)}[H^\theta(x_\tau,u_\tau) - c(x_\tau,u_\tau)]\, d\tau. \tag{5.79}$$

This is used to obtain a loss function Γ_n^ε analogous to (5.58b).

DQN

With $\theta_0 \in \mathbb{R}^d$ given, along with a sequence of positive scalars $\{\alpha_n\}$, define the following recursively:

$$\theta_{n+1} = \arg\min_\theta \Big\{ \Gamma_n^\varepsilon(\theta) + \frac{1}{\alpha_{n+1}} \|\theta - \theta_n\|^2 \Big\}, \tag{5.80a}$$

where for each n,

$$\Gamma_n^\varepsilon(\theta) = \tfrac{1}{2}\frac{1}{r_n}\int_{T_n}^{T_{n+1}} [\mathcal{D}_t^n(\theta)]^2 \, dt, \qquad \text{with } r_n = T_{n+1} - T_n. \tag{5.80b}$$

These algorithms are especially practical for a linear parameterization $H^\theta = \theta^{\intercal}\psi$, since, for example, $\mathcal{H}_t^\theta = \theta^{\intercal}\Psi_t$, where Ψ_t is obtained by filtering:

$$\Psi_t \stackrel{\text{def}}{=} \sigma \int_0^t e^{-\sigma(t-\tau)} \psi(x_\tau,u_\tau) d\tau.$$

5.7 Duality*

The ideas introduced here are based on an entirely different view of basic dynamic programming from Section 3.1. The main conclusion is an interesting dual for the DPLP (3.36).

This section might be regarded as a preview of techniques used in stochastic control and RL for Markovian models.

To keep notation simple, let's assume that X and U are finite. There are no special input constraints: $\mathsf{U}(x) = \mathsf{U}$ for each $x \neq x^e$, but we require $u(k) = u^e$ when $x(k) = x^e$, so that $\mathsf{U}(x^e) = \{u^e\}$. The equilibrium satisfies by definition $x^e = \mathrm{F}(x^e,u^e)$. The cost is nonnegative, with $c(x^e,u^e) = 0$.

The variables in the LP consist of nonnegative functions on $\mathsf{X} \times \mathsf{U}$. Justification requires a different perspective on optimal control. For any input sequence $\boldsymbol{u}$, we define what is known as the (conditional) *occupancy pmf*:

$$\varpi(x,u \mid x_0) = \sum_{k=0}^{\infty} \mathbb{1}\{x(k) = x\,,\, u(k) = u\}\,, \qquad (x,u) \in \mathsf{X} \times \mathsf{U}\,,\ x \neq x^e,$$

where $\boldsymbol{x}$ is the state process obtained with initial condition x_0 and input $\boldsymbol{u}$. For notational convenience, we set $\varpi(x^e,u \mid x_0) = 0$ for any u. A bit of accounting gives

$$\sum_{x,u} c(x,u)\varpi(x,u \mid x_0) = J(x_0) = \sum_{k=0}^{\infty} c(x(k),u(k))\,, \qquad x(0) = x_0.$$

Part of this accounting includes these assumptions: $c(x^e,u^e) = 0$ and $\mathsf{U}(x^e) = \{u^e\}$.

We then define the following for a given pmf ν on X:

$$\varpi(x,u) = \sum_{x_0} \nu(x_0)\varpi(x,u \mid x_0).$$

This has a very different interpretation than the steady-state probability measure introduced in (5.22). The function $\varpi\colon \mathsf{X} \times \mathsf{U} \to \mathbb{R}_+$ is an example of a feasible variable for the LP to be constructed, with the following objective function:

$$\langle \varpi, c\rangle \stackrel{\text{def}}{=} \sum_{x,u} c(x,u)\varpi(x,u) = \langle \nu, J\rangle.$$

The constraints in the LP require further effort. For any occupancy pmf and each x, denote

$$\varpi_{\mathsf{x}}(x) \stackrel{\text{def}}{=} \sum_{u} \varpi(x,u),$$

and whenever $\varpi_{\mathsf{x}}(x) > 0$, we denote

$$\breve{\phi}(u \mid x) \stackrel{\text{def}}{=} \frac{1}{\varpi_{\mathsf{x}}(x)}\varpi(x,u). \tag{5.81}$$

In stochastic control, this is viewed as a *randomized policy*: $\breve{\phi}(u \mid x)$ is the probability that $u(k) = u$ when $x(k) = x$. More notation from stochastic control is a mapping P: For any occupation measure ϖ, let $\varpi_{\mathsf{x}}^+ = \varpi P$ be defined by

$$\varpi_{\mathsf{x}}^+(x) \stackrel{\text{def}}{=} \sum_{x^-,u^-} \varpi(x^-,u^-)\mathbb{1}\{\mathrm{F}(x^-,u^-) = x\}.$$

The representation $\varpi_{\mathsf{x}} = \nu + \varpi P$ provides the constraint (5.82b) in the following LP:

$$\min_{\varpi} \ \langle \varpi, c \rangle \tag{5.82a}$$

$$\text{s.t.} \ \sum_u \varpi(x,u) = \nu(x) + \sum_{x^-,u^-} \varpi(x^-,u^-)\mathbb{1}\{\mathsf{F}(x^-,u^-) = x\}, \quad x \neq x^e, \tag{5.82b}$$

$$\sum_u \varpi(x^e,u) = 0, \tag{5.82c}$$

$$\varpi(x,u) \geq 0, \quad (x,u) \in \mathsf{X} \times \mathsf{U}. \tag{5.82d}$$

Proposition 5.11 *If $J^\star$ is finite valued, then the following hold:*

(i) *If ϖ satisfies Equations* (5.82b) *to* (5.82d)*, then $\langle \varpi, c \rangle \geq \langle \nu, J^\star \rangle$.*
(ii) *The LP* (5.82) *has a solution $\varpi^\star$ satisfying $\langle \varpi^\star, c \rangle = \langle \nu, J^\star \rangle$.*
(iii) *If $\phi^\star$ is an optimal policy, then one optimal solution admits the decomposition:*

$$\varpi^\star(x,u) = \mathbb{1}\{\phi^\star(x) = u\}\varpi^\star_{\mathsf{x}}(x). \tag{5.83}$$

Proof The proof of the proposition requires material from Part II. In particular, it requires familiarity with probability concepts beyond what was required up to this point in the book. If you have background in probability theory, then read on.

Parts (ii) and (iii) are by construction: Choose $\varpi^\star$ to be the occupancy pmf associated with $\phi^\star$. We move on to (i): For any feasible ϖ, we design an input sequence defined as a randomized function of the state using (5.81):

$$\mathsf{P}\{u(k) = u \mid x(0), \dots, x(k)\} = \breve{\phi}(u \mid x(k)).$$

We have $\varpi_{\mathsf{x}}(x^e) = 0$ by assumption, which is not a problem since we already impose $u(k) = u^e$ whenever $x(k) = x^e$. The policy is not defined for other states x satisfying $\varpi_{\mathsf{x}}(x) = 0$, which is not a problem for a different reason: Such states are never visited when this policy is used and the initial condition satisfies $\nu(x_0) > 0$.

We then define, for any initial condition satisfying $\nu(x_0) > 0$,

$$J^{\breve{\phi}}(x_0) = \mathsf{E}\Big[\sum_{k=0}^{\infty} c(x(k),u(k))\Big], \qquad x(0) = x_0.$$

The proof of (i) is completed on establishing that $\langle \varpi, c \rangle = \langle \nu, J^{\breve{\phi}} \rangle$, and that $J^{\breve{\phi}}(x_0) \geq J^\star(x_0)$ for any x_0. □

Every linear program has a dual. Here it is simplest to construct the dual following the steps in Section 4.4.4. The dual variable is a function $\lambda \colon \mathsf{X} \to \mathbb{R}$ associated with the equality constraint (5.82b), and the dual function is defined as follows: $\varphi^*(\lambda) =$

$$\min_{\varpi} \ \langle \varpi, c \rangle + \sum_x \lambda(x)\Big\{-\sum_u \varpi(x,u) + \nu(x) + \sum_{x^-,u^-} \varpi(x^-,u^-)\mathbb{1}\{\mathsf{F}(x^-,u^-) = x\}\Big\} \tag{5.84a}$$

$$\text{s.t.} \ \varpi(x,u) \geq 0, \quad (x,u) \in \mathsf{X} \times \mathsf{U}, \qquad \varpi_{\mathsf{x}}(x^e) = 0. \tag{5.84b}$$

We impose the constraint $\lambda(x^e) = 0$ since (5.82b) is imposed only for $x \neq x^e$.

The dual LP is by definition the maximum of φ^* over all λ. The main conclusion is that this dual is precisely the DPLP:

Proposition 5.12 *The dual function admits the representation*

$$\varphi^*(\lambda) = \begin{cases} \langle \nu, \lambda \rangle & \text{if } c(x,u) - \lambda(x) + \lambda(\mathrm{F}(x,u)) \geq 0 \quad \text{for all } x,u, \ x \neq x^e \\ -\infty & \text{else} \end{cases} . \tag{5.85}$$

If $J^\star$ is finite valued, then $\varphi^*(\lambda) \leq \langle \nu, J^\star \rangle$ for any λ, and this bound is achieved using $\lambda^\star = J^\star$.

Proof Using this identity:

$$\sum_x \lambda(x) \mathbb{1}\{\mathrm{F}(x^-,u^-) = x\} = \lambda(\mathrm{F}(x^-,u^-)),$$

it follows that the objective can be expressed

$$\varphi^*(\lambda) = \min_{\varpi} \ \langle \varpi, c - \lambda + P\lambda \rangle + \langle \nu, \lambda \rangle$$

subject to the constraints (5.84b), and where the function $\lambda^- = P\lambda$ is defined by

$$\lambda^-(x,u) = \lambda(\mathrm{F}(x,u))$$

This implies (5.85). The bound $\varphi^*(\lambda) \leq \langle \nu, J^\star \rangle$ holds because the constraint (5.82b) has been relaxed in (5.84) (this bound is known as weak duality). The fact that this upper bound is achieved using $\lambda^\star = J^\star$ is immediate from the dynamic programming equation that $J^\star$ satisfies.

□

5.8 Exercises

5.1 *Over-fitting*. Consider the curve fitting problem without noise: $y_i = H^*(z_i)$ in which $H^*(z) = z^2$ for $z \in \mathbb{R}$, and evenly spaced inputs $\{z_i = i/n : 1 \leq i \leq 2n\}$. Calculate the estimate h^* using RKHS function approximation, based on the solution (5.18). Plot h^* for various values of λ (be sure to include $\lambda = 0$). Also experiment with n and the choice of kernel.

5.2 For the linear system (2.13a) with scalar input, consider

$$u(k) = -Kx(k) + \xi(k). \tag{5.86}$$

The gain is chosen so that the eigenvalues of $F - GK$ lie within the open unit disk in $\mathbb{C}$, and the probing signal is a mixture of sinusoids:

$$\xi(k) = \sum_{i=1}^{p} a_i \sin(2\pi[\phi_i + \omega_i k]).$$

The question to be considered: *How large must we take p to ensure sufficient exploration?* To estimate d parameters you might answer $p = d$, but that intuition may fail because of nonlinearities in our "observations."

Consider a special case in which the input and state are scalar valued, and denote $\psi_{(k)} = (x(k)^2, u(k)^2, x(k)u(k))^\intercal$. This regression vector might be used in TD-learning for a scalar linear system. Denote

$$R^{\psi} = \lim_{N\to\infty} \frac{1}{N} \sum_{k=0}^{N-1} \psi_{(k)}\psi_{(k)}^{\intercal}.$$

Investigate the consequences of rank deficiency, and see if you can construct an example for which this matrix is full rank using $p = 1$ or 2.

It is essential to approximate the following:

$$x(k) = \sum_{i=1}^{p} a_i^x \sin(2\pi[\phi_i^x + \omega_i^x k]) + \varepsilon(k),$$

where $\varepsilon(k)$ converges to zero geometrically quickly, and $\{a_i^x, \phi_i^x, \omega_i^x\}$ are obtained by reviewing your lecture notes on signals and systems! You can ignore the vanishing term $\varepsilon(k)$ in your computation of R^{ψ}.

5.3 Obtain an expression for $A(\theta) = -\nabla_\theta^2 \Gamma_N(\theta)$ for the batch loss function (5.36b). Obtain conditions on $\{x^i(0), u^i(0)\}$ so that A is Hurwitz. For this, it will be helpful to represent $-A$ as the sum of M positive semidefinite matrices.

5.4 The ODE approximation for TD(λ) is linear $\frac{d}{dt}\vartheta = A(\vartheta - \theta^*)$, provided the function approximation architecture is linear (recall (5.48)). With $Q^\theta = \theta^{\intercal}\psi$, we have

$$A = \mathsf{E}_{\varpi}\big[\zeta_k[-\psi(x(k),u(k)) + \psi(x(k+1),\phi(x(k+1))]^{\intercal}\big].$$

The existence of a steady-state ϖ can be justified by considering an implementation with restart.

In this exercise, you will consider $\lambda = 0$ so that $\zeta_k = \psi_{(k)} = \psi(x(k),u(k))$, and consider the on-policy setting for which we may write

$$A = \mathsf{E}_{\varpi}\big[-\psi_{(k)}\psi_{(k)}^{\intercal} + \psi_{(k)}\psi_{(k+1)}^{\intercal}\big].$$

To simplify the calculations that follow, assume that $\mathsf{E}_{\varpi}\big[\psi_{(k)}\psi_{(k)}^{\intercal}\big] = I$, and also assume the nondegeneracy condition: $\mathsf{E}_{\varpi}\big[\{\theta^{\intercal}(\psi_{(k+1)} - \psi_{(k)})\}^2\big] > 0$ whenever $\theta \neq 0$.

Show that the matrix A is Hurwitz under these assumptions.

Suggested approach: Let (λ, v) denote an eigenvalue–eigenvector pair, with $\|v\| = 1$ (and remember that λ and v may be complex). You then have, by the eigenvector property,

$$v^{\dagger}Av = \lambda v^{\dagger}v = \lambda,$$

where "$\dagger$" denotes complex conjugate transpose. Consider next the result of our simplification:

$$A = -I + \mathsf{E}_{\varpi}\big[\psi_{(k)}\psi_{(k+1)}^{\intercal}\big],$$
$$\lambda = v^{\dagger}Av = -1 + \mathsf{E}_{\varpi}\big[(v^{\dagger}\psi_{(k)})(v^{\intercal}\psi_{(k+1)})\big].$$

The right-hand side is $-1 + \langle v^{\intercal}\psi_{(k)}, v^{\intercal}\psi_{(k+1)}\rangle_{\varpi}$ in the notation introduced in Section 5.4.1. Look up the *Cauchy–Schwarz inequality* to see how to bound the inner product, and conclude that the real part of λ is strictly negative.

5.5 Formulate TD(λ)-learning for the discounted-cost criterion, with a fixed-policy Q-function defined by

$$Q^{\phi}(x,u) = \sum_{k=0}^{\infty} \gamma^k c(x(k),u(k)), \qquad x(0) = x,\ u(0) = u \ \text{and}\ u(k) = \phi(x(k)) \text{ for } k \geq 1.$$

The key step is to obtain a new definition for the temporal difference.

Repeat Exercise 5.4 for the on-policy version of your algorithm.

5.6 *TD-Learning for the Inverted Pendulum.* Review Exercise 3.11 and see if you can find inspiration to obtain a basis for TD- or Q-learning with cost function $c(x,u) = \theta^2 + u^2$.

Apply TD-learning with a linear function class to estimate the total cost value function for your favorite policy ϕ from Exercise 3.11. Does the policy improvement step based on your estimate of Q^{ϕ} provide a sensible policy?

5.7 *TD-Learning for MagBall.* Take your favorite policy for MagBall, such as the nonlinear policy (2.74) (for suitable values of K and K_3). Apply TD-learning with a linear function class to estimate Q^{ϕ} with $c(x,u) = \tilde{y}^2 + u^2$ (see Exercise 4.14).

Use your intuition to devise a basis. For example, you expect the value function to grow very quickly when the position is near the magnet, or very far away.

Does the policy improvement step based on your estimate of Q^{ϕ} provide a sensible policy?

5.8 *Return to Rowing.* This and many other exercises in this chapter might be assigned over several weeks, and split into two parts:

Part 1: Prepare a proposal on how you would tackle the rowing problem using either approximate policy iteration or a version of Q-learning. Give rationale for your choice of algorithm. Give full details regarding exploration, step size, etc. (and explain your choices). Predict what might go wrong, and how you would modify your design.

Don't forget that this is a (cooperative) game. For simplicity, you might convert this into a "two-player game" as follows: Isolate one rower as "player 1," and then the collection 100 rowers that model "player 2." In a best response strategy, player 1 learns the best policy ϕ^n in response to the remaining 100 rowers playing policy ϕ^{n-1}.

Part 2: Experiment with your algorithm with a finite population of rowers. Make sure you choose diverse initial conditions for the population in each round.

5.9 *Convex Q with Binning.* If the input space is not too large, and binning of the state space is feasible, then there is a more intuitive relaxation of the DPLP:

$$\theta^* = \arg\max_{\theta} \ \{\langle \mu, Q^\theta \rangle \quad \text{s.t.} \quad \overline{\mathcal{D}}^{i,u}(\theta) \ge 0 \quad \text{for each } 1 \le i \le d \text{ and } u \in \mathsf{U}\}$$

$$\text{with} \quad \overline{\mathcal{D}}^{i,u}(\theta) = \frac{1}{\mathcal{N}} \sum_{k=0}^{\mathcal{N}-1} \big[-Q^\theta(x(k),u(k)) + c(x(k),u(k)) + Q^\theta(x(k+1),u)\big]\mathbb{1}\{x(k) \in B_i\}.$$

Observe that $\overline{\mathcal{D}}^{i,u}(\theta)$ is an affine function of θ when $\{Q^\theta\}$ is defined using a linear function approximation (not necessarily using binning).

Try this out with the mountain car example, taking note of the warnings in Example 5.5.1.

5.10 *ERM and Kernel Methods.* This exercise is intended to improve understanding of both kernel methods and batch algorithms. The integer $r_n \ge 1$ denotes the batch size, using the same interpretation as in DQN (see (5.58)), and the batch of data at stage n is denoted $\{z_i^n : 1 \le i \le r_n\}$.

Consider the recursive algorithm

$$h_{n+1} = \arg\min\{\Gamma_n(h) + \frac{1}{\alpha_{n+1}} \tfrac{1}{2}\|h - h_n\|_n^2 + \delta\|h\|_{\mathcal{H}}^2\},$$

$$\|h - h_n\|_n^2 = \frac{1}{r_n} \sum_{k=1}^{r_n} \big(h(z_i^n) - h^n(z_i^n)\big)^2$$

with $\{\alpha_n\}$ a sequence of positive scalars, and the objective has the form

$$\Gamma_n(h) = \Gamma(h(z_1^n), \dots, h(z_{r_n}^n)).$$

The Representer Theorem tells us that $h_{n+1}(z) = \sum \theta^*_{n+1}(i)\mathbb{k}(z,z^n_i)$ for an r_n-dimensional vector θ^*_{n+1}.

Obtain a recursive formula for $\{\theta^*_n : n \ge 1\}$ for the curve fitting problem, in which Γ_n is the quadratic function

$$\Gamma_n(h) = \sum_{i=1}^{r_n} [y^n_i - h(z^n_i)]^2$$

with $\{y^n_i\}$ scalars. Your solution will be similar to (5.18).

5.11 The loss function (5.58a) in DQN simplifies computation, but unfortunately does not address the many challenges with Q(λ)-learning. Consider the alternative:

$$\Gamma^{\varepsilon}_n(\theta) = \frac{1}{r_n} \sum_{k=T_n}^{T_{n+1}-1} \left[-Q^{\theta}(x(k),u(k)) + c(x(k),u(k)) + \widehat{\underline{Q}}^{\theta}_n(x(k+1))\right]^2, \tag{5.87}$$

in which $\widehat{\underline{Q}}^{\theta}_n(x) = \underline{Q}^{\theta_n}(x) + \nabla_\theta \underline{Q}^{\theta_n}(x) \cdot [\theta - \theta_n]$. For a linear function approximation, a subgradient is given by

$$\nabla_\theta \underline{Q}^{\theta_n}(x) = \nabla_\theta Q^{\theta_n}(x,u)\Big|_{u=\phi^{\theta_n}(x)}.$$

This is a true gradient whenever the minimizer of $Q^{\theta_n}(x,u)$ over u is unique.

(a) Obtain a version of Proposition 5.9 for this algorithm (a fixed point equation for θ_{n+1}). Based on this, propose a recursive algorithm similar to batch Q(0)-learning.

(b) Obtain a conjecture on how Proposition 5.10 should be modified using the new definition (5.87), and obtain an interpretation for a limit point of the algorithm. Feel free to assume a linear parameterization.

(c) Review Exercise 5.10, and consider the loss function defined on a RKHS: For $h \in \mathcal{H}$,

$$\Gamma^{\varepsilon}_n(h) = \frac{1}{r_n} \sum_{k=T_n}^{T_{n+1}-1} \left[-h(x(k),u(k)) + c(x(k),u(k)) + \widehat{\underline{h}}^{\theta}_n(x(k+1))\right]^2$$

and the associated batch Q-learning algorithm

$$h_{n+1} = \arg\min\{\Gamma^{\varepsilon}_n(h) + + \frac{1}{\alpha_{n+1}} \tfrac{1}{2}\|h - h_n\|^2_n + \delta\|h\|^2_{\mathcal{H}}\}.$$

Obtain a recursive representation for the optimizers $\{h_n : n \ge 1\}$ (similar to Exercise 5.10).

5.9 Notes

This chapter also covers a great deal of ground. These notes provide a few missing ingredients and offer sources for further reading.

5.9.1 Machine Learning

The vast literature on function approximation, model selection, and over-fitting is an indication of its importance.

There are many good references on machine learning. The *Elements of Statistical Learning* [156] and Murphy's *Machine Learning: A Probabilistic Perspective* [267] are great introductions, and MacKay's survey [233] is fast-paced but also good. References [262, 290] contain accessible treatments of kernels with statistical interpretations (and much more). See also the classics [80, 97, 365] for ways of quantifying model complexity and overfitting from various perspectives.

5.9.2 TD-Learning

A full history of temporal difference methods can be found in the second edition of the monograph of Sutton and Barto [338]. While these authors are considered major stars in RL and in particular TD methods, they are the first to point out an older history going back to Shannon in the 1950s. The TD(0) algorithm was introduced by Witten in the 1970s [377]. See chapter 1 of [338] for a scholarly and entertaining survey of the origins of the field.

The promise of TD-learning took a leap following Sutton's dissertation [339, 340] (based in part on collaboration with Charles Anderson and his advisor Andrew Barto [26, 342]). This early work contains substantial intuition regarding TD(λ) algorithms and their application, with emphasis on neural network approximation architecture for applications, and linear function approximation for much of the theory. The end of the decade was crowned by Watkins's dissertation that introduced the Q-learning algorithm [346, 371, 372].

It is surprising that there was so little synergy in the 1980s and 1990s between RL and *adaptive control* [83, 145, 202, 241]. There was significant outreach in one direction: Notable examples include the surveys by Sutton et al.: *Learning and Sequential Decision Making* [27], and "Reinforcement Learning Is Direct Adaptive Optimal Control" [343]. RL pioneers in the control systems research community include Frank Lewis [183, 222], who remains a leader at the intersection of RL and control systems, and John Tsitsiklis, whose contributions are surveyed in sections 9.11 and 10.10. An early example of off-policy TD learning is [74], which treats the LQR problem and is written for a control theory audience.

The TD-learning algorithm (5.34) is more similar to the (off-policy) LSQ algorithm of [206] than the original LSTD algorithm of [75]. The common acronym LSTD is used for both on- and off-policy implementations throughout the book.

The objective function Γ in (5.33) is known as the *mean-square Bellman residual* in Baird's 1995 paper [21]. It is pointed out there that the resulting SA approximation of the gradient flow is slow to converge. The paper goes on to investigate compromises between TD(0) and gradient descent to accelerate convergence. This paper also introduced the famous counterexample based on Figure 5.5. Around the same time, Gordon [146] presented examples of unstable function approximations for Q-learning.

The theoretical foundations of temporal difference methods took a significant leap one decade after Sutton's dissertation, following the realization that TD-learning can be cast as a stochastic approximation algorithm [169, 352]. This sparked Tsitsiklis's research program on reinforcement learning that has had enormous impact on the field and on my own appreciation of the discipline. Two dissertations supervised by Tsitsiklis were truly ground breaking in this domain: Ben Van Roy [363] and Vijaymohan Konda [188] provide elegant theory that explains the success (and potential failure) of TD-learning and actor-critic algorithms for stochastic control systems. Much of this theory is a foundation for material in Part II of this book.

Kernel methods in RL have a significant history, with most of the algorithms designed to approximate the value function for a fixed policy, so that the function approximation problem can be cast in a least-squares setting [131, 279] (the latter proposes extensions to Q-learning).

Left out of the book is any discussion on "safe RL," in which an attempt is made to enforce stability guarantees. The theory developed in this book should help you understand the literature, such as [94, 284], and help you to discover new techniques.

5.9.3 Q-Learning

First, *why Q*? The question of its origin was raised by Aaron Snoswell (then a graduate student at Queensland University of Technology) during the early days of the fall 2020 Simon's program on reinforcement learning. Csaba Szepesvari contacted Chris Watkins, who responded shortly after: "... which letter to choose? I realised I hadn't used Q, that enigmatic letter, and one could retro-fit 'quality' ...". An enigmatic letter is fitting for this mysterious class of algorithms!

The Q(λ) algorithm (5.52) is not commonly seen in textbooks, except for the special case $\lambda = 0$. Q(0)-learning, and variants are commonly applied because they are the natural extension of Watkins's Q-learning algorithm for controlled Markov chains. There is a firm theory for convergence of Q(0)-learning in the special case considered by Watkins, in part because it is assumed that the function class is "complete" (contains every possible function on $\mathsf{X} \times \mathsf{U}$). Convergence of Watkins's algorithm is established using ODE methods in Section 9.6.

Major success stories in DQN practice are described in [259–261], and [9] contains an insightful analysis. The limit theory for the algorithm (5.58) summarized in Proposition 5.10 is taken from [247]. The refinement of DQN introduced in Exercise 5.11 is inspired by the convex–concave optimization procedure of Hartman [155, 226]. Another approach to batch RL is based on empirical value iteration [153, 174, 317].

The origin of convex Q-learning is [245], where a family of LP approaches is formulated in continuous time. The challenge at the time was to find ways to create a reliable online algorithm. The algorithm challenges were addressed in [246, 247], which is the basis of much of Section 5.5.

For more on RL in continuous time, consider reviewing the research program of Lewis [184, 359], the volume [360], and the recent survey [220].

Recall from Section 3.11 that Manne introduced the linear programming approach to dynamic programming in the 1960 article [237]. A significant program on linear programming approaches to approximate dynamic programming for Markovian decision processes (MDPs) began in [102–104, 314] and continues today.

The algorithms and theory in Section 5.5 are based on [247], which builds on the first version of convex Q-learning [245] (designed for deterministic systems in continuous time). Improvements appeared in the following decade, primarily in a stochastic control setting. For example, the theory in [218] is based on a variant of the convex program (3.36), with the inequality in (3.36b) replaced by equality: It contains substantial theory for the tabular setting (recall (5.10)). More recent results in [28] obtain efficient algorithms based an LP formulation closely related to the DPLP (3.36).

Part II

Reinforcement Learning and Stochastic Control

6

Markov Chains

We begin Part II with a return to the foundations of state space models, but now in a stochastic setting. The notation is essentially the same as in previous chapters, except that we use upper case to denote random variables: $\boldsymbol{X} = \{X(0), X(1), X(2), \dots\}$ denotes a sample path of the state process. For each time $k \geq 0$, it is assumed that $X(k)$ takes values in a state space denoted X. As in previous chapters, the state space is a closed subset of $\mathbb{R}^n$ (recall (2.22)). We don't rule out a finite state space, but there is no reason to be bound to this special case.

6.1 Markov Models Are State Space Models

Recall from Section 2.3 that the state process in the nonlinear state space model is interpreted as a *sufficient statistic*. Consider the controlled model (2.6a), under a stationary Markov policy $u(k) = \phi(x(k))$ for $k \geq 0$. To compute future states $x(j)$ for $j \geq k$, we only need to know $x(k)$; the prior history $\{x(i), u(i) : i < k\}$ is irrelevant in determining future behavior.

The definition of a Markov chain is formulated to capture the same *memoryless property* in a stochastic environment. An example is an independent and identically distributed (i.i.d.) sequence $\boldsymbol{N}$, in which $N(0) \sim \pi$ for a probability measure π, and there is no memory:

$$\mathsf{P}\{N(k) \in S \mid N(0), \dots, N(k-1)] = \pi(S), \quad \text{for each } k \text{ and } S \subset \mathsf{X}. \tag{6.1}$$

These form a building block for more complex stochastic processes.

Here are two definitions of a Markov chain. The first makes precise the definition of "memoryless" in a form milder than (6.1).

(i) *Memoryless property:* The stochastic process $\boldsymbol{X}$ is a Markov chain if the following holds: For $S \subset \mathsf{X}$, any time k, and initial $X(0)$,

$$\mathsf{P}\{X(k+1) \in S \mid X(0), \dots, X(k)\} = \mathsf{P}\{X(k+1) \in S \mid X(k)\}. \tag{6.2}$$

(ii) *Nonlinear state space model*: A Markov chain is a stochastic process that evolves according to the nonlinear state space model,

$$X(k+1) = \mathsf{F}(X(k), N(k+1)), \tag{6.3}$$

where $\boldsymbol{N}$ is i.i.d., and the initial condition $X(0)$ is specified (if it is random, then it is assumed independent of the "disturbance" $\boldsymbol{N}$).

The first definition is slightly more general than the second, only because the dynamics defined by F do not depend upon time. We will restrict to such *time-homogeneous* Markov chains throughout the book. If an application demands a time-varying model, then we may resort to the state-augmentation tricks described in Section 3.3.

The distribution of $X(k)$ for $k \geq 0$ is defined by the initial distribution (the distribution of the potentially random $X(0)$) and the *transition kernel*. This defines the one-step transition probabilities,

$$P(x,S) = \mathsf{P}\{X(k+1) \in S \mid X(k) = x\}, \qquad x \in \mathsf{X},\ S \subset \mathsf{X}. \tag{6.4}$$

It is called the *transition matrix* if the state space X is finite. For the nonlinear state space model (6.3),

$$P(x,S) = \mathsf{P}\{X(1) \in S \mid X(0) = x\} = \mathsf{P}\{\mathsf{F}(x,N(1)) \in S\}.$$

For $j > 1$, the j-step transition probability from x to S is denoted as follows:

$$P^j(x,S) = \mathsf{P}\{X(k+j) \in S \mid X(k) = x\}. \tag{6.5}$$

In the majority of cases, we no longer think about equilibria $x^e \in \mathsf{X}$ when studying Markov chains. We seek instead an *equilibrium measure* π (more commonly called an *invariant measure*) satisfying the ergodic theorem:

$$\lim_{k\to\infty} P^k(x,S) = \pi(S), \qquad \text{for any } x \in \mathsf{X} \text{ and } S \subset \mathsf{X}. \tag{6.6}$$

We will see that this implies the existence of a *steady state*: If $X(0) \sim \pi$, then $\boldsymbol{X}$ is a stationary process (so that, in particular, $X(k) \sim \pi$ for all k). This is interpreted as a stability property for the Markov chain, much like global asymptotic stability for deterministic nonlinear state space models.

6.1.1 Notation and Conventions

If you have taken a course with an introduction to measure theory, then you know that care must be taken in defining the class of sets S for which (6.4) and the equations that follow are meaningful. For those of you with this background, keep in mind that X will be taken to be a *Borel* subset of Euclidean space (such as a closed subset), and any $S \subset \mathsf{X}$ will also be assumed to have this property. This is denoted $S \in \mathcal{B}(\mathsf{X})$. Examples of Borel sets in $\mathbb{R}$ include any interval $[a,b]$, $[a,b)$, $(a,b]$, or (a,b) with $b > a$, and any finite or countable union of intervals. Similarly, any function $h \colon \mathsf{X} \to \mathbb{R}$ is assumed to be Borel measurable. That is, the set $S_h(r) = \{x : h(x) \leq r\}$ is a Borel set for each constant r.

Never heard the word "Borel"? Don't worry. Measure theory is not important for understanding any of the concepts that follow. The notation is required because transition kernels cannot in general be defined on *every* subset of the state space, except when the state space is finite or countably infinite.

Integrals and Expectations

The symbols μ, ν, and π are reserved for probability measures on $\mathcal{B}(\mathsf{X})$. We opt for the term *probability mass function* (pmf) when X is finite or countable.

The state $X(k)$ at time k is a random variable. Its distribution is a probability measure denoted μ_k, defined for any Borel measurable function h via

$$\mathsf{E}[h(X(k))] = \int h(x)\,\mu_k(dx). \tag{6.7}$$

The notation may look strange to you, but I know of no better alternative when we don't know the form of μ_k. If there is a density, then by definition $\mu_k(dx) = p_k(x)dx$ for some nonnegative function p_k; if μ_k is discrete, then the integral becomes a sum. The Gaussian linear state space model discussed in Example 6.2.1 makes clear why we need this abstract notation.

Please keep in mind: *We don't know the form of* μ_k. We don't want to write one book for Markov chains with densities, another for those on a countable state space, and a third for when neither assumption applies (as found in Example 6.2.1). The notation (6.7) is agnostic to the form of μ_k.

Notation Surrounding Conditional Expectations

Conditional expectations of the form

$$\mathsf{E}[h(X(k+1)) \mid X(0),\dots,X(k)]$$

appear everywhere in the remainder of the chapter and the book (which is meaningful provided $\mathsf{E}[|h(X(k+1)|] < \infty$). *Never heard of conditional expectation?* Example 6.3 is provided as a mini-crash-course, with a longer crash-course in Section 9.2. You should review [154] or some other foundational source for a fuller understanding.

Fortunately, definitions are simplified when considering functions of a Markov chain, because the conditional expectation can be expressed in terms of the transition kernel: for any $x \in \mathsf{X}$, and any initial distribution for $X(0)$,

$$\begin{aligned}\mathsf{E}[h(X(k+1)) \mid X(0),\dots,X(k-1); X(k)=x]&\\ &= \mathsf{E}[h(X(k+1)) \mid X(k)=x]\\ &= \int P(x,dy)h(y).\end{aligned} \tag{6.8}$$

If X is finite, of size m, then P is interpreted as an $m \times m$ matrix. In this case, $P(x_0,x_1)$ is the probability of moving from x_0 to x_1 in one time-step. The conditional expectation is expressed as a sum:

$$\mathsf{E}[h(X(k+1)) \mid X(k)=x] = \sum_{x_1 \in \mathsf{X}} P(x,x_1)h(x_1).$$

Conditional expectations appear so frequently that we require shorthand notation: For a function $h\colon \mathsf{X} \to \mathbb{R}$ and integers $r,k \geq 0$,

$$\mathsf{E}_x[h(X(k)))] \stackrel{\text{def}}{=} \mathsf{E}[h(X(r+k)) \mid X(r)=x], \tag{6.9a}$$

$$P^k h\,(x) \stackrel{\text{def}}{=} \mathsf{E}[h(X(r+k)) \mid X(r)=x]\,, \qquad x \in \mathsf{X}. \tag{6.9b}$$

In the special case $k=1$, we write Ph rather than $P^1 h$.

In (6.9b), we view P^k as a mapping from functions to functions. This representation was introduced for finite state space models early on in this book, just above (3.17), where for emphasis we introduced the vector notation

$$\vec{h} = [h(x_1), \ldots, h(x_m)]^{\intercal}, \qquad \mathsf{X} = \{x_1, \ldots, x_m\},$$

and wrote $P^k\vec{h}$ rather than $P^k h$. This cumbersome vector notation will not appear again in this book.

If μ is a probability measure on X, and $X(r) \sim \mu$ (the state is distributed according to μ at time r), it then follows that $X(k+r) \sim \mu_k$ for any $k \geq 1$, with

$$\mu_k(S) = \int \mu(dx) P^k(x,S), \qquad S \in \mathcal{B}(\mathsf{X}). \tag{6.10}$$

This is expressed $\mu_k = \mu P^k$, which is also consistent with vector-matrix multiplication in the finite state space setting. This probability measure is precisely the same as used in (6.7) when $r = 0$.

We could go further, writing

$$\mu h = \int h(x)\mu(dx).$$

This is consistent with multiplication of a column vector h by a row vector μ to obtain a scalar (an inner product). However, "μh" can create ambiguity, so we introduce parentheses for emphasis:

$$\mu(h) = \int h(x)\mu(dx). \tag{6.11}$$

Please get used to these notational conventions! They will be used throughout the remainder of the book.

6.2 Simple Examples

We begin with a few basic examples. The linear model is standard in physics, systems theory, economics, and many other areas.

Example 6.2.1 (***The Linear State Space Model***) Suppose $\boldsymbol{X} = \{X(k)\}$ is a stochastic process for which there is an $n \times n$ matrix F and an i.i.d. sequence $\boldsymbol{N}$ taking values in $\mathbb{R}^n$ such that

$$X(k+1) = FX(k) + N(k+1), \qquad k \geq 0,$$

where $X(0) \in \mathbb{R}^n$ is independent of $\boldsymbol{N}$. Then $\boldsymbol{X}$ is called the (uncontrolled) linear state space model. It is precisely of the form (6.3) in which $\mathrm{F}(x,n) = Fx + n$.

We denote the state process using a lower case variable when $\boldsymbol{N} \equiv 0$, as in (2.42):

$$x(k+1) = Fx(k), \qquad k \geq 0. \tag{6.12}$$

The state process $\boldsymbol{x}$ is also Markovian: Given the full history of observations $\{x(i) : i \le k\}$, we can still predict $x(k+1)$ with exact accuracy, based only on knowledge of $x(k)$.

The transition kernel is easily described: For any $x \in \mathsf{X} = \mathbb{R}^n$ and set $S \subset \mathsf{X}$, we have

$$P(x,S) = \mathsf{P}\{X(1) \in S \mid X(0) = x\} = \mathsf{P}\{Fx + N(1) \in S\}.$$

If in particular $N(1)$ is Gaussian $N(0,\Sigma_N)$, then $P(x,\,\cdot\,)$ is also a Gaussian distribution, but with mean Fx rather than zero. If at some time $r \ge 0$ we observe $X(r) = x$, then for each $j \ge 0$,

$$X(r+j) = F^j x + \sum_{i=1}^{j} F^{j-i} N(r+i).$$

That is, conditioned on $X(r) = x$, the random vector $X(r+j)$ has a Gaussian distribution with mean $F^j x$ and covariance

$$\Sigma_{X_j} = \sum_{i=1}^{j} (F^{j-i})^{\intercal} \Sigma_N F^{j-i}.$$

If Σ_{X_j} is full rank (so its inverse exists), then P^j admits a transition density:

$$p_j(x,y) = \frac{1}{\sqrt{(2\pi)^n \det(\Sigma_{X_j})}} \exp\Bigl(-\tfrac{1}{2}(y - F^j x)^{\intercal} \Sigma_{X_j}^{-1} (y - F^j x)\Bigr),$$

$$P^j(x,S) = \int_S p_j(x,y)\,dy,$$

where the j-step transition kernel is defined in (6.5).

From this, we obtain our first ergodic theorem:

Proposition 6.1 *Suppose that the eigenvalues of F lie in the open unit disk in $\mathbb{C}$, and that $\boldsymbol{N}$ is i.i.d., with Gaussian marginal $N(0,\Sigma_N)$. Consider any factorization, $\Sigma_N = GG^{\intercal}$, with G an $n \times m$ matrix for some $m \ge 1$, and suppose that the rank condition holds:*

$$\text{rank}\bigl(\mathcal{C}\bigr) = n, \quad \text{where} \quad \mathcal{C} = [G \mid FG \mid \cdots \mid F^{n-1}G]. \tag{6.13}$$

Then the following conclusions hold:

(i) *The steady-state covariance Σ_{X_∞} has rank n, where*

$$\Sigma_{X_\infty} = \lim_{j\to\infty} \Sigma_{X_j} = \sum_{k=0}^{\infty} (F^k)^{\intercal} \Sigma_N F^k.$$

(ii) *The density p_k exists for $k \ge n$, and converges as $k \to \infty$: For any x,y,*

$$\lim_{k\to\infty} p_k(x,y) = p_\infty(y) = \frac{1}{\sqrt{(2\pi)^n \det(\Sigma_{X_\infty})}} \exp\Bigl(-\tfrac{1}{2} y^{\intercal} \Sigma_{X_\infty}^{-1} y\Bigr).$$

The limit defines the invariant measure: for $S \in \mathcal{B}(\mathsf{X})$,

$$\pi(S) \stackrel{\text{def}}{=} \int_S p_\infty(y)dy = \int_{\mathsf{X}} p_\infty(y)P^k(y,S)dy = \int_{\mathsf{X}} P^k(y,S)\,\pi(dy).$$

(iii) *For functions h satisfying $\int |h(y)|p_\infty(y)dy < \infty$, we have, for each initial condition $X(0) = x$,*

$$\lim_{k\to\infty} \mathsf{E}_x[h(X(k))] = \lim_{k\to\infty} P^k h\,(x) = \pi(h) = \int p_\infty(y)h(y)dy. \qquad \square$$

In state space control theory, the matrix $\mathcal{C}$ in (6.13) is called the *controllability matrix*, and Σ_{X_∞} the *controllability Grammian*. Part (i) is a consequence of the Cayley–Hamilton theorem [7, 76, 205].

An interesting special case is $\Sigma_N = GG^\intercal$, with G a column vector (Σ_N has rank 1). For any initial condition x, the probability measure $P^k(x,\cdot\,)$ does not have a density for $k < n$. The proposition tells us that there is a density for $k \geq n$, provided $\mathcal{C}$ has rank n.

There is no density for any k when $\mathcal{C}$ is rank deficient. Moreover, since Σ_{X_∞} is no longer invertible, the limits (ii) and (iii) are no longer valid. Example 6.10 is intended to explain how the proposition must be modified when Σ_{X_∞} is not full rank.

Recall from Figure 2.7 a comparison of the deterministic and stochastic models. The linear Gaussian model was chosen so that the assumptions of Proposition 6.1 are satisfied: The eigenvalues of F lie in the open unit disk in $\mathbb{C}$, and the rank condition (6.13) holds. The covariance for the disturbance was chosen to be rank deficient. This was through the choice $N(k) = GW(k)$ with $G \in \mathbb{R}^2$ and $W(k)$ scalar $N(0,1)$, resulting in $\Sigma_N = GG^\intercal$. The rank condition (6.13) is

$$\text{rank}([G \mid FG]) = 2.$$

Equivalently, G is not an eigenvector for F. ■

The Gaussian assumption is imposed only so that we can identify the invariant density. There is an ergodic steady state and some form of ergodicity, whenever $|\lambda(F)| < 1$ for every eigenvalue of F, regardless of the marginal distribution for the disturbance. In other words, the distribution of the noise is hardly relevant, so it is sufficient to consider the disturbance-free model with state process $\boldsymbol{x}$ to determine stability of this Markov chain (in the sense of the existence of a steady state). We will see in Chapter 7 that generalizations of this conclusion hold for more general nonlinear models, and that one explanation for the solidarity of deterministic and stochastic models is found through Lyapunov theory.

Random walks are defined by taking successive sums of independent and identically distributed (i.i.d.) random variables.

Example 6.2.2 (*Random Walks*) Suppose that $\boldsymbol{X} = \{X(k); k \geq 0\}$ is a sequence of random variables defined by

$$X(k+1) = X(k) + N(k+1), \qquad k \geq 0,$$

where $X(0) \in \mathbb{R}$ is independent of $\boldsymbol{N}$, and the sequence $\boldsymbol{N}$ is i.i.d., taking values in $\mathbb{R}$. Then $\boldsymbol{X}$ is called a *random walk* on $\mathbb{R}$. The random walk is a special case of the one-dimensional linear state space model in which $F = I$.

Suppose that the stochastic process $\boldsymbol{X}$ is defined by the following recursion:

$$X(k+1) = [X(k) + N(k+1)]_+ \stackrel{\text{def}}{=} \max(0, X(k) + N(k+1)), \qquad k \geq 0,$$

where again $X(0) \in \mathbb{R}$, and $\boldsymbol{N}$ is an i.i.d. sequence of random variables taking values in $\mathbb{R}$. Then $\boldsymbol{X}$ is called the *reflected random walk*. The reflected random walk is a special case of the one-dimensional nonlinear linear state space model in which $\mathrm{F}(x,d) = [x+d]_+$ for each $x, d \in \mathbb{R}$. ■

The reflected random walk is a model for storage systems and queueing systems. For all such applications, there are similar concerns: "we need to know whether a dam overflows, whether a queue ever empties, whether a computer network jams" [257, p. 13]. We are also interested in finer questions regarding performance, such as the mean and variance of delay.

One of the simplest reflected random walks is also the most famous model for a queue.

Example 6.2.3 (*The M/M/1 Queue*) The transition function for the *M/M/1 queue* is defined as

$$\mathsf{P}(X(k+1) = y \mid X(k) = x) = P(x,y) = \begin{cases} \alpha & \text{if } y = x+1 \\ \mu & \text{if } y = (x-1)_+ \end{cases}, \tag{6.14}$$

where α denotes the arrival rate to the queue, μ is the service rate, and these parameters are normalized so that $\alpha + \mu = 1$.

The parameter $\rho \stackrel{\text{def}}{=} \alpha/\mu$ is known as the *load* for the queue. If $\rho < 1$, then the arrival rate is strictly less than the service rate. In this case, the process is ergodic: There is a pmf π on the nonnegative integers such that for any initial queue length $X(0) = x$, and any integer $m \geq 0$,

$$\lim_{k \to \infty} \mathsf{P}_x\{X(k) = m\} = \pi(m).$$

The invariant pmf is geometric with parameter ρ, so that $\pi(m) = (1-\rho)\rho^m$. The existence of π is interpreted as a form of stability for the queueing model, so that the sample path behavior looks like that shown in the left-hand side of Figure 6.1 and in Figure 6.2. ■

6.3 Spectra and Ergodicity

This section is devoted to the finite state space model: X is finite with $m \geq 2$ elements. In this case, P is viewed as an $m \times m$ matrix, whose eigenvalues are the solution to the following characteristic equation:

$$\det[\lambda I - P] = 0. \tag{6.15}$$

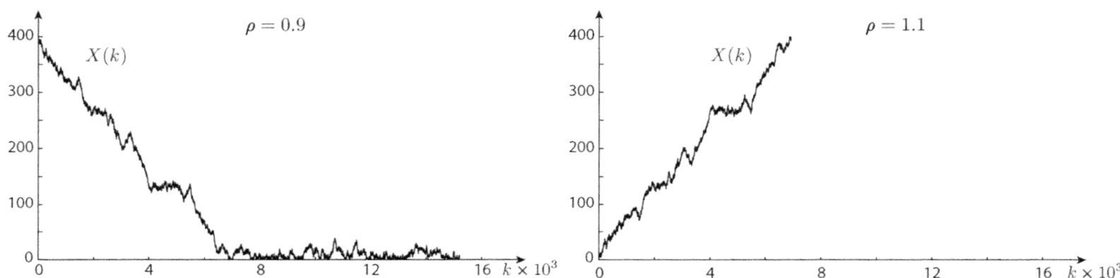

Figure 6.1 The M/M/1 queue: In the stable case on the left, we see that the process $X(k)$ appears piecewise linear, with a relatively small high-frequency "disturbance." The process explodes linearly in the unstable case shown on the right.

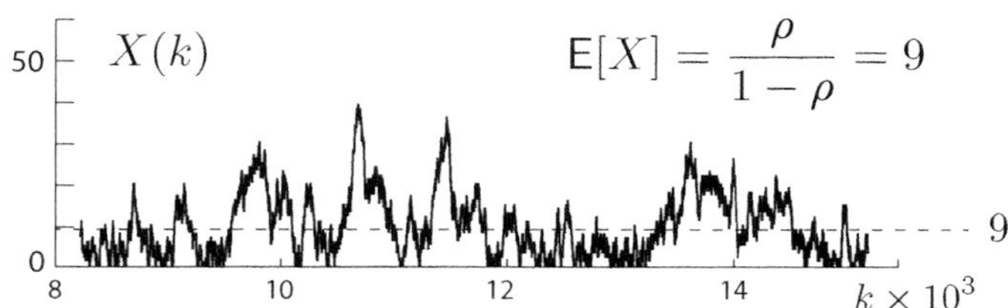

Figure 6.2 A close-up of the trajectory shown on the left-hand side of Figure 6.1 with load $\rho = 0.9 < 1$. After a transient period, the queue length oscillates around its steady-state mean of 9.

There are m solutions denoted $\{\lambda_1, \dots, \lambda_m\}$ (some may be repeated). By convention, we set $\lambda_1 = 1$.

Some immediate properties of eigenvalues:

(i) Why is $\lambda_1 = 1$ an eigenvalue? Because there is always an eigenvector: Define $v^1 \in \mathbb{R}^d$ to be the vector whose entries are all equal to one. Following the preceding conventions, the vector is also viewed as a function on X. The matrix-vector product Pv^1 is obtained using the usual definition:

$$Pv^1\,(x) = \sum_y P(x,y)v^1(y) = \sum_y P(x,y) = 1.$$

That is, $Pv^1 = v^1$.

(ii) Less obvious is that there is a left eigenvector π with eigenvalue $\lambda_1 = 1$ that has nonnegative entries. This is normalized so that $\sum_x \pi(x) = 1$. The eigenvector property is

$$\pi(y) = \sum_x \pi(x)P(x,y).$$

The pmf π is called *invariant*.

(iii) Every eigenvalue must satisfy $|\lambda| \leq 1$ (that is, λ lies in the closed unit disk in the complex plane). To see this, consider iterating the equation $Pv = \lambda v$ to obtain

$$P^n v = \lambda^n v, \qquad n \geq 1.$$

Remember that the left-hand side is a conditional expectation, so that

$$\mathsf{E}[v(X(n)) \mid X(0) = x] = \lambda^n v(x).$$

The left-hand side of this equation is bounded in n, which means that $|\lambda| \leq 1$ as claimed. $\square$

The Markov chain is called *ergodic* if for each $x,y \in \mathsf{X}$,

$$\lim_{n\to\infty} \mathsf{P}\{X(n) = y \mid X(0) = x\} \stackrel{\text{def}}{=} \lim_{n\to\infty} P^n(x,y) = \pi(y). \tag{6.16}$$

Consequently, for any function $c\colon \mathsf{X} \to \mathbb{C}$,

$$\lim_{n\to\infty} \mathsf{E}[c(X(n)) \mid X(0) = x] = \pi(c) = \sum_y c(y)\pi(y). \tag{6.17}$$

This leads to one more simple observation:

(iv) Suppose there is an eigenvalue $\lambda \neq 1$ but satisfying $|\lambda| = 1$ (the eigenvalue lies on the boundary of the unit disk). Then the Markov chain cannot be ergodic. To see this, let $v \in \mathbb{C}^d$ be an eigenvector (nonzero) and write $\lambda = e^{j\theta}$ with $0 < \theta < 2\pi$. Hence $P^n v = \lambda^n v = e^{jn\theta} v$ for each n. With $c = v$, we obtain

$$\mathsf{E}[c(X(n)) \mid X(0) = x] = \sum_{y\in\mathsf{X}} P^n(x,y)v(y) = e^{jn\theta} v(x).$$

The right-hand side does not converge as $n \to \infty$.

The following may be expected from the foregoing.

Theorem 6.2 (Spectral Conditions for Ergodicity) *Suppose that* $\lambda_1 = 1$ *is the only eigenvalue satisfying* $|\lambda| = 1$*, and this eigenvalue is not repeated. Then the chain is ergodic, and the convergence rate in* (6.16) *is geometric:*

$$\lim_{n\to\infty} \frac{1}{n} \log\Bigl(\max_{x,y} |P^n(x,y) - \pi(y)|\Bigr) = \log(\rho) < 0, \tag{6.18}$$

where $\rho = \max\{|\lambda_k| : k \geq 2\}$.

Proof The first step is to consider a modified matrix $\widetilde{P}$ defined by

$$\widetilde{P}(x,y) = P(x,y) - \pi(y), \qquad x,y \in \mathsf{X}. \tag{6.19}$$

This can be expressed $\widetilde{P} = P - \mathbf{1} \otimes \pi$, where $\mathbf{1} = v^1$ is a column vector of ones, π is the invariant pmf, and "$\otimes$" is an outer product. It can be shown by induction that

$$\widetilde{P}^n = P^n - \mathbf{1} \otimes \pi. \tag{6.20}$$

That is, for each x,y,

$$\widetilde{P}^n(x,y) = P^n(x,y) - \pi(y).$$

With a bit more effort, it can be shown that $\lambda(\widetilde{P}) = \{0,\lambda_2,\ldots,\lambda_m\}$. That is, all of the eigenvalues of $\widetilde{P}$ coincide with those of P, except the first eigenvalue, which is moved to the origin. A bit of linear algebra completes the proof of (6.18). $\square$

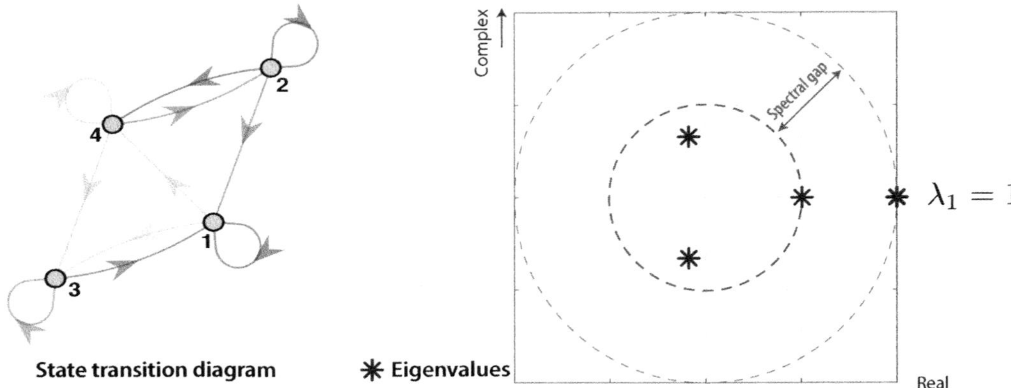

Figure 6.3 Communication diagram and eigenvalues for a four-state Markov chain.

6.3.1 Example

Matlab's `mcmix` command is a convenient way to randomly generate transition matrices with a given structure. Here is one example with $m = 4$ states, in which the five zeros in the transition matrix were imposed:

$$P = \begin{bmatrix} 0.0500 & 0 & 0.5536 & 0.3964 \\ 0.9094 & 0.0500 & 0 & 0.0406 \\ 0.1519 & 0 & 0.8481 & 0 \\ 0 & 0.1891 & 0.4302 & 0.3807 \end{bmatrix}. \tag{6.21}$$

The plot on the left in Figure 6.3 shows the *communication diagram* for this Markov chain. This is a directed graph in which nodes correspond to the four states, and there is a directed edge between states x and y if $P(x,y) > 0$. It is a generalization of the graph model for deterministic control systems introduced in Example 3.2.

The eigenvalues of P are $\{\lambda_1, \dots, \lambda_4\} = \{1, 0.5044, -0.0878 \pm 0.3295j\}$, and illustrated at the right in Figure 6.3. The *spectral gap* is defined by $1 - \max\{|\lambda_i| : i \geq 2\} = 1 - |\lambda_2|$. The plots were obtained using Matlab commands `graphplot` and `eigplot`.

Matlab can be used to find the eigenvectors of the transpose of P:

```
[V, L] = eig(P'),
```

which gives $L = \{\lambda_1, \dots, \lambda_4\}$, and the four columns of V are the corresponding eigenvectors of $P^{\intercal}$. From this we obtain the invariant pmf, $\pi = [0.1378, 0.0178, 0.7551, 0.0893]$.

Theorem 6.2 states that $P^n(x,y) \to \pi(y)$ at rate approximately $\lambda_2^n = \rho^n$ for all x,y. Shown in Figure 6.4 is a plot of $\log(|P^n(x,y) - P^n(y,y)|)$ for $y = 4$ and $x \neq 4$, along with a plot of $\log(\lambda_2^n) = n\log(\rho)$. Observe that the difference $\log|P^n(x,y) - P^n(y,y)| - n\log(\rho)$ is bounded in n (which is more than anticipated from (6.18)). This bound holds in this example because there is a single eigenvalue satisfying $|\lambda_2| = \rho$.

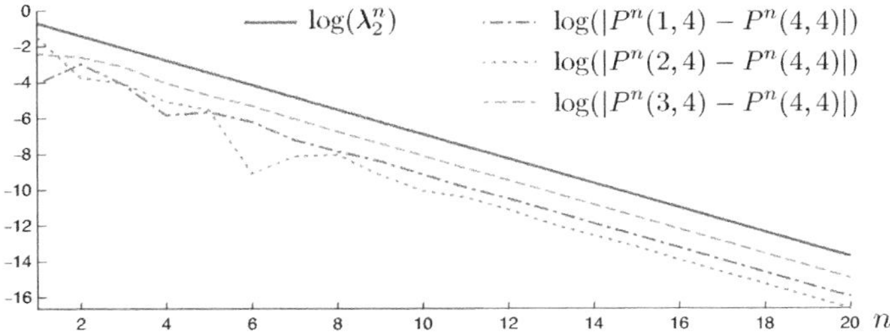

Figure 6.4 Rate of convergence of P^n to $\mathbf{1} \otimes \pi$ for the four-state Markov chain.

6.4 A Random Glance Ahead

For the linear state space model, the M/M/1 queue, and for finite state space Markov chains, we identified conditions under which there is a limiting probability measure π satisfying (6.6): For each initial condition $x \in \mathsf{X}$ and $S \in \mathcal{B}(\mathsf{X})$,

$$\lim_{k\to\infty} P^k(x,S) = \pi(S).$$

The limit π is invariant, in the sense that

$$\int_{\mathsf{X}} \pi(dx)P^k(x,S) = \pi(S), \qquad S \in \mathcal{B}(\mathsf{X}), \ k \geq 1.$$

That is, $\pi P^k = \pi$. Conditions for the existence of an invariant measure on an infinite state space will be surveyed later in the chapter, along with far stronger ergodic theorems.

The existence of an invariant measure is equivalent to the existence of a *steady-state* realization of the state process $\boldsymbol{X}$. That is, the state process satisfies the stationarity property:

$$\mathsf{P}\{X(k) \in A_0, \ X(k+1) \in A_1, \dots, X(k+m) \in A_n\} \qquad \text{is independent of } k \geq 0,$$

for any $m \geq 0$ and any sequence of sets $\{A_0, \dots, A_m\}$, each in $\mathcal{B}(\mathsf{X})$. Naturally, the stationary realization satisfies $X(k) \sim \pi$ for each k. While we don't expect to encounter true stationarity in the real world, this idealization is helpful for conceptualizing and analyzing algorithms.

6.4.1 Critic Methods

The term "critic" in RL refers to a value function h, which is defined with respect to a one-step cost function c. One example is defined by total discounted cost: For given $0 \leq \gamma < 1$,

$$h(x) = \mathsf{E}_x\Big[\sum_{k=0}^{\infty} \gamma^k c(X(k))\Big].$$

TD(λ) learning was introduced in the 1970s to obtain an approximate solution to the discounted-cost dynamic programming equation, based on a generalization of the temporal difference that is the core of TD-learning algorithms found in Part I. The stochastic setting gives new tools and insights. For example, it will be seen that the final output of the TD(1) algorithm solves the minimum norm problem:

$$\min\{\|\hat{h} - h\|_\pi^2 : \hat{h} \in \mathcal{H}\},$$

where $\mathcal{H}$ is the function class within which we seek an approximation, and the norm is defined with respect to the steady state:

$$\|\hat{h} - h\|_\pi^2 = \mathsf{E}\big[[\hat{h}(X(k)) - h(X(k))]^2\big] \qquad \text{when } X(k) \sim \pi. \tag{6.22}$$

6.4.2 Actor Methods

One formulation of RL begins with a parameterized family $\{P_\theta : \theta \in \mathbb{R}^d\}$, along with cost functions $\{c_\theta : \theta \in \mathbb{R}^d\}$. The "actor" methods are designed to find the parameter $\theta^* \in \mathbb{R}^d$ that minimizes the average cost $\eta_\theta = \int c_\theta(x)\, \pi_\theta(dx)$, with π_θ invariant for P_θ. See Theorem 6.8 for one technique to estimate the gradient of η_θ, so that $\theta^* \in \mathbb{R}^d$ can be estimated using stochastic gradient descent. *Actor-critic methods* make use of a combination of Theorem 6.8 and (6.22) to obtain model-free and unbiased estimates of the gradient.

6.5 Poisson's Equation

This little equation will appear in many forms later in the book:

$$c + Ph = h + \eta. \tag{6.23}$$

It is known as *Poisson's equation*. The function c is known as the *forcing function*, η is a constant, and the solution h is called the *relative value function*. The conditions imposed to establish a solution to (6.23) also imply that an invariant measure π exists, and that $\eta = \pi(c) \stackrel{\text{def}}{=} \int c(x)\, \pi(dx)$. In many cases, we obtain a solution by iteration or inversion:

$$h = \sum_{k=0}^{\infty} P^k \tilde{c}, \tag{6.24}$$

with $\tilde{c}(x) = c(x) - \eta$ (one rationale for the name *relative* value function). The solution to (6.23) is not unique: If h is a solution, then we obtain a new solution by adding a constant.

The abstract notation in (6.23) and (6.24) is based on (6.9b). For a finite state space model, Poisson's equation becomes

$$c(x) + \sum_{x'} P(x,x')h(x') = h(x') + \eta, \qquad x \in \mathsf{X}. \tag{6.25}$$

An equivalent representation is reminiscent of the fixed policy dynamic programming equation (2.25), based on the Markov model (6.3):

$$h(x) = \tilde{c}(x) + \mathsf{E}[h(\mathrm{F}(x,N(k+1))].$$

This implies sample path formulae similar to those discussed in Section 2.5.2 and throughout Section 5:

$$h(X(k)) = \tilde{c}(X(k)) + \mathsf{E}[h(X(k+1)) \mid X(0), \dots, X(k)].$$

Poisson's equation plays a starring role in later chapters:

(i) The relative value function of average-cost optimal control is the solution to a particular Poisson equation.
(ii) Recall that Poisson's *inequality* was the engine behind performance bounds in Section 2.4.3 (i.e., bounds on the value function J). The analogous inequality is used in Section 6.6 to obtain bounds on the steady-state mean η as well as the relative value function h.
(iii) The Central Limit Theorem (CLT) is used to obtain rates of convergence for algorithms in nearly every chapter. The covariance matrix appearing in the CLT has a representation in terms of the solution to (6.23), where the choice of c depends on the application. The first introduction to the CLT is in Section 6.7.
(iv) As previewed in Section 6.4, in some applications to control we have a family of transition kernels $\{P_\theta : \theta \in \mathbb{R}^d\}$. With $c\colon \mathsf{X} \to \mathbb{R}$ interpreted as a cost function, we would like to minimize the steady-state average cost η_θ over all θ. Many approximations of gradient descent are based on Poisson's equation and rooted in the sensitivity theory surveyed in Section 6.8.
(v) One application of the main result of Section 6.8 is to actor-critic methods for RL, which is the topic of Section 10.

The concepts in Section 6.3 provide conditions for existence of a solution to (6.23) when X is finite. The discussion in Section 3.2.3 provides an early introduction to the Perron–Frobenius theory behind Theorem 6.3.

Theorem 6.3 (Spectral Conditions for Poisson's Equation) *Suppose X is finite, and the assumptions of Theorem 6.2 are satisfied. Then the following hold:*

(i) *The function $h_1 = \sum_{k=0}^\infty P^k \tilde{c}$ is a solution to (6.23) (recall (6.24)).*
(ii) *Let $s\colon \mathsf{X} \to \mathbb{R}_+$ be a function satisfying $\pi(s) > 0$, and ν a pmf satisfying*

$$P(x,x') \ge s(x)\nu(x')\,, \qquad x,x' \in \mathsf{X},$$

also expressed $P \ge s \otimes \nu$. Then a solution to Poisson's equation is given by

$$h_2 = G_{s,\nu}\tilde{c}, \qquad \textit{where} \quad G_{s,\nu} = \sum_{n=0}^{\infty}(P - s\otimes\nu)^n = [I - (P - s \otimes \nu)]^{-1}.$$

(iii) *Let $x^\bullet \in \mathsf{X}$ denote any state for which $\pi(x^\bullet) > 0$. Another solution to Poisson's equation is defined by the following expectation:*

$$h_3(x) = \mathsf{E}_x\Big[\sum_{k=0}^{\tau_\bullet - 1} \tilde{c}(X(k))\Big], \tag{6.26}$$

where $\tau_\bullet$ is the first return time:

$$\tau_\bullet = \min\{k \ge 1 : X(k) = x^\bullet\}.$$

This solution satisfies $h_3(x^\bullet) = 0$.
(iv) *If a function g and constant β, solve $c + Pg = g + \beta$, then $\beta = \eta = \pi(c)$, and*

$$g(x) - g(x^\bullet) = h_1(x) - h_1(x^\bullet) = h_2(x) - h_2(x^\bullet) = h_3(x) \qquad \textit{for each } x \in \mathsf{X}. \quad \square$$

Proof The simplest of the three is (i), since

$$Ph_1 = \sum_{k=0}^{\infty} P^{k+1}\tilde{c},$$

where we used $P \cdot P^k = P^{k+1}$. The right-hand side is equal to $h_1 - \tilde{c}$.

The remainder of the proof is only a "roadmap." For the full details, see the appendix of [254].

For parts (ii) and (iii), recall that the invariant pmf π exists and is unique, due to Theorem 6.2. Poisson's equation combined with invariance of π implies the following:

$$\begin{aligned}\pi(h) &\stackrel{\text{def}}{=} \sum_x \pi(x)h(x) = \sum_x \sum_y \pi(x)P(x,y)h(y) \\ &= \sum_x \pi(x)\{h(x) - c(x) + \eta\} = \pi(h) - \pi(c) + \eta.\end{aligned}$$

Hence $\eta = \pi(c)$.

The proof that h_2 solves Poisson's equation follows arguments similar to Proposition 3.5. A full proof can be found in [257] or the appendix of [254]. This solution is related to h_1: We have $P^k\tilde{c} = \widetilde{P}^k\tilde{c}$ for any k, where $\widetilde{P} = P - \mathbf{1} \otimes \pi$ was introduced in (6.19). Hence $h_1 = G_{1,\pi}\tilde{c}$.

The third representation can be reduced to the second, starting with

$$h_3(x) = \sum_{k=0}^{\infty} \mathsf{E}_x\big[\mathbb{1}\{\tau_\bullet > k\}\tilde{c}(X(k))\big].$$

It can be shown that this is h_2 in the special case $s(x) = \mathbb{1}_{x^\bullet}(x)$, and $\nu(y) = P(x^\bullet,y)$.

We finally come to (iv): If $c + Pg = g + \beta$ and $c + Ph = h + \eta$, then let $\Delta = h - g$, giving

$$P\Delta = \Delta + \eta - \beta.$$

Using invariance of π gives

$$\pi(\Delta) \stackrel{\text{def}}{=} \sum_x \pi(x)\Delta(x) = \sum_{x,y} \pi(x)P(x,y)\Delta(y) = \sum_x \pi(x)\Delta(x) + \eta - \beta = \pi(\Delta) + \eta - \beta.$$

This gives $\eta = \beta$, and also the following eigenvector equation:

$$P\Delta = \Delta.$$

Under the assumptions of the theorem, it follows that $\Delta(x)$ does not depend on x. □

6.6 Lyapunov Functions

Much of the Lyapunov stability theory for deterministic dynamical systems can be adapted to the Markovian setting. Even for an irreducible Markov chain on a finite state space, for which the term "stability" may not be meaningful, Lyapunov functions are useful as a means to obtain performance bounds (generalizing the Comparison Theorem in Proposition 2.3).

Poisson's inequality for the Markovian model is the following extension of (2.31): For a function $V: \mathsf{X} \to \mathbb{R}_+$, a function $c: \mathsf{X} \to \mathbb{R}_+$, and a constant $\overline{\eta} < \infty$,

$$\mathsf{E}[V(X(k+1)) \mid X(k) = x] \le V(x) - c(x) + \overline{\eta}, \qquad x \in \mathsf{X}.$$

In the more compact operator-theoretic notation, this becomes

$$PV \le V - c + \overline{\eta}. \tag{6.27}$$

As in the deterministic case, the function c is usually interpreted as a cost function on the state space. It is frequently assumed that $c(x)$ is large for "large" x (recall the definition of *coercive* from Section 2.4.3). In this case, the Poisson inequality implies that $V(X(k))$ decreases on average whenever $X(k)$ is large. This is illustrated for a deterministic system in Figure 2.5, in which the set referred to in the caption is $S = \{x : c(x) \le \overline{\eta}\}$.

6.6.1 Average Cost

Let $\eta(x)$ denote the average cost:

$$\eta(x) = \limsup_{n\to\infty} \frac{1}{n} \sum_{k=0}^{n-1} \mathsf{E}[c(X(k)) \mid X(0) = x].$$

Using the operator-theoretic notation (6.9b) gives

$$\eta(x) = \limsup_{n\to\infty} \frac{1}{n} \sum_{k=0}^{n-1} P^k c\,(x)\,.$$

The dependency on x and the use of "limit supremum" rather than limit in the definition of $\eta(x)$ are both required because we are not imposing any particular structure on $\boldsymbol{X}$.

The average cost admits a simple bound under Poisson's inequality (6.27). This is an extension of Proposition 2.3 to the Markovian setting.

Proposition 6.4 *Suppose that* (6.27) *holds with* $V \ge 0$ *everywhere. Then the following transient bound holds for each* $n \ge 1$ *and each* $x \in \mathsf{X}$:

$$\frac{1}{n} \sum_{k=0}^{n-1} P^k c\,(x) \le \overline{\eta} + \frac{1}{n} V(x).$$

Consequently, the average cost admits the bound $\eta(x) \le \overline{\eta}$.

Proof Applying P to both sides gives $P^2V \le PV - Pc + P\overline{\eta}$, and since $\overline{\eta}$ is constant,

$$P^2V \le PV - Pc + \overline{\eta} \le V - c - Pc + 2\overline{\eta}.$$

By repeated multiplication by P, we conclude that, for any n,

$$P^n V \le V + n\overline{\eta} - \sum_{k=0}^{n-1} P^k c.$$

This gives the desired result on rearranging terms and using the assumption that $V \ge 0$. □

We have seen that the average-cost bound given in Proposition 6.4 is tight for a finite state space Markov chain, under the assumptions of Theorem 6.3: We can take $V = h + \text{const.}$, where the constant is chosen large enough so that $V \ge 0$.

The beauty of Lyapunov theory is that we can obtain performance bounds without knowing much about the model. This is illustrated in the next example.

Example: The Scalar Linear State Space Model

Consider the scalar model,

$$X(k+1) = \alpha X(k) + N(k+1), \qquad k \geq 0, \tag{6.28}$$

where $\boldsymbol{N}$ i.i.d., with zero mean and finite second moment σ_N^2 (not necessarily Gaussian). The cost function is the quadratic, $c(x) = \frac{1}{2}x^2$.

Let $V(x) = \frac{1}{2}\kappa x^2$, with $\kappa > 0$. We then have the following:

$$\begin{aligned} PV(x) &= \mathsf{E}[V(X(k+1)) \mid X(k) = x] \\ &= \tfrac{1}{2}\kappa \mathsf{E}[(\alpha x + N(1))^2] \\ &= V(x) + \tfrac{1}{2}\kappa(\alpha^2 - 1)x^2 + \tfrac{1}{2}\kappa\sigma_N^2. \end{aligned} \tag{6.29}$$

Provided $|\alpha| < 1$, we can set $\kappa = (1-\alpha^2)^{-1}$ in the definition of V to obtain a solution to Poisson's equation with forcing function c:

$$PV(x) = V(x) - c(x) + \overline{\eta}, \qquad \text{with} \quad \overline{\eta} = \tfrac{1}{2}(1-\alpha^2)^{-1}\sigma_N^2. \tag{6.30}$$

It follows from Proposition 6.4 that $\eta(x) \leq \overline{\eta}$ for each x. In fact, the preceding steps show that $\mathsf{E}[c(X(k))] \to \overline{\eta}$ for each initial condition, so that we have equality: $\eta(x) \equiv \overline{\eta}$.

If $\boldsymbol{N}$ is Gaussian, then $P^k(x, \cdot\,)$ converges to a Gaussian $N(0,\sigma_\infty^2)$ distribution as $k \to \infty$, with $\sigma_\infty^2 = (1-\alpha^2)^{-1}\sigma_N^2$.

6.6.2 Discounted Cost

In the long run we are all dead. This quote is attributed to John Maynard Keynes, and is commonly used to justify the use of discounting in optimal control. I believe this is a mistake in most control applications. The rush to discount is often based on a false impression – that the average cost $\eta(x)$ *only* reflects the cost "at infinity." Lyapunov bounds and their consequences, such as the elementary bounds in (6.4), indicate that a policy with good steady-state behavior will also have good transient behavior. In particular, if the average cost is finite, then there is a solution to (6.27), from which we obtain the transient bound presented in Proposition 6.4.

However, the discounted cost criterion is sometimes convenient because it is easier to analyze, and I am also forced to cover this performance criterion because it is preferred in many disciplines (in particular, operations research and economics).

The discounted-cost value function was introduced briefly in Section 6.4: Given a discount parameter $\gamma \in (0,1)$, the discounted cost from initial condition x is defined as the weighted sum:

$$h_\gamma(x) = \sum_{k=0}^{\infty} \gamma^k \mathsf{E}[c(X(k)) \mid X(0) = x]\,. \tag{6.31}$$

Once again, this has the operator-theoretic form:

$$h_\gamma = \sum_{k=0}^{\infty} \gamma^k P^k c, \tag{6.32}$$

and from this we obtain a dynamic programming equation:

$$h_\gamma = c + \gamma P h_\gamma \,. \tag{6.33}$$

If c is nonnegative valued, then the lower bound $h_\gamma(x) \ge c(x)$ holds, so that the discounted cost is unbounded whenever this is true of c. And, once again, we obtain a bound on h_γ under Poisson's inequality.

Proposition 6.5 *If* (6.27) *holds with* $V \ge 0$ *everywhere, then* $h_\gamma(x) \le V(x) + \overline{\eta}(1-\gamma)^{-1}$ *for each* x, *and* $\gamma \in (0,1)$.

Proof The bound (6.27) gives

$$\gamma P V \le V - g + \gamma\overline{\eta}, \tag{6.34}$$

where $g = (1-\gamma)V + \gamma c$: a convex combination of the Lyapunov function and the cost function. Applying γP to each side gives

$$(\gamma P)^2 V \le \gamma P V - \gamma P g + \gamma^2 \overline{\eta},$$

and then, using (6.34),

$$(\gamma P)^2 V \le V - g - \gamma P g + \gamma\overline{\eta} + \gamma^2\overline{\eta}.$$

As in the average-cost problem, we obtain the following by induction:

$$(\gamma P)^n V \le V - \sum_{k=0}^{n-1} \gamma^k P^k g + \overline{\eta} \sum_{k=0}^{n-1} \gamma^{k+1}.$$

From the definition $g = (1-\gamma)V + \gamma c$, we obtain

$$\sum_{k=0}^{\infty} \gamma^k \big(\gamma P^k c\,(x) + (1-\gamma) P^k V\,(x)\big) \le V(x) + \frac{\gamma}{1-\gamma}\overline{\eta}. \tag{6.35}$$

Using the fact that $V \ge 0$, we can drop all but one term involving V on the left-hand side of (6.35) to obtain the following:

$$(1-\gamma)V(x) + \gamma \sum_{k=0}^{\infty} \gamma^k P^k c\,(x) \le V(x) + \frac{\gamma}{1-\gamma}\overline{\eta}.$$

The bound $h_\gamma \le V + \overline{\eta}(1-\gamma)^{-1}$ follows on subtracting $(1-\gamma)V(x)$ from each side, and then dividing each side of the resulting inequality by γ. □

Example 6.6.1 (Discounted Cost for the Scalar Linear State Space Model) With cost function $c(x) = \frac{1}{2}x^2$, the solution to Poisson's equation was obtained in (6.30). Proposition 6.5 gives the bound $h_\gamma \le V + \eta(1-\gamma)^{-1}$, which in this case becomes

$$h_\gamma(x) \le \tfrac{1}{2}\frac{1}{1-\alpha^2}\Big[x^2 + \frac{1}{1-\gamma}\sigma_N^2\Big]. \tag{6.36}$$

We next compute h_γ to see if this bound is accurate. For this, we begin with the dynamic programming equation (6.33). Let $V(x) = A_\gamma + \frac{1}{2}\kappa_\gamma x^2$, with A_γ, κ_γ constants to be chosen. From (6.29), we have

$$PV \le \alpha^2 V + (1-\alpha^2)A_\gamma + \tfrac{1}{2}\kappa_\gamma\sigma_N^2.$$

Scaling by γ and adding c to each side gives

$$c + \gamma PV = c + \gamma\big(\alpha^2 V + (1-\alpha^2)A_\gamma + \tfrac{1}{2}\kappa_\gamma\big),$$

or, reintroducing the quadratic expressions,

$$c(x) + \gamma PV\,(x) = \tfrac{1}{2}(1 + \gamma\alpha^2\kappa_\gamma)x^2 + \gamma(\tfrac{1}{2}\kappa_\gamma\sigma_N^2 + A_\gamma).$$

To solve the dynamic programming equation, we require that the right-hand side coincide with V. This requires that we match coefficients: $1 + \gamma\alpha^2\kappa_\gamma = \kappa_\gamma$ and $\gamma(\frac{1}{2}\kappa_\gamma\sigma_N^2 + A_\gamma) = A_\gamma$, giving

$$h_\gamma(x) = A_\gamma + \tfrac{1}{2}\kappa_\gamma x^2 = \tfrac{1}{2}\frac{1}{1-\gamma\alpha^2}\Big[x^2 + \frac{\gamma}{1-\gamma}\sigma_N^2\Big].$$

In particular, the bound (6.36) does hold. ∎

6.7 Simulation: Confidence Bounds and Control Variates

In average-cost optimal control, we are faced not with a single Markov chain, but an entire family: one Markov chain for each in a family of policies. We would like to estimate the average cost $\eta = \pi(c)$ for many different policies so we can select the best in the family. Lyapunov functions can provide bounds, but it is rare to obtain bounds that are sufficiently tight so that we can determine which policy is optimal. Without alternatives, in the majority of cases we resort to simulation.

6.7.1 Asymptotic Statistics Made Finite

We are blessed by the fact that the Law of Large Numbers (LLN) holds whenever there is an invariant probability measure π. The *Monte Carlo estimate* based on n samples is denoted

$$\eta_n = \frac{1}{n}\sum_{k=0}^{n-1} c(X(k)). \tag{6.37}$$

The LLN tells us that this is asymptotically consistent:

$$\lim_{n\to\infty} \eta_n = \eta, \tag{6.38}$$

where the limit holds with probability one, for almost every (with respect to π) initial condition $X(0)$. In most cases, the limit holds for every initial condition.

The next question is the rate of convergence. For this it is most common to turn to the Central Limit Theorem, which tells us that

$$\lim_{n\to\infty} \mathsf{P}\{|\eta_n - \eta| \ge r/\sqrt{n}\} = \mathsf{P}\{\sigma_{\text{CLT}}|W| \ge r\}, \qquad r > 0, \tag{6.39}$$

where W is a standard Gaussian random variable ($W \sim N(0,1)$). The value σ^2_{CLT} is called the *asymptotic variance* and has several equivalent forms (subject to assumptions):

$$\sigma^2_{\text{CLT}} = \lim_{n\to\infty} n\mathsf{E}[(\eta_n - \eta)^2] \tag{6.40a}$$

$$= \sum_{k=-\infty}^{\infty} R(k) \tag{6.40b}$$

$$= 2\pi(\tilde{c}h) - \pi(\tilde{c}^2), \tag{6.40c}$$

where $\tilde{c}(x) = c(x) - \eta$ for any x, and for $k \geq 0$,

$$R(k) = \pi(\tilde{c}P^k\tilde{c}) = \mathsf{E}_\pi[\tilde{c}(X(0))\tilde{c}(X(k))], \quad \text{and} \quad R(-k) = R(k).$$

This is the autocorrelation sequence for $\tilde{c}(X(k))$ for the stationary version of $\boldsymbol{X}$. The function h in (6.40c) is the solution to Poisson's equation (6.23) [257].

In many control applications, the random variables $\{X(i), X(i+k)\}$ are positively correlated (at least for small k), which means that $R(k) > 0$. This is true for the M/M/1 queue (6.14), for example, and can be anticipated from the skip-free property of this Markov chain. For this reason, we usually expect σ^2_{CLT} to be much greater than the ordinary variance, which is $R(0)$.

To apply the LLN and CLT for performance approximation, it is necessary to estimate the asymptotic variance. Unfortunately, none of the preceding three expressions are useful for anything but analysis, or to inspire algorithms. The representation (6.40a) is inspiration for the batch means method:

Batch Means Method Perform M independent runs, each based on $\mathcal{N}$ observations, to obtain M estimates:

$$\eta_{\mathcal{N}}{}^i = \frac{1}{\mathcal{N}} \sum_{k=0}^{\mathcal{N}-1} c(X^i(k)), \qquad 1 \leq i \leq M. \tag{6.41a}$$

Estimates of the mean and asymptotic variance are then defined by

$$\eta_{\mathcal{N}} = \frac{1}{M} \sum_{i=1}^{M} \eta_{\mathcal{N}}{}^i, \qquad \widehat{\sigma}^2_{\text{CLT}} = \frac{\mathcal{N}}{M} \sum_{i=1}^{M} (\eta_{\mathcal{N}}{}^i - \eta_{\mathcal{N}})^2. \tag{6.41b}$$

See [133] for estimators thar are potentially more efficient.

The estimates in (6.41b) are used to obtain an approximate confidence bound: For given $\delta > 0$, choose $r > 0$ so that $\mathsf{P}\{\widehat{\sigma}_{\text{CLT}}|W| \geq r\} = \delta$. Then, for large $\mathcal{N}$, we have confidence that η lies in the interval $[\eta_{\mathcal{N}} - r/\sqrt{\mathcal{N}}, \eta_{\mathcal{N}} + r/\sqrt{\mathcal{N}}]$, with probability approximately δ. If $r/\sqrt{\mathcal{N}}$ is not very small, then the run length $\mathcal{N}$ should be increased.

Care with Histograms

The procedure (6.41b) to estimate the asymptotic variance is only effective if the variance is finite, and the initial conditions in the M independent trials are spaced widely apart.

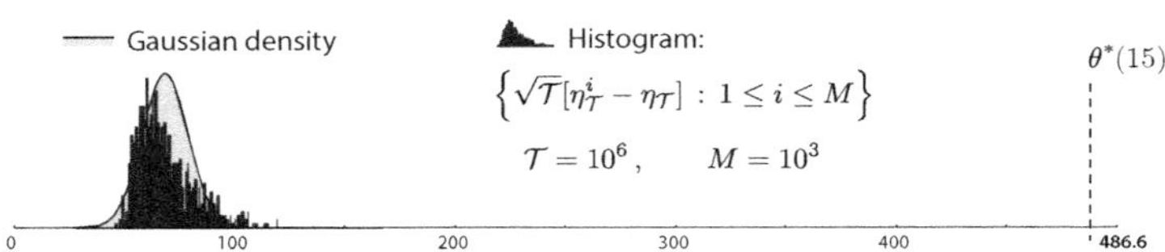

Figure 6.5 Histogram of $M = 10^3$ independent estimates of $\theta(15)$, with time horizon $\mathcal{N} = 10^6$ for the Watkins algorithm applied to the six-state example with discount factor $\gamma = 0.8$. In each of the M experiments, the algorithm was initialized with $\theta_0 = 0$.

Figure 6.5 is an illustration of what can go wrong. It is based on an example introduced in Section 9.7.2 for an RL algorithm rather than Monte Carlo, but the procedure to estimate variance remains the same.

With the time horizon of $\mathcal{N} = 10^6$ samples, one might expect that the algorithm has converged. Based on the histogram, many would believe that the estimates will converge to a value no greater than 100. The actual limit is nearly 500. In conclusion, *this experiment has no value for understanding how many iterations are required for an accurate estimate.*

In this particular example, it is known that the limit is positive, so it would make sense to sample the initial parameter uniformly on a widely spaced interval of the form $[0,\bar{\eta}]$.

Section 6.7.4 contains an example for which the CLT is highly predictive, and other examples will follow when we come to RL (recall the discussion surrounding Figure 1.3, or look ahead to Sections 8.4 and 9.8.2).

6.7.2 Asymptotic Variance and Mixing Time

The "mixing time" is informally defined as the number of iterations required for the Markov chain to approximately reach its steady-state distribution. This might be formalized with the introduction of $\varepsilon > 0$ to quantify "approximately," and let $T(\varepsilon) > 0$ denote the minimal time for which

$$|P^n(x,A) - \pi(A)| \le \varepsilon, \quad \text{for all } n \ge T(\varepsilon), \quad A \subset \mathsf{X}.$$

This implies the following bound for functions $f \colon \mathsf{X} \to \mathbb{R}$ satisfying $|f(x)| \le 1$ for all x:

$$\big|\mathsf{E}_x[f(X(n)) - \pi(f)]\big| \le 2\varepsilon, \quad \text{for all } n \ge T(\varepsilon).$$

This follows on observing that a function f maximizing the left-hand side can be taken of the form $f^*(x) = 2\mathbb{1}_A - 1$ for some $A \in \mathcal{B}(\mathsf{X})$. In the finite state space setting, we can take $A = \{y : P^n(x,y) \ge \pi(y)\}$.

Remaining in the finite state space setting, it is immediate from Theorem 6.2 and the surrounding discussion that the mixing time will be very large if there is an eigenvalue λ of P satisfying $\lambda \ne 1$ but $|\lambda| \sim 1$. In particular, if λ is on the unit circle, so that $|\lambda| = 1$, then the mixing time is infinite. An example of this is a two-state Markov chain with $\mathsf{X} = \{1,2\}$ and transition matrix $P(i,j) = 1$ if $i \ne j$:

$$P = \begin{bmatrix} 0 & 1 \\ 1 & 0 \end{bmatrix}.$$

The eigenvalues of P are $\lambda_1 = 1$ and $\lambda_2 = -1$. The Markov chain deterministically cycles between the two states; the second eigenvalue $\lambda_2 = e^{2\pi j/T}$ with $T = 2$ reflects the period-2 dynamics. Hence the mixing time is infinite. What does this say about simulation?

It is often taken for granted that a large mixing time implies that Monte Carlo methods will take a long time to converge. This is clearly *false* in the two-state example, since for any function $c\colon \mathsf{X} \to \mathbb{R}$,

$$\eta_n = \frac{1}{n}\sum_{k=0}^{n-1} c(X(k)) = \begin{cases} \eta & \text{if } n \text{ is even} \\ \frac{n}{n+1}\eta + \frac{1}{n+1}c(X(n)) & \text{else} \end{cases}.$$

The asymptotic variance is *zero* since η_n converges to zero at rate $1/n$. The fast convergence is explained by the fact that this is an instance of quasi–Monte Carlo.

Even in a highly volatile setting, the mixing time tells us little about the asymptotic variance. Proposition 6.6 tells us that we can expect a large asymptotic variance for some functions c when $|1 - \lambda_i|$ is close to zero for some i, and also reassures us that $|\lambda_i| \approx 1$ is not a problem in general.

Proposition 6.6 *Suppose that $c\colon \mathsf{X} \to \mathbb{R}$ can be expressed as a linear combination of eigenvectors:*

$$c(x) = \eta + \sum_{k=2}^{m} \beta_k v^k(x).$$

Then,

$$\sigma^2_{\text{CLT}} = \sum_{x,y\in\mathsf{X}} u(x)\Sigma_\Delta(x,y)u^*(y),$$

where u^* denotes complex conjugate transpose, and for each $x,y \in \mathsf{X}$,

$$u(x) = \sum_{i=2}^{m} \frac{1}{1-\lambda_i}\beta_i v^i(x),$$

$$\Sigma_\Delta(x,y) = \pi(x)\mathbb{1}\{x = y\} - \sum_{z\in\mathsf{X}} \pi(z)P(z,x)P(z,y).$$

Proof Note first that some of the coefficients $\{\beta_k\}$ may be complex if any of the eigenvectors $\{v^k\}$ are complex valued.

Consider for each $x \in \mathsf{X}$ the martingale difference sequence:

$$\begin{aligned}\Delta_k(x) &= \mathbb{1}\{X(k) = x\} - \sum_y \mathbb{1}\{X(k-1) = y\}P(y,x) \\ &= \mathbb{1}\{X(k) = x\} - \mathsf{P}\{X(k) = x \mid X(0),\dots,X(k-1)\},\end{aligned}$$

and let Δ_k denote the corresponding m-dimensional vector sequence. It is not difficult to establish that Σ_Δ is the steady-state covariance of this sequence. In matrix form, we have $\Sigma_\Delta = \Pi - P^{\intercal}\Pi P$, where $\Pi = \text{diag}\,(\pi)$ (the $m \times m$ diagonal matrix with entries $\pi(x)$).

Without any assumption of stationarity, we have for any $i \geq 2$,

$$\Delta_k^i \stackrel{\text{def}}{=} \sum_x v^i(x)\Delta_k(x) = v^i(X(k)) - \lambda_i v^i(X(k-1)).$$

Averaging each side gives

$$\begin{aligned}\frac{1}{n}\sum_{k=1}^{n}\Delta_k^i &= \frac{1}{n}\sum_{k=1}^{n}\{v^i(X(k)) - \lambda_i v^i(X(k-1))\}\\ &= (1-\lambda_i)\frac{1}{n}\sum_{k=0}^{n-1} v^i(X(k)) + \frac{1}{n}\big[v^i(X(n)) - v^i(X(0))\big].\end{aligned}$$

Multiplying each side by $\beta_i/(1-\lambda_i)$ and summing

$$\begin{aligned}\frac{1}{n}\sum_{k=1}^{n}\Delta_k^c &\stackrel{\text{def}}{=} \eta + \frac{1}{n}\sum_{k=1}^{n}\sum_{i=2}^{m}\frac{1}{1-\lambda_i}\beta_i\Delta_k^i\\ &= \eta_n + \frac{1}{n}\sum_{i=2}^{m}\frac{1}{1-\lambda_i}\beta_i\big[v^i(X(n)) - v^i(X(0))\big].\end{aligned}$$

It follows that the asymptotic variance σ^2_{CLT} coincides with the ordinary variance of the martingale difference sequence $\{\Delta_k^c\}$ in steady state. It can be expected to be very large if $|\beta_i/(1-\lambda_i)|$ is large for one i. The vector β depends entirely on the function c, and the quantity $|1/(1-\lambda_i)|$ is large if the eigenvalue λ_i is near unity. □

6.7.3 Sample Complexity

What if a random confidence interval gives you no confidence? A deterministic confidence interval requires what is known as a *finite-n bound*, such as

$$\mathsf{P}\{|\eta_n - \eta| \ge r/\sqrt{n}\} \le \bar{B}(n,r), \tag{6.42}$$

with computable right-hand side. It is more common to consider the probability of error exceeding a fixed value $\varepsilon > 0$, and a bound of the form

$$\mathsf{P}\{|\eta_n - \eta| \ge \varepsilon\} \le \bar{b}\exp(-n\bar{I}(\varepsilon)), \tag{6.43}$$

where $\bar{b}$ is a finite constant, and $\bar{I}(\varepsilon) > 0$ for $\varepsilon > 0$. This leads to *sample complexity bounds* for estimating the mean – the terminology is explained in Section 8.2 in a more general setting.

In the majority of applications, *you are out of luck*. If you want (6.42) or (6.43) with explicit values for the right-hand side, then you require substantial assumptions on the Markov model and the cost function. For example, bounds are available for a finite state space Markov chain, but the bounds are very loose unless there is substantial prior knowledge available. See the "Notes" section for background.

The example that follows illustrates what can go wrong.

6.7.4 A Simple Example?

The M/M/1 queue introduced in Example 6.2.3 should be the best-case scenario for efficient simulation. This Markov chain enjoys the following properties whenever $\rho < 1$:

(i) The unique invariant pmf is geometric: $\pi(x) = (1-\rho)\rho^x$, $x = 0,1,2,\ldots$.
(ii) It is skip-free: $|X(k+1) - X(k)| \le 1$ for all k.

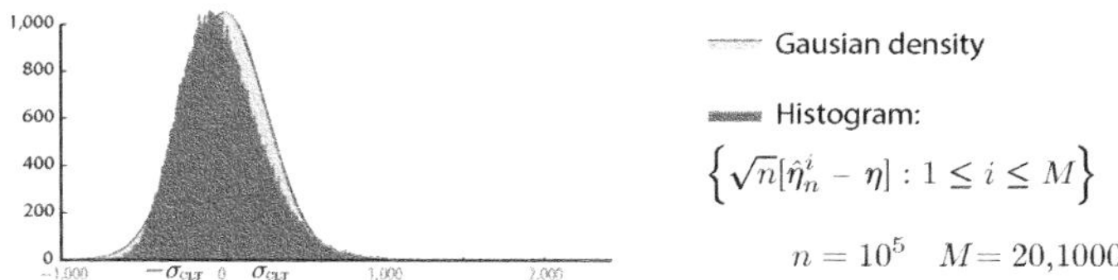

Figure 6.6 Histogram of estimates of the mean in the M/M/1 queue.

(iii) It is geometrically ergodic: The limit in (6.6) holds geometrically fast for all x,S.
(iv) It is reversible: This means that reversing the direction of time does not change the statistics of $\boldsymbol{X}$ in steady state. Equivalently, the detailed balance equations hold:

$$\pi(x)P(x,y) = \pi(y)P(y,x)\,, \qquad x,y \in \mathsf{X} = \{0,1,2,\dots\}.$$

These desirable properties should have positive implications for simulation.

In fact, the M/M/1 queue and other skip-free Markov chains pose challenges, as illustrated here for the simple task of estimating the steady-state mean $\eta = \pi(c)$ with $c(x) = x$. We don't need to simulate, since we know π:

$$\eta = (1-\rho)\sum_{n=0}^{\infty} n\rho^n = \frac{\rho}{1-\rho}.$$

The experiments that follow illustrate what can go wrong in even the simplest examples when the state space is not finite.

Challenges

#1 The asymptotic variance is massive.
#2 The CLT holds, but the empirical distribution appears skewed for finite-n.
#3 There is no known sample complexity bound.

The ordinary variance is $\sigma^2 = \pi(\tilde{c}^2) = \pi(c^2) - \eta^2 = \rho/(1-\rho)^2$. The asymptotic variance is, as stated in #1, *massive*:

$$\sigma^2_{\text{CLT}} = 8\frac{1+o(1)}{(1-\rho)^4} = \big(8 + o(1)\big)\sigma^4,$$

where $o(1) = O(1-\rho)$. This approximation follows from [254, prop. 11.3.1].

Figure 6.6 illustrates the CLT for this example with $\rho = 9/10$. The histogram shows results from 2×10^4 independent runs, with initial condition drawn independently from π. The asymptotic variance estimate $\sigma^2_{\text{CLT}} \approx 8(1-\rho)^{-4}$ results in the standard deviation approximation $\sigma_{\text{CLT}} \approx 283$ indicated in the figure.

Despite the skew observed in the histogram, the CLT remains a reliable predictor of algorithm performance in this example. In particular, we find that the time horizon is too short. Consider the approximation

$$\mathsf{P}\{|\eta_n - \eta| > 2\sigma_{\text{CLT}}/\sqrt{n}\} \approx \mathsf{P}\{|W| > 2\} \approx 0.05\,, \qquad W \sim N(0,1).$$

With $n = 10^5$, we have $2\sigma_{\text{CLT}}/\sqrt{n} \approx 1.8 = 0.2\eta$. That is, in 5% of our experiments, the error is over 20%. If we increase the time horizon to $n = 10^7$, then the error reduces to 2% with the same frequency.

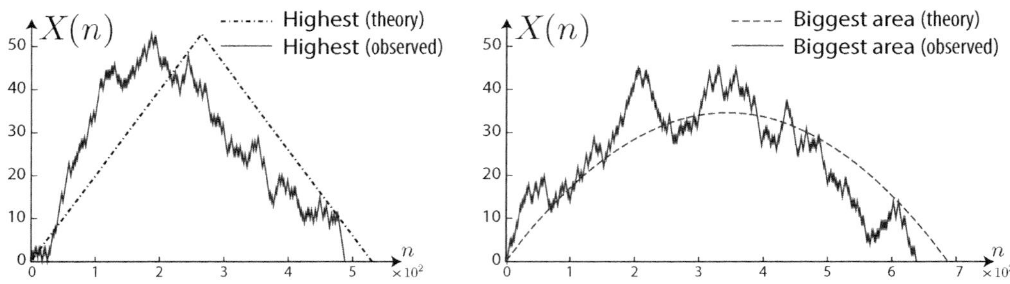

Figure 6.7 Sample paths of the M/M/1 queue: two large excursions.

A finite-n bound of the form (6.43) is not available, but we can establish the following (highly asymmetric) one-sided asymptotic bounds: For functions $I_-, I_+ : \mathbb{R}_+ \to \mathbb{R}_+$, and all $\varepsilon > 0$,

$$\lim_{n\to\infty} \frac{1}{n} \log \mathsf{P}\{\eta_n - \eta \le -\varepsilon\} = -I_-(\varepsilon) < 0, \tag{6.44a}$$

$$\lim_{n\to\infty} \frac{1}{n} \log \mathsf{P}\Big\{\eta_n - \eta \ge n\varepsilon\Big\} = -I_+(\varepsilon) < 0. \tag{6.44b}$$

The first limit is what is expected for a finite state space Markov chain.

The probability in the second limit (6.44b) is not a typo: It is the probability that the error exceeds n **times** ε. See the "Notes" section for history and resources.

It isn't difficult to explain the source of asymmetry: First observe that η_n is nonnegative for all n, so that $\mathsf{P}\{\eta_n - \eta \le -n\varepsilon\} = 0$ for all large n; this is consistent with (6.44a). To understand the upper tail (6.44b), write $\eta_n = n^{-1}S_n$ with $S_n = \sum_{k=0}^{n-1} X(k)$, so that

$$\mathsf{P}\Big\{\eta_n - \eta \ge n\varepsilon\Big\} = \mathsf{P}\Big\{S_n \ge \eta n + n^2\varepsilon\Big\}.$$

Examples of large excursions of the queue length process are illustrated in Figure 6.7. In each of the two sample paths shown, the maximal height of $\boldsymbol{X}$ is roughly proportional to the length of the time horizon. The partial sum S_n may be regarded as the area under the trajectory formed by $\{X(k) : 0 \le k \le n-1\}$, which is of order n^2 over much of the run in these two plots. This is consistent with (6.44b).

The performance criterion (6.43) is focused exclusively on rare events. That is, we know that $\mathsf{P}\{|\eta_n - \eta| \ge \varepsilon\}$ will go to zero very quickly. The asymptotic covariance is grounded in typical performance, which helps to explain why the CLT holds under very general conditions.

6.7.5 Combating Variance by Design

Here are a few techniques to cope with high variance.

Common Random Numbers

Suppose we have a family of Markov chains indexed by a parameter $\theta \in \mathbb{R}^d$:

$$X^\theta(k+1) = \mathrm{F}(X^\theta(k), N(k+1); \theta). \tag{6.45}$$

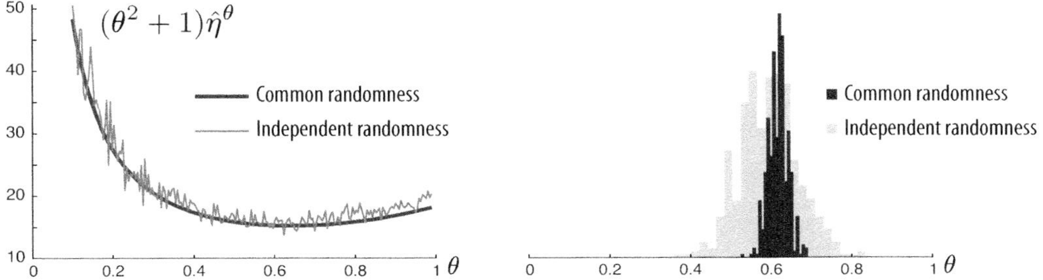

Figure 6.8 Common random numbers used to reduce relative variance.

The goal is to estimate the parameter $\theta^\star$ minimizing $\eta_\theta = \pi_\theta(c)$ for a function $c\colon \mathsf{X} \to \mathbb{R}$. If using (6.37) to estimate η_θ for several different values of θ, be sure to reuse the sample path $\{N(k) : 1 \le k \le n\}$ for each θ.

Consider, for example, a scalar linear system:

$$X^\theta(k+1) = (1-\theta)X^\theta + N(k+1),$$

with an i.i.d., zero mean disturbance $\boldsymbol{N}$, $c(x) = x^2$, and our interest is minimizing over $\theta \in \mathbb{R}$ the objective $\Gamma(\theta) = (\theta^2+1)\eta^\theta$. This is easily computed for this simple example:

$$\Gamma(\theta) = \frac{(\theta^2+1)}{1-(1-\theta)^2}\sigma_N^2.$$

The upper plots in Figure 6.8 compare estimates obtained with common random numbers, and those obtained with independent randomness (meaning that the samples of the disturbance $N(k)$ are chosen independently for each value of θ). The plot obtained using common random numbers is smooth as a function of θ.

Independent trials were performed, where in each of 500 experiments the minimizer was computed for each approach. The histograms shown in Figure 6.8 confirm that the estimate of $\theta^\star \approx 0.6$ is far more reliable when using common random numbers.

Split Sampling

Consider estimation of an expectation $\mathsf{E}[L(X(k), X(k+1))]$ where $\boldsymbol{X}$ is a finite state space Markov chain with unique invariant pmf π. The standard estimator is

$$\widehat{L}_N = \frac{1}{N}\sum_{k=0}^{N-1} L(X(k), X(k+1)). \tag{6.46}$$

If the second eigenvalue of the transition matrix P is close to unity, then the mixing time of the Markov chain $\boldsymbol{X}$ will be slow, and this will adversely affect the convergence rate. In this case, the following variant, known as *split sampling*, can be used. Let $\boldsymbol{X}^1$ denote an i.i.d. sequence with marginal π. Construct a second stochastic process as follows: For each $k = 1,2,\ldots$, the random variable $X^2(k)$ is chosen in two stages. First, the value $x = X^1(k-1)$ is observed. Next, the value of $X^2(k)$ is chosen according to the distribution $P(x,\cdot)$, independent of $\{X^1(j), X^2(j) : j \le k-1\}$. Based on this pair of stochastic processes, the estimate at iteration N is defined by

$$\widehat{L}_N = \frac{1}{N}\sum_{k=0}^{N-1} L(X^1(k),X^2(k+1)). \tag{6.47}$$

See Exercise 6.15 for instructions on how to obtain an expression for the asymptotic variance of this estimate, and how to compare it to the standard estimator. You can expect significant variance reduction when $\sigma^2_{\text{CLT}} \gg \sigma^2$.

Control Variates

Suppose that there is a d-dimensional stochastic process $\{\Delta(k)\}$ that is correlated with the sequence $\{c(X(k))\}$, and for which we know the steady-state mean is zero. That is, the following limit holds with probability one, for each $1 \le i \le d$:

$$\lim_{n\to\infty} \frac{1}{n}\sum_{k=0}^{n-1} \Delta_i(k) = 0.$$

For each $v \in \mathbb{R}^d$, denote $\Delta_v(k) = \sum v_i \Delta_i(k)$, and define the new sequence of estimates:

$$\eta_n^v = \frac{1}{n}\sum_{k=0}^{n-1}[c(X(k)) + \Delta_v(k)]. \tag{6.48}$$

Significant variance reduction is possible in some cases – see the "Notes" section for examples and resources.

State Weighting and Likelihood Ratios

Consider the mean-square error (6.22) defined with respect to the invariant probability measure π. Algorithms to minimize this loss function may suffer from very high variance. One way to reduce variance is to introduce a weighting function $w\colon \mathsf{X} \to \mathbb{R}_+$ (it might also be interpreted as an unnormalized likelihood ratio). The weighted mean-square error is denoted

$$\|\hat{h} - h\|^2_{\varpi,w} = \mathsf{E}\big[[\hat{h}(X(k)) - h(X(k))]^2 w(X(k))\big] \qquad \text{when } X(k) \sim \pi. \tag{6.49}$$

For example, in the M/M/1 example for which π is geometric, and h is a quadratic function of x, we might choose $w(x) = 1/(1+x^4)$, so that the product within the expectation is bounded.

6.8 Sensitivity and Actor-Only Methods

Let's turn now to a control problem. Rather than the feedback formulations developed in Part I, we are presented with a parameterized family $\{P_\theta, \pi_\theta, c_\theta, \eta_\theta : \theta \in \mathbb{R}^d\}$, subject to the following assumptions:

Assumptions for a Markov Family There is a common state space X, and for each θ:

- ▲ π_θ is invariant for P_θ.
- ▲ $c_\theta\colon \mathsf{X} \to \mathbb{R}$, and $\eta_\theta = \pi_\theta(c_\theta)$.

▲ There is a solution h_θ to Poisson's equation:

$$c_\theta + P_\theta h_\theta = h_\theta + \eta_\theta. \tag{6.50}$$

▲ The average cost η_θ and other functions of θ are continuously differentiable in θ.

The assumption that η_θ and h_θ are continuously differentiable functions of θ is not strong. See Example 6.21 for hints at how to obtain a representation of the gradient of h_θ, subject to mild assumptions on the parameterized model. The "Notes" section contains references with full details.

The control objective is to minimize the loss function $\Gamma(\theta) = \eta_\theta$ over all $\theta \in \mathbb{R}^d$ and, as in Section 4, our approach is to approximate gradient descent: $\frac{d}{dt}\vartheta_t = -\nabla\Gamma(\vartheta_t)$.

A formula from the 1960s provides one avenue for approximating the gradient, based on the so-called *score function*, defined for a finite state space model as follows:

$$S^\theta(x,x') = \nabla_\theta \log(P_\theta(x,x')), \qquad x,x' \in \mathsf{X}. \tag{6.51}$$

Lemma 6.7 is merely a restatement of this definition, recalling the chain rule for the gradient of a logarithm:

Lemma 6.7 *For a finite state space Markov chain, and any function $g\colon \mathsf{X} \to \mathbb{R}$,*

$$\nabla_\theta \Big\{ \sum_{x'} P_\theta(x,x') g(x') \Big\} = \sum_{x'} P_\theta(x,x') S^\theta(x,x') g(x'). \qquad \square$$

The proof of the following representation is found at the end of this section.

Theorem 6.8 (Sensitivity Theorem) *Suppose that the assumptions of this section hold, and in addition X is finite, $c_\theta(x)$ is continuously differentiable in θ for each x, and the score function is continuous at each value of θ for which $P_\theta(x,x') > 0$. Then,*

$$\nabla\Gamma(\theta) = \mathsf{E}_{\pi_\theta}\big[\nabla_\theta c_\theta(X(k)) + S^\theta(X(k),X(k+1)) h_\theta(X(k+1))\big], \tag{6.52}$$

where the expectation is in steady state.

The stochastic approximation theory of Section 8 invites the *stochastic gradient descent* (SGD) algorithm:

$$\begin{aligned} \theta_{n+1} &= \theta_n - \alpha_{n+1} \breve{\nabla}_\Gamma(n+1), \\ \breve{\nabla}_\Gamma(n+1) &\stackrel{\text{def}}{=} \big[\nabla_\theta c_\theta(X(n)) + S^\theta(X(n),X(n+1)) h_\theta(X(n+1))\big]\big|_{\theta=\theta_n} \end{aligned} \tag{6.53}$$

where $\{\alpha_n\}$ is a step-size sequence, as seen in many earlier chapters. In practice, it is likely that we have designed P_θ and c_θ, so the score function is available. A challenge with this algorithm is the computational complexity associated with computing h_{θ_n} at each iteration n.

The update equation for $\boldsymbol{\theta}$ is an example of the *actor* in the RL literature, and the relative value function h_{θ_n} is the critic at iteration n. The actor-critic methods surveyed in Section 10 provide a computationally feasible refinement of (6.53), in which the relative value function is estimated simultaneously with estimation of the parameter θ^* that minimizes Γ.

How is the score function defined for a general state space? Suppose that $\mathsf{X} = \mathbb{R}^n$ and there is a transition density:

$$P_\theta(x,A) = \int_{y\in A} p_\theta(x,y)dy\,, \qquad x\in\mathsf{X},\ A\in\mathcal{B}(\mathsf{X}).$$

In this case, the definition is analogous to the finite state space case

$$S^\theta(x,x') = \nabla_\theta \log(p_\theta(x,x'))\,, \qquad x,x'\in\mathsf{X}. \tag{6.54}$$

Lemma 6.7 continues to hold with this definition of the score function, subject to smoothness assumptions on the density, and growth conditions on g.

Consider, for example, the nonlinear model with additive noise, $X(k+1) = \mathrm{F}(X(k);\theta) + N(k+1)$, where the marginal of $\boldsymbol{N}$ has density p_N. For $g\colon\mathsf{X}\to\mathbb{R}$, we have

$$P_\theta g\,(x) = \int g(\mathrm{F}(x;\theta)+z)\,p_N(z)dz.$$

Consequently, it would appear that $\nabla P_\theta g$ requires differentiation of g. This is avoided through the change of variables $y = \mathrm{F}(x;\theta)+z$:

$$P_\theta g\,(x) = \int g(y)\,p_\theta(x,y)dy\,, \qquad p_\theta(x,y) = p_N(y-\mathrm{F}(x;\theta)),$$

and from this, we obtain a version of Lemma 6.7:

$$\begin{aligned}\nabla_\theta P_\theta g\,(x) &= \mathsf{E}[g(X(k+1))S^\theta(X(k),X(k+1)) \mid X(k)=x],\\ S^\theta(x,x') &= \nabla_\theta \log\{p_N(x'-\mathrm{F}(x;\theta))\}\,, \qquad x,x'\in\mathsf{X}.\end{aligned}\tag{6.55}$$

Proof of Theorem 6.8 Expanding Poisson's equation gives, for each x and θ,

$$c_\theta(x) + \sum_{x'} P_\theta(x,x')h_\theta(x') = h_\theta(x) + \Gamma(\theta).$$

We then take the gradient of each side, applying the product rule:

$$\nabla c_\theta(x) + \sum_{x'}\{[\nabla P_\theta(x,x')]h_\theta(x') + P_\theta(x,x')\nabla h_\theta\,(x')\} = \nabla h_\theta(x) + \nabla\Gamma(\theta).$$

The introduction of the score function is only so that we can bring P_θ outside of the brackets in the left-hand side (essentially an application of Lemma 6.7) to obtain

$$\nabla c_\theta(x) + \sum_{x'} P_\theta(x,x')\{S^\theta(x,x')h_\theta(x') + \nabla h_\theta\,(x')\} = \nabla h_\theta(x) + \nabla\Gamma(\theta).$$

Multiplying each side by $\pi_\theta(x)$ and summing then gives

$$\begin{aligned}&\mathsf{E}_{\pi_\theta}\big[\nabla c_\theta(X(k)) + S^\theta(X(k),X(k+1))h_\theta(X(k+1)) + \nabla h_\theta\,(X(k+1))\big]\\ &\quad = \mathsf{E}_{\pi_\theta}\big[\nabla h_\theta\,(X(k))\big] + \nabla\Gamma(\theta).\end{aligned}$$

The proof is completed on canceling $\mathsf{E}_{\pi_\theta}[\nabla h_\theta\,(X(k+1))] = \mathsf{E}_{\pi_\theta}[\nabla h_\theta\,(X(k))]$ from each side. $\square$

6.9 Ergodic Theory for General Markov Chains*

Spectral theory for Markov chains can be extended far beyond the finite state space setting. In particular, a full generalization of Theorem 6.2 is available, known as the *V-uniform ergodic theorem* [257]. Ergodic theory and bounds on solutions to Poisson's equation are important in the remainder of the book, but you will have to go to other sources for details: A survey with references can be found in the appendix of [254], and a high-level survey is provided here.

6.9.1 Classification

For a Markov chain on a general state space, it remains true that $\lambda_1 = 1$ is always a right eigenvalue. Recalling the notation in (6.9b), we have $P\mathbf{1} = \mathbf{1}$, where "$\mathbf{1}$" denotes a function: $\mathbf{1}(x) = 1$ for all $x \in \mathsf{X}$. More generally, for each $k \geq 1$ and $x \in \mathsf{X}$,

$$P^k\mathbf{1}\,(x) = \mathsf{E}[\mathbf{1}(X(r+k)) \mid X(r) = x] = 1.$$

The assumptions on eigenvalues appearing in Theorem 6.2 are traditionally replaced with the following notion of irreducibility and aperiodicity. A probability measure ψ on X is identified, and we then have the following classification:

Classification of Markov Chains

(i) The chain is ψ-irreducible if, for any set $A \in \mathcal{B}(\mathsf{X})$ satisfying $\psi(A) > 0$, and any $x \in \mathsf{X}$, there is $n \geq 1$ satisfying $P^n(x,A) > 0$.
(ii) The chain is aperiodic if, for any set $A \in \mathcal{B}(\mathsf{X})$ satisfying $\psi(A) > 0$, and any $x \in \mathsf{X}$, there is $n_0 \geq 1$ satisfying

$$P^n(x,A) > 0, \qquad n \geq n_0.$$

These definitions appear unverifiable: How can one test every $A \in \mathcal{B}(\mathsf{X})$? One approach is through verification of a minorization condition: A set $S \in \mathcal{B}(\mathsf{X})$ is called *small* if there is a probability measure ν, $\delta > 0$, and a time n such that

$$P^n(x,A) \geq \delta\nu(A), \qquad x \in S,\ A \in \mathcal{B}(\mathsf{X}). \tag{6.56}$$

This isn't as hard to verify as it might appear. For example, it is easy to construct small sets if $\mathsf{X} = \mathbb{R}^n$ and P^n has a continuous density.

Lemma 6.9 *Suppose that there is a pair (S,ν) satisfying* (6.56). *Then,*

(i) *Suppose that $\sum_{k=0}^{\infty} P^k(x_0,S) > 0$ for every $x_0 \in \mathsf{X}$. Then the chain is ψ-irreducible, with $\psi = \nu$.*
(ii) *Suppose that for any $x \in \mathsf{X}$, there is $n_0 \geq 1$ satisfying*

$$P^n(x,S) > 0, \qquad n \geq n_0.$$

Then the chain is also aperiodic. □

The situation is even simpler when X is countable, since every singleton is small (a set S consisting of just one element). Suppose that there is $x^\bullet \in \mathsf{X}$ satisfying

$$\sum_{k=0}^{\infty} P^k(x_0,x^\bullet) > 0 \qquad \text{for every } x_0 \in \mathsf{X}.$$

Applying Lemma 6.9, using $S = \{x^\bullet\}$, we see that the chain is ν-irreducible, with $\nu(\,\cdot\,) = P(x^\bullet,\,\cdot\,)$. In this case, the term *uni-chain* is substituted for ψ-irreducible (or we say the chain is $x^\bullet$-irreducible if we want to emphasize the particular reachable state $x^\bullet$). The definition of aperiodicity is also more easily verified: There is $n_0 \geq 1$ satisfying

$$P^n(x^\bullet,x^\bullet) > 0\,, \qquad n \geq n_0. \tag{6.57}$$

One celebrated representation of an invariant pmf π is known as Kac's theorem:

Proposition 6.10 (Kac's Theorem) *Suppose that $\boldsymbol{X}$ is a Markov chain on a countable state space. Suppose that $x^\bullet \in \mathsf{X}$ satisfies $\mathsf{E}_{x^\bullet}[\tau_{x^\bullet}] < \infty$. Then there is an invariant pmf satisfying $\pi(x^\bullet) > 0$, and for all functions g for which $\pi(|g|)$ is finite,*

$$\pi(g) \stackrel{\text{def}}{=} \sum \pi(x)g(x) = \pi(x^\bullet)\mathsf{E}_{x^\bullet}\Big[\sum_{k=0}^{\tau_{x^\bullet}-1} g(X(k))\Big]. \tag{6.58}$$

The invariant pmf is unique if $\boldsymbol{\Phi}$ is uni-chain. □

The connection with the finite state space setting is made clear in the following:

Proposition 6.11 *The following equivalences hold for a finite state space Markov chain:*

(i) *The eigenvalue $\lambda_1 = 1$ is not repeated $\Longleftrightarrow$ the uni-chain assumption holds.*
(ii) *The eigenvalue $\lambda_1 = 1$ is the only eigenvalue satisfying $|\lambda| = 1$, and this eigenvalue is not repeated $\Longleftrightarrow$ the chain is aperiodic.* □

6.9.2 Lyapunov Theory

Recall that the coercive assumption was a useful property for Lyapunov functions in a deterministic setting: V is coercive means that the sublevel set $S_V(r)$ is a bounded subset of X for any r. In the theory of ψ-irreducible Markov chains, the sublevel sets are small, either by direct assumption or a consequence of other assumptions. The two Lyapunov conditions (V3) and (V4) that follow are examples. Each of these bounds implies a "negative drift" whenever the state is outside of a small set:

$$\mathsf{E}[V(X(k+1)) \mid X(0),\dots,X(k)] < V(X(k)) \qquad \text{whenever } X(k) \notin S.$$

Assumption (V3) is a refinement of the Poisson inequality (6.27).

Theorem 6.12 (*Lyapunov Condition for Poisson's Equation*) *Suppose that the Markov chain is ψ-irreducible, and there exists a solution to the following Lyapunov bound: For a nonnegative-valued function V on X, a small set $S \in \mathcal{B}(\mathsf{X})$, $b < \infty$, and a function $f\colon \mathsf{X} \to [1,\infty)$,*

$$PV(x) \leq V(x) - f(x) + b\mathbb{1}_S(x), \qquad x \in \mathsf{X}. \tag{V3}$$

Then there exists a unique invariant probability measure π. It satisfies $\pi(f) < \infty$, and the following additional conclusions hold for any function $c\colon \mathsf{X} \to \mathbb{R}$ satisfying

$$\sup_x \frac{|c(x)|}{f(x)} < \infty.$$

(i) *There exists a solution to Poisson's equation* (6.23) *with $\eta = \pi(c)$ and*

$$\sup_x \frac{|h(x)|}{V(x)+1} < \infty.$$

(ii) *Suppose that the sublevel set $S_c(r)$ is small or empty for each r, where*

$$S_c(r) = \{x \in \mathsf{X} : c(x) \le r\}.$$

Then the function h in (i) can be chosen so that $h(x) \ge 0$ for each x. □

There are also ergodic theorems available under (V3) – for details, see [257].

In most cases, a far stronger drift condition is available, and from this we obtain a strong form of *geometric ergodicity*. The interpretation of a Lyapunov function as a weighting function is particularly useful in the definitions that follow. For this, we assume that $V(x) \ge 1$ for each x, and denote for $c\colon \mathsf{X} \to \mathbb{R}$,

$$\|c\|_V = \sup_x \frac{|c(x)|}{V(x)}.$$

Let L_∞^V denote the set of all Borel-measurable functions for which this is finite. We say that the Markov chain is V-uniformly ergodic if there exists an invariant measure π, along with constants $\rho < 1$, $B < \infty$ such that for any $c \in L_\infty^V$,

$$\big|\mathsf{E}_x[c(X(k))] - \pi(c)\big| \le B\rho^k \|c\|_V V(x), \qquad k \ge 0,\, x \in \mathsf{X}. \tag{6.59}$$

Or, in operator-theoretic notation, on denoting $\tilde{c} = c - \pi(c)$:

$$\|P^k \tilde{c}\|_V \le B\rho^k \|c\|_V, \qquad k \ge 0.$$

Theorem 6.13 (*Lyapunov Condition for V-Uniform Ergodicity*) *Suppose that the Markov chain is ψ-irreducible and aperiodic, and the following drift condition holds for a function $V\colon \mathsf{X} \to [1,\infty)$: for constants $\varepsilon > 0$, $b < \infty$, and a small set $S \in \mathcal{B}(\mathsf{X})$,*

$$PV(x) \le (1-\varepsilon)V(x) + b\mathbb{1}_S(x), \qquad x \in \mathsf{X}. \tag{V4}$$

Then the Markov chain is V-uniformly ergodic. □

The fact that we can identify the state dependency in the bound (6.59) is fantastic news. Unfortunately, obtaining bounds on B or ρ is not at all easy [232, 256, 302, 303].

6.10 Exercises

There are many exercises in this chapter: It is very important to understand this material and also the notation in order to follow the final chapters of this book.

6.1 Consider the two-state Markov chain on $\mathsf{X} = \{0,1\}$ with transition matrix

$$P = \begin{bmatrix} \frac{9}{10} & \frac{1}{10} \\ \frac{1}{4} & \frac{3}{4} \end{bmatrix}.$$

(a) First, think probabilistically: Explain why the first hitting time to $x = 1$ from the starting point $X(0) = 0$ has a geometric distribution on $\{1,2,\dots\}$. Compute the invariant pmf π using Proposition 6.10 (Kac's theorem).

The rest is algebra:

(b) Obtain the spectral representation of P,

$$P = \lambda_1 v^1 \mu^1 + \lambda_2 v^2 \mu^2,$$

where $\{\lambda_i\}$ are eigenvalues, $\{\mu^i\}$ are left eigenvectors (taken to be row vectors), and $\{v^i\}$ are right eigenvectors (taken to be column vectors).

(c) Find an expression for P^n based on (b). At what rate does $P^n(i,j)$ tend to $\pi(j)$?

(d) Choose a pair of two-dimensional vectors w and v. The product $wv^\intercal$ is then a 2×2 matrix (often written $w \otimes v$ in this book for emphasis). Compute the inverse,

$$G = [I - (P - wv^\intercal)]^{-1},$$

and verify that the row vector vG is proportional to π. If you are unlucky, and the inverse does not exist; if so, then try a different pair!

This is an example of the Perron–Frobenius construction from Section 3.2.3, for which there is theory available to ensure invertibility. See Example 6.20 for another example.

6.2 Let $\boldsymbol{X} = (X(0), X(1), X(2), \dots)$ denote a Markov chain on the state space of three elements $\mathsf{X} = \{1,2,3\}$. Its transition matrix is of the following form:

$$P = \begin{bmatrix} 1-\varepsilon_2 & \varepsilon_2 & 0 \\ \varepsilon_1 & 1-2\varepsilon_1 & \varepsilon_1 \\ 0 & \varepsilon_2 & 1-\varepsilon_2 \end{bmatrix} \qquad \text{(all elements are nonnegative).}$$

(a) Verify that $v = (\varepsilon_1, \varepsilon_2, \varepsilon_1)^\intercal$ is a left eigenvector:

$$v^\intercal P = v^\intercal,$$

and from this obtain π.

(b) Find all eigenvalues of P (perform your calculation by hand).

(c) Verify that that $P^k(i,j)$ converges to a limit $\pi(j)$, as $k \to \infty$, for any i,j.

(d) Fix numerical values for P; choose small, distinct values for $\varepsilon_1, \varepsilon_2$.

Plot $\log(\mathsf{P}\{X(k) = 1 \mid X(0) = 1\})$, for $0 \le k \le 100$. On the same figure, plot $\log(|\lambda_2|^k)$, where λ_2 is the "second eigenvalue" of P (the one with second largest magnitude).

Discuss your findings.

6.3 *Conditional Expectation and Preparation for Section 9.* Suppose that X,Y are scalar-valued random variables with finite second moments. The conditional expectation $\widehat{X} = \mathsf{E}[X \mid Y]$ is defined to be the solution to minimum norm problem: $\widehat{X} = g^\star(Y)$, with

$$g^\star = \arg\min_g \Gamma(g) \stackrel{\text{def}}{=} \arg\min_g \mathsf{E}[(X - g(Y))^2].$$

Consider $X = 1/(1+Y)$, with Y uniformly distributed on the interval $[0,1]$.

(a) Compute $\mathsf{E}[X \mid Y]$ by constructing $g^\star$, resulting in $\Gamma(g^\star) = 0$.

(b) In many applications, it isn't so easy, so we opt for an approximation. It is common to restrict to a finite-dimensional set of functions. That is, for dimension d, assume that we have d functions $\{\psi_1, \dots, \psi_d\}$, denote $g_\theta = \sum_k \theta_k \psi_k$ for $\theta \in \mathbb{R}^d$, and define $\widehat{X} = g_{\theta^*}(Y)$ with

$$\theta^* = \arg\min_\theta \Gamma(g_\theta).$$

Obtain an expression for θ^* based on expectations such as

$$R^\psi_{i,j} = \mathsf{E}[\psi_i(Y)\psi_j(Y)], \quad \bar{\psi}^X_i = \mathsf{E}[\psi_i(Y)X].$$

(c) Discuss how you would compute the solution to (b) using simulation. For example, how would you compute it, given i.i.d. samples $\{Y_k\}$ each with uniform distribution on $[0,1]$?

(d) Compute or approximate θ^* for a basis of your choice (Fourier or polynomial are acceptable) with $d = 1,2,3,4,5$. On the same figure, show the five plots of $g_{\theta^*}(y)$ as a function of $0 \le y \le 1$, and also include a plot of $g^\star$. You should get a good approximation if your basis is reasonable, and d isn't too small.

6.4 Let $\boldsymbol{X}$ be a time-homogeneous Markov chain on the finite state space $\mathsf{X} = \{1, \dots, N\}$, and let P denote the $N \times N$ transition matrix. For any function $h : \mathsf{X} \to \mathbb{R}$, review or recall the *smoothing property*:

$$\mathsf{E}[h(X(k+2)) \mid X(k)] = \mathsf{E}\big[\mathsf{E}[h(X(k+2)) \mid X(k), X(k+1)] \mid X(k)\big].$$

Explain how this implies the representation for the two-step transition matrix: For each $i \in \mathsf{X}$,

$$\mathsf{E}[h(X(k+2)) \mid X(k) = i] = \sum_j P^2(i,j)h(j),$$

where $P^2 \stackrel{\text{def}}{=} P \cdot P$ is the usual matrix product, and $P^2(i,j)$ is the (i,j)th entry of P^2.

6.5 *ODE Method for Lyapunov Function Construction.* Consider the nonlinear state space model

$$X(k+1) = X(k) + \mathrm{F}(X(k)) + sN(k+1),$$

where F is a scaling of the vector field in Example 2.13:

$$\mathrm{F}(x) = \delta \frac{1 - e^x}{1 + e^x} = -\delta \tanh(x/2), \qquad \text{with } \delta > 0.$$

The disturbance $\{N(k)\}$ is i.i.d., and uniform on $[-1,1]$. That is, its density is supported on this interval, with $f_N(x) = 1/2$ for $-1 \le x \le 1$.

Take the function V you obtained for the continuous time model in Example 2.13, and see if you can establish a similar bound: $PV \le V - c + \overline{\eta}_s$, where $\overline{\eta}_s$ will probably grow as the cube of s for any fixed δ. You may have to modify V slightly, depending on your choice.

You will test the resulting bound $\pi(c) \le \overline{\eta}_s$ in Example 6.14.

6.6 Let P be a transition kernel, $c\colon \mathsf{X} \to \mathbb{R}_+$ a cost function, and $\gamma \in (0,1)$ the discount factor, and recall the discounted cost value function that was defined in (6.33). To begin, provide a proof that the DP equation (6.33) holds based on the representation (6.32).

(a) In Example 6.6.1, we obtained h_γ for the linear state space model. Was stability required to obtain a solution? That is, do we require $|\alpha| < 1$?
(b) Consider a finite state space Markov chain that is uni-chain. Show that

$$h_\gamma(x) = \tilde{h}_\gamma(x) + k(\gamma), \quad x \in \mathsf{X},$$

in which $\sup_{0<\gamma<1} |\tilde{h}_\gamma(x)|$ is finite for each x, and $k(\gamma)$ does not depend upon x. For this you will find the following useful: $P^n(x,y) = \pi(y) + \widetilde{P}^n(x,y)$ (see (6.19)).
(c) Compute $\tilde{h}_\gamma$ and $k(\gamma)$ for the four-state Markov chain with transition matrix (6.21), and with $c(x) = x$.

6.7 We can extend the Poisson inequality to something more closely aligned with the discounted setting. Suppose that (P,c,γ) are as in Example 6.6. Suppose also that we have a solution $V : \mathsf{X} \to \mathbb{R}_+$ and $\overline{\eta} < \infty$ to the following "discounted" Poisson inequality:

$$\gamma PV \le V - c + \overline{\eta}.$$

(a) Show that $h_\gamma \le V + \text{const.}$, and identify the constant (this is easy once you review the average cost bound obtained using Poisson's inequality).
(b) Obtain a solution to the inequality for the M/M/1 queue with $c(x) = x$.
Is the load condition $\rho < 1$ necessary to obtain a solution?

6.8 *On Poisson's Equation.* This problem shows that a solution to a dynamic programming equation must be interpreted with care.
For the M/M/1 queue, with load $\rho = \alpha/\mu \in (0,1)$, perform the following computations:
(a) Let $V(x) = \rho^{-x}$, and compute the drift:

$$\Delta(x) = PV(x) - V(x), \qquad x = 0,1,2,\ldots.$$

(b) Compute the steady-state mean m of Δ. For this, recall that the invariant pmf is $\pi(x) = (1-\rho)\rho^x$, so that $m = \sum_x \pi(x)\Delta(x)$. Verify that the mean is *not* equal to zero. Also verify that the mean of V is not finite.
(c) Compute a solution h to Poisson's equation, with forcing function Δ:

$$Ph = h - \Delta + m.$$

6.9 Consider the following generalization of the M/M/1 queue on the nonnegative integers $\mathbb{Z}_+ = \{0,1,2,\ldots\}$. The transition matrix satisfies $P(n,m) = 0$ if $|n-m| > 1$. Equivalently, for the Markov chain $\boldsymbol{X}$,

$$|X(k+1) - X(k)| \le 1 \qquad \text{for each } X(0) \text{ and } k \ge 1.$$

This is called a *birth-death process*.
Verify that the detailed balance equations hold, whenever an invariant pmf π exists. That is,

$$\pi(i)P(i,j) = \pi(j)P(j,i).$$

Can you obtain an expression for π, similar to the M/M/1 queue?

6.10 Consider the two-dimensional linear state space model,

$$X(k+1) = FX(k) + GN(k+1),$$

where F is a 2×2 matrix, with eigenvalues satisfying $|\lambda| < 1$, and $G \in \mathbb{R}^2$. The disturbance $\boldsymbol{N}$ is i.i.d. on $\mathbb{R}$ with zero mean and finite variance. We have seen that $X(k)$ converges in distribution to the random variable

$$\widehat{X}_\infty = \sum_{i=0}^{\infty} F^i G N(i).$$

Convergence in distribution means that for any bounded and continuous function $g\colon \mathbb{R}^2 \to \mathbb{R}$,

$$\lim_{k\to\infty} \mathsf{E}[g(X(k))] = \mathsf{E}[g(\widehat{X}_\infty)].$$

This convergence holds for any given $X(0) \in \mathbb{R}^2$. Moreover, if $\boldsymbol{N}$ is Gaussian, then so is $\widehat{X}_\infty$, with covariance

$$\Sigma_{X_\infty} = \sigma_N^2 \sum_{i=0}^{\infty} F^i G G^{\intercal} F^{i\intercal}.$$

Find an example in which Σ_{X_∞} is rank one, choose your distribution for $\boldsymbol{N}$ so that $\sigma_N^2 = 1$, and proceed:

(a) Find a (discontinuous) function $g\colon \mathbb{R}^2 \to \mathbb{R}$ and an initial condition $X(0)$ for which $\mathsf{E}[g(X(k))] = 0$ for all k, yet $\mathsf{E}[g(\widehat{X}_\infty)] = 1$ (ergodicity fails).

(b) Solve Poisson's equation $PV = V - c + \overline{\eta}$ with $c(x) = x_1^2$.

The remaining two parts are based on simulation for this example.

(c) Average $\{c(X(k)) : 1 \le k \le T\}$ and observe that the value $\overline{\eta}_T$ does approximate $\overline{\eta}$. You might plot this as a function of T (the range of T should be much larger than trace (Σ_{X_∞})).

(d) Observe the evolution of $\boldsymbol{X}$ on $\mathbb{R}^2$. Choose two initial conditions: one proportional to G, and one satisfying $X(0)^{\intercal} G = 0$. And, choose $\|X(0)\| \gg$ trace (Σ_{X_∞}) (say, 10 times larger). Provide plots of $\boldsymbol{X}$ along with discussion.

6.11 *Criteria for Instability.* Let $\boldsymbol{X}$ be an *irreducible* Markov chain on the nonnegative integers $\mathsf{X} = \{0, 1, 2, \dots\}$. That is, the Markov chain is $x^\bullet$-irreducible for every $x^\bullet \in \mathsf{X}$.

Assume that there is a nonnegative function $V : \mathsf{X} \to \mathbb{R}_+$ satisfying $PV \le V$ (such functions are known as *superharmonic*).

(a) Verify that $M(k) = V(X(k))$ satisfies the *supermartingale* property:

$$\mathsf{E}[M(k+1) \mid M(0), \dots, M(k)] \le 0.$$

Suggestion: First condition on $X(0), \dots, X(k)$, and then apply the *smoothing property* of conditional expectation. If this language is not familiar, then skip to (b).

A useful fact about nonnegative supermartingales is that they are convergent:

$$M(\infty) \stackrel{\text{def}}{=} \lim_{k\to\infty} M(k),$$

where the limit exists with probability one, but may take on infinite values.

(c) If V is not identically constant, show that the Markov chain is *transient*. For this, you must show that there are two states x and y such that $\mathsf{P}\{\tau_y = \infty \mid X(0) = x\} > 0$.

6.12 Consider the M/M/1 queue, with load $\rho = \alpha/\mu > 1$, so that the system is not stable. Show that the function V of Example 6.11 defined by $V(x) = \rho^{-x}$ is superharmonic.

6.13 *Simulation Theory and Practice.* Consider the Markov chain with transition matrix (6.21).

(a) Obtain the invariant pmf π, and the solution to Poisson's equation h with $c(x) \equiv x$. For this, you might review Perron–Frobenius theory in Section 3.2.3 (see also Example 6.20).

(b) Compute σ_{CLT}^2 based on π, h, c (review Section 6.7.1).

(c) Test the predictive value of σ_{CLT}^2 through the batch means methods described in Section 6.7: Run $M = 500$ (or more) independent simulations to obtain the M estimates $\{\eta_{\mathcal{N}}{}^i : 1 \le$

$i \le M\}$ defined in (6.41a). Based on these data, obtain an approximation $\widehat{\sigma}^2_{\text{CLT}}(\mathcal{N})$ based on a histogram of $\{\sqrt{\mathcal{N}}(\eta_{\mathcal{N}}{}^i - \eta_{\mathcal{N}}) : 1 \le i \le M\}$.
Repeat for $\mathcal{N} = 10^m$ for $m = 2,3,4,\ldots$ (stop when your computer power can't keep up).
Discuss your findings. In particular, does your estimate for smaller values of $\mathcal{N}$ provide insight into how long you must simulate to obtain a good estimate of $\eta = \pi(c)$?

6.14 *Simulation Theory and Practice.* We return to the example in Example 6.5.
(a) If you haven't done so already, obtain the solution to Example 6.5, and review Section 6.6 to understand why $\pi(c) \le \overline{\eta}_s$.
(b) Solve Poisson's equation numerically for several values of δ and s, and plot your result.
(c) Estimate $\eta = \pi(c)$ through simulation for *at least* five values of δ (as small as 0.01 and as large as 0.5) and several values of s. Perform multiple independent runs to obtain estimates of the error in your estimates.

Suggestions and Warnings

Review Section 6.7.5 before you begin, especially the value of common random numbers. Keep in mind that the dynamics are similar to a queueing model, in that the mean drift

$$\mathsf{E}[X(k+1) - X(k) \mid X(k) = x] = \mathrm{F}(x)$$

is nearly constant (independent of x) when $|x|$ is large. The steady-state mean $\pi(c)$ grows as δ^{-1}, and the asymptotic variance σ^2_{CLT} grows as δ^{-4} for vanishing δ.

6.15 The M/M/1 queue has a geometric pmf with parameter ρ. Suppose that we wish to estimate the autocorrelation via

$$R_N(1) = \frac{1}{N}\sum_{k=0}^{N-1} X(k)X(k+1)$$

so that in the notation of (6.47) we have $L(X(k),X(k+1)) = X(k)X(k+1)$.
(a) Compute or bound the asymptotic covariance of this estimator–it will be huge for $\rho \sim 1$!
(b) Obtain a formula for the asymptotic covariance using split sampling, as defined in (6.46). This is easy, since the samples are i.i.d., and the marginal of $\boldsymbol{X}$ is geometric.
How do the asymptotic variances compare?

Sensitivity

6.16 This exercise provides an exploration of Schweitzer's formula (6.52) for the CRW queue:

$$X(k+1) = X(k) - U(k) + A(k+1),$$

in which there is a cost for control and a cost for queueing delay. A randomized policy is denoted

$$\breve{\phi}^{\theta}(1 \mid x) \stackrel{\text{def}}{=} \mathsf{P}\{U(k) = 1 \mid X_0^k,\, U_0^{k-1},\, A_0^{\infty}\}, \qquad X(k) = x.$$

Here we focus on a simple special case in which $\breve{\phi}^{\theta}(1 \mid x) = \theta\mathbb{1}\{x \ge 1\}$, with $\theta \in [0,1]$, and consider the cost function $c_\theta(x) = x + c_2\theta^p$, with $c_2 > 0$ and $p \ge 1$.
(a) Obtain an expression for $\frac{d}{d\theta}P_\theta g$, for an arbitrary function $g\colon \mathsf{X} \to \mathbb{R}$.
(b) Compute η_θ and the solution to Poisson's equation h_θ with forcing function c_θ. Compute η_θ' by directly differentiating your formula for η_θ. Verify that your answer is consistent with Schweitzer's formula.
(c) Plot η_θ' for $\theta \in (0,1)$ to find the best policy. Use your preferred value of $c_2 > 1, p > 1$, and take $\alpha = \mathsf{E}[A(t)] = \frac{1}{2}$.

6.17 Consider the one-dimensional dimensional linear state space model

$$X(k+1) = X(k) + U(k) + N(k+1), \qquad U(k) = -\theta X(k),$$

in which $\boldsymbol{N}$ is i.i.d., scalar valued, and with marginal $N(0,1)$. Consider the quadratic cost $c(x) = x^2$, and let η_θ denote the steady-state average cost. Our goal is to minimize the loss function

$$\Gamma(\theta) = \lim_{k\to\infty} \mathsf{E}[X(k)^2 + U(k)^2] = \eta_\theta[1+\theta^2].$$

(a) Obtain an expression for $\Gamma(\theta)$, including the range of $\theta \in \mathbb{R}$ for which it is finite, and a formula for the minimizer θ^*. Is Γ convex?

(b) Obtain an expression for $\nabla\Gamma(\theta)$ using Theorem 6.8 and verify that it agrees with (i). In particular, verify that $\nabla\Gamma(\theta) = 0$ when $\theta = \theta^*$.

6.18 Consider the generalization of Example 6.17 to the linear model with n-dimensional state process and scalar input:

$$X(k+1) = FX(k) + GU(k) + N(k+1), \qquad U(k) = -K_\theta X(k),$$

in which $\boldsymbol{N}$ is i.i.d., with marginal $N(0,\Sigma_N)$. Assume a linear parameterization for the gain: $K_\theta = \sum_{i=1}^d \theta_i K^i$ for $\theta \in \mathbb{R}^d$, where each K^i is $n \times 1$.

(a) Obtain an expression for the score function $S^\theta(x,y)$ for the special case (6.55).

(b) Find an expression for h_θ with forcing function $c(x) = \|x\|^2$, of the form $h_\theta(x) = x^\intercal M_\theta x$. Specification of $M_\theta \geq 0$ will involve a Lyapunov equation.

(c) Obtain an expression for $\nabla\Gamma(\theta)$ with

$$\Gamma(\theta) \stackrel{\text{def}}{=} \mathsf{E}_{\pi_\theta}\big[c(X(k)) + rU(k)^2\big], \qquad U(k) = K_\theta X(k)$$

for $r > 0$ fixed and where the expectation is in steady state.

Perron–Frobenius Theory

Section 3.2.3 contains a brief introduction to Perron–Frobenius theory. Application to finite state space Markov chains are surveyed in the exercises that follow. These concepts provide useful computational tools and insight.

In each of the problems that follow, we consider a Markov chain $\boldsymbol{X}$ on a countable state space X, with transition matrix P.

6.19 *An Introduction.* Suppose that P is “rank one.” This means that there exists a function s and a pmf ν on X satisfying $P = s \otimes \nu$ (that is, $P(x,y) = s(x)\nu(y)$ for each $x,y \in \mathsf{X}$.) Show that $s \equiv 1$, ν is an invariant pmf, and hence $\boldsymbol{X}$ is i.i.d. with marginal distribution ν.

6.20 *Perron–Frobenius Theory of Positive Matrices.* Suppose that P is not rank one, but rather dominates a rank-one matrix: There exists a nonnegative function s (not identically zero) and a pmf ν on X satisfying

$$P(x,y) \geq s(x)\nu(y) \qquad \text{for each } x,y \in \mathsf{X}. \tag{PF}$$

The following power series expansion always exists:

$$G = \sum_{k=0}^{\infty} (P - s \otimes \nu)^k$$

and satisfies $\nu G s \leq 1$. This is the starting point of Perron–Frobenius theory. Hence $G = [I - (P - s \otimes \nu)]^{-1}$ whenever the inverse exists.

(a) If π is an invariant pmf, so that $\pi P = \pi$, it then follows:

$$\pi[I - P + s \otimes \nu] = \delta \nu,$$

where $\delta \geq 0$. Provide a formula for δ in terms of π, s and ν.
Argue that $\mu = \nu G$ is a left eigenvector of P, provided the inverse $G = [I-(P-s\otimes\nu)]^{-1}$ exists, and $\delta > 0$.

(b) Postulate on a representation for a solution to Poisson's equation $Ph = h - \tilde{c}$, based on the matrix G.

6.21 *PF Theory and Sensitivity.* We now revisit the sensitivity formula in Theorem 6.8. You will obtain an expression for the gradient of h_θ at a particular value $\theta^0 \in \mathbb{R}^d$, subject to these local assumptions: For some $\varepsilon > 0$:

- $P_\theta(x,x')$ and $c_\theta(x)$ are continuously differentiable for θ in the region $B_\varepsilon = \{\theta : \|\theta - \theta^0\| \leq \varepsilon\}$.
- The Markov chain with transition matrix P_θ is uni-chain for each $\theta \in B_\varepsilon$, and satisfies the uniform minorization condition for θ in this domain:

$$P_\theta(x,x') \geq s(x)\nu(x'), \qquad x,x' \in \mathsf{X},$$

where ν is a pmf, and $\pi_\theta(s) > 0$.

Obtain a formula for ∇h_θ, using $h_\theta = G_\theta \tilde{c}_\theta$, where

$$G_\theta = [I - P_\theta + s \otimes \nu]^{-1}.$$

The following formula will be useful:

$$\frac{\partial}{\partial \theta_i} G_\theta = G_\theta [\frac{\partial}{\partial \theta_i} P_\theta] G_\theta.$$

6.22 *Risk-Sensitive Control [374].* Another application of PF theory is to infinite-horizon optimal control with the *risk-sensitive* criterion.

(a) The log moment generating function associated with a real-valued random variable Ξ is $\Lambda(r) = \log \mathsf{E}[\exp(r\Xi)]$, with $r \in \mathbb{R}$ a variable. Assume that Λ is finite valued in a neighborhood of the origin. Obtain the first and second derivatives of Λ at the origin, to justify the "small r approximation":

$$\Lambda(r) = m_\Xi r + \tfrac{1}{2}\sigma_\Xi^2 r^2 + O(r^3),$$

where the coefficients are the mean and variance of Ξ.

(b) One formulation of risk-sensitive control is motivated by this Taylor series approximation, with $r > 0$ and

$$\Xi = \sum_{k=0}^{\mathcal{N}-1} c(X(k)) + V_0(X(\mathcal{N})),$$

where $\mathcal{N} \geq 1$, c is a cost function, and V_0 is the terminal cost. Consider the finite state space Markov chain with $\mathsf{X} = \{1,\ldots,n\}$, introduce an $n \times n$ matrix with entries

$$R(i,j) = \exp(rc(i))P(i,j),$$

and let (v,λ) denote a solution to the eigenvector equation $Rv = \lambda v$. Show that for each $i \in \mathsf{X}$,

$$\lambda^n v_i = \sum_j R^n(i,j)v_j = \mathsf{E}\Big[r \sum_{k=0}^{\mathcal{N}-1} c(X(k)) + \mathcal{V}(X(\mathcal{N})) \mid X(0) = i\Big],$$

where $\mathcal{V}(i) = \log(v_i)$ for each i. Conclude that $\Lambda = \log(\lambda)$ is the infinite-horizon risk sensitive cost, defined by the following (using the notation (6.9)):

$$H_\infty(x) = \lim_{\mathcal{N}\to\infty} \frac{1}{\mathcal{N}} \log\Big\{\mathsf{E}_x\Big[\exp\Big(r\sum_{k=0}^{\mathcal{N}-1} c(X(k))\Big)\Big]\Big\}, \qquad X(0) = x \in \mathsf{X}.$$

(c) Solve the eigenvalue equation $Rv = \lambda v$ for the four-state Markov chain with transition matrix (6.21), using $c(i) = i$, and verify the following identities:

$$\tfrac{d}{dr}\Lambda(r)\Big|_{r=0} = \eta = \pi(c), \qquad \tfrac{d}{dr}\log(v_j(r)/v_1(r))\Big|_{r=0} = h_j, \quad 1 \le j \le 4,$$

where h is the unique solution to Poisson's equation satisfying $h_1 = 0$.

6.11 Notes

As in [257], in this book the word "chain" indicates that time is discrete, and the term *Markov process* is reserved for models in continuous time. The terminology is in honor of the Russian mathematician Andrey Markov. Good introductory texts include [138, 275], and for more advanced material, see [117, 257]. Some of the material in this chapter and Appendix B is adapted from [254, chapters 8, 9] and its appendix. Standard texts on Perron–Frobenius theory are [277, 315], and the appendix of [254] contains a survey aimed at readers with interest in control applications.

The reference [257] remains an up-to-date source for Lyapunov theory and Poisson's equation for Markov chains on a general state space. The book also contains spectral theory in the general state space setting, but this remains a rapidly evolving field [117, 196, 197, 378].

An encyclopedia for theory and practice of simulation is [12]. See [88, 194, 195, 253] for specialized theory on the CLT and other asymptotic statistics for Markov chains, written with attention to the applications of interest in this book.

It was first demonstrated in [253, prop. 1.1] that the finite-n bound (6.43) cannot be obtained for the M/M/1 queue and other "skip-free" Markov chains on a countable state space. Much more on this topic can be found in [254, chapter 11] (along with details on the histogram Figure 6.6), and [119, 120] for a complete explanation of $I_\pm(\varepsilon)$ appearing in Section 8.3.1.

Techniques to obtain finite-n bounds through the introduction of control variates can be found in [194, 253]. See [157–159] for applications of control variate techniques to network simulation, and Section 10.7 for applications in RL.

Schweitzer introduced his sensitivity formula in his doctoral thesis, which was subsequently published in 1968 [251, 313]. See Konda's thesis for early history of gradient free optimization for application in RL [188, 191], and Section 10.10 of this book for more history.

7

Stochastic Control

By *stochastic control*, we mean that random disturbances and measurement noise are accounted for explicitly in our control system model. Markov decision processes (MDP) are a very special case. While the theory in this part of the book will focus almost exclusively on MDPs, the title of the chapter is meant to emphasize our goals rather than a particular set of techniques to achieve them.

Before we dive straight into theory, it will be helpful (and perhaps more interesting) to first survey examples to explain the similarity and differences between deterministic and stochastic control. A short primer on MDP theory is contained in Appendix B.

The object of study in MDP theory is a state process $\boldsymbol{X} = \{X(k) : k \geq 0\}$ that takes values in a state space X. The evolution of $\boldsymbol{X}$ is influenced by disturbances, as in the nonlinear state space model (6.3), and also a control sequence $\boldsymbol{U} = \{U(k) : k \geq 0\}$ taking values in an input (or action) space U. As in deterministic control, our objective is to choose $U(k)$ for every $k \geq 0$, based on observations, so that the system behaves as desired – the meaning depends on the application, as we will see in the examples that follow.

7.1 MDPs: A Quick Introduction

In this short introduction, we assume that the state and input spaces are finite, or countably infinite. This greatly simplifies statements of the definitions, as in the uncontrolled setting.

The first ingredient in an MDP is the controlled transition matrix: Subject to an "admissibility" assumption defined later, the pair $(X(k),U(k))$ is a sufficient statistic in the following sense:

$$\mathsf{P}\{X(k+1) = x' \mid X(0),\dots,X(k),U(0),\dots,U(k); X(k) = x, U(k) = u\} = P_u(x,x'),$$

where the right-hand side is the controlled transition matrix, evaluated at the triple (u,x,x'). More generally, for any $m,k \geq 0$ and function $g\colon \mathsf{X}^{m+1} \to \mathbb{R}$,

$$\begin{aligned}\mathsf{E}[g\big(X(k),X(k+1),\dots,X(k+m)\big) \mid X(0),\dots,X(k),U(0),\dots,U(k)]\\ = \mathsf{E}[g\big(X(k),X(k+1),\dots,X(k+m)\big) \mid X(k),U(k)].\end{aligned}$$

The definition is far less abstract when we have a realization of the controlled Markov model:

$$X(k+1) = \mathsf{F}(X(k),U(k),N(k+1)), \tag{7.1}$$

where $\boldsymbol{N}$ is an i.i.d. sequence. The controlled transition matrix has the explicit form

$$P_u(x,x') = \mathsf{P}\{\mathsf{F}(x,u,N(1)) = x'\}, \qquad u \in \mathsf{U},\, x,x' \in \mathsf{X}.$$

Markov Decision Processes (MDP). The definition requires three ingredients:

(i) The controlled transition matrix, denoted $P_u(x,x')$ for $x,x' \in \mathsf{X}, u \in \mathsf{U}$.
(ii) A cost function $c\colon \mathsf{X} \times \mathsf{U} \to \mathbb{R}$, and input constraints represented by a set $\mathsf{U}(x) \subset \mathsf{U}$ for each $x \in \mathsf{X}$.
(iii) An objective, such as total cost: $h(x) = \sum_{k=0}^{\infty} \mathsf{E}_x[c(X(k),U(k))]$,

or average cost:

$$\eta = \lim_{n\to\infty} \frac{1}{n} \sum_{k=0}^{n-1} \mathsf{E}_x[c(X(k),U(k))]. \tag{7.2}$$

Once the objective is defined, the goal is to minimize over all "admissible" input sequences.

As in the deterministic control setting, stationary policies play an important role. For any such policy $\phi\colon \mathsf{X} \to \mathsf{U}$, if $U(k) = \phi(X(k))$ for each k, then the controlled process $\boldsymbol{X}$ is a Markov chain with transition matrix denoted P_ϕ:

$$P_\phi(x,x') = P_u(x,x')\big|_{u=\phi(x)}, \qquad x,x' \in \mathsf{X}. \tag{7.3}$$

Also similar to deterministic control is the role of DP equations. For the total-cost criterion, we have the following for each x:

$$h^\star(x) = \min_{u\in\mathsf{U}} \Big\{ c(x,u) + \sum_{x'} P_u(x,x')h^\star(x') \Big\}, \tag{7.4}$$

and the optimal policy is state feedback $\phi^\star$, in which $\phi^\star(x)$ is any minimizer of (7.4), for each x.

Minimization of the average-cost criterion (7.2) revolves around a very similar DP equation, whose origins are explained in Appendix B. Under mild assumptions, the minimal average cost $\eta^\star$ does not depend on the initial condition, and there is a solution to the *average-cost optimality equation* (ACOE):

$$h^\star(x) + \eta^\star = \min_u \{ c(x,u) + \sum_{x'} P_u(x,x')h^\star(x') \}. \tag{7.5}$$

The function $h^\star$ is known as the relative value function, and the optimal policy is again any minimizer:

$$\phi^\star(x) \in \arg\min \{ c(x,u) + \sum_{x'} P_u(x,x')h^\star(x') \}, \quad x \in \mathsf{X}. \tag{7.6}$$

The "Q-function" of Q-learning is the function within the brackets:

$$Q^\star(x,u) \stackrel{\text{def}}{=} c(x,u) + \sum_{x'} P_u(x,x')h^\star(x'), \quad x \in \mathsf{X},\, u \in \mathsf{U}. \tag{7.7}$$

Average-Cost and Transient Performance Bounds. The message from Section 6.6.2 deserves repeating here: Minimizing the average cost (7.2) does not mean we don't care about the present.

Theorem 6.12 tells us that we can expect to find a solution to the ACOE for which $h^\star$ takes on nonnegative values, even for a general state space. Proposition 6.4 then applies with $V = h^\star$ to obtain the following under the optimal policy:

$$\frac{1}{n}\sum_{k=0}^{n-1} \mathsf{E}[c(X^\star(k),U^\star(k)) \mid X(0)=x] \le \eta^\star + \frac{1}{n}h^\star(x), \qquad n\ge 1 \; x\in\mathsf{X}.$$

For a finite state space, geometric ergodicity follows from aperiodicity, from which we obtain $\mathsf{E}[c(X^\star(k),U^\star(k))] = \eta^\star + \varepsilon_k$, with $\varepsilon_k \to 0$ geometrically quickly.

7.1.1 Admissible Inputs

Before optimizing, it is necessary to first specify the class of allowable inputs. We already impose a hard constraint that $U(k) \in \mathsf{U}$ for each k, and occasionally have state-dependent constraints: $U(k) \in \mathsf{U}(x)$ when $X(k) = x$. We also impose causality, and to make this precise we require a bit more notation.

We could settle for the following definition: We only allow input sequences of the form

$$U(k) = \phi_k(X(0),\dots,X(k)), \qquad k\ge 0, \tag{7.8}$$

where $\phi_k : \mathsf{X}^{k+1} \to \mathsf{U}$ for each k (perhaps also subject to finer state-dependent constraints). However, theory requires that we sometimes allow *randomized* polices for which $U(k)$ depends on present and past state values, along with independent "noise" included for exploration, as discussed in Section 5.2.

Admissible Input Assumed given a sequence of independent and identically distributed random variables ξ, evolving on a countable set Ω. The sequence is exogenous to the control system in the following sense: For any input sequence of the form (7.8),

$$\begin{aligned}\mathsf{P}\{X(k+1) = x', \xi(k+1) = w' \mid \mathcal{X}(0),\dots,\mathcal{X}(k),U(0),\dots,U(k); X(k)=x, U(k)=u\}\\ = P_u(x,x')\nu(w') \qquad \text{for all } u\in\mathsf{U}, x,x'\in\mathsf{X},\ w'\in\Omega,\end{aligned} \tag{7.9}$$

where $\mathcal{X}(k) = (X(k),\xi(k))$, and ν is the pmf for $\xi(k)$ (independent of k by assumption).

We then say that an input sequence U is *admissible* if it is a causal function of the joint process:

$$U(k) = \phi_k(\mathcal{X}(0),\dots,\mathcal{X}(k)), \qquad k\ge 0. \tag{7.10}$$

We have essentially enlarged the state space to $\mathsf{X}\times\Omega$, with new state process $\mathcal{X}$. For any admissible input,

$$\begin{aligned}\mathsf{P}\{\mathcal{X}(k+1) = (x',w') \mid \mathcal{X}(0),\dots,\mathcal{X}(k),U(0),\dots,U(k);\\ \mathcal{X}(k) = (x,w), U(k)=u\} = P_u(x,x')\nu(w').\end{aligned}$$

The right-hand side is the controlled transition matrix for $\mathcal{X}$.

Notation and Conventions

The standard MDP terminology inserts "Markov" in the definition of a stationary policy:

- ▲ *Markov policy*: $U(k) = \phi_k(X(k))$ for a sequence of maps $\phi_k : \mathsf{X} \to \mathsf{U}$, $k \geq 0$.
- ▲ *Stationary Markov policy*: $U(k) = \phi(X(k))$.

We will usually opt for simply "stationary policy" or even "policy" for ϕ, which is also synonymous with the term *feedback law* introduced in Chapter 2.

These definitions extend to randomized policies by substituting $\mathcal{X}$ for $\boldsymbol{X}$. However, it is cumbersome to introduce ξ whenever we require randomization. We instead let $\breve{\phi}$ denote a randomized stationary policy, which is defined as a conditional probability: For each u and x,

$$\mathsf{P}\{U(k) = u \mid \mathcal{X}(0), \dots, \mathcal{X}(k-1), U(0), \dots, U(k-1); X(k) = x\} = \breve{\phi}(u \mid x). \quad (7.11)$$

Proposition 7.1 then follows from these definitions:

Proposition 7.1 *When the input sequence $\boldsymbol{U}$ is defined by a stationary (possibly randomized) policy $\breve{\phi}$, it follows that the state process $\boldsymbol{X}$ is a Markov chain, with transition matrix*

$$P_{\breve{\phi}}(x,x') = \sum_u \breve{\phi}(u \mid x) P_u(x,x'), \qquad x,x' \in \mathsf{X}. \quad (7.12)$$

□

For a function $h \colon \mathsf{X} \to \mathbb{R}$, we use the following compact notation for conditional expectations:

$$\begin{aligned} P_u h\,(x) &\stackrel{\text{def}}{=} \sum_{x'} \breve{\phi}(u \mid x) P_u(x,x') h(x') = \mathsf{E}[h(X(k+1)) \mid X(k) = x\,,\, U(k) = u], \\ P_{\breve{\phi}} h\,(x) &\stackrel{\text{def}}{=} \sum_{x'} \sum_u \breve{\phi}(u \mid x) P_u(x,x') h(x') = \mathsf{E}[h(X(k+1)) \mid X(k) = x], \end{aligned} \quad (7.13)$$

where $\boldsymbol{X}$ is controlled using policy $\breve{\phi}$ in the second definition.

For Those of You Who Know Something about Stochastic Processes

The expression (7.9) is an example of an equation that is begging for streamlined notation. It is common to introduce a nondecreasing sequence of σ-algebras (a *filtration*) as a way to model the history appearing in this equation:

$$\mathcal{F}_k = \sigma\{\mathcal{X}(0), \dots, \mathcal{X}(k), U(0), \dots, U(k)\}. \quad (7.14)$$

If the "σ" looks foreign to you, then simply take $\mathcal{F}_k$ as a notational convention.

We have under any admissible input

$$\mathsf{P}\{X(k+1) = x' \mid \mathcal{F}_k; X(k) = x, U(k) = u\} = P_u(x,x') \quad (7.15a)$$

and for any function $h \colon \mathsf{X} \to \mathbb{R}$,

$$\mathsf{E}[h(X(k+1)) \mid \mathcal{F}_k; X(k) = x\,,\, U(k) = u] = \sum_{x'} P_u(x,x') h(x'), \quad (7.15b)$$

which is also expressed using the matrix notation analogous to (6.9b),

$$P_u h\,(x) \stackrel{\text{def}}{=} \sum_{x'} P_u(x,x')h(x'). \tag{7.15c}$$

7.2 Fluid Models for Approximation

It is often best to initially ignore disturbances, as a means to obtain intuition regarding a good policy. Many of the examples in this chapter are designed to illustrate this point.

One approach is to consider the *averaged dynamics* associated with (7.1):

$$\overline{\mathsf{F}}(x,u) \stackrel{\text{def}}{=} \mathsf{E}[\mathsf{F}(x,u,N(k+1))], \qquad x \in \mathsf{X},\ u \in \mathsf{U}(x), \tag{7.16}$$

which is independent of k since $\boldsymbol{N}$ is i.i.d. The associated *fluid model* is the deterministic state space model

$$x(k+1) = \overline{\mathsf{F}}(x(k),u(k)). \tag{7.17}$$

It is sometimes simpler to introduce a model in continuous time, with vector field

$$\overline{\mathsf{f}}(x,u) \stackrel{\text{def}}{=} \overline{\mathsf{F}}(x,u) - x, \qquad x \in \mathsf{X},\ u \in \mathsf{U}(x), \tag{7.18}$$

so that (7.17) is expressed as

$$x(k+1) - x(k) = \overline{\mathsf{f}}(x(k),u(k)),$$

and this is then approximated by the nonlinear state space model in continuous time:

$$\tfrac{d}{dt} x_t = \overline{\mathsf{f}}(x_t,u_t). \tag{7.19}$$

These deterministic systems appear in approximating a large number of interacting stochastic systems, where they are called *mean-field models*. We will sometimes use this language here, even when we are only interested in a single system in isolation.

For either of the approximations (7.17) or (7.19) to be meaningful, we require that the state space X be a convex subset of Euclidean space, and typically also approximate U by a convex set. This can bring challenges with notation: In [254], which concerns control of queueing networks, two models are considered side by side. The state space $\mathsf{X}_\diamond$ is used for a countable-state space model, and X denotes a convex state space for a deterministic fluid model. It is simplest here to allow the definition of X and U to change with the context.

Deterministic and Stochastic Control Aren't So Different

One justification of this claim is provided in Proposition 9.6, but this result requires more background than is available to us at this stage in the book. Justification is provided here based on comparison of DP equations for stochastic and deterministic models.

Assume that the state and action spaces are convex subsets of Euclidean space, and consider any function $J\colon \mathsf{X} \to \mathbb{R}$ whose gradient ∇J is continuous. The mean value theorem (MVT) tells us that for any states $x,x' \in \mathsf{X}$, there is a scalar $\varrho \in [0,1]$ such that

$$J(x') = J(x) + \nabla J\,(\overline{x}) \cdot \{x' - x\}, \qquad \overline{x} = \varrho x' + (1-\varrho)x. \tag{7.20}$$

In the remainder of this subsection, we show how to interpret the MVT with $J = J^\star$ equal to the total-cost value function for either of the deterministic fluid models. It will be useful to impose a Lipschitz bound on the gradient: For a Lipschitz constant $L > 0$,

$$\|\nabla J(x') - \nabla J(x)\| \le L\|x' - x\|, \qquad x,x' \in \mathsf{X}. \tag{7.21}$$

Fluid Model in Discrete Time

Let's first consider the total-cost value function $J^\star$ associated with the (deterministic) fluid model (7.17). This satisfies the DP equation

$$J^\star(x) = \min_u \{c(x,u) + J^\star(\overline{\mathrm{F}}(x,u))\}. \tag{7.22}$$

Apply the MVT (7.20) using

$$x' = X(k+1) \qquad \text{and} \qquad x = \overline{\mathrm{F}}(x,u) \stackrel{\text{def}}{=} \mathsf{E}[X(k+1) \mid X(k) = x, U(k) = u].$$

This gives, for any continuously differentiable function J,

$$\begin{aligned} J(X(k+1)) &= J(\overline{\mathrm{F}}(x,u)) + \nabla J(\bar{X}) \cdot \widetilde{X}(k+1) \\ &\qquad \text{with } \widetilde{X}(k+1) \stackrel{\text{def}}{=} X(k+1) - \overline{\mathrm{F}}(x,u), \end{aligned} \tag{7.23}$$

and where $\bar{X} = \varrho X(k+1) + (1-\varrho)\overline{\mathrm{F}}(x,u)$, with ϱ a random variable taking values in the interval [0,1].

Lemma 7.2 provides a link between deterministic and stochastic dynamic programming equations. Denote

$$\eta(k+1) = \{\nabla J(\bar{X}) - \nabla J(\overline{\mathrm{F}}(x,u))\} \cdot \widetilde{X}(k+1).$$

We have $\bar{X} - \overline{\mathrm{F}}(x,u) = \varrho\widetilde{X}(k+1)$, so that (7.21) implies the bound on η given in (7.24a).

Lemma 7.2 *Suppose that $J\colon \mathsf{X} \to \mathbb{R}$ is differentiable, and its gradient satisfies the Lipschitz bound* (7.21)*. Then the following approximation holds for each k: Letting $x = X(k)$ and $u = U(k)$,*

$$\begin{aligned} J(X(k+1)) &= J(\overline{\mathrm{F}}(x,u)) + \nabla J(\overline{\mathrm{F}}(x,u)) \cdot \widetilde{X}(k+1) + \eta(k+1), \\ |\eta(k+1)| &\le L\|\widetilde{X}(k+1)\|^2. \end{aligned} \tag{7.24a}$$

Consequently, for any x,u, and k, in the notation of (7.15)*,*

$$\begin{aligned} P_u J(x) &= J(\overline{\mathrm{F}}(x,u)) + \bar{\eta}(x,u), \\ \bar{\eta}(x,u) &= \mathsf{E}[\eta(k+1) \mid X(k) = x,\, U(k) = u] \\ &= \mathsf{E}[J(X(k+1)) \mid X(k) = x,\, U(k) = u] - J(\overline{\mathrm{F}}(x,u)). \end{aligned} \tag{7.24b}$$

□

The function $\bar{\eta}$ can be expressed in the more compact notation

$$\bar{\eta}(x,u) = P_u J(x) - J(\overline{\mathrm{F}}(x,u)).$$

Suppose that the function J is convex. Jensen's inequality implies the bound

$$\begin{aligned}\mathsf{E}[J(X(k+1)) \mid X(k)=x\,,\,U(k)=u] &\geq J\big(\mathsf{E}[X(k+1) \mid X(k)=x\,,\,U(k)=u]\big)\\ &= J(\overline{\mathrm{F}}(x,u)).\end{aligned}$$

It follows from (7.24b) that $\bar{\eta}$ is a nonnegative function of (x,u) in this special case.

Consider application of the lemma with $J = J^\star$. Provided the value function satisfies the assumptions of the lemma, the DP equation (7.22) for the fluid model implies a DP equation for the MDP model:

$$J^\star(x) = \min_u\{c(x,u) - \bar{\eta}(x,u) + P_u J^\star\,(x)\}\,, \qquad x \in \mathsf{X}. \tag{7.25}$$

In many examples to follow, we find that $\bar{\eta}$ is small relative to c, so that $J^\star$ approximately solves the ACOE. In fact, we don't want this term to be small, but rather small in the *span seminorm*:

$$\|\bar{\eta}\|_{\mathsf{sp}} \stackrel{\mathsf{def}}{=} \min_{\varrho}\max_{x,u} |\bar{\eta}(x,u) - \varrho|.$$

Letting ϱ° denote the minimizer and $c^J(x,u) = c(x,u) - [\bar{\eta}(x,u) - \varrho^\circ]$, (7.25) becomes

$$\varrho^\circ + J^\star(x) = \min_u\{c^J(x,u) + P_u J^\star\,(x)\}. \tag{7.26}$$

Hence $J^\star$ solves the ACOE with this cost function, and average cost ϱ°.

Fluid Model in Continuous Time

The value function $J^\star$ for total cost in continuous time solves the HJB equation:

$$0 = \min_u\{c(x,u) + \bar{\mathrm{f}}(x,u)\cdot\nabla J^\star\,(x)\}. \tag{7.27}$$

Justification of the continuous time model requires a different application of the MVT (7.20). We take $x' = X(k+1)$ as before, but now $x = X(k)$ to obtain

$$J(X(k+1)) = J(X(k)) + \nabla J\,(\bar{X})\cdot\{X(k+1) - X(k)\},$$

where $\bar{X}$ lies on the line segment with endpoints $X(k)$ and $X(k+1)$. Denote

$$\eta(k+1) = \{\nabla J\,(\bar{X}) - \nabla J\,(X(k))\}\cdot\{X(k+1) - X(k)\}.$$

Lemma 7.3 *Suppose that* $J\colon \mathsf{X} \to \mathbb{R}$ *is differentiable, and its gradient satisfies the Lipschitz bound* (7.21). *Then the following approximation holds for each* k*:*

$$\begin{aligned}J(X(k+1)) &= J(X(k)) + \nabla J\,(X(k))\cdot\{X(k+1) - X(k)\} + \eta(k+1),\\ |\eta(k+1)| &\leq L\|X(k+1) - X(k)\|^2.\end{aligned} \tag{7.28a}$$

Consequently, for any x, u, *and* k,

$$\begin{aligned}P_u J\,(x) - J(x) &= \nabla J\,(x)\cdot\bar{\mathrm{f}}(x,u) + \bar{\eta}(x,u),\\ \bar{\eta}(x,u) &= \mathsf{E}[\eta(k+1) \mid X(k)=x\,,\,U(k)=u].\end{aligned} \tag{7.28b}$$

□

Applying the lemma with $J = J^\star$ solving (7.27), we again arrive at the representation (7.25), whenever $J^\star$ satisfies the assumptions of Lemma 7.3. In practice, these two lemmas are useful as motivation to initially ignore disturbances in control design. Simple applications can be found in the remainder of this chapter:

(i) The continuous time fluid model provides approximations for the ACOE in queueing networks. The single queue is considered next, and a generalization follows in Section 7.4. A significant part of the monograph [254] is dedicated to these approximations. The strongest theory relates stability of a Markov model and stability of its fluid model.

(ii) The discrete time fluid model predicts the solution to the ACOE *exactly* for the linear quadratic Gaussian (LQG) model considered in Section 7.5. This is because the function $\bar{\eta}(x,u)$ appearing in Lemma 7.2 does not depend on (x,u).

7.3 Queues

The reflected random walk, introduced in Example 6.2.2, is a common model for the evolution of workload in the single server queue. The *controlled random walk* (CRW) queue has the same form, but with the introduction of an input:

$$X(k+1) = X(k) - S(k+1)U(k) + A(k+1), \tag{7.29}$$

where $N(k) \stackrel{\text{def}}{=} (S(k), A(k))$ is an i.i.d. sequence, and $S(k)$ has a Bernoulli distribution. It is assumed that $\mathsf{X} = \mathbb{Z}_+ \stackrel{\text{def}}{=} \{0,1,2,\ldots\}$ and $\mathsf{U} = \{0,1\}$. The input process is interpreted as the sequences of times at which the server is busy. It is subject to the constraint $U(k) \in \mathsf{U}(X(k))$ for each k, where $\mathsf{U}(x) = \{0,1\}$ for $x \geq 1$, and $\mathsf{U}(0) = \{0\}$ (the server can't work if there is nobody in the queue).

Example 6.2.3 provides a simple example in which $\boldsymbol{A}$ is an i.i.d. Bernoulli process with parameter α. Setting $S(k) = 1 - A(k)$ for each k, it follows that $\boldsymbol{S}$ is also an i.i.d. Bernoulli process with parameter $\mu = 1 - \alpha$. The MDP in this special case is the controlled M/M/1 queue:

(i) The following is controlled transition matrix:

$$P_u(x,x') = \begin{cases} \alpha & x' = x+1 \\ \mu & x' = x - u\ . \\ 0 & \text{else} \end{cases} \tag{7.30}$$

(ii) A standard cost function is $c(x,u) = x$ for each x, so that $\mathsf{E}[c(X(k))] = \mathsf{E}[X(k)]$ is the mean queue length at time k.

(iii) A typical objective in queueing network applications is average cost (7.2), which requires $\rho = \alpha/\mu < 1$.

The M/M/1 queue is obtained with the *nonidling* policy, $U(k) = \phi^\star(X(k))$, with $\phi^\star(x) = 1$ for $x \geq 1$. This is average cost optimal, resulting in $\eta^\star = \rho/(1-\rho)$.

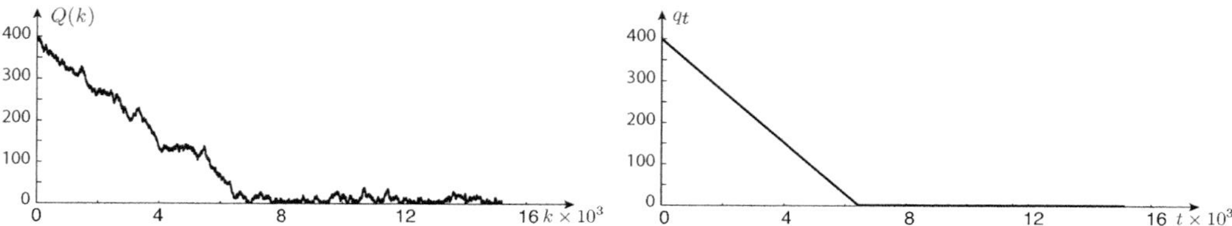

Figure 7.1 On the left is a sample path $X(k)$ of the M/M/1 queue with $\rho = \alpha/\mu = 0.9$, and $X(0) = 400$. On the right is a solution to the fluid model equation $\frac{d}{dt}q = (-\mu + \alpha)$ for $q > 0$, starting from the same initial condition.

7.3.1 Fluid Models and Value Functions

To define the fluid model for the CRW queue, we begin with a convex relaxation, taking $\mathsf{X} = \mathbb{R}_+$, and $\mathsf{U} = [0,1]$. The mean-field dynamics and mean-field vector field associated with (7.29) are

$$\begin{aligned}
\overline{\mathrm{F}}(x,u) &= \mathsf{E}[X(k) - S(k+1)U(k) + A(k+1) \mid X(k) = x\,,\, U(k) = u] \\
&= x - \mu u + \alpha, \\
\overline{\mathrm{f}}(x,u) &= -\mu u + \alpha.
\end{aligned}$$

Shown on the left-hand side of Figure 7.1 is a copy of the left-hand side of Figure 6.1, and on the right-hand side the evolution of the fluid model $\frac{d}{dt}q = \overline{\mathrm{f}}(q,u)$, under the nonidling policy $u = 1$ when $q > 0$, and $u = \rho = \alpha/\mu$ otherwise.

Let's now compare three value functions under the respective nonidling policies, and with cost function $c(x,u) = x$:

(i) It is easy to verify that a solution to the ACOE (7.5) is given by

$$h^\star(x) = \tfrac{1}{2}\frac{x^2 + x}{\mu - \alpha}. \tag{7.31}$$

(ii) The fluid value function in continuous time is easily obtained:

$$J^\star(x) = \int_0^\infty q_t\, dt = \int_0^W q_t\, dt = \tfrac{1}{2}W \times H \quad \text{(area of a triangle)},$$

where H refers to the height of the triangle defined by the linear path of q_t, and W the width, which is the time to reach zero. A glance at the plot on the right-hand side of Figure 7.1 should convince you that $H = q_0 = x$ and $W = x/(\mu - \alpha)$, so that

$$J^\star(x) = \tfrac{1}{2}\frac{x^2}{\mu - \alpha}.$$

We can compute the function $\bar{\eta}(x,u)$ appearing in (7.28b):

$$\begin{aligned}
\bar{\eta}(x,u) &= \mathsf{E}[J^\star(X(k+1)) - J^\star(X(k)) \mid X(k) = x\,,\, U(k) = u] - \nabla J^\star(x) \cdot \overline{\mathrm{f}}(x,u) \\
&= \tfrac{1}{2}\frac{u\mu + \alpha}{\mu - \alpha}.
\end{aligned}$$

This is bounded, and independent of x. It follows from Lemma 7.3 that $J^\star$ almost solves the ACOE for the MDP model.

(iii) Treatment of the fluid model in discrete time is a bit more complex:
 (a) The fluid model becomes $x(k+1) = \overline{\mathsf{F}}(x(k),u(k)) = x(k) - \mu u(k) + \alpha$.
 (b) The optimal policy is maximal, subject to the constraint that $x(k) \geq 0$ for each k,

$$\phi^\star(x) = \min\{1,(x+\alpha)/\mu\}.$$

 This results in $x(k+1) = 0$ when $x(k) \leq \mu - \alpha$.
 (c) The total cost is given by

$$J^\star(x) = \begin{cases} x & x \leq \mu - \alpha \\ \frac{1}{2}\dfrac{x^2}{\mu-\alpha} + \frac{1}{2}x & \text{otherwise} \end{cases}.$$

 This follows by direct computation, or verification that this function solves the DP equation $J^\star(x) = \min_u\{c(x,u) + J^\star(\overline{\mathsf{F}}(x,u))\}$, with boundary condition $J^\star(0) = 0$.

The strong solidarity of the value functions in this example is the product of two factors: The cost function c is Lipschitz continuous, and the MDP is "skip free" in a mean-square sense:

$$\max_{x,u} \mathsf{E}[\|X(k+1) - X(k)\|^2 \mid X(k) = x\,,\, U(k) = u] < \infty.$$

The example considered next violates the skip-free property. However, the continuous-time fluid model approximation is accurate because $\nabla J^\star$ vanishes as the state tends to infinity.

7.4 Speed Scaling

Dynamic speed scaling in computer processors uses algorithms that adjust processing speed in response to environment. While initially proposed for processor design [25], the ideas have impacted other application areas such as wireless communication.

Dynamic speed scaling is modeled as an MDP in discrete time, using a variation of the CRW queueing model. For each $k = 0,1,2,\ldots$, let $A(k)$ denote the job arrivals in this time slot, $X(k)$ the number of jobs in the queue awaiting service, and $U(k)$ the rate of service. The evolution of the state is then

$$X(k+1) = X(k) - U(k) + A(k+1), \qquad k \geq 0\,. \tag{7.32}$$

It is assumed that the arrival process $\boldsymbol{A}$ is i.i.d., so that this forms the dynamical system for an MDP model.

One source of complexity comes from integer constraints on the state and input: each evolve on the nonnegative integers $\mathsf{X} = \mathsf{U} = \mathbb{Z}_+ \stackrel{\text{def}}{=} \{0,1,2,3,\ldots\}$, and the constraint $U(k) \leq X(k)$ is also imposed, so that $\mathsf{U}(x) = \{u \in \mathbb{Z}_+ : u \leq x\}$.

The arrival process also evolves in $\mathbb{Z}_+$. The common mean and variance of $A(k)$ are assumed finite, with mean denoted α. Assume moreover that $\mathsf{P}\{A(1) = 0\} > 0$. Under this assumption, there is a stationary policy under which $\boldsymbol{X}$ becomes a Markov chain that is $x^\bullet$-irreducible with $x^\bullet = 0$ (see (6.57) and surrounding discussion). A simple example is

$$U(k) = \phi^0(X(k)) = X(k),$$

so that $X(k) = A(k)$ for $k \geq 1$.

The cost function we consider balances delay with power consumption:

$$c(x,u) = x + r\mathcal{P}(u),$$

where $\mathcal{P}$ denotes the power consumption as a function of the service rate u, and $r > 0$. We are then led to the ACOE to obtain an optimal policy,

$$\begin{aligned} h^\star(x) + \eta^\star &= \min_{u \in \mathsf{U}(x)} \{c(x,u) + P_u h^\star(x)\} \\ &= \min_{u \in \mathsf{U}(x)} \{x + r\mathcal{P}(u) + \mathsf{E}[h^\star(x - u + A(k))]\}. \end{aligned} \tag{7.33}$$

Here we will stick to quadratic cost for u, which is alleged to be a good approximation for computer processors.

7.4.1 Fluid Model

We cannot possibly solve the ACOE for the stochastic model (7.33) or even obtain any intuition in this discrete-stochastic world. In this example, we find that optimization of the fluid model in continuous time provides a near-perfect approximation of the ACOE solution.

We henceforth abandon integer constraints, and focus on the scalar state space model

$$\tfrac{d}{dt} x_t = -u_t + \alpha, \tag{7.34}$$

where α is the expectation of $A(k)$, and the processing speed u_t and queue length x_t are each nonnegative. For any cost function $c\colon \mathbb{R}_+ \times \mathbb{R}_+ \to \mathbb{R}_+$, the associated value function is denoted

$$J^\star(x) = \inf_{\boldsymbol{u}} \int_0^\infty c(x_t,u_t)\,dt, \qquad x_0 = x \in \mathbb{R}_+.$$

The HJB equation is then

$$0 = \min_{u \in \mathsf{U}(x)} \{c(x,u) + (-u + \alpha)\tfrac{d}{dx} J^\star(x)\}. \tag{7.35}$$

This is similar to the integrator model with polynomial cost considered in Section 3.9.4 (see (3.62)).

7.4.2 Computation and Solidarity

Consider the following choices for $\mathcal{P}(u)$ in the definition of $J^\star$:

Case 1: $\mathcal{P}(u) = u^2$.

In this case, $c(x,u)$ never vanishes, so that the total cost $J^\star(x)$ is never finite valued!

This challenge is resolved by considering instead the (weighted) *shortest path problem* (SPP):

$$K^\star(x) = \min_{\boldsymbol{u}} \int_0^{T_0} c(x_t,u_t)\,dt\,, \tag{7.36}$$

where $x_0 = x \in \mathbb{R}_+$, $T_0 \stackrel{\text{def}}{=} \min\{t : x_t = 0\}$ is the first time that x_t hits the origin, and the minimum is over $\boldsymbol{u}$ as before. The function $K^\star$ is finite valued and solves the HJB equation (7.35).

We next obtain bounds on $K^\star$ by considering simple policies. For example, if we take $u_t = \mu$ whenever $x_t > 0$, then (7.34) turns into the fluid model for the CRW queue. Assuming that $\mu > \alpha$, this policy is stabilizing, as seen by solving the state equation:

$$x_t = x_0 - (\mu - \alpha)t\,, \qquad 0 \le t \le T_0,$$

where $T_0 = (\mu - \alpha)^{-1}x_0$. Integrating gives the following:

$$K(x;\mu) \stackrel{\text{def}}{=} \int_0^{T_0} \big(x_t + ru_t^2\big)\,dt = \tfrac{1}{2}\frac{x^2}{\mu-\alpha} + r\mu^2\frac{x}{\mu-\alpha}\,, \qquad x_0 = x\,.$$

This implies that $K^\star(x)$ can grow no faster than a quadratic.

We can obtain a tighter bound by allowing the input to depend on more information: Consider the control law $u_t = \mu^\star(x)$ for $x_t > 0$ with $x_0 = x$, where $\mu^\star(x)$ is the minimum of the $K(x;\mu)$ overall $\mu > \alpha$. The first-order condition for optimality gives

$$\begin{aligned} 0 &= \frac{d}{d\mu}\Big\{\tfrac{1}{2}\frac{x^2}{\mu-\alpha} + r\mu^2\frac{x}{\mu-\alpha}\Big]\Big|_{\mu=\mu^\star} \\ &= -\big(\tfrac{1}{2}x^2 + rx[\mu^\star]^2\big)\frac{1}{(\mu^\star-\alpha)^2} + 2r\mu^\star\frac{x}{\mu^\star-\alpha}, \end{aligned}$$

where $\mu^\star = \mu^\star(x)$ in each appearance. This becomes a quadratic equation in μ after multiplying both sides by $(\mu^\star - \alpha)^2$, and can be solved to obtain

$$\mu^\star(x) = \alpha + \sqrt{\alpha^2 + x/r}\,, \qquad K(x;\mu^\star(x)) = \frac{1}{\sqrt{\alpha^2+x/r}}\big(\tfrac{1}{2}x^2 + rx[\mu^\star(x)]^2\big).$$

We have $K^\star(x) \le K(x;\mu^\star(x))$, which implies that the growth rate of $K^\star$ is no faster than $x^{3/2}$.

This bound is relatively tight, as we now see by solving the HJB equation (7.35): For $x > 0$,

$$0 = \min_{u\ge 0}\big(x + \tfrac{1}{2}u^2 + (-u+\alpha)\tfrac{d}{dx}K^\star(x)\big). \tag{7.37}$$

This is a first-order ODE with boundary condition $K^\star(0) = 0$. Its solution with $r = \frac{1}{2}$ is

$$K^\star(x) = \alpha x + \tfrac{1}{3}[(2x+\alpha^2)^{3/2} - \alpha^3]. \tag{7.38}$$

Assuming that $u^\star \ne 0$ in (7.37), the first-order optimality conditions give the optimal policy:

$$0 = \tfrac{d}{du}\big(x + \tfrac{1}{2}u^2 + (-u+\alpha)\tfrac{d}{dx}K^\star(x)\big).$$

$u^\star = \phi^{F\star}(x) = \frac{d}{dx}K^\star(x)$ is indeed the optimal policy for $x > 0$, as the derivative is nonnegative for all x.

Case 2: $\mathcal{P}(u) = (u-\alpha)^2$

This modification of the cost function leads to a far simpler expression for the SPP, which coincides with total cost: We now have $c(x^e,u^e) = 0$, where $x^e = 0$ and $u^e = \alpha$. For simplicity, we maintain $r = \frac{1}{2}$. The HJB equation (7.35) is similar to (7.37):

$$0 = \min_{u\ge 0}\big(x + \tfrac{1}{2}(u-\alpha)^2 + (-u+\alpha)\tfrac{d}{dx}J^\star(x)\big). \tag{7.39}$$

Assuming that $u^\star \neq 0$, we apply the first-order optimality conditions as before to obtain

$$0 = \tfrac{d}{du}\big(x + \tfrac{1}{2}(u-\alpha)^2 + (-u+\alpha)\tfrac{d}{dx}J^\star(x)\big) \Longrightarrow u^\star = \alpha + \tfrac{d}{dx}J^\star(x).$$

The closed-loop dynamics can be expressed as gradient descent:

$$\tfrac{d}{dt}x_t^\star = -u_t^\star + \alpha = -\tfrac{d}{dx}J^\star(x_t^\star).$$

Computation of $J^\star$ proceeds as before: Solving (7.39), subject to the boundary condition $J^\star(0) = 0$. Let's guess the solution as $J^\star(x) = bp^{-1}x^p$ for some $p \geq 1$ and $b > 0$. We obtain the following conclusions:

(i) The minimizer in the HJB equation (7.39) gives the policy for the fluid model:

$$\phi^{\text{F}\star}(x) = \alpha + \tfrac{d}{dx}J^\star(x) = \alpha + bx^{p-1}.$$

(ii) Substitution of $u^\star = \phi^{\text{F}\star}(x)$ into (7.39) gives the following:

$$0 = \big(x + \tfrac{1}{2}[\tfrac{d}{dx}J^\star(x)]^2 - [\tfrac{d}{dx}J^\star(x)]^2\big) = x - \tfrac{1}{2}b^2x^{2(p-1)}.$$

This is only possible for $b = \sqrt{2}$ and $p = 3/2$ (consistent with (7.38)).

(iii) For general $r > 0$, the value function and optimal policy for the fluid model are given by

$$J^\star(x) = \tfrac{4}{3}r^{1/2}x^{3/2} \qquad \text{and} \qquad \phi^{\text{F}\star}(x) = \alpha + \sqrt{x/r}\,. \tag{7.40}$$

Note that x and $[\phi^{\text{F}\star}(x) - \alpha]^2$ are each linear in x. This reflects the balance between state and control cost.

7.4.3 Solidarity

A numerical example illustrates the strong solidarity between the MDP model and its fluid model approximation.

Take $r = \frac{1}{2}$, and choose the marginal distribution of the arrival process to be a scaled geometric distribution:

$$A(k) = \Delta_A G(k), \qquad k \geq 1, \tag{7.41}$$

where $\Delta_A > 0$ and $\boldsymbol{G}$ is geometrically distributed on $\{0,1,\ldots\}$ with parameter p_A. The mean and variance of $A(k)$ are given by, respectively,

$$m_A = \Delta_A \frac{p_A}{1-p_A}, \qquad \sigma_A^2 = \frac{p_A}{(1-p_A)^2}\Delta_A^2, \tag{7.42}$$

with $p_A = 0.96$ and $\Delta_A = 1/24$ chosen so that the mean m_A is equal to unity:

$$1 = m_A = \Delta_A \frac{p_A}{1-p_A}. \tag{7.43}$$

You can read about the value iteration algorithm (VIA) in Appendix B.2, which is nearly identical to the definition for deterministic control systems seen in (3.8). In particular, the algorithm generates a sequence of functions $\{V_n\}$, each of which can be interpreted as a value function for a finite horizon optimal control problem:

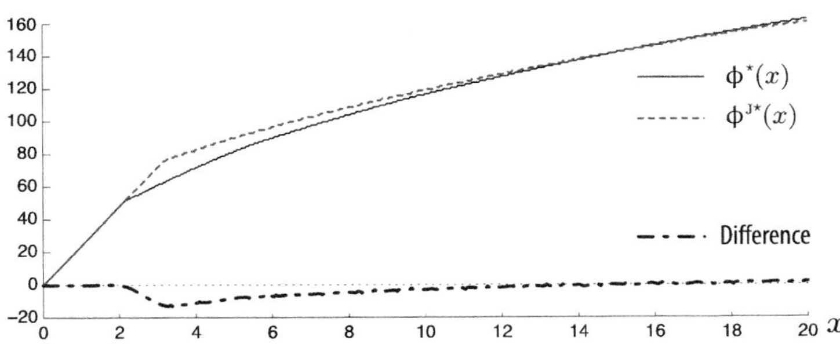

Figure 7.2 Comparison of optimal policies for the fluid and MDP models.

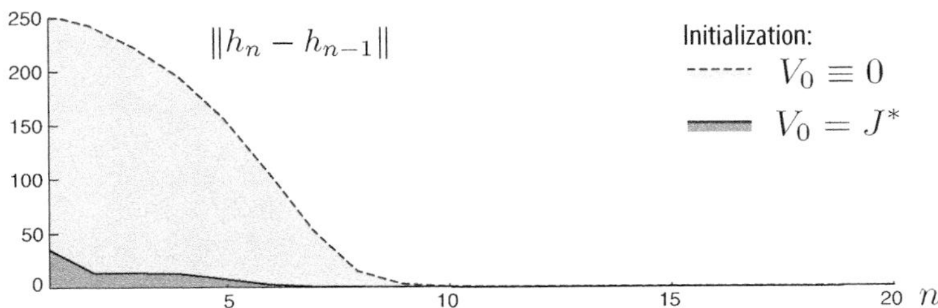

Figure 7.3 The convergence of value iteration for the quadratic cost function.

$$V_n(x) = \min_U \mathsf{E}\Big[\sum_{k=0}^{n-1} c(X(k),U(k)) + V_0(X(n)) \mid X(0) = x\Big]. \tag{7.44}$$

See (3.9) for the deterministic counterpart.

Shown in Figure 7.2 is a comparison of the optimal policy, computed numerically using value iteration, and the optimal policy for the fluid model. Recall that the constraint $U(k) \le X(k)$ is imposed in the stochastic model. This constraint is imposed in the policy shown in the figure, so that

$$\phi^{J^\star}(x) = \min(x, \phi^{F\star}(x)).$$

For MDP models, the sequence of differences $\{h_n(x) = V_n(x) - V_n(x^\bullet)\}$ consists of approximations of the relative value function. The convergence of $\{h_n\}$ to $h^\star$ is illustrated in Figure 7.3 using $x^\bullet = 0$. The error $\|h_{n+1} - h_n\|$ is *much smaller* for initial n when the algorithm is initialized using the fluid value function.

7.5 LQG

The discrete-time linear system equations are defined by the linear state space model of Section 2.3.3, with the introduction of disturbance process $\boldsymbol{N}$ and observation noise $\boldsymbol{W}$:

$$\begin{aligned} X(k+1) &= FX(k) + GU(k) + N(k+1), \\ Y(k) &= HX(k) + W(k). \end{aligned} \tag{7.45}$$

The joint process $\{N(k), W(k) : k \ge 0\}$ is assumed to be independent and identically distributed. The process $\boldsymbol{N}$ represents a system disturbance, in the sense that it is uncontrolled and impacts the state (whose entries represent physical quantities). The variable

$W(k)$ corrupts our measurement of $HX(k)$ at time k. It is assumed that each are zero mean processes, with finite covariances denoted Σ_N, Σ_W, respectively.

7.5.1 Fluid Model Dynamics

Under the assumption that the disturbance has zero mean, the fluid model in discrete time is the linear state space model introduced in (2.13a):

$$x(k+1) = Fx(k) + Gu(k), \quad k \ge 0.$$

Before turning to control comparisons, let's compare the dynamics of the two models without control:

$$x(k+1) = Fx(k) \quad \text{and} \quad X(k+1) = FX(k) + N(k+1), \qquad k \ge 0. \tag{7.46}$$

Consider the special case used as an example in Section 2.4.6, with

$$F = I + 0.02A, \qquad A = \begin{pmatrix} -0.2, & 1 \\ -1, & -0.2 \end{pmatrix}.$$

The fluid model in continuous time is defined by

$$\tfrac{d}{dt}x = \bar{\mathsf{f}}(x) = 0.02Ax \quad \text{(in this example, with } u \equiv 0\text{).}$$

This is entirely consistent with the construction of F (which was based on an Euler approximation).

We can now explain the nature of the disturbance process used to obtain the plots shown in Figure 2.7: $\boldsymbol{N}$ was chosen i.i.d. and Gaussian, with rank-deficient covariance: $N(k) = gV(k)$ with $V(k)$ scalar $N(0,1)$ and $g = 2.5\binom{1}{1}$. Trajectories of the two state processes are shown in Figure 2.7. A careful look at the figure on the right reveals the degeneracy of the noise, which influences the state directly in directions $\pm g$.

7.5.2 DP Equations

The linear dynamics in (7.45) are the explanation for the "L" in LQG, and the "Q" appears because we adopt the quadratic cost appearing in the deterministic LQR framework:

$$c(x,u) = x^{\intercal}Sx + u^{\intercal}Ru, \tag{7.47}$$

with $S \ge 0$ and $R > 0$. We postpone explanation of the "G" because it is irrelevant until we explain why we care about the measurements $\boldsymbol{Y}$.

The infinite horizon objective is typically infinite, so let's consider first the finite-horizon problem

$$J(x) = \mathsf{E}\Big[X(\mathcal{N})^{\intercal}R_0X(\mathcal{N}) + \sum_{k=0}^{\mathcal{N}-1}(X(k)^{\intercal}SX(k) + U(k)^{\intercal}RU(k)) \mid X(0) = x\Big] \tag{7.48}$$

with $R_0 \ge 0$. The minimization of J is easily obtained as linear state feedback:

Proposition 7.4 (i) *The minimization of* (7.48) *over all possibly nonlinear policies is obtained using linear state feedback* $U(k) = -K_kX(k)$, *in which the feedback gain matrix is*

$$K_k = [R + G^{\intercal} M_{k+1} G]^{-1} G^{\intercal} M_{k+1} F,$$

where $\{M_k\}$ *is determined by the matrix Riccati difference equation, which runs backward in time:*

$$M_k = F^{\intercal}\left(M_{k+1} - M_{k+1}G\left(G^{\intercal}M_{k+1}G + R\right)^{-1}G^{\intercal}M_{k+1}\right)F + S,$$

with terminal condition $M_{\mathcal{N}} = R_0$.

(ii) *The value function is quadratic:* $J^{\star}_{\mathcal{N}}(x) = J^{\star}_{\mathcal{N}}(0) + x^{\intercal} M_0 x$.

(iii) *The following limits exist:*

$$\eta^{\star} = \lim_{\mathcal{N}\to\infty} \frac{1}{\mathcal{N}} J^{\star}_{\mathcal{N}}(x) \qquad \text{(independent of } x\text{)}.$$

$$h^{\star}(x) = \lim_{\mathcal{N}\to\infty} [J^{\star}_{\mathcal{N}}(x) - J^{\star}_{\mathcal{N}}(0)], \qquad x \in \mathsf{X}.$$

The pair solve the ACOE (7.5), *for which* $\eta^{\star}$ *is the optimal average cost. The average-cost optimal policy* (7.6) *is linear state feedback:*

$$\phi^{\star}(x) = -K^{\star}x \quad \text{with} \quad K^{\star} = [R + G^{\intercal} M^{\star} G]^{-1} G^{\intercal} M^{\star} F,$$

where $M^{\star}$ *is the solution to the algebraic Riccati equation (ARE)* (3.40)*:*

$$M^{\star} = F^{\intercal}\left(M^{\star} - M^{\star}G(R + G^{\intercal}M^{\star}G)^{-1}G^{\intercal}M^{\star}\right)F + S. \qquad \square$$

A remarkable takeaway from this result is that the solution to the finite horizon and average-cost control problems does not depend in any way on the distribution of the disturbance, beyond the assumption that they are zero mean with finite variance, and the standing i.i.d. assumptions (even the independence assumption can be relaxed, subject to a restricted definition of optimality [7, 80]). In addition, the optimal policy for the average-cost optimal control problem coincides with the optimal policy for the associated fluid model (in discrete time) with total-cost criterion: Recall (3.39).

The only reason to impose assumptions on the distributions is when we come to the next topic.

7.5.3 Partial Observations

If only $\boldsymbol{Y}$ is observed, then we may attempt to minimize J over all functions of these observations. That is, restrict inputs to functions of current and past observations:

$$U(k) = \phi_k(Y(0), \dots, Y(k)). \tag{7.49}$$

An explicit solution can be obtained under the assumption that $(\boldsymbol{N}, \boldsymbol{W})$ is jointly Gaussian:

Proposition 7.5 *Suppose that* $(\boldsymbol{N}, \boldsymbol{W})$ *is jointly Gaussian, and independent of* $X(0)$*. Then:*

(i) *The solution to the finite horizon optimal control problem, in which* J *is minimized over all input sequences of the form* (7.49)*, is obtained using*

$$U(k) = -K_k \widehat{X}(k).$$

The gain K_k *is the same matrix sequence introduced in Proposition 7.4.*

The estimate $\widehat{X}(k)$ *is defined recursively as follows, based on this important fact: The conditional distribution of* $X(k)$ *given* Y_0^k *is Gaussian* $N(m_k, \Sigma_k)$ *in which*

(a) *The conditional mean* $m_k = \widehat{X}(k)$ *evolves as the time-varying linear system,*

$$\widehat{X}(k+1) = F\widehat{X}(k) + GU(k) + L_{k+1}[Y(k+1) - \widehat{Y}(k+1 \mid k)],$$
$$\widehat{Y}(k+1 \mid k) = H\widehat{X}(k+1 \mid k) = H[F\widehat{X}(k) + GU(k)], \qquad k \geq 0$$

with initial condition

$$\widehat{X}(0) = \mathsf{E}[X(0)] + L_0[Y(0) - H\mathsf{E}[X(0)]].$$

(b) *The filter gains are defined by*

$$L_k = \Sigma_{k+1|k} H^{\intercal}[\Sigma_W + H\Sigma_{k+1|k}H^{\intercal}]^{-1}, \qquad k \geq -1.$$

(c) *The conditional covariance does not depend on the observations, but evolves according to a deterministic Riccati recursion:*

$$\begin{aligned}\Sigma_{k+1|k} &= F\Sigma_k F^{\intercal} + \Sigma_N,\\ \Sigma_{k+1} &= \Sigma_{k+1|k} - \Sigma_{k+1|k}H^{\intercal}\left[H\Sigma_{k+1|k}H^{\intercal} + \Sigma_W\right]^{-1} H\Sigma_{k+1|k}\end{aligned} \tag{7.50}$$

with initial condition

$$\Sigma_{0|-1} = \mathsf{E}\big[\widetilde{X}(0)\widetilde{X}(0)^{\intercal}\big], \qquad \widetilde{X}(0) = X(0) - \widehat{X}(0).$$

(ii) *The solution to the average-cost optimal control problem, subject to the constraint* (7.49) *on the input sequence, is obtained using static linear feedback:*

$$U(k) = -K^{\star}\widehat{X}(k),$$

where $\widehat{X}(k)$ *is the conditional mean, as in (i).* □

One step in the proof of the proposition is that the cost can be expressed in terms of the new state $\widehat{\boldsymbol{X}}$ as follows:

$$\begin{aligned}\mathsf{E}[c(X(k),U(k)] &= \mathsf{E}[X(k)^{\intercal}SX(k) + U(k)^{\intercal}RU(k)]\\ &= \mathsf{E}[\widehat{X}(k)^{\intercal}S\widehat{X}(k) + U(k)^{\intercal}RU(k)] + \mathsf{E}[\widetilde{X}(k)^{\intercal}S\widetilde{X}(k)],\end{aligned}$$

in which the tilde denotes error: $\widetilde{X}(k) = X(k) - \widehat{X}(k)$. The last term is independent of control:

$$\mathsf{E}[\widetilde{X}(k)^{\intercal}S\widetilde{X}(k)] = \text{trace}\,(\Sigma_k S).$$

This leads to the *separation principle*: The optimal input is the naive "plug-in" control law:

$$U(k) = \phi^{\star}(\widehat{X}(k)) = K^{\star}\widehat{X}(k), \tag{7.51}$$

where K^* is the feedback gain obtained for the control problem with full observations.

This optimal control solution is known as *certainty-equivalent form*. Please don't forget that the certainty-equivalence conclusion is very particular to the assumptions imposed. It may be tempting to use the policy $U(k) = \phi^{\star}(\widehat{X}(k))$ in more general settings when the state is only partially observed. In general the optimal feedback law requires far more information regarding the conditional *distribution* of the state process. Appendix C contains a derivation of the optimal policy for more general partially observed control systems.

The next examples are intended to explore the role of partial information and the creation of a "belief state."

7.6 A Queueing Game

We return now to the two-station network model with four-dimensional queue-length processes introduced in Section 3.9.3.

An MDP model can be obtained by analogy with the fluid model described there. We might opt for an extension of the CRW model for the single queue (7.29), in which the four buffers evolve in discrete time as follows:

$$\begin{aligned} X_1(k+1) &= X_1(k) - S_1(k+1)U_1(k) + A_1(k+1), \\ X_2(k+1) &= X_2(k) - S_2(k+1)U_2(k) + S_1(k+1)U_1(k), \\ X_3(k+1) &= X_3(k) - S_3(k+1)U_3(k) + A_3(k+1), \\ X_4(k+1) &= X_4(k) - S_4(k+1)U_4(k) + S_3(k+1)U_3(k), \end{aligned}$$

in which each $S_i(k)$ is Bernoulli with parameter μ_i, and each $A_i(k)$ has mean α_i and finite variance. For this to be a controlled Markov chain, it is necessary to assume that the six-dimensional stochastic process $(\boldsymbol{S}, \boldsymbol{A})$ is i.i.d. The input process is subject to the same constraints as the fluid model, but in addition it is assumed that $U_i(k)$ takes on values zero or one for each i and k. Solidarity between the fluid model and this MDP model is investigated in [159], where you can find numerical results similar to what was obtained for the single queue.

We can now explain the simulation shown on the left-hand side of Figure 3.6: The random variables $S_i(k)$, $A_j(k)$ are each Bernoulli and highly dependent in the sense that only one is nonzero at each time k.

Let's consider a problem we *cannot solve* using the theory in this book: Restrict each input to be a function of only *local* information. This is a game, because the decision at a station is based on only the history of buffer levels at that station. We consider a *cooperative* setting, in which the two players (the stations) have a common goal of minimizing the long-run average cost.

By imposing symmetry, we can simplify the problem by imposing the following constraint: denote $X^{\mathrm{I}}(k) = (X_1(k), X_4(k))$, $X^{\mathrm{II}}(k) = (X_3(k), X_2(k))$, and assume the input is of the form

$$\begin{aligned} U_1(k) &= \phi_a(X^{\mathrm{I}}(k)), \qquad & U_2(k) &= \phi_b(X^{\mathrm{II}}(k)), \\ U_4(k) &= \phi_b(X^{\mathrm{I}}(k)), \qquad & U_3(k) &= \phi_a(X^{\mathrm{II}}(k)). \end{aligned}$$

Our goal is to obtain $\phi^\star = (\phi_a^\star, \phi_b^\star)$ that minimizes the average cost, with $c(x,u) = \sum x_i$. The information structure may be motivated by the desire to reduce communication cost, which is definitely the case in applications to global supply chains. In this case, the network models a single business, with geographically separated manufacturing. Noncooperative games can also be addressed using the concepts introduced here.

This is a crude approach. In particular, why not allow the $U_1(k)$ and $U_4(k)$ to depend on the history of local observations, $\{X^{\mathrm{I}}(i) : i \le k\}$? Appendix C contains hints at how one might construct a sufficient statistic for control.

The information constraints in this example destroy any justification for the application of the dynamic programming equations of MDP theory, but we may still apply MDP algorithms and see if we get lucky. In this simple example we do get lucky.

Here is an approach that leads to a successful control solution in this example: The goal is to obtain a sequence of approximating MDP models with state process $\boldsymbol{X}^{\mathrm{I}}$ and input process $\boldsymbol{U}^{\mathrm{I}}$, with $U^{\mathrm{I}}(k) = (U_1(k), U_4(k))$. We simultaneously obtain an identical sequence of MDP models with state process $\boldsymbol{X}^{\mathrm{II}}$ and input $U^{\mathrm{II}}(k) = (U_3(k), U_2(k))$.

The procedure requires initialization: Choose a randomized policy $\breve{\phi}^0 = (\breve{\phi}^0_a, \breve{\phi}^0_b)$ so that the resulting Markov chain $\boldsymbol{X}$ is positive recurrent. Then follow these steps for $m = 0$ to M, with $M > 1$ fixed, or determined by some stopping criterion:

(i) System identification: Simulate the Markov chain using policy $\breve{\phi}^m$ to obtain an estimate of the steady-state distribution:

$$\begin{aligned}\varpi^m_n(z,v,z') &= \frac{1}{n}\sum_{k=0}^{n-1}\Big(\mathbb{1}\{X^{\mathrm{I}}(k) = z, U^{\mathrm{I}}(k) = v, X^{\mathrm{I}}(k+1) = z'\Big)\\ &\quad + \frac{1}{n}\sum_{k=0}^{n-1}\Big(\mathbb{1}\{X^{\mathrm{II}}(k) = z, U^{\mathrm{II}}(k) = v, X^{\mathrm{II}}(k+1) = z'\Big)\end{aligned}$$

for each $z = (z_1, z_2)$, $z' = (z_1', z_2') \in \mathbb{Z}^2_+$, and $v \in \{v^0, v^1, v^2\} \stackrel{\text{def}}{=} \{\binom{0}{0}, \binom{1}{0}, \binom{0}{1}\}$. Based on this, define a controlled transition matrix:

$$P^{(m)}_v(z,z') = \frac{1}{\gamma_m(z,v)}\varpi^m_n(z,v,z'), \qquad \gamma_m(z,v) \stackrel{\text{def}}{=} \sum_{z'} \varpi^m_n(z,v,z'). \tag{7.52}$$

(ii) Cost identification: Include in your simulation the following estimate:

$$\begin{aligned}\mathcal{C}^m(z,v) &= \frac{1}{n}\sum_{k=0}^{n-1} c(X(k))\Big(\mathbb{1}\{X^{\mathrm{I}}(k) = z, U^{\mathrm{I}}(k) = v\Big)\\ &\quad + \frac{1}{n}\sum_{k=0}^{n-1} c(X(k))\Big(\mathbb{1}\{X^{\mathrm{II}}(k) = z, U^{\mathrm{II}}(k) = v\Big)\end{aligned}$$

for each $z \in \mathbb{Z}^2_+$, and $v \in \{0,1\}^2$. Based on this, define a cost function:

$$c^{(m)}(z,v) = \frac{1}{\gamma_m(z,v)}\mathcal{C}^m(z,v).$$

(iii) Policy update: Solve the ACOE with controlled transition matrix $P^{(m)}$ and cost function $c^{(m)}$ to obtain a policy ϕ^{m+1}.

Define $\breve{\phi}^{m+1}$ to be a randomized policy approximating ϕ^{m+1}, and go to step (i), with m incremented to $m+1$. □

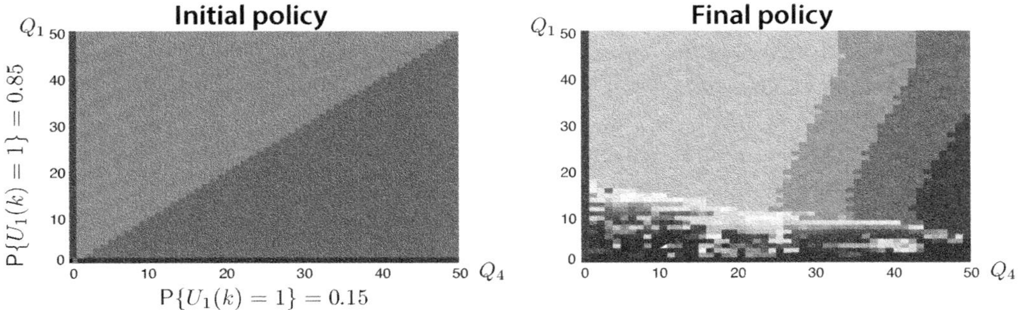

Figure 7.4 Distributed control in a two-station queueing network.

The system identification step is motivated by Bayes's rule. Suppose that $Z(k) = X^{\mathrm{I}}(k)$ were indeed an MDP model with input $V(k) = (U_1(k),U_4(k))$. Its controlled transition matrix is then defined by the ratio of probabilities:

$$\begin{aligned} P_v(z,z') &= \mathsf{P}\{Z(k+1) = z' \mid Z(k) = z\,,\, V(k) = v\} \\ &= \frac{1}{\mathsf{P}\{Z(k) = z\,,\, V(k) = v\}}\mathsf{P}\{Z(k+1) = z'\,,Z(k) = z\,,\, V(k) = v\}. \end{aligned}$$

The cost identification step has similar motivation. For large n, we have the approximation

$$c^{(m)}(z,v) \approx \mathsf{E}[c(X(k)) \mid Z(k) = z,\, V(k) = v], \tag{7.53}$$

so that the steady-state mean of $c^{(m)}(Z(k),V(k))$ approximates the steady-state average cost.

Shown on the right in Figure 7.4 is an illustration of a policy obtained using this approach. The initial policy was chosen to be a perturbation of the "serve the longest queue" policy:

$$\breve{\phi}^0(v^1 \mid z) = \begin{cases} 0.85 & \text{if } z_1 \geq z_2 \\ 0.15 & \text{else} \end{cases},$$

with $\breve{\phi}^0(v^2 \mid z) = 1 - \breve{\phi}^0(v^1 \mid z)$ (provided $z_2 \geq 1$).

The final policy shown on the right in the figure is more similar to a threshold policy of the form "Serve buffer 4 whenever $X_1 \leq \overline{x}_1$ and $X_4 \geq 1$," where $\overline{x}_1 \approx 10$. The resulting performance is close to that of the centralized optimal solution [255].

See the cover of this book for a clearer view of the policy, which shows the plot on the right in Figure 7.4 before it was converted to grayscale. The color indicates the probability that $U_1(k)$ is equal to one (which is one minus the probability that $U_4(k)$ is equal to one, provided $X_1(k) + X_4(k) \geq 1$). The dark blue indicates a value of approximately 0.1, and dark red approximately 0.9.

7.7 Controlling Rover with Partial Information

We now turn to a setting in which information is limited, but the theory and algorithms in this book are directly applicable. The ideas are illustrated with an extremely simple example.

In past stochastic control course offerings at the university of Florida, the following question is asked: *How can we control a rover on Planet Pluto?* Planetary exploration is frequently on our minds – the Kennedy Space Center is only about 150 miles away from Gainesville, Florida.

The setting: An autonomous rover on Pluto depends on its solar panels for energy, but there is not a lot of energy.[1] Its goal is to collect as much energy as possible, but it can be clumsy. It is close to a small hill and collects the most energy when it is at the top of the hill, but it has a tendency to roll off the hill, and it then takes energy to get back up.

The model: Rover can be in one of three states: top of the hill, rolling down the hill, or at the bottom of the hill: $\mathsf{X} = \{\mathtt{T},\mathtt{B},\mathtt{R}\}$. The input space is $\mathsf{U} = \{\mathtt{D},\not{\mathtt{D}}\}$, corresponding to the actions "drive" or "don't drive."

The state dynamics are summarized in the following three cases, distinguished by location:

(1) Rover on top. If driving, then it is still at the top of the hill in the next period with probability 0.8, and rolling down in the next period with probability 0.2. If not driving, these probabilities are 0.75 and 0.25, respectively.

(2) Rolling. If driving, then with probability 0.9 it is at the top of the hill in the next period, and with probability 0.1 it moves to the bottom.
If not driving, then with probability 1 it is at the bottom in the next period.

(3) Bottom. If driving, then it remains at the bottom with probability 0.9, and is rolling in the next period with probability 0.1. If not driving, it remains on the bottom with probability 1.

Cost: *Rover wants to maximize energy*. Energy collected (reward) depends on position and action:

Action: \ Position:	Top	Rolling	Bottom
Driving	1	0	0
Not driving	3	0	0

A realistic model would include energy storage. The example is simplistic for many obvious reasons beyond the lack of storage, but it is a good example to illustrate a few basic ideas.

7.7.1 Control with Partial Observations

The input $\boldsymbol{U}$ is limited to noisy observations of the state process $\boldsymbol{X}$. This is modeled by an *observation sequence* $\boldsymbol{Y}$, which takes on values zero or one. An observation can only can tell us if we are at the top of the hill: $Y(k) = 0$ if $X(k) = \mathtt{R}$ or $X(k) = \mathtt{B}$. If $X(k) = \mathtt{T}$, then $Y(k) = 1$ if $U(k-1) = \mathtt{D}$, and $Y(k) = 1$ with probability $\varrho \in (0,1)$ if $U(k-1) = \not{\mathtt{D}}$. In other words,

$$Y(k) = \mathbb{1}\{X(k) = \mathtt{T},\, U(k-1) = \mathtt{D}\} + \Gamma(k)\mathbb{1}\{X(k) = \mathtt{T},\, U(k-1) = \not{\mathtt{D}}\}, \qquad (7.54)$$

where $\{\Gamma(k)\}$ is an i.i.d. Bernoulli sequence with parameter ϱ.

This is known as a partially observed MDP (POMDP model). It is a remarkable fact that an optimal control solution is obtained by state feedback, provided we modify the definition of "state."

[1] https://science.nasa.gov/science-news/science-at-nasa/2002/08jan_sunshine.

In the POMDP literature, we introduce the *belief state* $\mathcal{X}(k)$, which is nothing more than the conditional pmf for the state $X(k)$, given observations up to time k. In the example considered here, the belief state evolves on the simplex $\mathcal{S}$ (a two-dimensional region in $\mathbb{R}^3_+$), with the interpretation

$$\mathcal{X}_x(k) = \mathsf{P}\{X(k) = x \mid Y(0), \dots, Y(k)\}, \qquad x \in \mathsf{X} = \{\mathtt{T},\mathtt{B},\mathtt{R}\}.$$

For the average- or discounted-cost criterion, the optimal policy can be represented as state feedback:

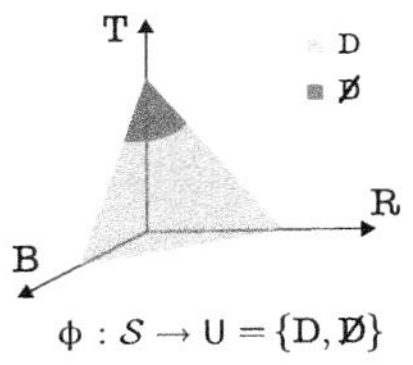

$$U^\star(k) = \phi^\star(\mathcal{X}(k)),$$

$\phi : \mathcal{S} \to \mathsf{U} = \{\mathtt{D}, \not{\mathtt{D}}\}$

Figure 7.5 A candidate policy for Rover with partial observations.

where $\phi^\star \colon \mathcal{S} \to \mathsf{U}$. The LQG solution described in Proposition 7.5 is an example of this construction in which the belief state can be summarized by the conditional mean and conditional covariance.

A brief survey of POMDP theory is found in Appendix C, where you can find a recursive update formula for the belief state:

$$\mathcal{X}(k+1) = \mathcal{M}(\mathcal{X}(k), Y(k+1), U(k)), \quad k \geq 0,$$

with the details of the update map $\mathcal{M}$ provided in Proposition C.3.

Computation of $\phi^\star$ is a major challenge in POMDP practice because the state space $\mathcal{S}$ is never finite. We are left to look for approximation techniques, and reinforcement learning provides many tools for this purpose.

Suppose that the solution to the fully observed problem is defined by $U(k) = \not{\mathtt{D}}$ if and only if $X(k) = \mathtt{T}$. The policy shown in Figure 7.5 is then well motivated in the partially observed setting. This was obtained based on the following threshold formula, given nonnegative constants a_T, a_R, a_B, r:

$$\phi(b) = \begin{cases} \not{\mathtt{D}} & \text{if } a_T[b_\mathtt{T} - 1]^2 + a_R b_\mathtt{R}^2 + a_B b_\mathtt{B}^2 \leq r \\ \mathtt{D} & \text{else} \end{cases}, \qquad b \in \mathcal{S}.$$

The degenerate case using $r = 0$ is not excluded, giving $\phi(b) = \not{\mathtt{D}}$ *only* if $b_\mathtt{T} = 1$.

This example and the example in Section 7.6 expose several challenges and opportunities:

(i) Information constraints on the input can render MDP theory inapplicable, but MDP algorithms may still lead to a useful policy.

(ii) If the POMDP assumptions are valid, then the theory is very rich, but direct application of computational tools such as VIA is a significant challenge. Reinforcement learning is a great alternative.

(iii) RL + POMDP is not model-free, since the nonlinear filter that generates the belief state depends crucially on a model. In practice, we either use a model, or replace the belief state with some other "features" to create a "pseudo state" that is believed to include enough information for reliable control.

7.8 Bandits

Our next partially observed control problem is known as a multi-armed bandit, which is a great vehicle to explain "exploitation" and "exploration" in reinforcement learning. As for the name *bandit*, consider a room full of slot machines, with different expected profit (or loss) on pulling an arm. This is called a K-armed bandit if there are a total of K distinct arms.

Other applications of varying degrees of usefulness are

▲ Game Playing
Exploitation: Play the move you believe is best.
Exploration: Play an experimental move.

▲ Restaurant Selection
Exploitation: Go to your favorite restaurant.
Exploration: Try a new restaurant.

▲ Oil Drilling
Exploitation: Drill at the best-known location.
Exploration: Drill at a new location.

▲ Online Banner Advertisements
Exploitation: Show the most successful advertisement.
Exploration: Show a different advertisement.

How would you play one of these bandit games?

7.8.1 Bandit Models

There are many models that capture the bandit theme. Here is one that may be regarded as a degenerate MDP model.

For the K-armed bandit, we assume the existence of something like a state process, denoted $\boldsymbol{Z}$, that evolves on $\mathbb{R}^K$. In the simple model described here, it is assumed that this sequence is i.i.d. with finite mean. The input evolves in the action space $\mathsf{U} = \{1, \dots, K\}$, and has no impact on $\boldsymbol{Z}$. The reward received at time k is

$$R(k) = \sum_{u=1}^{K} \mathbb{1}\{U(k) = u\} Z_u(k).$$

That is, $R(k) = Z_u(k)$ if $U(k) = u$. An input sequence $\boldsymbol{U}$ is admissible if $U(k)$ is a (possibly randomized) function of the observed rewards $\{R(j) : j < k\}$ for every time k. Our goal is to construct $\boldsymbol{U}$ for which the average reward is maximized.

Let's consider two extreme cases:

(i) If the "state" $Z(k)$ is observed at each time k, then obviously

$$U^\star(k) = \arg\max_{1 \le u \le K} Z_u(k).$$

This is optimal for any criterion: finite horizon, discounted, or average reward. However, we only observe the rewards received $\{R(j) : j < k\}$, so this policy is not feasible.

(ii) The infinite horizon optimal reward is defined by

$$\eta^\star = \max \lim_{N\to\infty} \frac{1}{N} \sum_{k=1}^{N} R(k).$$

Denote $\overline{r}_u = \mathsf{E}[Z_u(k)]$ (assumed independent of k), and $\overline{r}^\star = \max_u \overline{r}_u$. An optimizing policy is given by the open-loop strategy,

$$U^\star(k) = \arg\max_{1\le u\le K} \overline{r}_u.$$

This is not feasible unless the means are given.

We can of course estimate $\{\overline{r}_u : 1 \le u \le K\}$ using Monte Carlo, which is an example of exploration. However, for any action $u \in \{1,\dots,K\}$, an accurate estimate of $\overline{r}_u$ will likely require frequent selection of this action. In the big-money applications of bandit theory (such as in advertising), we are learning as we attempt to maximize profit. This means we must minimize the time spent exploring with inevitable suboptimal actions, which motivates a finer notion of optimal reward:

Regret: For a given time horizon $\mathcal{N}$, the regret is defined as the sum

$$L_{\mathcal{N}} = \sum_{k=1}^{\mathcal{N}} \{\overline{r}^\star - R(k)\}. \tag{7.55}$$

Under mild additional assumptions, its mean grows logarithmically in $\mathcal{N}$ for the best policies.

7.8.2 Bayesian Bandits

If we can formulate the bandit problem within an MDP setting, theory in Appendix C predicts that we can express an optimal policy as a form of state feedback:

$$U^\star(k) = \phi^\star_{\mathcal{N}-k}(\mathcal{X}(k)), \qquad 0 \le k \le \mathcal{N}. \tag{7.56}$$

The *belief state* $\mathcal{X}(k)$ coincides with the conditional distribution of the state at time k, given observations up to time k. This requires a Bayesian setting for which the reward is some randomized function of the state. As a hopefully simple starting point, let's turn to a linear-Gaussian model for which the belief state is finite dimensional.

In the *Gaussian bandit*, we create a state process evolving on $\mathbb{R}^K$ that is static: $X(k) = X(0)$ for each k. While static, the state can be modeled by the linear dynamics

$$X(k+1) = X(k), \qquad k \ge 0. \tag{7.57a}$$

The vector $X \stackrel{\text{def}}{=} X(0)$ is assumed random, with Gaussian distribution. The process $\boldsymbol{Z}$ is also assumed Gaussian:

$$Z(k) = X(k) + W(k),$$

in which $\boldsymbol{W}$ is an i.i.d. Gaussian stochastic process with zero mean, and independent of $\boldsymbol{X}$. The reward received at time k is interpreted as an observation equation:

$$Y(k) = R(k) = H_k X(k) + H_k W(k), \tag{7.57b}$$

where H_k is the K-dimensional row vector with entries $H_k(i) = \mathbb{1}\{U(k) = i\}$.

The pair of equations (7.57) looks like a special case of (7.45) in which the input $U(k)$ is hidden in the row vector H_k, and the observation noise has a slightly different form due to the multiplication by H_k in (7.57b). The conclusion of Proposition 7.5 stands: The conditional distribution of $X(k)$ given all observations up to time k is Gaussian, and the filtering equations simplify greatly.

For this model, we can replace the belief state by the conditional mean and covariance that define the conditional distribution. That is, we can take $\mathcal{X}(k) = \{\widehat{X}(k), \Sigma_k\}$ in the state feedback architecture (7.56). The dependency on both the conditional mean and covariance invites questions:

▸ Policy structure: *How might* $\phi^\star$ *depend upon the sufficient statistic* $\{\widehat{X}(k), \Sigma_k\}$ *at time* k*?* The certainty equivalent policy, generalizing (7.51), is

$$U(k) = \arg\max_u \widehat{X}_u(k). \tag{7.58}$$

This coincides with $\phi^\star_{\mathcal{N}-k}(\mathcal{X}(k))$ in a special case: $\Sigma_k \equiv 0$, so that $\widehat{X}_u(k) = X_u$ for each u.

Conversely, surely this is a *terrible* approach when the conditional covariance is far from zero, so there is significant uncertainty in the reward anticipated from one or more arms. We need to explore when there is high uncertainty.

▸ Exploration: *How much is required?* The following are anticipated for a good policy, in which the time horizon is not bounded:

(i) $\Sigma_k \to 0$ as $k \to \infty$ (uncertainty may lead to excessive suboptimal pulls).
(ii) The rate of convergence of $\Sigma_k(i,i)$ to zero will be slow if X_i is less than $X^\star \stackrel{\text{def}}{=} \max_j X_j$.

The regret grows logarithmically in $\mathcal{N}$ if and only if $n_i(k)\mathbb{1}\{X_i < X^\star\}$ grows logarithmically in k for each i, where

$$n_i(k) = \sum_{j=1}^{k} \mathbb{1}\{U(j) = i\}. \tag{7.59}$$

We might then ask, *is there a conflict between exploration and exploitation*? If $n_i(k)$ is constrained to grow logarithmically in k for "bad" i (exploitation), how can we be sure that $\Sigma_k(i,i)$ vanishes as $k \to \infty$ (exploration)? A careful look at the evolution of the conditional covariance shows that there is no conflict. Since $F = I$ and $\Sigma_N = 0$, the update equation for Σ_k is both simple and insightful:

Proposition 7.6 *The covariance evolution for the Gaussian bandit is summarized as follows:*

(i) $\Sigma_{k+1|k} = \Sigma_k$ *for each* $k \geq 0$.
(ii) *The inverse of the covariance has the representation*

$$\Sigma_k^{-1} = \Sigma_0^{-1} + D_k, \tag{7.60}$$

in which D_k is a diagonal matrix with entries

$$D_k(i,i) = \frac{1}{\sigma^2_{W_i}} n_i(k),$$

where $\sigma^2_{W_i}$ is the variance of the Gaussian random variable $W_i(k)$ (independent of k).

Consequently, $\Sigma_k \to 0$ as $k \to \infty$ if and only if each arm is pulled infinitely often.

Proof Part (i) follows from the first equation in (7.50), and from the second we obtain the update equation

$$\Sigma_k = \Sigma_{k-1} - \gamma^{-1} V V^\intercal, \qquad \textit{with} \quad V = \Sigma_{k-1} H_k^\intercal, \quad \gamma = H_k \Sigma_{k-1} H_k^\intercal + H_k \Sigma_W H_k.$$

The Matrix Inversion Lemma gives

$$\Sigma_k^{-1} = \Sigma_{k-1}^{-1} + \Sigma_{k-1}^{-1} V \big[\gamma - V^\intercal \Sigma_{k-1}^{-1} V\big]^{-1} V^\intercal \Sigma_{k-1}^{-1},$$

which simplifies dramatically when we insert the definition of V and γ:

$$\Sigma_k^{-1} = \Sigma_{k-1}^{-1} + \frac{1}{H_k \Sigma_W H_k^\intercal} H_k^\intercal H_k.$$

The second term is a matrix with all entries zero, except a signal term on the diagonal. Specifically, for all i,j,

$$\Sigma_k^{-1}(i,j) = \begin{cases} \Sigma_0^{-1}(i,j) & i \neq j \\ \Sigma_{k-1}^{-1}(i,i) + \frac{1}{\sigma^2_{W_i}} \mathbb{1}\{U(k) = i\} & i = j \end{cases},$$

which establishes (ii). □

The proposition implies that to compute the conditional covariance, it is sufficient to keep track of the number of times that we pull each arm. Moreover,

$$\lim_{k \to \infty} \Sigma_k^{-1}(i,i) = \Sigma_0^{-1}(i,i) + \frac{1}{\sigma^2_{W_i}} \sum_{k=1}^{\infty} \mathbb{1}\{U(k) = i\}.$$

Hence a logarithmic upper bound on $n_i(k)$ does not prevent convergence of $\Sigma_k(i,i)$ to zero.

7.8.3 Naive Optimism Can Be Successful

Bandit theory is typically posed in a setting far more general than Gaussian bandits, and algorithm design is often based on a frequentist setting. That is, algorithms are based on empirical pmfs, and there is no use for a prior distribution on the rewards.

A model is required for analysis. A typical choice is a parameterized model in which the vector-valued process $\boldsymbol{Z}$ is i.i.d., with

$$Z_u(k) \sim f(\,\cdot\,; \theta_u), \tag{7.61}$$

in which $f(\,\cdot\,; \theta_u)$ is a density on $\mathbb{R}$ for each $u \in \mathsf{U}$, with parameter $\theta \in \mathbb{R}^K$. Hence for each u,

$$\overline{r}_u = \mathsf{E}[Z_u(k)] = \int f(r; \theta_u) dr.$$

Once again, we are not interested in estimating θ_u if $\overline{r}_u < \overline{r}^\star$, but we don't know in advance which arms are suboptimal in this sense.

The frequentist will consider alternative representations of the regret (7.55). The following is most valuable in obtaining sharp bounds:

$$\mathsf{E}[L_{\mathcal{N}}] = \mathcal{N} \sum_u \mathsf{E}[\{\overline{r}^\star - \overline{r}_u\} \widehat{\upmu}_{\mathcal{N}}(u)],$$

in which $\widehat{\upmu}_{\mathcal{N}}(u)$ is the empirical pmf:

$$\widehat{\upmu}_{\mathcal{N}}(u) = \frac{1}{\mathcal{N}} n_u(\mathcal{N}) = \frac{1}{\mathcal{N}} \sum_{k=1}^{\mathcal{N}} \mathbb{1}\{U(k) = u\}, \qquad u \in \mathsf{U}. \tag{7.62}$$

The goal of optimal control is to steer the empirical pmf so that $\{\overline{r}^\star - \overline{r}_u\} \widehat{\upmu}_{\mathcal{N}}(u) \approx 0$ for each u.

To avoid taking expectations, we might use the representation

$$L_{\mathcal{N}} = \sum_u \{\overline{r}^\star - \hat{r}_u(\mathcal{N})\} n_u(\mathcal{N}), \tag{7.63}$$

in which the "reward estimates" are defined by

$$\hat{r}_u(k) = \frac{1}{n_u(k)} \sum_{j=1}^{k} \mathbb{1}\{U(j) = u\} Z_u(j).$$

The certainty equivalent policy $U(k+1) = \arg\max_u \hat{r}_u(k)$ is again doomed to failure. However, a small tweak results in a very good policy.

The idea is to define recursively a sequence of positive scalars $\{\varrho_u(k) : k \geq 1,\ 1 \leq u \leq K\}$, denote

$$\text{UCB}_u(k) = \hat{r}_u(k) + \varrho_u(k)$$

and ensure that the policy is designed so that these values serve as *upper confidence bounds* in the sense that

$$\lim_{k \to \infty} \mathsf{P}\{\text{UCB}_u(k) > \overline{r}_u\} = 1. \tag{7.64}$$

One version of the UCB algorithm is the simple optimistic rule:

$$\begin{aligned} U(k+1) &\in \arg\max_i \text{UCB}_i(k), && 0 \leq k \leq \mathcal{N} - 1, \\ \text{using} \quad \varrho_u(k) &= b_u \sqrt{\log(k)/[1 + n_u(k)]}, && 1 \leq u \leq K, \end{aligned} \tag{7.65}$$

where $\{b_u\}$ are positive constants chosen by the user. Regardless of their values, the decision rule (7.65) enforces $n_u(k) \to \infty$ as $k \to \infty$ for each u, and results in logarithmic regret under mild assumptions [216].

Figure 7.6 shows an example of this policy with $K = 4$. In this four-armed bandit, we have $\overline{r}^\star = \overline{r}_2$. The value $U(k+1) = 3$ is selected through the rule (7.65), even though $\overline{r}_3 < \overline{r}_2$. In this example, it is likely that $U(k+j) = 3$ for several consecutive values of $j > 1$, but the value of $\text{UCB}_3(k+j)$ is also likely to decrease each time this suboptimal arm is selected.

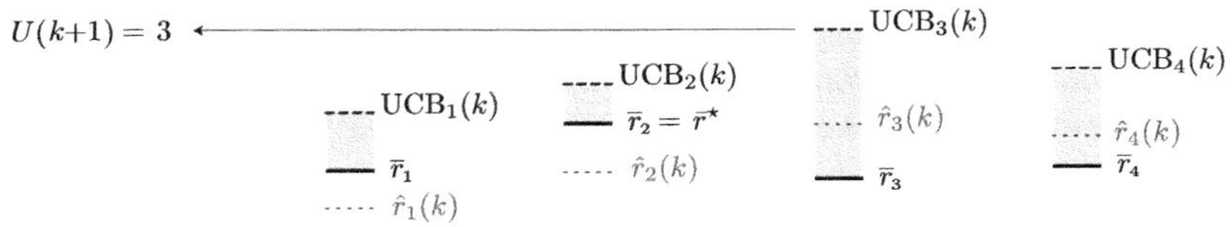

Figure 7.6 Four-armed bandit under the UCB policy (7.65).

Finer Bounds

Lai and Robbins in 1985 considered the special setting (7.61), and introduced a procedure to obtain a sharp logarithmic lower bound on the regret. It is based on the relative entropy (or Kullback–Leibler divergence) between the densities. For each $\theta,\xi \in \mathbb{R}^K$, this is defined by

$$D(\theta\|\xi) = \int \log\Big(\frac{f(r;\theta)}{f(r;\xi)}\Big) f(r;\theta)dr. \tag{7.66}$$

It is obviously zero for $\xi = \theta$, and is also known to be everywhere nonnegative. The bound obtained in [208] for an optimal algorithm, minimizing the mean regret, is expressed as an approximation:

$$\mathsf{E}[L_{\mathcal{N}}] \sim \Big(\sum_j \frac{1}{D(\theta_j\|\theta^\star)}[\overline{r}^\star - \overline{r}_j]\Big) \log(\mathcal{N}), \tag{7.67}$$

where the symbol $\sim$ means that the ratio tends to one as $\mathcal{N} \to \infty$.

7.9 Exercises

7.1 *Rover with Full Observations.*

(a) Sketch a graphical model of this MDP, as for an uncontrolled Markov chain (to make sense of the complex description of the rover).

(b) Obtain the solution to the ACOE $(h^\star,\eta^\star,\phi^\star)$ using VIA, or using common sense!

That is, it shouldn't be hard to guess $\phi^\star$, and then you simply solve Poisson's equation for a three-state Markov chain.

7.2 This problem is intended as preparation for Exercise 7.3. Consider the state space model

$$x(k+1) = (1+a)x(k) - u(k), \tag{7.68}$$

where $a > 0$. The state and input evolve on $\mathbb{R}_+$. Solve the total-cost Bellman equation with the cost function $c(x,u) = x + u$. *Suggestion:* Guess a polynomial representation for $J^\star$ and experiment.

7.3 Consider the MDP model in which the state evolves as follows:

$$X(k+1) = X(k) + \sum_{i=1}^{X(k)} A^i(k+1) - U(k) + N(k+1).$$

The state and input evolve on $\mathbb{Z}_+ = \{0,1,2,\ldots\}$. Assume the following:

(i) $\{A^i(k),\, N(k) \geq 1, i \geq 1\}$ are each i.i.d., with distributions supported on $\mathbb{Z}_+$.

(ii) The mean $\overline{n} = \mathsf{E}[N(1)]$ is finite.

(iii) $0 < \overline{a} < 1$, where $\overline{a} = \mathsf{E}[A^1(1)]$.
(iv) The cost function is $c(x,u) = x + u$.
(v) The input is subject to the hard constraints, $0 \le U(k) \le X(k)$.
Find $h^\star$ and $\eta^\star$ that solve the ACOE.

7.4 *Basic MDP Modeling.* Each quarter, the marketing manager of a retail store divides customers into two classes based on their purchase behavior in the previous quarter. Denote the classes as L for low and H for high. The manager wishes to determine to which classes of customers she should send quarterly catalogs.

The cost of sending a catalog is \$15 per customer, and the expected purchase depends on the customer's class and the manager's action. If a customer is in class L and receives a catalog, then the expected purchase in the current quarter is \$20, and if a class L customer does not receive a catalog her expected purchase is \$10. If a customer is in class H and receives a catalog, then her expected purchase is \$50, and if a class H customer does not receive a catalog her expected purchase is \$25.

The decision whether or not to send a catalog to a customer also affects the customer's classification in the subsequent quarter. If a customer is class L at the start of the present quarter, then the probability he is in class L at the subsequent quarter is 0.3 if he receives a catalog and 0.5 if he does not. If a customer is class H in the current period, then the probability that he remains in class H in the subsequent period is 0.8 if he receives a catalog and 0.4 if he does not.

Of course, the manager would like to maximize her average reward.

(a) Formulate this as an infinite horizon discounted Markov decision problem. Describe the controlled transition matrix and one-step "cost function" $c(x,u)$ (the negative of the reward function).
(b) Formulate an associated fluid model. Discrete time is best. This can be described as a one-dimensional model with state x, in which $x(k)$ denotes the number of class H customers at time k (relaxing integer constraints, as we always do for the fluid model).
(c) After reviewing Section B.2, describe the VIA for this MDP model. Explain in detail how V_{n+1} is obtained from V_n *for this specific model.*

7.5 Consider the speed-scaling model with *abandonment*, in which the arrival process takes values in $\{0,1\}$, and is conditionally independent:

$$\mathsf{P}\{A(k+1) = 1 \mid X_0^k, U_0^k; X(k) = x\} = \begin{cases} \beta^x & x \le 100 \\ 0 & x > 100 \end{cases}$$

with $0 < \beta < 1$ the abandonment rate.

The dynamics remain the same, $X(k+1) = X(k) - U(k) + A(k+1)$.

(aa) Provide a clear proof that $\boldsymbol{X}$ is a Markov chain on a finite state space, when $\boldsymbol{U}$ is defined by a stationary Markov policy satisfying $\phi(n) \ge 1$ if $n \ge 100$).

The remainder of the assignment is numerical, and requires algorithms from Section B.2. You will approximate the solution to the ACOE using $\beta = 0.99$, and $c(x,u) = x + u^2$. Given an approximation h, you have a policy denoted $\phi^h(x) = \arg\min_u\{c(x,u) + P_u h\,(x)\}$, and an estimate of $\eta^\star$. Stop the algorithm when the maximal normalized Bellman error $\bar{\mathcal{E}}(h)$ is less than $\varepsilon = 10^{-2}$, with

$$\bar{\mathcal{E}}(h) \stackrel{\text{def}}{=} \min_r \Bigl(\max_{0 \le x \le 100} \frac{1}{\max[1, c(x,\phi^h(x))]} \bigl| h(x) + r - \{c(x,\phi^h(x)) + P_{\phi^h} h\,(x)\} \bigr| \Bigr).$$

In all three cases, plot $\phi^\star(x)$ as a function of x (the answers may differ wildly!).

Comment on what you believe is the most efficient algorithm. You may want to explore the tolerance and see how total time depends on tolerance: $\varepsilon = 10^{-5}$, $10^{-7}, \dots$

(a) VIA with initial value function V_0 of your choosing. You might solve a fluid model optimal control problem for this model to obtain a useful initialization.

(b) PIA with initial policy of your choosing (review Perron–Frobenius for this).

(c) LP approach: Maximize η over all (h,η), subject to the set of inequality constraints:

$$c(x) - \eta + \sum_{y \in \mathsf{X}} P_u(x,y)h(y) - h(x) \geq 0 \qquad \text{[more than } 10^3 \text{ constraints on } h]$$

for each $x \in \mathsf{X} = \{0,1,\dots,100\}$ and $u \in \mathsf{U}(x) = \{0,1,\dots,x\}$.

7.6 Continuing with Exercise 7.4, let's now compute an optimal policy for varying customer populations. Let N denote the total number of customers, and solve the problem three times, for $N = 10^2$, 10^4, and 10^6 (reduce if necessary).

(a) Let's start with control of a fluid model in discrete time,

$$x(k+1) = x(k) + \overline{\mathrm{F}}(x(k),u(k)),$$

where $u(k)$ is the two-dimensional vector that indicates the number of catalogs sent to high/low customers, and $x(k)$ is the number of high-ranked customers.

An equilibrium is a triple $(x,u) = (x,u^H,u^L)$ such that $\overline{\mathrm{F}}(x,u) = 0$. Denote the cheapest equilibrium by

$$(x^\star,u^\star) = \mathop{\arg\min}_{(x,u)}\{c(x,u) : \text{such that } \overline{\mathrm{F}}(x,u) = 0\}.$$

You can easily compute this! The fluid value function might be defined as

$$K^\star(x) = \min \sum_{k=0}^{T^\star-1} [c(x(k),u(k)) - c(x^\star,u^\star)],$$

where $T^\star$ is the first time that the pair $(x^\star,u^\star)$ is reached. You might find this hard to compute, so use this:

$$J^\star(x) = \lim_{n\to\infty} [J_n^\star(x) - J_n^\star(x^\star)],$$

where $J_n^\star$ is the finite horizon value function, and $x^\star$ is defined as before.

Compute $J^\star$ and the optimal policy using value iteration.

(b) Compute the solution to the ACOE using value iteration. Try initializing with zero and with $J^\star$, and compare your results.

(c) Compute the solution to the ACOE using policy iteration (you must jump ahead to Section 9.1 or Appendix B). Try an initial policy that is completely stupid (your choice), and also a policy based on the optimal policy for the fluid model.

Provide plots of both policies and value functions in (a)–(c). Discuss your findings!

As a criterion for convergence, choose $\varepsilon = 10^{-2}$, and stop the algorithm when the span seminorm of the Bellman error is no greater than ε:

$$\varepsilon \geq \|\mathcal{E}\|_{\mathsf{sp}} \stackrel{\text{def}}{=} \tfrac{1}{2}[\max_x \mathcal{E}(x) - \min_x \mathcal{E}(x)].$$

As a criterion for performance of the algorithm, compute the number of `flops` required in each experiment (fluid and stochastic).

Figure 7.7 Single-station demand-driven model. The deficit buffer is nonempty, which means that $X(k) < 0$.

7.7 You are told that $(\boldsymbol{X},\boldsymbol{U})$ is the state-input sequence for a controlled Markov chain with finite state space and input space: $\mathsf{X} = \{1,2,3,4,5\}$ and $\mathsf{U} = \{0,1\}$. The controlled transition matrix P_u is not known. Explain how you would estimate it given a sequence of observations of the Markov chain $\{X(k) : 0 \le k \le 10^6\}$. As part of your answer, you must *explain how you would choose the input sequence* $\{U(k) : 0 \le k \le 10^6\}$.

7.8 Consider the average-cost optimal control problem with cost function c and relative value function $h^\star$, solving the ACOE,

$$\min_{u\in\mathsf{U}}\{c(x,u) + P_u h^\star(x)\} = \min_{u\in\mathsf{U}}\{c(x,u) + \sum_{y\in\mathsf{X}} P_u(x,y)h^\star(y)\} = h^\star(x) + \eta^\star.$$

Assume that the state space and action space are finite. Consider the value iteration algorithm designed to approximate the Q-function (7.7):

$$Q_{n+1}(x,u) = c(x,u) + P_u\underline{Q}_n(x), \qquad \text{where } \underline{Q}_n(y) = \min_{u\in\mathsf{U}} Q_n(y,u).$$

For each n, the function Q_n is the value function for a finite horizon optimal control problem, similar to what we saw for ordinary value iteration (see (7.44)). Conjecture on the form of this optimization problem, and see if you can justify your claim.

7.9 Consider the one-dimensional inventory model defined by the recursion

$$X(k+1) = X(k) + S(k+1)U(k) - A(k+1), \qquad k \ge 0,\ X(0) \in \mathsf{X} = \mathbb{R},$$

where $(\boldsymbol{S},\boldsymbol{A})$ is i.i.d. as in the CRW queue. However, in this model, $A(k)$ represents new demand for some product at time k, and $S(k)$ denotes a potential product completion at time k. A positive value of $X(k)$ corresponds to excess inventory and a negative value deficit. This is a simplified version of the model shown in Figure 7.7 since we are modeling only the inventory buffer and not the buffer representing storage of raw materials.

A piecewise linear cost function $c\colon \mathbb{R} \to \mathbb{R}_+$ is given, of the form $c(x) = c_- x_- + c_+ x_+$ with $0 < c_- < c_+$, $x_+ = \max(x,0)$, and $x_- = \max(-x,0)$.

In this exercise, you will restrict to a threshold policy of the following form: Given a constant $\overline{x} > 0$, define $\boldsymbol{U}$ so that $X'(k) \stackrel{\text{def}}{=} \overline{x} - X(k)$ is precisely the CRW queue under the nonidling policy. Hence $X(k)$ is restricted to the state space $\mathsf{X}_{\overline{x}} \stackrel{\text{def}}{=} \{\overline{x}, \overline{x}-1, \overline{x}-2, \dots\}$, and $U(k) = 1$ if and only if $X(k) \le \overline{x} - 1$.

For the same threshold, the fluid model is defined by

$$\frac{d}{dt}x_t = \begin{cases} \mu - \alpha & \text{if } x < \overline{x} \\ 0 & x = \overline{x} \end{cases}$$

for any initial condition $x_0 = x \le \overline{x}$, where μ and α are the mean values of $S(k)$ and $A(k)$ respectively. That is, for $x_0 < \overline{x}$, x_t increases linearly until it reaches the level $\overline{x}$, and thereafter stays at this level.

(a) Compute the fluid value function:

$$J_{\overline{x}}(x) = \int_0^\infty [c(x_t) - c(\overline{x})]\, dt, \qquad x \le \overline{x}.$$

Verify that $J_{\overline{x}}$ is continuously differentiable and satisfies the dynamic programming equation,

$$(\mu - \alpha)J'_{\overline{x}}(x) = -[c(x) - c(\overline{x})], \qquad x_0 = x \le \overline{x}.$$

(b) Using Lemma 7.3, show that the function $b \stackrel{\text{def}}{=} [P - I]J_{\overline{x}} + c$ is bounded on $\mathsf{X}_{\overline{x}}$. This approximation implies that $J_{\overline{x}}$ "almost" solves Poisson's equation for $\boldsymbol{X}$.

(c) Estimate the optimal value of $\overline{x}$ that minimizes the average cost using simulation. Take $c_+ = 10c_-$, $\rho = \alpha/\mu = 0.9$, and choose the distribution of (A,S) so that the variance of $A(k) - S(k)$ is between 1 and 5.

Perform two sets of simulation experiments. In each case, you will conduct 10 experiments with 10 different values of $\overline{x}$. Let $(\boldsymbol{S}^i, \boldsymbol{A}^i)$ denote the sample paths used in the ith experiment, $1 \le i \le 10$.

Experiment 1: Ten independent runs are called, so that $(\boldsymbol{S}^i, \boldsymbol{A}^i)$ is independent of $(\boldsymbol{S}^j, \boldsymbol{A}^j)$ for $i \neq j$.

Experiment 2: For this you must use a form of *coupling*: $(\boldsymbol{S}^i, \boldsymbol{A}^i) = (\boldsymbol{S}^1, \boldsymbol{A}^1)$ for each i. There is a way to set the "seed" in the random number generator to simplify this experiment, so that the code for Experiment 2 is similar to Experiment 1.

Discuss your findings. Do the plots of average cost versus $\overline{x}$ look better in Experiment 1 or 2? Explain why this can be expected.

7.10 Consider the one-dimensional inventory model Exercise 7.9:

$$X(k+1) = X(k) + S(k+1)U(k) - A(k+1), \qquad k \ge 0,\ X(0) \in \mathsf{X} = \mathbb{R},$$

where $(\boldsymbol{S}, \boldsymbol{A})$ is i.i.d. as in the CRW queue.

(a) Suppose that $h^\star$ is *convex*. Explain why the function

$$h^1(x) = \mathsf{E}[h^\star(x + A(k+1))]$$

is convex in x. Explain why this implies that there is a threshold policy, as defined in Exercise 7.9. *The following property of convex functions will be helpful*: If $g\colon \mathbb{R} \to \mathbb{R}$ is convex, then for any $y > 0$,

$$g(x+y) - g(x) \quad \text{is nondecreasing.}$$

Why? Because, g is convex if and only if its derivative $\frac{d}{dx}g(x)$ is nondecreasing.

(b) *Policy construction of Clark and Scarf.* Let π^0 denote the steady-state distribution for $\boldsymbol{X}$ obtained using $\overline{x} = 0$. Explain why it follows that for arbitrary $\overline{x}$, the resulting steady-state distribution π is characterized as follows: For any function $g\colon \mathbb{R} \to \mathbb{R}$,

$$\mathsf{E}_\pi[g(X)] = \mathsf{E}_{\pi^0}[g(X + \overline{x})].$$

Letting $g = c$, obtain a characterization of $\overline{x}^\star$ through differentiation.

(c) *Use value iteration* to approximate the optimal policy. Note that you will have to truncate the state space and return to an integer lattice. For example, take $\mathsf{X} = \{\overline{x} \pm m : 0 \le m \le M\}$ for some fixed M, with $\overline{x}$ an initial guess for a good threshold value.

Try two initializations: $V_0 \equiv 0$, and V_0 inspired by a fluid value function. Compare the speed of convergence of $V_{n+1}(0) - V_n(0)$ to $\eta^\star$ in the two cases.

7.11 Consider a modification of the "well-motivated but unstable" policy used for the queueing network considered in Section 3.9.3. The problem with this policy is the focus was entirely on draining from the two "exit buffers," without considering potential starvation of a station. In this exercise, you will consider the following modification for the CRW model: Given a pair of thresholds (τ_1, τ_2),

- The policy is assumed *nonidling*: $U_1(k) + U_4(k) = 1$ whenever $Q_1(k) + Q_4(k) \geq 1$, and $U_2(k) + U_3(k) = 1$ whenever $Q_2(k) + Q_3(k) \geq 1$.
  Subject to this constraint are priorities at each station:
- Priority is given to buffer 4 at Station 1 if $Q_2(k) + Q_3(k) \leq \tau_1$.
- Priority is given to buffer 2 at Station 2 if $Q_1(k) + Q_4(k) \leq \tau_2$.

Obtain a plot of average cost as a function of (τ_1, τ_2) via simulation. Perform multiple runs with at least one pair so you can estimate the variance of your cost estimates.

After you learn about actor-critic methods, you might try this to optimize (τ_1, τ_2) *using one of these algorithms.*

7.12 Consider a discrete-time scalar process initialized with $X(0) = 1$ and evolving according to

$$X(k+1) = \begin{cases} 2X(k) & \text{with probability } 2/3 \\ X(k)/2 & \text{with probability } 1/3 \end{cases}.$$

At each time t, we can opt to stop the process and receive a payoff of $G(X(k))$ or to continue. If the process is not stopped within 100 time steps, it terminates automatically and the payoff of $G(X(100))$ is received. The goal is to maximize the expected discounted payoff. Solve the problem using VIA, with discount factor $\gamma = 0.95$, $G(x) = \max(0, 1-x)$ and $G(x) = \min(0, 1-x)$. In each case, provide the maximal expected payoff.

7.13 *Risk-Sensitive Optimal Control.* This exercise is a follow-up to Exercise 6.22.

(a) Consider the finite horizon optimal control problem, with value function

$$h_{\mathcal{N}}{}^\star(x) = \min_{\boldsymbol{U}} \mathsf{E}_x[Z], \qquad Z = \sum_{k=0}^{\mathcal{N}-1} c(X(k), U(k)) + V_0(X_{\mathcal{N}}), \quad X(0) = x \in \mathsf{X}. \tag{7.69}$$

The corresponding risk-sensitive control problem is motivated by the need to penalize variance while minimizing the mean of Z: For fixed $r > 0$, the risk-sensitive value function is defined by

$$H_{\mathcal{N}}{}^\star(x) = \min_{\boldsymbol{U}} \log\big(\mathsf{E}_x[\exp(rZ)]\big), \qquad X(0) = x \in \mathsf{X}. \tag{7.70}$$

Obtain a dynamic programming equation for (7.70): Given $H^\star_{\mathcal{N}-1}$, obtain an update equation for $H_{\mathcal{N}}{}^\star$.

It will help to assume $\mathsf{X} = \{1, \ldots, n\}$ is finite, and your solution will depend on the matrix with nonnegative entries:

$$R_u(i,j) = \exp(rc(i,u))P_u(i,j).$$

(b) Postulate a dynamic programming equation for the infinite horizon problem with objective

$$H^{\star}_{\infty}(x) = \min_{U} \lim_{\mathcal{N}\to\infty} \frac{1}{\mathcal{N}} \log\Big\{\mathsf{E}_x\Big[\exp\Big(r\sum_{k=0}^{\mathcal{N}} c(X(k),U(k))\Big)\Big]\Big\}, \qquad X(0) = x \in \mathsf{X}.$$

See Exercise 6.22 for inspiration.

(c) Solve the risk-sensitive control problem numerically for the MDP in Exercise 7.1.

7.14 *Rover with Partial Information.* Review Proposition C.3 and write down the formula for the nonlinear filter for the POMDP described in Section 7.7:

$$\mathcal{X}(k+1) = \mathcal{M}(\mathcal{X}(k),Y(k+1),U(k)), \quad k \geq 0.$$

Take $\{\Gamma(k)\}$ in (7.54) to be i.i.d. Bernoulli with parameter $\varrho = 0.1$.

The fact that observations depend on the input doesn't cause any difficulties: You will need to define $q(y \mid x,u)$].

(a) The MAP estimator of $X(k)$ given observations up to time k is given by $\widehat{X}^{\mathsf{MAP}}(k) = \arg\max_x \mathcal{X}_x(k)$. Plot the evolution of the true state and its sequence of MAP estimates using two different policies: (i) degenerate and (ii) a policy of your choosing in which $\phi(b) = \not{p}$ for b in a neighborhood of $\mathtt{T}$. Plot the estimate $\widehat{X}^{\mathsf{MAP}}(k)$ and $X(k)$ on the same plot in each case, and estimate the mean-square error (MSE) over the run. *Please use the same random seed for cases (i) and (ii).* To estimate the MSE, you may want to run multiple independent trials with different seeds.

(b) Fix values of $\{a_T,a_R,a_B\}$ of your choosing, and plot the average cost as a function of r along with $\pm\sigma$ confidence bounds. It is even more important to use multiple runs in this case, since you need to estimate the variance σ^2 of your estimate.

This is another great example for testing Q-learning and actor-critical algorithms developed in later chapters.

7.15 *Parameter Estimation.* In Section 7.8.2, we saw that estimation can be cast as a state estimation problem. The purpose of this exercise is to look at a simpler estimation problem, with the "exploration" issue set aside.

We are given scalar measurements

$$Y(k) = \theta + W(k),$$

and wish to obtain an estimate $\hat{\theta}(n)$ of θ, based on n observations. If you are told that $\boldsymbol{W}$ is a zero mean sequence, a natural choice is Monte Carlo:

$$\hat{\theta}_{\mathrm{MC}}(n) = \frac{1}{n}\sum_{k=0}^{n-1} Y(k).$$

Suppose instead that it is known that $\boldsymbol{W}$ is the output of a stable filter: For some $1 \times n$ matrix G, and $n \times n$ matrix F, we have the following for $k \geq 0$:

$$Z(k+1) = FZ(k) + N(k+1), \qquad W(k) = GZ(k).$$

It is assumed that $\boldsymbol{N}$ is Gaussian white noise with marginal $N(0,\Sigma_N)$, and that θ has a known Gaussian distribution that is independent of $\boldsymbol{N}$.

(a) Write down state equations for this system with state $X(k) = (Z(k),\theta)^{\intercal}$, and write down the Kalman filter equations to estimate X and θ.

(b) Consider the scalar case $n = 1$. Do the equations simplify?

(c) When $F = 0$, the solution simplifies dramatically (follow the derivation of Σ_k for the Gaussian bandits). Compare the optimal estimator to $\hat{\theta}_{\mathrm{MC}}$ in this special case.

7.16 This exercise concerns the *Gaussian bandit* introduced in Section 7.8.2 with only two arms ($K = 2$). If the variance of the rewards is equal across arms, then we obtain a slightly simpler model:

$$R(k) = U(k)X_1 + (1 - U(k))X_2 + W(k), \qquad k \geq 0,$$

where $\{X_i\}$ are independent Gaussian random variables, the "arm" is defined by $U(k) \in \mathsf{U} = \{0,1\}$, and $\boldsymbol{W}$ is i.i.d., $N(0,\sigma_W^2)$, and independent of X. Recall this may be regarded as a POMDP with observation process $\boldsymbol{Y} = \boldsymbol{r}$.

For any choice of input, and each i, the conditional distribution of X_i given the observations up to time k is Gaussian: For all $S \subset \mathbb{R}$,

$$\mathsf{P}\{X_i \in S \mid Y_0^k, U_0^k\} = \int_S p_i(x;k)\,dx$$

$$\text{where} \qquad p_i(x;k) = \frac{1}{\sqrt{2\pi\sigma_i^2(k)}} \exp\Big\{-\frac{1}{2\sigma_i^2(k)}(x - m_i(k))^2\Big\}.$$

(a) Obtain expressions for $\{\sigma_i^2(k), m_i(k) : i = 1,2,\ k \geq 0\}$.
In the remaining numerical experiments, take $\sigma_W^2 = 1$, and $(X_1, X_2)^{\intercal} = \bar{r} = \binom{0}{1}$.

(b) Try out the certainty equivalent policy (7.58) over a fixed time horizon. Perform multiple independent runs, and present a histogram of the regret.

(c) Repeat (b), but with (7.58) replaced by a policy of your choice (such as the UCB rule (7.65)).

7.10 Notes

See [45, 46, 162, 291] and the collection [129] for much more on the foundations of MDP theory. In particular, [45, 46] also emphasizes the close parallels between deterministic and stochastic control theory (as does the earlier classic [43]). Other must-reads include [106, 123, 128].

See [80] for an encyclopedic treatment of stochastic linear systems, including many approaches to control, state estimation, and parameter estimation. Textbooks covering basic material include [7, 76, 205]. Section 7.2 and analysis of the speed-scaling model is adapted from the book chapter [165], based on a longer history, e.g., [8, 92, 141]. The article [92] was the outcome of a class project for stochastic control at the University of Illinois during the 2008 fall semester.

The "queueing game" introduced in Section 7.6 is based on [255], inspired by conversations regarding the "Mori–Zwanzig formalism" for model reduction. In this example, the four-dimensional control problem is replaced with one of dimension 2. The *soft state aggregation* approach to function approximation [324] is also based on the construction of a simple Markov model, defined via Bayes's rule as in (7.52). The origin of this idea can be found in remarks by Claude Shannon in his 1948 paper [316], regarded as the birth of modern information theory.

The concept of the *belief state* for optimal control of Markov chains with partial observations is credited to the 1960 paper of Stratonovich [334], followed shortly after by Åström [13]. Two valuable resources are available online: van Handel in [362] treats theory of nonlinear filtering (the recursion that generates the belief state), and Krishnamurthy [201] contains a nice survey and history of POMDPs, highlighting structural results for value functions that inspire function approximation architectures for RL (some conclusions most relevant to this book are discussed at the end of Section C.3).

See [178, 336, 337] for principled approaches to construct an approximate belief state in applications to RL, along with substantial history on the topic.

There was no time or space to include more examples and exercises related to games. Exercise 3.9 would provide a great example for RL algorithms to come, and for a large collection of interacting agents it is possible to predict the optimal solution through the theory of mean-field games [166, 167, 214]. Examples illustrating the application of mean-field theory to RL can be found in [245, 380–382].

The bandits literature has taken off in the past two decades, so just a few historical notes are provided here. See [78, 216] for comprehensive and recent treatments of bandit theory.

First, remember that UCB refers to upper confidence bound, a concept introduced by Lai and Robbins in their derivation of (7.67). The version (7.65) was introduced in [17], which contains an elegant proof of logarithmic regret in a strong sense, following the asymptotic analysis of a similar flavor in [3].

The reference to the empirical distributions (7.62) is intended to recall their use in information theory, where they together with relative entropy play a role in explaining channel capacity and error exponents [105], as well as the sharp bounds of Lai and Robbins. See [293, 295] for the use of similar information-theoretic techniques to obtain lower bounds on performance in system identification and optimization.

8

Stochastic Approximation

Quasistochastic approximation is the engine behind the gradient-free optimization algorithms surveyed in Section 4.6 and Q-learning algorithms introduced in Chapter 5. The history of stochastic approximation (SA) is far older, so that SA techniques are far more familiar to algorithm designers.

The goal is identical to the starting point of Section 4.5: We wish to solve the root-finding problem $\bar{f}(\theta^*) = 0$, where $\bar{f}\colon \mathbb{R}^d \to \mathbb{R}^d$ is defined as an expectation:

$$\bar{f}(\theta) \stackrel{\text{def}}{=} \mathsf{E}[f(\theta, \Phi)], \qquad \theta \in \mathbb{R}^d. \tag{8.1}$$

As in the deterministic setting, $f\colon \mathbb{R}^d \times \Omega \to \mathbb{R}^d$, and $\Phi \in \Omega$ is a random vector.

The SA recursion is entirely analogous to the QSA ODE (4.44):

Stochastic Approximation

For initialization $\theta_0 \in \mathbb{R}^d$, obtain the sequence of estimates recursively:

$$\theta_{n+1} = \theta_n + \alpha_{n+1} f_{n+1}(\theta_n), \tag{8.2}$$

where $f_{n+1}(\theta_n) = f(\theta_n, \Phi(n+1))$, $\Phi(n)$ has the same distribution as Φ for each n (or its distribution converges to that of Φ as $n \to \infty$), and $\{\alpha_n\}$ is a nonnegative scalar step-size sequence.

Analysis begins with a representation of (8.2) as a "noisy" Euler approximation,

$$\theta_{n+1} = \theta_n + \alpha_{n+1}[\bar{f}(\theta_n) + \Delta_{n+1}], \quad n \ge 0 \tag{8.3a}$$

$$\text{in which} \qquad \Delta_{n+1} = f_{n+1}(\theta_n) - \bar{f}(\theta_n) \qquad \text{and} \quad \Delta^{\infty}_{n+1} = f_{n+1}(\theta^*). \tag{8.3b}$$

Stability of the ODE and additional minor assumptions imply consistency:

$$\lim_{n\to\infty} \theta_n = \theta^* \qquad \text{with probability one.}$$

See Theorem 8.1 for a proof that follows theory in Section 4.5.

SA is one component of the ODE method applied in the remainder of the book:

ODE Method

(1) Formulate the algorithmic goal as a root-finding problem $\bar{f}(\theta^*) = 0$.
(2) Refine the design of $\bar{f}$, if necessary, to ensure that the associated ODE is globally asymptotically stable:

$$\tfrac{d}{dt}\vartheta = \bar{f}(\vartheta). \tag{8.4a}$$

The *Newton–Raphson flow* introduced in Section 4.3 is one example of this step.
(3) Is an Euler approximation appropriate?

$$\theta_{n+1} = \theta_n + \alpha_{n+1}\bar{f}(\theta_n), \quad n \geq 0. \tag{8.4b}$$

In particular, is $\bar{f}$ Lipschitz continuous?
(4) Design an SA algorithm to approximate (8.4b).

8.1 Asymptotic Covariance

The rate of convergence of the error sequence $\tilde{\theta}_n = \theta_n - \theta^*$ can be measured in terms of the error covariance

$$\Sigma_n = \mathsf{E}[\tilde{\theta}_n \tilde{\theta}_n^{\intercal}] \tag{8.5}$$

from which we obtain the mean-square error (MSE) $\sigma_n^2 \stackrel{\text{def}}{=} \mathsf{E}[\|\tilde{\theta}_n\|^2] = \text{trace}\,(\Sigma_n)$. When using the step-size $\alpha_n = g/(n+n_0)^\rho$ with $n_0 > 0$, $g > 0$, and $\rho \in (0,1]$, the asymptotic covariance is defined to be the limit:

$$\Sigma_\theta = \lim_{n\to\infty} n^\rho \Sigma_n. \tag{8.6}$$

The limit exists and is finite under mild assumptions. Moreover, it admits an expression in terms of simple algorithm primitives: The asymptotic covariance of $\{\Delta_n^\infty\}$ appearing in (8.3b), and the linearization of $\bar{f}$ at θ^*. See Section 8.2.5 for more details.

Similar to the definition (4.68), we say that σ_n^2 tends to zero at rate $1/n^\mu$ (with $\mu > 0$) if for each $\varepsilon > 0$,

$$\lim_{n\to\infty} n^{\mu-\varepsilon}\sigma_n^2 = 0 \qquad \text{and} \qquad \lim_{n\to\infty} n^{\mu+\varepsilon}\sigma_n^2 = \infty. \tag{8.7}$$

Hence when (8.6) holds with nonzero limit Σ_θ, we obtain (8.7) with $\mu = \rho$. For the applications considered in the remainder of this book, the optimal convergence rate is obtained using $\rho = 1$:

$$\sigma_n^2 = \mathsf{E}\big[\|\theta_n - \theta^*\|^2\big] = O(1/n). \tag{8.8}$$

However, in Section 8.2.5 we see that this fast convergence is only possible with $g > 0$ sufficiently large when using $\alpha_n = g/(n+n_0)$.

The theory of convergence rates for QSA surveyed in Section 4.5 was based on consideration of a scaled process in continuous time, $Z_t = \alpha_t^{-1}\widetilde{\Theta}_t$. The continuous time setting was useful for approximating its dynamics by a linear ODE. A similar approach is used for stochastic approximation, but with a few significant differences. First, the convergence rate is typically much slower: To be precise, we are forced to introduce a square root in the scaling:

$$Z_n = \alpha_n^{-1/2}\tilde{\theta}_n. \tag{8.9}$$

We also lose some of the simplicity of ODE analysis.

Along with these mean-square error approximations is a Central Limit Theorem (CLT), for which Σ_θ is the asymptotic covariance (under general assumptions):

$$\lim_{n\to\infty} Z_n \stackrel{\text{dist}}{=} W, \qquad W \sim N(0,\Sigma_\theta),$$

where the convergence is in distribution. Numerical results contained in Section 8.4 and in many examples later in the book show that the CLT is often a good predictor of algorithm performance in applications to optimization and RL.

It is possible to optimize the asymptotic covariance over all algorithms in a prescribed class: See Section 8.2.5, where a formula for the optimal covariance $\Sigma_\theta^\star$ may be found in (8.30). Three "ancient" approaches are, in chronological order, the following:

- Stochastic Newton–Raphson (SNR) of Chung [95].
- Stochastic quasi-Newton–Raphson of Ruppert [305].
- The averaging technique of Ruppert [306], and Polyak and Juditsky[1] [287, 288]: see Theorem 8.13.

The averaging technique is defined exactly as for QSA in (4.78):

Polyak-Juditsky-Ruppert Averaging

For initialization $\theta_0 \in \mathbb{R}^d$, obtain the sequence of estimates $\{\theta^\bullet_n\}$, and a final estimate θ^{PR}_N as follows:

$$\theta^\bullet_{n+1} = \theta^\bullet_n + \beta_{n+1} f_{n+1}(\theta_n), \qquad 0 \le n \le N-1, \tag{8.10a}$$

$$\theta^{\text{PR}}_N = \frac{1}{N-N_0}\sum_{k=N_0+1}^{N} \theta^{\text{PR}}_k, \tag{8.10b}$$

where $1 \ll N_0 \ll N$. The step-size sequence $\{\beta_n\}$ is square summable, and satisfies

$$\lim_{n\to\infty} n\beta_n = \infty. \tag{8.10c}$$

Two recent techniques to optimize the asymptotic covariance are

- Zap-SA: intended to approximate the Newton–Raphson flow (4.14a).
- Matrix momentum algorithms [108].

Zap SA algorithms are defined in Section 8.2; they stand out because they are stable under minimal assumptions on the model. Momentum methods are unfortunately beyond the scope

[1] As in Part I of the book, the "J" is omitted from the superscript in (8.10b); this is to keep notation compact, and also because of Polyak's independent work before Juditsky.

of this book, but the first-order version of Zap SA described in Section 8.5.2 is similar to the momentum algorithm NeSA of [108].

8.2 Themes and Roadmaps

This section is intended to provide an overview of SA theory, and how theoretical insights are used to create algorithms. It is a complex section that deserves its own roadmap:

(i) Section 8.2.1 simply recalls a basic message: It is often best to consider an ODE as a starting point in algorithm design. Both stability and rates of convergence of your algorithm will rest on properties of the ODE.

(ii) It is essential to understand what we mean by *ODE approximation* of a recursive algorithm. Section 8.2.2 provides an explanation that parallels the QSA theory of Section 4.9.

(iii) The choice of step-size is not at all obvious. A few minimal requirements are explained in Section 8.2.3, and discussion surrounding two time-scale SA algorithms (distinguished by two separate step-size sequences) is contained in Section 8.2.4.

(iv) Next, we need a way to distinguish between two SA designs and determine which is better. We first review in Section 8.2.5 the standard performance metric in machine learning and RL based on *sample complexity bounds*. Mean-square error is preferred in this book for many reasons surveyed in this subsection and later in the chapter. For example, the asymptotic covariance Σ_θ appearing in (8.6) solves a "Lyapunov equation," which leads to tools for algorithm design.

(v) By definition of "asymptotic," transient behavior is ignored in asymptotic analysis. The potential tension between asymptotic and transient performance is the topic of Section 8.2.6, which also shows how PJR averaging is a means to break this tension.

8.2.1 ODE Design

Consider first an ideal setting in which the distribution of Φ is known, and it is not costly to evaluate $\bar{f}(\theta)$ for $\theta \in \mathbb{R}^d$. In this case, estimates of θ^* might be obtained using the ODE

$$\frac{d}{dt}\vartheta = \bar{f}(\vartheta)$$

or an Euler approximation (an instance of successive approximation):

$$\theta_{n+1} = \theta_n + \alpha_{n+1}\bar{f}(\theta_n). \tag{8.11}$$

Convergence of the ODE or (8.11) is possible through careful design of the function f that determines $\bar{f}$.

The Newton–Raphson flow introduced in Section 4.3 is an ODE that is convergent under minimal conditions on $\bar{f}$ (see Proposition 4.4). Its Euler approximation is

$$\theta_{n+1} = \theta_n - \alpha_{n+1}\big[A(\theta_n)\big]^{-1}\bar{f}(\theta_n), \qquad A(\theta_n) = \big[\partial_\theta \bar{f}(\theta)\big]_{\theta=\theta_n}, \tag{8.12}$$

where $\partial_\theta \bar{f}$ denotes the Jacobian as in (4.13). Global convergence of the Newton–Raphson flow holds under very mild conditions. The same is true for (8.12) if the step-size is chosen with care – informed by a rich literature on ODEs. It may turn out that a more efficient and reliable approximation is obtained using a more sophisticated Runge–Kutta method.

When the step-size in (8.12) is set to unity, this becomes the Newton–Raphson algorithm:

$$\theta_{n+1} = \theta_n - \big[A(\theta_n)\big]^{-1} \bar{f}(\theta_n). \tag{8.13}$$

Under mild conditions, the estimates converge extremely rapidly to $\theta^\star$:

$$\lim_{n\to\infty} \frac{1}{n^2} \log(\|\theta_n - \theta^*\|) < 0.$$

That is, $\|\theta_n - \theta^*\| \le B\exp(-\varepsilon n^2)$ for some $B < \infty$ and $\varepsilon > 0$. However, this convergence is only local: valid for θ_0 in a neighborhood of θ^*.

8.2.2 ODE Approximation

Comparison of (8.3a) with an ODE requires a time transformation similar to the introduction of τ in (4.73) for analysis of QSA. Our first introduction to a standard Euler approximation was (4.8), in which the time points $\{\tau_k\}$ were assumed given. Here the step-size sequence $\{\alpha_k\}$ is given, and we define the time points via $\tau_0 = 0$, and $\tau_{k+1} = \tau_k + \alpha_{k+1}$ for $k \ge 0$.

The ODE approximation is based on a comparison of two processes in continuous time:

(i) $\Theta_t = \theta_k$ when $t = \tau_k$, for each $k \ge 0$, and defined for all t through piecewise linear interpolation. The notation is used to emphasize the similarity with the QSA parameter estimates considered in Section 4.5.

(ii) For each $n \ge 0$, let $\{\vartheta_t^{(n)} : t \ge \tau_n\}$ denote the solution to (8.4a), initialized according to the current parameter estimate:

$$\frac{d}{dt}\vartheta_t^{(n)} = \bar{f}(\vartheta_t^{(n)}), \quad t \ge \tau_n, \qquad \vartheta_{\tau_n}^{(n)} = \theta_n. \tag{8.14}$$

Expressed as a differential equation, it seems difficult to compare $\vartheta_{\tau_k}^{(n)}$ and θ_k for $k \ge n$. This is why the ODE approximation is obtained in integral form.

The *cumulative disturbance* is defined for any $K > n$ by

$$M_K^{(n)} = \sum_{i=n+1}^{K} \alpha_i \Delta_i, \tag{8.15}$$

with Δ_i defined in (8.3b). Iteration of (8.3a) then gives

$$\begin{aligned} \Theta_{\tau_K} &= \theta_n + \sum_{i=n+1}^{K} \alpha_{i+1} \bar{f}(\Theta_{t_i}) + M_K^{(n)} \\ &= \theta_n + \int_{\tau_n}^{\tau_K} \bar{f}(\Theta_\tau)\, d\tau + \mathcal{E}_{\tau_K}^{(n)}, \end{aligned} \tag{8.16}$$

where $\mathcal{E}_{\tau_K}^{(n)}$ is the sum of $M_K^{(n)}$ and the error resulting from the Riemann–Stieltjes approximation of the integral. This disturbance term will vanish with n, uniformly in K, subject to conditions on $\{\Delta_i\}$ and the step-size.

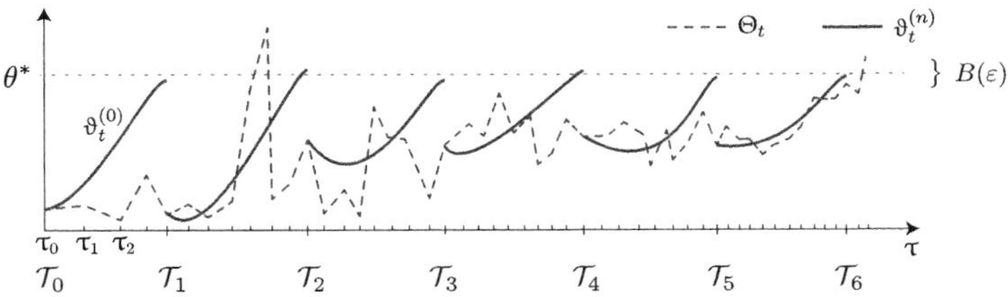

Figure 8.1 ODE approximation on time intervals $[\mathcal{N}_k, \mathcal{N}_{k+1})$ of width approximately T.

The integral representation of solutions to the ODE are identical, with the disturbance removed:

$$\vartheta_{\tau_K}^{(n)} = \theta_n + \int_{\tau_n}^{\tau_K} \bar{f}(\vartheta_\tau^{(n)}) d\tau. \tag{8.17}$$

Theory in Section 4.9 can then be applied to establish the following:

Theorem 8.1 *Suppose that the following hold:*

- $\bar{f}$ *is Lipschitz continuous.*
- *The parameter sequence* $\{\theta_n : n \geq 0\}$ *is bounded a.s.*
- *The disturbance vanishes in the following uniform sense: For each* $T > 0$,

$$\lim_{n\to\infty} \sup_K \|M_K^{(n)}\| = 0 \qquad a.s., \tag{8.18}$$

where the supremum is over K *satisfying* $K > n$ *and* $\tau_K - \tau_n \leq T$.

Then,

(i) *For each* T,

$$\lim_{n\to\infty} \sup_{\tau_n \leq t \leq \tau_n + T} \|\vartheta_t^{(n)} - \Theta_t\| = 0 \qquad a.s. \tag{8.19}$$

(ii) *If the ODE* (8.4a) *is globally asymptotically stable, with unique equilibrium* θ^*, *then*

$$\lim_{t\to\infty} \Theta_t = \lim_{n\to\infty} \theta_n = \theta^* \qquad a.s. \qquad \square$$

Proof Part (ii) of the theorem is illustrated in Figure 8.1 (see also Figure 8.5 and surrounding discussion).

Global asymptotic stability combined with boundedness of the parameter sequence implies the following: For any given $\delta > 0$, there is $T < \infty$ and $\varepsilon < \delta$ such that

(i) If $\|\vartheta_{\tau_n}^{(n)} - \theta^*\| \leq \varepsilon$, then $\|\vartheta_\tau^{(n)} - \theta^*\| \leq \delta$ for $\tau \geq \tau_n$.
(ii) $\|\vartheta_\tau^{(n)} - \theta^*\| \leq \varepsilon/2$ for each n and all $\tau \geq \tau_n + T$:

The sampling times indicated in the figure are defined by $\mathcal{N}_0 = 0$ and for $n \geq 1$,

$$\mathcal{N}_n = \min\{\tau_k : \tau_k \geq \mathcal{N}_{n-1} + T\}.$$

Each of these times can be expressed $\mathcal{N}_n = \tau_{n_n}$ for some integer $n_n \geq n$. They are constructed so that the ODE solution $\{\vartheta_\tau^{(n_n)}\}$ on $[\mathcal{N}_n, \infty)$ will satisfy $\|\vartheta_\tau^{(n_n)} - \theta^*\| \leq \varepsilon/2$ for $\tau \geq \mathcal{N}_{n+1}$.

Applying (i), we conclude that for some integer $n(\delta)$ and all $n \geq n(\delta)$,

$$\|\Theta_{\mathcal{N}_{n+1}} - \theta^*\| \leq \|\Theta_{\mathcal{N}_{n+1}} - \vartheta^{(n_n)}_{\mathcal{N}_{n+1}}\| + \|\vartheta^{(n_n)}_{\mathcal{N}_{n+1}} - \theta^*\| \leq \varepsilon.$$

By definition, $\vartheta^{(n_n+1)}_{\mathcal{N}_{n+1}} = \Theta_{\mathcal{N}_{n+1}}$ is the initialization for the next interval, which implies that

$$\|\vartheta^{(n_k)}_{\tau} - \theta^*\| \leq \delta \qquad \text{for all} \quad k \geq n(\delta)+1, \ \tau \geq \mathcal{N}_k.$$

From (8.19), we then obtain

$$\limsup_{n\to\infty} \|\theta_n - \theta^*\| = \limsup_{t\to\infty} \|\Theta_t - \theta^*\| \leq \delta.$$

This establishes convergence, since $\delta > 0$ is arbitrary. □

Projection and Restart

The introduction of $n_0 \geq 0$ in the step-size sequence $\alpha_n = g/(n+n_0)^\rho$ is to avoid excessive gain when n is small. Anyone who has experimented with SA has seen parameter estimates explode in the first few iterations. Without understanding of the asymptotic covariance, it is likely that a user will reduce the value of g, not realizing this might result in infinite asymptotic covariance. Increasing n_0 can tame the algorithm and has no impact on the asymptotic covariance.

Two alternatives are available, each based on a closed region $\mathsf{R} \subset \mathbb{R}^d$ satisfying $\theta^* \in \mathsf{R}$ (in practice, the choice of this set is much like the choice of n_0: through trial and error).

Projection

The definition requires some notion of distance: $\text{dist}(w,v) \geq 0$ for any $w,v \in \mathbb{R}^d$ with $\text{dist}(v,v) = 0$ for any v. It is typical to use either the standard Euclidean norm or the max norm: $\text{dist}(w,v) = \|w - v\|_\infty \stackrel{\text{def}}{=} \max_i |w_i - v_i|$. For any vector $v \in \mathbb{R}^m$, the vector $v' = \Pi_{\mathsf{R}}\{v\}$ satisfies

$$v' \in \arg\min\{\text{dist}(w,v) : w \in \mathsf{R}\}.$$

Projection applied to the basic algorithm (8.2) is defined by the following recursion:

$$\theta_{n+1} = \Pi_{\mathsf{R}}\{\theta_n + \alpha_{n+1} f_{n+1}(\theta_n)\}. \tag{8.20}$$

There are two difficulties with this approach: One is the potential computational complexity in updating the parameter estimate, and the other is complexity in an ODE analysis. How do we know that the parameter sequence doesn't become trapped on the boundary of R?

Restart

Whenever $\theta_{n+1} \notin \mathsf{R}$, we simply reset its value to a vector within the interior of R. For example, with $\mathsf{R} = \{\theta : \|\theta\| \leq r\}$, you might choose the reset parameter to be $\theta'_{n+1} \in \mathsf{R}$ by scaling the following:

$$\theta'_{n+1} = \frac{r}{2} \frac{\theta_{n+1}}{\|\theta_{n+1}\|}.$$

This procedure is far simpler than projection, and analysis is simpler.

8.2.3 Choice of Step-Size

The next question is how to choose the step-size appearing in (8.2). A constant step-size is often preferred in applications, though choice of the constant value remains an art form. Also, with a constant step-size we cannot expect convergence, unless the covariance matrix defined in (8.27) is identically zero. This degenerate special case is not found in the applications of interest in the remainder of this book, so we assume a vanishing step-size: $\lim_{n\to\infty} \alpha_n = 0$. Two further assumptions are imposed. First, the discrete-time version of Assumption (QSA1) of Section 4.5.4:

$$\sum_{n=1}^{\infty} \alpha_n = \infty.$$

This is imposed so that it is possible to reach θ^* from each initial θ_0.

The second assumption is more strongly rooted in probability theory:

$$\sum_{n=1}^{\infty} \alpha_n^2 < \infty. \tag{8.21}$$

In particular, it is used to establish (8.18), which is required for convergence of parameter estimates in Theorem 8.1. The proposition that follows makes clear why we require (8.21). The uniform bound on the second moment of $\{\Delta_k\}$ is relaxed in Proposition 8.7 (see (8.60b)).

Proposition 8.2 *Suppose that $\{\Delta_k\}$ is an uncorrelated sequence with bounded covariance: $\bar{\sigma}_\Delta^2 = \sup_k \mathsf{E}[\|\Delta_k\|^2] < \infty$. Then the second moment of $\{M_K^{(n)} : K \geq 1\}$ appearing in* (8.16) *admits the uniform bound*

$$\mathsf{E}[\|M_K^{(n)}\|^2] \leq \bar{\sigma}_\Delta^2 \sum_{j=n+1}^{\infty} \alpha_j^2.$$

The right-hand side vanishes as $n \to \infty$, provided (8.21) *holds.*

Proof If $\{\Delta_k\}$ is an uncorrelated sequence, then the covariance of $M_K^{(n)}$ satisfies

$$\mathsf{E}[M_K^{(n)} M_K^{(n)\intercal}] = \sum_{i=1}^{K} \alpha_{n+i}^2 \mathsf{E}[\Delta_{n+i} \Delta_{n+i}^\intercal]$$

and consequently

$$\mathsf{E}[\|M_K^{(n)}\|^2] = \operatorname{trace} \mathsf{E}[M_K^{(n)} M_K^{(n)\intercal}] \leq \bar{\sigma}_\Delta^2 \sum_{j=n+1}^{K} \alpha_j^2. \qquad \square$$

8.2.4 Multiple Time Scales

There are many examples in which it is valuable to use different step-sizes for different parameter estimates.

Consider the averaging technique (8.10). This is usually presented as a two time-scale recursion where (with $N_0 = 0$),

$$\theta_{n+1}^{\mathsf{PR}} = \theta_n^{\mathsf{PR}} + \alpha_{n+1}\big[\theta_{n+1}^{\bullet} - \theta_n^{\mathsf{PR}}\big], \qquad n \geq 0$$

and with $\alpha_n = 1/n$. A similar recursion holds for arbitrary $N_0 < N$, but the recursion begins at $n = N_0$ with $\theta^{\text{PR}}_{N_0} = 0$. The assumption (8.10c) is thus equivalently expressed

$$\lim_{n\to\infty} \frac{\beta_n}{\alpha_n} = \infty. \tag{8.22}$$

This means that the estimates $\{\theta^{\bullet}_n\}$ defined in (8.10a) evolve much more rapidly than $\{\theta^{\text{PR}}_n\}$.

The general two time-scale algorithm is described as follows:

$$\theta_{n+1} = \theta_n + \beta_{n+1} f_{n+1}(\theta_n, \omega_n), \tag{8.23a}$$

$$\omega_{n+1} = \omega_n + \alpha_{n+1} g_{n+1}(\theta_n, \omega_n), \tag{8.23b}$$

where $\{\theta_n\}$ evolves in $\mathbb{R}^d$ and $\{\omega_n\}$ evolves in $\mathbb{R}^m$. The assumption (8.22) is maintained, which is what makes this a two time-scale recursion.

The ODE approximation for these recursions will not be covered in any generality here, but the main message is something every user of SA should understand.

As always, we require the mean vector fields $\bar{f}(\theta,w) = \mathsf{E}_\varpi[f_{n+1}(\theta,w)]$ and $\bar{g}(\theta,w) = \mathsf{E}_\varpi[g_{n+1}(\theta,w)]$ (steady-state expectations). For each $\omega \in \mathbb{R}^m$, assume there is a unique vector $\theta^s(\omega)$ solving $\bar{f}(\theta^s(\omega),\omega) = \mathsf{0}$. Because the evolution of the second parameter sequence is so slow compared to the first, it is possible to prove under general conditions that $\theta_n \approx \theta^s(\omega_n)$ for all large n. This leads to the following ODE approximation for the second recursion:

$$\frac{d}{dt} w_t = \bar{g}(\theta^s(w_t), w_t). \tag{8.24}$$

See Theorem 8.3 for an example of convergence theory based on these concepts.

This insight is invaluable in algorithm design:

(i) It is critical in constrained optimization, where ω_n is an approximation of a dual variable (say, in the setting of Proposition 4.12).

(ii) The approximation (8.24) is essential for creating recursive algorithms that approximate the Newton–Raphson flow, as we have already seen in the QSA setting of Section 4.5.6.

(iii) The elegant theory of actor-critic methods is made possible through versions of the ODE approximation (8.24).

Stability theory for two time-scale SA can be found in other sources, such as [66], where the proof of the following companion to Theorem 8.1 can be found:

Theorem 8.3 *Consider the two time-scale algorithm* (8.23) *subject to the following assumptions:*

- $\bar{f}$ *and* $\bar{g}$ *are Lipschitz continuous, and the function* $\bar{g}(\theta^s(w),w)$ *is also Lipschitz continuous in* w.
- *The parameter sequences* $\{\theta_n, \omega_n : n \geq 0\}$ *are bounded a.s.*
- *The cumulative disturbances are bounded, in the sense that the following sums exist and are everywhere finite with probability one:*

$$\sum_{n=0}^{\infty} \beta_{n+1}\{f_{n+1}(\theta_n,\omega_n) - \bar{f}(\theta_n,\omega_n)\}, \qquad \sum_{n=0}^{\infty} \alpha_{n+1}\{g_{n+1}(\theta_n,\omega_n) - \bar{g}(\theta_n,\omega_n)\}. \tag{8.25}$$

▶ *The ODE* (8.24) *is globally asymptotically stable with unique equilibrium* w^*, *and for each* w *the following ODE is asymptotically stable with unique equilibrium* $\theta^s(w)$:

$$\frac{d}{dt}\vartheta_t = \bar{f}(\vartheta_t, w).$$

Then, $\lim_{n\to\infty} \theta_n = \theta^* \stackrel{\text{def}}{=} \theta^s(w^*)$ *and* $\lim_{n\to\infty} \omega_n = w^*$ $a.s.$ □

The remainder of this section contains much more on the important topic of step-size for the standard SA algorithm.

8.2.5 Algorithm Performance

An emphasis in these latter chapters of the book is consideration of covariance of parameter estimates, as defined in (8.5). The asymptotic covariance (8.6) exists under general conditions, and a representation is possible based on two matrices: the linearization matrix[2]

$$A = A(\theta^*) \stackrel{\text{def}}{=} \partial_\theta \bar{f}(\theta^*) \tag{8.26}$$

and the steady-state disturbance covariance:

$$\Sigma_\Delta \stackrel{\text{def}}{=} \lim_{n\to\infty} \frac{1}{n}\mathsf{E}[M_n M_n^\intercal], \qquad M_n = \sum_{k=1}^{n} \Delta_k^\infty, \tag{8.27}$$

where $\Delta_k^\infty \stackrel{\text{def}}{=} f_k(\theta^*)$. This is also known as the asymptotic covariance of $\{\Delta_k^\infty\}$, as it is the covariance that appears in the Central Limit Theorem for this sequence. If $\{\Delta_k^\infty\}$ is uncorrelated, then $\Sigma_\Delta = \mathsf{E}_\varpi[\Delta_k^\infty(\Delta_k^\infty)^\intercal]$.

The following conclusions are what can be expected, subject to additional conditions (such as stability of the ODE (8.4a)):

(i) For step-size $\alpha_n = g/(n+n_0)$, the asymptotic covariance (8.6) is finite provided each eigenvalue of A satisfies Real$(\lambda(gA)) < -\frac{1}{2}$, and in this case Σ_θ solves the Lyapunov equation

$$(gA + \tfrac{1}{2}I)\Sigma_\theta + \Sigma_\theta(gA + \tfrac{1}{2}I)^\intercal + g^2\Sigma_\Delta = 0. \tag{8.28a}$$

(ii) For $\alpha_n = g/(n+n_0)^\rho$ with $0.5 < \rho < 1$, the definition of the asymptotic covariance is modified:

$$\Sigma_\theta = \lim_{n\to\infty} n^\rho \Sigma_n.$$

This is finite provided Real$(\lambda(A)) < 0$ (A is Hurwitz), and in this case Σ_θ solves

$$A\Sigma_\theta + \Sigma_\theta A^\intercal + g\Sigma_\Delta = 0. \tag{8.28b}$$

There is of course no reason to restrict to a scalar step-size. With $\alpha_n = G/(n+n_0)$, it is necessary to verify that the ODE $\frac{d}{dt}\vartheta = G\bar{f}(\vartheta)$ is globally asymptotically stable, and in this case we typically conclude that the asymptotic covariance (8.6) is finite, provided each

[2] The linearization matrix $A(\theta^*)$ was denoted A^* in the first half of the book, starting in Section 4.3. It is convenient to abandon the superscript here.

eigenvalue of GA satisfies $\mathrm{Real}(\lambda(GA)) < -\frac{1}{2}$. The covariance matrix is the solution to the Lyapunov equation:

$$(GA + \tfrac{1}{2}I)\Sigma_\theta^G + \Sigma_\theta^G(GA + \tfrac{1}{2}I)^\intercal + G\Sigma_\Delta G^\intercal = 0. \tag{8.29}$$

The superscript G is introduced here so we can identify the optimal choice:

Optimizing the Asymptotic Covariance The Lyapunov equation (8.29) has a solution $\Sigma_\theta^G \geq 0$ provided the eigenvalue test is satisfied: $\mathrm{Real}(\lambda) < -\frac{1}{2}$ for each eigenvalue λ of GA.
The choice $G^\star = -A^{-1}$ passes this test, and results in

$$\Sigma_\theta^\star \stackrel{\text{def}}{=} A^{-1}\Sigma_\Delta\{A^{-1}\}^\intercal. \tag{8.30}$$

This is optimal, in the sense that the difference $\Sigma_\theta^G - \Sigma_\theta^\star$ is positive semidefinite.

See Proposition 8.10 for a special case, and the "Notes" section for resources.

The RL literature today has an entirely different emphasis: computation of a finite-time error bound of the form

$$\mathsf{P}\{\|\theta_n - \theta^*\| > \varepsilon\} \leq \overline{b}\exp(-n\overline{I}(\varepsilon)), \qquad n \geq 1, \tag{8.31}$$

where $\overline{b}$ is a constant, and $\overline{I}(\varepsilon) > 0$ for $\varepsilon > 0$. The bound is usually inverted: For a given $\delta > 0$, denote

$$\overline{n}(\varepsilon,\delta) = \frac{1}{\overline{I}(\varepsilon)}[\log(\overline{b}) + \log(\delta^{-1})]. \tag{8.32}$$

Then (8.31) implies the *sample complexity bound*: $\mathsf{P}\{\|\theta_n - \theta^*\| > \varepsilon\} \leq \delta$ for all $n \geq \overline{n}(\varepsilon,\delta)$.

The value of a finite-n bound is indisputable: We have assurance that the probability of error is below the desired value, provided we wait for $n \geq \overline{n}(\varepsilon,\delta)$ iterations of the algorithm.

There are also significant challenges:

(1) A sample complexity bound is typically very conservative. If the bound is very loose, then we will not be willing to wait for n to exceed the overestimate $\overline{n}$.
(2) The bound $\overline{n}$ may not offer guidance on how to improve the algorithm.

Counterparts for the parameter estimate covariance are not a challenge:

(1) $\sigma_n^2 = \mathrm{trace}\,(\Sigma_n)$ can be estimated using batch means methods based on a short run, and this gives approximate confidence bounds for a longer run. This is a standard technique in simulation (see (6.41b)).
(2) We will see that the asymptotic covariance can serve as a guide to algorithm design. Gain design for Watkins's Q-learning algorithm introduced in Section 9.6 is one simple example, where we conclude that $\alpha_n = (1-\gamma)^{-1}n^{-1}$ leads to the optimal $O(n^{-1})$ MSE convergence rate without any complex calculations.

There is a third criticism concerning any bound on the error metric $\|\tilde{\theta}_n\|$ (based on (8.31) or a bound on the error covariance): It is probably not what we care about! In the context of reinforcement learning, most valuable metric would be a measure of the performance of the policies associated with the parameter estimates, as in the theory of bandits surveyed in

Section 7.8. Fortunately, a CLT for the parameter estimates will likely imply approximations for more relevant statistics, such as average cost. In this case, we can borrow techniques from simulation theory to obtain approximate confidence bounds.

8.2.6 Asymptotic versus Transient Performance

As in the QSA theory of Section 4.9, there are trade-offs in choice of step-size: While $\alpha_n = g/n$ will typically yield the optimal convergence rate (8.8) (most crucially, $g > 0$ is chosen sufficiently large), this may also result in poor transient behavior.

Please review the summaries in both Section 8.2.2 and Section 4.5.4 to recall that convergence theory for SA and QSA rests on comparing Θ_t to what amounts to a time scaling of the ODE (8.4a) (recall (8.16) and (8.17)). Bounds on this time scaling are easily obtained:

Lemma 8.4 *Consider the step-size $\alpha_n = 1/n^\rho$. The following bounds hold for each $n \geq 1$:*

$$\tau_n^- \leq \tau_n \leq \tau_n^+,$$

where

$$\tau_n^- = \begin{cases} \log(n+1) & \rho = 1 \\ \frac{1}{1-\rho}[(n+1)^{1-\rho} - 1] & \rho < 1 \end{cases}, \qquad \tau_n^+ = \begin{cases} 1 + \log(n) & \rho = 1 \\ 1 + \frac{1}{1-\rho}[n^{1-\rho} - 1] & \rho < 1 \end{cases}.$$

Proof The following bounds hold for any $t \geq 0$:

$$\frac{1}{t+1} \leq \frac{1}{\lfloor t+1 \rfloor} \leq \frac{1}{\max(1,t)},$$

where $\lfloor t+1 \rfloor$ is the integer part of $t+1$; in particular, $\lfloor t+1 \rfloor = 1$ for $0 \leq t < 1$. The lemma follows from these bounds, combined with the integral representation

$$\tau_n = \int_0^n \Big(\frac{1}{\lfloor t+1 \rfloor}\Big)^\rho \, dt. \qquad \square$$

Let's revisit the uniform convergence obtained in (8.19) that motivated the lemma. Suppose that the ODE converges exponentially quickly to the optimal parameter: There exists $\varrho_0 > 0$, $B_0 < \infty$ such that for any solution to (8.4a), and any $t_0, t \geq 0$,

$$\|\vartheta_{t_0+t} - \theta^*\| \leq B_0 \|\vartheta_{t_0} - \theta^*\| \exp(-\varrho_0 t). \tag{8.33}$$

To apply (8.19), we set $t_0 = \tau_n$, so that $\vartheta^{(n)}_{\tau_n} = \theta_n$ by construction, and choose $t_0 + t = t_{n+k}$ for $k \geq 1$. If $\alpha_n = g/n$, then (8.19) gives, for a large range of $k \geq 1$,

$$\begin{aligned} \|\theta_{n+k} - \theta^*\| \approx \|\vartheta^{(n)}_{\tau_{n+k}} - \theta^*\| &\leq B_0 \|\theta_n - \theta^*\| \exp(-\varrho_0 g[\log(n+k) - 1 - \log(n)]) \\ &= B_0 \|\theta_n - \theta^*\| \exp(\varrho_0 g) \Big(\frac{n}{n+k}\Big)^{-\varrho_0 g}. \end{aligned} \tag{8.34}$$

If $\varrho_0 g$ is not sufficiently large, then the convergence of $\vartheta^{(n)}_{\tau_{n+k}}$ to θ^* may be very slow. In this case, it doesn't make much sense to worry about the variance of the parameter estimation error: *It is the slow transient behavior that we should worry about.*

Lemma 8.4 tells us that choice $\rho < 1$ leads to much faster convergence:

$$\|\vartheta^{(n)}_{\tau_n + k} - \theta^*\| \le B_0 \|\theta_n - \theta^*\| \exp\big(\varrho_0 g(1 + \tau_n)\big) \exp\Big(-\varrho_0 g \frac{1}{1-\rho}(n+k+1)^{1-\rho}\Big). \tag{8.35}$$

This is not geometrically quickly, but the right-hand side vanishes faster than k^{-R} for *any* $R \ge 1$. Does this mean we are forced to settle with a suboptimal convergence rate in order to cope with transients?

Fear not!

So far we have learned that each design choice for $\alpha_n = g/n^\rho$ faces challenges:

(i) We choose $\rho = 1$ to obtain the optimal convergence rate for the mean-square error. However, poor transient behavior might result in very slow convergence, unless $g > 0$ is sufficiently large (which creates its own problems).
(ii) The "high-gain" choice $\alpha_n = g/n^\rho$, with $\rho < 1$, results in the much better bound (8.35). However, the mean-square error of the parameter estimates converges to zero at a rate much slower than $1/n$.

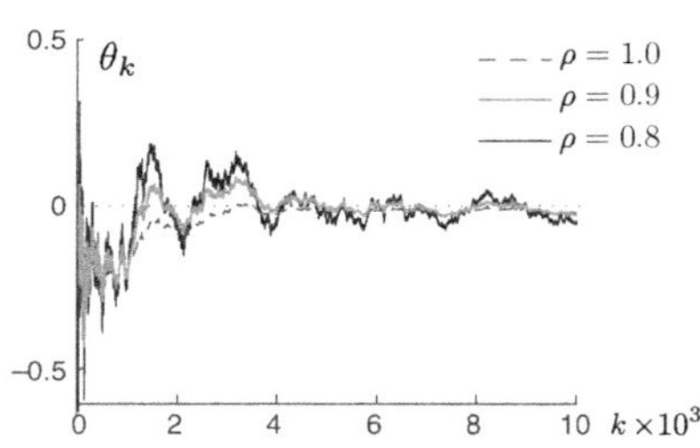

Figure 8.2 Comparison of three values of ρ for the step-size $\alpha_n = g/n^\rho$.

PJR averaging is a means to obtain the best features of each of these two cases. Motivation can be found in Figure 8.2, showing typical behavior of parameter estimates for a scalar SA algorithm, with three choices of ρ. All three estimates converge to the common limiting value $\theta^* = 0$. We see that the estimates show greater volatility for smaller values of ρ, as predicted by the theory. Note, however, that the estimates all appear to fluctuate about $\theta^* = 0$. This motivates additional smoothing in (8.10b), where the starting point N_0 is intended to be chosen "after the transients have settled down."

This simple smoothing of the estimates results in the optimal convergence rate under mild assumptions. The technique is illustrated with an example in Section 8.4, and analysis is postponed to Section 8.7.3.

8.3 Examples

The examples that follow are intended to make more concrete the themes outlined in the previous section.

8.3.1 Monte Carlo

Suppose we wish to estimate the mean $\theta^* = \mathsf{E}[c(\Phi)]$, where $c\colon \Omega \to \mathbb{R}^d$, and the random variable Φ has density p. That is,

$$\theta^* = \int c(x)\, p(x)\, dx.$$

Markov chain Monte carlo (MCMC) techniques include methods to construct a Markov chain $\boldsymbol{\Phi}$ whose steady-state distribution has density equal to the *target density* p [12, 115]. Computation of the mean θ^* is then an SA problem:

$$0 = \bar{f}(\theta^*) = \mathsf{E}[f(\theta^*, \Phi)] = \mathsf{E}[c(\Phi) - \theta^*].$$

Consider the SA recursion (8.2) in which $\alpha_n = g/n$, with $g > 0$:

$$\theta_{n+1} = \theta_n + \frac{g}{n+1}[c(\Phi(n+1)) - \theta_n], \quad n \geq 0. \tag{8.36}$$

This recursion and the associated ODE are linear:

$$\tfrac{d}{dt}\vartheta = -g[\vartheta - \theta^*].$$

This ODE is globally asymptotically stable for any $g > 0$. The case $g = 1$ is very special:

Proposition 8.5 *For the special case $g = 1$, the estimates obtained from* (8.36) *can be expressed as the sample path average:*

$$\theta_n = \frac{1}{n}\sum_{k=1}^{n} c(\Phi(k)). \tag{8.37}$$

This representation holds regardless of the initial condition θ_0.

Proof Multiplying each side of (8.36) by $(n+1)$ results in a recursive representation of the scaled parameter sequence $\{S_k = k\theta_k : k \geq 0\}$:

$$S_{n+1} = (n+1)\theta_n + [c(\Phi(n+1)) - \theta_n] = S_n + c(\Phi(n+1)), \qquad n \geq 0.$$

The representation of $\theta_n = S_n/n$ as a Monte Carlo average (8.37) follows, since $S_0 = 0$. □

Optimizing the Gain

The recursion (8.36) converges to θ^* subject to mild conditions on the Markov chain, and asymptotic statistics tell us something about the rate of convergence.

The covariance Σ_n in (8.5) is a scalar in this case:

$$\sigma_n^2 = \text{trace}\,(\Sigma_n) = \Sigma_n = \mathsf{E}[\tilde{\theta}_n^2],$$

which typically admits the approximation

$$\sigma_n^2 = n^{-1}\sigma_\theta^2 + o(n^{-1}),$$

where the asymptotic variance σ_θ^2 is the solution to (8.28a) with $A = -1$, and $\sigma_\Delta^2 = \Sigma_\Delta^2$ defined in (8.27). The Lyapunov equation admits the explicit solution shown in Figure 8.3 in this scalar setting.

However, *this solution is valid only if $g > 1/2$*. Assuming σ_Δ^2 is nonzero, the asymptotic variance is infinite for $g \leq 1/2$ and minimized using $g^* = 1$.

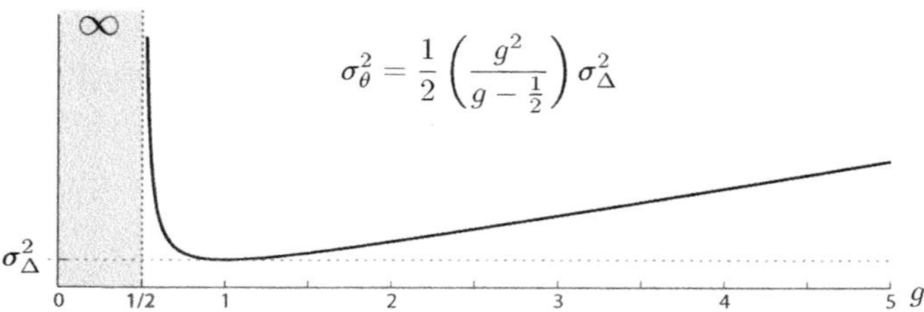

Figure 8.3 Asymptotic covariance for Monte Carlo estimates (8.36) for the scalar recursion.

8.3.2 Stochastic Gradient Descent

Consider the minimization problem $\theta^* = \arg\min_\theta \Gamma(\theta)$, with $\Gamma(\theta) = \mathsf{E}[\widetilde{\Gamma}(\theta,\Phi)]$, $\theta \in \mathbb{R}^d$. The gradient descent ODE is defined by

$$\tfrac{d}{dt}\vartheta = -\nabla\Gamma(\vartheta). \tag{8.38}$$

An approximation of gradient descent can be realized as SA, with

$$\bar{f}(\theta) = -\nabla_\theta \mathsf{E}[\widetilde{\Gamma}(\theta,\Phi)] = -\mathsf{E}[\nabla_\theta\widetilde{\Gamma}(\theta,\Phi)].$$

The exchange of derivative and expectation can be justified under mild conditions.

Suppose we are given samples $\mathbf{\Phi} = \{\Phi_n : n \geq 1\}$ for which the distribution of Φ_n converges to that of Φ, as $n \to \infty$, and denote $\Gamma_n(\theta) = \widetilde{\Gamma}(\theta,\Phi_n)$ for any n and θ. The basic algorithm (8.2) results in *stochastic gradient descent* (SGD):

$$\theta_{n+1} = \theta_n - \alpha_{n+1}\nabla_\theta\Gamma_{n+1}(\theta). \tag{8.39}$$

Stability of the Algorithm

Provided Γ is strongly convex (recall (4.25)), Proposition 4.7 tells us that the gradient flow (8.38) is exponentially asymptotically stable. In the proof, it is shown that $V(\theta) = \frac{1}{2}\|\theta - \theta^*\|^2$ serves as a Lyapunov function:

$$\tfrac{d}{dt}V(\vartheta_t) \leq -2\delta_0 V(\vartheta_t) \quad\Longrightarrow\quad \|\vartheta_t - \theta^*\| \leq \|\vartheta_0 - \theta^*\|\exp(-\delta_0 t). \tag{8.40}$$

Consequently, the bound (8.33) holds with $B_0 = 1$ and $\varrho_0 = \delta_0$. Conditions for exponential asymptotic stability without convexity can be obtained from Theorem 4.9.

What about stability of the SA algorithm? A sufficient condition is based on the ODE@∞, just as in the deterministic setting of Section 4.8.4: Define for $\theta \in \mathbb{R}^d$,

$$\Gamma^\infty(\theta) = \lim_{r\to\infty}\frac{1}{r^2}\Gamma(r\theta), \qquad \nabla\Gamma^\infty(\theta) = \lim_{r\to\infty}\frac{1}{r}\nabla\Gamma(r\theta).$$

Assuming these functions are finite valued, it follows that the first is radially quadratic, and the second is radially linear:

$$\Gamma^\infty(s\theta) = s^2\Gamma^\infty(\theta), \qquad \nabla\Gamma^\infty(s\theta) = s\nabla\Gamma^\infty(\theta), \qquad s > 0.$$

If Γ is strongly convex, then (4.25) implies the lower bounds:

$$\theta^\intercal\nabla\Gamma^\infty(\theta) \geq \delta_0\|\theta\|^2, \qquad \Gamma^\infty(\theta) \geq \tfrac{1}{2}\delta_0\|\theta\|^2.$$

The first bound follows directly from (4.25) and the definition of $\nabla\Gamma^\infty$. The second bound follows from the first and the following:

Lemma 8.6 *If Γ^∞ is continuously differentiable, then $\Gamma^\infty(\theta) = \frac{1}{2}\theta^\intercal\nabla\Gamma^\infty(\theta)$, $\theta \in \mathbb{R}^d$.*

Proof Differentiability justifies the chain rule in the following:

$$\Gamma^\infty(\theta) = \int_0^1 \tfrac{d}{dt}\Gamma^\infty(t\theta)\, dt = \int_0^1 \theta^\intercal\nabla\Gamma^\infty(t\theta)\, dt = \theta^\intercal\nabla\Gamma^\infty(\theta)\int_0^1 t\, dt.$$

The first equality is the fundamental theorem of calculus, and the identity $\Gamma^\infty(0) = 0$. The final equality follows from radial linearity of the gradient. □

The ODE@∞ is defined by $\frac{d}{dt}\vartheta^\infty = -g\nabla\Gamma^\infty(\vartheta^\infty)$. Convergence of the stochastic recursion follows from stability of two ODEs:

(i) If $\nabla\Gamma^\infty$ is continuous, and $\Gamma^\infty(\theta) > 0$ for $\theta \neq \mathsf{0}$, then the ODE@∞ is globally asymptotically stable. Theory in Section 8.7.1 implies that the sequence of parameter estimates from the SA algorithm (8.39) are bounded:

$$\sup_n \|\theta_n\| < \infty \qquad a.s.$$

(ii) If the assumptions of (i) hold, and in addition (8.38) is globally asymptotically stable, then the estimates are convergent to the unique root $\nabla\Gamma(\theta^*) = \mathsf{0}$.

Asymptotic Covariance

The asymptotic covariance defined in (8.6), or any of its variants, can all be expressed in terms of the linearization matrix $A = \partial_\theta \bar{f}$. For this class of algorithms, it is a symmetric matrix with entries:

$$A_{i,j}(\theta) = \frac{\partial}{\partial\theta_j}\bar{f}_i(\theta) = -\frac{\partial^2}{\partial\theta_i\partial\theta_j}\Gamma_i(\theta). \tag{8.41}$$

Variance theory requires that $A(\theta^*)$ is Hurwitz (recall (8.28a) and (8.28b)), which in this case means that the Hessian of Γ is positive definite at the optimizer: $-A(\theta^*) = \nabla^2\Gamma(\theta^*) > 0$.

Tension between Asymptotic and Transient Performance

Let's first consider a setting where the tension is not so severe: Γ is a quadratic, with $\Gamma(\theta) = \frac{1}{2}(\theta - \theta^*)^\intercal G(\theta - \theta^*)$, and $G > 0$ (positive definite). This is strongly convex, with $\delta_0 = \lambda_1$, the minimum eigenvalue of G.

Consider the step-size $\alpha_n = g/(n + n_0)$:

- *Transient bounds:* The right-hand side of the bound (8.34) will decay as $1/n$ when using the step-size $\alpha_n = g/n$ and $g = 1/\lambda_1$.
- *Asymptotic covariance:* The linearization matrix used to compute the asymptotic covariance is $A(\theta^*) = -G$. The gain $g = 1/\lambda_1$ will result in a finite asymptotic covariance since all eigenvalues of gA satisfy $\lambda(gA) \leq -1 < -\frac{1}{2}$.
- *ODE fidelity for small n:* We may require $n_0 \gg g$ to avoid massive transients for small n (or employ restart to keep the parameters within a predefined region R, as described at the close of Section 8.2.2).

Theory surrounding PJR averaging motivates the use of $\alpha_n = g/n^\rho$ with a smaller value of g (say, $g = \bar{\alpha}$ if a good choice is available), and $\rho < 1$. This approach requires far less "tinkering" with parameters. It is true that we are left with three: ρ, g, and the integer N_0 used to obtain the final estimate θ_N^{PR} via (8.10b). Theory and practice suggest that sensitivity to $\rho \leq 0.9$ and $g > 0$ is not so high, and choice of N_0 should be clear after observing sample paths from various large initial conditions.

Or, we might give up on SA entirely. An alternative to SGD is considered next.

8.3.3 Empirical Risk Minimization

Recall from Section 5.1 our brief survey of empirical risk minimization (ERM). This approach can be applied here, with the *empirical risk* equal to the *empirical mean*:

$$\bar{\Gamma}_N(\theta) = \frac{1}{N}\sum_{i=1}^{N} \Gamma_i(\theta). \tag{8.42}$$

Application of ERM means that we forego a recursive SA algorithm, and instead minimize $\bar{\Gamma}_N(\theta)$ to obtain the estimate θ_N^{ERM}. This approach has become popular in recent years for optimization in very high dimensions.

For sake of illustration, consider the special case of quadratic loss $\Gamma_i(\theta) = \frac{1}{2}\|M_i\theta - \xi_i\|^2$, in which the matrix M_i and vector ξ_i are random. We then have $\nabla\Gamma_i(\theta) = M_i^{\intercal}(M_i\theta - \xi_i)$, so the SA algorithm is defined by

$$\theta_{n+1} = \theta_n - \alpha_{n+1} M_{n+1}^{\intercal}\{M_{n+1}\theta_n - \xi_{n+1}\}. \tag{8.43}$$

The ERM solution can be obtained in closed form, by applying the first-order necessary condition for optimality $\nabla\bar{\Gamma}_N(\theta) = \mathsf{0}$, where

$$\nabla\bar{\Gamma}_N(\theta) = \frac{1}{N}\sum_{i=1}^{N} M_i^{\intercal}\{M_i\theta - \xi_i\}.$$

Consequently, provided the inverse exists,

$$\theta_N^{\text{ERM}} = \Big(\sum_{i=1}^{N} M_i^{\intercal} M_i\Big)^{-1} \sum_{i=1}^{N} M_i^{\intercal}\xi_i. \tag{8.44}$$

Proposition 8.8 shows that θ_N^{ERM} coincides exactly with a particular SA algorithm using a carefully constructed matrix gain:

$$\theta_{n+1} = \theta_n - \alpha_{n+1} G_{n+1} M_{n+1}^{\intercal}\{M_{n+1}\theta_n - \xi_{n+1}\}, \tag{8.45}$$

in which

$$G_{n+1}^{-1} = \frac{1}{n+1}\Big(\sum_{i=1}^{n+1} M_i^{\intercal} M_i\Big), \qquad n \geq 0.$$

It will follow from Proposition 8.8 that θ_N^{ERM} is in an estimate of θ^* with minimum covariance.

Outside of some special cases (such as very high dimension), ERM should be regarded as a last resort. ERM and Zap each have approximately the same covariance as the PJR estimate θ_N^{PR} defined in (8.10b). *Given the simplicity of the recursions defining* θ_N^{PR}, *this is probably the first algorithm to try in most applications.*

8.4 Algorithm Design Example

The purpose of this section is to illustrate algorithm design with a simple nonlinear example. We will eventually arrive at a very efficient algorithm for this test case based on PJR averaging.

The function appearing in the SA recursion (8.2) is defined by $f_{n+1}(\theta) = f(\theta, \Phi(n+1))$ with

$$f(\theta, \Phi) = -(\theta + 3\sin(\theta)) + 10\cos(\theta)\Phi,$$

where θ and Φ are scalar, so that $f\colon \mathbb{R}^2 \to \mathbb{R}$. With Φ zero mean, we have

$$\bar{f}(\theta) = \mathsf{E}[f(\theta, \Phi)] = -(\theta + 3\sin(\theta)).$$

The plot of $\bar{f}$ in Figure 8.4 shows that $\theta^* = 0$ is the unique root.

We can integrate this function to obtain the representation $\bar{f} = -\nabla\Gamma$. The function $\Gamma(\theta) = \frac{1}{2}\theta^2 - 3\cos(\theta)$ is also shown in Figure 8.4, where we see that it is quasiconvex and coercive. The SA algorithm is an instance of stochastic gradient descent to obtain the minimizer of Γ.

8.4.1 Gain Selection

For the choice of step-size $\alpha_n = g/n$, the gain minimizing the asymptotic variance is $g = -1/A(\theta^*)$ in this scalar example. We have $A(\theta) = \partial_\theta \bar{f}(\theta) = -(1 + 3\cos(\theta))$, giving $A(\theta^*) = -4$ and $g^* = 1/4$. When considering transient performance of the SA algorithm, we will see that this is a *terrible choice*.

The transient bound (8.34) is based on global exponential asymptotic stability in the form (8.33), which is obtained through Lyapunov theory: With $V(\theta) = \frac{1}{2}\theta^2$,

$$\frac{d}{dt}V(\vartheta_\tau) = -\vartheta_\tau(\vartheta_\tau + 3\sin(\vartheta_\tau)).$$

The right-hand side is negative whenever $\vartheta_\tau \neq 0$. To obtain a bound in terms of V, consider the worst case:

$$\begin{aligned}\min_{\theta \neq 0} \frac{1}{V(\theta)}[\theta(\theta + 3\sin(\theta))] &= 2\min_{\theta \neq 0} \frac{1}{\theta}(\theta + 3\sin(\theta)) \\ &= 2 + 6\big[\min_\theta \operatorname{sinc}(\theta)\big] \geq 0.68,\end{aligned}$$

where the final bound comes from $\operatorname{sinc}(\theta) \geq -0.22$ for all θ. Denoting $\varrho_0 = 0.68/2 = 0.34$, we obtain the Lyapunov drift condition $\frac{d}{dt}V(\vartheta_\tau) \leq -2\varrho_0 V(\vartheta_\tau)$, leading to $V(\vartheta_\tau) \leq V(\vartheta_0)\exp(-2\varrho_0 t)$, and by definition of V,

$$|\vartheta_t - \theta^*| \leq |\vartheta_0 - \theta^*| \exp(-\varrho_0 t). \tag{8.46}$$

Hence (8.33) holds with $B_0 = 1$. Figure 8.4 indicates that $\varrho_0 = 0.34$ is approximately equal to the largest value such that $\bar{f}(\theta) \geq -0.34\theta$ for $\theta \leq 0$, and $\bar{f}(\theta) \leq -0.34\theta$ for $\theta \geq 0$.

The bound (8.34) becomes

$$|\vartheta^{(n)}_{\tau_{n+k}} - \theta^*| \leq |\theta_n - \theta^*| \exp(0.34g)\Big(\frac{n}{n+k}\Big)^{-0.34g}.$$

The right-hand side converges to zero at rate $1/k$ with $g = 1/0.34 \approx 3$.

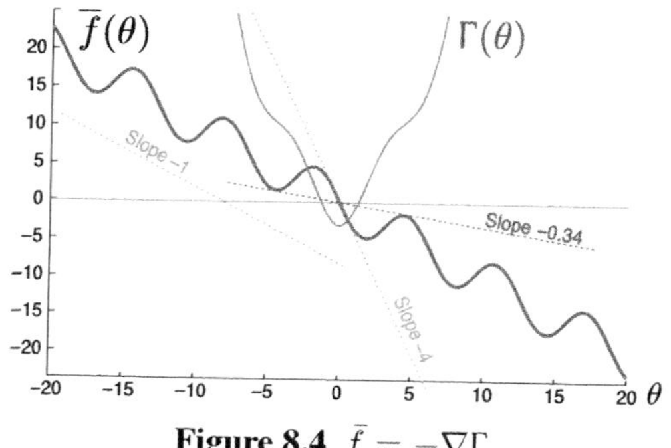

Figure 8.4 $\bar{f} = -\nabla\Gamma$.

The value $g = 1/4$ may lead to very slow transient performance, even if the mean-square error converges to zero at its optimal rate. This is illustrated in Figure 8.5. Before discussing the figure, we revisit the topic of asymptotic variance.

8.4.2 Variance Formulae

What can we expect if we increase the gain in the step-size rule $\alpha_n = g/n$? A variance formula for $g > g^*/2$ follows from (8.28a), and appears similar to the variance formula for Monte Carlo:

$$\sigma_\theta^2 = \tfrac{1}{2}\Big(\frac{g^2}{g/g^* - \frac{1}{2}}\Big)\sigma_\Delta^2. \tag{8.47}$$

The value $g = 1/0.34$ is nearly 12 times larger than the value $g^* = 1/4$ derived using asymptotic theory. The formula (8.47) can be applied to establish that σ_θ^2 is increased by more than six fold with the larger gain.

If we instead opt for $\alpha_n = g/n^\rho$, with $\rho < 1$, then the definition (8.6) results in

$$\sigma_\theta^2 = \lim_{n\to\infty} n^\rho \mathsf{E}\big[|\theta_n - \theta^*|^2\big]. \tag{8.48}$$

The formula is simpler in this case, and is valid for any $g > 0$, and any $\rho \in (0.5,1)$:

$$\sigma_\theta^2 = \tfrac{1}{2} g g^* \sigma_\Delta^2. \tag{8.49}$$

See Section 8.7.2 for details.

8.4.3 Simulations

Up until now, we have said nothing about the disturbance $\mathbf{\Phi}$, except that it has zero mean. The plots that follow used an i.i.d. Gaussian process with $\Phi_n \sim N(0,10)$. For i.i.d. disturbance, the variance term appearing on the right-hand side of (8.47) is defined by

$$\sigma_\Delta^2 = \mathsf{E}[\{f(\theta^*,\Phi_n)\}^2] = \mathsf{E}[\{10\cos(\theta^*)\Phi_n\}^2] = 100.$$

With step-size $\alpha_n = g/n$, the formula (8.47) gives

$$\sigma_\theta^2 = \begin{cases} g^2\sigma_\Delta^2 = (5/2)^2, & g = g^* = 1/4, \\ \frac{1}{2}\Big(\frac{g^2}{4g - \frac{1}{2}}\Big)\sigma_\Delta^2 \approx 6 \times (5/2)^2, & g = 1/0.34. \end{cases}$$

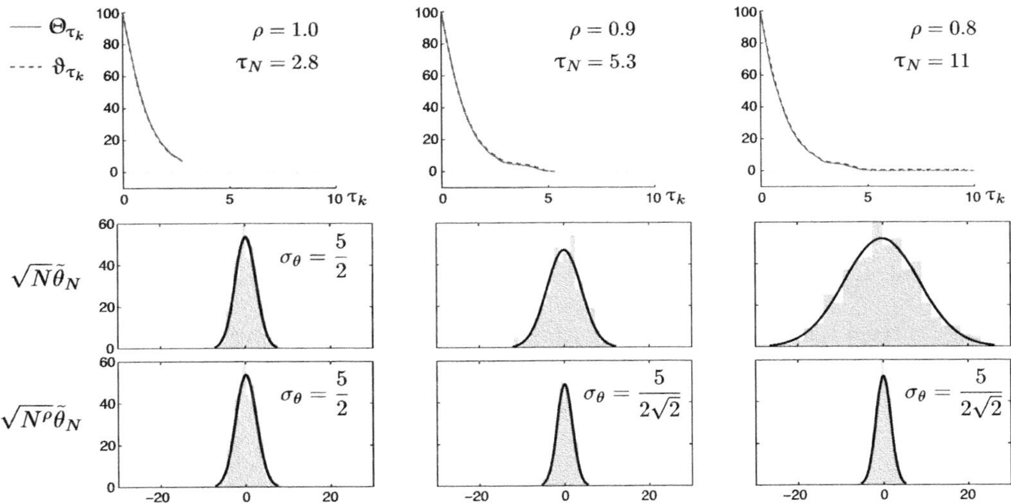

Figure 8.5 The first row shows a comparison of the parameter estimates from SA, and the sequence obtained from the Euler approximation (8.50), with common initial condition $\theta_0 = 100$. The second row shows that the CLT holds for $\rho = 1$, and the theoretical variance predicts what is observed in simulations. The third row illustrates the CLT for all three values of ρ, using the required scaling of the parameter error by $\sqrt{N^\rho}$.

Transient and Asymptotic Behavior

Figure 8.5 shows results from SA using $\alpha_n = g^*/n^\rho$ for three values of ρ. The columns are distinguished by the value of ρ. The plots shown in the first row compare the output of the algorithm $\Theta_{\tau_k} \stackrel{\text{def}}{=} \theta_k$ with the deterministic Euler approximation:

$$\vartheta_{\tau_{n+1}} = \vartheta_{\tau_n} + \alpha_{n+1}\bar{f}(\vartheta_{\tau_n}), \qquad n \geq 0, \quad \vartheta_0 = \theta_0. \tag{8.50}$$

The approximation $\Theta_{\tau_k} \approx \vartheta_{\tau_k}$ appears to be very accurate. The high accuracy is due in part to the large initial condition, since the fluctuations of θ_k are small compared to its magnitude (the plots shown in Figure 8.2 are for the same example, but with $\theta_0 = 1$). These plots are shown on the "ODE time scale": the x-axis is τ_k rather than k, so that the final time τ_N depends on the step-size:

$$\tau_N = \sum_{k=1}^{N} \alpha_k.$$

The value $N = 10^5$ was chosen in this experiment, so that $\alpha_k = g^*/k^\rho$ results in the values of τ_N shown in the top row of Figure 8.5. We see that ϑ_{τ_N} remains far from the equilibrium value $\theta^* = 0$ when using $\rho = 1$.

The histograms shown in Figure 8.5 were obtained based on 500 independent runs, time horizon $N = 10^6$, and with initial condition sampled independently $\theta_0 \sim N(0,1)$ (so that the transient behavior has less impact). The normalized error at the end of the run appears approximately Gaussian in all cases.

For the larger gain $g = 1/0.34$ the situation is very different: $|\vartheta_{\tau_n}|$ is very close to zero for $\tau_n \geq 3$, and for any value of $\rho \leq 1$. Figure 8.6 shows histograms obtained using this

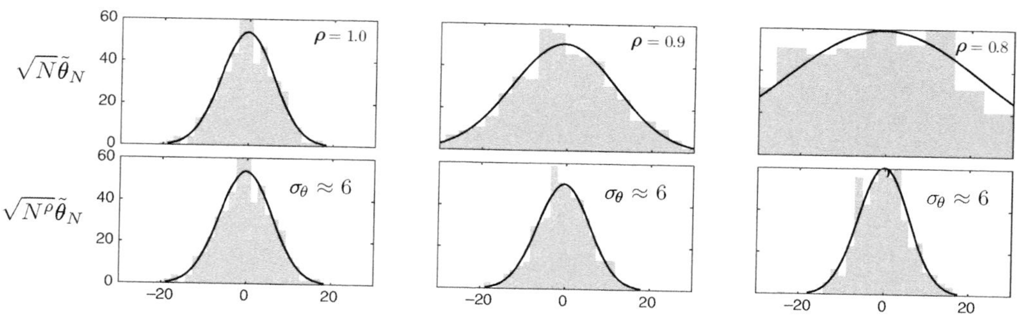

Figure 8.6 Histograms for the scaled parameter estimates using $g = 1/0.34$.

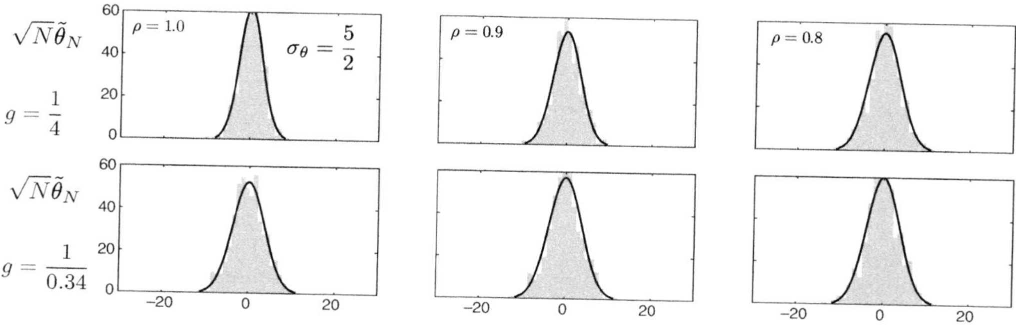

Figure 8.7 Histograms obtained using Polyak–Ruppert averaging, for two different choices of g.

larger gain. We observed earlier that (8.47) results in $\sigma_\theta \approx 6.2$ ($\rho = 1$). The formula (8.49) yields $\sigma_\theta \approx 6$ ($\rho < 1$).

PJR Averaging

We finally illustrate the value of averaging. The parameter estimates used to create the previous histograms were averaged according to the formula (8.10b), with $(N - N_0)/N = 0.4$. Figure 8.7 shows histograms of the normalized parameter estimation error for these smoothed estimates. As in the prior experiments, the columns are distinguished by ρ, and the two rows are distinguished by choice of gain g in the step-size rule $\alpha_n = g/n^\rho$.

The results are not so sensitive to choice of gain. Theory in Section 8.7.3 tells us that Polyak–Ruppert averaging will result in the optimal convergence rate for the MSE, provided the step-size $\alpha_n = g/n^\rho$ is used with $\rho \in (0.5,1)$ and $g > 0$.

8.5 Zap Stochastic Approximation

Given the amazing properties of the Polyak–Ruppert averaging technique, why would we ever consider a matrix gain algorithm? Three reasons can be found from a review of the book up to now:

(i) The most compelling motivation is Proposition 4.4, which suggests we obtain a consistent algorithm under very mild assumptions on $\bar{f}$.

(ii) The transient behavior is ideal: Recall from (4.12) we obtain $\bar{f}(\vartheta_t) = \bar{f}(\vartheta_0)e^{-t}$, which suggests good numerical properties for an SA algorithm.
(iii) What could not be predicted in the first part of this book is that the asymptotic covariance of this algorithm is also optimal (under mild assumptions on $\bar{f}$ and $\{f_n\}$).

8.5.1 Approximating the Newton–Raphson Flow

This algorithm is designed so that it approximates the regularized Newton–Raphson flow introduced in (4.15):

$$\frac{d}{dt}\vartheta_t = -[\varepsilon I + A(\vartheta_t)^{\intercal} A(\vartheta_t)]^{-1} A(\vartheta_t)^{\intercal} \mathrm{f}(\vartheta_t).$$

Zap Stochastic Approximation

Initialize $\theta_0 \in \mathbb{R}^d$, $\widehat{A}_0 \in \mathbb{R}^{d\times d}$, $\varepsilon > 0$. Update for $n \geq 0$:

$$\widehat{A}_{n+1} = \widehat{A}_n + \beta_{n+1}\big[A_{n+1} - \widehat{A}_n\big], \qquad A_{n+1} \stackrel{\text{def}}{=} \partial_\theta f_{n+1}(\theta_n), \tag{8.51a}$$

$$\theta_{n+1} = \theta_n + \alpha_{n+1} G_{n+1} f_{n+1}(\theta_n), \qquad G_{n+1} \stackrel{\text{def}}{=} -[\varepsilon I + \widehat{A}_{n+1}^{\intercal}\widehat{A}_{n+1}]^{-1}\widehat{A}_{n+1}^{\intercal}. \tag{8.51b}$$

The two step-size sequences $\{\alpha_n\}$ and $\{\beta_n\}$ satisfy (8.22):

$$\lim_{n\to\infty} \frac{\beta_n}{\alpha_n} = \infty.$$

Under the "high-gain" assumption (8.22), we expect that $\widehat{A}_{n+1}$ is a reasonable estimate of $A(\theta_n)$ for large n, with $A(\theta_n)$ defined in (8.13). This intuition is supported by the general theory of two time-scale SA, summarized briefly in Section 8.2.4. In particular, the high-gain assumption for (8.51a) tells us that we can expect the approximation $\widehat{A}_n \approx A(\theta_n)$ after a transient period. The ODE approximation for $\{\theta_n\}$ is precisely the regularized Newton–Raphson flow.

8.5.2 Zap Zero

In most of the algorithms considered in later chapters, the matrix A_{n+1} appearing in (8.51a) is of low rank. For the special case $\varepsilon = 0$, the matrix update for G_{n+1} is efficiently computed using the Matrix Inversion Lemma (A.1). This is particularly simple when the rank of A_{n+1} is equal to one, and defined in factored form $A_{n+1} = W_{n+1}V_{n+1}^{\intercal}$ with W_{n+1} and V_{n+1} column vectors. In this case, (A.1) gives the following update equation:

$$G_{n+1} = \big[G_n^{-1} - A_{n+1}\big]^{-1} = G_n - \frac{1}{1 - V_{n+1}^{\intercal} G_n W_{n+1}} G_n W_{n+1} V_{n+1}^{\intercal} G_n.$$

The right-hand side involves the two matrix-vector products, $G_n W_{n+1}$ and $V_{n+1}^{\intercal} G_n$, which introduces complexity of order $O(d^2)$.

An update of complexity $O(d)$ (and even $O(1)$) is possible under stronger conditions.

Zap Zero Stochastic Approximation

Initialize $\theta_0, \omega_0 \in \mathbb{R}^d$. Update for $n \ge 0$:

$$\theta_{n+1} = \theta_n + \alpha_{n+1}\omega_n, \tag{8.52a}$$

$$\omega_{n+1} = \omega_n + \beta_{n+1}\{A_{n+1}\omega_n + f_{n+1}(\theta_n)\}, \qquad A_{n+1} \stackrel{\text{def}}{=} \partial_\theta f_{n+1}(\theta_{n+1}). \tag{8.52b}$$

The two step-size sequences satisfy (8.22).

The multiplication $A_{n+1}\omega_n$ introduces additional complexity of order at most d. In applications, we often find that A_n is sparse. For example, in Watkins's algorithm (9.75) the matrix A_n is rank one, and also has at most two nonzero entries for each n. This is when we say that the additional complexity is zero or $O(1)$.

The fast time-scale recursion (8.52b) admits an ODE approximation with θ_n frozen:

$$\tfrac{d}{dt}\omega_t = A(\theta)\omega_t + \bar{f}(\theta).$$

Provided $A(\theta)$ is Hurwitz, the ODE is globally asymptotically stable, with equilibrium $\omega(\theta) = -A(\theta)^{-1}\bar{f}(\theta)$. Theory of two time-scale SA predicts that $\omega_n \approx \omega(\theta_n)$, and hence (8.52a) is approximated by an Euler approximation of the Newton–Raphson flow: For a vanishing vector-valued sequence $\{\varepsilon_n\}$,

$$\theta_{n+1} = \theta_n - \alpha_{n+1}[A(\theta_n)^{-1}\bar{f}(\theta_n) + \varepsilon_{n+1}].$$

Proposition 8.7 *Consider the algorithm* (8.52) *under the following assumptions:*

- $\bar{f}$ *is Lipschitz continuous, and* $A = \partial\bar{f}$ *is a bounded and Lipschitz continuous function of* θ.
- *The parameter sequences* $\{\theta_n, \omega_n : n \ge 0\}$ *are bounded a.s.*
- *The cumulative disturbance* (8.15) *vanishes in the uniform sense assumed in Theorem 8.1.*
- $A(\theta)$ *is Hurwitz for each* θ.

Then, $\lim_{n\to\infty} \bar{f}(\theta_n) = 0$. □

8.5.3 Stochastic Newton–Raphson

The algorithm (8.51) with $\beta_n = \alpha_n$ for each n, and $\varepsilon = 0$, is called stochastic Newton–Raphson (SNR). For the special case $\alpha_n = \beta_n = 1/n$, and $\varepsilon = 0$, the matrix sequence defined in (8.51a) reduces to the average of $\{A_n\}$. This uniform averaging is not desirable, and in particular hinders stability analysis. It is unlikely that this SNR ODE enjoys the same universal stability properties as the Newton–Raphson flow.

SNR for Linear SA

Consider the linear setting:

$$f_{n+1}(\theta) = A_{n+1}\theta - b_{n+1}, \qquad \bar{f}(\theta) = A\theta - b. \tag{8.53a}$$

The basic SA algorithm is defined by

$$\theta_{n+1} = \theta_n + \alpha_{n+1}\big[A_{n+1}\theta_n - b_{n+1}\big]. \tag{8.53b}$$

This is a very special case because $A(\theta) = \mathsf{E}[A_n]$ does not depend upon θ. It is the only situation for which relaxation of the assumption (8.22) can be easily justified.

The proposition that follows considers SNR using $\alpha_n = \beta_n = 1/n$, so that in particular (8.51a) becomes

$$\widehat{A}_{n+1} = \widehat{A}_n + \frac{1}{n+1}[A_{n+1} - \widehat{A}_n].$$

Recall from Section 8.3.1 that the solution to this recursion can be expressed as an average:

$$\widehat{A}_{n+1} = \frac{1}{n+1}\sum_{k=1}^{n+1} A_{n+1}.$$

Proposition 8.8 *Consider the SNR algorithm for the linear model* (8.53a) *in the following form:*

$$\begin{aligned}\theta_{n+1} &= \theta_n - \frac{1}{n+1}\widehat{A}_{n+1}^{-1}[A_{n+1}\theta_n - b_{n+1}],\\ \widehat{A}_{n+1} &= \frac{1}{n+1}\Big\{\widehat{A}_0 + \sum_{k=1}^{n+1} A_k\Big\}.\end{aligned} \tag{8.54}$$

Suppose that the $d \times d$ matrix $\widehat{A}_0$ is chosen so that $\widehat{A}_n$ is invertible for each n. Then for each $n \geq 1$, regardless of the initial condition θ_0,

$$\theta_n = \widehat{A}_n^{-1}\widehat{b}_n, \qquad \textit{where} \quad \widehat{b}_n = \frac{1}{n}\sum_{k=1}^{n} b_k.$$

An example is the minimization of a quadratic loss function with noisy observations, in the setting of Section 8.3.3. This is the linear SA algorithm (8.53b) with $A_n = -M_n^{\intercal}M_n$, $b_n = M_n^{\intercal}\xi_n$, and $A(\theta) = -\mathsf{E}[M_n^{\intercal}M_n] < 0$ by assumption. We also have $M_n^{\intercal}M_n \geq 0$ for all n, so any initialization $\widehat{A}_0 < 0$ will satisfy the assumption of the proposition. Proposition 8.8 implies that SNR is essentially equivalent to ERM.

For the more general (nonquadratic) optimization problem (8.42), we cannot claim that θ_n^{ERM} is identical to the solution obtained using SNR (we do not even know if stochastic gradient descent using SNR will be consistent). Algorithms can be obtained using Zap SA or PJR averaging to obtain the same asymptotic covariance as ERM.

Proof of Proposition 8.8 Multiply each side of the recursion for $\{\theta_n\}$ in (8.54) by $(n+1)\widehat{A}_{n+1}$ to obtain

$$(n+1)\widehat{A}_{n+1}\theta_{n+1} = (n+1)\widehat{A}_{n+1}\theta_n - [A_{n+1}\theta_n - b_{n+1}].$$

By definition, $(n+1)\widehat{A}_{n+1} = n\widehat{A}_n + A_{n+1}$, giving

$$\begin{aligned}(n+1)\widehat{A}_{n+1}\theta_{n+1} &= [n\widehat{A}_n + A_{n+1}]\theta_n - [A_{n+1}\theta_n - b_{n+1}]\\ &= n\widehat{A}_n\theta_n + b_{n+1}.\end{aligned}$$

Iterating this recursion gives $(n+1)\widehat{A}_{n+1}\theta_{n+1} = \sum_{k=1}^{n+1} b_k$ for each $n \geq 0$. □

8.6 Buyer Beware

Stochastic approximation can be difficult to apply because of exotic nonlinear dynamics. This is often resolved using Zap SA, while PJR averaging might fail. Two other potential curses are described here: condition number, and disturbances with long memory.

8.6.1 Curse of Condition Number

The *condition number* of the linearization matrix $A = \partial \bar{f}(\theta^*)$ is the ratio of maximal and minimal singular values:

$$\kappa(A) = \frac{\sigma_{\max}(A)}{\sigma_{\min}(A)}, \tag{8.55}$$

where the singular values $\{\sigma_i(A)\}$ are obtained by taking the square root of each of the eigenvalues of $AA^\intercal$. If the condition number is large, then the value of Polyak–Ruppert averaging may not be observed until after a very long run length.

The example and discussion here is early warning of what might go wrong in reinforcement learning. The standard Q-learning algorithm of Watkins typically has a linearization matrix A with a massive condition number, and examples in Section 9.6 reveal that PJR averaging may provide no benefit for time horizons less than 10 million.

This point is illustrated using the linear SA recursion

$$\theta_{n+1} = \theta_n + \alpha_{n+1}\{A\theta_n + \Delta_{n+1}\}, \tag{8.56}$$

in which $\boldsymbol{\Delta}$ is Gaussian and i.i.d., with marginal $N(0,I)$. The matrix is taken to be a simple form:

$$A = -[I + (\kappa - 1)vv^\intercal],$$

in which $\|v\| = 1$ and $\kappa > 1$. The matrix $-A$ has one eigenvalue at κ (with eigenvector v), and the remaining eigenvalues are unity. The condition number of A is κ.

Let's now compare two algorithms with optimal asymptotic covariance:

(i) Stochastic Newton–Raphson:

$$\theta^{\text{Zap}}_{n+1} = \theta^{\text{Zap}}_n + \tfrac{1}{n+1}\{\theta^{\text{Zap}}_n - A^{-1}\Delta_{n+1}\}. \tag{8.57}$$

(ii) PJR estimates with carefully selected step-size. One challenge with a large condition number is that the step-size must be reduced to avoid initial explosion of the parameter estimates. This is required even if there is no noise, so that $\bar{f} \equiv f_n$. This motivates the modification

$$\alpha_n = \min(\alpha_0, n^{-\rho}). \tag{8.58}$$

The value $\alpha_0 = 1/\kappa$ was reliable in all experiments, with $\rho \in (1/2, 1)$.

Either algorithm achieves the optimal asymptotic covariance,

$$\Sigma^\star_\theta = G\Sigma_\Delta G^\intercal = (A^2)^{-1} = (I + rvv^\intercal)^{-1} = I - \frac{r}{1+r}vv^\intercal,$$

with $r = \kappa^2 - 1$. In particular, either approach results in the optimal asymptotic variance for each component of the parameter:

$$\lim_{n\to\infty} n\mathsf{E}[\theta^{\text{Zap}}_n(i)^2] = \lim_{n\to\infty} n\mathsf{E}[\theta^{\text{PR}}_n(i)^2] = \Sigma^\star_\theta(i).$$

In fact, no limit is required for the Zap SA recursion. This is seen through a refinement of Proposition 8.8: First note that when $n = 0$ in (8.57), the initial condition is canceled:

$$\theta_1^{\text{Zap}} = \theta_0^{\text{Zap}} + \{\theta_0^{\text{Zap}} - A^{-1}\Delta_1\} = -A^{-1}\Delta_1.$$

It can be shown by induction that for each $n \geq 1$,

$$\theta_n^{\text{Zap}} = -A^{-1}\frac{1}{n}\sum_{k=1}^{n}\Delta_k.$$

Hence $\sqrt{n}\theta_n^{\text{Zap}} \sim N(0,\Sigma^*)$ for each n!

In the experimental results described here, the vector v was chosen as $v = z/\|z\|$, with z selected $N(0,d)$ with $d = 50$. It was found that $\Sigma_\theta^\star(i)$ was close to unity for each i for the values of κ considered.

The exponent for Polyak–Ruppert averaging was taken to be $\rho = 0.75$, with averaging over the recent 70% of samples:

$$\theta_n^{\text{PR}} = \frac{1}{0.7n}\sum_{0.3n\leq k\leq n}\theta_n.$$

Histograms were obtained for $\{Z_n^i = \sqrt{n}\theta_n^i : 1 \leq i \leq 500\}$ (500 independent runs), with initialization $\theta_0^i \sim N(0,\sigma^2 I)$ using $\sigma^2 = 25$.

For $\kappa = 100$, the behaviors of Zap and Polyak–Ruppert estimates are very similar after just 10^3 iterations. Increasing the value to $\kappa = 500$ revealed difficulties. The source of the problem is clear from Figure 8.8: The bound $\alpha_n \leq 1/\kappa$ was imposed to avoid explosion of the parameter estimates. The figure shows only the first three parameter estimates for each of the three parameter estimate sequences. In these close-ups, the estimates $\theta_n(1)$ and $\theta_n^{\text{PR}}(1)$ are not even visible since $\theta_0(1)$ is out of range and the step-size is so small.

Figure 8.9, showing histograms at $n = 10^3$, reveals significantly high variance when using Polyak–Ruppert averaging. With $n = 10^4$, the situation is improved, and the results from PJR averaging are more similar to SNR.

However, $n = 10^4$ samples is no longer sufficient if the condition number κ is increased from 500 to 1,000. The empirical variance of each parameter is found to be approximately 14 for $n = 10^4$ when using PJR averaging, while the optimal variance is slightly less than one.

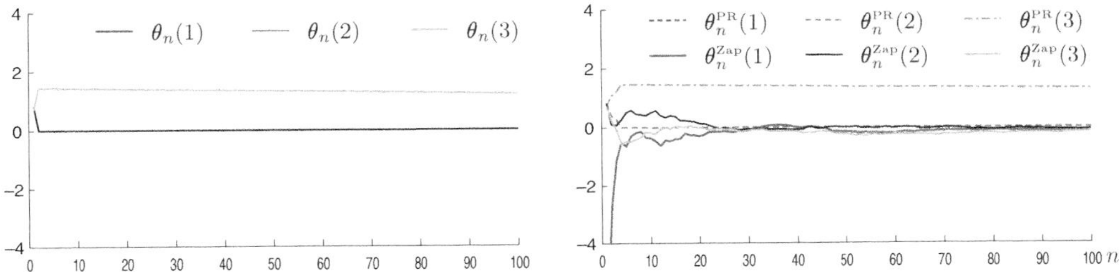

Figure 8.8 Comparison of the first three parameter estimates. The left-hand side shows parameter estimates using (8.56) with step-size $\alpha_n = \min(1/\kappa, 1/n)$. The right-hand side compares Zap SA and PJR-averaging.

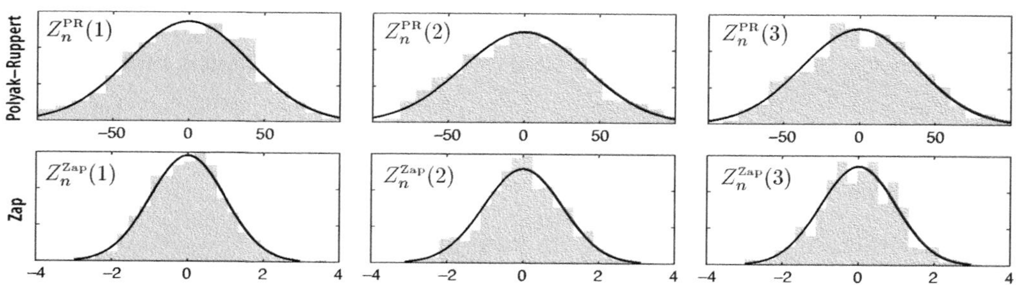

Figure 8.9 Histograms of the first three parameter estimates. For the Zap SA recursion, the estimates are Gaussian with distribution $N(0,\Sigma^*(i,i))$ for each $i = 1,2,3$.

8.6.2 Curse of Markovian Memory

The preceding example is special because the "noise" is i.i.d. rather than the Markovian noise that is typical in RL. To illustrate how memory can present challenges, we consider once more a linear algorithm, but this includes "multiplicative noise":

$$\theta_{n+1} = \theta_n + \alpha_{n+1}[A_{n+1}\theta_n + \Delta_{n+1}], \qquad \theta_0 \in \mathbb{R}, \tag{8.59}$$

in which $A_{n+1} = X(n+1) - \eta - 1$, where $\boldsymbol{X}$ is a sample of the M/M/1 queue (transition matrix given in (6.14)) and $\boldsymbol{\Delta}$ is i.i.d. $N(0,1)$ and independent of $\boldsymbol{X}$. Recall from Section 6.7.4 that the Markov chain $\boldsymbol{X}$ has many desirable properties, provided $\mu > \alpha$ (the load condition for the single server queue). In particular, it is reversible and geometrically ergodic, with geometric invariant pmf and $\eta \stackrel{\text{def}}{=} \mathsf{E}_\pi[X(n)] = \alpha/(\mu-\alpha)$.

The ODE approximation for (8.59) has linear vector field $\bar{f}(\theta) = -\theta$, so we expect convergence to $\theta^* = 0$ from each initial condition. Moreover, given that the estimates converge to zero, we might attempt to obtain a CLT and moment bounds through the following representation:

$$\theta_{n+1} = \theta_n + \alpha_{n+1}[-\theta_n + \widetilde{\Delta}_{n+1}], \qquad \theta_0 \in \mathbb{R},$$

where $\widetilde{\Delta}_{n+1} = \Delta_{n+1} + (X(n+1) - \eta)\theta_n$. Since θ_n converges to zero, this suggests we might attempt to treat this as a scalar version of the linear SA recursion (8.56) with $A = -1$, for which the CLT holds with asymptotic variance equal to one.

However, the difficulties discussed in Section 6.7.4 concerning estimation of the steady-state mean have a parallel here. If the load satisfies $\rho = \alpha/\mu \geq 1/2$, then $\mathsf{E}[\theta_n^2] \to \infty$ as $n \to \infty$ using $\alpha_n = 1/n$, which corresponds to Zap SA for this simple example (see the "Notes" for references). It is likely the second moment is also unbounded for estimates obtained using PJR averaging.

Figure 8.10 shows some positive news: Histograms of the normalized error $Z_n = \sqrt{n}\theta_n$ appear to be nearly Gaussian $N(0,1)$ even for high load. What is missing from these plots is outliers that were removed before plotting the histograms. For load $\alpha/\mu = 3/7$, the outliers were few and not large. For load $\alpha/\mu = 6/7$, nearly 1/3 of the samples were labeled as outliers for both PJR averaging and Zap, and in this case the outliers were massive: Values exceeding 10^{20} were observed in about 1/5 of runs.

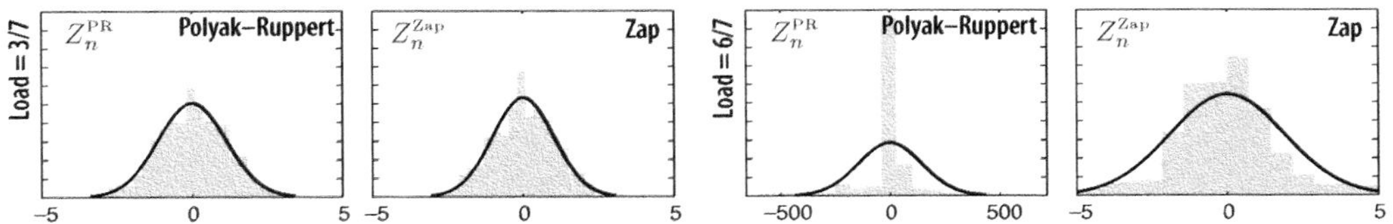

Figure 8.10 Histograms of the normalized error for the scalar SA recursion with Markovian multiplicative disturbance. The time horizon was 10^4 for the smaller load, and 10^5 for load 6/7.

8.7 Some Theory*

This chapter is technical, but intentionally incomplete. The main challenge is space – theory of stochastic approximation takes a sizable book of its own, as prior books will attest. The details of stability and convergence theory are skipped because these results follow the same steps as in the theory of quasistochastic approximation from Section 4.5.

The purpose of this section is to highlight the parallels between QSA and SA theory, and point out some differences (especially for analysis of PJR averaging, which takes up most of the space in this section).

To streamline discussion, we will impose strong assumptions:

(SA1) $\bar{f}$ is Lipschitz continuous.

(SA2) The sequence $\{\Delta_n : n \geq 1\}$ is a martingale difference sequence:

$$\mathsf{E}[\Delta_{n+1} \mid \mathcal{F}_n] = 0, \qquad n \geq 0, \tag{8.60a}$$

with $\mathcal{F}_n = \sigma\{\Phi(k) : k \leq n\}$. Moreover, for some $\bar{\sigma}^2_\Delta < \infty$,

$$\mathsf{E}[\|\Delta_{n+1}\|^2 \mid \mathcal{F}_n] \leq \bar{\sigma}^2_\Delta(1 + \|\theta_n\|^2). \qquad n \geq 0. \tag{8.60b}$$

(SA3) The sequence $\{\alpha_n : n \geq 1\}$ is deterministic, satisfies $0 < \alpha_n \leq 1$, and

$$\sum_{n=1}^{\infty} \alpha_n = \infty, \qquad \sum_{n=1}^{\infty} \alpha_n^2 < \infty. \tag{8.61}$$

□

See the "Notes" section to find sources for much stronger conclusions under weaker assumptions. Much of this theory is very recent.

In particular, Assumption (SA2) is imposed here for simplicity: It is not essential for the convergence theory for SA [39, 65, 66, 204]. This condition holds when $\boldsymbol{\Phi}$ is i.i.d., and also for TD-learning and Q-learning in special cases (see, for example, Proposition 9.16).

8.7.1 Stability and Convergence

If you have read Section 4.9, then you know that convergence of SA is not difficult to establish, once you have determined that the estimates $\{\theta_n : n \geq 0\}$ are bounded.

Conditions for boundedness follow the stability theory for QSA based on a Lyapunov function, or via the ODE@∞ recalled here:

$$\tfrac{d}{dt}\vartheta_t = \bar{f}_\infty(\vartheta_t), \tag{8.62}$$

with $\bar{f}_\infty$ defined in (4.138): $\bar{f}_\infty(\theta) \stackrel{\text{def}}{=} \lim_{r\to\infty} \bar{f}_r(\theta) = \lim_{r\to\infty} r^{-1}\bar{f}(r\theta)$ for any $\theta \in \mathbb{R}^d$.

The first row of Figure 8.5 might be viewed as illustration of the approximation of SA by the solution to the ODE $\frac{d}{dt}\vartheta = \bar{f}_r(\vartheta)$, with $r\theta = \theta_0 = 100$.

The Lyapunov criterion is (QSV1): For a differentiable Lyapunov function, this is equivalently expressed

$$\tfrac{d}{dt}V(\vartheta_t) \le -\delta_0\|\vartheta_t\|, \qquad \text{whenever } \|\vartheta_t\| > c_0.$$

Theorem 8.9 *Suppose that (SA1)–(SA3) hold, along with one of the following two conditions:*

(i) *(QSV1) holds with V Lipschitz continuous.*
(ii) *The origin is asymptotically stable for the ODE@∞.*

Then the SA recursion is ultimately bounded in the following sense: There exists $\bar{\sigma}_\theta < \infty$ such that for any initial condition,

$$\limsup_{n\to\infty} \|\theta_n\| \le \bar{\sigma}_\theta \quad a.s. \qquad \textit{and} \qquad \limsup_{n\to\infty} \mathsf{E}[\|\theta_n\|^2] \le \bar{\sigma}_\theta^2. \tag{8.63}$$

□

The proof of the almost sure bound in (8.63) is identical to the proofs obtained for QSA. The mean-square error bound requires more work.

8.7.2 Linearization and Convergence Rates

Section 8.7.3 contains a complete analysis of the asymptotic covariance when using PJR averaging, which begins with the following approximation:

$$f_{n+1}(\theta_n) = A(\theta_n - \theta^*) + \Delta_{n+1} + \mathcal{E}_f(\theta_n), \tag{8.64}$$

where

$$\mathcal{E}_f(\theta) = \bar{f}(\theta) - A[\theta - \theta^*] \quad \text{error in a first}-\text{order Taylor series approximation for } \bar{f}. \tag{8.65}$$

The difficult work involves mean-square bounds on the two terms $\left[\Delta_{n+1} - \Delta_{n+1}^\infty\right]$ and $\mathcal{E}_f(\theta_n)$.

To expose the most interesting concepts, we consider a special instance of the linear SA recursion (8.53a) for which $\mathcal{E}_f$ is eliminated. Consider the simplest setting:

$$f_{n+1}(\theta_n) = A\tilde{\theta}_n + \Delta_{n+1}, \tag{8.66}$$

with A Hurwitz, and $\tilde{\theta}_n = \theta_n - \theta^*$. For analysis, it is convenient to express the linear recursion in terms of the error:

$$\tilde{\theta}_{n+1} = \tilde{\theta}_n + \alpha_{n+1}\{A\tilde{\theta}_n + \Delta_{n+1}\}. \tag{8.67}$$

The scaled error is denoted

$$Z_n \stackrel{\text{def}}{=} \frac{1}{\sqrt{\alpha_n}}\tilde{\theta}_n, \text{ and } \Sigma_n^Z \stackrel{\text{def}}{=} \mathsf{E}[Z_n Z_n^{\intercal}] = \frac{1}{\alpha_n}\mathsf{E}[\tilde{\theta}_n\tilde{\theta}_n^{\intercal}]. \tag{8.68}$$

Proposition 8.10 *Suppose that $\{\Delta_n\}$ satisfies (SA2), and that the covariance is independent of n. Then the following approximations hold:*

(i) *With $\alpha_n = 1/(n+n_0)$,*

$$\Sigma_{n+1}^Z = \Sigma_n^Z + \frac{1}{n+n_0}\Big\{(A+\tfrac{1}{2}I+\mathcal{E}_n)\Sigma_n^Z + \Sigma_n^Z(A+\tfrac{1}{2}I+\mathcal{E}_n)^{\intercal} + \Sigma_\Delta\Big)\Big\}, \tag{8.69a}$$

with $\|\mathcal{E}_n\| = O(1/n)$. If in addition the matrix $A+\frac{1}{2}I$ is Hurwitz, then Σ_n^Z converges to Σ_θ, and this limit is the solution to the Lyapunov equation (8.28a).

(ii) *With $\alpha_n = 1/(n+n_0)^\rho$, using $\frac{1}{2} < \rho < 1$,*

$$\Sigma_{n+1}^Z = \Sigma_n^Z + \frac{1}{n+n_0}\Big\{(A+\mathcal{E}_n)\Sigma_n^Z + \Sigma_n^Z(A+\mathcal{E}_n)^{\intercal} + \Sigma_\Delta\Big)\Big\}, \tag{8.69b}$$

with $\|\mathcal{E}_n\| = O(1/n)$. If in addition the matrix A is Hurwitz, then Σ_n^Z converges to Σ_θ, and this limit is the solution to the Lyapunov equation (8.28b).

Proof In both parts, we simplify the calculations by setting $n_0 = 0$. This is justified since with $\rho \in (\frac{1}{2},1]$ and $n_0 > 0$ fixed, we have the following for any $n \geq 1$:

$$\frac{1}{(n+n_0)^\rho} = \frac{1}{n^\rho} + O\Big(\frac{1}{n^{1+\rho}}\Big).$$

(i) The approximation (8.69a) begins with the Taylor series approximation

$$\sqrt{n+1} = \sqrt{n} + \frac{1}{2\sqrt{n}} + O(n^{-1})\frac{1}{\sqrt{n}}.$$

Multiplying both sides of the recursion (8.67) by $\sqrt{n+1}$ results in a recursion for $\boldsymbol{Z}$:

$$Z_{n+1} = Z_n + \frac{1}{n+1}\Big\{(A+\tfrac{1}{2}I+\varepsilon_n I)Z_n + \sqrt{n+1}\Delta_{n+1}\Big\}, \tag{8.70}$$

with $\varepsilon_n = O(n^{-1})$. Taking outer products on both sides of the recursion, and then taking expectations, we obtain the recursion (8.69a) after simplifications. It is in this step that we use the fact that $\boldsymbol{\Delta}$ is a martingale difference sequence, so in particular,

$$\mathsf{E}[Z_n\Delta_{n+1}^{\intercal}] = \mathsf{E}[\Delta_{n+1}Z_n^{\intercal}] = 0.$$

The recursion (8.69a) can be viewed as a linear stochastic approximation algorithm of the form (8.53b), subject to multiplicative noise that is $O(1/n)$. Convergence follows under the Hurwitz assumption on $A+\frac{1}{2}I$.

The proof of (ii) is identical, following the Taylor series approximation

$$(n+1)^{\rho/2} = n^{\rho/2} + O(n^{-1})n^{\rho/2}.$$

Multiplying both sides of the recursion (8.67) by $(n+1)^{\rho/2}$ results in a recursion for Z:

$$Z_{n+1} = (1+\varepsilon_n)Z_n + \frac{1}{(n+1)^\rho}\Big\{A(1+\varepsilon_n)Z_n + (n+1)^{\rho/2}\Delta_{n+1}\Big\}, \tag{8.71}$$

where $\varepsilon_n = O(n^{-1})$. The conclusions of (ii) follow. □

8.7.3 Polyak–Ruppert Averaging

We conclude with an approximation of the error covariance obtained using PJR averaging, denoted

$$\Sigma_n^{\text{PR}} \stackrel{\text{def}}{=} \mathsf{E}[\{\theta_n^\bullet - \theta^*\}\{\theta_n^\bullet - \theta^*\}^\intercal].$$

The goal is to justify the approximation $n\Sigma_n^{\text{PR}} \approx \Sigma_\theta^\star$, where $\Sigma_\theta^\star \stackrel{\text{def}}{=} A^{-1}\Sigma_\Delta(A^{-1})^\intercal$ denotes the optimal asymptotic covariance matrix.

The following two simple lemmas are our starting point.

Lemma 8.11 *The Polyak–Ruppert estimate can be expressed*

$$\theta_N^{\text{PR}} = \theta^* - \frac{1}{N-N_0}A^{-1}\big[M_N^\infty - S_N^f + S_N^T + S_N^{\widetilde{\Delta}}\big], \tag{8.72}$$

where $A = A(\theta^*)$,

$$M_N^\infty = \sum_{n=N_0+1}^{N} f_{n+1}(\theta^*) = \sum_{n=N_0+1}^{N} \Delta_{n+1}^\infty, \tag{8.73a}$$

$$S_N^f = \sum_{n=N_0+1}^{N} f_{n+1}(\theta_n^\bullet), \tag{8.73b}$$

$$S_N^T = \sum_{n=N_0+1}^{N} \mathcal{E}_f(\theta_n^\bullet), \tag{8.73c}$$

$$S_N^{\widetilde{\Delta}} = \sum_{n=N_0+1}^{N} \{\Delta_{n+1} - \Delta_{n+1}^\infty\}, \tag{8.73d}$$

with $\mathcal{E}_f(\theta)$ *defined as in* (8.65), *and as in* (8.3b),

$$\Delta_{n+1} = f_{n+1}(\theta_n^\bullet) - \bar{f}(\theta_n^\bullet). \tag{8.74}$$

Proof By the definitions.

$$f_{n+1}(\theta_n^\bullet) = \bar{f}(\theta_n^\bullet) + \Delta_{n+1} = A[\theta_n^\bullet - \theta^*] + \Delta_{n+1}^\infty + \mathcal{E}_f(\theta_n^\bullet) + \{\Delta_{n+1} - \Delta_{n+1}^\infty\}.$$

The representation follows on multiplying each side of the equation by A^{-1}, summing over n, and rearranging terms. □

Under general conditions, the first term (8.73a) dominates, and from this we obtain

$$(N-N_0)\Sigma_N^{\text{PR}} = \frac{1}{N-N_0}A\mathsf{Cov}(M_N^\infty)A^\intercal + o(1) = \Sigma_\theta^\star + o(1). \tag{8.75}$$

It isn't difficult to see that two of the other terms should be relatively small:

(i) $\mathcal{E}_f(\theta^\bullet_n) = O(\|\theta^\bullet_n - \theta^*\|^2)$ when $\bar{f}$ is smooth.
(ii) We can only expect $\Delta_{n+1} - \Delta^\infty_{n+1} = O(\|\theta^\bullet_n - \theta^*\|)$ (without the square). It is the sum S^T_N that is small (compared to M_N) under (SA2).

It is a simple miracle that $\{S^f_N\}$ is small relative to $\{M^\infty_N\}$, given their very similar definitions. Bounds on $\{S^f_N\}$ are made possible by another representation, obtained by first rearranging the terms in (8.10a):

$$f_{n+1}(\theta^\bullet_n) = \frac{1}{\beta_{n+1}}[\tilde{\theta}^\bullet_{n+1} - \tilde{\theta}^\bullet_n], \tag{8.76}$$

with $\tilde{\theta}^\bullet_n = \theta^\bullet_n - \theta^*$. A useful representation for the sum is obtained using this simple transformation:

Lemma 8.12 (Summation by Parts) *For any two real-valued sequences* $\{x_n, y_n : n \ge 0\}$ *and integers* $0 \le N_0 < N$*,*

$$\sum_{n=N_0+1}^{N} x_n(y_n - y_{n-1}) = x_{N+1}y_N - x_{N_0+1}y_{N_0} - \sum_{n=N_0+1}^{N} (x_{n+1} - x_n)y_n. \qquad \square$$

Consequently,

$$\begin{aligned} S^f_N &= \sum_{n=N_0+1}^{N} \frac{1}{\beta_{n+1}}[\tilde{\theta}^\bullet_{n+1} - \tilde{\theta}^\bullet_n] \\ &= \frac{1}{\beta_{N+1}}\tilde{\theta}^\bullet_N - \frac{1}{\beta_{N_0+1}}\tilde{\theta}^\bullet_{N_0} - \sum_{n=N_0+1}^{N}\Big(\frac{1}{\beta_{n+1}} - \frac{1}{\beta_n}\Big)\tilde{\theta}^\bullet_n. \end{aligned} \tag{8.77}$$

The assumptions imposed in the following discussion imply strong bounds on each term.

Assumptions for PJR Averaging

For fixed constants b_Δ, b_f, b_Z, and every $n \ge 1$,

(PR1) The step-size sequence is $\beta_n = n^{-\rho}$ with $\frac{1}{2} < \rho < 1$.
(PR2) $\mathsf{E}[\Delta^\infty_n \Delta^{\infty\intercal}_n] = \Sigma_\Delta + O(\varrho^n)$ for some $\varrho \in (0,1)$.
$\mathsf{E}[\Delta_{n+1} \mid \mathcal{F}_n] = \mathsf{E}[\Delta^\infty_{n+1} \mid \mathcal{F}_n] = 0$, and

$$\mathsf{E}[\|\Delta_{n+1} - \Delta^\infty_{n+1}\|^2 \mid \mathcal{F}_n] \le b_\Delta \|\tilde{\theta}^\bullet_n\|^2.$$

(PR3) $\|\mathcal{E}_f(\theta^\bullet_n)\| \le b_f \|\tilde{\theta}^\bullet_n\|^2$.
(PR4) $\mathsf{E}[\|Z_n\|^4] \le b_Z$, with $Z_n = n^{\rho/2}\tilde{\theta}^\bullet_n$.

Once again, the martingale difference assumption in (PR2) is stronger than required, but allows for relatively simple calculations. The fourth moment for Z is not difficult to establish under a slight strengthening of (PR2):

$$\mathsf{E}[\|\Delta_{n+1} - \Delta^\infty_{n+1}\|^4 \mid \mathcal{F}_n] \le b'_\Delta \|\tilde{\theta}^\bullet_n\|^4$$

for a constant b'_Δ, along with either (i) or (ii) of Proposition 8.9.

The optimal convergence rate for PJR is now easily established. For simplicity, we take $N_0 = 0$ in Theorem 8.13.

Theorem 8.13 *Under (PR1)–(PR4), consider the PJR scheme obtained for arbitrary $N \ge 1$ and $N_0 = 0$. Then (8.75) holds in the form*

$$\Sigma_N^{\mathsf{PR}} = \frac{1}{N}\Sigma_\theta^\star + \Sigma_N^\varepsilon,$$

where $\Sigma_\theta^\star = A\Sigma_\Delta A^\intercal$, $\|\Sigma_N^\varepsilon\| \le O(N^{-1-\delta})$, and with $\delta = \min\big(\frac{1}{2}(1-\rho),\rho - \frac{1}{2},\rho/2\big) > 0$. Consequently, the asymptotic covariance for $\{\theta_N^{\mathsf{PR}}\}$ is optimal.

We require a simple companion to summation by parts:

Lemma 8.14 *The following bounds hold under (PR1):*

$$\sum_{n=1}^N \Big|\frac{1}{\beta_{n+1}} - \frac{1}{\beta_n}\Big|\sqrt{\beta_n} = 2N^{\rho/2} + O(1) \qquad \text{and} \qquad \sum_{n=1}^N \beta_n = \frac{1}{1-\rho}N^{1-\rho} + O(1).$$

Proof Each bound is obtained by comparing a sum to an integral. Details for the first bound follow:

$$\begin{aligned}\sum_{n=1}^N \Big|\frac{1}{\beta_{n+1}} - \frac{1}{\beta_n}\Big|\sqrt{\beta_n} &= \sum_{n=1}^N [(n+1)^\rho - n^\rho]n^{-\rho/2} \\ &= \rho\sum_{n=1}^N [n^{-1}n^\rho]n^{-\rho/2} + O(1) \\ &= \rho\int_{x=1}^N x^{-1+\rho/2}\,dx + O(1) \\ &= \rho\Big(\frac{1}{\rho/2}x^{\rho/2}\Big)\Big|_1^N + O(1) = 2N^{\rho/2} + O(1).\end{aligned}$$

The proof of the second bound is similar. □

It is convenient to use vector space notation through the remainder of the proof: For any vector-valued random variable Z,

$$\|Z\|_2 \stackrel{\mathsf{def}}{=} \Big(\sum_i \mathsf{E}[Z(i)^2]\Big)^{1/2}.$$

To refine the bound (8.75) (with $N_0 = 0$), we begin with (8.72), written as

$$\tilde\theta_N^{\mathsf{PR}} = \mathcal{V}_N - \mathcal{E}_N, \qquad \text{where} \quad \mathcal{V}_N = -\frac{1}{N}A^{-1}M_N^\infty \quad \text{and} \quad \mathcal{E}_N = \frac{1}{N}A^{-1}\big[S_N^f - S_N^T - S_N^{\tilde\Delta}\big].$$

Lemma 8.15 *The covariance admits the approximation*

$$\begin{aligned}\Sigma_N^{\mathsf{PR}} &= \mathsf{Cov}(\mathcal{V}_N) + \Sigma_N^\varepsilon \\ \text{where} \quad \mathsf{Cov}(\mathcal{V}_N) &= \frac{1}{N}\Sigma_\theta^\star + O(N^{-2}), \\ \Sigma_N^\varepsilon &\le \varepsilon_N I \qquad \text{with} \quad \varepsilon_N = 2\|\mathcal{V}_N\|_2\|\mathcal{E}_N\|_2 + \|\mathcal{E}_N\|_2^2.\end{aligned}$$

Proof Note first that the approximation for the covariance of $\mathcal{V}_N$ follows immediately from (PR2). Next we obtain by the definitions

$$\Sigma_N^{\mathsf{PR}} = \mathsf{E}[(\mathcal{V}_N - \mathcal{E}_N)(\mathcal{V}_N - \mathcal{E}_N)^\intercal] = \mathsf{Cov}(\mathcal{V}_N) + \Sigma_N^\varepsilon$$

with

$$\Sigma_N^\varepsilon = \mathsf{E}\big[\mathcal{E}_N \mathcal{V}_N^\intercal + \mathcal{V}_N \mathcal{E}_N^\intercal + \mathcal{E}_N \mathcal{E}_N^\intercal\big].$$

The remainder of the proof is concerned with a bound on the maximal eigenvalue of this error term:

$$\max_{\|v\|=1} v^\intercal \Sigma_N^\varepsilon v.$$

For any $v \in \mathbb{R}^d$, we have

$$v^\intercal \Sigma_N^\varepsilon v = \mathsf{E}\big[2(v^\intercal \mathcal{E}_N)(v^\intercal \mathcal{V}_N) + (v^\intercal \mathcal{E}_N)^2\big].$$

By the Cauchy–Schwarz inequality for vectors, we have $|v^\intercal \mathcal{E}_N| \le \|\mathcal{E}_N\|$ and $|v^\intercal \mathcal{V}_N| \le \|\mathcal{V}_N\|$ when $\|v\| = 1$, and then by the Cauchy–Schwarz inequality for expectation of products of random variables, we have

$$v^\intercal \Sigma_N^\varepsilon v \le 2\|\mathcal{V}_N\|_2 \|\mathcal{E}_N\|_2 + \|\mathcal{E}_N\|_2^2 = \varepsilon_N. \qquad \square$$

Proof of Theorem 8.13 We have the following from the definitions and the triangle inequality:

$$\varepsilon_N \le 2\|\mathcal{V}_N\|_2 \frac{1}{N} \| \big(\|S_N^f\|_2 + \|S_N^T\|_2 + \|S_N^{\widetilde{\Delta}}\|_2\big) + N^{-2}\big(\|S_N^f\|_2 + \|S_N^T\|_2 + \|S_N^{\widetilde{\Delta}}\|_2\big)^2$$

and also $\|\mathcal{V}_N\|_2 \le O(N^{-1/2})$, giving

$$\varepsilon_N \le O(N^{-3/2})\big(\|S_N^f\|_2 + \|S_N^T\|_2 + \|S_N^{\widetilde{\Delta}}\|_2\big) + N^{-2}\big(\|S_N^f\|_2 + \|S_N^T\|_2 + \|S_N^{\widetilde{\Delta}}\|_2\big)^2.$$

To complete the proof, we now show that

$$N^{-3/2}\big(\|S_N^f\|_2 + \|S_N^T\|_2 + \|S_N^{\widetilde{\Delta}}\|_2\big) \le O(N^{-1-\delta}),$$

where δ is defined in the proposition. It will then follow that $\varepsilon_N \le O(N^{-1-\delta})$.

▸ $N^{-3/2}\|S_N^f\|_2 \le O(N^{-1-\frac{1}{2}(1-\rho)}) \le O(N^{-1-\delta})$: Under (PR4), we have by the definition of Z_n and Jensen's inequality,

$$\mathsf{E}[\|\tilde{\theta}^\bullet_n\|^4] \le b_Z \beta_n^2, \qquad \mathsf{E}[\|\tilde{\theta}^\bullet_n\|^2] \le \sqrt{b_Z}\beta_n. \tag{8.78}$$

The triangle inequality applied to the representation (8.77) gives

$$\begin{aligned}
\|S_N^f\|_2 &\le \frac{1}{\beta_{N+1}}\|\tilde{\theta}^\bullet_N\|_2 + \frac{1}{\beta_1}\|\tilde{\theta}^\bullet_0\|_2 + \sum_{n=1}^\infty \Big|\frac{1}{\beta_{n+1}} - \frac{1}{\beta_n}\Big| \|\tilde{\theta}^\bullet_n\|_2 \\
&\le b_Z^{1/4}\Big[\frac{\sqrt{\beta_N}}{\beta_{N+1}} + \frac{\sqrt{\|\tilde{\theta}^\bullet_0\|_2}}{\beta_1} + \sum_{n=1}^\infty \Big|\frac{1}{\beta_{n+1}} - \frac{1}{\beta_n}\Big| \sqrt{\beta_n}\Big].
\end{aligned}$$

The right-hand side is bounded by a constant times $N^{\rho/2}$ by Lemma 8.14.

▸ $N^{-3/2}\|S_N^T\|_2 \le O(N^{-1-(\rho-\frac{1}{2})}) \le O(N^{-1-\delta})$: Applying (8.78) and Lemma 8.14,

$$\|S_N^T\|_2 \le \sum_{n=1}^N \|\mathcal{E}_f(\theta^\bullet_n)\|_2 \le b_f \sum_{n=1}^N \|\tilde{\theta}^\bullet_n\|_2^2 \le b_f\sqrt{b_Z}\sum_{n=1}^N \beta_n \le O(N^{1-\rho}).$$

► $N^{-3/2}\|S_N^{\widetilde{\Delta}}\|_2 \le O(N^{-1-\rho/2}) \le O(N^{-1-\delta})$: The sequence $\{\widetilde{\Delta}_{n+1} = \Delta_{n+1} - \Delta_{n+1}^{\infty}\}$ is uncorrelated, so that

$$\|S_N^{\widetilde{\Delta}}\|_2^2 = \Big\|\sum_{n=1}^{N} \widetilde{\Delta}_{n+1}\Big\|_2^2 = \sum_{n=1}^{N} \|\widetilde{\Delta}_{n+1}\|_2^2.$$

Applying (PR2) gives $\|\widetilde{\Delta}_{n+1}\|_2^2 \le b_\Delta \mathsf{E}[\|\tilde{\theta}^{\bullet}_n\|^2]$, and from (8.78) we obtain $\|\widetilde{\Delta}_{n+1}\|_2^2 \le b_\Delta\sqrt{b_Z}\beta_n$. Putting these together with Lemma 8.14,

$$\|S_N^{\widetilde{\Delta}}\|_2^2 \le \sqrt{b_Z}b_\Delta \sum_{n=1}^{N} \beta_n \le O(N^{1-\rho}). \qquad \square$$

8.8 Exercises

8.1 Consider the linear SA recursion (8.59), this time with Gaussian multiplicative disturbance:

$$\theta_{n+1} = \theta_n + \alpha_{n+1}[(-1 + \Xi_{n+1})\theta_n + \Delta_{n+1}],$$
$$\Xi_{n+1} = \sqrt{1-\delta}\,\Xi_n + \sqrt{\delta}\Delta_{n+1}$$

with $\delta \in (0,1]$ and $\boldsymbol{\Delta}$ i.i.d. $N(0,1)$. In some sense, this multiplicative noise has far less memory than the example of Section 8.6.2. The sense in which this statement is true is made precise in [88], where the example (8.59) was first introduced.

(a) Verify that Ξ is a Markov chain whose marginals are Gaussian for each deterministic Ξ_0, and ergodic in the sense that for any $r \in \mathbb{R}$,

$$\lim_{n\to\infty} \mathsf{P}\{\Xi_n \ge r\} = \mathsf{P}\{\Delta_1 \ge r\}.$$

Consequently, the ODE approximation for this SA recursion is again linear, with $\bar{f}(\theta) = -\theta$.

(b) Repeat the experiments in Section 8.6.2 to investigate whether or not the CLT holds for this example, by obtaining a histogram of $\{Z_n^i : 1 \le i \le M\}$ for $M = 10^3$ and $n = 10^m$ for $m = 3,4,5$ (recall (8.9) for the definition of Z_n). Test several values of δ, and in each case obtain histograms after removing outliers (say, estimates satisfying $|Z_n| > 5$).

8.2 *Avoidance of Traps*. We wish to minimize the function $\Gamma(x)$ over $x \in \mathbb{R}$. We have access only to noisy measurements of its gradient:

$$Y(k) = \nabla\Gamma(\,\cdot\,) + N(k),$$

where $\boldsymbol{N}$ is i.i.d., with zero mean, and unit variance. In this exercise, you will try out the SA algorithm using $\Gamma(x) = x^2(1 + (x+10)^2)$.

(a) Apply the stochastic approximation algorithm repeatedly, from various initial conditions, to obtain estimates $\{X(k)\}$ of $x^* = 0$. Obtain an estimate of the probability that $X(\infty) = 0$ when $X(0) = 20$. Repeat, with $X(0) = -20$.

(b) Compare the sample path behavior of the standard SA algorithm, with the algorithm obtained using Polyak's averaging technique (again for $X(0) = 20$, and $X(0) = -20$). You should present histograms for multiple runs, reviewing the advice and warnings in Section 6.7.1.

(c) Propose a modification the SA algorithm to ensure that your estimates converge to $x^* = 0$ with probability one, from each initial condition.

8.9 Notes

This chapter is distilled from many years of collaborations and discussions with Vivek Borkar, Ken Duffy, Ioannis Kontoyiannis, and Eric Moulines, as well as recent collaborations with students and colleagues. Some of the material in this chapter is adapted from the first half of the book chapter [110], coauthored by a recent graduate student Adithya Devraj and colleague Ana Bušić.

For a full history of stochastic approximation, it is best to go to the classic texts [39, 65, 66, 204]. In brief, a scalar version of the stochastic approximation algorithm was introduced by Robbins and Monro in [301]. Blum in [58] extended the theory to vector-valued recursions. Convergence theory for SA appeared to be mature by the end of the 1990s, marked by the ambitious work of Benaïm on the *dynamics of stochastic approximation algorithms* [37], which led to my favorite book on the subject [65]. As made clear in the second edition [66], the theory evolves and becomes stronger each year.

What follows is a bit more history on topics most relevant to RL.

8.9.1 SA and RL

One driving force behind the recent evolution of RL has been the need for new theory to support complex RL algorithms, and one person who has formed the strongest bridge between SA and RL is Bhatnagar [180, 296, 297, 379]. The fact that many RL algorithms can be cast as instances of SA was first observed in [169, 352]. Over the decade that followed, SA theory was a primary tool of the MIT RL school [192, 193, 353, 354, 356], which had tremendous impact on my own research. With increasing interest in RL, there has been an impressive wave in contributions to stochastic recursive algorithms, with particular attention on identification of sharp bounds on the rate of convergence.

8.9.2 Stability

The stability theory contained in Section 8.7.1 is taken from [69], which is expanded upon in Borkar's monograph [65, 66]. The recent work [88] provides conditions justifying Assumption (PR4) for nonlinear SA recursions. It is shown that $\sup \mathsf{E}[\|Z_n\|^4] < \infty$ subject to two significant assumptions: The ODE@∞ is stable in the sense of Lyapunov, and the underlying Markov chain satisfies a condition slightly stronger than geometric ergodicty.

Stability conditions for two time-scale SA can be found in [209], justifying the assumptions of Theorem 8.3.

Stability theory for Zap SA is a simple corollary to the general stability theory for two time-scale SA, provided the assumptions of the theory hold. Fortunately, the stability of the Newton–Raphson flow is almost universal, even when the function $\bar{f}$ is not everywhere smooth, and this leads to convergence of Zap SA under conditions more general than predicted by the general theory [90].

The two time-scale algorithm (8.52) that defines first order Zap SA is inspired by a similar architecture used in GQ learning [234]. An alternative approach to approximate the Newton–Raphson flow without matrix inversion was introduced in [108], based on ideas similar to the second-order techniques of Polyak and Nesterov (essentially in (4.155), in which $\{\delta_k\}$ is a carefully designed matrix sequence).

8.9.3 Asymptotic Statistics

Asymptotic statistical theory for SA is extremely rich. Large deviations or CLT limits hold under very general assumptions for both SA and related Monte Carlo techniques [39, 65, 66, 188, 204, 257]. The variance analysis in Section 8.7.2 is adapted from the surveys [109, 110, 112], which themselves are based on standard material [39, 65, 66, 193, 204].

The optimal asymptotic variance, and techniques to obtain the optimum for scalar recursions, was introduced by Chung [95] soon after the introduction of SA (see also [125, 309]). Chung's algorithm can be cast as a form of stochastic Newton–Raphson (described in Section 8.5.3).

Gradient-free methods known as *stochastic quasi-Newton–Raphson* (SqNR) appeared in later work: The first such algorithm was proposed by Venter in [366], which was shown to obtain the optimal variance for a one-dimensional SA recursion. The algorithm obtains estimates of the SNR gain $-A^{-1}$ through a procedure similar to the Kiefer–Wolfowitz algorithm [182]. Ruppert introduced an extension of Venter's algorithm for vector-valued functions in [305].

The averaging technique came decades later in the independent work of Ruppert [306] and Polyak and Juditsky [287, 288] ([193] provides an accessible treatment in a simplified setting). It is noted in [266] that the averaging approach often leads to very large transients, so that the algorithm should be modified (such as through projection of parameter updates). The brief introduction in Section 8.7.3 is inspired by the elegant summary of [288] contained in [266].

The more recent Zap SA algorithm can be regarded as a significant extension of Chung's original idea. It is often far more practical, since stability is essentially universal [109, 112, 113] (see also the dissertation [107]).

8.9.4 Less Asymptotic Statistics

The articles [20, 266, 272] had significant impact because they established similar finite-n bounds for stochastic gradient descent, and also obtained the optimal covariance by use of PJR averaging. These articles also compare SA with ERM, arriving at conclusions similar to those of Section 8.3.3: In many cases, ERM leads to significant complexity without clear benefit. However, this is only true if the SA algorithm is designed with care (meaning, attention to all of the potential traps surveyed in Section 8.2).

The article [20] suggests variants of PJR averaging using a constant step-size in (8.10a). In experiments, this often works very well. Unfortunately, theory is currently lacking outside of the special linear SA model (8.66) with martingale difference disturbance [265]. The example in Section 8.6.2 and the example in Exercise 4.18 each suggest that analysis will be more challenging for linear SA when $\{A_n\}$ is a random matrix sequence, rather than fixed as in (8.66).

The recent paper [351] presents new approaches to finite-n bounds based on a combination of perturbation theory for ODEs due to Alekseev [4] and approximation theory for martingales.

The literature on finite-n error bounds for SA recursions with Markovian noise has been recent. Bounds are obtained in [49] for both vanishing step-sizes, and for (carefully selected) constant step-size TD-learning, with projection. Finite time bounds for SA with constant step-size are obtained in [333] by considering the drift of an appropriately chosen Lyapunov function. In the recent work [89] (briefly surveyed in Section 8.7.2), the limit (8.6) is refined to obtain something approaching a finite time error bound, which provides further motivation for optimizing the asymptotic covariance Σ_θ. All of this theory is encouraging: These approximations justify the use of asymptotic bounds for algorithm design.

The asymptotic covariance also lies beneath the surface in the theory of finite-time error bounds such as (8.31). Here is what can be expected from the theory of large deviations [105, 196]: on denoting the *rate function* by

$$I_i(\varepsilon) \stackrel{\text{def}}{=} -\lim_{n\to\infty} \frac{1}{n} \log \mathsf{P}\{|\theta_n(i) - \theta^*(i)| > \varepsilon\}, \tag{8.79}$$

the second-order Taylor series approximation holds:

$$I_i(\varepsilon) = \tfrac{1}{2} \frac{1}{\Sigma_\theta(i,i)} \varepsilon^2 + O(\varepsilon^3). \tag{8.80}$$

Hence a small asymptotic covariance is a prerequisite for a large rate function, and hence also a large exponent $\bar{I}(\varepsilon)$ in (8.31).

9

Temporal Difference Methods

This chapter is a gentle introduction to temporal difference methods in a stochastic environment. The main challenge here is that we cannot directly apply the ideas in Chapter 5, because the Bellman equations for MDPs involve a conditional expectation.

The discounted-cost optimality equation (DCOE) is a focus in the second half of this chapter. The state-input value function $Q^\star$ admits a model-free representation entirely analogous to (3.46): for any admissible input, and each $k \geq 0$,

$$0 = \mathsf{E}\big[-Q^\star(X(k),U(k)) + c(X(k),U(k)) + \gamma \underline{Q}^\star(X(k+1)) \mid \mathcal{F}_k\big], \tag{9.1}$$

where $\underline{Q}^\star(x) \stackrel{\text{def}}{=} \min_u Q^\star(x,u)$, and $\mathcal{F}_k$ represents the "history up to time k." Section 9.2 contains a tutorial on conditional expectations that is intended to simultaneously demystify these abstractions and propose approximations of (9.1).

Asymptotic Statistics Algorithm design and performance analysis is centered around the asymptotic covariance, without forgetting warnings regarding transients (recall the examples in Section 8.4.3).

Figure 1.3 illustrates the power of asymptotic statistics for estimating confidence bounds in RL. The plots demonstrate that the covariance can be estimated based on data collected over a short run: as small as $N = 10^4$ in this example. The data were obtained from a Q-learning algorithm introduced in Section 9.7, and the *theoretical density* was computed based on the Lyapunov equation (8.28a).

This chapter may be regarded as a "part 1" on temporal difference methods. The first half of this chapter focuses on the simpler problem of approximating the value function or Q-function for a fixed (possibly randomized) policy. Algorithms to approximate $Q^\star$ are surveyed in Sections 9.6–9.8.

In addition to discounting, theory is restricted to finite state space and input space, but the notation should make it clear that these assumptions are not essential. Algorithm construction and analysis will be simplified further by focusing on the linear function approximation:

$$H^\theta = \theta^\intercal \psi, \qquad \psi \colon \mathsf{X} \times \mathsf{U} \to \mathbb{R}^d. \tag{9.2}$$

Chapter 10 contains extensions and a wealth of theory that forms a foundation for actor-critic methods.

The use of H^θ as an approximation of $Q^\star$ or a fixed-policy Q-function is a departure from the notational convention in Chapter 5, which used the more suggestive notation Q^θ. The motivation for the change will be clear in Chapter 10 when we consider a parameterized family of policies.

The following notational conventions will be followed in this chapter and the next:

Ergodicity for a Stationary Policy $\check{\phi}$ The Markov chain $\boldsymbol{X}$ has transition matrix $P_{\check{\phi}}$ defined in (7.12). The pair process $\boldsymbol{\Phi} = \{\Phi(k) \stackrel{\text{def}}{=} (X(k),U(k)) : k \geq 0\}$ is also Markovian, with state space $\mathsf{Z} = \mathsf{X} \times \mathsf{U}$, and transition matrix

$$T_{\check{\phi}}(z,z') = P_u(x,x')\check{\phi}(u' \mid x'), \qquad \text{for any } z = (x,u) \text{ and } z' = (x',u'). \tag{9.3a}$$

It is assumed that the invariant pmf π for $P_{\check{\phi}}$ is unique, and the invariant pmf for $T_{\check{\phi}}$ is then

$$\varpi(x,u) \stackrel{\text{def}}{=} \pi(x)\check{\phi}(u \mid x), \qquad x \in \mathsf{X},\ u \in \mathsf{U}. \tag{9.3b}$$

As in Chapter 5, in an attempt to streamline notation we denote

$$\psi_{(n)} \stackrel{\text{def}}{=} \psi(\Phi(n)) \quad \text{and} \quad c_n \stackrel{\text{def}}{=} c(\Phi(n)), \qquad n \geq 0 \tag{9.4}$$

with $\Phi(n) = (X(n),U(n))$ as before.

Another notational convention regarding a function $H \colon \mathsf{X} \times \mathsf{U} \to \mathbb{R}$ requires explanation. In Equations (3.7d) and (9.1) the function $\underline{Q}^\star$ is defined as a minimum. This notation will be modified, depending on the context:

Underbar notation explained. For $H \colon \mathsf{X} \times \mathsf{U} \to \mathbb{R}$,

$$\underline{H}(x) = H(x,\phi(x)) \qquad \text{Fixed-policy setting, } \phi \text{ deterministic,} \tag{9.5a}$$

$$\underline{H}(x) = \sum_u H(x,u)\check{\phi}(u \mid x) \qquad \text{Fixed-policy setting, } \check{\phi} \text{ randomized,} \tag{9.5b}$$

$$\underline{H}(x) = \min_u H(x,u) \qquad \text{Approximating a DP optimality equation.} \tag{9.5c}$$

The notation (9.5a) is a simplification of (5.28b), which stressed the particular policy of interest. The common notation is useful in this chapter and the next to stress the similarity of the various algorithms. The meaning will be clear from context.

We begin with control background and motivation for estimating the fixed-policy value function.

9.1 Policy Improvement

Let's begin with a quick recap of the fixed-policy value function. To simplify notation, we restrict to deterministic policies in this section, so that the convention (9.5a) is adopted to define $\underline{H}$.

9.1.1 Fixed-Policy Value Functions and DP Equations

Two value functions are of interest in this chapter:

$$h(x) = \sum_{k=0}^{\infty} \gamma^k \mathsf{E}[c(\Phi(k)) \mid X(0) = x], \qquad U(k) = \phi(X(k)),\ k \geq 0, \tag{9.6a}$$

$$Q(x,u) = \sum_{k=0}^{\infty} \gamma^k \mathsf{E}[c(\Phi(k)) \mid X(0) = x,\, U(0) = u], \qquad U(k) = \phi(X(k)),\ k \geq 1. \tag{9.6b}$$

The latter is known as the fixed-policy Q-function. Each satisfies a dynamic programming equation:

$$h(x) = c_\phi(x) + \gamma \sum_{x'} P_\phi(x,x')h(x'), \qquad Q(x,u) = c(x,u) + \gamma \sum_{x'} P_u(x,x')\underline{Q}(x') \tag{9.7}$$

with $c_\phi(x) = \underline{c}(x) = c(x,\phi(x))$ and $\underline{Q}(x) = Q(x,\phi(x))$ for $x \in \mathsf{X}$ (recall (9.5a)). The DP equation for h appeared in (6.33).

The chapter starts off with methods to approximate h. In this case, it is convenient to suppress dependency of the transition matrix and the cost function on ϕ. That is, we write P instead of P_ϕ, and c in place of c_ϕ. Subject to these conventions, the DP equation for h in (9.7) becomes $h = c + \gamma P h$, with the probabilistic implication

$$0 = \mathsf{E}\big[-h(X(k)) + c(X(k)) + \gamma h(X(k+1)) \mid X(0), \dots, X(k)\big], \qquad k \geq 0. \tag{9.8}$$

The fact that h solves a linear fixed-point equation makes the function approximation problem far simpler (compared to the nonlinear fixed-point equation (9.1)). The biggest challenge is, how do we devise a learning algorithm that takes into account the conditional expectation appearing in (9.8)? Approaches to answer this question are surveyed in Section 9.2.

We first answer the question: *What do we do with a value function?* The most common answer is the *policy improvement* step in the policy improvement algorithm (PIA) (also called the policy iteration algorithm). The definition isn't very different from the deterministic counterpart introduced in Section 3.2.2.

9.1.2 PIA and the Q-Function

For the discounted-cost criterion, the algorithm is defined as follows:

PIA *for Discounted Cost*

Given an initial policy ϕ_0, a sequence (ϕ_n, h_n) is defined as follows. At stage n, given ϕ_n, being these steps:

(i) Solve

$$c_{\phi_n} + \gamma P_n h_n = h_n, \tag{9.9a}$$

where $P_n = P_{\phi_n}$ is the transition matrix obtained when the chain is controlled using ϕ_n.

(ii) Construct a new policy:

$$\phi_{n+1}(x) = \arg\min_u \big(c(x,u) + \gamma P_u h_n(x)\big), \qquad x \in \mathsf{X}, \tag{9.9b}$$

where $P_u h_n(x)$ is defined in (7.15).

This algorithm is consistent, with $h_n(x) \downarrow h(x)$ for each x, as $n \to \infty$ (the fact that $h_n(x)$ is nonincreasing is a corollary to Proposition 9.2).

TD-learning algorithms are designed to approximate the solution to (9.9a). However, we cannot obtain the updated policy (9.9b) unless we have the model P_u, and are also prepared to solve the minimization over u for each x. A potential solution to both challenges is to approximate the function of two variables within the brackets in (9.9b), the fixed-policy Q-function associated with the policy ϕ_n:

$$Q_n(x,u) = c(x,u) + \gamma P_u h_n(x).$$

Any policy satisfying $\phi_n(x) \in \arg\min_u Q_n(x,u)$ for each x is called "Q_n-greedy."

The representation (9.6b) holds:

$$Q_n(x,u) = \sum_{k=0}^{\infty} \gamma^k \mathsf{E}[c(\Phi(k)) \mid \Phi(0) = (x,u)] \qquad \text{with } U(k) = \phi_n(X(k)) \text{ for } k \ge 1,$$

along with a fixed-point equation that is very similar to (9.9a):

$$0 = \mathsf{E}[-Q_n(\Phi(n)) + c(\Phi(n)) + \gamma Q_n(\Phi(n+1)) \mid \mathcal{F}_n], \text{ with } U(k) = \phi_n(X(k)) \text{ for each } k,$$

and with $\mathcal{F}_n$ shorthand for $\{\Phi(0),\dots,\Phi(n)\}$. Any TD-learning algorithm can be applied to approximate this Q-function, which is made possible by recognizing that the pair process $\boldsymbol{\Phi}$ is a time-homogeneous Markov chain, whenever $\boldsymbol{U}$ is defined using a stationary Markov policy.

A TD-learning algorithm designed to estimate a fixed-policy Q-function is commonly known as *SARSA*. However, as explained in Section 5.3, we will opt for the term *TD-learning* regardless of whether we are estimating h or Q.

9.1.3 Advantage Function

If we have computed exactly the Q-function for a policy ϕ, then the policy improvement step is given by $\phi^+(x) \stackrel{\text{def}}{=} \arg\min_u Q(x,u)$. Rather than estimate Q, we could estimate $Q - G$ for any function G that does not depend upon u. The Q-greedy policy is unchanged:

$$\phi^+(x) \in \arg\min_u \{Q(x,u) - G(x)\} = \arg\min_u Q(x,u). \tag{9.10}$$

A reasonable way to choose G is by minimizing the mean-square error:

$$G^* = \arg\min_G \|Q - G\|_\varpi^2 = \arg\min_G \mathsf{E}_\pi[\{Q(\Phi(n)) - G(X(n))\}^2],$$

where the subscript indicates that the expectation is in steady state.

The proofs of Propositions 9.1 and 9.2 are postponed to Section 9.9.1.

Proposition 9.1 *The optimizer is the value function:* $G^* = \mathsf{E}[Q(\Phi(n)) \mid X(n) = x] = h(x)$.

The difference $V = Q - h$ is known as the *advantage function*. The probabilistic implication holds:

$$0 = \mathsf{E}[-V(\Phi(k)) - h(X(k)) + c(\Phi(k)) + \gamma h(X(k+1)) \mid \Phi(0), \ldots, \Phi(k)]. \qquad (9.11)$$

Any of the TD algorithms can be adapted to approximate a solution, based on a joint parameterization $\{V^\theta, h^\theta : \theta \in \mathbb{R}^d\}$. Details can be found in Sections 9.5.4 and 10.2, as well as algorithms to approximate the advantage function without a joint parameterization.

The advantage function appears in actor-critic methods as a variance reduction technique, and also because of the following proposition, which provides a means to compare policies.

Proposition 9.2 *For any two policies* ϕ *and* $\bar{\phi}$*, let* h_ϕ *and* $h_{\bar{\phi}}$ *denote the associated value functions on* X*, and* V_ϕ *the advantage function for policy* ϕ*. Then,*

$$h_{\bar{\phi}}(x) = h_\phi(x) + \mathsf{E}^{\bar{\phi}}\Big[\sum_{k=0}^{\infty} \gamma^k V_\phi(\Phi(k)) \mid X(0) = x\Big], \qquad x \in \mathsf{X},$$

where the superscript on the expectation indicates that $\Phi(k)$ *is the Markov chain obtained with policy* $\bar{\phi}$*.* □

Consider for example the choice $\bar{\phi}(x) \stackrel{\text{def}}{=} \arg\min_u V_\phi(x,u)$, which represents the policy improvement step. We then have

$$V_\phi(x,\bar{\phi}(x)) = \min_u V_\phi(x,u) = -h_\phi(x) + \min_u Q_\phi(x,u) \le -h_\phi(x) + Q_\phi(x,\phi(x)) = 0, \; x \in \mathsf{X}.$$

It follows that $V_\phi(\Phi(k)) = V_\phi(X(k),\bar{\phi}(X(k))) \le 0$ under the policy $\bar{\phi}$, for any $k \ge 0$. Together with Proposition 9.2, this justifies the term policy *improvement*: $h_{\bar{\phi}}(x) \le h_\phi(x)$ for each x.

Example 9.1.1 (*Advantage for the M/M/1 Queue*) The value of the advantage function is most obvious in this example. To obtain an MDP model, we adopt a special case of the CRW model introduced in Section 7.3:

$$\mathsf{P}(X(k+1) = y \mid X(k) = x\,,\, U(k) = u) = P_u(x,y) = \begin{cases} \alpha & \text{if } y = x+1 \\ \mu & \text{if } y = (x-u)_+ \end{cases}, \qquad (9.12)$$

with $\mathsf{U} = \{0,1\}$. For any cost function that is nondecreasing on $\mathsf{X} = \mathbb{Z}_+$, the optimal policy is nonidling $\phi^\star(x) = \mathbb{1}\{x \ge 1\}$.

Consider the cost function $c(x) = x$ with the average-cost criterion. An expression for $V^\star = Q^\star - h^\star$ follows from the pair of identities:

$$\begin{aligned} h^\star(x) &= x - \eta + \mathsf{E}[h^\star(X(k+1)) \mid X(k) = x] && \text{(Poisson's equation).} \\ Q^\star(x,u) &= x + \mathsf{E}[h^\star(X(k+1)) \mid \Phi(k) = (x,u)] && \text{(definition).} \end{aligned}$$

The relative value function $h^\star$ appeared in (7.31), from which we obtain

$$\begin{aligned} h^\star(x) &= \tfrac{1}{2}\frac{x^2+x}{\mu-\alpha}, \\ V^\star(x,u) &= \eta + \mathsf{E}[h^\star(X(k+1)) \mid \Phi(k) = (x,u)] - \mathsf{E}[h^\star(X(k+1)) \mid X(k) = x] \\ &= \eta + \alpha h^\star(x+1) + \mu\{u h^\star(x-1) + (1-u)h^\star(x)\} - [h^\star(x) - x + \eta], \end{aligned} \qquad (9.13)$$

where $\eta = \pi(c) = \alpha/(\mu - \alpha)$ is the steady-state mean under $\phi^\star$.

A small amount of algebra gives

$$V^\star(x,u) = Q^\star(x,u) - h^\star(x) = \frac{\mu}{\mu - \alpha}(1-u)x.$$

Crucial conclusion: The growth rate of $Q^\star$ is quadratic in x, while $V^\star$ grows linearly. This is a tremendous benefit for variance reduction when applying TD learning or actor-critic algorithms (see Section 10.2 for algorithms to estimate $V^\star$).

Obviously, nobody cares about optimizing the M/M/1 queue! Fortunately, similar structure for value functions holds for Markovian queueing networks when c is a linear function of the state [252, 254]. ∎

9.2 Function Approximation and Smoothing

We first attempt to demystify the conditional expectations appearing in the previous section. It is best to start with an abstraction:

$$\widehat{Z} \stackrel{\text{def}}{=} \mathsf{E}[Z \mid Y], \tag{9.14}$$

where Z and $\widehat{Z}$ are each scalar-valued random variables, and Y is a vector-valued random variable. For example, $Y = (X(0),\dots,X(k))$ in (9.8). When convenient to emphasize dependence on k, we adopt the notation (7.14):

$$\mathsf{E}[Z \mid \mathcal{F}_k] \stackrel{\text{def}}{=} \mathsf{E}[Z \mid X(0),\dots,X(k)].$$

9.2.1 Conditional Expectation and Projection

Subject to the assumption that $\mathsf{E}[Z^2] < \infty$, the random variable $\widehat{Z}$ is the solution to a function approximation problem of the form surveyed in Section 5.1: $\widehat{Z} = \phi^\star(Y)$, where

$$\phi^\star = \operatorname*{arg\,min}_{\phi\in\mathcal{H}} \mathsf{E}[(Z - \phi(Y))^2] \tag{9.15}$$

and $\mathcal{H} = \{\phi : \mathsf{E}[\phi(Y)^2] < \infty\}$. So, keep the following in mind throughout the remainder of the book:

Conditional Expectation The conditional expectation $\widehat{Z}$, given the "data" Y, is the minimum mean-square error estimate of the random variable Z based on these data.

The solution to the optimization problem (9.15) can be characterized geometrically; see [154] for a proof of Proposition 9.3, along with much more theory and intuition on this topic.

Proposition 9.3 *A function $\phi^\circ \in \mathcal{H}$ solves the minimum in* (9.15) *if and only if the orthogonality property holds: For each $g \in \mathcal{H}$,*

$$0 = \mathsf{E}[\{Z - \phi^\circ(Y)\}g(Y)]. \qquad \square$$

A valuable corollary to Proposition 9.3 is the *smoothing property* of conditional expectation. If we have two random vectors X,Y, then we can take the conditional expectation based on the total data (X,Y) to obtain a better estimate of Z (we have increased the size of the function class (9.15) to all functions of the pair (x,y), so the optimal mean-square error cannot be worse). The smoothing property is then the consistency identity,

$$\mathsf{E}[Z \mid Y] = \mathsf{E}[\mathsf{E}[Z \mid X,Y] \mid Y]. \tag{9.16}$$

Computing a conditional expectation is obviously a lofty goal, given the size of the function class $\mathcal{H}$. How do we verify the characterization in Proposition 9.3, which requires evaluating an expectation for each $g \in \mathcal{H}$? The answer is, we *cannot* in most cases, so we resort to the approximation techniques introduced in Section 5.4.1.

Approximating the L_2 ***Projection*** Given d basis functions $\{\psi_i\}$, define a finite-dimensional function class by linear combinations $\widehat{\mathcal{H}} = \{\sum_i \theta_i \psi_i : \theta \in \mathbb{R}^d\}$. The estimate $\hat{\phi}^\star(Y)$ of Z, with $\hat{\phi}^\star \in \widehat{\mathcal{H}}$, is defined by either the Galerkin relaxation or a restricted projection:

- *Galerkin relaxation:* Define a second collection of functions $\widehat{\mathcal{G}} = \{\sum_i \theta_i \psi_i^G : \theta \in \mathbb{R}^d\}$, and select $\hat{\phi}^\star \in \widehat{\mathcal{H}}$ that solves

$$0 = \mathsf{E}[(Z - \hat{\phi}^\star(Y))g(Y)], \qquad g \in \widehat{\mathcal{G}}. \tag{9.17}$$

- *Projection onto* $\widehat{\mathcal{H}}$*:* Solve the following projection problem:

$$\hat{\phi}^\star \in \arg\min\{\mathsf{E}[(Z - \phi(Y))^2] : \phi \in \widehat{\mathcal{H}}\}. \tag{9.18}$$

We then write

$$\widehat{\mathsf{E}}[Z \mid Y] \stackrel{\text{def}}{=} \hat{\phi}^\star(Y). \tag{9.19}$$

Proposition 9.4 implies that the solution to (9.18) is identical to the Galerkin relaxation using $\widehat{\mathcal{G}} = \widehat{\mathcal{H}}$. Its proof is similar to (and simpler than) the derivation of (5.18):

Proposition 9.4 *A function* $\hat{\phi}^\star = \sum_i \theta_i^* \psi_i$ *solves the minimum in* (9.18) *if and only if*

$$0 = \mathsf{E}[(Z - \hat{\phi}^\star(Y))g(Y)], \qquad g \in \widehat{\mathcal{H}}. \tag{9.20}$$

Any solution satisfies $\hat{\phi}^\star = \psi^\intercal \theta^*$ *with*

$$R^\psi \theta^* = \bar{\psi}^Z, \tag{9.21}$$

where R^ψ *is a* $d \times d$ *matrix and* $\bar{\psi}^Z$ *is a d-dimensional vector, with entries*

$$R^\psi_{i,j} = \mathsf{E}[\psi_i(Y)\psi_j(Y)], \qquad \bar{\psi}^Z_i = \mathsf{E}[Z\psi_i(Y)]. \tag{9.22}$$

Consequently, if R^ψ *is full rank, then* $\theta^* = [R^\psi]^{-1}\bar{\psi}^Z$ *is the unique solution.* □

9.2.2 Linear Independence

In this chapter, we apply Galerkin relaxation techniques based on $Y = \psi_{(n)} \stackrel{\text{def}}{=} \psi(\Phi(n))$ for arbitrary n, where $\mathbf{\Phi}$ is the Markov chain with transition matrix (9.3a) (in Section 9.4, we briefly consider the restriction to $\boldsymbol{X}$ rather than the pair process $\mathbf{\Phi}$). For the purpose of analysis, it is assumed that $\mathbf{\Phi}$ is stationary, which implies that the d-dimensional stochastic process $\{\psi_{(n)} : n \in \mathbb{Z}_+\}$ is also stationary. Its autocorrelation sequence is denoted

$$R(j) = R(-j)^{\intercal} = \mathsf{E}_\pi[\psi_{(n+j)}\psi_{(n)}{}^{\intercal}], \qquad j \in \mathbb{Z}_+. \tag{9.23}$$

The matrix $R^\psi \stackrel{\text{def}}{=} R(0)$ is the steady-state version of the sample correlation matrix $\widehat{R}^\psi$ defined in (5.19), and a version of the matrix in (9.22).

The following definition appeared in Proposition 5.7:

The basis vectors are said to be *linearly independent* if the correlation matrix is full rank:

$$R^\psi = \mathsf{E}_\varpi[\psi_{(n)}\psi_{(n)}^{\intercal}] > 0. \tag{9.24}$$

An equivalent definition is $\mathsf{E}_\varpi[\{\theta^{\intercal}\psi_{(n)}\}^2] > 0$ for any nonzero $\theta \in \mathbb{R}^d$.

Consider, for example, the tabular setting (5.10): X and U are finite, $\mathsf{X} \times \mathsf{U} = \{(x^i,u^i) : 1 \le i \le d\}$, and $\psi_i(x,u) = \mathbb{1}\{(x,u) = (x^i,u^i)\}$ for each i. When using a deterministic policy $U(k) = \phi(X(k))$, it follows that $\psi_i(X(k),U(k)) = 0$ for every k if $u^i \neq \phi(x^i)$. The rank condition (9.24) is not satisfied in this case. For any randomized policy $\check{\phi}$, the matrix in (9.24) is diagonal, with

$$R^\psi(i,i) = \varpi(x^i,u^i) = \pi(x^i)\check{\phi}(u^i \mid x^i), \qquad 1 \le i \le d. \tag{9.25}$$

This matrix is full rank if and only if there is full exploration, in the sense that the right-hand side is positive for each i.

9.3 Loss Functions

In this section and the next, we seek approximations of the discounted-cost value function h defined in (9.6a). This is formulated as an approximate solution to (9.8) for each k, among a class of functions $\{h^\theta : \theta \in \mathbb{R}^d\}$. The *temporal difference* is defined as the error without the conditional expectation:

$$\mathcal{D}^\theta_{n+1} = -h^\theta(X(n)) + c(X(n)) + \gamma h^\theta(X(n+1)). \tag{9.26}$$

If there is $\theta^* \in \mathbb{R}^d$ giving $\mathsf{E}[\mathcal{D}^{\theta^*}_{n+1} \mid \mathcal{F}_n] = 0$ for all n, and if every state in X is visited, then h^{θ^*} solves (9.8). As in previous chapters, in most cases we can only hope to approximate.

For linear function approximation, we denote

$$h^\theta = \theta^{\intercal}\psi, \tag{9.27}$$

where ψ is a d-dimensional function on X rather than $\mathsf{Z} = \mathsf{X} \times \mathsf{U}$. To avoid risk of confusion, we abandon the simplified notation (9.4) in this case.

9.3.1 Mean-Square Bellman Error

For each θ, there is an associated Bellman error,

$$\mathcal{B}^\theta(x) = \mathsf{E}[\mathcal{D}^\theta_{n+1} \mid X(n) = x] = -h^\theta(x) + c(x) + \gamma P h^\theta(x), \quad x \in \mathsf{X}, \tag{9.28}$$

where the second equality is the definition of the transition matrix. The mean-square Bellman error (MSBE) is then defined by

$$\mathsf{E}_\pi[\{\mathcal{B}^\theta(X)\}^2]. \tag{9.29}$$

To minimize this objective function, we might apply first-order methods to find a stationary point: a vector θ° satisfying

$$0 = \tfrac{1}{2}\nabla_\theta \mathsf{E}_\pi[\{\mathcal{B}^\theta(X)\}^2] = \mathsf{E}_\pi[\{\mathcal{B}^\theta(X)\}\nabla_\theta \mathcal{B}^\theta(X)].$$

On substituting the definitions, we obtain representations that suggest algorithms.

Lemma 9.5 *The following holds for each $\theta \in \mathbb{R}^d$:*

$$-\tfrac{1}{2}\nabla_\theta \mathsf{E}_\pi[\{\mathcal{B}^\theta(X)\}^2] = \mathsf{E}_\pi[\mathcal{D}^\theta_{n+1}\zeta^\theta_n],$$

where

$$\zeta^\theta_n = \nabla_\theta \mathsf{E}[h^\theta(X(n)) - \gamma h^\theta(X(n+1)) \mid \mathcal{F}_n]. \tag{9.30}$$

Proof By the Markov property, we have

$$\mathcal{B}^\theta(X(n)) \stackrel{\text{def}}{=} \mathsf{E}[\mathcal{D}^\theta_{n+1} \mid X(n)] = \mathsf{E}[\mathcal{D}^\theta_{n+1} \mid \mathcal{F}_n].$$

The gradient of interest is thus

$$-\tfrac{1}{2}\nabla_\theta \mathsf{E}_\pi[\{\mathcal{B}^\theta(X(n))\}^2] = \mathsf{E}[\mathsf{E}[\mathcal{D}^\theta_{n+1} \mid \mathcal{F}_n]\zeta^\theta_n],$$

where ζ^θ_n is given in the statement of the lemma:

$$\zeta^\theta_n = -\nabla_\theta \mathsf{E}[\mathcal{D}^\theta_{n+1} \mid \mathcal{F}_n] = \nabla_\theta \mathsf{E}[h^\theta(X(n)) - \gamma h^\theta(X(n+1)) \mid \mathcal{F}_n].$$

The smoothing property of conditional expectation completes the proof:

$$\mathsf{E}[\mathsf{E}[\mathcal{D}^\theta_{n+1} \mid \mathcal{F}_n]\zeta^\theta_n] = \mathsf{E}[\mathcal{D}^\theta_{n+1}\zeta^\theta_n]. \qquad \square$$

The lemma suggests that it is possible to approximate the gradient flow for the objective $\Gamma(\theta) = \mathsf{E}_\pi[\{\mathcal{B}^\theta(X)\}^2]$ using stochastic approximation, such as

$$\theta_{n+1} = \theta_n + \alpha_{n+1}[\mathcal{D}^\theta_{n+1}\zeta^\theta_n]\big|_{\theta=\theta_n}.$$

However, the conditional expectation in (9.30) presents a challenge. Proposition 9.4 suggests many approximations based on the approximate conditional expectation (9.19). An alternative is suggested in the following:

Proposition 9.6

$$\mathsf{E}_\pi[\{\mathcal{B}^\theta(X(n))\}^2] = \mathsf{E}_\pi[\{\mathcal{D}^\theta_{n+1}\}^2] - \sigma^2_{\mathcal{B}}(\theta), \tag{9.31}$$

where $\sigma^2_{\mathcal{B}}(\theta)$ denotes the conditional variance:

$$\sigma^2_{\mathcal{B}}(\theta) \stackrel{\text{def}}{=} \mathsf{E}_\pi[\{\mathcal{D}^\theta_{n+1} - \mathsf{E}[\mathcal{D}^\theta_{n+1} \mid \mathcal{F}_n]\}^2]. \qquad \square$$

The objective function $\Gamma(\theta) = \tfrac{1}{2}\mathsf{E}_\pi[\{\mathcal{D}^\theta_{n+1}\}^2]$ is thus equal to the MSBE plus $\tfrac{1}{2}\sigma^2_{\mathcal{B}}(\theta)$, which is relatively small in many applications. An SA algorithm designed to approximate the gradient flow is straightforward:

$$\theta_{n+1} = \theta_n + \alpha_{n+1}\mathcal{D}_{n+1}\zeta_{n+1} \tag{9.32}$$

with $\mathcal{D}_{n+1} \stackrel{\text{def}}{=} \mathcal{D}^{\theta_n}_{n+1}$, and

$$\zeta_{n+1} = -\nabla \mathcal{D}^\theta_{n+1}\big|_{\theta=\theta_n} = \nabla_\theta[h^\theta(X(n)) - \gamma h^\theta(X(n+1))]\big|_{\theta=\theta_n}.$$

One can use any of the techniques in Chapter 8 to accelerate this algorithm.

9.3.2 Mean-Square Value Function Error

An alternative mean-square error is defined in terms of the value function:

$$\theta^* = \arg\min_{\theta} \|h^\theta - h\|, \tag{9.33}$$

in which the choice of norm is part of the design of the algorithm. Most common is

$$\|h^\theta - h\|_\pi^2 \stackrel{\text{def}}{=} \sum_{x \in \mathsf{X}} (h^\theta(x) - h(x))^2 \pi(x), \tag{9.34}$$

in which π is the steady-state pmf for $\boldsymbol{X}$.

It is a remarkable fact that this loss function can be minimized without observations of $\{h(X(k))\}$. One class of algorithms for this purpose is TD(1)-learning. The algorithm is defined in Section 9.4.1, and conditions under which it solves (9.33) are presented in Theorem 9.7.

9.3.3 Projected Bellman Error

Assumed given is a d-dimensional stochastic process ζ known as the sequence of *eligibility vectors*. The goal is to obtain the vector $\theta^* \in \mathbb{R}^d$ that solves the Galerkin relaxation of (9.8). The smoothing property of conditional expectation gives

$$0 = \mathsf{E}\big[\{-h^{\theta^*}(X(k)) + c(X(k)) + \gamma h^{\theta^*}(X(k+1))\}\zeta_k(i)\big]\,, \quad 1 \le i \le d\,. \tag{9.35}$$

It is usually assumed that the expectation is in steady state (so that $X(k)$ is distributed according to π). If $h = h^{\theta^\bullet}$ for some $\theta^\bullet \in \mathbb{R}^d$, and if the solution to (9.35) is unique, then the Galerkin approach will yield the exact solution h.

9.4 TD(λ) Learning

The goal of this algorithm is to solve (9.35) for a particular choice of eligibility vector. We begin with a special case for which there is a rich supporting theory.

9.4.1 Linear Function Class

In TD(λ) learning with linear function approximation, the eligibility vectors are defined by passing $\{\psi(X(n)\}$ through a first-order low-pass filter:

$$\zeta_{n+1} = \lambda\gamma\zeta_n + \psi(X(n+1))\,, \qquad n \ge 0. \tag{9.36}$$

It is always assumed that $\lambda \in [0,1]$.

TD(λ) Algorithm

For initialization $\theta_0, \zeta_0 \in \mathbb{R}^d$, the sequence of estimates are defined recursively:

$$\begin{aligned}
\theta_{n+1} &= \theta_n + \alpha_{n+1}\zeta_n \mathcal{D}_{n+1}, \\
\mathcal{D}_{n+1} &= \big(-h^\theta(X(n)) + c(X(n)) + \gamma h^\theta(X(n+1))\big)\Big|_{\theta=\theta_n}, \\
\zeta_{n+1} &= \lambda\gamma\zeta_n + \psi(X(n+1))\,.
\end{aligned} \tag{9.37}$$

The random variable $\mathcal{D}_{n+1}$ is the temporal difference introduced in Section 9.3: using the definition (9.26), we have simplified notation via

$$\mathcal{D}_{n+1} = \mathcal{D}_{n+1}^{\theta_n}.$$

The proofs of Theorem 9.7 and Proposition 9.8 are postponed to Section 9.9.2.

Theorem 9.7 *Suppose that θ^* solves (9.35), where the expectation is in steady state, and the eligibility vector is defined using TD(λ) with linear function approximation (9.27). The solution has the following interpretation for two choices of λ:*

(i) $\lambda = 0$: *In the notation of* (9.19),

$$\widehat{\mathsf{E}}[\mathcal{D}_{n+1}^{\theta^*} \mid Y_n] = 0,$$

with $Y_n = \psi(X(n))$ *and* $\mathcal{D}_{n+1}^{\theta^*} = -h^{\theta^*}(X(n)) + c(X(n)) + \gamma h^{\theta^*}(X(n+1))$.

(ii) $\lambda = 1$: θ^* *solves* (9.33), *with norm* (9.34). □

Subject to (9.27), we have

$$\mathcal{D}_{n+1} = c(X(n)) + \big[\gamma\psi(X(n+1)) - \psi(X(n))\big]^{\intercal}\theta_n,$$

and consequently (9.37) can be placed in the form of the linear SA recursion (8.53b), with

$$\begin{aligned} A_{n+1} &= \zeta_n\big[\gamma\psi(X(n+1)) - \psi(X(n))\big]^{\intercal}, \\ b_{n+1} &= -\zeta_n c(X(n)). \end{aligned} \tag{9.38}$$

Let $A = \mathsf{E}[A_n]$ and $b = \mathsf{E}[b_n]$, where the expectations are in steady state. If A is invertible, then $\theta^* = A^{-1}b$ is the unique solution to (9.35).

Proposition 9.8 (i) tells us that the matrix A is invertible and the TD(λ) algorithm is consistent under linear independence. Part (ii) is of interest when we come to the average-cost setting.

The definition of linear independence remains the same when ψ is a function of x only, and we continue to denote as in (9.24):

$$R^{\psi} = \mathsf{E}_{\pi}[\psi(X(n))\psi(X(n))^{\intercal}]. \tag{9.39}$$

Let Σ^{ψ} denote the steady-state covariance of the basis:

$$\Sigma^{\psi} = R^{\psi} - \bar{\psi}\bar{\psi}^{\intercal}, \tag{9.40}$$

where $\bar{\psi} = \mathsf{E}_{\pi}[\psi(X(n))]$.

Proposition 9.8 *The steady-state mean of the matrix A_n defined in* (9.38) *satisfies the following:*

(i) *If the linear independence condition* (9.24) *holds, then A is Hurwitz, and* $\theta^* = A^{-1}b$ *for any* $\gamma \in [0,1)$ *and* $\lambda \in [0,1]$.

(ii) *If* $\Sigma^{\psi} > 0$ *and* $\mathbf{\Phi}$ *is aperiodic, then A is Hurwitz for* $\gamma = 1$ *and* $\lambda < 1$. □

The following representation of A is required in the proofs of Theorem 9.7 and Proposition 9.8. See (9.23) to recall the definition of the autocorrelation sequence $\{R(i)\}$.

Lemma 9.9 *$A = -R^\psi$ if $\lambda = 0$ or $\lambda = 1$, for any $\gamma \in [0,1)$. Otherwise,*

$$A = -R(0) + (\lambda^{-1} - 1)\sum_{i=1}^{\infty}(\gamma\lambda)^i R(i)^\intercal \tag{9.41}$$

with autocorrelation sequence $\{R(i)\}$ defined in (9.23).

Proof We start with the steady-state representation of the eligibility vector:

$$\zeta_n = \sum_{i=0}^{\infty}(\lambda\gamma)^i \psi(X(n-i)).$$

Applying (9.38) then gives

$$\begin{aligned} A &= \mathsf{E}_\pi\big[\zeta_n\big[\gamma\psi(X(n+1)) - \psi(X(n))\big]^\intercal\big] \\ &= \sum_{i=0}^{\infty}(\lambda\gamma)^i \mathsf{E}_\pi\big[\psi(X(n-i))\big(-\psi(X(n)) + \gamma\psi(X(n+1))\big)^\intercal\big] \\ &= \sum_{i=0}^{\infty}(\lambda\gamma)^i\{-R(-i) + \gamma R(-i-1)\}. \end{aligned}$$

The representation (9.41) follows, using $R(-i) = R(i)^\intercal$. □

Although TD(λ) is convergent, the mean-square error may converge at a rate far slower than optimal. The optimal $O(1/n)$ rate can be achieved by using one of the techniques from Chapter 8: $\alpha_n = g/n$ with $g > 0$ sufficiently large, the use of Polyak–Ruppert averaging (8.10), or an appropriate matrix gain. One instance of the last approach is the stochastic Newton–Raphson algorithm (8.54), which is known as LSTD(λ) in the present context.

LSTD(λ)

With initialization $\theta_0, \zeta_0 \in \mathbb{R}^d$ and $\widehat{A}_0 \in \mathbb{R}^{d\times d}$:

$$\theta_{n+1} = \theta_n - \alpha_{n+1}\widehat{A}_n^{-1}\zeta_n\mathcal{D}_{n+1}, \tag{9.42a}$$

$$\mathcal{D}_{n+1} = c(X(n)) + \big[\gamma\psi(X(n+1)) - \psi(X(n))\big]^\intercal\theta_n, \tag{9.42b}$$

$$\zeta_{n+1} = \lambda\gamma\zeta_n + \psi(X(n+1)), \tag{9.42c}$$

$$\widehat{A}_{n+1} = \widehat{A}_n + \alpha_{n+1}[A_{n+1} - \widehat{A}_n], \tag{9.42d}$$

$$A_{n+1} = \zeta_n[\gamma\psi(X(n+1)) - \psi(X(n))]^\intercal. \tag{9.42e}$$

Proposition 8.8 can be applied, and suggests the simpler Monte Carlo implementation: After gathering all the data up to time N, define $\theta_N^{\text{LSTD}} = \widehat{A}_N^{-1}\widehat{b}_N$, where

$$\widehat{A}_N = \frac{1}{N}\sum_{k=0}^{N-1}A(k+1), \qquad \widehat{b}_N = -\frac{1}{N}\sum_{k=0}^{N-1}\zeta_k c(X(k)).$$

9.4.2 Nonlinear Parameterizations

Suppose $\{h^\theta : \theta \in \mathbb{R}^d\}$ are not linear functions of θ, but are differentiable. A generalization of the foregoing is based on the definition

$$\psi_i(x;\theta) = \frac{\partial}{\partial\theta_i} h^\theta(x)\,.$$

The temporal difference and eligibility sequence are redefined as follows:

$$\mathcal{D}_{n+1} = c(X(n)) + \gamma h^{\theta_n}(X(n+1)) - h^{\theta_n}(X(n)), \tag{9.43a}$$

$$\zeta_{n+1} = \lambda\gamma\zeta_n + \psi(X(n+1);\theta_n)\,, \qquad n \ge 0\,. \tag{9.43b}$$

The TD(λ) or LSTD(λ) algorithms can be defined using these definitions, but convergence theory is lacking.

The Zap TD(λ) algorithm is a potential alternative, which will be convergent under mild conditions. However, it is useful to go back to basics, and ask if there is good motivation for the choice of eligibility vector (9.43b).

If the algorithm is convergent, then the limit θ^* is expected to be solved as follows:

$$0 = \mathsf{E}\big[\big(c(X(n)) + \gamma h^{\theta_n}(X(n+1)) - h^{\theta_n}(X(n))\big)\zeta_{n+1}^{\theta^*}\big], \tag{9.44}$$

where $\zeta_{n+1}^{\theta^*} = \lambda\gamma\zeta_n^{\theta^*} + \psi(X(n+1);\theta^*)$, $n \ge 0$, and the expectation in (9.44) is taken with respect to the joint stationary process $(\boldsymbol{X},\boldsymbol{\zeta}^{\theta^*})$. The fixed-point equation (9.44) no longer has an interpretation as a Galerkin relaxation when the eligibility vector depends upon the parameter θ. It may be best to modify the definition of the loss function so that the solution is more easily understood. Examples include convex Q-learning and actor-critic methods.

9.5 Return to the Q-Function

In this section and the next, it is assumed that the input is defined by a (possibly randomized) stationary policy $\breve{\phi}$. For the sake of analysis, it is assumed throughout that $\boldsymbol{\Phi} = \{\Phi(k) \stackrel{\text{def}}{=} (X(k),U(k)) : k \ge 0\}$ is uni-chain, with unique invariant pmf given by (9.3b).

9.5.1 Exploration

It is time to discuss how to define $\breve{\phi}$ when our true goal is to estimate a value function for a deterministic policy ϕ. It may be useful to construct the randomized policy so that it can be regarded as an "ε-perturbation" of ϕ, where ε is a positive but small constant.

One approach is to start with any randomized policy $\breve{\phi}^\bullet$. This might be completely random, in the sense that $\breve{\phi}^\bullet(u \mid x)$ does not depend upon x. The ε-approximation is then defined as follows:

$$\breve{\phi}(u \mid x) = (1-\varepsilon)\mathbb{1}\{u = \phi(x)\} + \varepsilon\breve{\phi}^\bullet(u \mid x). \tag{9.45}$$

This is implemented using an i.i.d. Bernouli sequence $\{I_k\}$ with parameter ε, so that $\mathsf{P}\{I_k = 1\} = \varepsilon$. The policy ϕ is applied at time k if and only if $I_k = 0$; otherwise the input is determined by $\breve{\phi}^\bullet$.

An alternative approach is available in the context of policy iteration, as surveyed in Section 9.1. Suppose that ϕ is itself defined as a minimizer: For a function $G\colon \mathsf{X}\times\mathsf{U}\to\mathbb{R}$,

$$\phi(x)\in\arg\min_u G(x,u)=\arg\max_u\{-G(x,u)\}.$$

For given $\varepsilon>0$, the *soft-max* is defined as

$$\varepsilon\log\Bigl\{\sum_u \exp(-G(x,u)/\varepsilon)\Bigr\}.$$

As $\varepsilon\downarrow 0$, this is convergent to $\max_u\{-G(x,u)\}$.

This motivates a class of randomized policies:

Gibbs Policy Given $G\colon \mathsf{X}\times\mathsf{U}\to\mathbb{R}$ and $\varepsilon>0$,

$$\check{\phi}^{\varepsilon}(u\mid x)\stackrel{\text{def}}{=}\frac{1}{\kappa^{\varepsilon}(x)}\exp(-G(x,u)/\varepsilon), \tag{9.46a}$$

with κ^{ε} the normalizing constant, defined so that $\check{\phi}^{\varepsilon}(\cdot\mid x)$ is a pmf on U for each x:

$$\kappa^{\varepsilon}(x)\stackrel{\text{def}}{=}\sum_u\exp(-G(x,u)/\varepsilon). \tag{9.46b}$$

The parameter ε is called the *temperature*, justified because the policy is highly random if $\varepsilon>0$ is large (high entropy conjures the image of boiling water), while the policy typically becomes deterministic (freezes) as ε approaches zero. In particular, if G has a unique minimizer for each x, then

$$\lim_{\varepsilon\downarrow 0}\check{\phi}^{\varepsilon}(u\mid x)=\mathbb{1}\{\phi(x)=u\}.$$

9.5.2 On and Off Algorithms

Our main motivation for value function approximation is in application to approximate policy iteration, so we consider the fixed-policy Q-function (9.6b):

$$Q(x,u)=\sum_{k=0}^{\infty}\gamma^k\mathsf{E}[c(\Phi(k))\mid X(0)=x\,,\,U(0)=u].$$

When the policy $\check{\phi}$ is randomized, we require the definition (9.5b): $\underline{Q}(x)=\sum_u Q(x,u)\check{\phi}(u|x)$. The fixed-point equations (9.7) continue to hold, along with other expected relations:

Proposition 9.10 *The value functions h and Q obtained from a randomized policy $\check{\phi}$ satisfy*

$$h(x)=c_{\check{\phi}}(x)+\gamma\sum_{x'}P_{\check{\phi}}(x,x')h(x')\,,\qquad Q(x,u)=c(x,u)+\gamma\sum_{x'}P_u(x,x')\underline{Q}(x') \tag{9.47}$$

with $c_{\check{\phi}}(x)=\sum_u c(x,u)\check{\phi}(u\mid x)$, and $P_{\check{\phi}}$ defined in (7.12). *The two are related via*

$$h(x)=\underline{Q}(x)\quad\text{and}\quad Q(x,u)=c(x,u)+\gamma\sum_{x'}P_u(x,x')h(x')\,,\qquad\text{for each } x,u. \tag{9.48}$$

□

We obtain two model-free representations of the fixed-point equation for Q in (9.47), distinguished by the choice of input for learning. The following dichotomy was described in Section 5.3.1 for deterministic control systems:

- On-policy method: If $\boldsymbol{U}$ is chosen according to the policy $\breve{\phi}$, then

$$Q(\Phi(k)) = c(\Phi(k)) + \gamma \mathsf{E}[Q(\Phi(k+1)) \mid \mathcal{F}_k]. \tag{9.49}$$

- Off-policy method: If $\boldsymbol{U}$ is *any* admissible input, then the representation must be modified:

$$Q(\Phi(k)) = c(\Phi(k)) + \gamma \mathsf{E}[\underline{Q}(X(k+1)) \mid \mathcal{F}_k], \tag{9.50}$$

where $\mathcal{F}_k$ represents the history $\{\Phi(0),\dots,\Phi(k)\}$.

Consider now application of these representations for function approximation within a parameterized family $\{H^\theta : \theta \in \mathbb{R}^d\}$. The on-policy TD-learning algorithms surveyed in the previous pages are directly applicable on recognizing that $\boldsymbol{\Phi}$ is a Markov chain, and that Q is its discounted-cost value function. For example, here is the TD(λ) algorithm for a linear function approximation architecture: $H^\theta(x,u) = \theta^\intercal \psi(x,u)$ with $\psi\colon \mathsf{X}\times\mathsf{U} \to \mathbb{R}^d$:

TD(λ) Algorithm (On-Policy for Q)

For initialization $\theta_0, \zeta_0 \in \mathbb{R}^d$, the sequence of estimates are defined recursively:

$$\begin{aligned}
\theta_{n+1} &= \theta_n + \alpha_{n+1}\zeta_n \mathcal{D}_{n+1},\\
\mathcal{D}_{n+1} &= \big(-H^\theta(\Phi(n)) + c_n \gamma H^\theta(\Phi(n+1))\big)\Big|_{\theta=\theta_n},\\
\zeta_{n+1} &= \lambda\gamma\zeta_n + \psi_{(n+1)}, \qquad \psi_{(n+1)} \stackrel{\text{def}}{=} \psi(\Phi(n+1)),\ c_n \stackrel{\text{def}}{=} c(\Phi(n)).
\end{aligned} \tag{9.51}$$

The conclusions of Theorem 9.7 hold because we are simply replacing $\boldsymbol{X}$ with $\boldsymbol{\Phi}$ in the algorithm (9.51). The theorem is stated in this new notation for ease of reference. Equation (9.35) in this notation becomes

$$0 = \mathsf{E}\big[\{-H^{\theta^*}(X(k)) + c(X(k)) + \gamma H^{\theta^*}(X(k+1))\}\zeta_k(i)\big], \quad 1 \le i \le d. \tag{9.52}$$

Theorem 9.11 *Suppose that θ^* solves (9.52), where the expectation is in steady state, and the eligibility vector is defined using TD(λ) with linear function approximation. The solution has the following interpretation for two choices of λ:*

(i) $\lambda = 0$: *In the notation of* (9.19),

$$\widehat{\mathsf{E}}[\mathcal{D}^{\theta^*}_{n+1} \mid Y_n] = 0,$$

with $Y_n = \psi(\Phi(n)) = \psi_{(n)}$ *and* $\mathcal{D}^{\theta^*}_{n+1} = -H^{\theta^*}(\Phi(n)) + c_n + \gamma H^{\theta^*}(\Phi(n+1))$.

(ii) $\lambda = 1$: θ^* *solves*

$$\theta^* = \arg\min_\theta \|H^\theta - Q\|^2_\varpi \stackrel{\text{def}}{=} \sum_{x\in\mathsf{X},\, u\in\mathsf{U}} (H^\theta(x,u) - Q(x,u))^2 \varpi(x,u).$$

□

The off-policy setting is far more practical in many cases. In particular, for application to policy iteration the policies $\{\phi_n\}$ obtained through (9.9b) are deterministic. However, in most cases we require a randomized policy to ensure sufficient exploration.

TD(λ) Algorithm (Off-Policy for Q)

For initialization $\theta_0, \zeta_0 \in \mathbb{R}^d$, the sequence of estimates are defined recursively:

$$\begin{aligned}
\theta_{n+1} &= \theta_n + \alpha_{n+1}\zeta_n \mathcal{D}_{n+1}, \\
\mathcal{D}_{n+1} &= \left(-H^\theta(\Phi(n)) + c_n + \gamma \underline{H}^\theta(X(n+1))\right)\Big|_{\theta=\theta_n}, \\
\zeta_{n+1} &= \lambda\gamma\zeta_n + \psi_{(n+1)}, \qquad \psi_{(n+1)} \stackrel{\text{def}}{=} \psi(\Phi(n+1)),\ c_n \stackrel{\text{def}}{=} c(\Phi(n)).
\end{aligned} \tag{9.53}$$

A critical difference is in the form of the temporal difference term: To obtain $\mathcal{D}_{n+1}$, it is necessary to compute

$$\underline{H}^\theta(X(n+1)) = \Big(\sum_u Q(x,u)\breve{\phi}(u \mid x)\Big)\Big|_{x=X(n+1)}. \tag{9.54}$$

If this is too complex, an alternative is *split sampling* (recall (6.47)):

$$\mathcal{D}_{n+1} = \left(-H^\theta(\Phi(n)) + c_n + \gamma H^\theta(X(n+1), U'_{n+1})\right)\Big|_{\theta=\theta_n}, \tag{9.55}$$

in which U'_{n+1} is a random variable that is conditionally independent of $\mathcal{F}_{n+1}$ given $X(n+1)$, with conditional pmf defined as follows:

$$\mathsf{P}\{U'_{n+1} = u \mid \mathcal{F}_{n+1}\} = \phi(u \mid x') \qquad \text{when } x' = X(n+1).$$

The update equation is unchanged: $\theta_{n+1} = \theta_n + \alpha_{n+1}\zeta_n\mathcal{D}_{n+1}$. Theory for convergence using (9.55) is unchanged, but the algorithm will have higher variance (the covariance Σ_Δ appearing in Section 8.2.5 will be larger).

The geometry behind the proof of Theorem 9.7 breaks down in the off-policy setting. The off-policy algorithm is intended to solve

$$0 = \mathsf{E}_\pi\big[\big(-H^\theta(\Phi(n)) + c_n + \gamma H^\theta(X(n+1), U'_{n+1})\big)\zeta_n\big],$$

which can be expressed as the linear equation $A\theta = b$ with

$$A = \mathsf{E}_\pi\big[\zeta_n\big(-\psi(\Phi(n)) + \gamma\underline{\psi}(X(n+1))\big)^{\intercal}\big], \quad b = -\mathsf{E}_\pi\big[c_n\zeta_n\big], \quad \text{and } \underline{\psi}(x) = \sum_u \psi(x,u)\breve{\phi}(u \mid x).$$

We don't even know if A is invertible, so the linear equation may not have a solution.

The following result gives us some hope. The proposition looks at the entire range of $\gamma \in [0,1]$, so we write A_γ to emphasize the dependence.

Proposition 9.12 *Suppose that the linear independence condition* (9.24) *holds. We then have the following:*

(i) *For $\lambda = 0$, the matrix A_γ is invertible for all but at most d values of $\gamma \in [0,1]$.*
(ii) *For each $\lambda \in (0,1)$, the matrix A_γ is invertible for all but a finite number of values of $\gamma \in [0,1]$.*
(iii) *The matrix A_γ with $\lambda = 1$ is invertible for all but a finite number of values of $\gamma \in [0, 1-\delta]$ for each $\delta > 0$.* □

Proposition 9.12 *does not* claim that the matrix A_γ is Hurwitz, so stability of off-policy TD(λ) is *not resolved*. The proposition justifies application of LSTD(λ) in the off-policy setting since it is highly likely that A_γ is full rank.

9.5.3 Relative TD(λ)

We can expect numerical challenges with TD(λ) algorithms when γ is close to unity. The reason comes from the fact that either of the value functions defined in (9.6) is typically unbounded as $\gamma \uparrow 1$. Here we exploit the fact that the value functions are large only because of an additive constant.

This structure is illustrated via an example in Exercise 6.6 (b). For the general case, consider the fixed-policy Q-function:

$$Q_\gamma(z) \stackrel{\text{def}}{=} \sum_{k=0}^{\infty} \gamma^k \mathsf{E}[c(\Phi(k)) \mid \Phi(0) = z].$$

Let $\eta = \mathsf{E}_\varpi[c_n]$, $\tilde{c}(z) = c(z) - \eta$, $\tilde{c}_k = \tilde{c}(\Phi(k))$, and write

$$Q_\gamma(z) = \sum_{k=0}^{\infty} \gamma^k \mathsf{E}[\eta + \tilde{c}_k \mid \Phi(0) = z] = \frac{1}{1-\gamma}\eta + \sum_{k=0}^{\infty} \gamma^k \mathsf{E}[\tilde{c}_k \mid \Phi(0) = z].$$

For $\gamma \sim 1$, the right-hand side is a very large constant, plus a term that approximates the solution to Poisson's equation given in Theorem 6.3 (i) (for the Markov chain $\boldsymbol{\Phi}$ rather than $\boldsymbol{X}$). Consequently,

$$\lim_{\gamma \uparrow 1} \Big\{ Q_\gamma(z) - \frac{1}{1-\gamma}\eta \Big\} = \widetilde{Q}(z), \qquad z \in \mathsf{X} \times \mathsf{U},$$

where $\widetilde{Q}$ solves Poisson's equation:

$$\mathsf{E}[\tilde{c}_k + \widetilde{Q}(\Phi(k+1)) \mid \Phi(k) = z] = \widetilde{Q}(z). \tag{9.56}$$

The function $\widetilde{Q}_\gamma = Q_\gamma - \eta/(1-\gamma)$ solves the DP equation

$$c + \gamma P \widetilde{Q}_\gamma = \widetilde{Q}_\gamma + \eta. \tag{9.57}$$

We might use this to define a temporal difference sequence. In application to policy improvement, the new policy can be represented in terms of $\widetilde{Q}_\gamma$ instead of Q_γ:

$$\phi^+(x) \in \arg\min \widetilde{Q}_\gamma(x,u) = \arg\min Q_\gamma(x,u).$$

To avoid estimation of η, we opt for an alternative, known as the (fixed-policy) *relative dynamic programming equation*:

$$c + \gamma P H = H + \delta \langle \mu, H \rangle, \tag{9.58}$$

where $\delta > 0$ is a positive scalar, $\mu : \mathsf{X} \times \mathsf{U} \to [0,1]$ is a pmf (both design choices), and $\langle \mu, H \rangle = \sum_{x,u} \mu(x,u) H(x,u)$.

In the notation of Section 6.3, the DP equation (9.58) can be expressed

$$[I - (\gamma P - \delta 1 \otimes \mu)] H = c.$$

Lemma 9.13 tells us that H can be expressed as a power series under mild assumptions on P and δ. More important is that $H = Q +$ constant, so it is just as valuable as Q for application in policy improvement.

Lemma 9.13 *Suppose that $\boldsymbol{\Phi}$ is uni-chain. Then, for each $\gamma \in [0,1)$,*

(i) *The eigenvalues of the matrix* $\gamma P - \delta 1 \otimes \mu$ *coincide with those of* γP*, except for* $\lambda_1 = \gamma$ *which is moved to* $\gamma - \delta$.
(ii) *Provided* $|\gamma - \delta| < 1$*, we have*

$$H = [I - (\gamma P - \delta 1 \otimes \mu)]^{-1} c = \sum_{n=0}^{\infty} (\gamma P - \delta 1 \otimes \mu)^n c. \tag{9.59}$$

The sum is convergent because $(\gamma P - \delta 1 \otimes \mu)^n \to 0$ *geometrically quickly as* $n \to \infty$.
(iii) $H = Q - k$*, with*

$$k = \frac{\delta}{1+\delta-\gamma} \langle \mu, Q \rangle = \frac{\delta}{1-\gamma} \langle \mu, H \rangle. \tag{9.60}$$

The big step in establishing part (iii) is an application of the Matrix Inversion Lemma (A.1) to obtain the representation

$$[I - (\gamma P - \delta 1 \otimes \mu)]^{-1} = (I - \gamma P)^{-1} - \frac{\delta}{1+\delta-\gamma} [1 \otimes \mu](I - \gamma P)^{-1}. \tag{9.61}$$

The relative DP equation (9.58) has the probabilistic interpretation

$$\mathsf{E}_{\varpi}\big[-H(\Phi(n)) - \delta \langle \mu, H \rangle + c_n + \gamma \underline{H}(X(n+1)) \mid \mathcal{F}_n\big] = 0, \qquad n \geq 0, \tag{9.62}$$

where $\underline{H}(x) = \sum_u H(x,u) \check{\phi}(u \mid x)$ as in (9.54). Suppose that $\{H^\theta : \theta \in \mathbb{R}^d\}$ is a parameterized family of functions on $\mathsf{X} \times \mathsf{U}$. The goal in relative TD(λ) learning is to find θ^* satisfying $\bar{f}(\theta^*) = 0$, with

$$\bar{f}(\theta) \stackrel{\text{def}}{=} \mathsf{E}_{\varpi}\big[\{-H(\Phi(n)) - \delta \langle \mu, H \rangle + c_n + \gamma \underline{H}(X(n+1))\} \zeta_n\big], \tag{9.63}$$

where $\{\zeta_n\}$ are the eligibility vectors – defined via (9.53) if the parameterization is linear. An SA algorithm to estimate θ^* is described next in this special case:

Relative TD(λ) Algorithm (Off-Policy)

For initialization $\theta_0, \zeta_0 \in \mathbb{R}^d$, the sequence of estimates are defined recursively:

$$\begin{aligned}
\theta_{n+1} &= \theta_n + \alpha_{n+1} \zeta_n \mathcal{D}_{n+1}, \\
\mathcal{D}_{n+1} &= \big(-H^\theta(\Phi(n)) - \delta \langle \mu, H^\theta \rangle + c_n + \gamma \underline{H}^\theta(X(n+1))\big)\Big|_{\theta=\theta_n}, \\
\zeta_{n+1} &= \lambda \gamma \zeta_n + \psi_{(n+1)}, \qquad \psi_{(n+1)} \stackrel{\text{def}}{=} \psi(\Phi(n+1)).
\end{aligned} \tag{9.64}$$

This is a linear SA recursion based on the ODE $\frac{d}{dt}\vartheta = \bar{f}(\vartheta) = A\vartheta - b$, in which

$$A = \mathsf{E}_{\varpi}\big[\zeta_n(-\psi(\Phi(n)) - \delta \bar{\psi}^{\mu} + \gamma \underline{\psi}(X(n+1)))^{\intercal}\big], \qquad b = -\mathsf{E}_{\varpi}\big[c_n \zeta_n\big],$$

where $\bar{\psi}^{\mu}$ is a d-dimensional column vector, whose ith component is the mean $\langle \mu, \psi_i \rangle$. Conditions to ensure that A is Hurwitz can be obtained in the on-policy setting.

A challenge remains for $\lambda = 1$ in which case $b = -\mathsf{E}_{\varpi}[c_n \zeta_n]$ may be very large when $\gamma \sim 1$, and this suggests high variance in the algorithm. The regeneration technique introduced in Section 10.3 is one approach to obtain algorithms that are reliable when both γ and λ are close to unity.

An alternative is to abandon approximation of Q and turn to the advantage function.

9.5.4 TD(λ) for Advantage

The advantage function introduced in Section 9.1.3 admits the following equivalent forms:

Proposition 9.14 *The following representations hold for the advantage function:*

$$\begin{aligned} V(x,u) &= Q(x,u) - h(x) && (9.65a)\\ &= -h(x) + c(x,u) + \gamma\mathsf{E}[h(X(k+1)) \mid \Phi(k) = (x,u)] && (9.65b)\\ &= c(x,u) - c_{\breve{\phi}}(x) + \gamma\{\mathsf{E}[h(X(k+1)) \mid \Phi(k) = (x,u)] - \mathsf{E}[h(X(k+1)) \mid X(k) = x]\} && (9.65c) \end{aligned}$$

for each $x \in \mathsf{X}$, $u \in \mathsf{U}$, *and with* $c_{\breve{\phi}}(x) = \sum_u c(x,u)\breve{\phi}(u \mid x)$. □

The proof is postponed to Section 9.9.1.

The motivation for the advantage function is in part the desire to reduce variance in the estimate of the function used in policy improvement. This brings a question, *can we estimate* V *directly with reduced variance* (as compared to estimating Q and h separately, and then subtracting)? It might not be surprising that the answer is *yes*, but full justification won't come until Section 10.2. We provide here a heuristic and an algorithm.

For the heuristic, we have $\mathsf{E}[V(\Phi(k)) \mid X(k)] = 0$ for each k, so it is reasonable to choose a function class for which the same holds for any approximation within this class. This is not difficult to arrange.

The following notation is used throughout Chapter 10:

$$\underline{\psi}(x) = \sum_u \psi(x,u)\breve{\phi}(u \mid x) \quad \text{and} \quad \widetilde{\psi}(x,u) = \psi(x,u) - \underline{\psi}(x), \qquad x \in \mathsf{X},\, u \in \mathsf{U} \quad (9.66)$$

We search for an approximation within the function class:

$$\widetilde{\mathcal{H}} = \{H^\theta \stackrel{\text{def}}{=} \theta^\intercal \widetilde{\psi} : \theta \in \mathbb{R}^d\}. \qquad (9.67)$$

We have by definition $\mathsf{E}[H(\Phi(k)) \mid X(k)] = 0$ for any $H \in \widetilde{\mathcal{H}}$. With a bit more work, we learn in Section 10.2 that the best estimate of V within $\widetilde{\mathcal{H}}$ coincides with the best estimate of Q within the same function class.

Stability of any algorithm based on this finding requires linear independence of the basis $\widetilde{\psi}$. For a deterministic policy, we have $\widetilde{\psi}(\Phi(k)) = 0$ for every k, so we are out of luck! Even for a randomized policy, the covariance matrix $\Sigma^{\widetilde{\psi}}$ may be rank deficient even when Σ^{ψ} is full rank. In this case, the basis can be trimmed by writing $\Sigma^{\widetilde{\psi}} = C^\intercal C$, where C is an $m \times d$ matrix with rank $m < d$, and then we can replace $\widetilde{\psi}$ with the m-dimensional basis:

$$\widetilde{\psi}^\circ = [CC^\intercal]^{-1}C\widetilde{\psi}.$$

The covariance of $\widetilde{\psi}^\circ$ is the $m \times m$ identity matrix, and the function class is unchanged:

$$\widetilde{\mathcal{H}}^\circ = \{\omega^\intercal \widetilde{\psi}^\circ : \omega \in \mathbb{R}^m\} = \widetilde{\mathcal{H}}.$$

TD(λ) Algorithm (On-Policy for Advantage)

For initialization $\omega_0, \zeta_0 \in \mathbb{R}^m$, the sequence of estimates are defined recursively:

$$\begin{aligned} \omega_{n+1} &= \omega_n + \alpha_{n+1}\zeta_n \mathcal{D}_{n+1}, \\ \mathcal{D}_{n+1} &= \left(-H^{\omega}(\Phi(n)) + c_n + \gamma H^{\omega}(\Phi(n+1))\right)\Big|_{\omega=\omega_n}, \\ \zeta_{n+1} &= \lambda\gamma\zeta_n + \widetilde{\psi}^{\circ}(\Phi(n+1)), \qquad H^{\omega}(\Phi(n)) = \omega^{\intercal}\widetilde{\psi}^{\circ}(\Phi(n)). \end{aligned} \tag{9.68}$$

Is it a problem if $d = 10^4$ and $m = 1$? Just the opposite: Complexity is reduced, and for $\lambda = 1$ the optimal estimate $\omega^* \in \mathbb{R}^m$ defines the optimal L_2 approximation of V. See Section 10.2 for details. The only remaining challenge may be computation of $\underline{\psi}$. See the discussion surrounding (9.54) for a solution using split sampling.

In the following sections, we exit the fixed-policy setting, returning to (9.1).

9.6 Watkins's Q-Learning

9.6.1 Optimal Control Essentials

Two value functions are of interest to us here:

$$\begin{aligned} h^\star(x) &= \min_{U(0),U(1),\dots} \sum_{k=0}^{\infty} \gamma^k \mathsf{E}[c(\Phi(k)) \mid X(0) = x], \\ Q^\star(x,u) &= \min_{U(1),U(2),\dots} \sum_{k=0}^{\infty} \gamma^k \mathsf{E}[c(\Phi(k)) \mid X(0) = x,\, U(0) = u], \end{aligned} \tag{9.69}$$

where $\Phi(k) = (X(k),U(k))$, and in the optimal control setting we denote $\underline{Q}^\star(x) \stackrel{\text{def}}{=} \min_u Q^\star(x,u)$, following the convention (9.5c). Given one value function, we have the other: For each x and u,

$$h^\star(x) = \underline{Q}^\star(x) \qquad \text{and} \qquad Q^\star(x,u) = c(x,u) + \gamma \sum_{x'} P_u(x,x')h^\star(x'). \tag{9.70}$$

The advantage function is defined as the difference $V^\star = Q^\star - h^\star$, which is a function on $\mathsf{X} \times \mathsf{U}$ taking nonnegative values: $\min_u V^\star(x,u) = 0$ for each x.

Q-learning algorithms are often based on a Galerkin relaxation that mirrors TD(λ): Given a parameterized family $\{H^\theta : \theta \in \mathbb{R}^d\}$, and a sequence of d-dimensional eligibility vectors $\{\zeta_n\}$, the goal is to find a solution θ^* to

$$0 = \bar{f}(\theta^*) = \mathsf{E}[\{-H^\theta(\Phi(n)) + c_n + \gamma \underline{H}^\theta(X(n+1))\}\zeta_n]\Big|_{\theta=\theta^*}. \tag{9.71}$$

The ODE method (8.4) leads quickly to an algorithm:

(1) Formulate the goal as a root-finding problem $\bar{f}(\theta^*) = 0$, with $\bar{f}$ defined in (9.71).
(2) Refine the design of $\bar{f}$ to ensure that the associated ODE is globally asymptotically stable.
(3) Is an Euler approximation appropriate? Is $\bar{f}$ Lipschitz continuous?

(4) If step (2) is skipped (no modification is needed), and step (3) is answered in the affirmative, then we arrive at the SA algorithm:

$$\theta_{n+1} = \theta_n + \alpha_{n+1}\{-H^{\theta_n}(\Phi(n)) + c(\Phi(n)) + \gamma \underline{H}^{\theta_n}(X(n+1))\}\zeta_n. \tag{9.72}$$

Q(0)-*Learning* The recursion (9.72) using $\zeta_n = \nabla H^\theta(\Phi(n))\Big|_{\theta=\theta_n}$.
For a linear parameterization $H^\theta = \theta^\intercal \psi$, this gives $\zeta_n = \psi_{(n)}$.

In general, the ODE method fails at step (3) when the state space is not finite. An example is the LQG problem in which $\{H^\theta : \theta \in \mathbb{R}^d\}$ is a linearly parameterized family of quadratic functions on $\mathsf{X} \times \mathsf{U}$. In this case, $\underline{H}^\theta$ is rarely Lipschitz continuous as a function of θ – see Exercise 9.4 for an example.

In the finite state space setting, we can expect Lipschitz continuity, but conditions ensuring stability of the ODE are not easily verified.

9.6.2 *Watkins's Algorithms*

One great success story is found in the special case called *tabular Q-learning*, with the basis previously defined in (5.10): $\psi_i(x,u) = \mathbb{1}\{(x,u) = (x^i,u^i)\}$ for each i, with $\mathsf{X} \times \mathsf{U} = \{(x^i,u^i) : 1 \le i \le d\}$. We continue to write $\theta \in \mathbb{R}^d$, but in the tabular setting $d = |\mathsf{X}| \times |\mathsf{U}|$, and the function class spans all possible functions on $\mathsf{X} \times \mathsf{U}$. For this architecture, the stability theory of TD learning admits extension to the nonlinear SA algorithm (9.72).

A simple stochastic-shortest-path problem will be used to illustrate theory, in which the state space $\mathsf{X} = \{1,\dots,6\}$ coincides with the six nodes on the un-directed graph shown on the left-hand side of Figure 9.1. The input space coincides with the edges shown: $\mathsf{U} = \{e_{x,x'}\}$, $x,x' \in \mathsf{X}$. The controlled transition matrix is defined as follows: If $X(n) = x \in \mathsf{X}$, and $U(n) = e_{x,x'} \in \mathsf{U}$, then $X(n+1) = x'$ with probability 0.8, and with probability 0.2, the next state is randomly chosen between the other neighboring nodes. The goal is to reach the state $x^* = 6$ and maximize the time spent there. The cost function is designed with this goal in mind, and also a cost for movement from any node:

$$c(x,u) = \begin{cases} 0 & u = e_{x,x}\,, \quad x \neq 6, \\ 5 & u = e_{x,x'}\,, \quad x' \neq 6, x \neq x', \\ -100 & u = e_{x,6}. \end{cases}$$

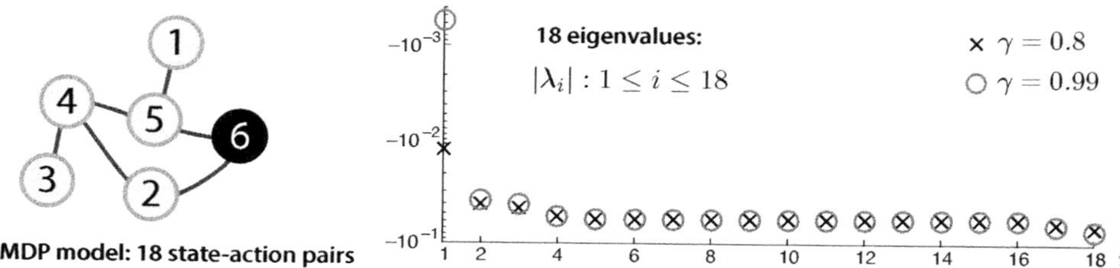

Figure 9.1 Six-state directed graph for a finite state action MDP example.

In the tabular setting, it is common to write H^n rather than H^{θ_n} (identifying the function approximation with the parameter). This is justified by the following representation: For each i and θ,

$$H^\theta(x^i,u^i) = \sum_{j=1}^{d} \theta(j)\psi_j(x^i,u^i) = \theta(i), \tag{9.73}$$

where the final equality holds because of the tabular basis.

Two versions of tabular Q-learning are distinguished by the way in which samples of $\mathbf{\Phi} = (\boldsymbol{X},\boldsymbol{U})$ are obtained.

Either of the following algorithms is commonly known as *Watkins's Q-learning.*

(i) *Asynchronous*: access to a single sample path of $\mathbf{\Phi}$.
$H^{n+1}(x,u) = H^n(x,u)$ if $\Phi(n) \neq (x,u)$, and otherwise

$$H^{n+1}(x,u) = H^n(x,u) + a_{n+1}\big[-H^n(x,u) + c(x,u) + \gamma \underline{H}^n\,(X(n+1))\big].$$

Asynchronous Q-learning can be implemented without a model: $Q^\star$ is approximated based on observations of the system.

(ii) *Synchronous*: access to a simulator to generate from the conditional pmf $P_u(x,\cdot)$ an i.i.d. sequence $\mathbf{\Xi}$ on X^d, with $\Xi^i_{n+1} \sim P_{u^i}(x^i,\cdot)$.
At iteration $n+1$ each entry of H^{n+1} is updated: for $i = 1,\ldots,d$,

$$H^{n+1}(x^i,u^i) = H^n(x^i,u^i) + a_{n+1}\big[-H^n(x^i,u^i) + c(x^i,u^i) + \gamma \underline{H}^n\,(\Xi^i_{n+1})\big].$$

In either case, given the estimate of the Q-function at iteration n, we obtain the H^n-greedy policy as any solution to

$$\phi_n(x) \in \arg\min_u H^n(x,u)\,, \quad x \in \mathsf{X}. \tag{9.74}$$

This section restricts to the asynchronous case (only to avoid repetition of equations and concepts in the theoretical development). Given the definition of the basis, asynchronous Q-learning is expressed as Q(0)-learning:

$$\begin{aligned} \theta_{n+1} &= \theta_n + \alpha_{n+1}\mathcal{D}_{n+1}\zeta_n, \\ \mathcal{D}_{n+1} &= -H^n(\Phi(n)) + c_n + \gamma \underline{H}^n(X(n+1)), \\ \zeta_n &= \nabla_\theta\{H^\theta(\Phi(n))\}\big|_{\theta=\theta_n} = \psi_{(n)}. \end{aligned} \tag{9.75}$$

The recursion (9.75) for the Q-learning algorithm can be written in a form similar to the linear recursion (8.53b). On denoting $\underline{\psi}_{(n+1)} = \psi(X(n+1),\phi_n(X(n+1)))$, with ϕ_n any H^n-greedy policy,

$$\begin{aligned} \theta_{n+1} &= \theta_n + \alpha_{n+1}\big[A_{n+1}\theta_n - b_{n+1}\big] \\ \text{with}\quad A_{n+1} &= \psi_{(n)}\{\gamma\underline{\psi}_{(n+1)} - \psi_{(n)}\}^{\intercal}, \\ b_{n+1} &= -c_n\psi_{(n)}. \end{aligned} \tag{9.76}$$

This is not a linear SA algorithm since the policy ϕ_n depends upon θ_n.

It should be clear that the algorithm (9.76) can be implemented with an arbitrary basis. The restriction to the tabular setting is made in this section only because there is a complete and accessible stability theory for Watkins's algorithms and refinements to come.

9.6.3 Exploration

It is common to employ the Gibbs policy (9.46a) using $G = H^n$:

$$\mathsf{P}\{U(n) = u \mid X(n) = x\} \stackrel{\text{def}}{=} \frac{1}{\kappa^{\varepsilon,n}(x)} \exp\bigl(-H^n(x,u)/\varepsilon\bigr), \tag{9.77}$$

where $\kappa^{\varepsilon,n}(x)$ is a normalizing constant, and $\varepsilon > 0$ is typically fixed (but it too may depend upon n, possibly vanishing as $n \to \infty$). This is often highly successful, but avoided in the theoretical development of this chapter. While SA theory now has matured to the point where it can be applied to establish stability of Q-learning with a time-varying policy such as this, there is no space in this book for a proper treatment.

Instead we assume that $\boldsymbol{U}$ is defined using a randomized Markov policy $\breve{\phi}$, so that $\boldsymbol{\Phi} = \{\Phi(k) \stackrel{\text{def}}{=} (X(k),U(k)) : k \geq 0\}$ is a Markov chain. Recall from (9.3b) that its invariant pmf can be expressed $\varpi(x,u) = \pi(x)\breve{\phi}(u \mid x)$, where π is invariant for the Markov chain $\boldsymbol{X}$. It is assumed throughout that $\boldsymbol{X}$ is uni-chain, so that π is unique.

Linear independence of the basis is defined by the rank condition $R^\psi > 0$, with matrix $R^\psi > 0$ defined in (9.24). For the tabular setting, this reduces to the diagonal matrix (9.25):

$$R^\psi(i,i) = \varpi(x^i,u^i), \qquad 1 \leq i \leq d. \tag{9.78}$$

It follows that the tabular basis is full rank if and only if the Markov chain $\boldsymbol{\Phi}$ is irreducible in the usual sense, so that $\varpi(x^i,u^i)$ is nonzero for each i.

9.6.4 ODE Analysis

Watkins' algorithm (9.75) admits a simple ODE approximation.

Proposition 9.15 *The ODE approximation for the Q-learning algorithm* (9.75) *takes the form* $\frac{d}{dt}\theta_t = \bar{f}^0(\theta_t)$, *with vector field*

$$\bar{f}^0_i(\theta) = \varpi(x^i,u^i)[-H^\theta(x^i,u^i) + c(x^i,u^i) + \sum_{x'} \gamma P_{u^i}(x^i,x')\underline{H}^\theta\,(x')].$$

For each i, the function $\bar{f}^0_i$ is concave and piecewise linear as a function of θ. □

Concavity of $\bar{f}^0_i$ for each i follows because $\underline{H}^\theta(x')$ is concave in θ for each x', as it is a minimum of linear functions. This fact is useful when we come to Zap Q-learning.

Proposition 9.15 raises concerns: The premultiplication by $\varpi(x^i,u^i)$ in the vector field $\bar{f}^0$ introduces "low gain" for state-input pairs that are rarely visited, and suggests that the "curse of condition number" will be severe if ϖ is far from the uniform pmf (see Section 8.6.1).

The path-finding problem provides an example of this curse. The eigenvalues of $A = \partial_\theta \bar{f}^0(\theta)$ are real and negative in this example. The right-hand side of Figure 9.1 shows $\{-\lambda_i\}$ on a semilog scale for two values of γ. Because A is Hurwitz, when using the step-size $\alpha_n = g/n$, the asymptotic covariance of the resulting algorithm is obtained as a solution to the Lyapunov equation (8.28a), provided each eigenvalue of gA is strictly less than $-1/2$. This translates to the bound $g > 45$ for $\gamma = 0.8$, and $g > 900$ for $\gamma = 0.99$.

These observations inspire the state-dependent step-size rule: $\alpha_n^v(x^i,u^i) \stackrel{\text{def}}{=} 0$ for any i satisfying $\Phi(k) \neq (x^i,u^i)$ for $k \leq n$, and otherwise

$$\alpha_n^v(x,u) = \big[\text{number of times } (x,u) \text{ has been visited up to time } n\,\big]^{-1}. \tag{9.79}$$

Proposition 9.16 *The following hold for Watkins's Q-learning with step-size rule* (9.79)*, under the assumption that* ϖ *is everywhere positive:*

(i) *It is equivalently expressed as the Q(0)-learning algorithm* (9.75) *with* $\alpha_n = 1/n$*, and modified using a diagonal matrix gain:*

$$\theta_{n+1} = \theta_n + \frac{1}{n+1} G_n \mathcal{D}_{n+1}\zeta_n\,, \qquad G_n^{-1} = \frac{1}{n+1}\sum_{k=0}^{n} \zeta_k \zeta_k^{\intercal}, \tag{9.80}$$

with the exception $G_n(i,i) \stackrel{\text{def}}{=} 0$ *if* $\Phi(k) \neq (x^i,u^i)$ *for* $k \leq n$.

(ii) *Its ODE approximation has vector field with components*

$$\bar{f}_i(\theta) = -H^\theta(x^i,u^i) + c(x^i,u^i) + \gamma \sum_{x'} P_{u^i}(x^i,x')\underline{H}^\theta\,(x'). \tag{9.81}$$

(iii) *The parameter recursion in* (9.80) *admits the representation*

$$\theta_{n+1} = \theta_n + \alpha_{n+1}\{G_n\zeta_n\zeta_n^{\intercal}\bar{f}(\theta_n) + \Delta_{n+1}\},$$

in which $\{\Delta_n : n \geq 1\}$ *is a martingale difference sequence.*

Proof The representation for $\bar{f}$ follows immediately from the definitions (especially the special structure for ψ). The irreducibility assumption for $\boldsymbol{\Phi}$ is required here: If this assumption is violated, then there is an index i for which $\varpi(x^i,u^i) = 0$, and hence $\Phi(k) \neq (x^i,u^i)$ for all sufficiently large k. This results in $\bar{f}_i(\theta) = 0$ for any θ.

The sequence $\{\Delta_n\}$ is taken of the form $\Delta_{n+1} = \Delta_{n+1}^\circ G_n\zeta_n$, in which $\{\Delta_n^\circ\}$ is a scalar martingale difference sequence satisfying

$$\mathsf{E}[\Delta_{n+1}^\circ \mid \mathcal{F}_n] = 0,$$

where $\mathcal{F}_n$ represents the history $\{\Phi(0),\dots,\Phi(n)\}$. The martingale difference property for $\{\Delta_n\}$ follows, since

$$\mathsf{E}[\Delta_{n+1} \mid \mathcal{F}_n] = \mathsf{E}[\Delta_{n+1}^\circ \mid \mathcal{F}_n]G_n\zeta_n.$$

Let i_n denote the unique index for which $\zeta_n(i_n) = 1$ (that is, $\Phi(n) = (X(n),U(n)) = (x^i,u^i)$ with $i = i_n$), and denote

$$\begin{aligned}\Delta_{n+1}^\circ &\stackrel{\text{def}}{=} -H^{\theta_n}(x^{i_n},u^{i_n}) + c(x^{i_n},u^{i_n}) + \gamma\underline{H}^{\theta_n}(X(n+1)) - \bar{f}_{i_n}(\theta_n)\\ &= \gamma\{\underline{H}^{\theta_n}(X(n+1)) - \sum_{x'} P_{u^i}(x^i,x')\underline{H}^\theta\,(x')\}\big|_{i=i_n},\end{aligned}$$

where the final equation follows from (9.81). The conclusion $\mathsf{E}[\Delta_{n+1}^\circ \mid \mathcal{F}_n] = 0$ follows from the interpretation of the controlled transition matrix as a conditional expectation:

$$\Delta_{n+1}^\circ = \gamma\underline{H}^{\theta_n}(X(n+1)) - \mathsf{E}[\gamma\underline{H}^{\theta_n}(X(n+1)) \mid \mathcal{F}_n]. \qquad \square$$

The notation $H^n \stackrel{\text{def}}{=} H^{\theta_n}$, and consequently $H^n(x^i,u^i) = \theta_n(i)$ is extended to the ODE approximation, using the notation q_t rather than ϑ_t. The ODE with vector field (9.81) defines the dynamics:

$$\tfrac{d}{dt} q_t(x,u) = -q_t(x,u) + c(x,u) + \gamma P_u \underline{q}_t\,(x), \tag{9.82}$$

with $\underline{q}_t(x) = \min_u q_t(x,u)$ and where the matrix notation is used:

$$P_u \underline{q}_t\,(x) \stackrel{\text{def}}{=} \sum_{x'} P_u(x,x') \underline{q}_t(x').$$

We expect $H^n(x,u) \approx q_{\tau_n}(x,u)$ for large n, and each pair (x,u) (subject to stability and consistent initialization – review Section 8.2.2 if the ODE approximation is not familiar).

The ODE@∞ (8.62) for the vector field (9.81) has a simple form. For any $r > 0$ and $1 \le i \le d$, we have

$$r^{-1}\bar{f}_i(r\theta) = -H^\theta(x^i,u^i) + r^{-1}c(x^i,u^i) + \gamma \sum_{x'} P_{u^i}(x^i,x') \underline{H}^\theta\,(x').$$

Letting $r \uparrow \infty$ gives

$$[\bar{f}_\infty(\theta)]_i = -H^\theta(x^i,u^i) + \gamma \sum_{x'} P_{u^i}(x^i,x') \underline{H}^\theta\,(x').$$

That is, the cost function is removed from the vector field. Stability is easily verified.

Proposition 9.17 can be extended to Q(0)-learning with basis defined by binning – see Exercise 9.3.

Proposition 9.17 *For Watkins's algorithm* (9.80),

(i) *The function* $V(\theta) = \|\tilde{\theta}\|_\infty$ *is a Lyapunov function for the ODE with vector field* (9.81)*:*

$$\frac{d^+}{dt} V(\vartheta_t) \le -(1-\gamma) V(\vartheta_t).$$

(ii) *The function* $V_\infty(\theta) = \|\theta\|_\infty$ *is a Lyapunov function for the ODE@*∞*:*

$$\frac{d^+}{dt} V_\infty(\vartheta_t^\infty) \le -(1-\gamma) V(\vartheta_t^\infty),$$

where the superscript "+" indicates right derivative.

It follows that either of the stability criteria of Proposition 8.9 hold: V is a Lipschitz-continuous solution to (QSV1), and the drift condition for V_∞ implies that the origin is asymptotically stable for the ODE@∞.

Proof of Proposition 9.17 A proof is presented only for the simpler ODE@∞, whose ODE is expressed

$$\tfrac{d}{dt} q_t^\infty(z) = -q_t^\infty(z) + \gamma P_u \underline{q}_t^\infty\,(x), \qquad z = (x,u) \in \mathsf{X} \times \mathsf{U}.$$

The Lyapunov function can be expressed

$$V_\infty(q_t^\infty) = \max\Bigl\{\max_i q_t^\infty(z^i),\ -\min_i q_t^\infty(z^i)\Bigr\},$$

where $z^i = (x^i, u^i)$ for each i. Based on this, we obtain a bound on the right derivative

$$\tfrac{d^+}{dt} V_\infty(q_t^\infty) \le \max\Big\{ \max_{i \in I_t^+} \tfrac{d^+}{dt} q_t^\infty(z^i),\ -\min_{i \in I_t^-} \tfrac{d^+}{dt} q_t^\infty(z^i) \Big\},$$

where I_t^+ is the set of indices satisfying $q_t^\infty(z^i) = \max_j |q_t^\infty(z^j)|$ if and only if $i \in I_t^+$, and I_t^- is the set of indices that are minimizers: $q_t^\infty(z^i) = -\max_j |q_t^\infty(z^j)|$ if and only if $i \in I_t^-$. At a given time t, either one of these sets can be empty, but not both.

If I_t^+ is nonempty and $i^+ \in I_t^+$ then

$$\tfrac{d^+}{dt} q_t^\infty(z^{i^+}) = -q_t^\infty(z^{i^+}) + \gamma \sum_{x'} P_u(x,x') \min_{u'} q_t^\infty(x',u') \Big|_{(x,u)=z^{i^+}}.$$

Applying the definitions gives

$$\tfrac{d^+}{dt} q_t^\infty(z^{i^+}) \le -q_t^\infty(z^{i^+}) + \gamma \max_i q_t^\infty(z^i) = -(1-\gamma) V_\infty(q_t^\infty).$$

The same arguments imply the analogous bound for $i^- \in I_t^-$ (when it is nonempty):

$$\tfrac{d^+}{dt} q_t^\infty(z^{i^-}) \ge -q_t^\infty(z^{i^-}) + \gamma \min_i q_t^\infty(z^i) = -(1-\gamma) \min_i q_t^\infty(z^i) = (1-\gamma) V_\infty(q_t^\infty).$$

Putting these bounds together establishes the bound $\tfrac{d^+}{dt} V_\infty(q_t^\infty) \le -(1-\gamma) V_\infty(q_t^\infty)$. □

9.6.5 Variance Matters

While stability of Watkins's algorithm is easily established, it should also be clear that the asymptotic covariance of this algorithm is typically infinite.

To apply the general SA theory, we require the Jacobian of $\bar f$ at θ^*. Existence of a derivative requires one more assumption:

Lemma 9.18 *Suppose that the optimal policy $\phi^\star$ is unique. Then the Jacobian $A = \partial \bar f\,(\theta^*)$, with $\bar f$ given in* (9.81), *is given by*

$$A = -I + \gamma T^\star, \tag{9.83}$$

where $T^\star$ defines the transition matrix for $\boldsymbol{\Phi}$ under the optimal policy:

$$T^\star(i,j) \stackrel{\text{def}}{=} P_{u^i}(x^i, x^j) \mathbb{1}\{u^j = \phi^\star(x^j)\}, \qquad 1 \le i,j \le d.$$

Proof The uniqueness assumption implies that there exists $\varepsilon > 0$ such that whenever $\theta \in \mathbb{R}^d$ satisfies $\|\theta - \theta^*\| < \varepsilon$,

$$\phi^\star(x) = \arg\min_{u \in \mathsf{U}} H^\theta(x,u), \qquad x \in \mathsf{X},$$

$$\bar f_i(\theta) = -H^\theta(x^i,u^i) + c(x^i,u^i) + \gamma \sum_{x'} P_{u^i}(x^i,x') H^\theta(x', \phi^\star(x')), \qquad i \ge 1.$$

It follows that $\bar f$ is linear in a neighborhood of the optimal parameter and

$$\begin{aligned} A_{i,j}(\theta) \stackrel{\text{def}}{=} \frac{\partial}{\partial \theta_j} \bar f_i\,(\theta) &= -\frac{\partial}{\partial \theta_j} H^\theta(x^i,u^i) + \gamma \sum_{x'} P_{u^i}(x^i,x') \frac{\partial}{\partial \theta_j} H^\theta\,(x', \phi^\star(x')) \\ &= -\mathbb{1}\{i = j\} + \gamma P_{u^i}(x^i,x^j) \mathbb{1}\{u^j = \phi^\star(x^j)\}, \qquad \text{whenever } \|\theta - \theta^*\| < \varepsilon. \end{aligned}$$

□

Lemma 9.18 suggests trouble, since A has an eigenvalue at $-(1-\gamma)$ with eigenvector $v=\mathbf{1}$. It is fortunate that this "worst" eigenvalue is known, so we can design the step-size rule to ensure a finite asymptotic covariance Σ_θ (as defined in (8.6), with $\rho=1$):

Proposition 9.19 *Suppose that the uniqueness assumption of Lemma 9.18 holds, and the step-size rule is modified:* $\alpha_n=\min\{\alpha_0, g\alpha_n^v\}$ *with* $\alpha_0>0$, $g\geq 1/(1-\gamma)$, *and* α_n^v *defined in* (9.79). *Then* $\{\theta_n\}$ *is consistent, and the asymptotic covariance of the resulting algorithm is obtained as a solution to the Lyapunov equation* (8.28a), *in which the noise covariance is diagonal, with entries*

$$\Sigma_\Delta(i,i)=\gamma^2\mathsf{E}\Big[\big(h^\star(X(n+1))-P_{u^i}h^\star(x^i)\big)^2\mid\Phi(n)=(x^i,u^i)\Big], \tag{9.84}$$

where $h^\star$ *is the value function* (9.69). □

Many improvements are possible based on theory in previous sections. Relative TD-learning is easily extended to Q-learning and is far more reliable when $\gamma\sim 1$. This is explained next.

9.7 Relative Q-Learning

The motivation for relative Q-learning is identical to the fixed-policy setting of Section 9.5.3, and the DP equation (9.62) is unchanged except for a change of interpretation:

$$0=\mathsf{E}_\varpi\big[-H^\star(\Phi(n))-\delta\langle\upmu,H^\star\rangle+c_n+\gamma\underline{H}^\star(X(n+1))\mid\mathcal{F}_n\big],\qquad n\geq 0, \tag{9.85}$$

where $\underline{H}^\star(x)=\min_u H^\star(x,u)$. The final conclusion of Lemma 9.13 holds in this more complex setting: $H^\star=Q^\star-k$, with k defined in (9.60):

$$k=\frac{\delta}{1+\delta-\gamma}\langle\upmu,Q^\star\rangle=\frac{\delta}{1-\gamma}\langle\upmu,H^\star\rangle.$$

We maintain the tabular basis in this section and the next, and restrict to the asynchronous setting, for which $\mathbf{\Phi}$ is a single sample path of $(\boldsymbol{X},\boldsymbol{U})$. Following the same steps as in Watkins's algorithm (9.75), we arrive at the following.

Relative Q-Learning

For initialization $\theta_0,\zeta_0\in\mathbb{R}^d$, the sequence of estimates is defined recursively:

$$\begin{aligned}\theta_{n+1}&=\theta_n+\alpha_{n+1}\mathcal{D}_{n+1}\psi_{(n)},\\ \mathcal{D}_{n+1}&=-H^{\theta_n}(\Phi(n))-\delta\langle\upmu,H^{\theta_n}\rangle+c_n+\gamma\underline{H}^{\theta_n}(X(n+1)).\end{aligned} \tag{9.86}$$

We opt for the step-size sequence (9.79) with scaling, and use the notation h_t rather than ϑ_t, as in (9.82). We obtain from the foregoing $\frac{d}{dt}h_t(x^i,u^i)=\bar{f}_i(h_t)$ with

$$\bar{f}_i(h)=-h(x^i,u^i)+c(x^i,u^i)+\gamma P_{u^i}\underline{h}(x^i)-\delta\langle\upmu,h\rangle, \tag{9.87}$$

in which $\underline{h}(x^i)=\min_u h(x^i,u)$, and $P_{u^i}\underline{h}(x^i)=\sum_{x'}P_{u^i}(x^i,x')\underline{h}(x')$.

Proposition 9.17 extends to the relative Q-learning algorithm with a slightly different ODE analysis:

Proposition 9.20 *The ODE@∞ for relative Q-learning is obtained using the vector field* (9.87) *with cost set to zero:*

$$\tfrac{d}{dt} h_t^\infty(z) = -h_t^\infty(z) + \gamma P_u \underline{h}_t^\infty(x) - \delta\langle \mu, h_t^\infty \rangle, \qquad z = (x,u) \in \mathsf{X} \times \mathsf{U}.$$

The origin is globally asymptotically stable for any choice of $\gamma \in [0,1)$ and $\delta > 0$.

Proof We cannot directly apply the Lyapunov function used previously, but instead opt for the span seminorm:

$$V(\theta) = \|\theta\|_{\mathrm{sp}} = \tfrac{1}{2}\{\max_i \theta_i - \min_i \theta_i\} = \min_r \max_i |\theta_i - r|.$$

Following the same steps as in the proof of Proposition 9.17, we obtain

$$\tfrac{d^+}{dt} V(h_t^\infty) \le -(1-\gamma) V(h_t^\infty).$$

Separate arguments show that on setting $r_t = \langle \mu, h_t^\infty \rangle$, there is $\kappa > 0$ such that

$$\tfrac{d^+}{dt} r_t \le -(1+\delta-\gamma) r_t + \kappa V(h_t^\infty).$$

Given the bound $V(h_t^\infty) \le e^{-(1-\gamma)t} V(h_0^\infty)$, it follows that $r_t \to 0$ exponentially fast as well. □

9.7.1 Gain Selection

Lemma 9.18 is more easily extended, which is the first step in a variance analysis:

Lemma 9.21 *Suppose that the optimal policy $\phi^\star$ is unique. Then the Jacobian $A_h = \partial \bar{f}(\theta^*)$, with $\bar{f}$ given in* (9.87)*, is given by*

$$A_h = -I + \gamma T^\star - \delta 1 \otimes \mu. \tag{9.88}$$

□

Analysis of the eigenvalues is simplified under the following assumption, which is actually a restatement of the assumption that π is unique.

> The Markov chain with transition matrix $T^\star$ is uni-chain: the eigenspace corresponding to the eigenvalue $\lambda = 1$ is one dimensional. (9.89)

Under this assumption, we denote by $\{\lambda_i\}$ the eigenvalues of $T^\star$, ordered so that $\lambda_1 = 1$, and denote

$$\rho^* = \max\{\mathrm{Re}(\lambda_i) : i \ge 2\}, \quad \rho^*_+ = \max\{\rho^*, 0\}, \tag{9.90a}$$

$$\rho = \max\{|\lambda_i| : i \ge 2\}. \tag{9.90b}$$

The value $1 - \rho$ appeared in Section 6.3, where it was designated the *spectral gap* of the transition matrix.

Lemma 9.22 *The quantities defined in* (9.90) *satisfy $\rho^*_+ \le \rho$.*

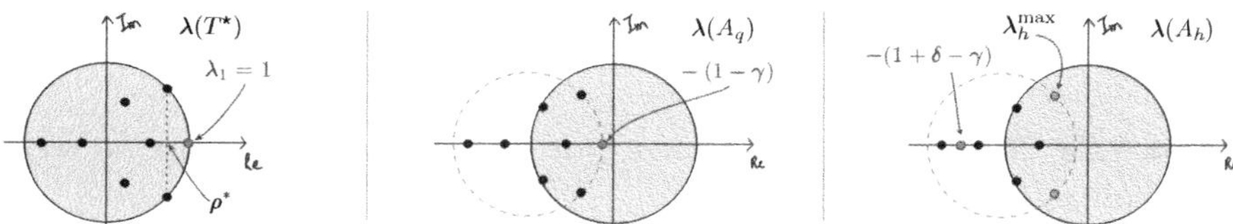

Figure 9.2 Relationship between the eigenvalues of the matrices $T^\star$, A_q, and A_h.

Proposition 9.23 is a companion to Proposition 9.19, with a big improvement:

Uniformly Bounded Asymptotic Covariance The choice of gain g in relative Q-learning can be fixed, independent of $\gamma < 1$, subject to a lower bound on δ, resulting in asymptotic covariance that is uniformly bounded for $0 \le \gamma < 1$. One choice is $\delta = \gamma$ and $g = 1/(1 - \rho_+^*)$.

A positive spectral gap is *not necessary* for stability of relative Q-learning, or uniform boundedness of the asymptotic covariance. This observation is illustrated in Figure 9.2, comparing the spectra of $T^\star$, A_h, and A_q (the Jacobian obtained with $\delta = 0$). The plot of eigenvalues for $T^\star$ indicates complex eigenvalues on the unit circle, so that $\rho = 1$: *The spectral gap is zero.* The plot on the left-hand side shows that $\rho^* = \rho_+^* < 1$.

Proposition 9.23 *For the relative Q-learning algorithm* (9.86) *with step-size rule* (9.79)*, the matrix A_h in* (9.88) *is equal to the Jacobian $A_h = \partial_\theta \bar{f}(\theta)\big|_{\theta=\theta^*}$. If $\delta \ge \gamma(1 - \rho_+^*)$, then each eigenvalue of A_h satisfies* $\text{Re}\,(\lambda(A_h)) \le -(1 - \gamma\rho_+^*)$. *Consequently, if the step-size is scaled via $\alpha_n(x,u) = g\alpha_n^v(x,u)$ with $g \ge 1/(1-\gamma\rho_+^*)$, then each eigenvalue of A_h satisfies*

$$\text{Re}\,(\lambda(gA_h)) = -g\text{Re}\,\big(\lambda(I - [\gamma T^\star - \delta\cdot\mathbf{1}\otimes\mu])\big) \le -1.$$

The asymptotic covariance of the resulting algorithm is obtained as a solution to the Lyapunov equation (8.28a). □

9.7.2 Honest Conclusions

Proposition 9.23 suggests that we should abandon Watkins's algorithm for its relative counterpart. In fact, a more detailed analysis reveals that we may view this proposition as a guide to gain selection for Q-learning in its standard form – that is, the recursion (9.86) with $\delta = 0$.

With a bit more work, we can show that while the asymptotic covariance of Watkins's algorithm is typically infinite if $g < \frac{1}{2}(1-\gamma)^{-1}$, it is only infinite on a one-dimensional subspace spanned by $\mathbf{1}$, provided $g > 0$ satisfies the assumption of Proposition 9.23.

Let $\widehat{Q}^n$ denote the estimate of $Q^\star$ at iteration n, obtained using either Q-learning or relative Q-learning. The span seminorm of the error is denoted

$$\|\widehat{Q}^n - Q^\star\|_{\text{sp}} = \min_r \max_{x,u} |\widehat{Q}^n(x,u) - Q^\star(x,u) - r|.$$

Proofs of the following claims can be found in [114]:

Proposition 9.24 *Fix $g \ge 1/(1-\gamma\rho_+^*)$, and let $\Sigma_\theta \ge 0$ be the solution to the Lyapunov equation* (8.28a) *using this g, $A = -I + \gamma[T^\star - \mathbf{1}\otimes\mu]$, and Σ_Δ the diagonal matrix* (9.84).

The following then hold for any $\delta \geq 0$ (not excluding $\delta = 0$), with step-size sequence $g\alpha_n^v$:

(i) *For any vector $v \in \mathbb{R}^d$ satisfying $\sum_i v_i = 0$,*

$$\lim_{n\to\infty} n\mathsf{E}[(v^\intercal \tilde{\theta}_n)^2] = \lim_{n\to\infty} nv^\intercal \mathsf{E}[\tilde{\theta}_n \tilde{\theta}_n^\intercal]v = v^\intercal \Sigma_\theta v < \infty. \tag{9.91}$$

(ii) *The scaled mean-square span seminorm vanishes at rate $1/n$:*

$$\sup_n n\,\mathsf{E}[\|\widehat{Q}^n - Q^\star\|_{\text{sp}}^2] < \infty.$$

□

These conclusions are illustrated using the example of Figure 9.1. Figure 9.3 compares three algorithms, with two different discount factors, $\gamma = 1 - 10^{-3}$ and $\gamma = 1 - 10^{-4}$. The three algorithms are distinguished by step-size (the value of g in $\alpha_n = g\alpha_n^v$) and the value of δ:

(1) Relative Q-learning with gain $g_h \stackrel{\text{def}}{=} 1/(1 - \rho_+^*\gamma)$ and $\delta = 1$.
(2) Watkins's Q-learning ($\delta = 0$) with gain g_h, and (3) Watkins's Q-learning with $g_q \stackrel{\text{def}}{=} 1/(1 - \gamma)$.

Consider first relative Q-learning. Figure 1.3 shows histograms of $\tilde{\theta}_n(i)$ from this algorithm for $i = 10$ and $\gamma = 1 - 10^{-3}$ (based on 10^3 independent runs); the value of i chosen is not important – similar results are observed for each component. The CLT approximation is nearly perfect for $n \geq 10^4$. The curse of condition number is solved in this example: The condition number $\kappa(A_h)$ is less than 30 for all $\gamma < 1$, while $\kappa(A_q)$ is of order $1/(1 - \gamma)$, tending to infinity as $\gamma \uparrow 1$ (recall (8.55) for the definition of κ).

It is also found that Watkins's algorithm works great with gain g_h, when performance is measured in the span seminorm: Figure 9.3a illustrates the behavior of each of the three algorithms on a single sample path. Figure 9.3b shows the average error, obtained by averaging 10^3 independent runs of each algorithm. The evolution of $\|\widehat{Q}^n - Q^\star\|_{\text{sp}}$ is nearly identical using either Watkins's algorithm or relative Q-learning, with common step-size gain $g_h = 1/(1 - \rho_+^*\gamma)$.

Figure 6.5 shows results for Watkins's algorithm with the standard step-size $\alpha_n = \alpha_n^v$ ($g = 1$), and $\gamma = 0.8$ for which the asymptotic variance is infinite. The infinite variance is not apparent because of the poor design of the experiment, using $\theta_0^i = 0$ for each i. Remember the advice given after the figure: *It is known that the limit is positive, so it would make sense to sample the initial parameter uniformly on a widely spaced interval of the form $[0,\bar{\eta}]$.*

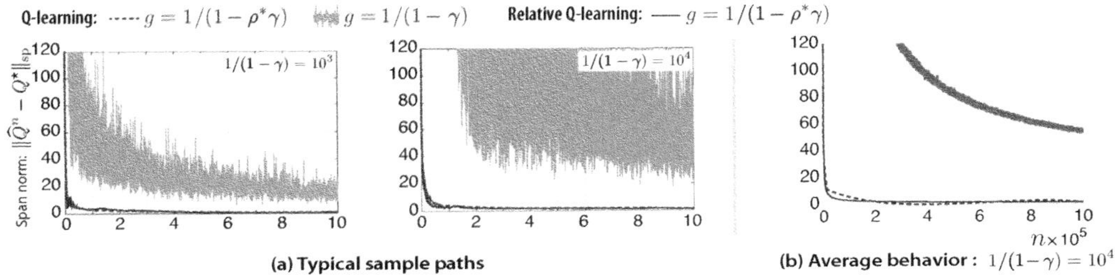

Figure 9.3 (a) Span norm error for Q-learning and relative Q-learning are similar for $\gamma \sim 1$. (b) Average error for the three algorithms, with $1/(1 - \gamma) = 10^4$.

9.8 GQ and Zap

This section contains more ideas to accelerate Watkins's Q-learning, and also inspire new techniques for use outside of the tabular setting. However, theory in this section is restricted to the tabular basis.

An understanding of the matrix gain algorithms described here requires a closer look at the vector field $\bar{f}^0$ given in Proposition 9.15.

When the state space and input space are finite as assumed here, there are only a finite number of deterministic stationary policies. Denote these by $\{\phi^m : 1 \le m \le M\}$, where M is the number of possible functions from X to U. For each m, denote

$$\Theta^m = \{\theta \in \mathbb{R}^d : \phi^m(x) \in \arg\min_u H^\theta(x,u) \text{ for each } x\}.$$

Each set Θ^m is a convex cone: $r_1\theta^1 + r_2\theta^2 \in \Theta^m$ whenever $\theta^i \in \Theta^m$ and $r_i \in \mathbb{R}_+$ for $i = 1,2$. Figure 9.4 provides an illustration of these sets.

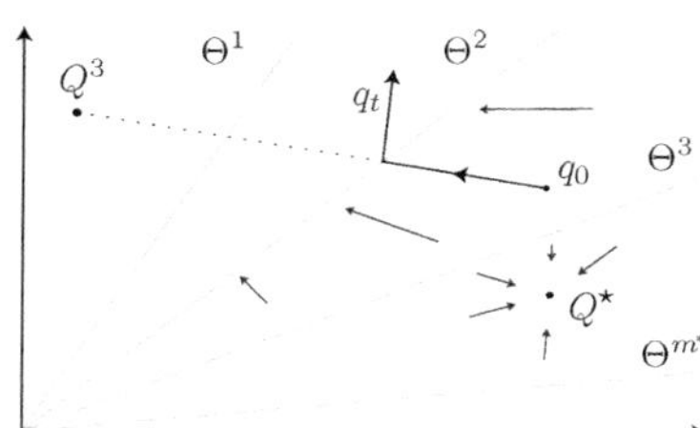

Figure 9.4 Parameter space decomposition for Watkins' Q-learning. The path $\{q_t\}$ is one trajectory of the Newton–Raphson flow associated with $\bar{f}^0$.

Let Q^m denote the fixed-policy Q-function obtained with policy ϕ^m. On denoting by T_m the transition matrix for the resulting Markov chain $\boldsymbol{\Phi}$ with control ϕ^m, we have

$$Q^m = [I - \gamma T_m]^{-1} c.$$

These Q-functions are also indicated in Figure 9.4, which is justified by the identity (9.73). The index m^* shown in the figure is special because $Q^{m^*} \in \Theta^{m^*}$, which implies the fixed-point equation:

$$\phi^{m^*}(x) \in \arg\min_u Q^{m^*}(x,u) \text{ for each } x \in \mathsf{X}.$$

That is, this step of policy iteration returns the same policy, which implies that $Q^{m^*} = Q^\star$.

Let Π denote the diagonal matrix $\Pi = \text{diag}(\varpi)$ (also equal to R^ψ as defined in (9.78)).

Lemma 9.25 *The Jacobian $A = \partial \bar{f}^0$ is piecewise constant, with $A(\theta)$ independent of θ within the interior of Θ^m for each m. If $\theta \in \mathbb{R}^d$ satisfies $\theta \in$ interior (Θ^m) for any m, then at this value the Jacobian is given by*

$$\begin{aligned} A(\theta) &= -\Pi[I - \gamma T_m] \\ \text{with} \quad T_m(i,j) &\stackrel{\text{def}}{=} P_{u^i}(x^i,x^j)\mathbb{1}\{u^j = \phi^m(x^j)\}, \qquad 1 \le i,j \le d. \end{aligned} \tag{9.92a}$$

The function $\bar{f}^0$ is thus continuous and piecewise linear, and for each θ,

$$\bar{f}^0(\theta) = A(\theta)\theta - \Pi b, \qquad \text{where } b_i = -c(x^i,u^i) \text{ for each } i. \tag{9.92b}$$

9.8.1 GQ-Learning

This algorithm is defined exactly as in the deterministic setting of Section 5.4.4, with the same objective: solve

$$\min_\theta \Gamma(\theta) = \min_\theta \tfrac{1}{2}\{\bar{f}^0(\theta)\}^\intercal M \bar{f}^0(\theta),$$

where once again $M^{-1} = \mathsf{E}_\varpi[\zeta_n\zeta_n^\intercal]$ with $\zeta_n = \psi_{(n)}$ (recall (9.4) for notation). For the tabular basis, this reduces to $M^{-1} = \Pi$, and $\Gamma(\theta^*) = 0$.

The ODE method based on gradient descent will provide a recursive algorithm, as in the deterministic setting considered previously (recall (5.55)). First we must interpret the ODE. The following representations are implied by (9.92b).

Lemma 9.26 *If $\theta \in \mathbb{R}^d$ satisfies $\theta \in$ interior(Θ^m) for any m, then Γ is quadratic in a neighborhood of θ, with partial derivatives*

$$\nabla\Gamma(\theta) = A(\theta)^\intercal M \bar{f}^0(\theta) = -[I - \gamma T_m]^\intercal \bar{f}^0(\theta),$$
$$\nabla^2\Gamma(\theta) = [I - \gamma T_m]^\intercal \Pi [I - \gamma T_m].$$

GQ-learning is the two-time scale SA algorithm, designed to approximate $\frac{d}{dt}\vartheta = -\nabla\Gamma(\vartheta)$, with $-\nabla\Gamma(\theta) = \bar{f}^0(\theta) - \gamma T_m^\intercal \bar{f}^0(\theta)$. A challenge is to interpret the product:

$$T_m^\intercal \bar{f}^0(\theta)\Big|_i = \sum_j \bar{f}_j^0(\theta) T_m(j,i), \qquad \theta \in \text{interior}(\Theta^m).$$

For the tabular basis, this can be expressed

$$T_m^\intercal \bar{f}^0(\theta)\Big|_i = \sum_{j,k} \bar{f}_j^0(\theta) T_m(j,k)\psi_i(x^k,u^k) = \sum_j \bar{f}_j^0(\theta)\mathsf{E}[\underline{\psi}_{(n+1)} \mid \Phi(n) = (x^j,u^j)]\Big|_i, \tag{9.93}$$

where $\underline{\psi}_{(n+1)} = \psi(X(n+1),\phi^m(X(n+1)))$ for $\theta \in$ interior(Θ^m).

This representation lends itself to algorithm design. Recall from (9.74) that ϕ_n denotes the greedy policy associated with H^n.

GQ-Learning

For initialization θ_0, $\omega_0 \in \mathbb{R}^d$,

$$\theta_{n+1} = \theta_n + \alpha_{n+1}\{\mathcal{D}_{n+1}\psi_{(n)} - \gamma\omega_{n+1}^\intercal\psi_{(n)}\underline{\psi}_{(n+1)}\}, \tag{9.94a}$$
$$\omega_{n+1} = \omega_n + \beta_{n+1}\psi_{(n)}\{\mathcal{D}_{n+1} - \psi_{(n)}^\intercal\omega_n\}, \tag{9.94b}$$

where
$$\underline{\psi}_{(n+1)} = \psi(X(n+1),\phi_n(X(n+1))),$$
$$\mathcal{D}_{n+1} = -H^n(\Phi(n)) + c_n + \gamma\underline{H}^n(X(n+1)),$$

where the two step-size sequences satisfy (8.22).

The analysis that follows concludes with Proposition 9.27, which implies that the condition number for the linearized ODE dynamics can be expected to be of order $O(1/(1-\gamma)^2)$. Consequently, GQ learning is probably not the best option in a tabular setting. It is presented here because it may be useful in function approximation settings for which it is not known if $\bar{f}^0(\theta) = 0$ has a solution.

GQ Analysis

The fast time-scale recursion (9.94b) is designed so that $\omega_n \approx M\bar{f}^0(\theta_n)$ for large n. Theory for two time-scale SA provides an approximation of (9.94a):

$$\theta_{n+1} \approx \theta_n + \alpha_{n+1}\{\mathcal{D}_{n+1}\zeta_n - \gamma\bar{f}^0(\theta_n)^{\intercal} M\zeta_n \underline{\psi}_{(n+1)}\}.$$

We conclude that the ODE approximation of this recursion is gradient descent on applying Lemma 9.26 and (9.93).

The curse of condition number is potentially worse when using this algorithm:

Proposition 9.27 *Suppose that the optimal policy $\phi^\star$ is unique. Then the linearization matrix for GQ-learning is given by*

$$A_{\text{GQ}} = -\nabla^2\Gamma(\theta^*) = -[I-\gamma T^\star]^{\intercal}\Pi[I-\gamma T^\star].$$

Consequently, the eigenvalues of the matrix A_{GQ} are real and nonpositive, and its condition number admits the lower bound

$$\kappa(A_{\text{GQ}}) \geq \frac{d}{(1-\gamma)^2}\{\max((1-\lambda\gamma)^2 v^{\intercal}\Pi v)\},$$

where the max is over all eigenvalue-eigenvector pairs (λ, v) for $T^\star$ satisfying $\|v\| = 1$.

Proof Because $A_{\text{GQ}} = -\nabla^2\Gamma(\theta^*)$ is symmetric, its condition number is the ratio of eigenvalues:

$$\kappa(A_{\text{GQ}}) = \frac{\lambda_{\max}(\nabla^2\Gamma(\theta^*))}{\lambda_{\min}(\nabla^2\Gamma(\theta^*))}.$$

It remains to establish the following bounds:

$$\lambda_{\min}(\nabla^2\Gamma(\theta^*)) \leq (1-\gamma)^2/d, \tag{9.95a}$$

$$\lambda_{\max}(\nabla^2\Gamma(\theta^*)) \geq (1-\lambda\gamma)^2 v^{\intercal}\Pi v\,, \text{ for any eigenvalue}-\text{eigenvector pair } (\lambda, v) \text{ for } T^\star, \tag{9.95b}$$

where in (9.95b) the eigenvectors are normalized, with $\|v\| = 1$.

The proof is based on the pair of inequalities

$$\lambda_{\min}(\nabla^2\Gamma(\theta^*)) = \min v^{\intercal}\nabla^2\Gamma(\theta^*)v,$$
$$\lambda_{\max}(\nabla^2\Gamma(\theta^*)) = \max v^{\intercal}\nabla^2\Gamma(\theta^*)v,$$

where the max and min are over all $v \in \mathbb{R}^d$ satisfying $\|v\| = 1$. To obtain bounds, we restrict to eigenvectors of $T^\star$, normalized by $\|v\| = 1$, from which we obtain

$$v^{\intercal}\nabla^2\Gamma(\theta^*)v = v^{\intercal}[I-\gamma T^\star]^{\intercal}\Pi[I-\gamma T^\star]v = (1-\lambda\gamma)^2 v^{\intercal}\Pi v$$

and hence the pair of bounds

$$\lambda_{\min}\big(\nabla^2 \Gamma(\theta^*)\big) \le (1-\lambda\gamma)^2 v^\intercal \Pi v \le \lambda_{\max}\big(\nabla^2 \Gamma(\theta^*)\big).$$

The lower bound (9.95b) follows.

To obtain the bound (9.95a) on the minimal eigenvector, take $v = \mathbf{1}/\sqrt{d}$, which is an eigenvector of $T^\star$ with eigenvalue $\lambda = 1$:

$$\lambda_{\min}(\nabla^2 \Gamma(\theta^*)) \le (1-\lambda\gamma)^2 v^\intercal \Pi v = (1-\gamma)^2/d.$$

□

9.8.2 Zap Q-Learning

To crush the condition number curse, there is no better approach than Zap SA. This is easily adapted to Q-learning, even in nonlinear function approximation settings. For analysis, we continue to restrict to the tabular setting.

The quasilinear SA representation of Watkins's algorithm in (9.76) is most easily adapted to create an algorithm.

Zap Q-Learning

For initialization $\theta_0 \in \mathbb{R}^d$ and $\widehat{A}_0 \in \mathbb{R}^{d\times d}$, with $\{A_n, b_n\}$ defined in (9.76),

$$\begin{aligned}\widehat{A}_{n+1} &= \widehat{A}_n + \beta_{n+1}\{-\widehat{A}_n + A_{n+1}\},\\ \theta_{n+1} &= \theta_n + \alpha_{n+1} G_{n+1}\big[A_{n+1}\theta_n - b_{n+1}\big], \quad G_{n+1} = -\widehat{A}_{n+1}^{-1},\end{aligned} \tag{9.96}$$

where the two step-size sequences satisfy (8.22).

This algorithm is intended to approximate the Newton–Raphson flow:

$$\frac{d}{dt}\vartheta = G(\vartheta)\bar{f}^0(\vartheta),$$

with $G(\vartheta) = -[\partial_\theta \bar{f}^0(\vartheta)]^{-1}$. Based on the representation for $\bar{f}^0$ in (9.92) along with Lemma 9.25, which gives $A(\theta)$, and using the suggestive notation q_t in place of ϑ_t, this becomes

$$\frac{d}{dt}q_t = -q_t - A(q_t)^{-1}\Pi b = -\vartheta + Q^m, \quad q_t \in \text{interior}(\Theta^m).$$

On denoting $\tilde{q}_t^m = q_t - Q^m$, we obtain linear error dynamics in the region Θ^m:

$$\frac{d}{dt}\tilde{q}_t^m = -\tilde{q}_t^m. \tag{9.97}$$

These dynamics are illustrated in Figure 9.4 with $m = 3$.

Testing the CLT

Zap Q-learning has minimal asymptotic covariance, given by (8.30):

$$\Sigma_\theta^\star \stackrel{\text{def}}{=} A^{-1}\Sigma_\Delta(A^{-1})^\intercal.$$

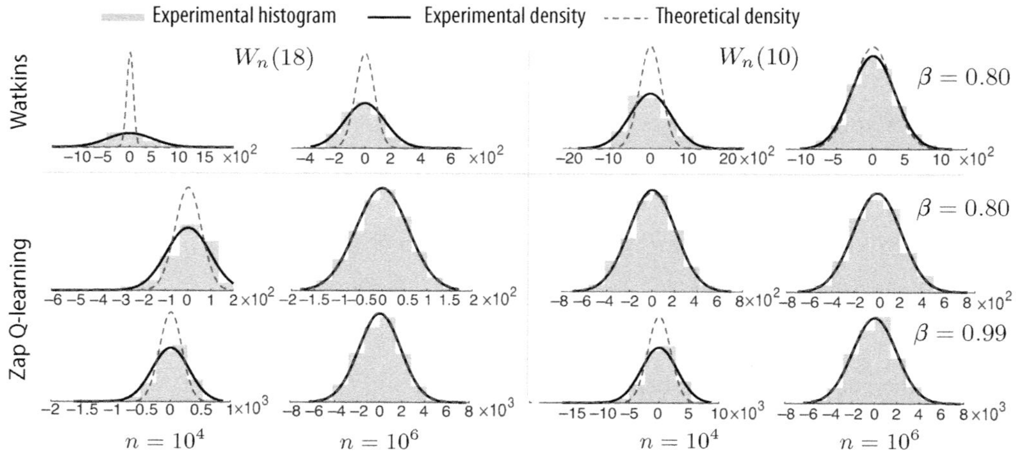

Figure 9.5 Comparison of theoretical and empirical asymptotic variance for Q-learning applied to the six-state example. Row 1: Watkins's algorithm with gain $g = 70$, $\gamma = 0.8$. Row 2: Zap Q-learning with $\gamma = 0.8$. Row 3: Zap Q-learning with $\gamma = 0.99$.

For illustration, consider the six-state example shown in Figure 9.1, for which it is possible to compute both A and Σ_Δ [110]. With $M = 10^3$ independent runs, histograms of the normalized error are obtained:

$$W_n^i = \sqrt{n}[\theta_n^i - \overline{\theta}_n], \qquad \overline{\theta}_n \stackrel{\text{def}}{=} \frac{1}{M}\sum_{i=1}^{M} \theta_n^i. \tag{9.98}$$

Figure 1.1 shows a single sample path of Zap Q-learning, compared with several other algorithms using the step-size $\alpha_n = 1/n$ (a poor choice, since in this plot the discount factor was taken to be $\gamma = 0.99$).

Figure 9.5 shows histograms obtained using Zap Q-learning, and also Watkins's algorithm using step-size $\alpha_n = g/n$ with $g = 70$ (resulting in a finite asymptotic covariance for the discount factor $\gamma = 0.8$ chosen).

The first row shows the histogram for Watkins's algorithm, and the second and third rows for Zap Q-learning, with $\beta_n = (\alpha_n)^{0.85} = 1/n^{0.85}$. Data in the third row were obtained with the discount factor $\gamma = 0.99$. The covariance estimates and the Gaussian approximations match the theoretical predictions well for $n \geq 10^4$.

Analysis of this algorithm falls way outside of the scope of this book, because $A(\theta)$ is not continuous, so there is no "off the shelf" theory to justify an ODE approximation. Exploiting concavity of the entries of $\bar{f}^0$, it is possible to justify an ODE approximation, and this can be extended to general nonlinear function approximation (with substantial effort) [90].

Zap Zero

Zap Q-learning is blindly fast in practice, but the update equation for θ_{n+1} in (9.96) is complex. We have a solution to this complexity using the first-order Zap SA algorithm (8.52).

The algorithm is applicable because one crucial assumption of Proposition 8.7 holds: $A(\theta)$ is Hurwitz for each θ. With $\{A_n, b_n\}$ defined in (9.76), the algorithm (8.52) is expressed as follows:

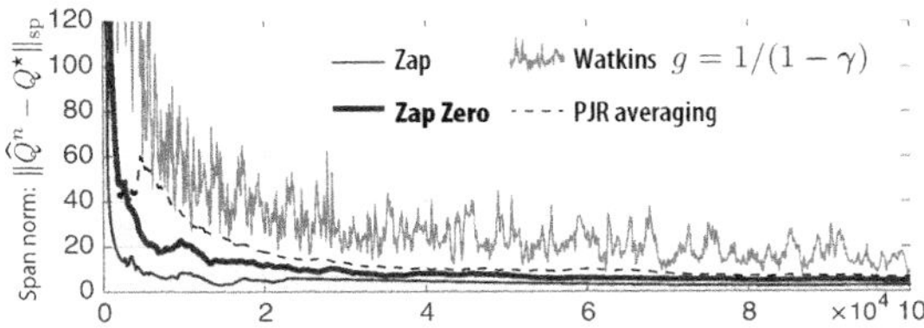

Figure 9.6 Span norm error for Zap Zero Q-learning.

Zap Zero Q-Learning

Initialize $\theta_0, \omega_0 \in \mathbb{R}^d$. Update for $n \geq 0$:

$$\theta_{n+1} = \theta_n + \alpha_{n+1}\omega_n, \tag{9.99a}$$

$$\omega_{n+1} = \omega_n + \beta_{n+1}\{A_{n+1}\omega_n + (A_{n+1}\theta_n - b_{n+1})\}, \tag{9.99b}$$

where the two step-size sequences satisfy (8.22).

The fast time-scale recursion (9.99b) is designed to obtain the approximation

$$\omega_n \approx -A(\theta_n)^{-1}\{A(\theta_n)\theta_n - b\}. \tag{9.100}$$

The Zap Zero algorithm is not much more complex than Watkins's original algorithm. We have doubled the number of parameter elements since we must update θ_n and ω_n at each stage, but the updates are not at all complex.

When this and Zap Q-learning are compared for the example considered in Figure 9.3 we observe that the span seminorm errors for the respective parameter estimates $\{\theta_n\}$ are very similar. Results are shown in Figure 9.6, alongside results using PJR averaging and Watkins's algorithm with gain $\alpha_n = g\alpha_n^v$, and $g = 1/(1-\gamma)$. The transient behavior of Zap Zero Q-learning is better than what is obtained using averaging, and a bit worse than Zap Q-learning.

For Zap Q-learning, any value $0.6 \leq \rho \leq 0.9$ for $\beta_n = n^{-\rho}$ in (9.96) gives similar performance.

However, for both Zap Zero and PJR averaging, it was found in this example that a very large step-size is required for the fast time scale. These results were obtained using $\beta_n = n^{-\rho}$ with $\rho = 0.1$. Performance was terrible for Zap Zero and PJR averaging with $\rho \geq 0.5$. *New theory is needed to explain these findings.*

9.9 Technical Proofs*

9.9.1 Advantage Function

Proof of Proposition 9.1 The conclusion $G^*(x) = \mathsf{E}[Q(\Phi(n)) \mid X(n) = x] = \sum_u \breve{\phi}(u \mid x)Q(x,u) = \underline{Q}(x)$ is obtained upon recalling the definition of the conditional expectation in (9.15). Recall that $\underline{Q} = h$ is the value function (9.6a). □

Proof of Proposition 9.2 Equation (9.11) can be extended to show that for each $x \in \mathsf{X}$ and $k \geq 0$,

$$\mathsf{E}^{\bar{\Phi}}\Big[V_\Phi(\Phi(k)) \mid X(0)=x\Big] = \mathsf{E}^{\bar{\Phi}}\Big[c(\Phi(k)) + \gamma h_\Phi(X(k+1)) - h_\Phi(X(k)) \mid X(0)=x\Big].$$

Consequently,

$$\begin{aligned}
&\mathsf{E}^{\bar{\Phi}}\Big[\sum_{k=0}^{\infty}\gamma^k V_\Phi(\Phi(k)) \mid X(0)=x\Big] \\
&= \mathsf{E}^{\bar{\Phi}}\Big[\sum_{k=0}^{\infty}\gamma^k \{c(\Phi(k)) + \gamma h_\Phi(X(k+1)) - h_\Phi(X(k))\} \mid X(0)=x\Big] \\
&= \mathsf{E}^{\bar{\Phi}}\Big[-h_\Phi(X(0)) + \sum_{k=0}^{\infty}\gamma^k c(\Phi(k)) \mid X(0)=x\Big] \\
&= -h_\Phi(x) + h_{\bar{\Phi}}(x).
\end{aligned}$$

□

Proof of Proposition 9.14 The representation (9.65a) is the definition of V, and (9.65b) follows from (9.65a) since (in the compact notation) $Q(x,u) = c(x,u) + \gamma P_u h\,(x)$. The final representation (9.65c) follows from (9.65b) and the dynamic programming equation $h = c_{\breve{\Phi}} + \gamma P_{\breve{\Phi}} h$. □

9.9.2 TD Stability Theory

Bounds on the eigenvalues of A for on-policy TD(λ) are established by careful consideration of the autocorrelation sequence (9.23). This can be expressed

$$R(j) = \Sigma(j) + \bar{\psi}\bar{\psi}^{\intercal}, \qquad j \in \mathbb{Z}_+, \tag{9.101}$$

where $\bar{\psi} = \mathsf{E}_\pi[\psi(X(n))]$, and letting $\widetilde{\psi} = \psi - \bar{\psi}$,

$$\Sigma(j) = \mathsf{E}_\pi[\widetilde{\psi}(X(n+j))\widetilde{\psi}(X(n))^{\intercal}].$$

Eigenvalue bounds are obtained in terms of the scalars

$$\varrho_\gamma = \gamma\frac{1-\lambda}{1-\gamma\lambda}\varrho, \qquad \varrho = \max_{i\geq 1}\max_{y\in\mathbb{C}}\frac{|y^\dagger R(i) y|}{y^\dagger R^\psi y}, \tag{9.102}$$

where $y^\dagger$ denotes complex conjugate transpose, $R^\psi = R(0)$, and the maximum excludes $y = 0$.

Lemma 9.28 *We have $\varrho \leq 1$ and $\varrho_\gamma \leq \gamma\varrho \leq \gamma$. If $\Sigma^\psi > 0$ and $\mathbf{\Phi}$ is aperiodic, then $\varrho < 1$.*

Proof It is obvious that $\varrho_\gamma \leq \gamma\varrho$ whenever $0 \leq \lambda \leq 1$. We proceed to bound ϱ.

We have from the Cauchy–Schwarz inequality, for any nonzero $y \in \mathbb{C}$,

$$\begin{aligned}
|y^\dagger R(i) y| &= |\mathsf{E}_\pi[y^\dagger \psi(X(n+i))\psi(X(n))^{\intercal} y]| \\
&\leq \sqrt{\mathsf{E}_\pi[|y^\dagger\psi(X(n+i))|^2]}\sqrt{\mathsf{E}_\pi[|\psi(X(n))^{\intercal} y|^2]}.
\end{aligned}$$

The right-hand side is precisely $\mathsf{E}_\pi[|\psi(X(n))^{\intercal} y|^2] = y^\dagger R^\psi y$, from which we conclude that $\varrho \leq 1$.

To complete the proof, we obtain a strict inequality under aperiodicity and the full rank condition $\Sigma^\psi > 0$. It is sufficient to restrict to $i = 1$, and show that $|y^\dagger R(1)y| < y^\dagger R^\psi y$ for any nonzero $y \in \mathbb{C}$ when $\Sigma^\psi > 0$ and $\mathbf{\Phi}$ is aperiodic.

The Cauchy–Schwarz inequality tells us more: If equality holds, then there is a complex number w satisfying $|w| = 1$ and $y^\dagger \psi(X(n+1)) = w y^\dagger \psi(X(n))$ with probability one. Since n is arbitrary, we can iterate to obtain the following with probability 1:

$$y^\dagger \psi(X(n+i)) = w^i y^\dagger \psi(X(n)), \qquad i \in \mathbb{Z}_+.$$

Multiplying each side by $\psi(X(n))^\intercal$ on the right and taking expectations gives

$$y^\dagger R(i) y = w^i y^\dagger R^\psi y.$$

Aperiodicity tells us that $\lim_{i\to\infty} R(i) = \lim_{i\to\infty} \mathsf{E}[\psi(X(i))\psi(X(0))^\intercal] = \bar\psi\bar\psi^\intercal$. If $\bar\psi = 0$, it follows that $y^\dagger R^\psi y = 0$, which contradicts the assumption $R^\psi > 0$.

Otherwise, we take expectations to obtain $y^\dagger\bar\psi = w^i y^\dagger\bar\psi$, giving $w = 1$, and hence

$$|y^\dagger\bar\psi|^2 = \lim_{i\to\infty} y^\dagger R(i) y = y^\dagger R^\psi y.$$

However, on applying (9.101),

$$|y^\dagger\bar\psi|^2 = y^\dagger R^\psi y = y^\dagger[\Sigma^\psi + \bar\psi\bar\psi^\intercal] y = y^\dagger \Sigma^\psi y + |y^\dagger\bar\psi|^2.$$

This implies that $y^\dagger\Sigma^\psi y = 0$, violating the assumption that $\Sigma^\psi > 0$. □

Proof of Theorem 9.7 Part (i) is from the definitions, since we have

$$\mathsf{E}_\pi[\mathcal{D}^{\theta^*}_{n+1}\psi_i(X(n))] = 0, \qquad 1 \le i \le d.$$

Part (ii) requires interpretation of θ^* for TD(1). Lemma 9.9 tells us that $A = -R^\psi$, and (9.38) then gives

$$-R^\psi\theta^* + \mathsf{E}_\pi[\zeta_n c(X(n))] = 0, \qquad \zeta_n = \sum_{i=0}^\infty \gamma^i \psi(X(n-i)). \tag{9.103}$$

To complete the proof, we show that (9.103) coincides with the necessary and sufficient condition for optimality of (9.33) with norm (9.34).

Let $\theta^\circ \in \mathbb{R}^d$ denote a solution to (9.33). Recalling that $\nabla_\theta h^\theta = \psi$, the first-order condition for optimality is expressed

$$\begin{aligned}0 = \tfrac{1}{2}\nabla_\theta\|h^\theta - h\|^2\Big|_{\theta=\theta^\circ} &= \sum_{x\in\mathsf{X}} (h^\theta(x) - h(x))\nabla_\theta h^\theta(x)\pi(x)\Big|_{\theta=\theta^\circ} \\ &= R^\psi\theta^\circ - \mathsf{E}_\pi[h(X(n))\psi(X(n))].\end{aligned}$$

In view of (9.103), it remains to show that

$$\mathsf{E}_\pi[h(X(n))\psi(X(n))] = \mathsf{E}_\pi[\zeta_n c(X(n))]. \tag{9.104}$$

This is obtained from the definition of the value function:

$$\mathsf{E}_\pi[h(X(n))\psi(X(n))] = \mathsf{E}_\pi\Big[\mathsf{E}\Big[\sum_{i=0}^\infty \gamma^i c(X(n+i)) \mid X(n)\Big]\psi(X(n))\Big].$$

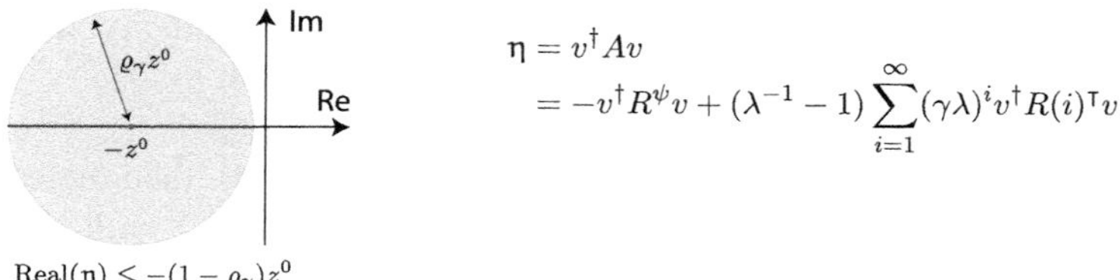

Figure 9.7 Left: Eigenvalues of A satisfy $\text{Real}(\eta) \le -(1-\varrho_\gamma)z^0$. Right: Eigenvalue expressed in terms of eigenvector and autocorrelation sequence.

The identity (9.104) then follows from the smoothing property of conditional expectation:

$$\begin{aligned}
\mathsf{E}_\pi[h(X(n))\psi(X(n))] &= \mathsf{E}_\pi\Big[\sum_{i=0}^{\infty}\gamma^i c(X(n+i))\psi(X(n))\Big] \\
&= \sum_{i=0}^{\infty}\gamma^i \mathsf{E}_\pi[c(X(n+i))\psi(X(n))] \\
&= \sum_{i=0}^{\infty}\gamma^i \mathsf{E}_\pi[c(X(n))\psi(X(n-i))] = \mathsf{E}_\pi[\zeta_n c(X(n))]. \qquad \square
\end{aligned}$$

Proof of Proposition 9.8 We confront a notational clash in analysis of TD(λ), since a focus is bounding the eigenvalues of a matrix A. In the remainder of this section, an eigenvalue–eigenvector pair is denoted (η, v) for which v is not zero, and $Av = \eta v$.

Let (η, v) denote any eigenvalue–eigenvector pair for A, satisfying $\|v\| = 1$. The eigenvector equation $Av = \eta v$ together with Lemma 9.9 give the formula for η shown on the right-hand side of Figure 9.7.

Let $z^0 = v^\dagger R^\psi v > 0$ and $w = \eta + z^0 \in \mathbb{C}$, so that $\eta = -z^0 + w$. It remains to show that $|w| \le \varrho_\gamma z^0$, so that η lies within the closed disc shown in Figure 9.7. This follows from Lemma 9.28:

$$|w| \le (\lambda^{-1} - 1)\sum_{i=1}^{\infty}(\gamma\lambda)^i |v^\dagger R(i)^\intercal v| \le \varrho[v^\dagger (R^\psi)^\intercal v](\lambda^{-1} - 1)\sum_{i=1}^{\infty}(\gamma\lambda)^i \le \varrho_\gamma z^0. \qquad \square$$

Proof of Proposition 9.12 Each part of the proof is based on properties of the function $p(\gamma) = \det(A_\gamma)$, which requires an alternative representation of A_γ.

Following the proof of Lemma 9.9, we write $\zeta_n = \sum_{i=0}^{\infty}(\lambda\gamma)^i \psi_{(n-i)}$, and hence

$$A_\gamma = \sum_{i=0}^{\infty}(\lambda\gamma)^i \mathsf{E}_\pi\big[\psi_{(n-i)}\big(-\psi_{(n)} + \gamma\underline{\psi}_{(n+1)}\big)^\intercal\big].$$

We always have $A_0 = -R^\psi$, so that $p(0) = \det(R^\psi) \neq 0$ for any value of λ.

For $\lambda = 0$ this simplifies to

$$A_\gamma = -R^\psi + \gamma B, \qquad \text{with } B \stackrel{\text{def}}{=} \mathsf{E}_\pi\big[\psi(X(n))\underline{\psi}(X(n+1))^\intercal\big].$$

Part (i) is established on recognizing that $p(\gamma)$ is a polynomial function of degree d that is not identically zero, and is therefore zero for at most d values of γ.

The proof of (ii) is similar: In this case, the representation for A_γ implies that we can extend the domain of p to the interval $(-\varepsilon, 1+\varepsilon)$ on which p is an analytic function of γ. It therefore can have at most a finite number of zeros on the interval $[0,1] \subset (-\varepsilon, 1+\varepsilon)$ [304].

The proof of (iii) is the same as (ii), with one exception: The domain of p can be extended to define an analytic function on the smaller interval $(-\varepsilon, 1)$. Hence it has a finite number of roots on each closed interval $[0, 1-\delta] \subset (-\varepsilon, 1)$. □

Proof of Lemma 9.13 Denote $W_\gamma = \gamma P - \delta \mathbf{1} \otimes \mu$.

For (i), first note that $\mathbf{1}$ remains a right eigenvector of the matrix W_γ, with eigenvalue $\gamma - \delta$. To characterize the remaining eigenvalues of W_γ, observe that if $\eta \neq \gamma - \delta$ is an eigenvalue, then an associated left eigenvector $v \in \mathbb{R}^d$ must be orthogonal to $\mathbf{1}$. Consequently,

$$\eta v^\intercal = v^\intercal (\gamma P - \delta \mathbf{1} \otimes \mu) = \gamma v^\intercal P.$$

Hence v is also a left eigenvector of P.

Part (ii) then follows from (i) since the eigenvalues of W_γ lie within the open unit disc in $\mathbb{C}$.

For (iii), we obtain a representation of

$$[I - W_\gamma]^{-1} = (A + UV)^{-1}, \qquad \text{with } A = (I - \gamma P),\, U = \delta \mathbf{1},\, V = \mu.$$

The Matrix Inversion Lemma (A.1) gives

$$[I - W_\gamma]^{-1} = A^{-1} - A^{-1}U\left(1 + VA^{-1}U\right)^{-1} VA^{-1} = A^{-1} - \frac{1}{\varrho} A^{-1}UVA^{-1},$$

where $\varrho = 1 + VA^{-1}U = 1 + \langle \mu, \delta(I - \gamma P)^{-1}\mathbf{1}\rangle = 1 + \delta/(1-\gamma)$,

$$A^{-1}U = \delta(I - \gamma P)^{-1}\mathbf{1} = \delta/(1-\gamma), \qquad VA^{-1} = \mu(I - \gamma P)^{-1}.$$

Substituting these identities gives (9.61):

$$[I - W_\gamma]^{-1} = (I - \gamma P)^{-1} - \frac{\delta}{1 + \delta - \gamma}[\mathbf{1} \otimes \mu](I - \gamma P)^{-1}$$

and consequently

$$H = [I - W_\gamma]^{-1} c = (I - \gamma P)^{-1} c - \frac{\delta}{1 + \delta - \gamma}\langle \mu, (I - \gamma P)^{-1} c\rangle = Q - \frac{\delta}{1 + \delta - \gamma}\langle \mu, Q\rangle.$$

This gives one representation of k, and the other is obtained on taking the mean of each side of this expression with respect to μ. □

9.10 Exercises

There are not many exercises in this chapter, and none in the next. What follows is intended to fill some theoretical gaps.

9.1 Consider the M/M/1 queue with controlled transition matrix (7.30) and cost function $c(x,u) = x$ for all x, u. The relative value function was derived in Section 7.3, based on the fact that the optimal policy is $\phi^\star(x) = \mathbb{1}\{x \geq 1\}$ (it is "nonidling"). The policy remains nonidling for the discounted-cost criterion, but the value function $h^\star$ is no longer quadratic.

(a) Show that $h^\star(x) = ax + b + r\beta^x$ for $x \in \mathsf{X}$, where a,b,r, and β are constants. For this, you should solve the DP equation (9.6a) with the knowledge that $\phi^\star$ is nonidling.

(b) Compute $Q^\star$ using (9.70) together with your formula for $h^\star$ in (a), and verify that $\phi^\star$ is obtained as its minimizer.

9.2 The approximation (9.100) begs the question: why approximate $-A(\theta_n)^{-1}A(\theta_n)\theta_n = -\theta_n$? The following algorithm is designed so that $\omega_n \approx A(\theta_n)^{-1}b$, with $-\theta_n$ moved to the slow recursion:

$$\theta_{n+1} = \theta_n + \alpha_{n+1}\{-\theta_n + \omega_n\}, \tag{9.105a}$$

$$\omega_{n+1} = \omega_n + \beta_{n+1}\{A_{n+1}\omega_n - b_{n+1}\}. \tag{9.105b}$$

(a) Show that for TD-learning, (9.2) is precisely PJR averaging when $\alpha_n = 1/n$.

(b) Compare (9.2) and (9.99) on a tabular Q-learning example, such as the six-state example shown in Figure 9.1. Obtain plots and histograms to compare both the transient behavior and the asymptotic covariance. *Review warnings at the close of Section 9.8.2 regarding the choice of* $\{\beta_n\}$.

9.3 Q(0)-learning is defined by (9.72) using $\zeta_n = \nabla_\theta H^{\theta_n}(\Phi(n))$. Consider this algorithm with linear function approximation, using the basis (5.11) defined by binning. Assume that the Markov policy for exploration is chosen so that $\varpi(B_i) > 0$ for each bin B_i.

The algorithm is stable in this very special case through an extension of Proposition 9.15:

(a) Obtain the vector field for the ODE approximation. It will be similar to the form $\frac{d}{dt}\theta_t = \bar f^0(\theta_t)$ obtained in Proposition 9.15.

(b) Obtain the ODE approximation with matrix gain designed to approximate $[R^\psi]^{-1}$, which is diagonal for this basis.

(c) Show that the function $V(\theta) = \|\tilde\theta\|_\infty$ used in Proposition 9.17 remains a Lyapunov function for Q(0)-learning with this basis.

9.4 Find an example for which step (3) of the ODE method fails in the case of Q(0)-learning for LQG. Take $\{H^\theta : \theta \in \mathbb{R}^d\}$ to be a linearly parameterized family of quadratic functions on $\mathsf{X} \times \mathsf{U}$, and verify in your example that $\underline{H}^\theta$ is not Lipschitz continuous as a function of θ.

Propose a method to modify the algorithm so that the Lipschitz condition is satisfied.

9.5 The following is an example from [355] for which TD-learning may be unstable:

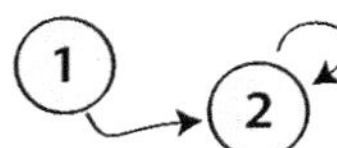

The setting is similar to Baird's counterexample, illustrated in Figure 5.5, except there are only two states with $\mathsf{X} = \{1,2\}$. There is no control, and the dynamics are deterministic, with state 2 absorbing. The cost is zero, so that $h^\star(x) = Q^\star(x,u) = 0$ for all x,u.

We would like to estimate $h^\star$ using TD-learning with $d = 1$ and $\psi(x) = 1 + \mathbb{1}\{x = 2\}$. Like Baird's example, this violates our convention that $\psi(x^e) = 0$, but we do have $h^\star = h^{\theta^*}$ with $\theta^* = 0$.

Obtain a formula for the temporal difference, similar to (5.51), and perform the following tasks:

(a) Verify that TD(0) is not stable for some values of $\gamma \in [0,1]$ when "perfect exploration" is adopted (for this you must review discussion surrounding (5.51)). *Approach*: The linearization matrix A is a scalar in this case. Show that $A > 0$ for some values of γ.

(b) Show that a less uniform sampling will lead to a stable algorithm: Choose $\boldsymbol{X}$ i.i.d., with $\varepsilon = \mathsf{P}\{X(n) = 1\}$ positive but small. This is similar to an "ε-greedy policy," even though there is no control.

9.11 Notes

9.11.1 Temporal Difference Methods

As surveyed earlier in Section 5.9, the TD-learning algorithms developed by Sutton and Barto in the 1980s were designed to obtain approximations of value functions within a finite-dimensional parameterized class, with emphasis on both linear function classes and neural networks. Sutton's dissertation contains early insights on temporal difference methods and some of the first TD algorithms [26, 339, 340] (see also Williams [376] for more early references). A fuller history of RL origins can be found in [338, 347].

The seeds planted by the early RL explorers prompted a flurry of analysis in the 1990s (much of it led by Tsitsiklis and his students at MIT), along with many new algorithms and analytical techniques; more on the contributions of the MIT school can be found in Section 10.10.

The terminology *split sampling* is due to Borkar [64], but the use of multiple sampling in RL, such as in (9.55), has a longer history in RL [21].

The interpretation Theorem 9.7 (i) can be found in [338, 347], and part (ii) is due to [356] (more history on minimum norm solutions can be found in Section 10.10).

Proposition 9.12 is adapted from [187, theorem 4.1].

Baird introduced the advantage function in [22], and soon after he proposed application to policy gradient methods in [23]. In Baird's work and more recent research, estimation of the advantage function requires a parallel algorithm to estimate the value function. The algorithm (9.68) and refinements in Section 10.2 avoid parallel estimation of the value function without sacrificing accuracy – see Proposition 10.7. These algorithms and supporting theory appear to be new.

Finite-n performance of single time-scale SA algorithms with application to TD-learning was studied in [210, 351], and bounds for two time-scale SA algorithms were obtained in [101]. However, these works rest on a critical assumption: that the noise is a martingale difference sequence. Extensions to Markovian noise presents a significant challenge [88, 89].

9.11.2 Q-Learning

Watkins's algorithm was introduced in his dissertation [371], with further analysis following in [372]. It was soon understood that the ODE approximation is easily analyzed in this tabular setting through Lyapunov techniques, as seen in Proposition 9.17. Similar techniques are available to establish stability of Q-learning for optimal stopping with linear function approximation [353].

Proposition 9.20 and the variance Analysis is taken from [114]. The paper [111] addresses high variance for large discounting by estimating the gradient of the value function (so the theory is applicable only when X is Euclidean space).

Soon after stability was established, Szepesvári investigated the rate of convergence. Using a clever coupling argument introduced in [227], the following upper bound is obtained in [346] for Watkins's algorithm with the state-dependent step-size α_n^v:

$$|H^n(x,u) - Q^\star(x,u)| \le B\frac{1}{n^{(1-\gamma)r}}, \qquad n \ge 1,\, x \in \mathsf{X},\, u \in \mathsf{U},$$

with B a constant and $r = \underline{\varpi}/\bar{\varpi}$ (the ratio of the minimum and maximum of ϖ). The bound is only valid for sufficient large γ (it is not realistic to have $(1-\gamma)r > 1/2$). While only an upper bound, this suggests that performance is very poor when the discount factor is close to unity. See [18, 124] for extensions and refinements.

It was first established in [112, 113] that the convergence rate of the MSE $\mathsf{E}\big[\|\theta_n - \theta^*\|^2\big]$ of Watkins's Q-learning can be slower than $O(1/n^{2(1-\gamma)})$, if the discount factor satisfies $\gamma > \frac{1}{2}$. It was also shown that the optimal convergence rate (8.8) is obtained by using a step-size of the form $\alpha_n = g/n$ or $\alpha_n = g\alpha_n^v$, for $g > 0$ sufficiently large.

Stability theory is not well developed outside of very special cases, such as the use of binning in Exercise 9.3. This exercise is inspired by Gordon [146], who describes this and other successful function approximation architectures for Q-learning. A generalization of binning called *soft state aggregation* was introduced in [324]. Stability theory for off-policy TD-learning faces similar challenges as Q-learning [219, 249, 345]. Counterexamples show that conditions on the function class are required in general, even in a linear function approximation setting [21, 147, 341, 355].

9.11.3 GQ and Zap

The GQ-learning algorithm of Section 9.8.1 was introduced in [345] for linear function approximation (see also [234]). Convergence theory was extended to nonlinear function approximation in [55].

The LSTD(λ) algorithm (9.42) was introduced in [75] (see also [70, 271]). It is an instance of stochastic Newton–Raphson, but the original motivation had nothing to do with minimizing the asymptotic covariance.

Recall from Section 4.11 that the Newton–Raphson flow was introduced by Smale [325]. The Zap Q-learning algorithm was introduced in [112, 113] without knowledge of Smale's theory – the matrix gain was motivated by minimizing the asymptotic covariance, rather than creating a general tool for the creation of consistent algorithms.

The proof of convergence based on Figure 9.4 first appeared in [112], and soon after It was realized that the ODE approximation (9.97) was valid outside of the tabular setting [90, 107, 110].

The discontinuity of the vector field $\bar{f}^0$ initially presented a challenge in analysis of Zap Q-learning: It wasn't obvious that the ODE approximation could be justified. In [90], this open question was resolved by appealing to special structure in Q-learning. The theory in [90] is completely general (applicable even to nonlinear function approximation architecture, such as neural networks). A central idea can be explained within the context of the tabular setting. The matrix A_{n+1} appearing in (9.96) is a subgradient of f_{n+1} at the value θ_n in the following sense:

$$\{f_{n+1}(\theta) - f_{n+1}(\theta_n)\}_i \le \sum_j A_{n+1}(i,j)[\theta(j) - \theta_n(j)]\,, \qquad 1 \le i \le d\,,\ \theta \in \mathbb{R}^d.$$

This holds for the algorithm (9.76) with linear function approximation, provided the basis vector has nonnegative entries, $\psi\colon \mathsf{X} \times \mathsf{U} \to \mathbb{R}^d_+$. It is not difficult to show that a similar inequality is preserved in any ODE limit, which is all that is needed to show that $V(\theta) \stackrel{\text{def}}{=} \|\bar{f}^0(\theta)\|^2$ serves as a Lyapunov function for the SA algorithm.

Relaxing the positivity assumption was a bigger challenge than confronting a nonlinear function approximation architecture.

The article [90] also contains many numerical examples illustrating the application of Zap Q-learning with neural network function approximation.

9.11.4 Convex Q-Learning

Extensions of the convex Q algorithms of Section 5.5 are described in [246, 247]. The main challenge in algorithm design is that the constraints involve a conditional expectation. For example, (5.63) would be modified as follows:

$$\begin{aligned} &\max_\theta\ \langle \mu, H^\theta \rangle \\ &\text{s.t.}\ \ H^\theta(x,u) \le c(x,u) + \mathsf{E}[\underline{H}^\theta(\Phi(k+1)) \mid \Phi(k) = (x,u)], \qquad x \in \mathsf{X},\ u \in \mathsf{U}(x). \end{aligned} \tag{9.106}$$

The conditional expectation can be approximated to obtain an algorithm, as discussed in Section 9.2. The use of *experience replay* is another approach based on empirical distributions (see [338, ch. 16] and [211]). Theory for convex Q-learning remains immature, so best left to a sequel or second edition.

The recent paper [218] is based on a variant of the convex program (9.106) in the tabular setting, and [224] contains an algorithm very similar to convex Q-learning (see [224, (6)]). The more recent RL survey [269] has a version of convex Q-learning, and explains the importance of regularization. Also related to (9.106) is the *logistic Q-learning* algorithm of [28], which may represent an opening for more practical algorithms, as well as more elegant theory.

10

Setting the Stage, Return of the Actors

This chapter introduces techniques to improve TD-learning, along with algorithms for the average-cost optimality criterion. There is an emphasis on geometry surrounding minimum norm problems, as first discussed in the paragraphs surrounding (6.22). Alternative proofs of Theorems 9.7 and 9.11 that expose the underlying geometry will lead to new tools for algorithm design.

You should be asking yourself, why do we care about solving the minimum norm problems posed in Theorems 9.7 and 9.11? In particular, what is your motivation to solve the following optimization problem?

$$\theta^* = \arg\min_\theta \|H^\theta - Q\|^2_{\varpi} \stackrel{\text{def}}{=} \sum_{z \in \mathsf{Z}} (H^\theta(z) - Q(z))^2 \varpi(z), \tag{10.1}$$

with $\mathsf{Z} = \mathsf{X} \times \mathsf{U}$. Mathematical elegance may provide ample motivation, but up to now there is no evidence that this is a useful metric for success in control design.

Put on your "control hat" and look back to the inverse dynamic programming (IDP) discussion in Section 3.4. Our goal there was not to approximate a value function but to ensure that any approximating function J we choose comes with a cost function c^J with desirable properties: Namely, it is coercive, and $c^J \approx c$. In the stochastic setting, the average-cost criterion is most closely related to the total-cost setting of Section 3.4, as made precise through examples and some analysis in Section 7.2. In particular, recall the approximation (7.26):

$$\varrho^\circ + J^\star(x) = \min_u \{c^J(x,u) + P_u J^\star\,(x)\},$$

in which $J^\star$ denotes a value function for the *fluid model*, and $c^J \approx c$ if and only if the Bellman error is small in the span seminorm.

To understand the practical value of the optimization criterion (10.1) requires an entirely different control-theoretic "wardrobe," which is the topic of Section 10.5 and beyond. It is explained there why the first half of this chapter sets the stage for actor-critic methods. The *actors* are defined by a family of randomized policies $\{\check{\phi}^\theta : \theta \in \mathbb{R}^d\}$. The goal is to create an efficient algorithm that estimates the "best" policy within this family, where the notion of "best" can be defined in terms of discounted cost, total cost, or average cost.

We discover in Section 10.4.1 that most optimality criteria can be converted to average cost through design of the framework for simulation or experimentation. For this reason, the theoretical development of actor-critic methods focuses entirely on the average-cost criterion. The relative value function plays the role of *critic*, and theory surrounding TD(1) for average cost is used to construct stochastic gradient descent algorithms; these algorithms are designed to eliminate the bias that is inherent in the actor-only methods surveyed in Section 4.6.

One conclusion from Section 10.6 is that actor-critic methods may be regarded as a disciplined approach to Q-learning. For comparison:

▲ Q-learning seeks to solve the Galerkin relaxation (9.71), which is not easily justified outside of the tabular setting.
▲ Actor-critic methods use (as a subroutine) a variant of Q-learning, which is an essential ingredient to obtain an unbiased gradient estimate.

10.1 The Stage, Projection, and Adjoints

The geometry developed in this chapter requires a linearly parameterized function class. If space permitted, we might allow an RKHS for this purpose. Since this is not an option, a d-dimensional basis $\psi\colon \mathsf{Z} \to \mathbb{R}^d$ is chosen, and any approximation is expressed $H^\theta = \theta^{\intercal}\psi$ with $\theta \in \mathbb{R}^d$.

Regardless of the interpretation of Q in (10.1), the approximation H^{θ^*} is known as the *projection* of Q onto the linear subspace $\mathcal{H} = \{H^\theta : \theta \in \mathbb{R}^d\}$, and can be expressed

$$H^{\theta^*}(\Phi(k)) = \widehat{\mathsf{E}}[Q(\Phi(k)) \mid Y]$$

with $Y = \psi(\Phi(k))$ (recall (9.19) for the definitions). These interpretations were discussed in Section 5.4.1, so we adopt the notation from Chapter 5: For any two functions $g,h\colon \mathsf{Z} \to \mathbb{R}$, the inner product is defined by

$$\langle g,h\rangle_{\varpi} \stackrel{\text{def}}{=} \mathsf{E}_{\varpi}[g(\Phi(k))h(\Phi(k))] = \sum_{z\in\mathsf{Z}} g(z)h(z)\varpi(z)$$

so that

$$\|H^\theta - Q\|_{\varpi}^2 = \langle H^\theta - Q, H^\theta - Q\rangle_{\varpi}.$$

Recall that we write $g \in L_2(\varpi)$ whenever $\|g\|_{\varpi} < \infty$. This comes for free since we assume in this chapter that X and U are finite.

The conclusions of Propositions 5.7 and 9.4 are restated here for ease of reference:

Proposition 10.1 *Suppose that $\{\psi_i\}$ are linearly independent in $L_2(\varpi)$: $\|\theta^{\intercal}\psi\|_{\varpi} = 0$ implies that $\theta = 0$. Then, for any function $G \in L_2(\varpi)$, the projection exists, is unique, and is given by $\widehat{G} = \theta^{*\intercal}\psi$ with $\theta^* = R(0)^{-1}\bar{\psi}^G$, where $\bar{\psi}^G \in \mathbb{R}^d$ and the $d \times d$ matrix $R(0) = R^\psi$ are defined by*

$$\bar{\psi}_i^G = \langle \psi_i, G\rangle_{\varpi}, \qquad R^\psi_{i,j} = \langle \psi_i, \psi_j\rangle_{\varpi}, \qquad 1 \le i,j \le d. \tag{10.2}$$

□

Some mystery comes when G is the Q-function. For the discounted-cost criterion, the vector $\bar{\psi}^Q \in \mathbb{R}^d$ can be expressed

$$\bar{\psi}^Q = \mathsf{E}_{\varpi}[\psi(\Phi(0))Q(\Phi(0))] = \sum_{k=0}^{\infty} \gamma^k \mathsf{E}_{\varpi}[\psi(\Phi(0))c(\Phi(k))]. \tag{10.3}$$

where the second equation follows from the definition (9.6b) together with the smoothing property of conditional expectation. Estimation of the right-hand side using Monte Carlo methods is challenging because it involves the state-input trajectory over the infinite future.

The mystery is unmasked with the use of a bit of linear algebra.

10.1.1 Linear Operators and Adjoints

Let $T\colon L_2(\varpi) \to L_2(\varpi)$ be a linear operator. That is, for any $g,h \in L_2(\varpi)$ and scalars $\alpha,\beta \in \mathbb{R}$,

$$T(\alpha g + \beta h) = \alpha T(g) + \beta T(h).$$

It is customary to write Tg rather than $T(g)$ when there is no risk of confusion.

For TD-learning with discounted-cost criterion, the linear operator of interest is defined by

$$T_\gamma g\,(z) \stackrel{\text{def}}{=} \sum_{k=0}^{\infty} \gamma^k \mathsf{E}[g(\Phi(k)) \mid \Phi(0) = z], \qquad \text{for any } g \in L_2(\varpi) \text{ and } z \in \mathsf{Z}, \tag{10.4}$$

so that $Q = T_\gamma c$. Basic theory of linear operators provides tools to efficiently estimate the vector $\bar{\psi}^G$ appearing in (10.2) with $G = Q$.

The main concept is the *adjoint* of a linear operator T, denoted $T^\dagger$. This is defined by the simple identity,

$$\langle Tg,h\rangle_\varpi = \langle g,T^\dagger h\rangle_\varpi\,, \qquad \text{for all } g,h \in L_2(\varpi). \tag{10.5}$$

In this finite setting there is a simple formula, obtained on expressing T as a matrix:

$$Tg\,(z) = \sum_{z' \in \mathsf{Z}} T(z,z')g(z').$$

Lemma 10.2 *The adjoint of T is equal to its transpose, followed by a similarity transformation:*

$$T^\dagger(z,z') = \frac{1}{\varpi(z)} T(z',z)\varpi(z'), \qquad z,z' \in \mathsf{Z}.$$

Consequently, for any $h \in L_2(\varpi)$,

$$T^\dagger h\,(z') = \sum_{z} T^\dagger(z',z)h(z) = \sum_{z \in \mathsf{Z}} T(z,z')\tfrac{\varpi(z)}{\varpi(z')}h(z), \qquad z' \in \mathsf{Z}. \tag{10.6}$$

Proof We have the following by definition:

$$\langle Tg,h\rangle_\varpi = \sum_{z \in \mathsf{Z}} \{Tg\,(z)\}h(z)\varpi(z) = \sum_{z \in \mathsf{Z}} \{\sum_{z' \in \mathsf{Z}} T(z,z')g(z')\}h(z)\varpi(z).$$

Reversing the order of summation and introducing $1 = \varpi(z')/\varpi(z')$ gives (10.6):

$$\langle Tg,h\rangle_\varpi = \sum_{z' \in \mathsf{Z}} g(z')\Big(\sum_{z \in \mathsf{Z}} T(z,z')h(z)\tfrac{\varpi(z)}{\varpi(z')}\Big)\varpi(z').$$

□

While (10.6) conforms with undergraduate linear algebra intuition, it is not obviously useful for our purposes.

10.1.2 Adjoints and Eligibility Vectors

The probabilistic representation of T_γ provides a more useful representation of its adjoint.

Proposition 10.3 *The adjoint of T_γ admits the representation, for any $h \in L_2(\varpi)$ and $z \in \mathsf{Z}$,*

$$T_\gamma^\dagger h\,(z) = \sum_{k=0}^{\infty} \gamma^k \mathsf{E}[h(\Phi(-k)) \mid \Phi(0) = z],$$

where $\mathbf{\Phi}$ is the stationary process on the two-sided time interval.

Proof Based on the definition (10.4), we have

$$\langle T_\gamma g, h\rangle_\varpi = \sum_{z\in\mathsf{Z}} \varpi(z)\Big(\sum_{k=0}^{\infty} \gamma^k \mathsf{E}[g(\Phi(k)) \mid \Phi(0) = z]\Big) h(z) = \sum_{k=0}^{\infty} \gamma^k \mathsf{E}_\varpi[h(\Phi(0))g(\Phi(k))].$$

We have by stationarity $\mathsf{E}_\varpi[h(\Phi(0))g(\Phi(k))] = \mathsf{E}_\varpi[h(\Phi(-k))g(\Phi(0))]$, so that

$$\langle T_\gamma g, h\rangle_\varpi = \sum_{k=0}^{\infty} \gamma^k \mathsf{E}_\varpi[h(\Phi(-k))g(\Phi(0))].$$

The proof is completed on applying the smoothing property:

$$\begin{aligned}\mathsf{E}_\varpi[h(\Phi(-k))g(\Phi(0))] &= \mathsf{E}_\varpi[\mathsf{E}[h(\Phi(-k))g(\Phi(0)) \mid \Phi(0)]] \\ &= \sum_{z\in\mathsf{Z}} \mathsf{E}_\varpi[h(\Phi(-k)) \mid \Phi(0) = z] g(z)\varpi(z).\end{aligned}$$ □

Theorem 9.11 (ii) Revisited This result follows from Proposition 10.1 with only notational changes.

The vector $\bar{\psi}^Q$ in (10.3) has components

$$\bar{\psi}_i^Q = \mathsf{E}_\varpi[\psi_i(\Phi(0))Q(\Phi(0))] = \langle T_\gamma c, \psi_i\rangle_\varpi = \langle c, T_\gamma^\dagger \psi_i\rangle_\varpi\,, \quad 1 \le i \le d. \tag{10.7}$$

Proposition 10.3 provides a more familiar formula: For any n,

$$\bar{\psi}^Q = \mathsf{E}_\varpi[c_n\zeta_n], \qquad \text{with} \quad c_n = c(\Phi(n)) \quad \text{and} \quad \zeta_n = \sum_{k=0}^{\infty} \gamma^k \psi(\Phi(n-k)), \tag{10.8}$$

with $\mathbf{\Phi}$ stationary, and defined on the two-sided time axis. The sequence $\{\zeta_n : n \in \mathbb{Z}\}$ is the stationary version of the eligibility vectors for the TD(1) algorithm. Hence, the formula $\theta^* = R(0)^{-1}\bar{\psi}^Q$ given in Proposition 10.1 corresponds to the equilibrium condition for TD(1):

$$0 = \bar{f}(\theta^*) = -R^\psi \theta^* + \mathsf{E}_\varpi[c_n\zeta_n].$$

10.1.3 Weighted Norms and Weighted Eligibility

The use of state weighting was introduced in Section 6.7.5 as a means to reduce variance in algorithms based on Monte Carlo methods. Let $w\colon \mathsf{Z} \to \mathbb{R}_+$ denote the weighting function used to define the norm

$$\|H\|^2_{\varpi,w} \stackrel{\text{def}}{=} \mathsf{E}_\varpi[H(\Phi(n))^2 w(\Phi(n))]. \tag{10.9}$$

We write $H \in L_2(\varpi,w)$ if this is finite (a vacuous assumption when Z is finite, as assumed in the theoretical development here). The inner product is redefined consistently:

$$\langle G,H\rangle_{\varpi,w} \stackrel{\text{def}}{=} \mathsf{E}_\varpi[G(\Phi(n))H(\Phi(n))w(\Phi(n))], \qquad G,H \in L_2(\varpi,w).$$

The adaptation of (6.49) to the current setting is minimization of the weighted mean-square error:

$$\|H^\theta - Q\|^2_{\varpi,w} = \mathsf{E}_\varpi\big[\big(H^\theta(\Phi(n)) - Q(\Phi(n))\big)^2 w(\Phi(n))\big]. \tag{10.10}$$

The Galerkin approach to on-policy TD(λ)-learning is modified analogously:

$$0 = \mathsf{E}_\varpi\big[\{-H^{\theta^*}(\Phi(n)) + c_n + \gamma H^{\theta^*}(\Phi(n+1))\}w(\Phi(n))\zeta_n\big], \tag{10.11}$$

with $\zeta_n = \sum_{k=0}^\infty (\lambda\gamma)^k \psi(\Phi(n-k))$, and with $\boldsymbol{\Phi}$ stationary on $\mathbb{Z}$.

The development of Section 10.1 carries over to the new vector space $L_2(\varpi,w)$, beginning with the following:

Proposition 10.4 *The following hold for any function $G \in L_2(\varpi,w)$, with the following notation:*

$$\begin{aligned} \bar\psi_i^G &= \langle \psi_i, G\rangle_{\varpi,w}, & 1 \le i \le d,\\ R^\psi_{i,j} &= \langle \psi_i,\psi_j\rangle_{\varpi,w}, & 1 \le i,j \le d. \end{aligned} \tag{10.12}$$

(i) *The projection $\widehat{G}$ exists, given by $\widehat{G} = \theta^{*\intercal}\psi$, with $\theta^* \in \mathbb{R}^d$ any solution to the linear equation $R^\psi\theta^* = \bar\psi^G$.*

(ii) *Suppose that $\{\psi_i\}$ are linearly independent in $L_2(\varpi,w)$: $\|\theta^\intercal\psi\|_{\varpi,w} = 0$ only when $\theta = 0$. Then $\theta^\star = [R^\psi]^{-1}\bar\psi^G$ is unique.* □

When applied to minimize the objective (10.10), we still have $Q = T_\gamma c$, and hence

$$\bar\psi_i^Q = \langle \psi_i, T_\gamma c\rangle_{\varpi,w} = \langle T_\gamma^\dagger \psi_i, c\rangle_{\varpi,w}, \qquad 1 \le i,j \le d.$$

However, the definition of the adjoint depends on the choice of norm:

Lemma 10.5 *We have for all $g,h \in L_2(\varpi,w)$,*

$$\begin{aligned} \langle T_\gamma g,h\rangle_{\varpi,w} &= \sum_{k=0}^\infty \gamma^k \mathsf{E}_\varpi[w(\Phi(0))h(\Phi(0))g(\Phi(k))]\\ &= \sum_{k=0}^\infty \gamma^k \mathsf{E}_\varpi[w(\Phi(-k))h(\Phi(-k))g(\Phi(0))]. \end{aligned}$$

Consequently, the adjoint of T_γ in $L_2(\varpi,w)$ admits the following representation:

$$T_\gamma^\dagger h\,(z) = \frac{1}{w(z)} \sum_{k=0}^\infty \gamma^k \mathsf{E}[w(\Phi(-k))h(\Phi(-k)) \mid \Phi(0) = z], \qquad z \in \mathsf{Z}.$$ □

This motivates a new algorithm and consistency result:

LSTD(1) with Weighting (On-Policy)

With initialization $\zeta_0 \in \mathbb{R}^d$, $\widehat{\Sigma}_0 \in \mathbb{R}^{d\times d}$ (positive definite), and time horizon N,

$$\theta_N = \widehat{\Sigma}_N^{-1} \bar{\psi}_N^Q \tag{10.13a}$$

$$\text{with} \quad \widehat{\Sigma}_N = \frac{1}{N}\Big(\widehat{\Sigma}_0 + \sum_{n=1}^N w_n \psi_{(n)} \psi_{(n)}^{\intercal}\Big), \tag{10.13b}$$

$$\bar{\psi}_N^Q = \frac{1}{N}\sum_{n=1}^N c_n \zeta_n, \tag{10.13c}$$

$$\zeta_n = \gamma \zeta_{n-1} + w_n \psi_{(n)}, \quad w_n = w(\Phi(n)), \qquad 1 \le n \le N. \tag{10.13d}$$

The Law of Large Numbers then gives the following proposition:

Proposition 10.6 *Under the linear independence assumption of Proposition 10.4, the LSTD(1) algorithm* (10.13) *is consistent:* $\lim_{N\to\infty} \theta_N = \theta^* = R(0)^{-1}\bar{\psi}^Q$ *with probability one, where* $R(0) = R^{\psi}$ *and* $\bar{\psi}^Q$ *are defined in* (10.12) *with* $G = Q$ *equal to the fixed policy Q-function* (9.47)*. Consequently,* θ^* *minimizes the* L_2 *objective* (10.10). □

10.2 Advantage and Innovation

Recall from Section 9.1.3 one motivation for the advantage function: In policy iteration, we don't need a precise estimate of Q, since we are only interested in computing its minimum over u for each x. Instead of Q, we seek to estimate the difference $Q - G$, where $G\colon \mathsf{X} \to \mathbb{R}$ (the function G does not depend upon u). Proposition 9.14 tells us that the best choice is $G^* = \underline{Q} = h$.

By "best," we mean that h is the minimal MSE estimate of Q over all functions on X. Consequently, the error $V = Q - h$ is orthogonal to any function on X. In statistics, it is common to call V the *innovations* associated with the approximation of Q by h. This interpretation of the advantage function is tremendously useful for approximation of both Q and V, as it inspires better approximation architectures.

Throughout this section, we remain in the discounted-cost setting, so that h and Q are defined via (9.47). Extension of theory and algorithms to average cost is taken for granted in the remainder of the chapter.

10.2.1 Projection of Advantage and Value

Let's step back and reconsider estimation of Q within a function class defined by a given basis $\psi\colon \mathsf{X}\times\mathsf{U} \to \mathbb{R}^d$, expanding the function class in one of two forms:

$$\mathcal{H} = \{\theta^{\intercal}\psi + \xi^{\intercal}\underline{\psi} : \theta, \xi \in \mathbb{R}^d\} \quad \text{or} \quad \mathcal{H}^X = \{\theta^{\intercal}\psi + g : \theta \in \mathbb{R}^d,\, g\colon \mathsf{X} \to \mathbb{R}\}, \tag{10.14}$$

where $\underline{\psi}$ and $\widetilde{\psi}$ were introduced in (9.66), followed by the function class $\widetilde{\mathcal{H}}$. We have $\mathcal{H} \subset \mathcal{H}^X$, where the latter contains every function that depends only on $x \in \mathsf{X}$. In particular, $h \in \mathcal{H}^X$.

Here we also require the two d-dimensional function classes

$$\underline{\mathcal{H}} = \{\theta^{\intercal}\underline{\psi} : \theta \in \mathbb{R}^d\} \quad \text{and} \quad \widetilde{\mathcal{H}} = \{\theta^{\intercal}\widetilde{\psi} : \theta \in \mathbb{R}^d\}.$$

The interpretation $\underline{\psi}(X(k)) = \mathsf{E}[\psi(\Phi(k)) \mid X(k)]$ implies orthogonality of these two function classes, and much more.

Denote the projections of Q onto the function spaces $\{\mathcal{H},\underline{\mathcal{H}},\widetilde{\mathcal{H}}\}$ by, respectively, $\widehat{Q}$, $\widehat{Q}^{-}$ and $\widehat{Q}^{\sim}$. The projections of h and $V = Q - h$ are denoted similarly.

Proposition 10.7 (i) *Any $G \in \widetilde{\mathcal{H}}$ is orthogonal to any function $g\colon \mathsf{X} \to \mathbb{R}$:*

$$\langle G,g\rangle_{\varpi} \stackrel{\text{def}}{=} \mathsf{E}[G(\Phi(k))g(X(k))] = 0.$$

Consequently, $\widetilde{\mathcal{H}}$ and $\underline{\mathcal{H}}$ are orthogonal in $L_2(\varpi)$.

(ii) *For each $g \in \underline{\mathcal{H}}$ and $G \in \widetilde{\mathcal{H}}$,*

$$\|G+g-Q\|_{\varpi}^2 = \|G-V\|_{\varpi}^2 + \|g-h\|_{\pi}^2. \tag{10.15}$$

(iii) $\widehat{V} = \widehat{V}^{\sim} = \widehat{Q}^{\sim}$ *and* $\hat{h} = \hat{h}^{-} = \widehat{Q}^{-}$.

(iv) $\widehat{Q} = \widehat{V} + \hat{h}$.

(v) $\widehat{Q}^X \stackrel{\text{def}}{=} \widehat{V} + h$ *is the projection of Q onto $\mathcal{H}^X$.* □

It is part (iii) that justifies the TD(λ) algorithm (9.68). The proof of Theorem 10.8 is simply a restatement of Theorem 9.11 with the new basis.

Theorem 10.8 *The algorithm* (9.68) *is consistent: The estimates converge to the parameter ω^* that defines the projection $\widehat{V} = \{\omega^*\}^{\intercal}\widetilde{\psi}^{\circ}$.* □

10.2.2 Weighted Norm

If we seek an approximation in a weighted norm, then a convenient choice for G is the solution to the L_2 optimization problem,

$$G^w = \arg\min_G \|Q-G\|_{\varpi,w}^2 = \arg\min_G \mathsf{E}_{\varpi}[\{Q(\Phi(n)) - G(X(n))\}^2 w(\Phi(n))],$$

where the minimum is over all $G\colon \mathsf{X} \to \mathbb{R}$. The optimizer is characterized by orthogonality:

$$\langle Q - G^w, G\rangle_{\varpi,w} = 0 \qquad \text{for all } G\colon \mathsf{X} \to \mathbb{R}.$$

The proof of Proposition 10.9 is obtained on setting $G = G^i$, where $G^i(x) = \mathbb{1}\{x = x^i\}$ for each i, where $\{x^i\}$ is an enumeration of the state space X.

Proposition 10.9 *The optimizer is given by*

$$G^w(x) = \frac{1}{\kappa(x)} \sum_u \breve{\phi}(u \mid x)Q(x,u)w(x,u)\,, \quad \kappa(x) = \sum_u \breve{\phi}(u \mid x)w(x,u)\,, \qquad x \in \mathsf{X}.$$

If w does not depend upon u, this gives

$$G^w(x) = \underline{Q}(x) \stackrel{\text{def}}{=} \sum_u \breve{\phi}(u \mid x)Q(x,u)\,, \quad x \in \mathsf{X}.$$

Hence, in this case, $G^w = \underline{Q} = h$, so that $V = Q - h$ exactly as in (9.65a). □

The proposition tells us that the choice of basis $\widetilde{\psi}$ remains valid for approximating the advantage function, provided w does not depend upon u. The Law of Large Numbers motivates an algorithm as seen in Proposition 10.6. Recall Section 9.5.4 for explanation of the basis $\widetilde{\psi}^{\circ}$.

LSTD(1) for Advantage with Weighting (On-Policy)

With weighting function $w\colon \mathsf{X} \to (0,\infty)$, initialization $\zeta_0 \in \mathbb{R}^m$, $\widehat{\Sigma}_0 \in \mathbb{R}^{m\times m}$, and time horizon N,

$$\omega_N = \widehat{\Sigma}_N^{-1}\bar{\psi}_N^Q \tag{10.16a}$$

$$\text{with}\quad \widehat{\Sigma}_N = \frac{1}{N}\Big(\widehat{\Sigma}_0 + \sum_{n=1}^{N} w_n \widetilde{\psi}_{(n)} \widetilde{\psi}_{(n)}^{\intercal}\Big), \tag{10.16b}$$

$$\bar{\psi}_N^Q = \frac{1}{N}\sum_{n=1}^{N} c_n \zeta_n, \tag{10.16c}$$

$$\zeta_n = \gamma\zeta_{n-1} + w_n\widetilde{\psi}_{(n)}, \quad w_n = w(X(n)), \quad \widetilde{\psi}_{(n)} = \widetilde{\psi}^{\circ}(\Phi(n)), \qquad 1 \le n \le N. \tag{10.16d}$$

10.3 Regeneration

The representation (6.26) for Poisson's equation admits a partial generalization to the discounted-cost criterion. Let $z^{\bullet} = (x^{\bullet},u^{\bullet}) \in \mathsf{X}\times\mathsf{U}$ denote any state with positive steady-state probability: $\varpi(z^{\bullet}) > 0$. Consider the function introduced before (9.57):

$$\widetilde{Q}_\gamma(z) = \mathsf{E}\Big[\sum_{k=0}^{\tau_\bullet - 1} \gamma^k \tilde{c}(\Phi(k)) \mid \Phi(0) = z\Big] + \mathsf{E}\Big[\gamma^{\tau_\bullet}\sum_{k=0}^{\infty}\gamma^k\tilde{c}(\Phi(k+\tau_\bullet)) \mid \Phi(0) = z\Big].$$

Apply the strong Markov property (see Section A.2.3) to obtain

$$\begin{aligned}\mathsf{E}\Big[\gamma^{\tau_\bullet}\sum_{k=0}^{\infty}\gamma^k\tilde{c}(\Phi(k+\tau_\bullet)) \mid \Phi(0) = z\Big] &= \mathsf{E}\big[\gamma^{\tau_\bullet}\widetilde{Q}_\gamma(\Phi(\tau_\bullet)) \mid \Phi(0) = z\big] \\ &= \widetilde{Q}_\gamma(z^{\bullet})\mathsf{E}\big[\gamma^{\tau_\bullet} \mid \Phi(0) = z\big].\end{aligned}$$

A similar decomposition holds for Q_γ:

Lemma 10.10 *The following hold for* $\gamma \in [0,1)$*:*

$$\widetilde{Q}_\gamma(z) = \mathsf{E}\Big[\sum_{k=0}^{\tau_\bullet - 1}\gamma^k\tilde{c}(\Phi(k)) \mid \Phi(0) = z\Big] + \widetilde{Q}_\gamma(z^{\bullet})\mathsf{E}\big[\gamma^{\tau_\bullet} \mid \Phi(0) = z\big],$$

$$Q_\gamma(z) = \mathsf{E}\Big[\sum_{k=0}^{\tau_\bullet - 1}\gamma^k c(\Phi(k)) \mid \Phi(0) = z\Big] + Q_\gamma(z^{\bullet})\mathsf{E}\big[\gamma^{\tau_\bullet} \mid \Phi(0) = z\big].$$

Consequently, $\lim_{\gamma\uparrow 1} \widetilde{Q}_\gamma(z) = H_3(z) + \widetilde{Q}_1(z^\bullet)$, *where* H_3 *is the solution to Poisson's equation:*

$$H_3(z) = \mathsf{E}\Big[\sum_{k=0}^{\tau_\bullet - 1} \tilde{c}(\Phi(k)) \mid \Phi(0) = z\Big]. \tag{10.17}$$

□

For $\gamma \sim 1$ we might opt to estimate the finite horizon objective to obtain an algorithm with reduced variance. Consider for fixed-policy $\breve{\phi}$:

$$J_\gamma(z) = \mathsf{E}\Big[\sum_{k=0}^{\tau_\bullet - 1} \gamma^k c(\Phi(k)) \mid \Phi(0) = z\Big].$$

On writing $J_\gamma(z) = c(z) + \mathsf{E}\Big[\mathbb{1}\{\tau_\bullet \geq 2\} \sum_{k=1}^{\tau_\bullet - 1} \gamma^k c(\Phi(k)) \mid \Phi(0) = z\Big]$, the following DP equation is obtained:

$$\begin{aligned} J_\gamma(z) &= c(z) + \gamma \sum_{z' \neq z^\bullet} P(z,z') J_\gamma(z') \\ &= \mathsf{E}[c_n + \gamma \mathbb{1}\{\Phi(n+1) \neq z^\bullet\} J_\gamma(\Phi(n+1)) \mid \Phi(n) = z]. \end{aligned} \tag{10.18}$$

The finite horizon objective invites a new eligibility vector: For $n \geq 0$,

$$\zeta_n = \sum_{\tilde{\sigma}_\bullet^{[n]} \leq k \leq n} (\lambda\gamma)^{n-k} \psi_{(k)} \tag{10.19a}$$

$$\text{where} \quad \tilde{\sigma}_\bullet^{[n]} = \max\{k \leq n : \Phi(k) = z^\bullet\}. \tag{10.19b}$$

In the special case $\Phi(k) \neq z^\bullet$ for $k = 0, \ldots, n$ (i.e., the maximum in (10.19b) is over an empty set), we define $\tilde{\sigma}_\bullet^{[n]} = 0$. The sequence of eligibility vectors has a recursive form, which together with (10.18) motivates the regenerative TD(λ) algorithm:

Regenerative TD(λ) Algorithm (On-Policy)

For initialization $\theta_0, \zeta_0 \in \mathbb{R}^d$, the sequence of estimates are defined recursively:

$$\begin{aligned} \theta_{n+1} &= \theta_n + \alpha_{n+1} \zeta_n \mathcal{D}_{n+1}, \\ \mathcal{D}_{n+1} &= \big(-H^\theta(\Phi(n)) + c_n + \gamma \mathbb{1}\{\Phi(n+1) \neq z^\bullet\} H^\theta(\Phi(n+1))\big)\Big|_{\theta=\theta_n}, \\ \zeta_{n+1} &= \lambda\gamma \mathbb{1}\{\Phi(n+1) \neq z^\bullet\} \zeta_n + \psi_{(n+1)}, \qquad n \geq 0. \end{aligned} \tag{10.20}$$

With the introduction of regeneration, the algorithm remains practical even when $\gamma = \lambda = 1$. For a linear function approximation, this is a linear SA recursion $\theta_{n+1} = \theta_n + \alpha_{n+1}[A_{n+1}\theta_n - b_{n+1}]$ with

$$\begin{aligned} A_{n+1} &= \zeta_n \big[-\psi_{(n)} + \gamma \mathbb{1}\{\Phi(n+1) \neq z^\bullet\} \psi_{(n+1)}\big]^\intercal, \\ b_{n+1} &= -\zeta_n c_n. \end{aligned} \tag{10.21}$$

The value of $\lambda = 1$ is explained in Theorem 10.11, whose proof can be found in Section 10.9.

Theorem 10.11 (L_2 Optimality of TD(1)) *Consider the algorithm* (10.20) *with linear function approximation $H^\theta = \theta^\intercal \psi$. Assume that $\boldsymbol{\Phi}$ is uni-chain and that $\varpi(z^\bullet) > 0$.*

Then, in the special case $\lambda = 1$,

(i) $A \stackrel{\text{def}}{=} \mathsf{E}_\varpi[A_n] = -R(0)$ *and* $b \stackrel{\text{def}}{=} \mathsf{E}_\varpi[b_n] = -\mathsf{E}_\varpi[J_\gamma(\Phi(n))\psi(\Phi(n))]$.
(ii) *Any solution to* $0 = \bar{f}(\theta^*) = \mathsf{E}_\varpi[\zeta_n \mathcal{D}_{n+1}]$ *solves the minimum norm problem:*

$$\theta^* \in \arg\min_\theta \|H^\theta - J_\gamma\|^2_\varpi \stackrel{\text{def}}{=} \arg\min_\theta \mathsf{E}_\varpi\big[\big(H^\theta(\Phi(n)) - J_\gamma(\Phi(n))\big)^2\big]. \tag{10.22}$$

□

As in all TD(1) algorithms with linear function approximation, the characterization of A strongly motivates the use of LSTD(1). One formulation is given by

$$\theta^{\text{LSTD}}_N = \widehat{A}^{-1}\widehat{b}, \tag{10.23}$$

where N denotes the time horizon, and for given $\widehat{R}_0 > 0$,

$$\widehat{A} = -\frac{1}{N}\Big\{\widehat{R}_0 + \sum_{k=1}^N \psi_{(k)}\psi^\intercal_{(k)}\Big\}, \qquad \widehat{b} = -\frac{1}{N}\sum_{k=1}^N \zeta_n c_n.$$

10.4 Average Cost and Every Other Criterion

10.4.1 Every Other Criterion

When we optimize over a family of policies, as described at the start of this chapter, we cannot expect to find a single policy in the family that minimizes the discounted- or total-cost criterion from each initial condition. It is customary to instead choose a pmf μ on $\mathsf{Z} = \mathsf{X} \times \mathsf{U}$, and define the objective for optimization as follows:

$$\Gamma(\breve{\phi}) = \sum_z h_{\breve{\phi}}(z)\,\mu(z),$$

where $h_{\breve{\phi}}$ is the value function associated with the policy $\breve{\phi}$ for the chosen optimality criterion. In Section 10.5, the family is defined through a finite-dimensional parameterization $\{\breve{\phi}^\theta : \theta \in \mathbb{R}^d\}$, and we write $\Gamma(\theta)$ rather than $\Gamma(\breve{\phi}^\theta)$.

In the following, we show how to translate from one optimality criterion to another. Translation is accomplished by the creation of a Markov chain $\boldsymbol{\Psi}$, a strictly increasing sequence of times $\{\mathcal{N}_n : n \ge 1\}$, and a modified cost function $\widehat{c}$, all designed so that the partial sums

$$S_n = \sum_{k=\mathcal{N}_n}^{\mathcal{N}_{n+1}-1} \widehat{c}(\Psi(k)), \qquad n \ge 1 \tag{10.24}$$

are i.i.d., with common mean $\Gamma(\breve{\phi})$. It will follow by construction that $\Gamma(\breve{\phi})$ is proportional to average cost for the newly constructed stochastic process.

There is no need to identify which policy is under consideration in the constructions that follow, so we write Γ instead of $\Gamma(\breve{\phi})$, and let T denote the transition matrix for the Markov chain $\boldsymbol{\Phi}$.

Discounted Cost

Take h equal to the discounted-cost value function obtained with a policy $\breve{\phi}$, and denote

$$\Gamma = \sum_z h(z)\mu(z) = \mathsf{E}\Big[\sum_{k=0}^{\infty} \gamma^k c(\Phi(k))\Big], \quad \Phi(0) \sim \mu. \tag{10.25}$$

The construction is defined through regeneration: $\Psi(k) = (\widehat{\Phi}(k), B(k))$, in which $B(k) \in \{0,1\}$ for each k, with $B(k) = 1$ indicating that a regeneration occurred at time k, and $\widehat{\Phi}(k)$ evolves according to the transition matrix T in between regeneration times.

We begin with the construction of the first regeneration time along with an alternative representation of (10.25). Let $\boldsymbol{B}$ be a Bernoulli process with parameter $1-\gamma$, independent of $\boldsymbol{\Phi}$:

$$\mathsf{P}\{B(k) = 0 \mid \Phi_0^\infty\} = \gamma,$$

where the aforementioned conditioning is on the entire trajectory of the Markov chain $\boldsymbol{\Phi}$. On denoting $T_\bullet = \min\{k \geq 1 : B(k) = 1\}$, we have $\mathsf{P}\{T_\bullet > k \mid \Phi_0^\infty\} = \gamma^k$ for $k \geq 0$, and by independence

$$\mathsf{E}[\mathbb{1}\{T_\bullet > k\} c(\Phi(k))] = \mathsf{E}[\mathbb{1}\{T_\bullet > k\}]\mathsf{E}[c(\Phi(k))] = \gamma^k \mathsf{E}[c(\Phi(k))].$$

Summing each side removes the discounting from (10.25), converting it to a stochastic shortest path problem:

$$h(z) = \mathsf{E}\Big[\sum_{k=0}^{T_\bullet - 1} c(\Phi(k)) \mid \Phi(0) = z\Big]. \tag{10.26}$$

To define $\boldsymbol{\Psi}$, we let $\mathcal{N}_1 = T_\bullet$ define the first regeneration time, and $\widehat{\Phi}(k) = \Phi(k)$ for $0 \leq k \leq T_\bullet - 1$. The random variable $\widehat{\Phi}(T_\bullet)$ is sampled independently of the past, with distribution μ. This construction is repeated, with $\{\mathcal{N}_n\}$ a renewal process, defined inductively by

$$\mathcal{N}_{n+1} = \min\{k \geq \mathcal{N}_n + 1 : B(k) = 1\}, \qquad n \geq 1$$

with $\widehat{\Phi}(k)$ defined as before on the interval $\{\mathcal{N}_n \leq k \leq \mathcal{N}_{n+1}\}$ for each n.

The following is a variant of Kac's theorem for this Markov chain (see Proposition 6.10):

Proposition 10.12 *For the Markov chain $\boldsymbol{\Psi}$ with cost function $\widehat{c}(\Psi(k)) = c(\widehat{X}(k))$, $k \geq 0$, the partial sums $\{S_n\}$ in* (10.24) *are i.i.d. with common mean Γ defined in* (10.25). *Consequently, the average cost is given by*

$$\lim_{N\to\infty} \frac{1}{N} \sum_{k=0}^{N-1} c(\widehat{\Phi}(k)) = \lim_{M\to\infty} \frac{M}{\mathcal{N}_M} \frac{1}{M} \sum_{m=1}^{M-1} S_m = (1-\gamma)\Gamma. \qquad \square$$

Finite-Horizon

Let $\mathcal{N} \geq 1$ and $z^\bullet \in \mathsf{Z}$ be given, and consider the finite horizon criterion

$$\Gamma = \mathsf{E}\Big[\sum_{k=0}^{\mathcal{N} \wedge \mathcal{N}_\bullet} \gamma^k c(\Phi(k))\Big], \quad \Phi(0) \sim \mu, \tag{10.27}$$

where $\mathcal{N}_\bullet = \min\{k \geq 1 : \Phi(k) = z^\bullet\}$, $\mathcal{N} \wedge \mathcal{N}_\bullet = \min(\mathcal{N},\mathcal{N}_\bullet)$, and $\gamma > 0$ is arbitrary. This is the weighted shortest path problem when $\mathcal{N} = \infty$ and $\gamma = 1$.

To construct a Markov chain $\boldsymbol{\Psi}$ for which (10.27) is proportional to average cost requires a different regeneration construction. We again define $\boldsymbol{\Psi}$ as a pair process $\Psi(k) = (\widehat{\Phi}(k),\iota(k))$, where in this setting $\boldsymbol{\iota}$ is defined to be deterministic and periodic: $\iota(k) = k$ (mod $\mathcal{N}$). The regeneration times are also deterministic: $\mathcal{N}_n = n\mathcal{N}$ for $n \geq 1$, and the construction is defined so that the sequence $\{\widehat{\Phi}(\mathcal{N}_n) : n \geq 1\}$ is i.i.d. with marginal μ.

We borrow ideas from the discounted cost setting to construct $\boldsymbol{\Psi}$: The state space Z is enlarged to include a *graveyard state* denoted $\blacktriangle$. Hence the state space for $\boldsymbol{\Psi}$ is $\{\mathsf{Z} \cup \blacktriangle\} \times \{0, \dots, \mathcal{N} - 1\}$. The dynamics on each interval $\mathcal{N}_n < k < \mathcal{N}_{n+1}$ are defined as follows:

(i) $\mathsf{P}\{\widehat{\Phi}(k) = \blacktriangle \mid \widehat{\Phi}(k-1) = z^\bullet\} = \mathsf{P}\{\widehat{\Phi}(k) = \blacktriangle \mid \widehat{\Phi}(k-1) = \blacktriangle\} = 1$.
(ii) $\mathsf{P}\{\widehat{\Phi}(k) = z' \mid \widehat{\Phi}(k-1) = z\} = T(z,z')$ for $z,z' \in \mathsf{Z}$, whenever $z \neq z^\bullet$.

As in the discounted setting, there is a simple interpretation that lends itself to simulation or experimental design: For each n, initialize $\widehat{\Phi}(\mathcal{N}_n) \sim \mu$, independent of $\{\widehat{\Phi}(k) : k < \mathcal{N}_n\}$. Obtain samples of the state process according to the natural dynamics for $\mathcal{N}_n < k < \mathcal{N}_{n+1}$, stopping the experiment or simulation if $z^\bullet$ is reached during this interval.

The cost function is defined by $\widehat{c}(\blacktriangle,\iota) \stackrel{\text{def}}{=} 0$, and $\widehat{c}(z,\iota) \stackrel{\text{def}}{=} \gamma^\iota c(z)$ for $z \in \mathsf{Z}$ and $\iota \in \{0, \dots, \mathcal{N} - 1\}$.

An analog of Proposition 10.12 is obtained through this construction:

Proposition 10.13 *The partial sums* $\{S_n\}$ *in* (10.24) *are i.i.d. with common mean* Γ*, now defined in* (10.27)*. Consequently, the average cost is given by*

$$\lim_{N\to\infty} \frac{1}{N} \sum_{k=1}^{N} \mathsf{E}[c(\widehat{\Phi}(k))] = \frac{1}{\mathcal{N}}\Gamma. \qquad \square$$

Proposition 10.13 also applies to the truncated discounted-cost criterion:

$$\Gamma = \mathsf{E}\Big[\sum_{k=0}^{\mathcal{N}} \gamma^k c(\Phi(k))\Big], \quad \Phi(0) \sim \mu.$$

This may be preferred to the infinite horizon objective (10.25), since the use of deterministic regeneration times will likely lead to lower variance.

10.4.2 Average-Cost Algorithms

Both regeneration and relative DP equations are used next to construct algorithms designed to estimate the solution to Poisson's equation (9.56). Regeneration motivates the particular representation H_3 given in (10.17), which is the unique solution satisfying $H_3(z^\bullet) = 0$.

We begin with an algorithm inspired by the regenerative algorithm (10.20) and Theorem 10.11:

Regenerative TD(λ) Algorithm for Average Cost (On-Policy)

For initialization $\theta_0, \zeta_0 \in \mathbb{R}^d$, the sequence of estimates are defined recursively:

$$\begin{aligned}
\theta_{n+1} &= \theta_n + \alpha_{n+1}\zeta_n \mathcal{D}_{n+1}, \\
\mathcal{D}_{n+1} &= \big(-H^\theta(\Phi(n)) + \tilde{c}_n + \mathbb{1}\{\Phi(n+1) \neq z^\bullet\}H^\theta(\Phi(n+1))\big)\Big|_{\theta=\theta_n}, \\
\zeta_{n+1} &= \lambda\mathbb{1}\{\Phi(n+1) \neq z^\bullet\}\zeta_n + \psi_{(n+1)}, \\
\eta_{n+1} &= \eta_n + \tilde{c}_n/(n+1), \qquad \tilde{c}_n = c(\Phi(n)) - \eta_n, \qquad n \geq 0.
\end{aligned} \tag{10.28}$$

This is a linear SA algorithm based on a slight modification of (10.21): $\gamma = 1$ in the definition of A_{n+1} and $b_{n+1} = -\zeta_n[c_n - \eta_n]$. The associated ODE is thus linear, with vector field

$$\bar{f}(\vartheta) = A\vartheta + b, \qquad A = \mathsf{E}_\varpi[A_n],\ b = -\mathsf{E}_\varpi[\zeta_n \tilde{c}(\Phi(n))].$$

Theorem 10.14 (L_2 Optimality of TD(1) for Average Cost) *Consider the algorithm (10.28) with linear function approximation $H^\theta = \theta^\intercal\psi$. Assume that $\boldsymbol{\Phi}$ is uni-chain and that $\varpi(z^\bullet) > 0$.*

Then, in the special case $\lambda = 1$,

(i) $A = -R(0)$.

(ii) *Any solution to* $0 = \bar{f}(\theta^*) = \mathsf{E}_\varpi[\zeta_n \mathcal{D}_{n+1}]$ *solves the minimum norm problem:*

$$\theta^* \in \arg\min_\theta \|H^\theta - H_3\|^2_\varpi = \arg\min_\theta \mathsf{E}_\varpi\big[\big(H^\theta(\Phi(n)) - H_3(\Phi(n))\big)^2\big], \tag{10.29}$$

where H_3 is the solution to Poisson's equation given by

$$H_3(z) = \mathsf{E}\Big[\sum_{k=0}^{\tau_\bullet - 1} \tilde{c}(\Phi(k)) \mid \Phi(0) = z\Big].$$ □

Once again, in most cases it is best to use the LSTD(1) formulation (10.23) if the function class is linear.

It is anticipated that an algorithm derived from a relative DP equation will have lower variance. Consider

$$0 = \mathsf{E}[-H(\Phi(k)) - \delta\langle\mu, H\rangle + c(\Phi(k)) + H(\Phi(k+1)) \mid \Phi(k) = z], \qquad z \in \mathsf{X} \times \mathsf{U}. \tag{10.30}$$

The function H is the unique solution to Poisson's equation for which $\delta\langle\mu, H\rangle = \eta$. Consequently,

$$H(z) - H(z^\bullet) = H_3(z), \qquad z \in \mathsf{X} \times \mathsf{U}. \tag{10.31}$$

Given the foregoing, we have a natural candidate for approximation, in which estimation of η is abandoned:

Regenerative Relative TD(λ) Algorithm for Average Cost (On-Policy)

For initialization $\theta_0, \zeta_0 \in \mathbb{R}^d$, the sequence of estimates is defined recursively:

$$\begin{aligned} \theta_{n+1} &= \theta_n + \alpha_{n+1}\zeta_n \mathcal{D}_{n+1}, \\ \mathcal{D}_{n+1} &= \big(-H^\theta(\Phi(n)) - \delta\langle \mu, H^\theta\rangle + c_n + H^\theta(\Phi(n+1))\big)\Big|_{\theta=\theta_n}, \qquad (10.32) \\ \zeta_{n+1} &= \lambda \mathbb{1}\{\Phi(n+1) \neq z^\bullet\}\zeta_n + \psi_{(n+1)}. \end{aligned}$$

We now have $\theta_{n+1} = \theta_n + \alpha_{n+1}[A_{n+1}\theta_n - b_{n+1}]$ with

$$A_{n+1} = \zeta_n\big[-\psi_{(n)} - \delta\bar{\psi}^\mu + \psi_{(n+1)}\big]^\intercal, \qquad b_{n+1} = -\zeta_n c_n, \qquad (10.33)$$

where $\bar{\psi}_i^\mu = \langle \mu, \psi_i\rangle$ for each i. We have the following companion to Theorem 10.14:

Theorem 10.15 (L_2 Optimality of TD(1) for Average Cost) *Consider the algorithm (10.32) with linear function approximation $H^\theta = \theta^\intercal \psi$. Assume that Φ is uni-chain, that $\varpi(z^\bullet) > 0$, and that for some parameter vector $\theta^\bullet \in \mathbb{R}^d$,*

$$\sum \theta_i^\bullet \psi_i(z) = \mathbb{1}\{z = z^\bullet\}, \qquad z \in \mathsf{X} \times \mathsf{U}.$$

Then, in the special case $\lambda = 1$, for any solution to $\bar{f}(\theta^*) = 0$,

(i) $\eta = \delta\langle \mu, H^{\theta^*}\rangle$.
(ii) *The "projected Poisson's equation" holds: with $Y = \psi(\Phi(n))$,*

$$H^{\theta^*}(\Phi(n)) = \widehat{\mathsf{E}}[\tilde{c}(\Phi(n)) + H^{\theta^*}(\Phi(n+1)) \mid Y].$$

(iii) *Suppose in addition that $\mathbf{1}$ is in the span of the basis: For some $\theta^1 \in \mathbb{R}^d$,*

$$\sum \theta_i^1 \psi_i(z) = 1, \qquad z \in \mathsf{X} \times \mathsf{U}.$$

Then, $H^{\theta^*}(\Phi(n)) = \widehat{\mathsf{E}}[H_3(\Phi(n)) + H^{\theta^*}(z^\bullet) \mid Y]$, and the minimum norm problem is solved in the following span seminorm: With $r^* = H^{\theta^*}(z^\bullet)$,

$$(\theta^*, r^*) \in \operatorname*{arg\,min}_{(\theta, r)} \mathsf{E}_\varpi\big[\big(H^\theta(\Phi(n)) - r - H_3(\Phi(n))\big)^2\big]. \qquad (10.34)$$

□

Unfortunately we lose the elegant expression $A = -R(0)$ for this algorithm. A glance at the proof reveals that instead,

$$\begin{aligned} A &= \mathsf{E}_\varpi\big[\zeta_n\big[-\psi_{(n)} - \delta\bar{\psi}^\mu + \psi_{(n+1)}\big]^\intercal\big] \\ &= -\delta\mathsf{E}_\varpi\big[\zeta_n\big]\{\bar{\psi}^\mu\}^\intercal + \mathsf{E}_\varpi\big[\psi_{(n)}\{-\psi_{(n)} + \psi(z^\bullet)\}^\intercal\big]. \end{aligned}$$

It can be shown that A is invertible for sufficiently small $\delta > 0$ provided $\bar{\psi}^\intercal R(0)^{-1}\psi(z^\bullet) < 1$. Moreover,

$$\bar{\psi}^\intercal R(0)^{-1}\psi(z^\bullet) < \sqrt{\psi(z^\bullet)^\intercal R(0)^{-1}\psi(z^\bullet)},$$

which might lead to choices for basis selection to ensure the right-hand side is no greater than one. Conditions to ensure that A is Hurwitz are not yet available, so this approach may be best implemented using stochastic Newton–Raphson, implemented as LSTD(1). The estimate at final time N would then be defined by (10.23) where the "hats" represent sample path averages of $\{A_n, b_n\}$ defined in (10.33).

10.5 Gather the Actors

We met the actors briefly at the start of this chapter, defined to be a family of randomized policies $\{\breve{\phi}^{\theta} : \theta \in \mathbb{R}^d\}$. It is assumed henceforth that they are continuously differentiable in θ. Examples include the Gibbs policy (9.46a), and the linear family:

$$\phi^{\theta}(u \mid x) = \sum_{i=1}^{d} \theta_i \phi^i(x), \tag{10.35}$$

where $\{\phi^i : 1 \le i \le d\}$ is a preselected family of deterministic policies, and the parameter is constrained to be nonnegative and sum to unity: $\theta \in \mathbb{R}^d_+$ and $\sum_i \theta_i = 1$. The linear family (10.35) can be regarded as a compression of the input space, replacing U with the set of d indices $I = \{1, \dots, d\}$, with θ_i interpreted as the probability of choosing index i.

Theory in Section 10.4.1 allows us to restrict exclusively to the average-cost criterion throughout the remaining sections of this chapter, since other optimality criteria can be converted to average cost through the introduction of regeneration. This is convenient to simplify discussion, and also because we can build on ideas from Section 6.8 concerning "Sensitivity and Actor-Only Methods."

10.5.1 Actor-Critic for Average Cost

To apply the sensitivity formula in Theorem 6.8 requires the representations

$$\begin{aligned} c_\theta(x) &= \sum_u \breve{\phi}^{\theta}(u \mid x) c(x,u), \\ P_\theta(x,x') &= \sum_u \breve{\phi}^{\theta}(u \mid x) P_u(x,x'), \qquad x,x' \in \mathsf{X},\ \theta \in \mathbb{R}^d. \end{aligned} \tag{10.36}$$

We also require notation for the pair process $\boldsymbol{\Phi} = (\boldsymbol{X}, \boldsymbol{U})$. Its transition matrix and invariant pmf are again given by (9.3). In the current notation, these become

$$T_\theta(z,z') = P_u(x,x')\breve{\phi}^{\theta}(u' \mid x'), \qquad \varpi_\theta(z) \stackrel{\text{def}}{=} \pi_\theta(x)\breve{\phi}^{\theta}(u \mid x) \tag{10.37}$$

for any $z = (x,u)$ and $z' = (x',u')$. Our goal is to minimize average cost:

Actor-Critic Objective

$$\Gamma(\theta) = \sum_{x \in \mathsf{X}} c_\theta(x)\, \pi_\theta(x) = \sum_{z \in \mathsf{Z}} c(z) \varpi_\theta(z).$$

It is assumed throughout that the invariant pmf π_θ is unique for each θ.

In view of the definitions of c_θ and P_θ, the sensitivity formula (6.52) in Theorem 6.8 requires partial derivatives of $\breve{\phi}^{\theta}$ with respect to θ. The gradient of the logarithm of $\breve{\phi}^{\theta}$ plays an essential role:

$$\Lambda^\theta(x,u) = \nabla_\theta \log[\breve{\phi}^\theta(u \mid x)]. \tag{10.38}$$

In particular, we have

$$\begin{aligned} \nabla_\theta c_\theta(x) &= \sum_u \breve{\phi}^\theta(u \mid x)\Lambda^\theta(x,u)c(x,u), \\ \nabla_\theta P_\theta(x,x') &= \sum_u \breve{\phi}^\theta(u \mid x)\Lambda^\theta(x,u)P_u(x,x'), \qquad x,x' \in \mathsf{X},\ \theta \in \mathbb{R}^d. \end{aligned} \tag{10.39}$$

Perhaps more fundamental is that Λ^θ is the score function for the transition matrix on Z:

$$\Lambda^\theta(z') = \nabla_\theta \log(T_\theta(z,z')), \qquad z,z' \in \mathsf{Z}. \tag{10.40}$$

The reason that actor-critic methods appear here, right after TD(1)-learning for average cost, is that the sensitivity formula in Theorem 6.8 can be expressed in terms of the fixed-policy Q-function. Denote for any θ,

$$Q_\theta(x,u) \stackrel{\text{def}}{=} c(x,u) + P_u h_\theta\,(x) = c(x,u) + \sum_{x' \in \mathsf{X}} P_u(x,x')h_\theta(x'), \qquad x \in \mathsf{X},\ u \in \mathsf{U}, \tag{10.41}$$

where h_θ solves Poisson's equation, $c_\theta + P_\theta h_\theta = h_\theta + \Gamma(\theta)$.

Theorem 10.16 *Under the assumptions of this section, for each $\theta \in \mathbb{R}^d$,*

$$\nabla\Gamma(\theta) = \mathsf{E}_{\varpi_\theta}\big[\Lambda^\theta(\Phi(k))Q_\theta(\Phi(k))\big]. \tag{10.42}$$

Proof The function Q_θ solves Poisson's equation for $\boldsymbol{\Phi}$, with cost function $c\colon \mathsf{Z} \to \mathbb{R}$:

$$\begin{aligned} \mathsf{E}[Q_\theta(\Phi(k+1))\,|\,\Phi(k) = (x,u)] &= \sum_{x'}\sum_{u'} P_u(x,x')\breve{\phi}^\theta(u' \mid x')\{c(x',u') + P_{u'}h_\theta\,(x')\} \\ &= \sum_{x'} P_u(x,x')\{c_\theta(x') + P_\theta h_\theta\,(x')\} \\ &= \sum_{x'} P_u(x,x')\{h_\theta(x') + \Gamma(\theta)\} = Q_\theta(x,u) - c(x,u) + \Gamma(\theta). \end{aligned}$$

Written in matrix notation, this is $T_\theta Q_\theta = Q_\theta - c + \Gamma(\theta)$.

This combined with (10.40) and Theorem 6.8 completes the proof. □

The theorem invites many questions:

(i) How can this be used for optimization? Stochastic approximation is an option:

$$\theta_{n+1} = \theta_n - \alpha_{n+1}\breve{\nabla}_\Gamma(n), \qquad \breve{\nabla}_\Gamma(n) \stackrel{\text{def}}{=} \Lambda^{\theta_n}(\Phi(n))Q_{\theta_n}(\Phi(n)).$$

This is a version of stochastic gradient descent (SGD). The function Λ^θ is known, since we have constructed the policy. The Q-function is not known, and a poor estimate would mean poor approximation of θ^*.

(ii) Even if Q_θ were known, the stochastic approximation algorithm can be expected to have large variance. How can the variance be tamed?

The questions are addressed one by one, and justify new conclusions and algorithms. Each algorithm requires two function classes: one to define the family of randomized policies

$\{\check{\phi}^\theta : \theta \in \mathbb{R}^d\}$, and a second function class $\{\mathcal{H}^\theta : \theta \in \mathbb{R}^d\}$ to define the approximations for the Q functions. The following assumptions are imposed so the L_2 theory from the previous section will be available:

Actor-Critic Basis A linear parameterization for $\{\mathcal{H}^\theta : \theta \in \mathbb{R}^d\}$ is assumed, with fixed dimension d'. The basis functions may depend upon θ, so that a generic function in $\mathcal{H}^\theta$ can be expressed

$$H^\omega_\theta = \omega^\intercal \psi_\theta, \qquad \omega \in \mathbb{R}^{d'}, \ \theta \in \mathbb{R}^d. \tag{10.43}$$

It is assumed that ψ_θ is continuously differentiable and Lipschitz continuous in θ.

We will see shortly that $d' \geq d$ is usually desirable.

Actor-Critic Algorithm

For initialization $\theta_0 \in \mathbb{R}^d$ and $\omega_0, \zeta_0 \in \mathbb{R}^{d'}$,

$$\theta_{n+1} = \theta_n - \alpha_{n+1}\breve{\nabla}_\Gamma(n), \qquad \breve{\nabla}_\Gamma(n) \stackrel{\text{def}}{=} \Lambda^{\theta_n}(\Phi(n))H^{\omega_n}_{\theta_n}(\Phi(n)), \tag{10.44a}$$

$$\Phi(n+1) \sim T_{\theta_n}(z, \cdot\,), \ \text{ with } z = \Phi(n), \tag{10.44b}$$

$$\left.\begin{aligned} \mathcal{D}_{n+1} &= \{-H^\omega_\theta(\Phi(n)) + \tilde{c}_n + \mathbb{1}\{\Phi(n+1) \neq z^\bullet\}H^\omega_\theta(\Phi(n+1))\}\Big|_{\substack{\theta=\theta_n \\ \omega=\omega_n}} \\ \omega_{n+1} &= \omega_n + \beta_{n+1}\zeta_n\mathcal{D}_{n+1} \\ \zeta_{n+1} &= \lambda\mathbb{1}\{\Phi(n+1) \neq z^\bullet\}\zeta_n + \psi_{\theta_{n+1}}(\Phi(n+1)) \\ \eta_{n+1} &= \eta_n + \beta_{n+1}\tilde{c}_n, \qquad \tilde{c}_n = c(\Phi(n)) - \eta_n \end{aligned}\right\}. \tag{10.44c}$$

The set of equations in (10.44c) is based on the TD(1) algorithm (10.28) (on setting $\lambda = 1$). This version of TD(1) is favored because there is a firmer stability theory as compared to (10.32).

The algorithm has two different step-sizes, satisfying the standard assumptions:

$$\sum_{n=1}^\infty \alpha_n = \sum_{n=1}^\infty \beta_n = \infty, \qquad \sum_{n=1}^\infty \{\alpha_n^2 + \beta_n^2\} < \infty.$$

It is assumed that the latter is much larger than the former, so that it is possible for H^{ω_n} to track the estimate of the fixed-policy Q-function Q_{θ_n} (associated with the policy $\check{\phi}^{\theta_n}$).

The following would be expected from the theory of two time-scale SA:

Proposition 10.17 *Suppose that* $\lambda = 1$ *and the step-size sequences satisfy assumption* (8.22)*:*

$$\lim_{n\to\infty} \frac{\beta_n}{\alpha_n} = \infty.$$

Assume moreover that the parameter estimates are bounded, and the following consistency condition holds:

$$\text{For each } \theta \in \mathbb{R}^n \text{ there is a } \omega_\theta^* \in \mathbb{R}^{d'} \text{ satisfying } H_\theta^{\omega_\theta^*} = Q_\theta. \tag{10.45}$$

Then, the ODE approximation of (10.44) *is gradient descent* $\frac{d}{dt}\vartheta = -\nabla\Gamma(\vartheta)$. □

The consistency assumption (10.45) is unrealistic outside of the tabular setting. Removing this assumption is possible through an application of Theorem 10.14 – details are provided in Section 10.6.

10.5.2 A Few Warnings and Remedies

It is time to say a few words about the focus on randomization here, which wasn't required in Sections 4.6 and 4.7. Randomization is required if we want to apply sensitivity theory for Markov chains, which brings in the score functions S^θ and Λ^θ. In particular, there is no meaningful definition of Λ^θ for deterministic threshold policies, such as the policy proposed for the mountain car in Section 4.7.1.[1] In most applications, it is reasonable to abandon randomization in the final step of policy design: Once we have our parameter estimate $\hat\theta \approx \theta^*$, construct a deterministic policy:

$$\phi^{\mathsf{final}}(x) \stackrel{\mathsf{def}}{=} \arg\max_u \breve{\phi}^{\hat\theta}(u \mid x)\,, \qquad x \in \mathsf{X}\,.$$

We might expect that $\breve{\phi}^{\hat\theta}$ will be nearly deterministic if it is nearly optimal, in which case ϕ^{final} is a small perturbation of $\breve{\phi}^{\hat\theta}$. The example that follows illustrates this point.

Example 10.5.1 (***The Best Parameter Is Probably*** ∞) Consider an entirely ideal setting in which $d = 1$ and θ plays the role of "inverse temperature" in the Gibbs policy (9.46a):

$$\breve{\phi}^{\theta}(u \mid x) \stackrel{\mathsf{def}}{=} \frac{1}{\kappa(x,\theta)} \exp\bigl(-\theta H(x,u)\bigr),$$

where $H\colon \mathsf{X}\times\mathsf{U} \to \mathbb{R}$, and $\kappa(x,\theta)$ is a normalizing constant. Suppose that we are so fortunate that the optimal policy is obtained from H:

$$\phi^\star(x) = \arg\min_u H(x,u)\,, \qquad x \in \mathsf{X},$$

and that $\phi^\star$ is unique (no other policy is optimal). Unfortunate conclusions follow:

(i) $\breve{\phi}^{\theta}$ is not an optimal policy for any θ, and (ii) $\lim_{\theta\to\infty} \breve{\phi}^{\theta} = \phi^\star$. ■

This example might seem contrived, but Gibbs policies will be featured in the coming sections, and we will see in Section 10.6 that that there is good reason to include an approximation to the Q-function in a Gibbs policy.

The example suggests that a good algorithm must allow for θ_n to converge to ∞. This may not be practical, so instead we introduce regularization: choose a convex regularizer

[1] See [323] for alternative formulations of actor-critic methods for deterministic policies.

$\mathcal{R}\colon \mathbb{R}^d \to \mathbb{R}_+$, and modify the actor-critic algorithm to approximate regularized gradient descent:

$$\tfrac{d}{dt}\vartheta = -\nabla\Gamma(\vartheta) - \nabla\mathcal{R}(\vartheta) \tag{10.46}$$

so that (10.44a) is replaced with

$$\theta_{n+1} = \theta_n - \alpha_{n+1}\{\breve{\nabla}_\Gamma(n) + \nabla\mathcal{R}_n(\theta_n)\},$$

where $\mathcal{R}_n : \mathbb{R}^d \to \mathbb{R}_+$ is potentially random, with $\mathsf{E}[\nabla\mathcal{R}_n(\theta)] \approx \nabla\mathcal{R}(\theta)$ for each θ and all large n.

10.6 SGD without Bias

The ODE approximation in Proposition 10.17 can be obtained under assumptions far weaker than (10.45).

A function class $\{\mathcal{H}^\theta : \theta \in \mathbb{R}^d\}$ of candidate approximations to the Q-functions is said to satisfy the *compatible features property* (CFP) if

$$\Lambda_i^\theta \in \mathcal{H}^\theta \qquad \text{for each } \theta \in \mathbb{R}^d \text{ and } 1 \le i \le d. \tag{10.47}$$

Proposition 10.18 *Suppose that* $\{\mathcal{H}^\theta : \theta \in \mathbb{R}^d\}$ *satisfies the CFP* (10.47). *For given* $\theta \in \mathbb{R}^d$, *let* $\widehat{Q}$ *denote a solution to the minimum norm problem:*

$$\widehat{Q} \in \arg\min\{\|H - Q_\theta\|^2_{\varpi_\theta} : H \in \mathcal{H}^\theta\}.$$

Then,

$$\nabla\Gamma(\theta) = \mathsf{E}_{\varpi_\theta}\big[\Lambda^\theta(\Phi(k))Q_\theta(\Phi(k))\big] = \mathsf{E}_{\varpi_\theta}\big[\Lambda^\theta(\Phi(k))\widehat{Q}(\Phi(k))\big]. \tag{10.48}$$

Proof L_2 optimality is equivalent to the orthogonality property:

$$0 = \mathsf{E}_{\varpi_\theta}\big[\{Q_\theta(\Phi(k)) - \widehat{Q}(\Phi(k))\}H(\Phi(k))\big], \qquad \text{for all } H \in \mathcal{H}^\theta.$$

The identity (10.48) is obtained on setting $H = \Lambda_i^\theta$ for each i. □

The practical importance of the proposition is seen on revisiting Theorem 10.14: For fixed θ and with $U(k) = \breve{\phi}^\theta(X(k))$ for all k, the identity (10.48) will hold for the approximation obtained using TD(1), whenever the linear function class satisfies the CFP.

This assumption is not restrictive. In practice, we might start with a function class $\mathcal{H}^0$, and then for each θ define

$$\mathcal{H}^\theta = \Big\{h = h^0 + \sum_{i=1}^d \omega_i\Lambda_i^\theta : h^0 \in \mathcal{H}^0,\ \omega \in \mathbb{R}^d\Big\}. \tag{10.49}$$

While Theorem 10.14 as stated is only valid when θ is independent of n, the theory of two time-scale SA gives us the following extension of Proposition 10.17:

Proposition 10.19 *Suppose that the assumptions of Proposition 10.17 hold, but with* (10.45) *replaced with the compatible features assumption* (10.47).

Then, the ODE approximation of (10.44) *is unchanged:* $\tfrac{d}{dt}\vartheta = -\nabla\Gamma(\vartheta)$. □

We can disregard any part of Λ_i^θ that does not depend upon u. Let $\mathcal{F}_k^-$ denote the partial history up to time k:

$$\mathcal{F}_k^- = \{X(k), \Phi(i) : 0 \le i \le k-1\}. \tag{10.50}$$

This is the entire history up to k, except that $U(k)$ is disregarded.

Lemma 10.20 *For any initial distribution for $X(0)$, we have $\mathsf{E}[\Lambda^\theta(\Phi(k)) \mid \mathcal{F}_k^-] = 0$. Consequently,*

(i) *$\{\Lambda^\theta(\Phi(k)) : k \ge 0\}$ is a martingale difference sequence.*
(ii) *For any function $g \colon \mathsf{X} \to \mathbb{R}$,*

$$0 = \mathsf{E}[g(X(k))\Lambda^\theta(\Phi(k))].$$

Proof From the definitions, we have the following for any k and $x \in \mathsf{X}$:

$$\mathsf{E}[\Lambda^\theta(\Phi(k)) \mid \mathcal{F}_k^-;\, X(k) = x] = \sum_u \Lambda^\theta(x,u)\phi^\theta(u \mid x).$$

Given the definition $\Lambda^\theta(x,u) = \nabla_\theta \breve{\phi}^\theta(u \mid x)/\breve{\phi}^\theta(u \mid x)$, it follows that

$$\mathsf{E}[\Lambda^\theta(\Phi(k)) \mid \mathcal{F}_k^-;\, X(k) = x] = \sum_u \nabla_\theta \breve{\phi}^\theta(u \mid x) = \nabla_\theta \sum_u \breve{\phi}^\theta(u \mid x) = 0,$$

where the final equality holds because $\breve{\phi}^\theta(\cdot \mid x)$ is a pmf on U for each x.

The smoothing property of conditional expectation gives

$$\mathsf{E}[g(X(k))\Lambda^\theta(\Phi(k))] = \mathsf{E}\big[g(X(k))\mathsf{E}[\Lambda^\theta(X(k),U(k)) \mid \mathcal{F}_k^-]\big] = 0. \qquad \square$$

Lemma 10.20 implies that we can relax the definition of compatible features to read as follows: For each $\theta \in \mathbb{R}^d$ and $1 \le i \le d$, there is a function $G_i^\theta : \mathsf{X} \to \mathbb{R}$ such that

$$\Lambda_i^\theta - G_i^\theta \in \mathcal{H}^\theta. \tag{10.51}$$

Gibbs Policy

Given a d-dimensional basis vector ψ^0, consider for each θ the policy

$$\breve{\phi}^\theta(u \mid x) = \frac{1}{\kappa(\theta,x)} \exp\big(\theta^\intercal \psi^0(x,u)\big), \tag{10.52}$$

where κ is a normalizing constant (recall (9.46)). We then have the following from the definitions:

Lemma 10.21 *For the Gibbs policy,*

$$\Lambda^\theta(x,u) = \widetilde{\psi}_\theta(x,u) \stackrel{\text{def}}{=} \psi^0(x,u) - \underline{\psi}_\theta^0(x), \qquad \underline{\psi}_\theta^0(x) \stackrel{\text{def}}{=} \sum_v \breve{\phi}^\theta(v \mid x)\psi^0(x,v). \qquad \square$$

Consequently, for this policy we can take $d' = d$ and $\mathcal{H}^\theta = \{\omega^\intercal \psi^0 : \omega \in \mathbb{R}^d\}$ to ensure the CFP is satisfied in the relaxed form (10.51). However, in the next subsection we see that it may be best to use $\mathcal{H}^\theta = \{\omega^\intercal \widetilde{\psi}_\theta : \omega \in \mathbb{R}^d\}$.

10.7 Advantage and Control Variates

First, *and most important*: Don't be fooled by the beauty of unbiased gradient observations. The ideal algorithm using TD(1) may come with massive variance. In practice, you are likely to resort to the introduction of $\lambda < 1$ in TD(λ) along with the application of state weighting, so that the eligibility vector in (10.44c) is replaced with

$$\zeta_{n+1} = \lambda \mathbb{1}\{\Phi(n) \neq z^\bullet\}\zeta_n + w_{n+1}\psi_{\theta_{n+1}}(\Phi(n+1)),$$

where $w_{n+1} = w(X(n+1))$ for the weighting function $w\colon \mathsf{X} \to \mathbb{R}_+$.

You may go further and experiment with the discounted-cost value function as an approximation for Q_θ. This is unfortunate, but bias/variance trade-offs are a theme in machine learning that appears to be inescapable.

The following pages describe techniques to reduce variance without bias.

10.7.1 Variance Reduction through Advantage

Lemma 10.20 tells us that we can construct a second family of functions $\mathcal{G}$, where $G\colon \mathsf{X} \to \mathbb{R}$ for each $G \in \mathcal{G}$, and replace (10.44a) with the following:

$$\theta_{n+1} = \theta_n - \alpha_{n+1}\Lambda^{\theta_n}(\Phi(n))\{H^{\omega_n}_{\theta_n}(\Phi(n)) - G_n(X(n))\}. \qquad (10.44a')$$

Provided that the CFP holds, we will maintain the ODE approximation as gradient descent, regardless of how $\{G_n\}$ are defined (subject to continuous dependency on parameter estimates). The favored choice of G is the same as identified in Section 9.1.3:

$$G^\omega_\theta(x) = \mathsf{E}[H^\omega_\theta(\Phi(n)) \mid X(n) = x] = \sum_u H^\omega_\theta(x,u)\breve{\phi}^\theta(u \mid x).$$

The difference $Q_\theta - h_\theta$ was designated the *advantage function* associated with policy $\breve{\phi}^\theta$.

A modified function class $\mathcal{H}^\theta_V$ is defined such that any $V_\theta \in \mathcal{H}^\theta_V$ can be expressed:

$$V_\theta(x,u) = H_\theta(x,u) - \underline{H}_\theta(x), \quad \text{for some } H_\theta \in \mathcal{H}^\theta, \text{ with } \underline{H}_\theta(x) \stackrel{\text{def}}{=} \sum_u H_\theta(x,u)\breve{\phi}^\theta(u \mid x).$$

And for any ω, we write $V^\omega_\theta(x,u) \stackrel{\text{def}}{=} H^\omega_\theta(x,u) - \underline{H}^\omega_\theta(x) = \omega^\intercal \widetilde{\psi}_\theta(x,u)$, with

$$\widetilde{\psi}_\theta(x,u) = \psi_\theta(x,u) - \underline{\psi}_\theta(x), \qquad \underline{\psi}_\theta(x) = \sum_u \psi_\theta(x,u)\breve{\phi}^\theta(u \mid x).$$

We arrive at an update equation that is preferred in recent research:

$$\theta_{n+1} = \theta_n - \alpha_{n+1}\breve{\nabla}^v_\Gamma(n), \qquad \breve{\nabla}^v_\Gamma(n) \stackrel{\text{def}}{=} \Lambda^{\theta_n}(\Phi(n))V^{\omega_n}_{\theta_n}(\Phi(n)). \qquad (10.44a^\star)$$

This form comes for free when using $\psi_\theta = \Lambda^\theta$, since in this case $\underline{\psi}_\theta \equiv 0$ is obtained as an application of Lemma 10.20.

The introduction of $\{\Lambda^{\theta_n}(\Phi(n))\underline{H}^{\omega_n}_{\theta_n}(X(n)) : n \geq 0\}$ to obtain ($10.44a^\star$) from (10.44a) is an example of the *control variate* technique that was introduced in Section 6.7.5.

10.7.2 A Better Advantage

Consider a function class satisfying the CFP. Suppose that the input space is not large, so that it is practical to compute $\underline{H}^{\omega}_{\theta}(x)$ based on $H^{\omega}_{\theta}(x,u)$ for each observed $x \in \mathsf{X}$. In this case, there is an alternative control variate available, defined by a different sort of smoothing. It is no more complex and has lower variance.

For any θ, ω and x denote

$$\underline{\Lambda H}^{\omega}_{\theta}(x) = \mathsf{E}[\Lambda^{\theta}(\Phi(n))H^{\omega}_{\theta}(\Phi(n)) \mid \mathcal{F}^{-}_{n}\,;\, X(n) = x],$$

with $\{\mathcal{F}^{-}_{k}\}$ defined in (10.50). Applying the definition of the conditional mean using $\check{\phi}^{\theta}$ gives

$$\underline{\Lambda H}^{\omega}_{\theta}(x) = \sum_{u} \nabla\check{\phi}^{\theta}(u \mid x)H^{\omega}_{\theta}(x,u)\,, \qquad x \in \mathsf{X}.$$

From the smoothing property of conditional expectation, we obtain a new unbiased SGD algorithm by "smoothing" (10.44a):

$$\theta_{n+1} = \theta_n - \alpha_{n+1}\check{\nabla}^{s}_{\Gamma}(n)\,, \qquad \check{\nabla}^{s}_{\Gamma}(n) \stackrel{\text{def}}{=} \underline{\Lambda H}^{\omega_n}_{\theta_n}(X(n)). \tag{10.44a^{**}}$$

We will see that $\check{\nabla}^{s}_{\Gamma}(n)$ has lower variance when compared to $\check{\nabla}^{v}_{\Gamma}(n)$ in (10.44$a^{\star}$).

More important is a comparison of the respective asymptotic covariance matrices Σ_{Δ}, as defined in (8.27). The first step in this comparison is to consider the gradient estimates evaluated at the optimal parameters. Since $\nabla\Gamma(\theta^*) = 0$ for any limit θ^* of either algorithm, the following two processes have zero mean for the process $\mathbf{\Phi}$ in steady state:

$$\Delta^{v,\infty}_{n}(n) = \check{\nabla}^{v,\infty}_{\Gamma}(n) \stackrel{\text{def}}{=} \Lambda^{\theta^*}(\Phi(n))V^{\omega^*}_{\theta^*}(\Phi(n)),$$
$$\Delta^{s,\infty}_{n}(n) = \check{\nabla}^{s,\infty}_{\Gamma}(n) \stackrel{\text{def}}{=} \underline{\Lambda H}^{\omega^*}_{\theta^*}(X(n)).$$

The respective asymptotic covariance matrices are denoted

$$\Sigma^{v,\infty}_{\Delta} = \sum_{n=-\infty}^{\infty} \mathsf{E}_{\varpi}[\check{\nabla}^{v,\infty}_{\Gamma}(n)\{\check{\nabla}^{v,\infty}_{\Gamma}(0)\}^{\intercal}] \text{ and } \Sigma^{s,\infty}_{\Delta} = \sum_{n=-\infty}^{\infty} \mathsf{E}_{\varpi}[\check{\nabla}^{s,\infty}_{\Gamma}(n)\{\check{\nabla}^{s,\infty}_{\Gamma}(0)\}^{\intercal}].$$

Proposition 10.22 *We have, for any n,*

$$\check{\nabla}^{v,\infty}_{\Gamma}(n) = \check{\nabla}^{s,\infty}_{\Gamma}(n) + \Delta^{A}_{n},$$

where $\{\Delta^{A}_{n}\}$ is a martingale difference sequence, satisfying $\mathsf{E}[\Delta^{A}_{n} \mid \mathcal{F}^{-}_{n}] = 0$. Consequently,

(i) *The covariances are ordered:*

$$\mathsf{Cov}(\check{\nabla}^{v,\infty}_{\Gamma}(n)) = \mathsf{Cov}(\check{\nabla}^{s,\infty}_{\Gamma}(n)) + \mathsf{Cov}(\Delta^{A}_{n}) \geq \mathsf{Cov}(\check{\nabla}^{s,\infty}_{\Gamma}(n)).$$

(ii) *The asymptotic covariances are also ordered:* $\Sigma^{v,\infty}_{\Delta} = \Sigma^{s,\infty}_{\Delta} + \mathsf{Cov}(\Delta^{A}_{n})$.

Part (i) is not helpful for understanding variance of the respective actor-critic algorithms: The ordinary covariance is not of primary interest in convergence theory for stochastic approximation. Part (ii) tells us that the alternative control variate approach is preferable whenever $\mathsf{Cov}(\Delta^{A}_{k})$ is large.

Proof of Proposition 10.22 We have by definition

$$\Delta_n^A \stackrel{\text{def}}{=} \Lambda^{\theta^*}(\Phi(n))V_{\theta^*}^{\omega^*}(\Phi(n)) - \underline{\Lambda H}_{\theta^*}^{\omega^*}(X(n)).$$

The conditional expectation is zero:

$$\begin{aligned}
\mathsf{E}[\Delta_n^A \mid \mathcal{F}_n^-] &= \mathsf{E}[\Lambda^{\theta^*}(\Phi(n))V_{\theta^*}^{\omega^*}(\Phi(n)) \mid \mathcal{F}_n^-] - \underline{\Lambda H}_{\theta^*}^{\omega^*}(X(n)) \\
&= \mathsf{E}[\Lambda^{\theta^*}(\Phi(n))H_{\theta^*}^{\omega^*}(\Phi(n)) \mid \mathcal{F}_n^-] - \underline{\Lambda H}_{\theta^*}^{\omega^*}(X(n)) \\
&= 0,
\end{aligned}$$

where the second equality follows from Lemma 10.20. The conclusion $\mathsf{E}[\Delta_n^A \mid \mathcal{F}_n^-] = 0$ implies that $\{\Delta_n^A\}$ is a martingale difference sequence. Part (i) follows because $\breve{\nabla}_\Gamma^{s,\infty}(n) = \underline{\Lambda H}_{\theta^*}^{\omega^*}(X(n))$ is measurable with respect to $\mathcal{F}_n^-$, so that Δ_n^A and $\breve{\nabla}_\Gamma^{s,\infty}(n)$ are uncorrelated.

For (ii), observe that the martingale difference property implies that Δ_n^A and $\breve{\nabla}_\Gamma^{s,\infty}(0)$ are uncorrelated for $n \geq 1$, giving

$$\mathsf{E}_\varpi[\breve{\nabla}_\Gamma^{v,\infty}(n)\{\breve{\nabla}_\Gamma^{v,\infty}(0)\}^\intercal] = \mathsf{E}_\varpi[\breve{\nabla}_\Gamma^{s,\infty}(n)\{\breve{\nabla}_\Gamma^{s,\infty}(0)\}^\intercal].$$

Taking transposes of each side, we obtain the same identity for $n \leq -1$. Hence the two auto-covariance sequences are identical for $n \neq 0$. □

10.8 Natural Gradient and Zap

What about the Newton–Raphson flow? If we had direct observations of the gradient, this would become

$$\tfrac{d}{dt}\vartheta = -G(\vartheta)\nabla\Gamma(\vartheta), \tag{10.53}$$

with $G = [\nabla^2\Gamma]^{-1}$. Theorem 10.16 might provide a means to obtain unbiased estimates, but a tractable Zap-SA algorithm is not yet available. Moreover, this approach could compute a local maximum rather than local minimum of Γ.

There is an alternative choice of matrix gain that is popular, and defines the *natural gradient* algorithm.

To set up notation, let's first review theory surrounding approximation of the critic Q_θ. For the fixed-policy setting with linear function approximation, Theorem 10.14 tells us that the optimal matrix gain is given by $-A^{-1} = R(0)^{-1}$, with $R(0)$ the autocorrelation matrix for the basis.

Consider the minimal function class with compatible features using $\psi_\theta = \Lambda^\theta(x,u)$. We have seen that this has mean zero for each θ, so that the autocorrelation coincides with the autocovariance, and the notation $R(0)$ is abandoned in favor of

$$F(\theta) \stackrel{\text{def}}{=} \sum_{x,u} \Lambda^\theta(x,u)\Lambda^\theta(x,u)^\intercal \varpi_\theta(x,u). \tag{10.54}$$

This is known as the *Fisher information matrix* because of its association with a matrix of this name appearing in statistics (see the close of Section 10.10 for further discussion).

For fixed-policy TD-learning with linear function approximation, the asymptotic covariance can be optimized using stochastic Newton–Raphson, and the same is true here for this two time-scale algorithm. The matrix gain $G(\theta) \stackrel{\text{def}}{=} F^{-1}(\theta)$ is also used in the definition of the *natural gradient* algorithm, whose ODE approximation is (10.53) with this choice of G.

Look over the next algorithm carefully: The matrix gain G_n that approximates $F^{-1}(\theta_n)$ appears twice. Its first appearance is used to approximate the natural gradient, and it appears again in the update for ω_n (a version of stochastic Newton–Raphson).

The variance might be reduced using the control variate technique described in Section 10.7.2, replacing $\breve{\nabla}^v_\Gamma(n)$ in (10.55a) by $\breve{\nabla}^s_\Gamma(n)$.

Natural Actor-Critic Algorithm with Zap

The function class is defined using $\psi_\theta = \Lambda^\theta$.
For initialization $R_0 > 0$ $(d \times d)$, $\eta_0 \in \mathbb{R}$, and $\theta_0, \omega_0, \zeta_0 \in \mathbb{R}^d$,

$$\theta_{n+1} = \theta_n - \alpha_{n+1} G_n \breve{\nabla}^v_\Gamma(n), \qquad \breve{\nabla}^v_\Gamma(n) \stackrel{\text{def}}{=} \Lambda_n H^{\omega_n}_{\theta_n}(\Phi(n)), \quad G_n = R_n^{-1}, \tag{10.55a}$$

$$\Lambda_n = \Lambda^{\theta_n}(\Phi(n)), \tag{10.55b}$$

$$\Phi(n+1) \sim T_{\theta_n}(z, \cdot\,), \ \text{ with } z = \Phi(n), \tag{10.55c}$$

$$\left.\begin{aligned}
\mathcal{D}_{n+1} &= -H^{\omega_n}_{\theta_n}(\Phi(n)) + \tilde{c}_n + \mathbb{1}\{\Phi(n+1) \neq z^\bullet\} H^{\omega_n}_{\theta_n}(\Phi(n+1)) \\
\omega_{n+1} &= \omega_n + \beta_{n+1} G_n \zeta_n \mathcal{D}_{n+1} \\
\zeta_{n+1} &= \lambda \mathbb{1}\{\Phi(n+1) \neq z^\bullet\}\zeta_n + \psi_{\theta_{n+1}}(\Phi(n+1)) \\
\eta_{n+1} &= \eta_n + \beta_{n+1}\tilde{c}_{n+1}, \qquad \tilde{c}_{n+1} = c(\Phi(n+1)) - \eta_n \\
R_{n+1} &= R_n + \beta_{n+1}[\Lambda_{n+1}\Lambda_{n+1}^{\intercal} - R_n]
\end{aligned}\right\} . \tag{10.55d}$$

The inverse that defines the gain matrix $G_n = R_n^{-1}$ can be computed efficiently using the Matrix Inversion Lemma (A.1), or an algorithm can be obtained without matrix inversion by adapting the first-order Zap algorithm (8.52).

Do not forget the warnings in Section 9.5.4: If R_n is never invertible, then you will need to either prune the basis, or use a pseudo inverse to define G_n.

10.9 Technical Proofs*

The proofs of Theorems 10.11 and 10.15 are similar to the proof of Theorem 9.7, except that we need to understand the impact of regeneration. Recall that $\boldsymbol{\Phi}$ is assumed defined on the two-sided time axis. For $\lambda = 1$, the steady-state realization of the eligibility vectors is defined by

$$\zeta_n = \sum_{\tilde{\sigma}^{[n]}_\bullet \le k \le n} \gamma^{n-k}\psi(\Phi(k)), \qquad n \in \mathbb{Z}. \tag{10.56}$$

That is, we allow negative values of n and k (recall (10.19)).

The following solves half of the "regeneration puzzle." For any function $g\colon \mathsf{X} \times \mathsf{U} \to \mathbb{R}$ and $\gamma \in [0,1]$, denote $\hat{g} = T^{\bullet}_{\gamma} g$, with

$$\hat{g}(z) = \mathsf{E}\Big[\sum_{k=0}^{\tau_{\bullet}-1} \gamma^k g(\Phi(k)) \mid \Phi(0) = z\Big].$$

We have $\hat{g} = J_\gamma(z)$ if $g = c$, and $\hat{g} = H_3$ if $g = \tilde{c}$ and $\gamma = 1$.

Lemma 10.23 *The adjoint of $T^{\bullet}_{\gamma}$, satisfying $\langle T^{\bullet}_{\gamma} g, h\rangle_{\varpi} = \langle g, [T^{\bullet}_{\gamma}]^{\dagger} h\rangle_{\varpi}$ for each $g,h \in L_2(\varpi)$, is given by*

$$[T^{\bullet}_{\gamma}]^{\dagger} h\,(z) = \mathsf{E}\Big[\sum_{\tilde{\sigma}^{[n]}_{\bullet} \le k \le n} \gamma^{n-k} h(\Phi(n)) \mid \Phi(n) = z\Big], \qquad z \in \mathsf{X} \times \mathsf{U},\, n \in \mathbb{Z},$$

where $\{\Phi(k) : k \in \mathbb{Z}\}$ is a stationary version of the Markov chain. In particular, with ζ_n defined in (10.56),

$$\mathsf{E}_{\varpi}[\hat{g}(\Phi(n))\psi(\Phi(n))] = \mathsf{E}_{\varpi}[g(\Phi(n))\zeta_n].$$

Proof It is enough to establish the identity for $n = 0$. From the definitions,

$$\langle T^{\bullet}_{\gamma} g, h\rangle_{\varpi} = \mathsf{E}_{\varpi}[h(\Phi(0))\hat{g}(\Phi(0))] = \mathsf{E}_{\varpi}\Big[h(\Phi(0))\mathsf{E}\Big[\sum_{k=0}^{\tau_{\bullet}-1} \gamma^k g(\Phi(k)) \mid \Phi(0)\Big]\Big].$$

The smoothing property of conditional expectation gives

$$\mathsf{E}_{\varpi}[h(\Phi(0))\hat{g}(\Phi(0))] = \mathsf{E}_{\varpi}\Big[h(\Phi(0)) \sum_{k=0}^{\tau_{\bullet}-1} \gamma^k g(\Phi(k))\Big]$$

and then by stationarity and the definition of $\tau_{\bullet}$,

$$\begin{aligned}
&\mathsf{E}_{\varpi}[h(\Phi(0))\hat{g}(\Phi(0))] \\
&= \mathsf{E}_{\varpi}[h(\Phi(0))g(\Phi(0))] + \sum_{k=1}^{\infty} \gamma^k \mathsf{E}_{\varpi}\Big[\mathbb{1}\{\Phi(j) \neq z^{\bullet} : 1 \le j \le k\} h(\Phi(0)) g(\Phi(k))\Big] \\
&= \mathsf{E}_{\varpi}[h(\Phi(0))g(\Phi(0))] + \sum_{k=1}^{\infty} \gamma^k \mathsf{E}_{\varpi}\Big[\mathbb{1}\{\Phi(j-k) \neq z^{\bullet} : 1 \le j \le k\} h(\Phi(-k)) g(\Phi(0))\Big].
\end{aligned}$$

Make the change of variables $\ell = j - k$, so that $\mathbb{1}\{\Phi(j-k) \neq z^{\bullet} : 1 \le j \le k\} = \mathbb{1}\{\Phi(\ell) \neq z^{\bullet} : -k+1 \le \ell \le 0\}$. Adopting this change, and then returning the sum and the coefficient γ^k within the expectation gives

$$\begin{aligned}
&\mathsf{E}_{\varpi}[h(\Phi(0))\hat{g}(\Phi(0))] \\
&= \mathsf{E}_{\varpi}[h(\Phi(0))g(\Phi(0))] + \mathsf{E}_{\varpi}\Big[g(\Phi(0)) \sum_{k=1}^{\infty} \gamma^k \mathbb{1}\{\Phi(\ell) \neq z^{\bullet} : -k+1 \le \ell \le 0\} h(\Phi(-k))\Big] \\
&= \mathsf{E}_{\varpi}[h(\Phi(0))g(\Phi(0))] + \mathsf{E}_{\varpi}\Big[g(\Phi(0)) \sum_{\tilde{\sigma}^{[0]}_{\bullet} \le k \le 1} \gamma^{-k} h(\Phi(-k))\Big],
\end{aligned}$$

where the sum is defined to be zero when $\tilde{\sigma}^{[0]}_{\bullet} = 0$. This establishes the desired result for $n = 0$.

□

The second half of the puzzle is solved next:

Lemma 10.24 *For any* $\gamma \in [0,1]$ *and function* $H\colon \mathsf{X} \times \mathsf{U} \to \mathbb{R}$,

(i) $\mathsf{E}_\varpi\big[\big(-H(\Phi(n)) + \gamma \mathbb{1}\{\Phi(n+1) \neq z^\bullet\} H(\Phi(n+1))\big)\zeta_n\big] = -\mathsf{E}_\varpi\big[H(\Phi(0))\psi(\Phi(0))\big]$.
(ii) $\mathsf{E}_\varpi\big[\big(-H(\Phi(n)) + \gamma H(\Phi(n+1))\big)\zeta_n\big] = \mathsf{E}_\varpi\big[\{-H(\Phi(0)) + \gamma^{\tau_\bullet} H(z^\bullet)\}\psi(\Phi(0))\big]$.

Proof The proof of (i) is obtained as a corollary to the previous lemma, using

$$g(z) = -H(z) + \gamma \mathsf{E}\big[\mathbb{1}\{\Phi(n+1) \neq z^\bullet\} H(\Phi(n+1)) \mid \Phi(n) = z\big],$$

so that by the smoothing property,

$$\mathsf{E}_\varpi\big[\big(-H(\Phi(n)) + \mathbb{1}\{\Phi(n+1) \neq z^\bullet\} H(\Phi(n+1))\big)\zeta_n\big] = \mathsf{E}_\varpi\big[g(\Phi(n))\zeta_n\big].$$

It remains to prove that $\mathsf{E}_\varpi[g(\Phi(n))\zeta_n] = -\mathsf{E}_\varpi[H(\Phi(n))\psi(\Phi(n))]$.

Lemma 10.23 gives

$$\begin{aligned}\mathsf{E}_\varpi[g(\Phi(n))\zeta_n] = \mathsf{E}_\varpi[g(\Phi(0))\zeta_0] &= \mathsf{E}_\varpi[\psi(\Phi(0))\hat{g}(\Phi(0))] \\ &= \mathsf{E}_\varpi\Big[\psi(\Phi(0)) \sum_{k=0}^{\tau_\bullet - 1} \gamma^k g(\Phi(k))\Big] \\ &= \sum_{k=0}^{\infty} \gamma^k \mathsf{E}_\varpi[\psi(\Phi(0)) g(\Phi(k)) \mathbb{1}\{k < \tau_\bullet\}].\end{aligned}$$

The smoothing property of the conditional expectation provides a useful representation for each expectation:

$$\begin{aligned}&\mathsf{E}_\varpi[\psi(\Phi(0))\mathbb{1}\{k < \tau_\bullet\} g(\Phi(k))] \\ &\quad = \mathsf{E}_\varpi\big[\psi(\Phi(0))\mathbb{1}\{k < \tau_\bullet\}\big\{-H(\Phi(k)) + \gamma \mathsf{E}\big[\mathbb{1}\{\Phi(k+1) \neq z^\bullet\} H(\Phi(k+1)) \mid \mathcal{F}_k\big]\big\}\big] \\ &\quad = \mathsf{E}_\varpi\big[\psi(\Phi(0))\mathbb{1}\{k < \tau_\bullet\}\big\{-H(\Phi(k)) + \gamma \mathbb{1}\{\Phi(k+1) \neq z^\bullet\} H(\Phi(k+1))\big\}\big],\end{aligned}$$

so that on substitution,

$$\begin{aligned}\mathsf{E}_\varpi[g(\Phi(n))\zeta_n] &= -\sum_{k=0}^{\infty} \gamma^k \mathsf{E}_\varpi\big[\psi(\Phi(0))\mathbb{1}\{k < \tau_\bullet\} H(\Phi(k))\big] \\ &\quad + \sum_{k=0}^{\infty} \gamma^k \mathsf{E}_\varpi\big[\psi(\Phi(0))\mathbb{1}\{k < \tau_\bullet\}\big\{\gamma \mathbb{1}\{\Phi(k+1) \neq z^\bullet\} H(\Phi(k+1))\big\}\big] \\ &= -\mathsf{E}_\varpi\Big[\psi(\Phi(0)) \sum_{k=0}^{\tau_\bullet - 1} \gamma^k H(\Phi(k)) \\ &\qquad - \psi(\Phi(0)) \sum_{k=0}^{\tau_\bullet - 1} \gamma^{k+1} \mathbb{1}\{\Phi(k+1) \neq z^\bullet\} H(\Phi(k+1))\Big].\end{aligned}$$

The difference of sums reduces to $\psi(\Phi(0))H(\Phi(0))$ (all other terms cancel), giving (i).

The proof of (ii) is the same, except that all but two terms cancel. □

Proof of Theorem 10.11 Applying (10.21), we have

$$A \stackrel{\text{def}}{=} \mathsf{E}_\varpi[A_{n+1}] = \mathsf{E}_\varpi\big[\zeta_n\big\{-\psi_{(n)} + \gamma \mathbb{1}\{\Phi(n+1) \neq z^\bullet\}\psi_{(n+1)}\big\}^{\intercal}\big].$$

Next apply Lemma 10.24 (i) using with $H = \psi_i$, for arbitrary i. Letting A^i denote the ith column of A, the lemma implies

$$\begin{aligned} A^i &= \mathsf{E}_\varpi\big[\{-\psi_i(\Phi(n)) + \gamma\mathbb{1}\{\Phi(n+1) \neq z^\bullet\}\psi_i(\Phi(n+1))\}\zeta_n\big] \\ &= -\mathsf{E}_\varpi\big[\psi_i(\Phi(0))\psi(\Phi(0))\big]. \end{aligned}$$

This establishes part (i): $A = -R^\psi$.

For (ii), consider the first-order condition for optimality for a parameter $\theta^\circ \in \mathbb{R}^d$:

$$0 = \nabla_\theta \tfrac{1}{2}\mathsf{E}_\varpi\big[\big(H^\theta(\Phi(n)) - J_\gamma(\Phi(n))\big)^2\big]\big|_{\theta=\theta^\circ} = \mathsf{E}_\varpi\big[\big(H^{\theta^\circ}(\Phi(n)) - J_\gamma(\Phi(n))\big)\psi_{(n)}\big].$$

By definition, $\mathsf{E}_\varpi\big[H^{\theta^\circ}(\Phi(n))\psi_{(n)}\big] = R(0)\theta^\circ = -A\theta^\circ$. Applying Lemma 10.23,

$$-\mathsf{E}_\varpi\big[J_\gamma(\Phi(n))\psi_{(n)}\big] = -\mathsf{E}_\varpi[c_n\zeta_n] = b,$$

where $b = \mathsf{E}[b_{n+1}]$ (see (10.21)). Hence the first-order condition for optimality becomes $-A\theta^\circ + b = 0$ as claimed. □

Proof of Theorem 10.15 We first establish (i): $\eta = \delta\langle \mu, H^{\theta^*}\rangle$ for any solution to $\bar{f}(\theta^*) = 0$. For this, we take $g(z) = c(z) - \delta\langle \mu, H^{\theta^*}\rangle$ and apply Lemma 10.24 (ii):

$$\begin{aligned} 0 = \bar{f}(\theta^*) &= \mathsf{E}_\varpi\big[\{g(\Phi(n)) - H^\theta(\Phi(n)) + H^\theta(\Phi(n+1))\}\zeta_n\big]\Big|_{\theta=\theta^*} \\ &= \mathsf{E}_\varpi\big[\{\hat{g}(\Phi(0)) - H^{\theta^*}(\Phi(0)) + H^{\theta^*}(z^\bullet)\}\psi(\Phi(0))\big], \end{aligned} \tag{10.57}$$

where

$$\hat{g}(z) = \mathsf{E}\Big[\sum_{k=0}^{\tau_\bullet - 1}\big[c(\Phi(k)) - \delta\langle \mu, H^{\theta^*}\rangle\big] \mid \Phi(0) = z\Big].$$

We next use the special property of $\theta^\bullet$:

$$\begin{aligned} 0 = \sum_i \theta_i^\bullet \bar{f}_i(\theta^*) &= \sum_i \theta_i^\bullet \mathsf{E}_\varpi\big[\psi_i(\Phi(0))\{\hat{g}(\Phi(0)) - H^{\theta^*}(\Phi(0)) + H^{\theta^*}(z^\bullet)\}\big] \\ &= \mathsf{E}_\varpi\big[\mathbb{1}\{\Phi(0) = z^\bullet\}\{\hat{g}(\Phi(0)) - H^{\theta^*}(\Phi(0)) + H^{\theta^*}(z^\bullet)\}\big]. \end{aligned}$$

Substituting the definitions,

$$\begin{aligned} 0 &= \mathsf{E}_\varpi\big[\mathbb{1}\{\Phi(0) = z^\bullet\}\{\hat{g}(\Phi(0)) - H^{\theta^*}(\Phi(0)) + H^{\theta^*}(z^\bullet)\}\big] \\ &= \varpi\{z^\bullet\}\hat{g}(z^\bullet). \end{aligned}$$

Under the assumptions of the theorem, it follows that $\hat{g}(z^\bullet) = 0$ and hence $\eta = \delta\langle \mu, H^{\theta^*}\rangle$ by Proposition 6.10 (Kac's theorem), which is (i).

We also conclude that $\hat{g} = H_3$, so that (10.57) implies (ii).

The remainder of the proof follows the proof of Theorem 10.11. First, revisiting (10.57) with the knowledge that $g = \tilde{c}$,

$$0 = \mathsf{E}\big[\{H^{\theta^*}(\Phi(0)) - r^* - H_3(\Phi(0))\}\psi(\Phi(0))\big] \tag{10.58}$$

with $r^* = H^{\theta^*}(z^\bullet)$. We next show that this equation characterizes optimality of (10.34).

The first-order condition for optimality of $(\theta^\circ, r^\circ) \in \mathbb{R}^{d+1}$ for the minimization (10.34) is

$$\begin{aligned} 0 &= \mathsf{E}_\varpi\big[\big(H^{\theta^\circ}(\Phi(0)) - r^\circ - H_3(\Phi(0))\big)\psi(\Phi(0))\big], \\ 0 &= \mathsf{E}_\varpi\big[H^{\theta^\circ}(\Phi(0)) - r^\circ - H_3(\Phi(0))\big]. \end{aligned}$$

The first equation is obtained on taking the gradient with respect to θ, and the second by taking the derivative with respect to r. The second equation follows from the first under the assumption that $\mathbf{1}$ is in the span of $\{\psi_i\}$. Hence (10.58) implies that (θ^*, r^*) satisfies the first-order optimality condition. □

10.10 Notes

10.10.1 Adjoints and TD-Learning

Most of this theory in this chapter was developed by the MIT group led by John Tsitsiklis in a single decade starting in the early 1990s.

The wonderful geometry surrounding TD learning is part of the dissertation of Ben Van Roy [363], which summarizes several remarkable papers, including [353–356]. Proposition 10.1 appears as [356, Theorem. 1], along with bounds for any value of λ: with $\theta^*(\lambda)$ the solution to TD(λ),

$$\|H^{\theta^*(\lambda)} - Q\|_{\varpi}^2 \leq \frac{1-\lambda\gamma}{1-\gamma}\|\widehat{Q} - Q\|_{\varpi}^2, \qquad \widehat{Q} = H^{\theta^*(1)}.$$

The use of regeneration to define the eligibility sequence (10.19a), inspired by the older representation of Poisson's equation H_3 in (10.17), was introduced in [192] upon realizing that TD(1) learning could be used to obtained unbiased gradient estimates. Nummelin's monograph [277] has had great impact in both statistics and Markov chain theory. One significant contribution of his research, highlighted in his book, is how regeneration times can be constructed for a Markov chain on a continuous state space. This may be valuable in future research.

10.10.2 Actor-Critic Methods

Glynn's research in the 1980s [142, 143] introduced likelihood ratio methods for stochastic gradient descent without bias, based in part on [313] (i.e., the sensitivity theory surveyed in Section 6.8). Just over one decade later, this was extended and applied to obtain the first unbiased stochastic gradient descent approach for reinforcement learning [238, 239] (see also [31, 32]), followed soon after with new insights in [344]. This work was the start of the actor-critic revolution that followed.

Two time-scale stochastic approximation and associated variance theory was still evolving in the late 1990s. Konda's research with Borkar [189, 190] and then Tsitsiklis [188, 193] helped to shed light on this topic, and [188, 192] introduced a major advancement in actor-critic theory and application: the compatible features property (10.47) was introduced in this work, based on the prior L_2 theory surveyed above [353–356].

The introduction of the advantage function as a means to accelerate actor-critic algorithms was proposed in [172], following [23]. Proposition 9.2 of [172] was later applied to obtain the *trust region policy optimization* (TRPO) algorithm of [311], which spawned many other approaches.

The regenerative structure leading to the i.i.d. samples $\{S_n\}$ appearing in (10.24) suggests that the policy should be frozen between regeneration times in algorithm implementation, similar to the way qSGD was applied for the mountain car example in Section 4.7.1. This was one approach in [238, 239], and similar "episodic" approaches are used in [311, 312].

The *better advantage* control variate technique is new, along with the covariance comparison Proposition 10.22.

The natural actor-critic algorithm was introduced in [173] (see also [53, 56, 151, 285]). The value of the natural gradient in terms of acceleration is explained in [2]; also, in this work and the concurrent research [48, 248] it is shown that a large class of policy gradient algorithms are globally convergent with appropriate regularization (recall $\mathcal{R}_n$ discussed after (10.46)). The recent article [368] provides an elegant Lyapunov analysis for bandit problems, and [236] contains a survey of actor-critic methods.

Absent from this chapter is any discussion on how to choose the regularizer in (10.46) for application to gradient descent. See [270] for an approach intended to improve both policy and value function approximation.

Left out of this chapter is any mention of the application of the gradient-free techniques emphasized in Sections 4.6 and 4.7 based on SPSA: The algorithms presented there were actually first proposed in a stochastic setting – a history can be found in Section 4.11. Williams's REINFORCE algorithm [376] may be the first to apply these techniques to MDPs to create *actor-only* algorithms of the form described in Section 4.6.

More recently, in [236] it is argued that SPSA is sometimes more efficient than any of the actor-critic algorithms introduced to date. Algorithm 1 of [236] is a version of SPSA, and essentially the same as the original Kiefer–Wolfowitz algorithm [182]. However, the efficiency results of [236] deserve a warning label: *Any technique involving multiple function evaluations for a single gradient estimate must take into account observation noise.* This concern is the reason for emphasis on qSGD methods #1 and #2 in Section 4.6 of this book.

10.10.3 Some Ancient History

Many in the RL community have lost track of the elegant control theory for Markov chains pioneered by Mandl [235] and Borkar [60–62]. This work is easy to miss because the language and notation is so different from what is used today in the RL literature. The authors begin with a family of transition matrices $\{T_\theta : \theta \in \mathbb{R}^d\}$ on a state space Z (in later papers, the theory is extended to general state spaces and continuous time). One goal is to find the parameter θ^* that minimizes the average cost.

A reader might dismiss this as being far from RL, since the family of models is assumed known. A closer look reveals that the observations are log-likelihoods, $L_\theta = \log(T_\theta/T_{\theta^0})$, where θ^0 is fixed but arbitrary (it plays no essential role in the theory). The setting is thus far more general than this chapter. For the very special case (10.37),

$$L_\theta(z,z') = \log \frac{T_\theta(z,z')}{T_{\theta^0}(z,z')} = \log \frac{\check{\phi}^{\theta}(u' \mid x')}{\check{\phi}^{\theta^0}(u' \mid x')}, \qquad z,\, z' = (x',u') \in \mathsf{Z}.$$

This "ancient history" deserves closer inspection, as well as the substantial concurrent work in the USSR [136].

10.10.4 Fisher Information

The interpretation of (10.54) *as Fisher information is not easily justified.*

The term arises in the theory of parameter estimation [6, 361]. In the context of this chapter, the estimation problem is the same as in Borkar's thesis [61, 62]: The input is chosen according to ϕ^{θ° for some $\theta^\circ \in \mathbb{R}^d$. Given samples $\{\Phi(k) : 0 \le k \le n\}$, the maximum likelihood estimate θ_n^{ML} of the true parameter θ° is a solution to

$$0 = \nabla_\theta \log\Big(\prod_{k=0}^{n-1} T_\theta(\Phi(k),\Phi(k+1))\Big)\Big|_{\theta=\theta_n^{\text{ML}}} = \sum_{k=1}^{n} \Lambda^\theta(\Phi(k))\Big|_{\theta=\theta_n^{\text{ML}}}.$$

In this context, the Fisher information is the normalized covariance of this statistic, evaluated at $\theta = \theta^\circ$:

$$F_n(\theta^\circ) = \frac{1}{n}\text{Cov}\Big(\sum_{k=1}^{n} \Lambda_{(k)}^{\theta^\circ}\Big).$$

Due to the martingale difference property established Lemma 10.20,

$$\lim_{n\to\infty} F_n(\theta^\circ) = \frac{1}{n}\sum_{k=1}^{n} \text{Cov}(\Lambda_{(k)}^{\theta^\circ}) = F(\theta^\circ),$$

with the right-hand side defined in (10.54).

The matrix $F_n(\theta^\circ)$ is a measure of the sensitivity of the first n observations to the parameter θ°, and from this limit we can justify the interpretation of $F(\theta^\circ)$ as the sensitivity with respect to the entire history of observations. This is an elegant conclusion for applications to parameter estimation, but doesn't explain why the inverse of $F(\theta_n)$ is a good gain for applications to actor-critic algorithms.

Appendices

Appendix A

Mathematical Background

A.1 Notation and Math Background

This section reviews basic notation and concepts from calculus and real analysis.

A.1.1 Generalities

Concerning functions and sequences:

- $\mathbb{1}_A$: Indicator function of a set A. This means that $\mathbb{1}_A(x) = 1$ when $x \in A$ and 0 otherwise.
- $J(\,\cdot\,)$: The "dot" is used to stress that J is a function of some variable.
- $\boldsymbol{u}$: Boldface is compact notation used to designate a sequence. Alternative notation: $\boldsymbol{u} = \{u_0, u_1, \ldots\} = u_{[0,\infty)}$.
- For a function $J\colon \mathbb{R}^n \to \mathbb{R}$, do not forget that the gradient ∇J is *not the same* as the derivative ∂J. The gradient is a column vector, and the derivative a row vector (the linear approximation of the scalar valued function J).

A.1.2 Topology

Concerning sets and sequences in $\mathbb{R}^n$.

- Neighborhood of $x \in \mathbb{R}^n$: a set containing x that is open.
- A set $S \subset \mathbb{R}^n$ is called compact if it is closed and bounded.
- A collection of sets $\{O_\nu : \nu \in \mathcal{N}\}$ (where the index $\mathcal{N}$ may be uncountably infinite) is called a *covering* of a set $S \subset \mathbb{R}^n$ if $O_\nu \subset \mathbb{R}^n$ for each $\nu \in \mathcal{N}$, and $S \subset \bigcup O_\nu$. Many proofs in the book make implicit use of the following characterization: A set S is compact if and only if every covering by open sets admits a finite *subcovering* (there is a finite collection of indices $\{\nu_i : 1 \le i \le N\}$ satisfying $S \subset \bigcup_{i=1}^{N} O_{\nu_i}$).
- For a function $g\colon \mathsf{Z} \to \mathbb{R}$, the span seminorm is defined by

$$\|g\|_{\mathrm{sp}} = \min_r \max_z |g(z) - r| = \tfrac{1}{2}[\max_z g(z) - \min_z g(z)].$$

  Equation (10.34) shows an example of a variation of this norm.

The following notation refers to a collection of vectors or scalars indexed by a variable $t \in \mathbb{T}$ interpreted either as time, or the number of iterations in an algorithm. Examples: $\mathbb{Z}_+ = \{0,1,2,\ldots\}$ and $\mathbb{R}_+$.

- $\sup_t a_t$: *Supremum* of the scalars $\{a_t : t \in \mathbb{T}\}$, also known as the least upper bound (LUB). Denote the set of *all* upper bounds by $S = \{r \in \mathbb{R} : a_t \le r \textit{ for each } t \in \mathbb{T}\}$. If $\{a_t\}$ is bounded from above, then this set is nonempty and can be expressed $[s_0, \infty)$ for some $s_0 \in \mathbb{R}$. This is by definition the supremum: $\sup_t a_t = \min\{s : s \in S\} = s_0$.
- The *infimum* is the greatest lower bound, or $\inf\{\alpha_t\} = -\sup\{-\alpha_t\}$.
- $\limsup_{t\to\infty} \delta_t$: *Limit supremum*, defined as follows for a scalar-valued function of t. First denote

  $$\bar{\delta}_r = \sup\{\delta_t : t \ge r\}, \qquad r \in \mathbb{T}.$$

  As r increases, $\bar{\delta}_r$ cannot increase (the supremum is taken over a smaller set). The limit as $r \to \infty$ is the limit supremum:

  $$\limsup_{t\to\infty} \delta_t = \lim_{r\to\infty} \bar{\delta}_r.$$

- $\liminf_{t\to\infty} \delta_t = -\limsup_{t\to\infty}(-\delta_t)$: *limit infimum.*
- We say the limit exists if $\liminf_{t\to\infty} \delta_t = \limsup_{t\to\infty} \delta_t$.
- For two scalar-valued functions of time $\{a_t, b_t : t \in \mathbb{T}\}$:
  - $a_t = O(b_t)$: The ratio is bounded, so that $|a_t| \le B|b_t|$ for some constant B and all $t \in \mathbb{T}$.
  - $a_t = o(b_t)$: $\lim_{t\to\infty} a_t/b_t = 0$.
- We also consider the parameter tending to zero rather than infinity. For example, this bound might be anticipated in Section 4.6:

  $$\Gamma(\theta + \varepsilon\xi) = \Gamma(\theta) + \varepsilon\xi^{\intercal}\nabla\Gamma(\theta) + o(\varepsilon), \qquad \varepsilon > 0.$$

  This is shorthand for the following limit:

  $$\lim_{\varepsilon\downarrow 0} \frac{1}{\varepsilon}\Big|\Gamma(\theta + \varepsilon\xi) - \Big\{\Gamma(\theta) + \varepsilon\xi^{\intercal}\nabla\Gamma(\theta)\Big\}\Big| = 0.$$

A.1.3 Linear Algebra

Concerning n-dimensional vectors and $n \times n$ matrices:

- $v \cdot w$: For two vectors of the same dimension, this is the inner product. Written as column vectors: $v \cdot w = v^{\intercal} w$.
- Singular values of a matrix R: $\{\sigma_1, \dots, \sigma_n\}$. First obtain the n eigenvalues $\{\lambda_i\}$ of $RR^{\intercal}$, and then define $\sigma_i = \sqrt{\lambda_i}$.
- Condition number of R: The ratio of the maximum and minimum singular values.
- Positive definite: $R > 0$ means that $x^{\intercal} R x > 0$ whenever $x \in \mathbb{R}^n$ with $x \neq 0$.
- Positive semidefinite: $R \ge 0$ means that $x^{\intercal} R x \ge 0$ whenever $x \in \mathbb{R}^n$.

  Note: In this book, the statement that R is positive definite, or positive semidefinite, carries with it the hidden assumption that the matrix is symmetric: $R = R^{\intercal}$.

▸ Matrix Inversion Lemma: For matrices A, U, and V of compatible dimension,

$$(A+UCV)^{-1} = A^{-1} - A^{-1}U\left(C^{-1}+VA^{-1}U\right)^{-1}VA^{-1}. \tag{A.1}$$

A.2 Probability and Markovian Background

A prerequisite of Part II of the book is some understanding of stochastic processes, which means you need to know the meaning of $(\Omega,\mathcal{F},\mathsf{P})$ and related machinery.

A.2.1 Events and Sample Space

Here we make precise the meaning of a probability space, and introduce the shift-operator that formally defines the Markov property.

Events

What is $(\Omega,\mathcal{F},\mathsf{P})$? First, recall that the σ-field $\mathcal{F}$ denotes the set of *events*. Each event $A \in \mathcal{F}$ must be a subset of Ω, and $\mathcal{F}$ defines the domain of the probability measure P. By "domain," we mean that $\mathsf{P}(A)$ is defined only if $A \in \mathcal{F}$, and not for any other subset $A \subset \Omega$.

To be a σ-field, $\mathcal{F}$ must be closed under countable unions and finite intersections. Please review this material, along with the definition of sub-σ-fields and conditional expectation. The first chapter of Hajek's textbook [154] is a great reference.

A (real-valued) random variable H is a mapping $H\colon \Omega \to \mathbb{R}$ that is measurable with respect to $\mathcal{F}$. That is, the set $E_c = \{\omega : H(\omega) \le c\}$ is an event (i.e., $E_c \in \mathcal{F}$) for each $c \in \mathbb{R}$. When we write $\mathsf{P}\{H \le c\}$, this is shorthand for the probability of the event: $\mathsf{P}\{E_c\}$.

A *stochastic process* is a family of random variables indexed by time. If we take discrete time, and restrict to times $k \ge 0$, then a stochastic process is a sequence of random variables denoted $\boldsymbol{X} = \{X_k : k \in \mathbb{Z}_+\}$. Subscripts are adopted in this appendix to save space, and because we need to stress that X_k is a function on Ω for each k.

Suppose that each random variable takes values in a discrete set X. For an integer $N \ge 1$, denote by $\mathcal{F}_N \subset \mathcal{F}$ the smallest σ-field that contains events of the form

$$E_{(x_0,\dots,x_N)} \stackrel{\text{def}}{=} \{\omega \in \Omega : X_k(\omega) = x_k, \quad 0 \le i \le N\} \tag{A.2}$$

for any collection $\{x_i\} \subset \mathsf{X}$. If H is a random variable on $(\Omega,\mathcal{F}_N,\mathsf{P})$, then there is a function $h\colon \mathsf{X}^{N+1} \to \mathbb{R}$ such that

$$H(\omega) = h(X_0(\omega),X_1(\omega),\dots,X_N(\omega)), \qquad \omega \in \Omega.$$

Sample Space

The set Ω is called the sample space, whose definition is a modeling choice. When studying a single stochastic process, it is convenient to choose the set of all possible state sequences. That is, each $\omega \in \Omega$ is a sequence of states:

$$\omega = (\omega_0,\omega_1,\omega_2,\dots) \quad \text{with } \omega_i \in \mathsf{X} \text{ for each } i.$$

It is interpreted as a possible realization of the stochastic process, so that $X_k(\omega) = \omega_k$. When Ω is defined in this way, the event defined in (A.2) becomes

$$E_{(x_0,\dots,x_N)} \stackrel{\text{def}}{=} \{\omega \in \Omega : \omega_i = x_i, \quad 0 \le i \le N\}. \tag{A.3}$$

And in this case, we typically take $\mathcal{F}$ to be the *smallest* σ-field that contains all events of the form (A.3), where N ranges over all integers $N \ge 0$, and the $\{x_i\}$ can take on any value in X. This σ-field contains any event of interest, including

$$\Big\{\omega \in \Omega : \lim_{T\to\infty} \frac{1}{T}\sum_{i=0}^{T-1} c(\omega_i) = \eta\Big\},$$

where $c\colon \mathsf{X} \to \mathbb{R}$ is any function, and $\eta \in \mathbb{R}$ any constant.

A.2.2 Markov Chain Basics

We will keep things simple and assume that the state space X for the Markov chain is finite or countably infinite. The transition matrix is denoted P.

For each pmf μ on X, there is a probability measure P_μ on $\mathcal{F}$ defined so that μ is the initial distribution for the chain. Consistent with definitions in Chapter 6,

$$\begin{aligned}
\mathsf{P}_\mu\{X_0 = x\} &= \mu(x), \\
\mathsf{P}_\mu\{X_k = x\} &= \sum_{x'\in\mathsf{X}} \mu(x')P^k(x',x), \qquad && x \in \mathsf{X}, \\
\mathsf{E}_\mu[g(X_k)] &= \sum_x \mathsf{P}_\mu\{X_k = x\}g(x) && \text{for any } g\colon \mathsf{X}\to\mathbb{R}.
\end{aligned}$$

When μ is degenerate, in the sense that $\mu(x) = 1$ for some x, then we write P_x and E_x.

The *shift operators* are mappings on Ω that provide compact language for complex concepts. For each k, the shift operator θ^k maps an element $\omega = \{x_0,x_1,\dots,x_n,\dots\} \in \Omega$ to a new value via

$$\theta^k\omega = \{x_k, x_{1+k},\dots,x_{n+k},\dots\}.$$

It defines a transformation on random variables H by

$$(\theta^k H)(w) = H(\theta^k\omega)\,.$$

Hence if the random variable H is of the form $H = h(X_0,X_1,\dots)$ for a function h, then

$$\theta^k H = h(X_k, X_{k+1},\dots).$$

Specializing to $H = h(X_n)$ for some n and some $h\colon \mathsf{X}\to\mathbb{R}$ gives

$$\theta^k H = h(X_{n+k})$$

and hence

$$\begin{aligned}
\mathsf{E}_\mu[\theta^k H \mid \mathcal{F}_k] &= \mathsf{E}_\mu[h(X_{n+k}) \mid \mathcal{F}_k] \\
&= \mathsf{E}_\mu[h(X_{n+k}) \mid X_k] && \text{by the Markov property} \\
&= \sum_{x'} P^n(x,x')h(x')\Big|_{x=X_k} && \text{by definition of the transition matrix.}
\end{aligned}$$

This can be generalized: For any initial distribution $X_0 \sim \mu$, any bounded random variable H, and fixed $k,n \in \mathbb{Z}_+$:

$$\mathsf{E}_\mu[\theta^k H \mid \mathcal{F}_k] = \mathsf{E}_x[H]\Big|_{x=X_k} \qquad \text{a.s. } [\mathsf{P}_\mu]. \tag{A.4}$$

This describes the (time-homogeneous) *Markov property* in a succinct way.

Note that we are viewing $\mathsf{E}_x[H]$ as a real-valued function on the state space. Henceforth, we will substitute the following:

$$\mathsf{E}_{X_k}[H] \equiv \mathsf{E}_x[H]\Big|_{x=X_k}.$$

A.2.3 Strong Markov Property

The strong Markov property is described by a significant extension of the formula (A.4). The definition of this property requires these three ingredients:

(i) A function $\tau\colon \Omega \to \mathbb{Z}_+ \cup \{\infty\}$ is a *stopping time* for $\boldsymbol{X}$ if the event $\{\tau = n\}$ lies in $\mathcal{F}_n$ for each $n \in \mathbb{Z}_+$. That is, for each n there is a function f_n such that

$$\mathbb{1}\{\tau = n\} = f_n(X_0,\dots,X_n).$$

(ii) The associated shift operator θ^τ is defined exactly as before:

$$\theta^\tau H = h(X_\tau, X_{\tau+1},\dots).$$

(iii) An associated σ-field is also defined:

$$\mathcal{F}_\tau \stackrel{\text{def}}{=} \{A \in \mathcal{F} : \{\tau = n\} \cap A \in \mathcal{F}_n \ \text{ for each } \ n \in \mathbb{Z}_+\}. \tag{A.5}$$

This is interpreted as the events that happen "up to time τ."

Two important examples of stopping times are, for any set $A \subset \mathsf{X}$,

$$\begin{aligned}\tau_A &\stackrel{\text{def}}{=} \min\{n \ge 1 : X_n \in A\},\\ \sigma_A &\stackrel{\text{def}}{=} \min\{n \ge 0 : X_n \in A\},\end{aligned}$$

known as the *first return* and *first hitting* times on A, respectively.

Proposition A.1 *For any set $A \subset \mathsf{X}$, the variables τ_A and σ_A are stopping times for $\boldsymbol{X}$.*

Proof The random variables τ_A and σ_A have this representation, for any $n \ge 1$,

$$\begin{aligned}\mathbb{1}\{\tau_A = n\} &= f_n(X_0,\dots,X_n) \stackrel{\text{def}}{=} \mathbb{1}\{X_n \in A\} \prod_{i=1}^{n-1} \mathbb{1}\{X_i \notin A\},\\ \mathbb{1}\{\sigma_A = n\} &= g_n(X_0,\dots,X_n) \stackrel{\text{def}}{=} f_n(X_0,\dots,X_n)\mathbb{1}\{X_0 \notin A\},\end{aligned}$$

where $\prod_{i=1}^0 \stackrel{\text{def}}{=} 1$ (handles the case $n=1$).

For $n=0$, we have $\mathbb{1}\{\tau_A = 0\} = f_0(X_0) \equiv 0$, and $\mathbb{1}\{\sigma_A = 0\} = g_0(X_0) \stackrel{\text{def}}{=} \mathbb{1}\{X_0 \in A\}$. $\square$

A finite-valued random variable H that is $\mathcal{F}_\tau$-measurable can be expressed as an infinite sum:

$$H = \sum_{n=0}^{\infty} h_n(X_0, \ldots, X_n)\mathbb{1}\{\tau = n\}$$

for a sequence of functions $\{h_n\}$. This is true so that we have the required property:

$$H\mathbb{1}\{\tau = k\} = h_k(X_0, \ldots, X_k)\mathbb{1}\{\tau = k\} \quad \text{is } \mathcal{F}_k\text{-measurable for each } k.$$

An example is the random variable X_τ, defined by setting $X_\tau = X_n$ on the event $\{\tau = n\}$:

$$X_\tau = \sum_{n=0}^{\infty} X_n \mathbb{1}\{\tau = n\}.$$

Finally, we come to a key definition:

Strong Markov Property $\boldsymbol{X}$ has the strong Markov property if for any initial distribution μ, any real-valued bounded random variable H, and any stopping time τ,

$$\mathsf{E}_\mu[\theta^\tau H \mid \mathcal{F}_\tau] = \mathsf{E}_{X_\tau}[H] \quad \text{a.s. } [\mathsf{P}_\mu], \quad \text{on the event } \{\tau < \infty\}. \tag{A.6}$$

Proposition A.2 *For a Markov chain* $\boldsymbol{X}$ *with a discrete time parameter, the strong Markov property always holds.*

Proof This is a consequence of decomposing the expectations on both sides of (A.6) over the set where $\{\tau = n\}$, and using the ordinary Markov property, in the form of equation (A.4), at each of these fixed times n. □

Appendix B

Markov Decision Processes

This section mirrors the optimal control theory surveyed in Chapter 3. See Section 7.1 for the definition of an MDP and surrounding notation. Throughout the remainder of the appendix, it is assumed that the state space X and action space U are finite.

B.1 Total Cost and Every Other Criterion

The definition of the total-cost value function $J^\star$ defined in (3.2) is unchanged, except that we introduce an expectation and change the notation:

$$h^\star(x) = \min_{U} \sum_{k=0}^{\infty} \mathsf{E}_x[c(\Phi_k)], \tag{B.1}$$

where $\Phi_k = (X_k, U_k)$, the minimum is over all admissible policies, and the subscript indicates that $X_0 = x$.

When finite, this value function solves the Bellman equation

$$h^\star(x) = \min_u \Big\{ c(x,u) + \sum_{x'} P_u(x,x') h^\star(x') \Big\}, \qquad x \in \mathsf{X}.$$

This is very similar to the dynamic programming equation (3.5) for $J^\star$, especially when expressed in the equivalent sample path form:

$$h^\star(X_k) = c(\Phi_k) + \mathsf{E}[h^\star(X_{k+1}) \mid \mathcal{F}_k] \qquad \text{when } U_k = \phi^\star(X_k).$$

Also similar to the deterministic setting, the optimal policy is any minimizer:

$$\phi^\star(x) \in \arg\min_u \Big\{ c(x,u) + \sum_{x'} P_u(x,x') h^\star(x') \Big\}, \qquad x \in \mathsf{X}.$$

There is, however, a significant difference in the stochastic control formulation: In most cases, we find that $\mathsf{E}_x[c(\Phi_k)]$ converges to a *strictly positive* constant, as $k \to \infty$, meaning that $h^\star$ is not finite. *Why then should we care about* (B.1)*?*

B.1.1 Total Cost in Many Flavors

What follows are several examples of optimization criteria for MDPs, and how they can be transformed to the total-cost criterion.

Shortest Path Problem (SPP) Given a target set $S \subset \mathsf{X}$ and a terminal cost $V_0 \colon S \to \mathbb{R}$, define for each $x \in S^c$:

$$h^\star(x) = \min_{\boldsymbol{U}} \mathsf{E}_x\Big[\sum_{k=0}^{\tau_S - 1} c(\Phi_k) + V_0(X_{\tau_S})\Big].$$

This is transformed to the total-cost problem through the enlargement of X to include a *graveyard state* denoted $\blacktriangle$. The "graveyard property" indicates that $P_u(\blacktriangle,\blacktriangle) = 1$ for each u, and we also impose $P_u(x,\blacktriangle) = 1$, for $x \in S$ and any u. The cost function is also modified: $c(x,u) = V_0(x)$ for $x \in S$, and $c(\blacktriangle,u) = 0$ for each u. Under these conventions, the value function for the SPP can be represented as (B.1).

Discounted-Cost Value Function For a discount factor $\gamma \in [0,1)$,

$$h^\star(x) = \min_{\boldsymbol{U}} \sum_{k=0}^{\infty} \gamma^k \mathsf{E}_x[c(\Phi_k)]. \tag{B.2}$$

Enlarge the state space for the MDP with a geometric random variable T with parameter γ, and independent of everything:

$$\mathsf{P}\{T \ge k \mid \Phi_0^\infty\} = \gamma^k.$$

Then $\Psi_k = (X_k, B_k)$ is a Markovian state, with $B_k = \mathbb{1}\{T \ge k\}$. Independence of $\boldsymbol{X}$ and $\boldsymbol{B}$ implies that

$$\gamma^k \mathsf{E}_x[c(\Phi_k)] = \mathsf{E}_x[c(\Phi_k) B_k].$$

Consequently,

$$h^\star(x) = \min_{\boldsymbol{U}} \mathsf{E}_x\Big[\sum_{k=0}^{\infty} \widehat{c}(\Psi_k, U_k)\Big]$$

with $\widehat{c}(z,u) = c(x,u)b$ when $z = (x,b)$.

Most surprising is the transformation of the *average-cost* criterion:

Average Cost Optimal Control Denote the following for any input sequence:

$$\eta_{\boldsymbol{U}}(x) = \limsup_{n\to\infty} \frac{1}{n} \sum_{k=0}^{n-1} \mathsf{E}_x[c(\Phi_k)]. \tag{B.3}$$

The minimum over all admissible inputs is denoted $\eta^\star(x)$.

The minimum is typically independent of x, and the solution is obtained via an SPP with modified cost. Consider

$$h^\star(x) = \min_{\boldsymbol{U}} \mathsf{E}_x\Big[\sum_{k=0}^{\tau_S - 1} \{c(\Phi_k) - \eta^*\}\Big] \tag{B.4}$$

with $S = \{x^\bullet\}$ a singleton, so this is the first return time used in Theorem 6.3:

$$\tau_\bullet = \min\{k \geq 1 : X_k = x^\bullet\}. \tag{B.5}$$

If $\pi^\star(x^\bullet) > 0$, with $\pi^\star$ the invariant pmf under the optimal policy, then $h^\star$ solves the *average-cost optimality equation* (ACOE):

$$\min_u \{c(x,u) + P_u h^\star(x)\} = h^\star(x) + \eta^\star. \tag{B.6}$$

The function $h^\star$ is known as the *relative value function*, and the minimizer is a stationary policy that achieves the optimal average cost:

$$\phi^\star(x) = \arg\min_u \{c(x,u) + P_u h^\star(x)\}.$$

B.2 Computational Aspects of MDPs

The value iteration and policy iteration (or improvement) algorithms each have extensions to the MDP setting. These techniques are reviewed here, along with a linear programming approach that is related to the LPs introduced in Section 3.5.

This section is devoted to the ACOE (B.6). The relative value function $h^\star$ is not unique – we can always add a constant to obtain a new solution. It is convenient here to impose the additional constraint $h^\star(x^\bullet) = \eta^\star$, where $x^\bullet$ is some distinguished state. Under mild conditions, the solution is then unique, and we eliminate $\eta^\star$ from the ACOE:

$$\min_u \{c(x,u) + P_u h^\star(x)\} = h^\star(x) + h^\star(x^\bullet). \tag{B.7}$$

Algorithm design begins with the representation of (B.7) as a fixed-point equation: Let T denote the *functional* that takes any function $h\colon \mathsf{X} \to \mathbb{R}$, and creates a new function via the following:

$$T(h)\Big|_x = \min_u \{c(x,u) + P_u h(x)\} - h(x^\bullet), \qquad x \in \mathsf{X}.$$

The ACOE can be expressed as the fixed-point equation:

$$h^\star = T(h^\star). \tag{B.8}$$

There are two common approaches to solve a fixed-point equation: The first one is successive approximation, which leads to value iteration algorithm (VIA). The second approach is the Newton–Raphson method, which leads to the policy improvement algorithm (PIA) method.

B.2.1 Value Iteration and Successive Approximation

In successive approximation, we initialize with a function $h_0\colon \mathsf{X} \to \mathbb{R}$, and then for $n \geq 0$,

$$h_{n+1}(x) = T(h_n)\Big|_x = \min_u \{c(x,u) + P_u h_n(x)\} - h_n(x^\bullet), \qquad x \in \mathsf{X}. \tag{B.9}$$

The value iteration algorithm is obtained by disregarding the constant $h_n(x^\bullet)$.

Value Iteration Algorithm (VIA)

VIA is initialized with a function $V_0 \colon \mathsf{X} \to \mathbb{R}$. Then, for each $n \geq 0$,

$$V_{n+1}(x) = \min_u \{c(x,u) + P_u V_n(x)\}. \tag{B.10}$$

A policy at stage n is defined as the minimizer:

$$\phi_n(x) = \arg\min_u \{c(x,u) + P_u V_n(x)\}.$$

VIA solves a finite horizon optimal control problem:

Proposition B.1 *At stage n, we have a sequence of policies $(\phi_0, \dots, \phi_{n-1})$. The function V_n can be expressed as*

$$V_n(x) = \min \mathsf{E}_x \Big[\sum_{k=0}^{n-1} c(X_k, U_k) + V_0(X_n)\Big], \tag{B.11}$$

where the minimum is over all admissible inputs. There is a minimizer that is Markov, but not necessarily stationary:

$$U_k^\star = \phi_{n-k}(X_k^\star), \quad 0 \leq k \leq n-1. \tag{B.12}$$

□

Suppose that $\{V_n\}$ are obtained using VIA, and $\{h_n\}$ are obtained using successive approximation, with common initialization $h_0 \equiv V_0$. It can be shown by induction on n that

$$h_n(x) - h_n(x^\bullet) = V_n(x) - V_n(x^\bullet) \quad \text{for each } x \text{ and each } n \geq 0.$$

Consequently, we have convergence under mild assumptions [45]:

$$\lim_{n\to\infty} [V_n(x) - V_n(x^\bullet)] = h^\star(x). \tag{B.13}$$

It is argued in [126] that the rate of convergence can be improved by introducing additional "control loops" in the VIA recursion (B.10).

B.2.2 Policy Improvement and Newton–Raphson

The second well-known algorithm is far more complex per iteration, but often converges very quickly.

Policy Improvement Algorithm (PIA)

Given an initial policy ϕ_0, a sequence (ϕ_n, h_n) is constructed as follows: At stage n, given ϕ_n,

(i) solve Poisson's equation

$$P_n h_n = h_n - c_n + \eta_n,$$

where $c_n(x) = c(x,\phi_n(x))$ for each x, η_n is the steady-state cost using the policy ϕ_n, and P_n is the transition matrix obtained when the chain is controlled using ϕ_n;

(ii) construct a new policy:

$$\phi_{n+1}(x) \in \arg\min_u \{c(x,u) + P_u h_n(x)\}, \qquad x \in \mathsf{X}. \tag{B.14}$$

The PIA is in fact a special case of the Newton–Raphson method, in which the function T appearing in (B.8) is replaced by its linearization $\widehat{T}_n$ to obtain a sequence of approximations to $h^\star$.

Given some function h_n, the mapping $\widehat{T}_n$ is defined via a first-order Taylor expansion,

$$\widehat{T}_n(h) \stackrel{\text{def}}{=} T(h_n) + D_n(h - h_n), \tag{B.15}$$

where $D_n = \nabla T\,(h_n)$ is a $d \times d$ matrix when X consists of d elements. The Newton–Raphson method then defines h_{n+1} to be a solution of the linear equation,

$$h = \widehat{T}_n(h) = T(h_n) + D_n(h - h_n). \tag{B.16}$$

This is illustrated in Figure B.1

The functional T may not be differentiable, but we can always find a *subgradient* D_n. This means that for any h_n and any other function g,

$$T(h_n + g) \leq T(h_n) + D_n(g),$$

where the inequality is interpreted pointwise (remember, $T(h)$ and $D(g)$ are functions on X). The existence of subgradients is assured because T is a concave function of its arguments: For any two functions g,h,

$$T(\alpha h + (1-\alpha)g) \geq \alpha T(h) + (1-\alpha)T(g), \qquad 0 \leq \alpha \leq 1.$$

The function $h - T(h)$ is *convex*, as illustrated in Figure B.1.

The following lemma shows how to obtain the gradient of $T(h)$.

Lemma B.2 *For any function $h\colon \mathsf{X} \to \mathbb{R}$, let ϕ_+ denote a policy satisfying*

$$\phi_+(x) \in \arg\min_u \{c(x,u) + P_u h\,(x)\}, \qquad x \in \mathsf{X}.$$

Let $P_+ = P_{\phi_+}$ and let $S_\bullet$ denote the substitution operator, defined for any function $g\colon \mathsf{X} \to \mathbb{R}$ by

$$S_\bullet g\big|_x = g(x^\bullet), \qquad x \in \mathsf{X}.$$

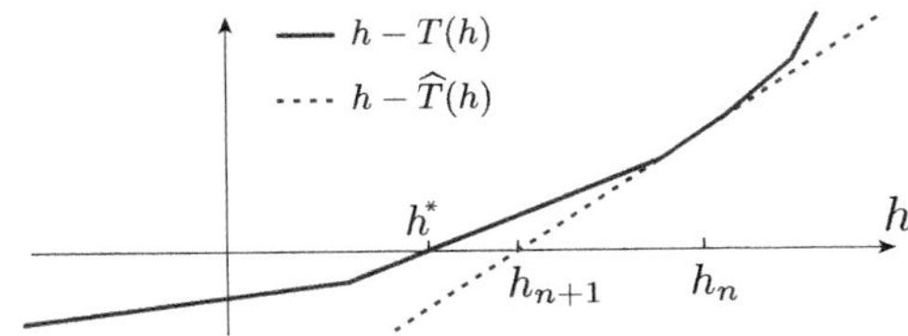

Figure B.1 PIA interpreted as an application of Newton–Raphson. The functional T is piecewise linear for a finite-state/finite-action MDP.

Then a subgradient of T at h is given by $D_h = P_+ - S_\bullet$.

Proof To prove the lemma, we must establish the following pointwise bound for any function g:

$$T(h+g) \leq T(h) + P_+ g - g(x^\bullet).$$

It will then follow that $D_h(g) = P_+ g - g(x^\bullet)$.

Denote the evaluation $T(h+g)$ at x by $T(h+g)\big|_x$. The notation $Ph\,(x)$ and $Ph\big|_x$ both denote the evaluation of Ph at x. Then, on setting $c_+(x) = c(x,\phi_+(x))$,

$$\begin{aligned} T(h+g)\Big|_x &= \min_u \{c(x,u) + P_u(h+g)\Big|_x\} - h(x^\bullet) - g(x^\bullet) \\ &\leq c_+(x) + P_+(h+g)\,(x) - h(x^\bullet) - g(x^\bullet) \\ &= \{c_+(x) + P_+ h\,(x) - h(x^\bullet)\} - g(x^\bullet) + P_+ g\,(x) \\ &= T(h)\Big|_x - g(x^\bullet) + P_+ g\,(x), \end{aligned} \tag{B.17}$$

which is the desired bound (the inequality is obtained on replacing the minimum over u with the particular value $u = \phi_+(x)$). □

Given the function h_n, denote $\phi_{n+1}(x) \in \arg\min_u\{c(x,u) + P_u h_n\,(x)\}$, and denote the resulting transition law and cost function as follows:

$$P_{n+1} = P_{\phi_{n+1}}, \qquad c_{n+1}(x,u) = c(x,\phi_{n+1}(x)).$$

That is, ϕ_{n+1} is the feedback law ϕ_+ given in the lemma with $h = h_n$, and P_{n+1} is precisely P_+. Letting $g = h_{n+1} - h_n$, the lemma provides the following representation of the Newton–Raphson update (B.16):

$$\begin{aligned} h_{n+1}(x) &= T(h_n)\Big|_x + P_{n+1}(h_{n+1} - h_n)\,(x) - h_{n+1}(x^\bullet) + h_n(x^\bullet) \\ &= \{c_{n+1}(x) + P_{n+1} h_n\,(x) - h_n(x^\bullet)\} \\ &\qquad + P_{n+1}(h_{n+1} - h_n)\,(x) - h_{n+1}(x^\bullet) + h_n(x^\bullet). \end{aligned} \tag{B.18}$$

Canceling terms, we conclude that h_{n+1} satisfies the following fixed-point equation,

$$P_{n+1} h_{n+1}\,(x) = h_{n+1}\,(x) - c_{n+1}(x) + h_{n+1}(x^\bullet). \tag{B.19}$$

On writing $\eta_{n+1} = h_{n+1}(x^\bullet)$, the identity (B.19) becomes Poisson's equation:

$$P_{n+1} h_{n+1} = h_{n+1} - c_{n+1} + \eta_{n+1}.$$

This is precisely the PIA.

B.2.3 LP Formulations

The basic idea of the LP approach is as follows. Let ϖ denote a pmf on state-action pairs $(x,u) \in \mathsf{X} \times \mathsf{U}$. We denote by $\mathcal{G}$ the set of all possible limits of the empirical pmf:

$$\widetilde{\varpi}_N(x,u) = \frac{1}{N}\sum_{k=0}^{N-1} \mathbb{1}\{X_k = x,\, U_k = u\}, \qquad x \in \mathsf{X},\, u \in \mathsf{U}.$$

That is, $\varpi \in \mathcal{G}$ if there is an admissible input $\boldsymbol{U}$ and a subsequence $\{N_i\}$ such that

$$\lim_{i\to\infty} \widetilde{\varpi}_{N_i}(x,u) = \varpi(x,u) \qquad \text{all } x,u. \tag{B.20}$$

It is known that $\mathcal{G}$ is a polyhedron for which a simple characterization is easily obtained:

(1) Any $\varpi \in \mathcal{G}$ is a pmf on $\mathsf{X} \times \mathsf{U}$.
A factorization is obtained via Bayes's rule:

$$\varpi(x,u) = \pi(x)\breve{\phi}(u|x), \tag{B.21}$$

where $\pi(x) = \sum_u \varpi(x,u), \quad \breve{\phi}(u \mid x) = \dfrac{\varpi(x,u)}{\pi(x)}, \qquad \text{all } x,u.$
Let $P_{\breve{\phi}}$ denote the transition matrix

$$P_{\breve{\phi}}(x,x') = \sum_u \breve{\phi}(u \mid x) P_u(x,x').$$

(2) π is an invariant pmf for $P_{\breve{\phi}}$. The main step in the proof is the following consequence of (B.20):

$$\lim_{i\to\infty} \varpi_{N_i+1}(x,u) = \varpi(x,u) \qquad \text{all } x,u.$$

We arrive at a DPLP for the ACOE:

ACOE Linear Program

$$\eta^\star = \min \quad \sum_{u,x} \varpi(x,u)c(x,u) \tag{B.22a}$$

$$\text{s.t.} \quad \sum_{u,x} \varpi(x,u)P_u(x,x') = \sum_u \varpi(x',u), \quad x' \in \mathsf{X}, \tag{B.22b}$$

$$\sum_{u,x} \varpi(x,u) = 1, \qquad \varpi \geq 0. \tag{B.22c}$$

Justification is provided in the following. See [63] or [254, section 9.2] for details.

Proposition B.3 *The set $\mathcal{G}$ is the convex set characterized by (B.22b, B.22c). The optimizer $\varpi^\star$ defines an optimal policy $\phi^\star$ via the factorization* (B.21). □

The LP approach is more flexible to extensions, such as to multi-objective optimal control: Given a collection of functions $\{c^i\}$ and bounds $\{\eta^i\}$, we can consider the following:

$$\min \quad \langle \varpi, c\rangle \qquad \text{s.t.} \quad \varpi \in \mathcal{G}.$$
$$\langle \varpi, c^i\rangle \leq \eta^i \qquad \text{each } i.$$

For Those of You Who Know Something about Linear Programs

First, the extreme points of this LP admit the factorization (B.21) with $\check{\phi}$ deterministic ($\phi(u \mid x)$ is zero or one for each x,u) and π "ergodic" (the chain restricted to the support of π is irreducible).

There is something called the *dual* of an LP:

$$\min c^{\intercal} x \quad \text{s.t. } Ax \leq b, x \geq 0 \qquad \longleftrightarrow \qquad \max b^{\intercal} \xi \quad \text{s.t. } A^{\intercal} \xi \geq c, \xi \geq 0.$$

The dual of (B.22) can be reduced to a version of the ACOE:

$$\begin{aligned} \max \quad & z \\ \text{s.t.} \quad & c(x) - z + \sum_{y \in \mathsf{X}} P_u(x,y) h(y) - h(x) \geq 0, \qquad x \in \mathsf{X},\ u \in \mathsf{U}. \end{aligned} \tag{B.23}$$

This looks very much like the DPLP (3.36), and its dual (5.82) resembles (B.22).

Appendix C

Partial Observations and Belief States

We now have an observation process $\boldsymbol{Y}$, and no direct measurements of the state process $\boldsymbol{X}$. This short survey concerns a model in which $\boldsymbol{X}$, $\boldsymbol{Y}$, and the input process $\boldsymbol{U}$ take values in finite sets, denoted X, Y, and U.

We continue to write $\Phi_n = (X_n, U_n)$ when convenient.

C.1 POMDP Model

The state process is a controlled Markov chain as before. The observation Y_n is assumed to be a noisy, memoryless measurement of the state X_n, in the following sense: A family of pmfs on Y is given, denoted $\{q(\cdot \mid x) : x \in \mathsf{X}\}$. For each $y \in \mathsf{Y}$ and $x \in \mathsf{X}$,

$$\mathsf{P}\{Y_n = y \mid \Phi_k, k \le n\} = q(y \mid x) \qquad \text{on the event } X_n = x. \tag{C.1}$$

Our goal remains the same: We wish to optimize some performance criterion. This may be discounted cost, finite horizon, or the average cost, which has been the focus of the appendices up to now:

$$\eta = \limsup_{T \to \infty} \frac{1}{T} \sum_{k=0}^{T-1} c(\Phi_n).$$

The optimization problem becomes more complex when only $\boldsymbol{Y}$ is available for choosing $\boldsymbol{U}$.

It is rarely true that the optimal input is of the form $U_n = \phi(Y_n)$. We need the full history in general: For a sequence of functions $\{\phi_n\}$,

$$U_n = \phi_n(Y_0, \dots, Y_n). \tag{C.2}$$

This sounds horrible, but we will soon discover beautiful structure.

The combined dynamics can be realized through coupled system equations:

$$\begin{aligned} X_{n+1} &= f(X_n, U_n, N_{n+1}), \\ Y_{n+1} &= g(X_{n+1}, W_{n+1}), \qquad n \ge 0, \end{aligned} \tag{C.3}$$

where $(\boldsymbol{N}, \boldsymbol{W})$ is i.i.d., and mutually independent. This gives

$$p(x' \mid x, u) \stackrel{\text{def}}{=} P_u(x, x') = \mathsf{P}\{f(x, u, N(1)) = x'\} \quad \text{and} \quad q(y' \mid x') = \mathsf{P}\{g(x', W(1)) = y'\}.$$

It is sometimes useful to view the pair $(\boldsymbol{X},\boldsymbol{Y})$ as the state process for an MDP model:

$$
\begin{aligned}
P\{X_{n+1} = x', Y_{n+1} = y' \mid X_n = x, Y_n = y, U_n = u\} \\
&= \mathsf{P}\{f(x,u,N_{n+1}) = x' \quad \text{and} \quad g(x',W_{n+1}) = y'\} \\
&= p(x' \mid x, u) q(y' \mid x').
\end{aligned}
\tag{C.4}
$$

This gives the controlled transition matrix for the joint state-observation process:

$$
T_u(z,z') = p(x' \mid x, u) q(y' \mid x'), \qquad \text{with } z = (x,y) \text{ and } z' = (x',y'). \tag{C.5}
$$

Given observations of $(\boldsymbol{X},\boldsymbol{Y})$, we can apply our machinery to compute or approximate an optimal policy $U_n = \phi^\star(X_n,Y_n)$.

However, the *PO* in POMDP stands for *partial observations*. This means that inputs are restricted to the form (C.2) We need to develop new tools to respect the limited information for control that is captured in (C.2).

C.2 A Fully Observed MDP

Belief State The partially observed MDP can be recast as fully observed, provided we change our definition of "state."

The new state process $\{b_n : n \geq 0\}$ is also called the *belief state*, and coincides with the conditional distribution of the state given the observations: For each $x \in \mathsf{X}$,

$$
b_n(x) = \mathsf{P}\{X_n = x \mid \mathcal{Y}_n\}, \tag{C.6}
$$

in which $\mathcal{Y}_n = \sigma(Y_k : k \leq n)$.

The belief state evolves on what is called the *simplex* of pmfs on X, denoted $\mathcal{S}$. If X consists of *d* states, then

$$
\mathcal{S} = \Big\{ b \in \mathbb{R}^d_+ : \sum_i b(i) = 1 \Big\}.
$$

The definition implies that for any function h,

$$
\mathsf{E}[h(X_n) \mid \mathcal{Y}_n] = \sum_{x \in \mathsf{X}} b_n(x) h(x).
$$

In this short survey, we restrict to the finite horizon optimal control problem to explain the MDP construction. The extension to average cost and discounted cost will be obvious.

For fixed $N \geq 1$ and $0 \leq n < N$, assume that some input has been applied for $k < n$, and denote the *cost to go* function,

$$
V^\star_{n,N} = \min_{U_n^{N-1}} \mathsf{E}\Big[\sum_{k=n}^{N-1} c(\Phi_k) + V_0(X_N) \mid \mathcal{Y}_n \Big]. \tag{C.7}
$$

This is *random* and grows in complexity with increasing n, since $V^\star_{n,N}$ is a function of $Y_0, \ldots, Y_n$. In order to mimic the characterization of optimal policies from the fully observed setting, we require a *sufficient statistic* $\boldsymbol{I} = \{I_0, \dots, I_n, \dots\}$ evolving on some fixed space, such that for some function $\mathcal{V}^\star_{n,N}$,

$$V^\star_{n,N} = \mathcal{V}^\star_{n,N}(I_n).$$

Since this is a time-homogeneous model, we might hope to have $\mathcal{V}^\star_{n,N} = \mathcal{V}^\star_{N-n}(I_n)$ for a sequence of functions $\{\mathcal{V}^\star_m : m \geq 0\}$.

The amazing conclusion is this: A sufficient statistic does exist, with $I_n = b_n$. For this reason, the belief state b_n is sometimes called the *information state*. Moreover, the stochastic process $\boldsymbol{b} = \{b_0, b_1, \dots\}$ *is itself a controlled Markov model that is fully observed.* The Markov property is explained in Proposition C.1. A deterministic stationary Markov policy is defined via a feedback law $U_n = \Phi(b_n)$, where $\Phi\colon \mathcal{S} \to \mathsf{U}$.

Proposition C.1 states that there is a mapping $\mathcal{M}\colon \mathcal{S} \times \mathsf{Y} \times \mathsf{U} \to \mathcal{S}$ such that for each $n \geq 0$,

$$b_{n+1} = \mathcal{M}(b_n, Y_{n+1}, U_n), \qquad n \geq 0. \tag{C.8}$$

From this, a specific formula for the controlled transition kernel for $\{b_n\}$ is obtained in (C.9). The proof is postponed to Section C.3

Proposition C.1 (Transition Law for the Belief State) *The following Markov properties hold: For any admissible input $\boldsymbol{U}$, any set $S \subset \mathcal{S}$, and any $y' \in \mathsf{Y}$,*

$$\mathsf{P}\{b_{n+1} \in S\,,\, Y_{n+1} = y' \mid \mathcal{Y}_n\} = \mathsf{P}\{b_{n+1} \in S\,,\, Y_{n+1} = y' \mid b_n, U_n\},$$
$$\mathsf{P}\{b_{n+1} \in S \mid \mathcal{Y}_n\} = \mathsf{P}\{b_{n+1} \in S \mid b_n, U_n\}.$$

The transition kernel for the belief state is given as follows: For any $b \in \mathcal{S}$, $u \in \mathsf{U}$, and any $S \subset \mathcal{S}$:

$$\begin{aligned} &\mathsf{P}\{b_{n+1} \in S\,, \mid b_n = b,\, U_n = u\} \\ &\qquad = \sum_{y'} \mathbb{1}\{\mathcal{M}(b, y', u) \in S\} \mathsf{P}\{\, Y_{n+1} = y' \mid b_n = b,\, U_n = u\} \\ &\qquad = \sum_{y'} \mathbb{1}\{\mathcal{M}(b, y', u) \in S\} \Big(\sum_{x, x' \in \mathsf{X}} b(x) P_u(x, x') q(y' \mid x') \Big). \end{aligned} \tag{C.9}$$

Moreover, for any function $F\colon \mathcal{S} \times \mathsf{Y} \to \mathbb{R}$,

$$\begin{aligned} &\mathsf{E}[F(b_{n+1}, Y_{n+1}) \mid \mathcal{Y}_n\,;\, b_n = b,\, U_n = u\}] \\ &\qquad = \sum_{y'} \sum_{x, x'} b(x) P_u(x, x') q(y' \mid x') F(\mathcal{M}(b, y', u), y'). \end{aligned}$$

□

The representation of the cost to go is given in the following:

Proposition C.2 *For any $b \in \mathcal{S}$ and $u \in \mathsf{U}$, denote the following:*

$$\mathcal{C}(b, u) \stackrel{\text{def}}{=} \sum_x b(x) c(x, u)\,, \qquad \mathcal{V}_0(b) \stackrel{\text{def}}{=} \sum_x b(x) V_0(x). \tag{C.10}$$

Then the cost to go admits the representation

$$V^\star_{n,N} = \mathcal{V}^\star_{N-n}(b_n) \stackrel{\text{def}}{=} \min_{U_n^{N-1}} \mathsf{E}\Big[\sum_{k=n}^{N-1} \mathcal{C}(b_k, U_k) \; + \; \mathcal{V}_0(b_N) \mid b_n\Big]. \tag{C.11}$$

Proof The cost function $c\colon \mathsf{X}\times\mathsf{U} \to \mathbb{R}$ and the terminal cost V_0 are replaced with functions of the belief state by applying the smoothing property of conditional expectation: For any admissible input $\boldsymbol{U}$ and $k, N \geq n$,

$$\begin{aligned}
\mathsf{E}[c(X_k, U_k) \mid \mathcal{Y}_n] &= \mathsf{E}\big[\mathcal{C}(b_k, U_k) \mid \mathcal{Y}_n\big],\\
\mathcal{C}(b_k, U_k) &\stackrel{\text{def}}{=} \sum_x b_k(x) c(x, U_k) = \mathsf{E}\big[c(X_k, U_k) \mid \mathcal{Y}_k\big].
\end{aligned}$$

$$\begin{aligned}
\mathsf{E}[V_0(X_N) \mid \mathcal{Y}_n] &= \mathsf{E}\big[\mathcal{V}_0(b_N) \mid \mathcal{Y}_n\big],\\
\mathcal{V}_0(b_N) &\stackrel{\text{def}}{=} \sum_x b_N(x) V_0(x) = \mathsf{E}[V_0(X_N) \mid \mathcal{Y}_N].
\end{aligned}$$

Consequently, the (possibly nonoptimal) cost to go admits the representation

$$\begin{aligned}
V_{n,N} &= \mathsf{E}\Big[\sum_{k=n}^{N-1} c(X_k, U_k) \; + \; V_0(X_N) \mid \mathcal{Y}_n\Big]\\
&= \mathsf{E}\Big[\sum_{k=n}^{N-1} \mathcal{C}(b_k, U_k) \; + \; \mathcal{V}_0(b_N) \mid \mathcal{Y}_n\Big]\\
&= \mathsf{E}\Big[\sum_{k=n}^{N-1} \mathcal{C}(b_k, U_k) \; + \; \mathcal{V}_0(b_N) \mid b_n \,, U_n\Big],
\end{aligned}$$

where the final equality follows from Proposition C.1. On minimizing over admissible inputs, we obtain the representation (C.11). □

Besides the remaining work involved in establishing Proposition C.1, the biggest open question is, *can we ever solve a POMDP?* A solution can be found for the special case of linear Gaussian models because in this case b_n is Gaussian and hence characterized by the conditional mean and covariance.

We could potentially apply value iteration to obtain the optimal policy. Given an initial value function $\mathcal{V}_0\colon \mathcal{S} \to \mathbb{R}$, we define the following by induction:

$$\mathcal{V}_n(b) = \min_u \Big\{\mathcal{C}(b,u) + \sum_{y'} \sum_{x,x'} b(x) P_u(x,x') q(y' \mid x') \mathcal{V}_{n-1}(\mathcal{M}(b,y',u))\Big\}, \quad b \in \mathcal{S}.$$

Or, if you are interested in the average-cost optimization problem you would solve the dynamic programming equation:

$$\eta^\star + H^\star(b) = \min_u \Big\{\mathcal{C}(b,u) + \sum_{y'} \sum_{x,x'} b(x) P_u(x,x') q(y' \mid x') H^\star(\mathcal{M}(b,y',u))\Big\},$$

where $H^\star\colon \mathcal{S} \to \mathbb{R}$ and $\eta^\star$ is the optimal average cost for the partially observed optimal control problem.

While it is unfortunate that we have to move from the finite state space X to the simplex of pmfs $\mathcal{S}$, we are fortunate that the value functions have simple structure: It can be shown by induction that $\mathcal{V}_n$ is concave and piecewise linear as a function of $b \in \mathcal{S}$ [201, 326]. You would rightly conclude that $H^\star$ is also concave as a function of b. This opens the door to simple approximation architectures for approximate dynamic programming or reinforcement learning.

The next section contains the proof of Proposition C.1.

C.3 Belief State Dynamics

A more complete and detailed exposition of much of these notes can be found in Hajek's book [154] or Van Handel's *Lecture Notes on Hidden Markov Models* [362]. However, Proposition C.1 giving the transition law for the belief state is more difficult to find (this is usually taken for granted).

Recall that $(\boldsymbol{X}, \boldsymbol{Y})$ is regarded as the state process for an MDP model with transition law given in (C.5). This notation is too complex for our purposes. Our interest is in constructing a recursive algorithm that generates the belief state – a function of x – so we suppress the role of observations. For each n, given the observed quantities $y_n = Y_n$ and $u_{n-1} = U_{n-1}$, denote (following the notation of (C.5))

$$\rho_n(x_n \mid x_{n-1}) = p(x_n \mid x_{n-1}, u_{n-1}) q(y_n \mid x_n), \tag{C.12}$$

where it is understood that x_{n-1} and x_n are *variables*. In contrast, y_n and u_{n-1} appearing in (C.12) are *not variables*: They are observed quantities.

We first consider a (seemingly) more complex problem: Given a sequence $x_0^n \in \mathsf{X}^{n+1}$, we want to find the conditional probability that $X_0^n \stackrel{\text{def}}{=} (X_0, \dots, X_n) = x_0^n$, denoted

$$\beta_n(x_0^n) \stackrel{\text{def}}{=} \mathsf{P}\{X_0^n = x_0^n \mid \mathcal{Y}_n\}.$$

This is known as a *smoothing problem* since we wish to estimate past states given past and present observations. The pmf β_n can be expressed in terms of the observed input and output sequences u_0^{n-1}, y_0^n: This is obtained using Bayes's rule:

$$\begin{aligned}
\beta_n(x_0^n) &= \mathsf{P}\{X_0^n = x_0^n \mid Y_0^n = y_0^n, U_0^{n-1} = u_0^{n-1}\} \\
&= \frac{\mathsf{P}\{X_0^n = x_0^n \text{ and } Y_0^n = y_0^n, U_0^{n-1} = u_0^{n-1}\}}{\mathsf{P}\{Y_0^n = y_0^n, U_0^{n-1} = u_0^{n-1}\}}.
\end{aligned}$$

The denominator can be regarded as a normalizing constant (it does not depend on x_0^n). Letting $\beta_n^\bullet$ denote the numerator gives

$$\begin{aligned}
\beta_n^\bullet(x_0^n) &= \mathsf{P}\{X_0^n = x_0^n \text{ and } Y_0^n = y_0^n, U_0^{n-1} = u_0^{n-1}\} \\
&= \rho_n(x_n \mid x_{n-1}) \times \cdots \times \rho_1(x_1 \mid x_0) \times \mu(x_0),
\end{aligned}$$

where the pmf μ defines the distribution for X_0.

This is true for any n, so that we obtain a recursive relationship,

$$\beta_n^\bullet(x_0^n) = \rho_n(x_n, \mid x_{n-1}) \beta_{n-1}^\bullet(x_0^{n-1}). \tag{C.13}$$

We then obtain β_n through normalization, since we know it is a pmf:

$$\beta_n(x_0^n) = \kappa_n \beta_n^\bullet(x_0^n), \qquad \kappa_n^{-1} = \sum_{x'_0,\dots,x'_n} \beta_n^\bullet(x'_0,\dots,x'_n).$$

What about the original problem? We again have Bayes's rule:

$$\begin{aligned} b_n(x_n) &= \mathsf{P}\{X_n = x_n \mid Y_0^n = y_0^n, U_0^{n-1} = u_0^{n-1}\} \\ &= \frac{\mathsf{P}\{X_n = x_n \text{ and } Y_0^n = y_0^n, U_0^{n-1} = u_0^{n-1}\}}{\mathsf{P}\{Y_0^n = y_0^n, U_0^{n-1} = u_0^{n-1}\}}. \end{aligned}$$

The numerator, denoted $b_n^\bullet(x_n)$, is obtained from $\beta_n^\bullet$ as follows:

$$\begin{aligned} b_n^\bullet(x_n) &= \mathsf{P}\{X_n = x_n \text{ and } Y_0^n = y_0^n, U_0^{n-1} = u_0^{n-1}\} \\ &= \sum_{x'_0,\dots,x'_{n-1}} \beta_n^\bullet(x'_0,\dots,x'_{n-1},x_n). \end{aligned}$$

Applying (C.13) gives a recursive formula for the unnormalized belief state:

$$\begin{aligned} b_n^\bullet(x_n) &= \sum_{x'_0,\dots,x'_{n-1}} \rho_n(x_n \mid x'_{n-1}) \beta_{n-1}^\bullet(x'_0,\dots,x'_{n-1}) \\ &= \sum_{x'_{n-1}} \rho_n(x_n \mid x'_{n-1}) \Big[\sum_{x'_0,\dots,x'_{n-2}} \beta_{n-1}^\bullet(x'_0,\dots,x'_{n-1}) \Big]. \end{aligned}$$

From this, we obtain the linear dynamics:

$$b_n^\bullet(x') = \sum_x \rho_n(x' \mid x) b_{n-1}^\bullet(x), \quad n \ge 1, \ x' \in \mathsf{X}.$$

From Proposition C.3, we obtain the transition matrix for the belief state process given in Proposition C.1.

Proposition C.3 (Nonlinear Filter) *The belief state dynamics are nonlinear:*

$$\begin{aligned} b_0(x') &= \kappa_0 \mu(x') q(Y_0 \mid x'), \\ b_n(x') &= \mathcal{M}(b_{n-1}, Y_n, U_{n-1}) \stackrel{\text{def}}{=} \kappa_n \sum_x \rho_n(x' \mid x) b_{n-1}(x), \qquad x' \in \mathsf{X}, \ n \ge 1, \end{aligned}$$

where ρ_n *is defined in* (C.12), *and* κ_n *is determined by the constraint* $\sum_{x'} b_n(x') = 1$. □

References

[1] A. Agarwal and O. Dekel. Optimal algorithms for online convex optimization with multi-point bandit feedback. In *Proc. COLT*, pages 28–40, 2010.

[2] A. Agarwal, S. M. Kakade, J. D. Lee, and G. Mahajan. Optimality and approximation with policy gradient methods in Markov decision processes. In *Proc. COLT*, pages 64–66, 2020.

[3] R. Agrawal. Sample mean based index policies with O(log n) regret for the multi-armed bandit problem. *Advances in Applied Probability*, pages 1054–1078, 1995.

[4] V. M. Alekseev. An estimate for the perturbations of the solutions of ordinary differential equations (Russian). *Westnik Moskov Unn. Ser*, 1:28–36, 1961.

[5] F. Alvarez, H. Attouch, J. Bolte, and P. Redont. A second-order gradient-like dissipative dynamical system with Hessian-driven damping: application to optimization and mechanics. *Journal de mathématiques pures et appliquées*, 81(8):747–779, 2002.

[6] S.-I. Amari and S. C. Douglas. Why natural gradient? In *ICASSP'98*, volume 2, pages 1213–1216. IEEE, 1998.

[7] B. D. O. Anderson and J. B. Moore. *Optimal Control: Linear Quadratic Methods*. Prentice Hall, Englewood Cliffs, NJ, 1990.

[8] L. L. Andrew, M. Lin, and A. Wierman. Optimality, fairness, and robustness in speed scaling designs. *SIGMETRICS Perform. Eval. Rev.*, 38(1):37–48, June 2010.

[9] O. Anschel, N. Baram, and N. Shimkin. Averaged-DQN: Variance reduction and stabilization for deep reinforcement learning. In *Proc. ICML*, pages 176–185. JMLR.org, 2017.

[10] A. Arapostathis, V. S. Borkar, E. Fernandez-Gaucherand, M. K. Ghosh, and S. I. Marcus. Discrete-time controlled Markov processes with average cost criterion: a survey. *SIAM J. Control Optim.*, 31:282–344, 1993.

[11] K. B. Ariyur and M. Krstić. *Real Time Optimization by Extremum Seeking Control*. John Wiley & Sons, Inc., New York, NY, 2003.

[12] S. Asmussen and P. W. Glynn. *Stochastic Simulation: Algorithms and Analysis*, volume 57 of *Stochastic Modelling and Applied Probability*. Springer-Verlag, New York, NY, 2007.

[13] K. J. Åström. Optimal control of Markov processes with incomplete state information I. *J. of Mathematical Analysis and Applications*, 10:174–205, 1965.

[14] K. J. Åström and K. Furuta. Swinging up a pendulum by energy control. *Automatica*, 36(2):287–295, 2000.

[15] K. J. Åström and R. M. Murray. *Feedback Systems: An Introduction for Scientists and Engineers*. Princeton University Press, Princeton, NJ, 2nd ed., 2020.

[16] H. Attouch, X. Goudou, and P. Redont. The heavy ball with friction method, I. the continuous dynamical system: global exploration of the local minima of a real-valued function by asymptotic analysis of a dissipative dynamical system. *Communications in Contemporary Mathematics*, 2(01):1–34, 2000.

[17] P. Auer, N. Cesa-Bianchi, and P. Fischer. Finite-time analysis of the multiarmed bandit problem. *Machine Learning*, 47(2-3):235–256, 2002.

[18] M. G. Azar, R. Munos, M. Ghavamzadeh, and H. Kappen. Speedy Q-learning. In *Proc. Advances in Neural Information Processing Systems*, pages 2411–2419, 2011.

[19] F. Bach. *Learning Theory from First Principles*. `www.di.ens.fr/~fbach/ltfp_book.pdf`, 2021.

[20] F. Bach and E. Moulines. Non-strongly-convex smooth stochastic approximation with convergence rate $o(1/n)$. In *Proc. Advances in Neural Information Processing Systems*, volume 26, pages 773–781, 2013.

[21] L. Baird. Residual algorithms: reinforcement learning with function approximation. In A. Prieditis and S. Russell, editors, *Proc. Machine Learning*, pages 30–37. Morgan Kaufmann, San Francisco, CA, 1995.

[22] L. C. Baird. Reinforcement learning in continuous time: advantage updating. In *Proc. of Intl. Conference on Neural Networks*, volume 4, pages 2448–2453. IEEE, 1994.

[23] L. C. Baird III. *Reinforcement Learning through Gradient Descent.* PhD thesis, US Air Force Academy, 1999.

[24] F. Ball, C. Larédo, D. Sirl, and V. C. Tran. *Stochastic Epidemic Models with Inference*, volume 2255. Springer Nature, Cham, 2019.

[25] N. Bansal, T. Kimbrel, and K. Pruhs. Speed scaling to manage energy and temperature. *J. ACM*, 54(1):1–39, March 2007.

[26] A. Barto, R. Sutton, and C. Anderson. Neuron-like adaptive elements that can solve difficult learning control problems. *IEEE Trans. on Systems, Man and Cybernetics*, 13(5):835–846, 1983.

[27] A. G. Barto, R. S. Sutton, and C. J. C. H. Watkins. Learning and sequential decision making. In M. Gabriel and J. W. Moore, editors *Learning and Computational Neuroscience: Foundations of Adaptive Networks*, pages 539–602, MIT Press, Cambridge, MA, 1989.

[28] J. Bas Serrano, S. Curi, A. Krause, and G. Neu. Logistic Q-learning. In A. Banerjee and K. Fukumizu, editors, *Proc. of the Intl. Conference on Artificial Intelligence and Statistics*, volume 130, pages 3610–3618, April 13–15 2021.

[29] T. Basar, S. Meyn, and W. R. Perkins. Lecture notes on control system theory and design. *arXiv e-print 2007.01367*, 2010.

[30] N. Baumann. Too fast to fail: is high-speed trading the next Wall Street disaster? *Mother Jones*, January/February 2013.

[31] J. Baxter and P. L. Bartlett. Direct gradient-based reinforcement learning: I. gradient estimation algorithms. Technical report, Australian National University, 1999.

[32] J. Baxter and P. L. Bartlett. Infinite-horizon policy-gradient estimation. *Journal of Artificial Intelligence Research*, 15:319–350, 2001.

[33] J. Beck. *Strong Uniformity and Large Dynamical Systems.* World Scientific, Hackensack, NJ, 2017.

[34] R. Bellman. The stability of solutions of linear differential equations. *Duke Math. J.*, 10(4):643–647, 1943.

[35] R. Bellman. *Dynamic Programming*. Princeton University Press, Princeton, NJ, 1957.

[36] R. Bellman, J. Bentsman, and S. M. Meerkov. Stability of fast periodic systems. In *Proc. of the American Control Conf.*, volume 3, pages 1319–1320. IEEE, 1984.

[37] M. Benaïm. Dynamics of stochastic approximation algorithms. In *Séminaire de Probabilités, XXXIII*, pages 1–68. Springer, Berlin, 1999.

[38] A. Benveniste, M. Métivier, and P. Priouret. *Adaptive Algorithms and Stochastic Approximations*, volume 22 of *Applications of Mathematics (New York)*. Springer-Verlag, Berlin, 1990. Translated from the French by Stephen S. Wilson.

[39] A. Benveniste, M. Métivier, and P. Priouret. *Adaptive Algorithms and Stochastic Approximations*. Vol. 22. Springer Science & Business Media, Berlin, Heidelberg, 2012.

[40] A. Bernstein, Y. Chen, M. Colombino, E. Dall'Anese, P. Mehta, and S. Meyn. Optimal rate of convergence for quasi-stochastic approximation. *arXiv:1903.07228*, 2019.

[41] A. Bernstein, Y. Chen, M. Colombino, E. Dall'Anese, P. Mehta, and S. Meyn. Quasi-stochastic approximation and off-policy reinforcement learning. In *Proc. of the Conf. on Dec. and Control*, pages 5244–5251, March 2019.

[42] D. Bertsekas. Multiagent rollout algorithms and reinforcement learning. *arXiv preprint arXiv:1910.00120*, 2019.

[43] D. Bertsekas and S. Shreve. *Stochastic Optimal Control: The Discrete-Time Case*. Athena Scientific, Belmont, MA 1996.

[44] D. Bertsekas and J. N. Tsitsiklis. *Neuro-Dynamic Programming*. Athena Scientific, Cambridge, MA, 1996.

[45] D. P. Bertsekas. *Dynamic Programming and Optimal Control*, volume II. Athena Scientific, Belmont, MA, 4th ed., 2012.

[46] D. P. Bertsekas. *Dynamic Programming and Optimal Control*, volume 1. Athena Scientific, Belmont, MA, 4th ed., 2017.

[47] D. P. Bertsekas. *Reinforcement Learning and Optimal Control*. Athena Scientific, Belmont, MA, 2019.

[48] J. Bhandari and D. Russo. Global optimality guarantees for policy gradient methods. *arXiv preprint arXiv: 1906.01786*, 2019.

[49] J. Bhandari, D. Russo, and R. Singal. A finite time analysis of temporal difference learning with linear function approximation. In *Proc. COLT*, pages 1691–1692, 2018.

[50] S. Bhatnagar. Simultaneous perturbation and finite difference methods. *Wiley Encyclopedia of Operations Research and Management Science*, `https://onlinelibrary.wiley.com/doi/10.1002/9780470400531.eorms0784`, 2010.

[51] S. Bhatnagar and V. S. Borkar. Multiscale chaotic SPSA and smoothed functional algorithms for simulation optimization. *Simulation*, 79(10):568–580, 2003.

[52] S. Bhatnagar, M. C. Fu, S. I. Marcus, and I.-J. Wang. Two-timescale simultaneous perturbation stochastic approximation using deterministic perturbation sequences. *ACM Transactions on Modeling and Computer Simulation (TOMACS)*, 13(2):180–209, 2003.

[53] S. Bhatnagar, M. Ghavamzadeh, M. Lee, and R. S. Sutton. Incremental natural actor-critic algorithms. In *Proc. Advances in Neural Information Processing Systems*, pages 105–112, 2008.

[54] S. Bhatnagar, H. Prasad, and L. Prashanth. *Stochastic Recursive Algorithms for Optimization: Simultaneous Perturbation Methods*. Lecture Notes in Control and Information Sciences. Springer, London, 2013.

[55] S. Bhatnagar, D. Precup, D. Silver, R. S. Sutton, H. R. Maei, and C. Szepesvári. Convergent temporal-difference learning with arbitrary smooth function approximation. In *Proc. Advances in Neural Information Processing Systems*, pages 1204–1212, 2009.

[56] S. Bhatnagar, R. S. Sutton, M. Ghavamzadeh, and M. Lee. Natural actor–critic algorithms. *Automatica*, 45(11):2471–2482, 2009.

[57] C. M. Bishop. *Pattern Recognition and Machine Learning*. Springer, 2006.

[58] J. R. Blum. Multidimensional stochastic approximation methods. *The Annals of Mathematical Statistics*, 25(4): 737–744, 1954.

[59] V. Borkar and S. P. Meyn. Oja's algorithm for graph clustering, Markov spectral decomposition, and risk sensitive control. *Automatica*, 48(10):2512–2519, 2012.

[60] V. Borkar and P. Varaiya. Adaptive control of Markov chains, i: finite parameter set. *IEEE Trans. Automat. Control*, 24(6):953–957, 1979.

[61] V. Borkar and P. Varaiya. Identification and adaptive control of Markov chains. *SIAM J. Control Optim.*, 20(4):470–489, 1982.

[62] V. S. Borkar. *Identification and Adaptive Control of Markov Chains*. PhD thesis, University of California, Berkeley, 1980.

[63] V. S. Borkar. Convex analytic methods in Markov decision processes. In *Handbook of Markov Decision Processes*, volume 40 of *Internat. Ser. Oper. Res. Management Sci.*, pages 347–375. Kluwer Acad. Publ., Boston, MA, 2002.

[64] V. S. Borkar. Reinforcement learning – a bridge between numerical methods and Markov Chain Monte Carlo. In N. S. N. Sastry, B. Rajeev, M. Delampady, and T. S. S. R. K. Rao, editors, *Perspectives in Mathematical Sciences*, pages 71–91. World Scientific, Singapore, 2009.

[65] V. S. Borkar. *Stochastic Approximation: A Dynamical Systems Viewpoint*. Hindustan Book Agency and Cambridge University Press (jointly), Delhi, India, and Cambridge, UK, 2008.

[66] V. S. Borkar. *Stochastic Approximation: A Dynamical Systems Viewpoint (2nd ed., to appear)*. Hindustan Book Agency, Delhi, India, and Cambridge, UK, 2020.

[67] V. S. Borkar and V. Gaitsgory. Linear programming formulation of long-run average optimal control problem. *Journal of Optimization Theory and Applications*, 181(1):101–125, 2019.

[68] V. S. Borkar, V. Gaitsgory, and I. Shvartsman. LP formulations of discrete time long-run average optimal control problems: the non ergodic case. *SIAM Journal on Control and Optimization*, 57(3):1783–1817, 2019.

[69] V. S. Borkar and S. P. Meyn. The ODE method for convergence of stochastic approximation and reinforcement learning. *SIAM J. Control Optim.*, 38(2):447–469, 2000.

[70] J. A. Boyan. Technical update: Least-squares temporal difference learning. *Mach. Learn.*, 49(2–3): 233–246, 2002.

[71] S. Boyd, L. El Ghaoui, E. Feron, and V. Balakrishnan. *Linear Matrix Inequalities in System and Control Theory*, volume 15. SIAM, 1994.

[72] S. Boyd, N. Parikh, and E. Chu. *Distributed Optimization and Statistical Learning via the Alternating Direction Method of Multipliers*. Now Publishers Inc, Norwell, MA, 2011.

[73] S. Boyd and L. Vandenberghe. *Convex Optimization*, 1st edition. Cambridge University Press, New York, 1st ed., 2004.

[74] S. Bradtke, B. Ydstie, and A. Barto. Adaptive linear quadratic control using policy iteration. In *Proc. of the American Control Conf.*, volume 3, pages 3475–3479, 1994.

[75] S. J. Bradtke and A. G. Barto. Linear least-squares algorithms for temporal difference learning. *Machine Learning*, 22(1-3):33–57, 1996.

[76] W. L. Brogan. *Modern Control Theory*. Pearson, 3rd ed., 1990.

[77] J. Bu, A. Mesbahi, M. Fazel, and M. Mesbahi. LQR through the lens of first order methods: discrete-time case. *arXiv e-prints*, page arXiv:1907.08921, 2019.

[78] S. Bubeck and N. Cesa-Bianchi. Regret analysis of stochastic and nonstochastic multi-armed bandit problems. *Machine Learning*, 5(1):1–122, 2012.

[79] J. C. Butcher. *Numerical Methods for Ordinary Differential Equations*. John Wiley & Sons, New York, NY 2016.

[80] P. E. Caines. *Linear Stochastic Systems*. John Wiley & Sons, New York, NY, 1988.

[81] P. E. Caines. Mean field games. In J. Baillieul and T. Samad, editors, *Encyclopedia of Systems and Control*, pages 706–712. Springer London, London, UK, 2015.

[82] D. Chatterjee, A. Patra, and H. K. Joglekar. Swing-up and stabilization of a cart–pendulum system under restricted cart track length. *Systems & Control Letters*, 47(4):355–364, 2002.

[83] H. Chen and L. Guo. *Identification and Stochastic Adaptive Control*. Birkhauser, Boston, MA, 1991.

[84] R. T. Chen, Y. Rubanova, J. Bettencourt, and D. Duvenaud. Neural ordinary differential equations. In *Proc. Advances Neural Information Processing Systems*, volume 32, pages 6572–6583, 2018.

[85] S. Chen, A. Bernstein, A. Devraj, and S. Meyn. Stability and acceleration for quasi stochastic approximation. *arXiv:2009.14431*, 2020.

[86] S. Chen, A. Devraj, A. Bernstein, and S. Meyn. Accelerating optimization and reinforcement learning with quasi stochastic approximation. In *Proc. of the American Control Conf.*, pages 1965–1972, May 2021.

[87] S. Chen, A. Devraj, A. Bernstein, and S. Meyn. Revisiting the ODE method for recursive algorithms: fast convergence using quasi stochastic approximation. *Journal of Systems Science and Complexity. Special Issue on Advances on Fundamental Problems in Control Systems, in Honor of Prof. Lei Guo's 60th birthday*, 34(5):1681–1702, 2021.

[88] S. Chen, A. Devraj, V. Borkar, I. Kontoyiannis, and S. Meyn. The ODE method for asymptotic statistics in stochastic approximation and reinforcement learning. *Submitted for publication*, 2021.

[89] S. Chen, A. M. Devraj, A. Bušić, and S. Meyn. Explicit mean-square error bounds for Monte-Carlo and linear stochastic approximation. In S. Chiappa and R. Calandra, editors, *Proc. of AISTATS*, volume 108, pages 4173–4183, 2020.

[90] S. Chen, A. M. Devraj, F. Lu, A. Busic, and S. Meyn. Zap Q-Learning with nonlinear function approximation. In H. Larochelle, M. Ranzato, R. Hadsell, M. F. Balcan, and H. Lin, editors, *Advances in Neural Information Processing Systems, and arXiv e-prints 1910.05405*, volume 33, pages 16879–16890, 2020.

[91] T. Chen, Y. Hua, and W.-Y. Yan. Global convergence of Oja's subspace algorithm for principal component extraction. *IEEE Trans. Neural Networks*, 9(1):58–67, January 1998.

[92] W. Chen, D. Huang, A. A. Kulkarni, et al. Approximate dynamic programming using fluid and diffusion approximations with applications to power management. In *Proc. of the 48th IEEE Conf. on Dec. and Control; Held Jointly with the 2009 28th Chinese Control Conference*, pages 3575–3580, 2009.

[93] Y. Chen, A. Bernstein, A. Devraj, and S. Meyn. Model-free primal-dual methods for network optimization with application to real-time optimal power flow. In *Proc. of the American Control Conf.*, pages 3140–3147, September 2019.

[94] Y. Chow, O. Nachum, E. Duenez-Guzman, and M. Ghavamzadeh. A Lyapunov-based approach to safe reinforcement learning. In S. Bengio, H. Wallach, H. Larochelle, K. Grauman, N. Cesa-Bianchi, and R. Garnett, editors, *Proc. Advances in Neural Information Processing Systems*, pages 8092–8101, 2018.

[95] K. L. Chung et al. On a stochastic approximation method. *The Annals of Mathematical Statistics*, 25(3):463–483, 1954.

[96] M. Colombino, E. Dall'Anese, and A. Bernstein. Online optimization as a feedback controller: stability and tracking. *Trans. on Control of Network Systems*, 7(1):422–432, 2020.

[97] T. M. Cover and J. A. Thomas. *Elements of Information Theory*. John Wiley & Sons Inc., New York, NY, 1991.

[98] J. G. Dai. On positive Harris recurrence of multiclass queueing networks: a unified approach via fluid limit models. *Ann. Appl. Probab.*, 5(1):49–77, 1995.

[99] J. G. Dai and S. P. Meyn. Stability and convergence of moments for multiclass queueing networks via fluid limit models. *IEEE Trans. Automat. Control*, 40:1889–1904, 1995.

[100] J. G. Dai and J. H. Vande Vate. The stability of two-station multi-type fluid networks. *Operations Res.*, 48:721–744, 2000.

[101] G. Dalal, B. Szörényi, G. Thoppe, and S. Mannor. Concentration bounds for two timescale stochastic approximation with applications to reinforcement learning. *Proc. of the Conference on Computational Learning Theory*, pages 1–35, 2017.

[102] D. P. de Farias and B. Van Roy. The linear programming approach to approximate dynamic programming. *Operations Res.*, 51(6):850–865, 2003.

[103] D. P. de Farias and B. Van Roy. On constraint sampling in the linear programming approach to approximate dynamic programming. *Math. Oper. Res.*, 29(3):462–478, 2004.

[104] D. P. de Farias and B. Van Roy. A cost-shaping linear program for average-cost approximate dynamic programming with performance guarantees. *Math. Oper. Res.*, 31(3):597–620, 2006.

[105] A. Dembo and O. Zeitouni. *Large Deviations Techniques and Applications*. Springer-Verlag, New York, NY, 2nd ed., 1998.

[106] C. Derman. *Finite State Markovian Decision Processes*, volume 67 of *Mathematics in Science and Engineering*. Academic Press, Inc., Orlando, FL, 1970.

[107] A. M. Devraj. *Reinforcement Learning Design with Optimal Learning Rate*. PhD thesis, University of Florida, 2019.

[108] A. M. Devraj, A. Bušić, and S. Meyn. On matrix momentum stochastic approximation and applications to Q-learning. In *Allerton Conference on Communication, Control, and Computing*, pages 749–756, September 2019.

[109] A. M. Devraj, A. Bušić, and S. Meyn. Zap Q-Learning – a user's guide. In *Proc. of the Fifth Indian Control Conference*, `https://par.nsf.gov/servlets/purl/10211835`, January 9–11 2019.

[110] A. M. Devraj, A. Bušić, and S. Meyn. Fundamental design principles for reinforcement learning algorithms. In K. G. Vamvoudakis, Y. Wan, F. L. Lewis, and D. Cansever, editors, *Handbook on Reinforcement Learning and Control*, Studies in Systems, Decision and Control (SSDC) series (volume 325). Springer, 2021.

[111] A. M. Devraj, I. Kontoyiannis, and S. P. Meyn. Differential temporal difference learning. *IEEE Trans. Automat. Control*, 66(10): 4652–4667, doi: 10.1109/TAC.2020.3033417. October 2021.

[112] A. M. Devraj and S. P. Meyn. Fastest convergence for Q-learning. *ArXiv e-prints*, July 2017.

[113] A. M. Devraj and S. P. Meyn. Zap Q-learning. In *Proc. of the Intl. Conference on Neural Information Processing Systems*, pages, 2232–2241, 2017.

[114] A. M. Devraj and S. P. Meyn. Q-learning with uniformly bounded variance: large discounting is not a barrier to fast learning. *arXiv e-prints*, pages arXiv:2002.10301 (and to appear, IEEE Trans Auto Control), February 2020.

[115] P. Diaconis. The Markov chain Monte Carlo revolution. *Bull. Amer. Math. Soc. (N.S.)*, 46(2): 179–205, 2009.

[116] D. Ding and M. R. Jovanović. Global exponential stability of primal-dual gradient flow dynamics based on the proximal augmented Lagrangian. In *Proc. of the American Control Conf.*, pages 3414–3419. IEEE, 2019.

[117] R. Douc, E. Moulines, P. Priouret, and P. Soulier. *Markov Chains*. Springer, Cham, 2018.

[118] R. Douc, É. Moulines, and D. Stoffer. *Nonlinear Time Series : Theory, Methods and Applications with R Examples*. Texts in Statistical Science. Chapman et Hall–CRC Press, 2014.

[119] K. Duffy and S. Meyn. Large deviation asymptotics for busy periods. *Stochastic Systems*, 4(1): 300–319, 2014.

[120] K. R. Duffy and S. P. Meyn. Most likely paths to error when estimating the mean of a reflected random walk. *Performance Evaluation*, 67(12):1290–1303, 2010.

[121] K. Dupree, P. M. Patre, M. Johnson, and W. E. Dixon. Inverse optimal adaptive control of a nonlinear Euler–Lagrange system, Part I: Full state feedback. In *Proc. of the Conference on Decision and Control, Held Jointly with Chinese Control Conference*, pages 321–326, 2009.

[122] R. Durrett. Stochastic spatial models. *SIAM Review*, 41(4):677–718, 1999.

[123] E. B. Dynkin and A. A. Yushkevich. *Controlled Markov Processes*, volume 235 of *Grundlehren der Mathematischen Wissenschaften [Fundamental Principles of Mathematical Sciences]*. Springer-Verlag, Berlin, 1979. Translated from the Russian original by J. M. Danskin and C. Holland.

[124] E. Even-Dar and Y. Mansour. Learning rates for Q-learning. *J. of Machine Learning Research*, 5:1–25, 2003.

[125] V. Fabian et al. On asymptotic normality in stochastic approximation. *The Annals of Mathematical Statistics*, 39(4):1327–1332, 1968.

[126] A.-M. Farahmand and M. Ghavamzadeh. PID accelerated value iteration algorithm. In M. Meila and T. Zhang, editors, *Proc. ICML*, volume 139, pages 3143–3153, July 18–24 2021.

[127] M. Fazlyab, A. Ribeiro, M. Morari, and V. M. Preciado. Analysis of optimization algorithms via integral quadratic constraints: nonstrongly convex problems. *SIAM Journal on Optimization*, 28(3):2654–2689, 2018.

[128] E. Feinberg and A. Shwartz, editors. *Markov Decision Processes: Models, Methods, Directions, and Open Problems*. Kluwer Acad. Publ., Holland, 2001.

[129] E. A. Feinberg and A. Shwartz, editors. *Handbook of Markov Decision processes*. Intl. Series in Operations Research & Management Science, 40. Kluwer Academic Publishers, Boston, MA, 2002. Methods and applications.

[130] A. Feintuch and B. Francis. Infinite chains of kinematic points. *Automatica*, 48(5):901–908, 2012.

[131] Y. Feng, L. Li, and Q. Liu. A kernel loss for solving the Bellman equation. In *Proc. Advances in Neural Information Processing Systems*, pages 15456–15467, 2019.

[132] L. Finlay, V. Gaitsgory, and I. Lebedev. Duality in linear programming problems related to deterministic long run average problems of optimal control. *SIAM Journal on Control and Optimization*, 47(4):1667–1700, 2008.

[133] J. M. Flegal and G. L. Jones. Batch means and spectral variance estimators in Markov chain Monte Carlo. *Annals of Statistics*, 38(2):1034–1070, 04 2010.

[134] G. Fort, E. Moulines, S. P. Meyn, and P. Priouret. ODE methods for Markov chain stability with applications to MCMC. In *Valuetools '06: Proceedings of the 1st International Conference on Performance Evaluation Methodolgies and Tools*, page 42, ACM Press, New York, NY, 2006.

[135] F. G. Foster. On Markoff chains with an enumerable infinity of states. *Proc. Cambridge Phil. Soc.*, 47:587–591, 1952.

[136] A. Fradkov and B. T. Polyak. Adaptive and robust control in the USSR. *IFAC–PapersOnLine*, 53(2):1373–1378, 2020. 21th IFAC World Congress.

[137] K. Furuta, M. Yamakita, and S. Kobayashi. Swing up control of inverted pendulum. In *Proc. Intl. Conference on Industrial Electronics, Control and Instrumentation*, pages 2193–2198. IEEE, 1991.

[138] P. A. Gagniuc. *Markov Chains: From Theory to Implementation and Experimentation*. John Wiley & Sons, New York, NY, 2017.

[139] V. Gaitsgory, A. Parkinson, and I. Shvartsman. Linear programming formulations of deterministic infinite horizon optimal control problems in discrete time. *Discrete and Continuous Dynamical Systems – Series B*, 22(10):3821–3838, 2017.

[140] V. Gaitsgory and M. Quincampoix. On sets of occupational measures generated by a deterministic control system on an infinite time horizon. *Nonlinear Analysis: Theory, Methods and Applications*, 88:27–41, 2013.

[141] J. M. George and J. M. Harrison. Dynamic control of a queue with adjustable service rate. *Operations Res.*, 49(5):720–731, September 2001.

[142] P. W. Glynn. Stochastic approximation for Monte Carlo optimization. In *Proc. of the 18th Conference on Winter Simulation*, pages 356–365, 1986.

[143] P. W. Glynn. Likelihood ratio gradient estimation: an overview. In *Proc. of the Winter Simulation Conference*, pages 366–375, 1987.

[144] P. W. Glynn and S. P. Meyn. A Liapounov bound for solutions of the Poisson equation. *Ann. Probab.*, 24(2):916–931, 1996.

[145] G. C. Goodwin and K. S. Sin. *Adaptive Filtering Prediction and Control*. Prentice Hall, Englewood Cliffs, NJ, 1984.

[146] G. J. Gordon. Stable function approximation in dynamic programming. In *Proc. ICML* (see also the full-length technical report, CMU-CS-95-103), pages 261–268. Elsevier, Netherlands, 1995.

[147] G. J. Gordon. Reinforcement learning with function approximation converges to a region. In *Proc. of the 13th Intl. Conference on Neural Information Processing Systems*, pages 996–1002, Cambridge, MA, 2000.

[148] A. Gosavi. *Simulation-Based Optimization*. Springer, Berlin, 2015.

[149] R. L. Graham, D. E. Knuth, and O. Patashnik. *Concrete Mathematics: A Foundation for Computer Science*. Addison-Wesley Longman Publishing Co., Inc., Boston, MA, 2nd ed., 1994.

[150] L. Greenemeier. AI versus AI: self-taught AlphaGo Zero vanquishes its predecessor. *Scientific American*, 371(4), `www.scientificamerican.com/article/ai-versus-ai-self-taught-alphago-zero-vanquishes-its-predecessor/`, October 2017.

[151] E. Greensmith, P. L. Bartlett, and J. Baxter. Variance reduction techniques for gradient estimates in reinforcement learning. *Journal of Machine Learning Research*, 5:1471–1530, 2004.

[152] P. Guan, M. Raginsky, and R. Willett. Online Markov decision processes with Kullback–Leibler control cost. *IEEE Trans. Automat. Control*, 59(6):1423–1438, June 2014.

[153] A. Gupta, R. Jain, and P. W. Glynn. An empirical algorithm for relative value iteration for average-cost MDPs. In *Proc. of the Conf. on Dec. and Control*, pages 5079–5084, 2015.

[154] B. Hajek. *Random Processes for Engineers*. Cambridge University Press, Cambridge, UK, 2015.

[155] P. Hartman. On functions representable as a difference of convex functions. *Pacific Journal of Mathematics*, 9(3):707–713, 1959.

[156] T. Hastie, R. Tibshirani, and J. Friedman. *The Elements of Statistical Learning*. Springer Series in Statistics. Springer-Verlag, New York, NY, 2nd ed., 2001. Corr. 3rd printing, 2003.

[157] S. Henderson. *Variance Reduction via an Approximating Markov Process*. PhD thesis, Stanford University, 1997.

[158] S. G. Henderson and P. W. Glynn. Regenerative steady-state simulation of discrete event systems. *ACM Trans. on Modeling and Computer Simulation*, 11:313–345, 2001.

[159] S. G. Henderson, S. P. Meyn, and V. B. Tadić. Performance evaluation and policy selection in multiclass networks. *Discrete Event Dynamic Systems: Theory and Applications*, 13(1–2):149–189, 2003. Special issue on learning, optimization and decision making (invited).

[160] D. Hernández-Hernández, O. Hernández-Lerma, and M. Taksar. The linear programming approach to deterministic optimal control problems. *Applicationes Mathematicae*, 24(1):17–33, 1996.

[161] O. Hernández-Lerma and J. B. Lasserre. The linear programming approach. In *Handbook of Markov Decision Processes*, volume 40 of *Internat. Ser. Oper. Res. Management Sci.*, pages 377–407. Kluwer Acad. Publ., Boston, MA, 2002.

[162] O. Hernández-Lerma and J. B. Lasserre. *Discrete-Time Markov Control Processes: Basic Optimality Criteria*, volume 30. Springer Science & Business Media, New York, NY, 2012.

[163] B. Hu and L. Lessard. Dissipativity theory for Nesterov's accelerated method. In *Proc. ICML*, pages 1549–1557, 2017.

[164] B. Hu, S. Wright, and L. Lessard. Dissipativity theory for accelerating stochastic variance reduction: a unified analysis of SVRG and Katyusha using semidefinite programs. In *Proc. ICML*, pages 2038–2047, 2018.

[165] D. Huang, W. Chen, P. Mehta, S. Meyn, and A. Surana. Feature selection for neuro-dynamic programming. In F. Lewis, editor, *Reinforcement Learning and Approximate Dynamic Programming for Feedback Control*. Wiley, Hoboken, NJ, 2011.

[166] M. Huang, P. E. Caines, and R. P. Malhame. Large-population cost-coupled LQG problems with nonuniform agents: individual-mass behavior and decentralized ε-Nash equilibria. *IEEE Trans. Automat. Control*, 52(9):1560–1571, 2007.

[167] M. Huang, R. P. Malhame, and P. E. Caines. Large population stochastic dynamic games: closed-loop McKean–Vlasov systems and the Nash certainty equivalence principle. *Communications in Information and Systems*, 6(3):221–251, 2006.

[168] A. Iserles. *A First Course in the Numerical Analysis of Differential Equations*, volume 44. Cambridge University Press, 2009.

[169] T. Jaakola, M. Jordan, and S. Singh. On the convergence of stochastic iterative dynamic programming algorithms. *Neural Computation*, 6:1185–1201, 1994.

[170] K. G. Jamieson, R. Nowak, and B. Recht. Query complexity of derivative-free optimization. In *Proc. Advances in Neural Information Processing Systems*, pages 2672–2680, 2012.

[171] C. Jin, Z. Allen-Zhu, S. Bubeck, and M. I. Jordan. Is Q-learning provably efficient? *Proc. Advances in Neural Information Processing Systems*, 31:4863–4873, 2018.

[172] S. Kakade and J. Langford. Approximately optimal approximate reinforcement learning. In *Proc. ICML*, pages 267–274, 2002.

[173] S. M. Kakade. A natural policy gradient. In *Proc. Advances in Neural Information Processing Systems*, pages 1531–1538, 2002.

[174] D. Kalathil, V. S. Borkar, and R. Jain. Empirical Q-value iteration. *Stochastic Systems*, 11(1):1–18, 2021.

[175] R. E. Kalman. Contribution to the theory of optimal control. *Bol. Soc. Mat. Mexicana*, 5:102–119, 1960.

[176] R. E. Kalman. When is a linear control system optimal? *Journal of Basic Engineering*, 86:51, 1964.

[177] A. Kamoutsi, T. Sutter, P. Mohajerin Esfahani, and J. Lygeros. On infinite linear programming and the moment approach to deterministic infinite horizon discounted optimal control problems. *IEEE Control Systems Letters*, 1(1):134–139, July 2017.

[178] A. D. Kara and S. Yuksel. Convergence of finite memory Q-learning for POMDPs and near optimality of learned policies under filter stability. *arXiv preprint arXiv:2103.12158*, 2021.

[179] H. Karimi, J. Nutini, and M. Schmidt. Linear convergence of gradient and proximal-gradient methods under the Polyak–Łojasiewicz condition. In *European Conference on Machine Learning and Knowledge Discovery in Databases*, volume 9851, pages 795–811, Springer-Verlag, Berlin, Heidelberg, 2016.

[180] P. Karmakar and S. Bhatnagar. Two time-scale stochastic approximation with controlled Markov noise and off-policy temporal-difference learning. *Math. Oper. Res.*, 43(1):130–151, 2018.

[181] H. K. Khalil. *Nonlinear Systems*. Prentice Hall, Upper Saddle River, NJ, 3rd ed., 2002.

[182] J. Kiefer and J. Wolfowitz. Stochastic estimation of the maximum of a regression function. *Ann. Math. Statist.*, 23(3):462–466, September 1952.

[183] Y. H. Kim and F. L. Lewis. *High-Level Feedback Control with Neural Networks*, volume 21. World Scientific, Hackensack, NJ, 1998.

[184] B. Kiumarsi, K. G. Vamvoudakis, H. Modares, and F. L. Lewis. Optimal and autonomous control using reinforcement learning: a survey. *Transactions on Neural Networks and Learning Systems*, 29(6):2042–2062, 2017.

[185] G. Kohs. *AlphaGo*, Ro*co Films, 2017.

[186] P. Kokotović, H. K. Khalil, and J. O'Reilly. *Singular Perturbation Methods in Control: Analysis and Design*. Society for Industrial and Applied Mathematics, Philadelphia, PA, 1999.

[187] D. Koller and R. Parr. Policy iteration for factored MDPs. In *Proc. of the 16th conference on Uncertainty in Artificial Intelligence*, pages 326–334, 2000.

[188] V. Konda. *Actor-Critic Algorithms*. PhD thesis, Massachusetts Institute of Technology, 2002.

[189] V. R. Konda. Learning algorithms for Markov decision processes. Master's thesis, Indian Institute of Science, Dept. of Computer Science and Automation, 1997.

[190] V. R. Konda and V. S. Borkar. Actor-critic–type learning algorithms for Markov decision processes. *SIAM Journal on Control and Optimization*, 38(1):94–123, 1999.

[191] V. R. Konda and J. N. Tsitsiklis. Actor-critic algorithms. In *Proc. Advances in Neural Information Processing Systems*, pages 1008–1014, 2000.

[192] V. R. Konda and J. N. Tsitsiklis. On actor-critic algorithms. *SIAM J. Control Optim.*, 42(4): 1143–1166 (electronic), 2003.

[193] V. R. Konda and J. N. Tsitsiklis. Convergence rate of linear two-time-scale stochastic approximation. *Ann. Appl. Probab.*, 14(2):796–819, 2004.

[194] I. Kontoyiannis, L. A. Lastras-Montaño, and S. P. Meyn. Relative entropy and exponential deviation bounds for general Markov chains. In *Proc. of the IEEE Intl. Symposium on Information Theory*, pages 1563–1567, September 2005.

[195] I. Kontoyiannis, L. A. Lastras-Montaño, and S. P. Meyn. Exponential bounds and stopping rules for MCMC and general Markov chains. In *Proc. of the 1st Intl. Conference on Performance Evaluation Methodolgies and Tools*, Valuetools '06, pages 1563–1567, Association for Computing Machinery, New York, NY, 2006.

[196] I. Kontoyiannis and S. P. Meyn. Spectral theory and limit theorems for geometrically ergodic Markov processes. *Ann. Appl. Probab.*, 13:304–362, 2003.

[197] I. Kontoyiannis and S. P. Meyn. Large deviations asymptotics and the spectral theory of multiplicatively regular Markov processes. *Electron. J. Probab.*, 10(3):61–123 (electronic), 2005.

[198] N. B. Kovachki and A. M. Stuart. Continuous time analysis of momentum methods. *J. of Machine Learning Research*, 22(17):1–40, 2021.

[199] A. Krener. Feedback linearization. In J. Baillieul and J. C. Willems, editors, *Mathematical Control Theory*, pages 66–98. Springer, 1999.

[200] W. Krichene and P. L. Bartlett. Acceleration and averaging in stochastic descent dynamics. *Proc. Advances in Neural Information Processing Systems*, 30:6796–6806, 2017.

[201] V. Krishnamurthy. Structural results for partially observed Markov decision processes. *ArXiv e-prints*, page arXiv:1512.03873, 2015.

[202] M. Krstic, P. V. Kokotovic, and I. Kanellakopoulos. *Nonlinear and Adaptive Control Design*. John Wiley & Sons, Inc., New York, NY, 1995.

[203] P. R. Kumar and T. I. Seidman. Dynamic instabilities and stabilization methods in distributed real-time scheduling of manufacturing systems. *IEEE Trans. Automat. Control*, AC-35(3):289–298, March 1990.

[204] H. J. Kushner and G. G. Yin. *Stochastic Approximation Algorithms and Applications*, volume 35 of *Applications of Mathematics (New York)*. Springer-Verlag, New York, 1997.

[205] H. Kwakernaak and R. Sivan. *Linear Optimal Control Systems*. Wiley-Interscience, New York, NY, 1972.

[206] M. G. Lagoudakis and R. Parr. Model-free least-squares policy iteration. In *Proc. Advances in Neural Information Processing Systems*, pages 1547–1554, 2002.

[207] T. L. Lai. Information bounds, certainty equivalence and learning in asymptotically efficient adaptive control of time-invariant stochastic systems. In L. Gerencséer and P. E. Caines, editors, *Topics in Stochastic Systems: Modelling, Estimation and Adaptive Control*, pages 335–368. Springer Verlag, Heidelberg, Germany, 1991.

[208] T. L. Lai and H. Robbins. Asymptotically efficient adaptive allocation rules. *Adv. in Appl. Math.*, 6(1):4–22, 1985.

[209] C. Lakshminarayanan and S. Bhatnagar. A stability criterion for two timescale stochastic approximation schemes. *Automatica*, 79:108–114, 2017.

[210] C. Lakshminarayanan and C. Szepesvari. Linear stochastic approximation: how far does constant step-size and iterate averaging go? In *Intl. Conference on Artificial Intelligence and Statistics*, pages 1347–1355, 2018.

[211] S. Lange, T. Gabel, and M. Riedmiller. Batch reinforcement learning. In *Reinforcement learning*, pages 45–73. Springer, Freiberg, Germany, 2012.

[212] B. Lapeybe, G. Pages, and K. Sab. Sequences with low discrepancy generalisation and application to Robbins–Monro algorithm. *Statistics*, 21(2):251–272, 1990.

[213] S. Laruelle and G. Pagès. Stochastic approximation with averaging innovation applied to finance. *Monte Carlo Methods and Applications*, 18(1):1–51, 2012.

[214] J. M. Lasry and P. L. Lions. Mean field games. *Japan. J. Math.*, 2:229–260, 2007.

[215] J.-B. Lasserre. *Moments, Positive Polynomials and Their Applications*, volume 1. World Scientific, Hackensack, NJ, 2010.

[216] T. Lattimore and C. Szepesvari. *Bandit Algorithms*. Cambridge University Press, Cambridge, UK, 2020.

[217] M. Le Blanc. Sur l'electrification des chemins de fer au moyen de courants alternatifs de frequence elevee [On the electrification of railways by means of alternating currents of high frequency]. *Revue Generale de l'Electricite*, 12(8):275–277, 1922.

[218] D. Lee and N. He. Stochastic primal-dual Q-learning algorithm for discounted MDPs. In *Proc. of the American Control Conf.*, pages 4897–4902, July 2019.

[219] D. Lee and N. He. A unified switching system perspective and ODE analysis of Q-learning algorithms. *arXiv*, page arXiv:1912.02270, 2019.

[220] J. Lee and R. S. Sutton. Policy iterations for reinforcement learning problems in continuous time and space – fundamental theory and methods. *Automatica*, 126:109421, 2021.

[221] F. L. Lewis and D. Liu. *Reinforcement Learning and Approximate Dynamic Programming for Feedback Control*, volume 17. Wiley-IEEE Press, Hoboken, NJ, 2013.

[222] F. L. Lewis, D. Vrabie, and K. G. Vamvoudakis. Reinforcement learning and feedback control: using natural decision methods to design optimal adaptive controllers. *Control Systems Magazine*, 32(6):76–105, December 2012.

[223] M. Lewis. *Flash Boys: A Wall Street Revolt*. W. W. Norton & Company, New York, NY, 2014.

[224] L. Li and J. Fu. Topological approximate dynamic programming under temporal logic constraints. In *Proc. of the Conf. on Dec. and Control*, pages 5330–5337, 2019.

[225] T. M. Liggett. *Stochastic Interacting Systems: Contact, Voter and Exclusion Processes*, volume 324. Springer Science & Business Media, New York, NY, 2013.

[226] T. Lipp and S. Boyd. Variations and extension of the convex–concave procedure. *Optimization and Engineering*, 17(2):263–287, 2016.

[227] M. L. Littman and C. Szepesvári. A generalized reinforcement-learning model: convergence and applications. In *Proc. ICML*, volume 96, pages 310–318, 1996.

[228] S. Liu and M. Krstic. Introduction to extremum seeking. In *Stochastic Averaging and Stochastic Extremum Seeking*, Communications and Control Engineering. Springer, London, UK, 2012.

[229] L. Ljung. Analysis of recursive stochastic algorithms. *Trans. on Automatic Control*, 22(4):551–575, 1977.

[230] D. Luenberger. *Linear and Nonlinear Programming*. Kluwer Academic Publishers, Norwell, MA, 2nd ed., 2003.

[231] D. G. Luenberger. *Optimization by Vector Space Methods*. John Wiley & Sons Inc., New York, NY, 1969. Reprinted 1997.

[232] R. B. Lund, S. P. Meyn, and R. L. Tweedie. Computable exponential convergence rates for stochastically ordered Markov processes. *Ann. Appl. Probab.*, 6(1):218–237, 1996.

[233] D. J. C. MacKay. *Information Theory, Inference, and Learning Algorithms*. Cambridge University Press, Cambridge, UK, 2003. Available from `www.inference.phy.cam.ac.uk/mackay/itila/`.

[234] H. R. Maei, C. Szepesvári, S. Bhatnagar, and R. S. Sutton. Toward off-policy learning control with function approximation. In *Proc. ICML*, pages 719–726, Omnipress, Madison, WI, 2010.

[235] P. Mandl. Estimation and control in Markov chains. *Advances in Applied Probability*, 6(1):40–60, 1974.

[236] H. Mania, A. Guy, and B. Recht. Simple random search provides a competitive approach to reinforcement learning. In *Proc. Advances in Neural Information Processing Systems*, pages 1800–1809, 2018.

[237] A. S. Manne. Linear programming and sequential decisions. *Management Sci.*, 6(3):259–267, 1960.

[238] P. Marbach and J. N. Tsitsiklis. Simulation-based optimization of Markov reward processes: implementation issues. In *Proc. of the Conf. on Dec. and Control*, volume 2, pages 1769–1774. IEEE, 1999.

[239] P. Marbach and J. N. Tsitsiklis. Simulation-based optimization of Markov reward processes. *IEEE Trans. Automat. Control*, 46(2):191–209, 2001.

[240] I. M. Mareels, B. D. Anderson, R. R. Bitmead, M. Bodson, and S. S. Sastry. Revisiting the MIT rule for adaptive control. In K.J. Aström and B. Wittenmark, editors *Adaptive Systems in Control and Signal Processing 1986*, pages 161–166. Elsevier, Netherlands, 1987.

[241] N. Matni, A. Proutiere, A. Rantzer, and S. Tu. From self-tuning regulators to reinforcement learning and back again. In *Proc. of the Conf. on Dec. and Control*, pages 3724–3740, 2019.

[242] D. Mayne, J. Rawlings, C. Rao, and P. Scokaert. Constrained model predictive control: stability and optimality. *Automatica*, 36(6):789–814, 2000.

[243] D. Q. Mayne. Model predictive control: recent developments and future promise. *Automatica*, 50(12):2967–2986, 2014.

[244] E. Mazumdar, A. Pacchiano, Y.-a. Ma, P. L. Bartlett, and M. I. Jordan. On Thompson sampling with Langevin algorithms. *arXiv e-prints*, pages arXiv–2002, 2020.

[245] P. G. Mehta and S. P. Meyn. Q-learning and Pontryagin's minimum principle. In *Proc. of the Conf. on Dec. and Control*, pages 3598–3605, December 2009.

[246] P. G. Mehta and S. P. Meyn. Convex Q-learning, part 1: deterministic optimal control. *ArXiv e-prints:2008.03559*, 2020.

[247] P. G. Mehta, S. P. Meyn, G. Neu, and F. Lu. Convex Q-learning. In *Proc. of the American Control Conf.*, pages 4749–4756, 2021.

[248] J. Mei, C. Xiao, C. Szepesvari, and D. Schuurmans. On the global convergence rates of softmax policy gradient methods. *arXiv eprint 2005.06392*, 2020.

[249] F. S. Melo, S. P. Meyn, and M. I. Ribeiro. An analysis of reinforcement learning with function approximation. In *Proc. ICML*, pages 664–671, ACM, New York, NY, 2008.

[250] M. Metivier and P. Priouret. Theoremes de convergence presque sure pour une classe d'algorithmes stochastiques a pas decroissants. *Prob. Theory Related Fields*, 74:403–428, 1987.

[251] C. D. Meyer, Jr. The role of the group generalized inverse in the theory of finite Markov chains. *SIAM Review*, 17(3):443–464, 1975.

[252] S. P. Meyn. Workload models for stochastic networks: value functions and performance evaluation. *IEEE Trans. Automat. Control*, 50(8):1106–1122, August 2005.

[253] S. P. Meyn. Large deviation asymptotics and control variates for simulating large functions. *Ann. Appl. Probab.*, 16(1):310–339, 2006.

[254] S. P. Meyn. *Control Techniques for Complex Networks*. Cambridge University Press, 2007. Pre-publication ed. available online.

[255] S. P. Meyn and G. Mathew. Shannon meets Bellman: feature based Markovian models for detection and optimization. In *Proc. of the Conf. on Dec. and Control*, pages 5558–5564, 2008.

[256] S. P. Meyn and R. L. Tweedie. Computable bounds for convergence rates of Markov chains. *Ann. Appl. Probab.*, 4:981–1011, 1994.

[257] S. P. Meyn and R. L. Tweedie. *Markov Chains and Stochastic Stability*. Cambridge University Press, Cambridge, UK, 2nd ed., 2009. Published in the Cambridge Mathematical Library. 1993 ed. online.

[258] D. Michie and R. A. Chambers. Boxes: an experiment in adaptive control. *Machine Intelligence*, 2(2):137–152, 1968.

[259] V. Mnih, A. P. Badia, M. Mirza, A. Graves, T. P. Lillicrap, T. Harley, D. Silver, and K. Kavukcuoglu. Asynchronous methods for deep reinforcement learning. *CoRR*, abs/1602.01783, 2016.

[260] V. Mnih, K. Kavukcuoglu, D. Silver, A. Graves, I. Antonoglou, D. Wierstra, and M. A. Riedmiller. Playing Atari with deep reinforcement learning. *ArXiv*, abs/1312.5602, 2013.

[261] V. Mnih, K. Kavukcuoglu, D. Silver, etc. Human-level control through deep reinforcement learning. *Nature*, 518:529–533, 2015.

[262] M. Mohri, A. Rostamizadeh, and A. Talwalkar. *Foundations of Machine Learning*. MIT Press, Cambridge, MA, 2018.

[263] D. K. Molzahn, F. Dörfler, H. Sandberg, S. H. Low, S. Chakrabarti, R. Baldick, and J. Lavaei. A survey of distributed optimization and control algorithms for electric power systems. *Trans. on Smart Grid*, 8(6):2941–2962, November 2017.

[264] A. W. Moore. *Efficient Memory-Based Learning for Robot Control.* PhD thesis, University of Cambridge, Computer Laboratory, 1990.

[265] W. Mou, C. Junchi Li, M. J. Wainwright, P. L. Bartlett, and M. I. Jordan. On linear stochastic approximation: fine-grained Polyak–Ruppert and non-asymptotic concentration. *arXiv e-prints*, page arXiv:2004.04719, April 2020.

[266] E. Moulines and F. R. Bach. Non-asymptotic analysis of stochastic approximation algorithms for machine learning. In *Advances in Neural Information Processing Systems 24*, pages 451–459, 2011.

[267] K. P. Murphy. *Machine Learning: A Probabilistic Perspective.* MIT Press, Cambridge, MA, 2012.

[268] R. Murray. Feedback control theory: architectures and tools for real-time decision making. Tutorial series at the Simons Institute Program on Real-Time Decision Making. `https://simons.berkeley.edu/talks/murray-control-1`, January 2018.

[269] O. Nachum and B. Dai. Reinforcement learning via Fenchel–Rockafellar duality. *arXiv preprint arXiv:2001.01866*, 2020.

[270] O. Nachum, M. Norouzi, K. Xu, and D. Schuurmans. Bridging the gap between value and policy based reinforcement learning. In *Proc. Advances Neural Information Processing Systems*, volume 10, page 8, 2017.

[271] A. Nedic and D. Bertsekas. Least squares policy evaluation algorithms with linear function approximation. *Discrete Event Dynamic Systems: Theory and Applications*, 13(1-2):79–110, 2003.

[272] A. Nemirovski, A. Juditsky, G. Lan, and A. Shapiro. Robust stochastic approximation approach to stochastic programming. *SIAM Journal on Optimization*, 19(4):1574–1609, 2009.

[273] Y. Nesterov. *Lectures on Convex Optimization.* Springer Optimization and Its Applications 137. Springer Intl. Publishing, New York, NY, 2018.

[274] Y. Nesterov and V. Spokoiny. Random gradient-free minimization of convex functions. *Foundations of Computational Mathematics*, 17(2):527–566, 2017.

[275] J. Norris. *Markov Chains.* Cambridge Series in Statistical and Probabilistic Mathematics. Cambridge University Press, Cambridge, UK, 1997.

[276] M. A. Nowak. *Evolutionary Dynamics: Exploring the Equations of Life.* Harvard University Press, Cambridge, MA, 2006.

[277] E. Nummelin. *General Irreducible Markov Chains and Nonnegative Operators.* Cambridge University Press, Cambridge, UK, 1984.

[278] E. Oja. A simplified neuron model as a principal component analyzer. *J. Math. Biol.*, 15(3):267–273, 1982.

[279] D. Ormoneit and P. Glynn. Kernel-based reinforcement learning in average-cost problems. *Trans. on Automatic Control*, 47(10):1624–1636, October 2002.

[280] J. S. Orr and C. J. Dennehy. Analysis of the X-15 flight 3-65-97 divergent limit-cycle oscillation. *Journal of Aircraft*, 54(1):135–148, 2017.

[281] I. Osband, B. Van Roy, and Z. Wen. Generalization and exploration via randomized value functions. In *Proc. ICML*, pages 2377–2386, 2016.

[282] N. Parikh and S. Boyd. *Proximal Algorithms.* Foundations and Trends in Optimization. Now Publishers, Norwell, MA, 2013.

[283] J. B. Park and J. Y. Lee. Nonlinear adaptive control based on Lyapunov analysis: overview and survey. *Journal of Institute of Control, Robotics and Systems*, 20(3):261–269, 2014.

[284] T. J. Perkins and A. G. Barto. Lyapunov design for safe reinforcement learning. *J. Mach. Learn. Res.*, 3:803–832, 2003.

[285] J. Peters, S. Vijayakumar, and S. Schaal. Reinforcement learning for humanoid robotics. In *Proc. of the IEEE-RAS International Conference on Humanoid Robots*, pages 1–20, 2003.

[286] B. T. Polyak. Gradient methods for minimizing functionals. *Zhurnal Vychislitel'noi Matematiki i Matematicheskoi Fiziki*, 3(4):643–653, 1963.

[287] B. T. Polyak. A new method of stochastic approximation type. *Avtomatika i telemekhanika (in Russian). translated in Automat. Remote Control, 51 (1991)*, pages 98–107, 1990.

[288] B. T. Polyak and A. B. Juditsky. Acceleration of stochastic approximation by averaging. *SIAM J. Control Optim.*, 30(4):838–855, 1992.

[289] W. B. Powell. *Reinforcement Learning and Stochastic Optimization*. John Wiley & Sons, Hoboken, NJ, 2021.

[290] J. C. Principe. *Information Theory, Machine Learning, and Reproducing Kernel Hilbert Spaces*, pages 1–45. Springer New York, New York, NY, 2010.

[291] M. L. Puterman. *Markov Decision Processes: Discrete Stochastic Dynamic Programming*. John Wiley & Sons, New York, NY, 2014.

[292] G. Qu and N. Li. On the exponential stability of primal-dual gradient dynamics. *Control Systems Letters*, 3(1):43–48, 2018.

[293] M. Raginsky. Divergence-based characterization of fundamental limitations of adaptive dynamical systems. In *Conference on Communication, Control, and Computing*, pages 107–114, 2010.

[294] M. Raginsky and J. Bouvrie. Continuous-time stochastic mirror descent on a network: variance reduction, consensus, convergence. In *Proc. of the Conf. on Dec. and Control*, pages 6793–6800, 2012.

[295] M. Raginsky and A. Rakhlin. Information-based complexity, feedback and dynamics in convex programming. *Transactions on Information Theory*, 57(10):7036–7056, 2011.

[296] A. Ramaswamy and S. Bhatnagar. A generalization of the Borkar–Meyn theorem for stochastic recursive inclusions. *Math. Oper. Res.*, 42(3):648–661, 2017.

[297] A. Ramaswamy and S. Bhatnagar. Stability of stochastic approximations with "controlled Markov" noise and temporal difference learning. *Trans. on Automatic Control*, 64:2614–2620, 2019.

[298] L. Rastrigin. Extremum control by means of random scan. *Avtomat. i Telemekh*, 21(9):1264–1271, 1960.

[299] L. A. Rastrigin. Random search in problems of optimization, identification and training of control systems. *Journal of Cybernetics*, 3(3):93–103, 1973.

[300] Research Staff. Experience with the X-15 adaptive flight control system. TN D-6208, NASA Flight Research Center, Edwards, CA, 1971.

[301] H. Robbins and S. Monro. A stochastic approximation method. *Annals of Mathematical Statistics*, 22:400–407, 1951.

[302] J. S. Rosenthal. Correction: "Minorization conditions and convergence rates for Markov chain Monte Carlo." *J. Amer. Statist. Assoc.*, 90(431):1136, 1995.

[303] J. S. Rosenthal. Minorization conditions and convergence rates for Markov chain Monte Carlo. *J. Amer. Statist. Assoc.*, 90(430):558–566, 1995.

[304] W. Rudin. *Real and Complex Analysis*. McGraw-Hill, New York, NY, 2nd ed., 1974.

[305] D. Ruppert. A Newton–Raphson version of the multivariate Robbins–Monro procedure. *The Annals of Statistics*, 13(1):236–245, 1985.

[306] D. Ruppert. Efficient estimators from a slowly convergent Robbins–Monro processes. Technical Report Tech. Rept. No. 781, Cornell University, School of Operations Research and Industrial Engineering, Ithaca, NY, 1988.

[307] D. J. Russo, B. Van Roy, A. Kazerouni, I. Osband, and Z. Wen. *A Tutorial on Thompson Sampling*. Now Publishers Inc., Norwell, MA, 2018.

[308] A. N. Rybko and A. L. Stolyar. On the ergodicity of random processes that describe the functioning of open queueing networks. *Problemy Peredachi Informatsii*, 28(3):3–26, 1992.

[309] J. Sacks. Asymptotic distribution of stochastic approximation procedures. *The Annals of Mathematical Statistics*, 29(2):373–405, 1958.

[310] J. Schrittwieser, I. Antonoglou, T. Hubert, et al. Mastering Atari, Go, chess and Shogi by planning with a learned model. *ArXiv*, abs/1911.08265, 2019.

[311] J. Schulman, S. Levine, P. Abbeel, M. Jordan, and P. Moritz. Trust region policy optimization. In *Intl. Conference on Machine Learning*, pages 1889–1897, 2015.

[312] J. Schulman, F. Wolski, P. Dhariwal, A. Radford, and O. Klimov. Proximal policy optimization algorithms. *ArXiv*, abs/1707.06347, 2017.

[313] P. J. Schweitzer. Perturbation theory and finite Markov chains. *J. Appl. Prob.*, 5:401–403, 1968.

[314] P. J. Schweitzer and A. Seidmann. Generalized polynomial approximations in Markovian decision processes. *Journal of Mathematical Analysis and Applications*, 110(2):568–582, 1985.

[315] E. Seneta. *Non-Negative Matrices and Markov Chains*. Springer, New York, NY, 2nd ed., 1981.

[316] C. Shannon. A mathematical theory of communication. *Bell System Tech. J.*, 27:379–423, 623–656, 1948.

[317] H. Sharma, R. Jain, and A. Gupta. An empirical relative value learning algorithm for non-parametric MDPs with continuous state space. In *European Control Conference*, pages 1368–1373. IEEE, 2019.

[318] B. Shi, S. S. Du, W. Su, and M. I. Jordan. Acceleration via symplectic discretization of high-resolution differential equations. In H. Wallach, H. Larochelle, A. Beygelzimer, F. d'Alché-Buc, E. Fox, and R. Garnett, editors, *Proc. Advances in Neural Information Processing Systems*, pages 5744–5752, 2019.

[319] S. Shirodkar and S. Meyn. Quasi stochastic approximation. In *Proc. of the American Control Conf.*, pages 2429–2435, July 2011.

[320] S. Shivam, I. Buckley, Y. Wardi, C. Seatzu, and M. Egerstedt. Tracking control by the Newton–Raphson flow: applications to autonomous vehicles. *CoRR*, abs/1811.08033, 2018.

[321] R. Sikora and W. Skarbek. On stability of Oja algorithm. In L. Polkowski and A. Skowron, editors, *Rough Sets and Current Trends in Computing*, volume 1424 of *Lecture Notes in Computer Science*, pages 354–360. Springer Verlag, Berlin 2009.

[322] D. Silver, T. Hubert, J. Schrittwieser, et al. A general reinforcement learning algorithm that masters chess, Shogi, and Go through self-play. *Science*, 362(6419):1140–1144, 2018.

[323] D. Silver, G. Lever, N. Heess, T. Degris, D. Wierstra, and M. Riedmiller. Deterministic policy gradient algorithms. In *Proc. ICML*, pages 387–395, 2014.

[324] S. P. Singh, T. Jaakkola, and M. Jordan. Reinforcement learning with soft state aggregation. *Proc. Advances in Neural Information Processing Systems*, 7:361, 1995.

[325] S. Smale. A convergent process of price adjustment and global Newton methods. *Journal of Mathematical Economics*, 3(2):107–120, July 1976.

[326] R. D. Smallwood and E. J. Sondik. The optimal control of partially observable Markov processes over a finite horizon. *Oper. Res.*, 21(5):1071–1088, October 1973.

[327] J. C. Spall. Multivariate stochastic approximation using a simultaneous perturbation gradient approximation. *IEEE Transactions on Automatic Control*, 37(3):332–341, 1992.

[328] J. C. Spall. A stochastic approximation technique for generating maximum likelihood parameter estimates. In *Proc. of the American Control Conf.*, pages 1161–1167. IEEE, 1987.

[329] J. C. Spall. A one-measurement form of simultaneous perturbation stochastic approximation. *Automatica*, 33(1):109–112, 1997.

[330] M. W. Spong and D. J. Block. The pendubot: a mechatronic system for control research and education. In *Proc. of the Conf. on Dec. and Control*, pages 555–556. IEEE, 1995.

[331] M. W. Spong and L. Praly. Control of underactuated mechanical systems using switching and saturation. In A. S. Morse, editor, *Control Using Logic-Based Switching*, pages 162–172. Springer, Berlin, Heidelberg 1997.

[332] M. W. Spong and M. Vidyasagar. *Robot Dynamics and Control*. John Wiley & Sons, Chichester, UK, 2008.

[333] R. Srikant and L. Ying. Finite-time error bounds for linear stochastic approximation and TD learning. In *Proc. COLT*, pages 2803–2830, 2019.

[334] R. L. Stratonovich. Conditional Markov processes. *SIAM J. Theory Probab. and Appl.*, 5:156–178, 1960.

[335] W. Su, S. Boyd, and E. Candes. A differential equation for modeling nesterov's accelerated gradient method: theory and insights. In *Proc. Advances in Neural Information Processing Systems*, pages 2510–2518, 2014.

[336] J. Subramanian and A. Mahajan. Approximate information state for partially observed systems. In *Proc. of the Conf. on Dec. and Control*, pages 1629–1636. IEEE, 2019.

[337] J. Subramanian, A. Sinha, R. Seraj, and A. Mahajan. Approximate information state for approximate planning and reinforcement learning in partially observed systems. *arXiv:2010.08843*, 2020.

[338] R. Sutton and A. Barto. *Reinforcement Learning: An Introduction*. MIT Press, Cambridge, MA. Online ed. at `www.cs.ualberta.ca/~sutton/book/the-book.html`, Cambridge, MA, 2nd ed., 2018.

[339] R. S. Sutton. *Temporal Credit Assignment in Reinforcement Learning*. PhD thesis, University of Massachusetts, Amherst, 1984.

[340] R. S. Sutton. Learning to predict by the methods of temporal differences. *Mach. Learn.*, 3(1):9–44, 1988.

[341] R. S. Sutton. Generalization in reinforcement learning: successful examples using sparse coarse coding. In *Proc. of the Intl. Conference on Neural Information Processing Systems*, pages 1038–1044, 1995.

[342] R. S. Sutton and A. G. Barto. Toward a modern theory of adaptive networks: expectation and prediction. *Psychological Review*, 88(2):135, 1981.

[343] R. S. Sutton, A. G. Barto, and R. J. Williams. Reinforcement learning is direct adaptive optimal control. *Control Systems Magazine*, 12(2):19–22, 1992.

[344] R. S. Sutton, D. A. McAllester, S. P. Singh, and Y. Mansour. Policy gradient methods for reinforcement learning with function approximation. In *Proc. Advances in Neural Information Processing Systems*, pages 1057–1063, 2000.

[345] R. S. Sutton, C. Szepesvári, and H. R. Maei. A convergent $O(n)$ algorithm for off-policy temporal-difference learning with linear function approximation. In *Proc. of the Intl. Conference on Neural Information Processing Systems*, pages 1609–1616, 2008.

[346] C. Szepesvári. The asymptotic convergence-rate of Q-learning. In *Proc. of the Intl. Conference on Neural Information Processing Systems*, pages 1064–1070, 1997.

[347] C. Szepesvári. *Algorithms for Reinforcement Learning*. Synthesis Lectures on Artificial Intelligence and Machine Learning. Morgan & Claypool Publishers, San Raphael, CA, 2010.

[348] Y. Tan, W. H. Moase, C. Manzie, D. Nešić, and I. Mareels. Extremum seeking from 1922 to 2010. In *Proc. of the 29th Chinese Control Conference*, pages 14–26. IEEE, 2010.

[349] A. Tanzanakis and J. Lygeros. Data-driven control of unknown systems: a linear programming approach. *ArXiv*, abs/2003.00779, 2020.

[350] G. Tesauro. TD-Gammon, a self-teaching backgammon program, achieves master-level play. *Neural Computation*, 6(2):215–219, 1994.

[351] G. Thoppe and V. Borkar. A concentration bound for stochastic approximation via Alekseev's formula. *Stochastic Systems*, 9(1):1–26, 2019.

[352] J. Tsitsiklis. Asynchronous stochastic approximation and Q-learning. *Machine Learning*, 16:185–202, 1994.

[353] J. Tsitsiklis and B. van Roy. Optimal stopping of Markov processes: Hilbert space theory, approximation algorithms, and an application to pricing high-dimensional financial derivatives. *IEEE Trans. Automat. Control*, 44(10):1840 –1851, 1999.

[354] J. N. Tsitsiklis and B. V. Roy. Average cost temporal-difference learning. *Automatica*, 35(11): 1799–1808, 1999.

[355] J. N. Tsitsiklis and B. Van Roy. Feature-based methods for large scale dynamic programming. *Machine Learning*, 22(1-3):59–94, 1996.

[356] J. N. Tsitsiklis and B. Van Roy. An analysis of temporal-difference learning with function approximation. *IEEE Trans. Automat. Control*, 42(5):674–690, 1997.

[357] Y. Z. Tsypkin and Z. J. Nikolic. *Adaptation and Learning in Automatic Systems*. Academic Press, New York, NY, 1971.

[358] B. Tzen and M. Raginsky. Theoretical guarantees for sampling and inference in generative models with latent diffusions. In A. Beygelzimer and D. Hsu, editors, *Proc. COLT*, volume 99, pages 3084–3114, 2019.

[359] K. G. Vamvoudakis, F. L. Lewis, and D. Vrabie. Reinforcement learning with applications in autonomous control and game theory. In P. Angelov, editor, *Handbook on Computer Learning and Intelligence*. World Scientific, Hackensack, NJ, 2nd ed., 2021.

[360] K. G. Vamvoudakis, Y. Wan, F. L. Lewis, and D. Cansever, editors. *Handbook on Reinforcement Learning and Control*. Studies in Systems, Decision and Control (SSDC), volume 325. Springer, Princeton, NJ, 2021.

[361] A. W. van der Vaart. *Asymptotic Statistics*. Cambridge Series in Statistical and Probabilistic Mathematics. Cambridge University Press, Cambridge, UK, 1998.

[362] R. van Handel. Lecture notes on hidden Markov models. `https://web.math.princeton.edu/~rvan/`, 2008.

[363] B. Van Roy. *Learning and Value Function Approximation in Complex Decision Processes.* PhD thesis, Massachusetts Institute of Technology, 1998. AAI0599623.

[364] L. Vandenberghe and S. Boyd. Applications of semidefinite programming. *Applied Numerical Mathematics*, 29(3):283–299, 1999.

[365] V. Vapnik. *Estimation of Dependences Based on Empirical Data.* Springer Science & Business Media, New York, NY, 2006.

[366] J. Venter et al. An extension of the Robbins–Monro procedure. *The Annals of Mathematical Statistics*, 38(1):181–190, 1967.

[367] R. Vinter. Convex duality and nonlinear optimal control. *SIAM Journal on Control and Optimization*, 31(2):518–21, 03 1993.

[368] N. Walton. A short note on soft-max and policy gradients in bandits problems. *arXiv preprint arXiv:2007.10297*, 2020.

[369] Y. Wang and S. Boyd. Performance bounds for linear stochastic control. *Systems Control Lett.*, 58(3):178–182, 2009.

[370] Y. Wardi, C. Seatzu, M. Egerstedt, and I. Buckley. Performance regulation and tracking via lookahead simulation: preliminary results and validation. In *Proc. of the Conf. on Dec. and Control*, pages 6462–6468, 2017.

[371] C. J. C. H. Watkins. *Learning from Delayed Rewards.* PhD thesis, King's College, Cambridge, UK, 1989.

[372] C. J. C. H. Watkins and P. Dayan. Q-learning. *Machine Learning*, 8(3-4):279–292, 1992.

[373] B. Weber. Swift and slashing, computer topples Kasparov. *New York Times*, 12:262, 1997.

[374] P. Whittle. *Risk-Sensitive Optimal Control.* John Wiley and Sons, Chichester, NY, 1990.

[375] A. Wibisono, A. C. Wilson, and M. I. Jordan. A variational perspective on accelerated methods in optimization. *Proc. of the National Academy of Sciences*, 113:E7351–E7358, 2016.

[376] R. J. Williams. Simple statistical gradient-following algorithms for connectionist reinforcement learning. *Machine Learning*, 8(3-4):229–256, 1992.

[377] I. H. Witten. An adaptive optimal controller for discrete-time Markov environments. *Information and Control*, 34(4):286–295, 1977.

[378] L. Wu. Essential spectral radius for Markov semigroups. I. Discrete time case. *Prob. Theory Related Fields*, 128(2):255–321, 2004.

[379] V. G. Yaji and S. Bhatnagar. Stochastic recursive inclusions with non-additive iterate-dependent Markov noise. *Stochastics*, 90(3):330–363, 2018.

[380] H. Yin, P. Mehta, S. Meyn, and U. Shanbhag. Synchronization of coupled oscillators is a game. *IEEE Transactions on Automatic Control*, 57(4):920–935, 2012.

[381] H. Yin, P. Mehta, S. Meyn, and U. Shanbhag. Learning in mean-field games. *IEEE Transactions on Automatic Control*, 59(3):629–644, March 2014.

[382] H. Yin, P. G. Mehta, S. P. Meyn, and U. V. Shanbhag. On the efficiency of equilibria in mean-field oscillator games. *Dynamic Games and Applications*, 4(2):177–207, 2014.

[383] J. Zhang, A. Koppel, A. S. Bedi, C. Szepesvari, and M. Wang. Variational policy gradient method for reinforcement learning with general utilities. *Proc. Advances in Neural Information Processing Systems*, 33:4572–4583, 2020.

[384] J. Zhang, A. Mokhtari, S. Sra, and A. Jadbabaie. Direct Runge–Kutta discretization achieves acceleration. In *Proc. of the Intl. Conference on Neural Information Processing Systems*, pages 3904–3913, 2018.

[385] J. Zhao and M. Spong. Hybrid control for global stabilization of the cart–pendulum system. *Automatica*, 37(12):1941–1951, 2001.

[386] K. Zhou, J. C. Doyle, and K. Glover. *Robust and Optimal Control.* Prentice Hall, Englewood Cliffs, NJ, 1996.

Glossary of Symbols and Acronyms

$\mathbb{1}_A$: Indicator function, 395
ϕ : (Stationary) Policy, 9, 247
π : Invariant pmf for X, 205, 319
ϖ, 169
Invariant pmf for X,U, 319
Occupancy pmf, 194
ξ: Exploration signal, 31
$\psi_{(n)} \stackrel{\text{def}}{=} \psi(\Phi(n))$, 178, 319
$c_n \stackrel{\text{def}}{=} c(\Phi(n))$, 178, 319
ζ_n : Eligibility vector, 163, 327
Γ : Loss function, 31, 90
Γ^ε : Bellman error loss, 31, 188
$\underline{H}$: Minimum or evaluation, 319
Λ^θ : Score function for rand. policy, 377
λ : Discounting in TD(λ), 178
λ or η : Eigenvalue, 26, 212, 356
Θ : State for QSA ODE, 98
$\overline{\Theta}$: Time-scaled ODE, 107
ϑ : State for ODE approximation, 85
$\tau = s_t$: ODE change of variables, 107

ACOE : Average-cost optimality equation, 245
ARE : Algebraic Riccati equation, 66, 77

$\mathcal{B}$: Bellman error, 63

C^1 : Continuously differentiable, 23
CLT : Central Limit Theorem, 222

$\mathcal{D}$: Temporal difference, 162, 325
DCOE : Discounted-cost optimality equation, 59, 318
DP : Dynamic programming, 53
DPLP : Dynamic programming LP, 65, 407
Dual, 193

ERM : Empirical risk minimization, 161, 296
ESC : Extremum-seeking control, 114
E_x, 207, 398
E_μ, 398

$\mathcal{F}_k$: Filtration, 247, 397
$\overline{f}$: QSA/SA vector field, 98, 280

$\mathcal{H}$: Function class, 160

IDP : Inverse dynamic programming, 63
inf : Infimum, 396

$\Bbbk$: Kernel, 165

liminf, 396
limsup, 396
LQR, 52
LSTD, 173, 371
LTI, 12

MDP : Markov decision process, 245
MSBE : Mean-square Bellman error, 325
MSE : Mean-square error, 281

PIA, 404
PJR : Polyak–Juditsky–Ruppert, 108
pmf : Probability mass function, 206
P_μ, P_x, 398
P_u : Controlled transition matrix, 245

Q : Q-function, 53, 246, 318
Fixed policy, 103, 320
qSGD : Quasistochastic gradiant descent, 114

RKHS, 166

S^θ : Score function for Markovian family, 231
$S_V(r)$: Sublevel set, 19
SGD : Stochastic gradient descent, 114, 231, 294
SNR : Stochastic Newton–Raphson, 302
SPP, 60, 402

SPSA : Simultaneous perturbation stochastic approximation, 157
sup : Supremum, 396

U : Input space, 12

(V3) : Lyapunov drift condition, 234
(V4) : Lyapunov drift condition, 235

VIA, 54, 403

X : State space, 12
x^e : Equilibrium state, 17

Z_t : Scaled QSA error, 107
Z_n : Scaled SA error, 282

Index